101 BASIC Computer Games

edited by

David H. Ahl

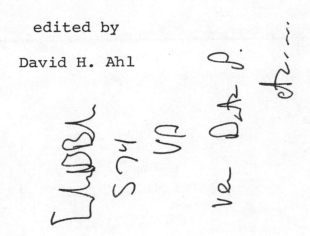

Digital Equipment Corporation
Maynard, Massachusetts

Additional copies of 101 BASIC Computer Games
are available for $5.00 plus .50 postage from:

Software Distribution Center
Digital Equipment Corporation
Maynard, Massachusetts 01754

Write for discount schedule on quantities over 30.

Two supplemental guides are available for use with
this book. They are:

Understanding Mathematics and Logic Using
BASIC Computer Games, $1.50. Grades 7-12.

Getting Started in Classroom Computing,
$1.50. Grades 2-7.

1st Printing -- July 1973
2nd Printing -- April 1974

Contents

Appendices

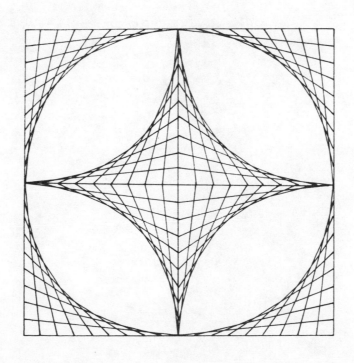

Preface

This is not the first collection of computer games and simulations nor will it by any means be the last. However, in many
ways it is unique. It is the <u>first</u> collection of games all
in BASIC. It is also the only collection that I have seen con-
taining both a complete listing <u>and</u> a sample run of each game
along with a descriptive write-up.

Educational Value of Games

Educators have widely different opinions as to the educational
value of games. There tends to be agreement that games are
highly motivational and frequently very addictive. Most
educators agree that games generally foster learning by
discovery--i.e., the player doesn't sit down at the terminal
with the purpose of learning a principle of logic but after
playing BAGLES three or four times he most assuredly has
learned something about logic. Newton's second law is probably
the furthest thing from the mind of a person sitting down to
play ROCKET. However, when the player finally lands his LEM
successfully on the moon, the chances are very good that he
has discovered something about gravity varying inversely with
the mass of the LEM and the distance from the moon.

The main objection to games as a learning tool seems to be the
fact that it's largely unguided learning and potentially waste-
ful of computer time. In fact, when I was discussing the distribution of this book with Art Leuhrmann of Dartmouth, he
joked that some computer center directors might be willing to
pay to <u>not</u> have the book sold on campus because of the computer
time that would be burned up by playing the games!

I personally believe that the educational value of games can
be enormous - not only in their playing but in their creation.
I know any number of both high school and college computer
science courses where the writing of a game or simulation is
the major course project. Indeed, many of the games in this
book were done as such projects.

Sources of Games

The games in this book were collected on my travels to schools
as well as from submittals in response to an advertisement in
EDU, a newsletter published by Digital Equipment Corporation.
Game authors range from seventh graders in Massachusetts and
California to PhDs in England and Canada.

Over 300 games were submitted in response to the ad in EDU.
Even after weeding out duplications or very similar games,
there were over 150 unique games. Hence, a second volume is
a possibility, assuming, of course, that this one sells a
few copies. A word to budding game authors: If you want to
submit a game for a future book, please pay careful attention
to Appendix C, "Instructions to Game Authors."

The majority of games submitted tend to simulate a sport, card or board game, a game of chance or something which already exists. Only a few games begin to use the logical and computational capabilities of the computer to come up with something new and truly unique. Some that do are STARS, BULCOW, ROCKET, and LIFE-2. I'd like to predict that we see more of these games in the future, at least I certainly hope so.

Certain games are, of course, more popular with game authors than others. There were no less than ten versions of NIM submitted, nine versions each of HORSES (Horse Race) and TICTAC (Tic-Tac-Toe), and eight versions of CRAPS. Other popular ones were simulations of baseball, basketball, football, blackjack, and hangman.

Families of Games

A word about the title of the book. The astute, quantitatively-oriented reader might notice that there seem to be more than 101 games in the book. In fact, there are 108 individual games; 7 are different versions of another game. There are 101 separate write-ups; thus, the title of the book.

Perhaps it is a disease of using the computer or perhaps it is just a compulsion of man that he must categorize things. The games in this book could be categorized by level of difficulty as is often the case in collections of puzzles. Tney could also be categorized in an educational sense, for example, those that could be used to teach logic principles, those that foster learning by discovery, those that require the user to solve an algebra problem, etc.

Faced with this categorization dilemma and the sure feeling that no way would please all the critics, I chose to simply put the programs in the book in alphabetical order. However, I have also put the games in some rough groupings shown in Appendix A. In the first two groups, Number or Letter Guessing and Piles of Objects, you will probably get more enjoyment if you play the games in the numbered order as there is a definite sequential nature to their difficulty. In the other fourteen categories, the games may be played in any order; one does not generally build upon another except in a few cases. In particular, you should play:

```
BAGLES before BULCOW
HI-Q   before 1CHECK
BATTLE before SALVO
GUNNER before GUNER1
ROCKET before ROCKT2
HMRABI before KING
```

Equipment to Play, Computer and Otherwise

Most of the games in this book require no special knowledge, tools or equipment to play, except, of course, a BASIC-speaking computer. Four of the matrix games will probably be more enjoyable if you use a grid or quadrille paper to play. Unless you have a photographic memory, QUBIC almost certainly requires a diagram. There is a page included as Appendix B which contains some supplemental diagrams; you may wish to reproduce it if you become addicted to the games on it.

With few exceptions, the games all run in "standard" BASIC. Any exceptions are noted in the write-ups under the heading, "Computer Limitations." The major difference between various computer systems appears to be in the handling of alphabetic strings. On Digital systems a subscripted string variable, for example, A$(8) or C1$(15), refers to a variable in an array or matrix. Other BASIC compilers may not have string arrays.

On some systems, in particular, Digital's Edusystems 20, 25, and 50, strings are limited to 6 characters. Several strings may, of course, be combined in an array to permit longer than 6-letter words to be used.

Many programs use the RANDOMIZE command to start the random number generator at a random point. Some BASIC compilers do not recognize RANDOMIZE and it must be removed in order for the program to run.

Digital BASIC permits more than one statement on each program line. Statement separators on the line may be one of three characters -- \ or : or ◊ .

I have tested and run almost every program in the book. About 65% of them I've rewritten, modified or cleaned up. Naturally, I can't guarantee that they'll run on every different BASIC compiler in the world, but they should be pretty reliable and bug-free.

Have fun!

Maynard, Massachusetts   David H. Ahl
July 1973

ACKNOWLEDGEMENTS

I'd like to acknowledge eight major sources of games for this book. While not all of the games from each source were published, they all submitted or offered to submit 10 or more games:

Rusty Whitney
Oregon Museum of Science and Industry
Portland, Oregon

Bob Albrecht
People's Computer Company
Menlo Park, California

Walt Koetke
Lexington High School
Lexington, Massachusetts

Charles Lund
The American School of the International Schools
The Hague, Netherlands

Mary C. Jones
Southwest High School
Fort Worth, Texas

Victor Nahigian (student)
Weston High School
Weston, Massachusetts

Keiwit Computation Center
Dartmouth College
Hanover, New Hampshire

Education and DECsystem-10 Groups
Digital Equipment Corporation
Maynard, Massachusetts

Illustrations courtesy of:

MAD Magazine
Scott, Foresman & Co.
Bob Barner
Creative Publications
Peoples Press
and several other sources.

Cover by Bob Barner.

The Games....

ACEYDU

ACEY DUCEY CARD GAME

Description

This is a simulation of the Acey Ducey card game. In the
game, the dealer (the computer) deals two cards face up.
You have an option to bet or not to bet depending on whether
or not you feel the next card dealt will have a value between
the first two.

Your initial money (Q) is set to $100; you may alter Statement
170 if you want to start with more or less than $100. The
game keeps going on until you lose all your money or interrupt
the program.

Program Author

Bill Palmby
Adlai E. Stevenson High School
Prairie View, Illinois   60069

PROGRAM LISTING

```
LISTNH
10 REM *** GAME OF ACEY-DUCEY WRITTEN BY BILL PALMBY
20 REM *** ADLAI STEVENSON HIGH SCHOOL, PRAIRE VIEW, ILL
30 REM *** TRANSLATED TO RSTS/E BY DAVE AHL, DIGITAL
100 RANDOMIZE
101 PRINT "ACEY-DUCEY IS PLAYED IN THE FOLLOWING MANNER:"
102 PRINT "THE DEALER (COMPUTER) DEALS TWO CARDS FACE UP."
103 PRINT "YOU HAVE THE OPTION TO BET OR NOT TO BET DEPENDING"
104 PRINT "ON WHETHER OR NOT YOU FEEL THE NEXT CARD WILL HAVE"
105 PRINT "A VALUE BETWEEN THE FIRST TWO."
106 PRINT "IF YOU DO NOT WANT TO BET, INPUT A 0."
110 PRINT
160 N=100:Q=100
190 PRINT "YOU NOW HAVE"Q"DOLLARS."
195 PRINT
200 GOTO 260
210 Q=Q+M
220 GOTO 190
240 Q=Q-M
250 GOTO 190
260 PRINT "HERE ARE YOUR NEXT TWO CARDS..."
270 A=INT(14*RND)+2
280 IF A<2 THEN 270
290 IF A>14 THEN 270
300 B=INT(14*RND)+2
310 IF B<2 THEN 300
320 IF B>14 THEN 300
330 IF A>=B THEN 270
350 IF A<11 THEN 400
360 IF A=11 THEN 420
370 IF A=12 THEN 440
380 IF A=13 THEN 460
390 IF A=14 THEN 480
400 PRINT A
410 GOTO 500
420 PRINT "JACK"
430 GOTO 500
440 PRINT "QUEEN"
450 GOTO 500
460 PRINT "KING"
470 GOTO 500
480 PRINT "ACE"
500 IF B<11 THEN 550
510 IF B=11 THEN 570
520 IF B=12 THEN 590
530 IF B=13 THEN 610
540 IF B=14 THEN 630
550 PRINT B
560 GOTO 650
570 PRINT "JACK"
580 GOTO 650
590 PRINT "QUEEN"
600 GOTO 650
610 PRINT "KING"
620 GOTO 650
630 PRINT "ACE"
650 PRINT
660 INPUT "WHAT IS YOUR BET";M
670 IF M<>0 THEN 680
675 PRINT "CHICKEN!!":PRINT
677 GOTO 260
680 IF M<=Q THEN 730
690 PRINT "SORRY, MY FRIEND, BUT YOU BET TOO MUCH"
700 PRINT "YOU HAVE ONLY"Q"DOLLARS TO BET."
710 GOTO 650
730 C=INT(14*RND)+2
740 IF C<2 THEN 730
750 IF C>14 THEN 730
760 IF C<11 THEN 810
770 IF C=11 THEN 830
780 IF C=12 THEN 850
790 IF C=13 THEN 870
800 IF C=14 THEN 890
810 PRINT C
820 GOTO 910
830 PRINT "JACK"
840 GOTO 910
850 PRINT "QUEEN"
860 GOTO 910
870 PRINT "KING"
880 GOTO 910
890 PRINT "ACE"
910 IF C>A THEN 930
920 GOTO 970
930 IF C>=B THEN 970
950 PRINT "YOU WIN!!!"
960 GOTO 210
970 PRINT "SORRY, YOU LOSE."
980 IF M<Q THEN 240
1000 PRINT
1010 PRINT "SORRY, FRIEND, BUT YOU BLEW YOUR WAD."
1020 INPUT "TRY AGAIN (YES OR NO)";A$
1030 IF A$="YES" THEN 110
1040 PRINT:PRINT "O.K. HOPE YOU HAD FUN!!"
1050 END

READY
```

SAMPLE RUN

```
RUNNH
ACEY-DUCEY IS PLAYED IN THE FOLLOWING MANNER:
THE DEALER (COMPUTER) DEALS TWO CARDS FACE UP.
YOU HAVE THE OPTION TO BET OR NOT TO BET DEPENDING
ON WHETHER OR NOT YOU FEEL THE NEXT CARD WILL HAVE
A VALUE BETWEEN THE FIRST TWO.
IF YOU DO NOT WANT TO BET, INPUT A 0.

YOU NOW HAVE 100 DOLLARS.
HERE ARE YOUR NEXT TWO CARDS...
  6
  10

WHAT IS YOUR BET? 10
  6
SORRY, YOU LOSE.
YOU NOW HAVE 90 DOLLARS.
HERE ARE YOUR NEXT TWO CARDS...
  6
QUEEN

WHAT IS YOUR BET? 20
JACK
YOU WIN!!!
YOU NOW HAVE 110 DOLLARS.
HERE ARE YOUR NEXT TWO CARDS...
  10
KING

WHAT IS YOUR BET? 0
CHICKEN!!

HERE ARE YOUR NEXT TWO CARDS...
  2
  9

WHAT IS YOUR BET? 30
  10
SORRY, YOU LOSE.
YOU NOW HAVE 80 DOLLARS.
HERE ARE YOUR NEXT TWO CARDS...
  3
  8

WHAT IS YOUR BET? 20
  3
SORRY, YOU LOSE.
YOU NOW HAVE 60 DOLLARS.
HERE ARE YOUR NEXT TWO CARDS...
  9
QUEEN

WHAT IS YOUR BET? 0
CHICKEN!!

HERE ARE YOUR NEXT TWO CARDS...
  2
  4

WHAT IS YOUR BET? 0
CHICKEN!!

HERE ARE YOUR NEXT TWO CARDS...
  8
  10

WHAT IS YOUR BET? 0
CHICKEN!!

HERE ARE YOUR NEXT TWO CARDS...
  2
ACE

WHAT IS YOUR BET? 100
SORRY, MY FRIEND, BUT YOU BET TOO MUCH
YOU HAVE ONLY 60 DOLLARS TO BET.

WHAT IS YOUR BET? 60
  5
YOU WIN!!!
YOU NOW HAVE 120 DOLLARS.
HERE ARE YOUR NEXT TWO CARDS...
  5
  9

WHAT IS YOUR BET? 20
  2
SORRY, YOU LOSE.
YOU NOW HAVE 100 DOLLARS.
HERE ARE YOUR NEXT TWO CARDS...
  3
  8

WHAT IS YOUR BET? 90
  10
SORRY, YOU LOSE.
YOU NOW HAVE 10 DOLLARS.
HERE ARE YOUR NEXT TWO CARDS...
  2
JACK

WHAT IS YOUR BET? 10
QUEEN
SORRY, YOU LOSE.

SORRY, FRIEND, BUT YOU BLEW YOUR WAD.
TRY AGAIN (YES OR NO)? NO

O.K. HOPE YOU HAD FUN!!
```

AMAZIN

DRAW A MAZE

Description

This program will print out a different maze every time it
is run and guarantees only one path through. You can choose
the dimensions of the maze--i.e. the number of squares wide
and long.

Computer Limitations

The amount of memory available will determine the maximum
size maze that may be constructed. An 8K EduSystem 20
initialized for one user can draw a 13x13 maze. RSTS/E
can draw a 23 (width of paper limit) x 50 maze, even larger
using virtual memory.

Experiment on your system with the maze dimensions in
Statement 110.

Program Author

Jack Hauber
Loomis School
Windsor, CT 06095

PROGRAM LISTING

AMAZIN EDUSYSTEM 30

```
100 RANDOMIZE
110 DIM W(25,103),V(25,103)
120 PRINT "WHAT ARE YOUR WIDTH AND LENGTH?"
121 INPUT H,V
122 PRINT
130 IF H<>1 THEN 150
131 IF V<>1 THEN 150
132 PRINT "MEANINGLESS DIMENSIONS, TRY AGAIN"
140 PRINT
141 GO TO 120
150 PRINT
151 PRINT
160 LET Q=0
161 LET Z=0
162 LET X=INT(RND(0)*H+1)
163 FOR I=1 TO H
170 IF I=X THEN 173
171 PRINT ":--";
172 GO TO 180
173 PRINT ":   ";
180 NEXT I
190 PRINT":"
191 LET C=1
192 LET W(X,1)=C
193 LET C=C+1
200 LET R=X
201 LET S=1
202 GO TO 260
210 IF R<>H THEN 240
211 IF S<>V THEN 230
220 LET R=1
221 LET S=1
222 GO TO 250
230 LET R=1
231 LET S=S+1
232 GO TO 250
240 LET R=R+1
250 IF W(R,S)=0 THEN 210
260 IF R-1=0 THEN 530
261 IF W(R-1,S)<>0 THEN 530
270 IF S-1=0 THEN 390
280 IF W(R,S-1)<>0 THEN 390
290 IF R=H THEN 330
300 IF W(R+1,S)<>0 THEN 330
310 LET X=INT(RND(0)*3+1)
320 IF X=1 THEN 790
321 IF X=2 THEN 820
323 IF X=3 THEN 860
330 IF S<>V THEN 340
331 IF Z=1 THEN 370
332 LET Q=1
333 GO TO 350
340 IF W(R,S+1)<>0 THEN 370
350 LET X=INT(RND(0)*3+1)
360 IF X=1 THEN 790
361 IF X=2 THEN 820
362 IF X=3 THEN 910
370 LET X=INT(RND(0)*2+1)
380 IF X=1 THEN 790
381 IF X=2 THEN 820
390 IF R=H THEN 470
400 IF W(R+1,S)<>0 THEN 470
401 IF S<>V THEN 420
410 IF Z=1 THEN 450
411 LET Q=1
412 GO TO 430
420 IF W(R,S+1)<>0 THEN 450
430 LET X=INT(RND(0)*3+1)
440 IF X=1 THEN 790
441 IF X=2 THEN 860
442 IF X=3 THEN 910
450 LET X=INT(RND(0)*2+1)
460 IF X=1 THEN 790
461 IF X=2 THEN 860
470 IF S<>V THEN 490
480 IF Z=1 THEN 520
481 LET Q=1
482 GO TO 500
490 IF W(R,S+1)<>0 THEN 520
500 LET X=INT(RND(0)*2+1)
510 IF X=1 THEN 790
511 IF X=2 THEN 910
520 GO TO 790
530 IF S-1=0 THEN 670
540 IF W(R,S-1)<>0 THEN 670
541 IF R=H THEN 610
542 IF W(R+1,S)<>0 THEN 610
550 IF S<>V THEN 560
551 IF Z=1 THEN 590
552 LET Q=1
553 GO TO 570
560 IF W(R,S+1)<>0 THEN 590
570 LET X=INT(RND(0)*3+1)
580 IF X=1 THEN 820
581 IF X=2 THEN 860
582 IF X=3 THEN 910
590 LET X=INT(RND(0)*2+1)
600 IF X=1 THEN 820
601 IF X=2 THEN 860
610 IF S<>V THEN 630
620 IF Z=1 THEN 660
621 LET Q=1
622 GO TO 640
630 IF W(R,S+1)<>0 THEN 660
640 LET X=INT(RND(0)*2+1)
650 IF X=1 THEN 820
651 IF X=2 THEN 910
660 GO TO 820
670 IF R=H THEN 740
680 IF W(R+1,S)<>0 THEN 740
681 IF S<>V THEN 700
690 IF Z=1 THEN 730
691 LET Q=1
692 GO TO 830
700 IF W(R,S+1)<>0 THEN 730
710 LET X=INT(RND(0)*2+1)
720 IF X=1 THEN 860
721 IF X=2 THEN 910
730 GO TO 860
740 IF S<>V THEN 760
750 IF Z=1 THEN 780
751 LET Q=1
752 GO TO 770
760 IF W(R,S+1)<>0 THEN 780
770 GO TO 910
780 GO TO 1000
790 LET W(R-1,S)=C
800 LET C=C+1
801 LET V(R-1,S)=2
802 LET R=R-1
810 IF C=H*V+1 THEN 1010
811 LET Q=0
812 GO TO 260
820 LET W(R,S-1)=C
830 LET C=C+1
840 LET V(R,S-1)=1
841 LET S=S-1
842 IF C=H*V+1 THEN 1010
850 LET Q=0
851 GO TO 260
860 LET W(R+1,S)=C
870 LET C=C+1
871 IF V(R,S)=0 THEN 880
872 LET V(R,S)=3
873 GO TO 890
880 LET V(R,S)=2
890 LET R=R+1
900 IF C=H*V+1 THEN 1010
902 GO TO 530
910 IF Q=1 THEN 960
920 LET W(R,S+1)=C
921 LET C=C+1
922 IF V(R,S)=0 THEN 940
930 LET V(R,S)=3
931 GO TO 950
940 LET V(R,S)=1
950 LET S=S+1
951 IF C=H*V+1 THEN 1010
952 GO TO 260
960 LET Z=1
970 IF V(R,S)=0 THEN 980
971 LET V(R,S)=3
972 LET Q=0
973 GO TO 1000
980 LET V(R,S)=1
981 LET Q=0
982 LET R=1
990 LET S=1
991 GO TO 250
1000 GO TO 210
1010 FOR J=1 TO V
1011 PRINT"I";
1012 FOR I=1 TO H
1013 IF V(I,J)<2 THEN 1030
1020 PRINT"   ";
1021 GO TO 1040
1030 PRINT"   I";
1040 NEXT I
1041 PRINT
1043 FOR I=1 TO H
1045 IF V(I,J)=0 THEN 1060
1050 IF V(I,J)=2 THEN 1060
1051 PRINT":  ";
1052 GO TO 1070
1060 PRINT ":--";
1070 NEXT I
1071 PRINT":"
1072 NEXT J
1073 END
```

SAMPLE RUN

AMAZIN EDUSYSTEM 30

WHAT ARE YOUR WIDTH AND LENGTH?
?9,7

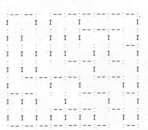

READY

16

ANIMAL

COMPUTER GUESSES YOUR ANIMAL

Description

Unlike other computer games in which the computer picks a
number or letter and you must guess what it is, in this
game you think of an animal and the computer asks you
questions and tries to guess the name of your animal. If
the computer guesses incorrectly, it will ask you for a
question that differentiates the animal it guessed from the
one you were thinking of. In this way the computer "learns"
new animals. Questions to differentiate new animals should
be input without a question mark.

IMPORTANT: At the end of a playing session, to the question,
"ARE YOU THINKING OF AN ANIMAL," you must respond "SAVE"
in order that the computer save all the new animals you have
introduced. To that same question, at any point in the game,
if you respond "LIST," the computer will tell you all the
animals it knows so far.

The program starts originally by knowing only "FISH" and
"BIRD." Additional animals are stored in the file "ANIMAL.GME."

Computer Limitations

This program was written for a DIGITAL RSTS-11 and uses several
unique features, in particular, multiple user access to a
common data file and several advanced string handling functions.
It has been converted with some minor changes to OS/8 BASIC
and could be adapted to other systems as well.

Program Author

Nathan Teichholtz
Digital Equipment Corporation
Maynard, MA 01754

PROGRAM LISTING

```
                        CREATED 06-APR-73   04:44 PM

100 &"PLAY 'GUESS THE ANIMAL' WITH RSTS
150 &"THINK OF AN ANIMAL AND THE COMPUTER WILL TRY TO GUESS IT..."!&
500 DIM A$(200)
525 F$="ANIMAL.GME"
        !ON ERROR GOTO 700
550 OPEN F$ FOR INPUT AS FILE 1%
        !INPUT #1%,N%
        !INPUT #1,A$(I%) FOR I%=1%TO N%
        !CLOSE 1%
        !A$(0%)=NUM$(N%)
        !ON ERROR GOTO 0
        !GOTO 1300
700 ON ERROR GOTO 1050
        !F$="$"+F$
        !RESUME 550
1050 READ A$(I%) FOR I%=0% TO 3%
1100 DATA "4","\QDOES IT SWIM\Y2\N3\","\AFISH","\ABIRD"
1300 INPUT "ARE YOU THINKING OF AN ANIMAL";Z9$
        !GOTO 1350 IF LEFT(Z9$,1%)="Y"
        !GOTO 1300 IF LEFT(Z9$,1%)=="N"
1310 IF Z9$="SAVE" THEN
                OPEN "ANIMAL.GME" FOR OUTPUT AS FILE 1%
                !PRINT #1%,A$(I%) FOR I%=0% TO VAL(A$(0%))
                !PRINT #1,CHR$(26%)
                !CLOSE 1%
                !GOTO 1300
1320 IF Z9$="LIST" THEN
        PRINT "ANIMALS I ALREADY KNOW ARE:"
        !PRINT RIGHT(A$(I%),3%), IF INSTR(1%,A$(I%),"\A") FOR I%=1% TO 200%
        !PRINT
        !GOTO 1300
1350 K%=1%
1400 K%=FNA%(A$(K%))
        !GOTO 3000 IF LEN(A$(K%))=0%
        !GOTO 1400 IF LEFT(A$(K%),2%)="\Q"
        !PRINT "IS IT A "RIGHT(A$(K%),3%)
        !INPUT Z7$
        !Z7$=LEFT(Z7$,1%)
1450 IF Z7$="Y" THEN
        PRINT "WHY NOT TRY ANOTHER ANIMAL"
        !GOTO 1300
2000 INPUT "THE ANIMAL YOU WERE THINKING OF WAS A ";Z9$
2050 PRINT "PLEASE TYPE IN A QUESTION THAT WOULD DISTINGUISH A "
        Z9$ " FROM A "RIGHT(A$(K%),3%)
        !INPUT Z8$
2100 PRINT "FOR A "Z9$" THE ANSWER WOULD BE";
        !INPUT Z7$
        !Z7$=LEFT(Z7$,1%)
        !IF Z7$="Y" THEN Z6$="N"
                ELSE IF Z7$="N" THEN Z6$="Y"
                ELSE PRINT "PLEASE ANSWER 'YES' OR 'NO'"
                !GOTO 2100
2200 Z1%=VAL(A$(0%))
        !A$(0%)=NUM$(Z1%+2%)
        !A$(Z1%)=A$(K%)
        !A$(Z1%+1%)="\A"+Z9$
        !A$(K%)="\Q"+Z8$+"\"+Z7$+NUM$(Z1%+1%)+"\"+Z6$+NUM$(Z1%)+"\"
2300 GOTO 1300
3000 DEF FNA%(Q$)
        !PRINT MID(Q$,3%,INSTR(3%,Q$,"\")-3%);
        !INPUT Z9$
        !Z9$=LEFT(Z9$,1%)
        !Z9$="N" IF Z9$<>"Y"
        !Z1%=INSTR(3%,Q$,"\"+Z9$)+2%
        !Z2%=INSTR(Z1%,Q$,"\")
        !FNA%=VAL(MID(Q$,Z1%,Z2%-Z1%))
        !FNEND
9999 END
```

SAMPLE RUN

```
PLAY 'GUESS THE ANIMAL' WITH RSTS
THINK OF AN ANIMAL AND THE COMPUTER WILL TRY TO GUESS IT...

ARE YOU THINKING OF AN ANIMAL? YES
DOES IT SWIM? YES
IS IT A FISH? NO
THE ANIMAL YOU WERE THINKING OF WAS A ? SEAL
PLEASE TYPE IN A QUESTION THAT WOULD DISTINGUISH A SEAL FROM A FISH
? DOES IT HAVE FLIPPERS
FOR A SEAL THE ANSWER WOULD BE? YES
ARE YOU THINKING OF AN ANIMAL? YES
DOES IT SWIM? NO
IS IT A BIRD? NO
THE ANIMAL YOU WERE THINKING OF WAS A ? ELEPHANT
PLEASE TYPE IN A QUESTION THAT WOULD DISTINGUISH A ELEPHANT FROM A BIRD
? DOES IT HAVE A TRUNK
FOR A ELEPHANT THE ANSWER WOULD BE? YES
ARE YOU THINKING OF AN ANIMAL? YES
DOES IT SWIM? NO
DOES IT HAVE A TRUNK? NO
IS IT A BIRD? NO
THE ANIMAL YOU WERE THINKING OF WAS A ? DOG
PLEASE TYPE IN A QUESTION THAT WOULD DISTINGUISH A DOG FROM A BIRD
? DOES IT GO 'ARF, ARF'
FOR A DOG THE ANSWER WOULD BE? YES
ARE YOU THINKING OF AN ANIMAL? YES
DOES IT SWIM? NO
DOES IT HAVE A TRUNK? NO
DOES IT GO 'ARF? NO
IS IT A BIRD? NO
THE ANIMAL YOU WERE THINKING OF WAS A ? CAT
PLEASE TYPE IN A QUESTION THAT WOULD DISTINGUISH A CAT FROM A BIRD
? DOES IT HAVE RETRACTIBLE CLAWS
FOR A CAT THE ANSWER WOULD BE? YES
ARE YOU THINKING OF AN ANIMAL? YES
DOES IT SWIM? NO
DOES IT HAVE A TRUNK? NO
DOES IT GO 'ARF? NO
DOES IT HAVE RETRACTIBLE CLAWS? YES
IS IT A CAT? NO
THE ANIMAL YOU WERE THINKING OF WAS A ? TIGER
PLEASE TYPE IN A QUESTION THAT WOULD DISTINGUISH A TIGER FROM A CAT
? DOES IT LIVE IN THE JUNGLE
FOR A TIGER THE ANSWER WOULD BE? YES
ARE YOU THINKING OF AN ANIMAL? YES
DOES IT SWIM? NO
DOES IT HAVE A TRUNK? NO
DOES IT GO 'ARF? NO
DOES IT HAVE RETRACTIBLE CLAWS? NO
IS IT A BIRD? NO
THE ANIMAL YOU WERE THINKING OF WAS A ? COW
PLEASE TYPE IN A QUESTION THAT WOULD DISTINGUISH A COW FROM A BIRD
? DOES IT GIVE MILK AND GO 'MOO'
FOR A COW THE ANSWER WOULD BE? YES
ARE YOU THINKING OF AN ANIMAL? YES
DOES IT SWIM? NO
DOES IT HAVE A TRUNK? NO
DOES IT GO 'ARF? NO
DOES IT HAVE RETRACTIBLE CLAWS? NO
DOES IT GIVE MILK AND GO 'MOO'? NO
IS IT A BIRD? NO
THE ANIMAL YOU WERE THINKING OF WAS A ? GOAT
PLEASE TYPE IN A QUESTION THAT WOULD DISTINGUISH A GOAT FROM A BIRD
? DOES IT GIVE MILK AND EAT TIN CANS AND ALMOST ANYTHING ELSE
FOR A GOAT THE ANSWER WOULD BE? YES
ARE YOU THINKING OF AN ANIMAL? YES
DOES IT SWIM? YES
DOES IT HAVE FLIPPERS? NO
IS IT A FISH? NO
THE ANIMAL YOU WERE THINKING OF WAS A ? WHALE
PLEASE TYPE IN A QUESTION THAT WOULD DISTINGUISH A WHALE FROM A FISH
? IS IT THE LARGEST KNOWN MAMMAL
FOR A WHALE THE ANSWER WOULD BE? YES
ARE YOU THINKING OF AN ANIMAL? LIST
ANIMALS I ALREADY KNOW ARE:
SEAL            ELEPHANT        DOG             CAT             TIGER
COW             BIRD            GOAT            FISH            WHALE

ARE YOU THINKING OF AN ANIMAL? YES
DOES IT SWIM? NO
DOES IT HAVE A TRUNK? NO
DOES IT GO 'ARF? NO
DOES IT HAVE RETRACTIBLE CLAWS? NO
DOES IT GIVE MILK AND GO 'MOO'? NO
DOES IT GIVE MILK AND EAT TIN CANS AND ALMOST ANYTHING ELSE? NO
IS IT A BIRD? NO
THE ANIMAL YOU WERE THINKING OF WAS A ? SHEEP
PLEASE TYPE IN A QUESTION THAT WOULD DISTINGUISH A SHEEP FROM A BIRD
? DOES IT HAVE A WOOLY COAT AND SAY 'BAA, BAA'
FOR A SHEEP THE ANSWER WOULD BE? YES
ARE YOU THINKING OF AN ANIMAL? YES
DOES IT SWIM? NO
DOES IT HAVE A TRUNK? NO
DOES IT GO 'ARF? NO
DOES IT HAVE RETRACTIBLE CLAWS? YES
DOES IT LIVE IN THE JUNGLE? YES
IS IT A TIGER? NO
THE ANIMAL YOU WERE THINKING OF WAS A ? LION
PLEASE TYPE IN A QUESTION THAT WOULD DISTINGUISH A LION FROM A TIGER
? IS IT THE KING OF THE JUNGLE
FOR A LION THE ANSWER WOULD BE? YES
ARE YOU THINKING OF AN ANIMAL? SAVE
ARE YOU THINKING OF AN ANIMAL? NO
ARE YOU THINKING OF AN ANIMAL? ^C

READY
```

AWARI

also known as Kahla (we have)

REMOVE BEANS FROM THE PITS

Description

                              My SIDE

6	5	4	3	2	1
ooo	ooo	ooo	ooo	ooo	ooo

My   Your
HOME   HOME

ooo	ooo	ooo	ooo	ooo	ooo
1	2	3	4	5	6

                             Your SIDE

AWARI game is played with seven sticks and thirty-six stones
(beans) laid out as shown above. The board is divided into six
compartments (PITS) on 'my SIDE' and six on 'your SIDE'. In
addition, there are two special PITS at the ends: 'my HOME'
and 'your HOME'.

A MOVE is made by taking all of the beans from any (non-empty)
PIT on your own SIDE. Starting from the PIT to the right of
this one, these beans are 'SOWN' one in each PIT working around
the board anticlockwise.

A TURN consists of one or two MOVEs. If the last bean of your
MOVE is SOWN in your own HOME you may take a second MOVE.

If the last bean SOWN in a MOVE lands in an empty PIT, provided
that the opposite PIT is not empty, all the beans in the opposite
PIT, together with the last bean SOWN are 'captured' and moved
to the player's HOME.

When either side is empty, the game is finished. The player
with most beans in his HOME has won.

In the computer version, the board is printed as 14 numbers representing the 14 PITS.

```
        3  3  3  3  3  3
    0                      0
        3  3  3  3  3  3
```

The PITS on your (lower) SIDE are numbered 1-6 from left to right. The PITS on my (the computer's) SIDE are numbered from my left (your right).

To make a MOVE you type in the number of a PIT. If the last bean lands in your HOME, the computer types 'AGAIN?' and you then type in your second move.

The computer's MOVE is typed, followed by a diagram of the board in its new state. The computer always offers you the first move. This is considered to be a slight advantage.

There is a learning mechanism in the program that causes the play of the computer to improve as it plays more games.

Computer Limitations

This program is written in DIGITAL PDP-11 BASIC. The only unusual feature is that an IF statement may have the form:

    IF (CONDITION) THEN (STATEMENT)

Whenever the IF condition fails, the program branches to the next line.

Program Author

A version of AWARI, called KALAH, was submitted by Christopher Stolz of Lexington High School. The version published (also known as BEANS) along with the description above was written by:

Geoff Wyvill
Bradford University
Bradford, Yorkshire, England

PROGRAM LISTING

```
5 DATA0
10 DIMB(13),G(13),F(50):READN
15 FORI=0TON-1:READF(I):NEXTI
20 PRINT\PRINT "GAME OF *** AWARI ***"\E=0
25 FORI=0TO12:LETB(I)=3:NEXTI
30 LETC=0:LETF(N)=0:LETB(13)=0:LETB(6)=0
35 GOSUB500
40 PRINT"YOUR MOVE";:GOSUB110
45 IFE=0GOTO80
50 IFM=HTHENGOSUB100
55 IFE=0GOTO80
60 PRINT"MY MOVE IS ";:GOSUB800
65 IFE=0GOTO80
70 IFM=HTHENPRINT",";:GOSUB800
75 IFE>0GOTO35
80 PRINT:PRINT"GAME OVER"
85 LET D=B(6)-B(13):IF D<0 THEN PRINT "I WIN BY";-D"POINTS":GOTO 20
90 LETN=N+1:IFD=0THENPRINT"DRAWN GAME":GOTO 20
95 PRINT"YOU WIN BY"D"POINTS":GOTO20
100 PRINT"AGAIN"
110 INPUTM:IFM<7THENIFM>0THENLETM=M-1:GOTO130
120 PRINT"ILLEGAL MOVE":GOTO100
130 IFB(M)=0GOTO120
140 LETH=6:GOSUB200
150 GOTO500
200 LETK=M:GOSUB600
205 LETE=0:IFK>6THENLETK=K-7
210 LETC=C+1:IFC<9THENLETF(N)=F(N)*6+K
215 FORI=0TO5:IFB(I)<>0THEN230
220 NEXTI
225 RETURN
230 FORI=7TO12:IFB(I)<>0THENLETE=1:RETURN
235 GOTO 220
500 PRINT:PRINT"   "
505 FORI=12TO7STEP-1:GOSUB580
510 NEXTI
515 PRINT:LETI=13:GOSUB580
520 PRINT,"       ";:PRINTB(6):PRINT"   ";
525 FORI=0TO5:GOSUB580
530 NEXTI
535 PRINT:PRINT:RETURN
580 IFB(I)<10THENPRINT" ";
585 PRINTB(I);:RETURN
600 LETP=B(M):LETB(M)=0
605 FORP=PTO1STEP-1:LETM=M+1:IFM>13THENLETM=M-14
610 LETB(M)=B(M)+1:NEXTP
615 IFB(M)=1THENIFM<>6THENIFM<>13THENIFB(12-M)<>0GOTO625
620 RETURN
625 LETB(H)=B(H)+B(12-M)+1:LETB(M)=0:LETB(12-M)=0:RETURN
800 LETD=-99:LETH=13
805 FORI=0TO13:LETG(I)=B(I):NEXTI
810 FORJ=7TO12:IFB(J)=0THEN885
815 LETG=0:LETM=J:GOSUB600
820 FORI=0TO5:IFB(I)=0GOTO845
825 LETL=B(I)+I:LETR=0
830 IFL>13THENLETL=L-14:LETR=1:GOTO830
835 IFB(L)=0THENIFL<>6THENIFL<>13THENLETR=B(12-L)+R
840 IFR>QTHENLETQ=R
845 NEXTI
850 LETQ=B(13)-B(6)-Q:IFC<8GOTO875
855 LETK=J:IFK>6THENLETK=K-7
860 FORI=0TON-1:IFF(N)*6+K=INT(F(I)/6^(7-C)+.1)THENLETQ=Q-2
870 NEXTI
875 FORI=0TO13:LETB(I)=G(I):NEXTI
880 IFQ>=DTHENLETA=J:LETD=Q
885 NEXTJ
890 LETM=A:PRINTCHR$(42+M);:GOTO200
900 FORI=0TON-1:PRINTF(I):NEXTI
999 END
```

21

SAMPLE RUN

```
RUN
AWARI     01:23 PM          16-MAY-73

GAME OF *** AWARI ***

      3   3   3   3   3   3
  0                           0
      3   3   3   3   3   3

YOUR MOVE? 5

      3   3   3   3   3   4
  0                           1
      3   3   3   3   0   4

MY MOVE IS 2
      3   4   4   4   0   4
  0                           1
      3   3   3   3   0   4

YOUR MOVE? 4

      3   4   4   4   0   4
  0                           2
      3   3   3   0   1   5

AGAIN? 1

      3   4   4   0   0   4
  0                           7
      0   4   4   0   1   5

MY MOVE IS 4
      0   5   0   0   0   4
  6                           7
      0   4   4   0   1   5

YOUR MOVE? 3

      0   5   0   0   0   4
  6                           8
      0   4   0   1   2   6

AGAIN? 5

      0   5   0   0   0   4
  6                           9
      0   4   0   1   0   7

MY MOVE IS 5
      1   0   0   0   0   4
  7                           9
      1   5   1   1   0   7

YOUR MOVE? 2

      1   0   0   0   0   4
  7                           10
      1   0   2   2   1   8

AGAIN? 3

      1   0   0   0   0   4
  7                           10
      1   0   0   3   2   8

MY MOVE IS 6,1
      0   1   1   1   1   0
  8                           10
      1   0   0   3   2   8

YOUR MOVE? 5

      0   1   1   1   1   0
  8                           11
      1   0   0   3   0   9

AGAIN? 4

      0   1   1   1   1   0
  8                           12
      1   0   0   0   1   10

MY MOVE IS 5
      0   0   1   1   1   0
 10                           12
      0   0   0   0   1   10

YOUR MOVE? 6

 11   1   0   2   2   2   1
                              15
      1   0   0   0   1   0

MY MOVE IS 6,4
      0   1   0   2   2   1
 14                           15
      0   0   0   0   1   0

YOUR MOVE? 5

      0   1   0   2   2   0
 14                           17
      0   0   0   0   0   0


GAME OVER
YOU WIN BY 3 POINTS
```

21

BAGLES

Description

The computer picks a 3-digit secret number and you attempt
to guess what it is. You are allowed up to twenty guesses.
No digit is repeated. After each guess the computer will
give you clues about your guess as follows:

PICO   One digit is correct, but in the wrong place
FERMI   One digit is in the correct place
BAGLES   No digit is correct

You will learn to draw inferences from the clues and, with
practice, you'll learn to improve your score. There are
several good strategies for playing BAGLES. After you have
found a good strategy, see if you can improve it. Or try
a different strategy altogether and see if it is any better.

This program was submitted from several sources including
Dartmouth and U.C.-Berkeley. The one published here is
from U.C.

Program Authors

D. Resek, P. Rowe
Lawrence Hall of Science
University of California
Berkeley, CA 94700

PROGRAM LISTING

```
LISTNH
5   REM *** BAGLES NUMBER GUESSING GAME
10  REM *** ORIGINAL SOURCE UNKNOWN BUT SUSPECTED TO BE LAWRENCE HALL
15  REM *** OF SCIENCE, U.C. BERKELEY.   MODIFIED FOR TIMESHARED-8
20  REM *** BY STUDENTS OF LEXINGTON HIGH SCHOOL, MA AND MODIFIED FOR
25  REM *** RSTS/E BY DAVE AHL OF DIGITAL 11/45 GROUP
30  DIM A1(6),A(3),B(3)
40  RANDOMIZE:Y=0:T=255
70  INPUT "GAME OF BAGLES.   WOULD YOU LIKE THE RULES (YES OR NO)";A$
90  IF A$="NO" THEN 150
100 PRINT:PRINT "I AM THINKING OF A THREE-DIGIT NUMBER.   TRY TO GUESS"
110 PRINT "MY NUMBER AND I WILL GIVE YOU CLUES AS FOLLOWS:"
120 PRINT "   PICO   - ONE DIGIT CORRECT BUT IN THE WRONG POSITION"
130 PRINT "   FERMI  - ONE DIGIT CORRECT AND IN THE RIGHT POSITION"
140 PRINT "   BAGLES - NO DIGITS CORRECT"
150 FOR I=1 TO 3
160 A(I)=INT(10*RND)
170 FOR J=1 TO I-1
180 IF A(I)=A(J) THEN 160
190 NEXT J
200 NEXT I
210 PRINT:PRINT "O.K.   I HAVE A NUMBER IN MIND."
220 FOR I=1 TO 20
230 PRINT "GUESS #"I;
240 INPUT A$
250 CHANGE A$ TO A1
255 IF A1(0)<>3 THEN 630
260 FOR J=1 TO 3
270 IF A1(J)<48 THEN 300
280 IF A1(J)>57 THEN 300
285 B(J)=A1(J)-48
290 NEXT J
295 GOTO 320
300 PRINT "WHAT?"
310 GOTO 230
320 IF B(1)=B(2) THEN 650
330 IF B(2)=B(3) THEN 650
340 IF B(3)=B(1) THEN 650
350 C=0:D=0
360 FOR J=1 TO 2
370 IF A(J)<>B(J+1) THEN 390
380 C=C+1
390 IF A(J+1)<>B(J) THEN 410
400 C=C+1
410 NEXT J
420 IF A(1)<>B(3) THEN 440
430 C=C+1
440 IF A(3)<>B(1) THEN 460
450 C=C+1
460 FOR J=1 TO 3
470 IF A(J)<>B(J) THEN 490
480 D=D+1
490 NEXT J
500 IF D=3 THEN 680
520 FOR J=1 TO C
530 PRINT "PICO ";
540 NEXT J
550 FOR J=1 TO D
560 PRINT "FERMI ";
570 NEXT J
580 IF C+D<>0 THEN 600
590 PRINT "BAGLES";
600 PRINT
605 NEXT I
610 PRINT "OH WELL"
615 PRINT "THAT'S 20 GUESSES. MY NUMBER WAS "100*A(1)+10*A(2)+A(3)
620 GOTO 700
630 PRINT "TRY GUESSING A THREE-DIGIT NUMBER. ":GOTO 230
650 PRINT "OH, I FORGOT TO TELL YOU THAT THE NUMBER I HAVE IN"
660 PRINT "MIND HAS NO TWO DIGITS THE SAME. ":GOTO 230
680 PRINT "YOU GOT IT!!!":PRINT
690 Y=Y+1
700 INPUT "PLAY AGAIN (YES OR NO)";A$
720 IF A$="YES" THEN 150
730 IF Y=0 THEN 750
740 PRINT:PRINT "A"Y"- POINT BAGLES BUFF!!"
750 PRINT "HOPE YOU HAD FUN.   BYE. "
999 END

READY
```

SAMPLE RUN

```
RUNNH
GAME OF BAGLES.   WOULD YOU LIKE THE RULES (YES OR NO)? YES

I AM THINKING OF A THREE-DIGIT NUMBER.   TRY TO GUESS
MY NUMBER AND I WILL GIVE YOU CLUES AS FOLLOWS:
   PICO   - ONE DIGIT CORRECT BUT IN THE WRONG POSITION
   FERMI  - ONE DIGIT CORRECT AND IN THE RIGHT POSITION
   BAGLES - NO DIGITS CORRECT

O.K.   I HAVE A NUMBER IN MIND.
GUESS # 1 ? 123
PICO PICO
GUESS # 2 ? 412
PICO PICO
GUESS # 3 ? 215
PICO PICO FERMI
GUESS # 4 ? 251
YOU GOT IT!!!

PLAY AGAIN (YES OR NO)? YES

O.K.   I HAVE A NUMBER IN MIND.
GUESS # 1 ? 123
PICO PICO
GUESS # 2 ? 412
PICO FERMI
GUESS # 3 ? 215
PICO
GUESS # 4 ? 432
FERMI FERMI
GUESS # 5 ? 431
YOU GOT IT!!!

PLAY AGAIN (YES OR NO)? YES

O.K.   I HAVE A NUMBER IN MIND.
GUESS # 1 ? 123
PICO
GUESS # 2 ? 451
BAGLES
GUESS # 3 ? 267
BAGLES
GUESS # 4 ? 389
PICO PICO PICO
GUESS # 5 ? 893
PICO PICO PICO
GUESS # 6 ? 938
YOU GOT IT!!!

PLAY AGAIN (YES OR NO)? YES

O.K.   I HAVE A NUMBER IN MIND.
GUESS # 1 ? 123
BAGLES
GUESS # 2 ? 456
PICO
GUESS # 3 ? 478
PICO
GUESS # 4 ? 578
PICO PICO
GUESS # 5 ? 957
PICO FERMI
GUESS # 6 ? 750
PICO
GUESS # 7 ? 985
YOU GOT IT!!!

PLAY AGAIN (YES OR NO)? YES

O.K.   I HAVE A NUMBER IN MIND.
GUESS # 1 ? 123
PICO
GUESS # 2 ? 145
BAGLES
GUESS # 3 ? 267
PICO
GUESS # 4 ? 376
BAGLES
GUESS # 5 ? 892
FERMI FERMI
GUESS # 6 ? 802
PICO FERMI
GUESS # 7 ? 092
YOU GOT IT!!!

PLAY AGAIN (YES OR NO)? NO

A 5 - POINT BAGLES BUFF!!
HOPE YOU HAD FUN.   BYE.

READY
```

BANNER

PRINTS A LARGE BANNER

Description

This program creates a large banner on a terminal of any
message you input (up to 54 characters in length). The
letters may be any dimension you wish although the letter
height plus distance from left-hand side should not exceed
6 inches. Also, the letter height should be somewhat more
than the width. Adhering to these rules will generally produce
a very attractive banner.

Computer Limitations

BANNER was written for a DIGITAL EduSystem 50. For other
computers, the character string line input (LINPUT) statement
at Line 240 would have to be changed.

Program Author

Daniel R. Vernon
Butler Senior High School
Butler, PA 16001

```
100 REM        PROGRAM WRITTEN BY DANIEL R. VERNON
110 REM        SENIOR AT  BUTLER SENIOR HIGH SCHOOL
120 REM        BUTLER, PENNSYLVANIA 16001
130 REM        DATE: 2/1/73
140 REM        COMPUTER SUPERVISION- MR. WILLIAM ELLIS
150 REM        COMPUTER TOPICS INSTRUCTION- MR. ALBERT STEWART
160 REM
170 REM        THIS PROGRAM IS DESIGNED TO CREATE POSTERS
180 REM
190 DIMGS(6),HS(6),BS(9),G(6),A(54)
200 PRINT"INPUT HEIGHTH, WIDTH IN INCHES"J\INPUTL,R\S=0\A=R*2\C=A
210 PRINT"HOW FAR, IN INCHES FROM THE LEFT HAND SIDE, DO YOU WANT TO PLACE "
220 PRINT"THE LETTERS"J\INPUTS\S=12*S
230 PRINT"INPUT MESSAGE HERE"
240 LINPUTBS(1),BS(2),BS(3),BS(4),BS(5),BS(6),BS(7),BS(8),BS(9)
250 FORX=9TO1STEP=1\CHANGEBS(X)TOA\FORY=1TO6\A(X*6=6+Y)=A(Y)\NEXTY\NEXTX
260 FORX=1TO6\READHS(X)\NEXTX\HS=HS(L)\GOSUB 940
270 F=F+1\IFA(F)=0THEN990\G(0)=L\FORX=1TO6\G(X)=A(F)\NEXTX\CHANGEGTOGS
280 FORX=1TO6\G(0)=X\CHANGEGTOGS(X)\NEXTX
290 FORX=1TOA/2\PRINT\NEXTX
300 IFA(F)=46THEN345\IFA(F)=36THEN990\IFA(F)=32THEN630\IFA(F)<48THEN270
305 IFA(F)>57THEN310\ONA(F)=47GOTO500,440,620,625,635,550,615,605,595,585
310 IFA(F)<65THEN270\IFA(F)>79THEN330
320 ONA(F)=64GOTO350,360,370,380,390,400,410,430,440,450,460,470,480,490,500
330 IFA>90THEN270\ONA(F)=79GOTO510,520,540,550,560,570,580,590,600,610,620
340 GOTO270
345 FORX=1TOA\PRINTTAB(S)JGSJGS\NEXTX\GOTO270
350 GOSUB640\GOSUB690\GOSUB640\GOTO270
360 GOSUB640\GOSUB650\A=C*.5\GOSUB640\A=C\GOSUB810\GOTO270
370 GOSUB640\GOSUB700\GOSUB700\GOTO270
380 GOSUB640\GOSUB700\A=C*.5\GOSUB640\A=C\GOSUB840\GOTO270
390 GOSUB640\GOSUB650\GOSUB650\GOTO270
400 GOSUB640\GOSUB690\GOSUB690\GOTO270
410 GOSUB640\A=C*.75\GOSUB700\A=C*.25\GOSUB650\A=C\GOSUB760
420 A=C*.25\GOSUB710\A=C\GOTO270
430 GOSUB640\GOSUB710\GOSUB640\GOTO270
440 GOSUB640\GOTO270
450 GOSUB750\GOSUB640\GOSUB640\GOTO270
460 GOSUB640\GOSUB860\GOTO270
470 GOSUB640\GOSUB740\GOSUB740\GOTO270
480 GOSUB640\GOSUB890\GOSUB880\GOSUB640\GOTO270
490 GOSUB640\GOSUB890\GOSUB640\GOTO270
500 GOSUB640\GOSUB700\GOSUB640\GOTO270
510 GOSUB640\GOSUB690\GOSUB790\GOTO270
520 GOSUB640\A=C*.75\GOSUB700\A=.25=C\GOSUB650\A=C\GOSUB640
530 A=C*.25\GOSUB710\A=C\GOTO270
540 GOSUB640\GOSUB690\A=C*.5\GOSUB640\GOSUB810\A=C\GOTO270
550 GOSUB770\GOSUB650\GOSUB780\GOTO270
560 GOSUB780\GOSUB740\GOSUB640\GOTO270
570 GOSUB640\GOSUB740\GOSUB640\GOTO270
580 GOSUB890\GOSUB880\GOTO270
585 GOSUB790\GOSUB710\GOSUB640\GOTO270
590 GOSUB640\GOSUB880\GOSUB890\GOSUB640\GOTO270
595 GOSUB640\GOSUB650\GOSUB640\GOTO270
600 GOSUB900\GOTO270
605 GOSUB640\GOSUB780\GOSUB640\GOTO270
610 GOSUB970\GOSUB800\GOSUB960\GOTO270
615 GOSUB640\GOSUB650\GOSUB760\GOTO270
620 GOSUB920\GOTO270
625 GOSUB700\GOSUB650\A=C*.5\GOSUB640\A=C\GOSUB810\GOTO270
630 GOSUB940\GOTO270
635 GOSUB790\GOSUB710\GOSUB640\GOTO270
640 FORY=1TOA\PRINTTAB(S)J\FORX=1TO10\PRINTGSJ\NEXTX\PRINT\NEXTY\RETURN
653 IFA<1THEN660\GOTO670
660 LETA=1
670 FORX=1TOA\PRINTTAB(S)JGSJGSJHSJHSJGSJGSJHSJHSJGSJGS\NEXTX\RETURN
680 PRINTTAB(S)J
690 FORX=1TOA\PRINTTAB(4+L+S)JGSJGSJHSJHSJGSJGS\NEXTX\RETURN
700 FORX=1TOA\PRINTTAB(S)JGSJGSJ\PRINTTAB(8+L+S)JGSJGS\NEXTX\RETURN
710 IFA<1THEN720\GOTO730
720 LETA=1
730 FORX=1TOA\PRINTTAB(4+L+S)JGSJGS\NEXTX\RETURN
740 FORX=1TOA\PRINTTAB(S)JGSJGS\NEXTX\RETURN
750 FORX=1TOA\PRINTTAB(S)JGSJGSJGSJGS\NEXTX\RETURN
760 FORY=1TOA\PRINTTAB(S)JGSJGSJHSJHSJGSJGSJ\HSJHSJGSJGS\NEXTY\RETURN
770 FORX=1TOA\PRINTTAB(S)JGSJGSJHSJHSJGSJGSJGSJGSJGSJGS\NEXTX\RETURN
780 FORX=1TOA\PRINTTAB(8+L+S)JGSJGS\NEXTX\RETURN
790 FORX=1TOA\PRINTTAB(4+L+S)JGSJGSJGSJGSJGS\NEXTX\RETURN
800 FORX=1TOA\PRINTTAB(S)JGSJGSJGSJGSJGSJGS\NEXTX\RETURN
810 FORX=1TOC/2\PRINTTAB(S)J\FORY=1TO2\FORZ=1TO(5+L)=X\PRINTGSJ(1)J\NEXTZ
820 IFX>3THEN950\V=X
830 PRINTHS(2+V)J\NEXTY\PRINT\NEXTX\RETURN
840 FORX=1TOC/2\PRINTTAB(S)JHS(X)J\FORY=1TO10+L=(2+X)\PRINTGSJ(1)J\NEXTY\PRINT
850 NEXTX\RETURN
860 FOR X=4+LTO7+LSTEP14+L/(C*6)\PRINTTAB(X+S)JGSJGSJGSJ
870 PRINTTAB(7+L=X+S)JGSJGSJGS\NEXT X\RETURN
880 FORX=0TO6+LSTEP6+L/C\PRINTTAB(X+S)JGSJGSJGS\NEXTX\RETURN
890 FORX=6+LTO0STEP=6+L/C\PRINTTAB(X+S)JGSJGSJGSJGS\NEXTX\RETURN
900 FORX=0TO7+LSTEP(14+L)/(C*6)\PRINTTAB(X+S)JGSJGSJGSJ
910 PRINTTAB(7+L=X+S)JGSJGSJGS\NEXT X\RETURN
920 FORX=0TO7+LSTEP(7+L)/(C*3)\PRINTTAB(S)JGSJGSJTAB(X+S)JGSJGSJGSJ
930 PRINTTAB(8+L+S)JGSJGS\NEXTX\RETURN
940 FORX=1TOA+3\PRINT\NEXTX\RETURN
950 FORW=1TOX=3\PRINT"   "J\NEXTW\V=3\GOTO830
960 FORX=4+LTO7+LSTEPL+4/C\PRINTTAB(X+S)JGSJGSJGS\NEXTX\RETURN
970 FOR X=7+LTO4+LSTEP=4+L/C\PRINTTAB(X+S)JGSJGSJGS\NEXTX\RETURN
980 DATA" "," "," "," "," "," "," "," "," "
990 FORX=1TOC+3\PRINT\NEXTX
1000 END
```

SAMPLE RUN

BASEBL

BASEBALL GAME

Description

This is a simulation of a nine-inning baseball game with you
controlling the pitcher when your team has the field and
controlling the batter when you are up to bat. The simulation
stops at nine innings, hence, it may be a tie game; however,
that has proved to occur remarkably few times.

Computer Limitations

The game published was written for DIGITAL EduSystem 15/30/35
and actually consists of two programs, one which prints the
rules chained to the second program which plays the game.
"NOLINE" must be given before running to prevent overflow.
Other BASIC compilers will require conversion of the alphabetic
string input statements to a compatible format.

Source

Another version of baseball was submitted for Timeshared-8
by Jeff Moskow and Brad Golden of Lexington High School.
This is available from DECUS as BASIC 8-562. A second version
was submitted by another Lexington High School student, Les
Servie. A FORTRAN version was submitted by David Benepe of
Fort Worth, Texas. These versions are not printed herein.

Jack Huisman
Oregon Museum of Science and Industry
Portland, Oregon   97200

PROGRAM LISTING

```
BASBAL  EDUSYSTEM-35

100 DIMT(50),C(19),F(19),Z(19)
110 FORX=1TO19\READC(X),Z(X),F(X)\NEXTX\LETX=1
120 PRINT"WELCOME TO HUISMAN STADIUM FOR TODAY'S GREAT GAME BETWEEN"
130 PRINT"THE PDP-8 PANTHERS AND (YOUR NAME PLEASE) THE ";
140 FOR A=1 TO 99\INPUT ST(A)\IF T(A)=141 THEN 150\NEXT A
150 LETT=A\PRINT\PRINT"A HIGHLY PARTISAN CROWD OF";
160 FORA=1TOT\LETB=2*RND(0)\NEXTA
170 LET A=INT(70000*RND(1))\PRINTA;
180 PRINT"FANS IS ANXIOUSLY AWAITING THE"\PRINT"START OF THE GAME."
190 PRINT"HERE IS MY TEAM!","AND HERE IS YOURS!"
200 PRINT"NAME","AVERAGE","NAME","AVERAGE"
210 PRINT"----","-------","----","-------"
220 GOSUB 400
230 PRINT\PRINT
240 PRINT"THE PANTHERS ARE TAKING THE FIELD NOW AS ANDREWS OF THE"
250 FOR A=1 TO T-1\PRINT CHR$(T(A));\NEXT A
260 PRINT"ADVANCES TO THE PLATE.  PLEASE WAIT AS THE COMPUTER SINGS"
270 PRINT"OUR NATIONAL ANTHEM TO ITSELF - 2 OR 3 TIMES!  JUST SING"
280 PRINT"ALONG UNTIL ASKED FOR YOUR PLAY."\PRINT
290 GOTO580
300 DATA.05,.412001,.05,.02,.263001,.03
310 DATA-.02,.236001,.02,.03,.316001,-.01
320 DATA.01,.241001,.03,.02,.321001,.02
330 DATA-.02,.367001,.02,-.02,.386001,-.01
340 DATA.01,.295001,.03,-.01,.296001,.02
350 DATA-.02,.319001,.02,-.02,.285001,.02
360 DATA-.03,.295001,.01,.02,.295001,.03
370 DATA.02,.218001,.02,.02,.139001,-.02
380 DATA.03,.238001,.01,.03,.231001,-.02
390 DATA 0,0,0
400 PRINT"HUISMAN",Z(1),"KLOOS",Z(2)
410 PRINT"HOEREN",Z(3),"ANDREWS",Z(4)
420 PRINT"BACCUS",Z(5),"MAYER",Z(8)
430 PRINT"SMITH",Z(7),"HANSEN",Z(6)
440 PRINT"SCHNEIDER",Z(9),"MICHEL",Z(10)
450 PRINT"ROSENBAUM",Z(11),"P. D. PEATE",Z(12)
460 PRINT"POULSEN",Z(13),"WILLIAMS",Z(14)
470 PRINT"KILGOUR",Z(15),"NELSON",Z(16)
480 PRINT "JOHNSON",Z(17),"ANKCORN",Z(18)
490 PRINT"WHITNEY"," MANAGER","IVEY"," MANAGER"\PRINT
500 PRINT"PITCHER'S OPTIONS ARE!"\PRINT"FASTBALL"
510 PRINT"BEANBALL"\PRINT"BRUSHBACK"\PRINT"BALL"\PRINT"CURVE"
520 PRINT"SLIDER"\PRINT"KNUCKLE"\PRINT"GREASEBALL (ILLEGAL)"
530 PRINT"SPITBALL (ILLEGAL)"\PRINT"CHECK"\PRINT
540 PRINT"BATTER'S OPTIONS ARE!"\PRINT"BUNT"\PRINT"SWING"
550 PRINT"HIT-AWAY"\PRINT"SACRIFICE"\PRINT"GROUNDER"\PRINT"FLY"
560 PRINT"KILL"\PRINT
570 RETURN
580 CHAIN"BASBL1"
590 END



BASBL1  EDUSYSTEM-35

100 DIMB(16)
110 LETZ(0)=.5\LETZ=.5
120 LETI=1
130 LETB1=0\LETB2=0\LETB3=0\LETI1=0\LETI2=0\LETI3=0
140 LETC1=0\LETC2=0\PRINT
150 IFC2<>4THEN160\PRINT"THE BATTER WALKS."\GOSUB920\GOTO140
160 IFC1<>3THEN180\PRINT"THE BATTER STRUCK OUT."\LET C3=C3+1\GOTO140
170 IF S1=1THEN180\LETX=X+1
180 IFC3<3THEN270\IFS1=1THEN190\LETS1=1\GOTO200
190 PRINT"AFTER";I;"INNINGS"\LETI=I+1\LETS1=0
200 PRINTI2;"RUNS,";I1;"HITS,";I3;"ERRORS AND";B1+B2+B3;"LEFT ON BASE."
210 IFI=5THEN1420\IFS1=0THEN230\PRINT"I'M";\GOTO240
220 IFS1=0THEN230\PRINT"I'M";\GOTO240
230 PRINT"YOU'RE";
240 PRINT" UP NOW."\PRINT"SCORE: ME";S2;"YOU";S3
250 PRINT\LETC3=0
260 GOTO130
270 PRINT"YOUR PLAY? ";
280 FORA=1TO20\INPUTSB(A)\IFB(A)=141THEN290\NEXTA
290 LETD=1*RND(5)\PRINT
300 LETC=100*B(1)+B(2)\IF S1=0THEN420
310 IFC<>19713THEN320\LETD=D+C(X)\GOTO1280
320 IFC<>19993THEN330\LETD=D+F(X)\GOTO1280
330 IFC=19597THEN1280
340 IFC=19610THEN1280
350 IFC=21304THEN1280
360 IFC=20506THEN1280
370 IFC<>20110THEN380\IFD<.8THEN1280\GOTO1270
380 IFC<>21308THEN390\IFD<.8THEN1280\GOTO1280
390 IFC<>19700THEN400\PRINT"RUNNERS ARE STICKING."\GOTO270
400 IFC<>19593THEN410\PRINT"MY BATTER";\GOTO1300
410 FORA1=ATOA-1\PRINTCHR$(B(A1));\NEXTA1\PRINT" 2"\GOTO270
420 IFC<>19613THEN430\PRINT"YOUR BATTER";\GOSUB570\GOTO140
430 IFC=21315THEN1280
440 IFC<>19700THEN450\PRINT"CHECK NOT YET IN."\GOTO270
450 IFC=20201THEN1280
460 IFC<>21312THEN470\PRINT"STEAL NOT YET IN."\GOTO270
470 IFC=21293THEN1280
480 IFC=20110THEN1280
490 IFC=20004THEN1280
500 IFC=20501THEN1280
510 GOTO410
520 LETA=9*RND(6)\IFS1=0THEN530\PRINT"MY BATTER";\GOTO540
530 PRINT"YOUR BATTER";
540 IFA>1THEN550\PRINT" LINED OUT TO THE THIRD BASEMAN."\GOTO840
550 IFA>2THEN560\PRINT" POPPED OUT IN SHALLOW LEFT."\GOTO840
560 IFA>3THEN580
570 PRINT" GROUNDED TO THE PITCHER";\GOTO590
580 IFA>4THEN680\PRINT" GROUNDED TO SHORTSTOP";
590 PRINT" WHO THREW OUT THE MAN";\IFC3=2THEN670
600 IFB1=0THEN670\IFB2=0THEN630\IFB3=0THEN620\PRINT" FORCED HOME."
610 GOTO850
620 PRINT" FORCED TO THIRD."\GOTO850
630 LETA1=INT(3*RND(0))\PRINT" FORCED TO SECOND";\IFA1<>1THEN650
640 PRINT"."\GOTO850
650 PRINT\PRINT"AND THEN TO FIRST FOR A DOUBLE PLAY!"
660 LETC3=C3+1\LETB1=0\GOTO840
670 PRINT" AT FIRST,"\GOTO840
680 IFA>5THEN700\PRINT" HIT A FLY INTO DEEP CENTER WHERE IT WAS";
690 PRINT" CAUGHT,"\GOTO710
700 IFA>6THEN880\PRINT" HIT TO LEFT FIELD FOR AN OUT."
710 IFC3=2THEN840\IFB1+B2+B3=0THEN840
720 PRINT"THE MAN ON";\IFB1=1THEN750\GOTO790
730 PRINT" THIRD MADE IT HOME,";\GOSUB930\LETB3=0
740 IFB2=0THEN780
750 PRINT" SECOND";\IFA1=0THEN760\PRINT" STAYED PUT."\GOTO780
760 IFA1>1THEN770\PRINT" MADE IT TO THIRD,"\LETB3=1\LETB2=0\GOTO780
770 PRINT" WAS OUT TRYING TO TAKE THIRD,"\LETC3=C3+1\LETB2=2
780 IFB1<>1THEN840
790 IFB2<>1THEN800\PRINT" FIRST STUCK,"\GOTO840
800 PRINT" ON FIRST";\IFB2<>2THEN820
810 PRINT" MADE IT TO SECOND,"\LETB2=1\LETB1=0\GOTO840
820 LETW=2*RND(0)\IFW>1THEN810\PRINT" WAS OUT GOING,"\LETC3=C3+1
830 LETB2=0
840 LETZ(Y)=Z(Y)-(Z(Y)/100)\GOTO860
850 LETZ(Y)=Z(Y)+(Z(Y)/100)
860 LETC3=C3+1\PRINT"THAT WAS OUT NUMBER";C3
870 GOTO1260
880 IFA>7THEN890\PRINT" HIT OVER THE PITCHER'S HEAD FOR A";\GOTO910
890 IFA>8THEN900\PRINT" HIT THROUGH THE HOLE INTO RIGHT FOR A";\GOTO910
900 PRINT" HIT INTO LEFT FIELD FOR A";
910 IFZ>4THEN920\IFZ>3=DTHEN1130\IFZ>2=DTHEN1040\PRINT" SINGLE."
920 IFB3=0THEN970\GOSUB930\LETB3=0\GOTO960
930 IFS1=1THEN940\LETS3=S3+1\GOTO950
940 LETS2=S2+1
950 LETI2=I2+1\RETURN
960 PRINT"THE MAN ON THIRD SCORED,"
970 IFB2=0THEN1000\PRINT"THE MAN ON SECOND";\IFA>8THEN990\PRINT" SCORED."
980 GOSUB930\LETB2=0\GOTO1000
990 PRINT" WENT TO THIRD,"\LETB2=0\LETB3=1
1000 IFB1=0THEN1030\PRINT"THE MAN ON FIRST";\IFA>8THEN1020
1010 IFC2=4THEN1020\LETB1=0\GOTO990
1020 PRINT" TO SECOND,"\LETB2=1
1030 LETB1=1\GOTO1240
1040 LETW=3*RND(0)\IFW>1THEN1050\PRINT"N OFF THE WALL";
1050 IFA2=1THEN1060\PRINT" STAND UP";
1060 PRINT" DOUBLE,"\IFB3=0THEN1080\PRINT"THE MAN ON THIRD SCORED."
1070 GOSUB930\LETB3=0
1080 IFB2=0THEN1090\PRINT"THE MAN ON SECOND SCORED."\GOSUB930\LETB2=0
1090 IFB1=0THEN1120\PRINT"THE MAN ON FIRST";\IFA>8THEN1110\PRINT" SCORED."
1100 GOSUB930\LETB1=0\GOTO1120
1110 PRINT" WENT TO THIRD,"\LET B1=0\LETB3=1
1120 LETB2=1\GOTO1240
1130 PRINT" TRIPLE!"\LETA3=B1+B2+B3\IFA3=0THEN1200\PRINT"THE MAN ON";
1140 IFB1=0THEN1150\PRINT" FIRST"\GOSUB930
1150 IFB2=0THEN1170\IFB1=0THEN1160\PRINT", AND";
1160 PRINT" SECOND"\GOSUB930
1170 IFB3=0THEN1190\IFB1+B2=0THEN1180\PRINT", AND";
1180 PRINT" THIRD"\GOSUB930
1190 PRINT" SCORED,"\LETB1=0\LETB2=0
1200 LETB3=1\GOTO1240
1210 IFB1+B2+B3<3THEN1220\PRINT" GRAND SLAM";
1220 PRINT" HOME RUN!!"\FORA1=1TO(B1+B2+B3+1)\GOSUB930\NEXTA1
1230 LETB1=0\LETB2=0\LETB3=0
1240 IFC2=4THEN1260\LETZ(Y)=Z(Y)+(Z(Y)/100)
1250 LETI1=I1+1
1260 RETURN
1270 PRINT"PITCHER THROWN OUT FOR THROWING ILLEGAL PITCH."\GOTO270
1280 LETA=5*RND(0)\IFA<3THEN1320
1290 IFA>4THEN1300\PRINT"INSIDE - ";\GOTO1310
1300 PRINT"OUTSIDE - ";
1310 LETC2=C2+1\PRINT"BALL";C2\GOTO150
1320 IFZ(Y)<DTHEN1340\GOSUB520\IFA<6THEN1330\LETC(Y)=C(Y)+1\GOTO140
1330 LETC(Y)=C(Y)-1\GOTO140
1340 LETC(Y)=C(Y)-1\LETB=3*RND(7)
1350 IFB>4THEN1360\PRINT"A SWING & A MISS = ";\GOTO1390
1360 IFB>2THEN1380\PRINT"INSIDE CORNER - CALL ";
1370 GOTO1390
1380 PRINT"FOUL - ";\IFC1=2THEN1400
1390 LETC1=C1+1\PRINT" STRIKE";C1\GOTO150
1400 PRINT"COUNT STAYS AT";C2;"BALLS AND";C1;
1410 PRINT" STRIKES,"\GOTO150
1420 PRINT"FINAL SCORE: ME";S2;"YOU";S3
1430 IFS2>S3THEN1450\IFS3=S2THEN1440\PRINT"YOU WON,"\GOTO1460
1440 PRINT"A DRAW!"\GOTO1460
1450 PRINT"I WON!"
1460 CHAIN"DEMON "
1470 END
```

SAMPLE RUN

```
RUN
BASEBL   01:38 PM          16-MAY-73
WELCOME TO HUISMAN STADIUM FOR TODAY'S GREAT GAME BETWEEN
THE PDP-8 PANTHERS AND (YOUR NAME PLEASE) THE ? RSTS/E ROCKETS

A HIGHLY PARTISAN CROWD OF 53971 FANS IS ANXIOUSLY AWAITING THE
START OF THE GAME.
HERE IS MY TEAM:             AND HERE IS YOURS:
NAME        AVERAGE         NAME         AVERAGE
----        -------         ----         -------
HUISMAN     .412001         KLOOS        .263001
HOEREN      .236001         ANDREWS      .316001
BACCUS      .241001         MAYER        .336001
SMITH       .367001         HANSEN       .321001
SCHNEIDER   .295001         MICHEL       .296001
ROSENBAUM   .319001         P. D. PEATE  .285001
POULSEN     .295001         WILLIAMS     .295001
KILGOUR     .218001         NELSON       .139001
JOHNSON     .233001         ANKCORN      .231001
WHITNEY     MANAGER         IVEY         MANAGER

PITCHER'S OPTIONS ARE:
FASTBALL
BEANBALL
BRUSHBACK
BALL
CURVE
SLIDER
KNUCKLE
GREASEBALL (ILLEGAL)
SPITBALL (ILLEGAL)
CHECK

BATTER'S OPTIONS ARE:
BUNT
SWING
HIT-AWAY
SACRIFICE
GROUNDER
FLY
KILL


THE PANTHERS ARE TAKING THE FIELD NOW AS ANDREWS OF THE
RSTS/E ROCKETS ADVANCES TO THE PLATE.  PLEASE WAIT AS THE COMPUTER SINGS
OUR NATIONAL ANTHEM TO ITSELF - 2 OR 3 TIMES!  JUST SING
ALONG UNTIL ASKED FOR YOUR PLAY.


YOUR PLAY? SWING
YOUR BATTER GROUNDED TO SHORTSTOP WHO THREW OUT THE MAN AT FIRST.
 THAT WAS OUT NUMBER 1

YOUR PLAY? SWING
INSIDE - BALL 1
YOUR PLAY? SWING
INSIDE - BALL 2
YOUR PLAY? HIT-AWAY
INSIDE CORNER - CALL   STRIKE 1
YOUR PLAY? KILL
INSIDE CORNER - CALL   STRIKE 2
YOUR PLAY? KILL
YOUR BATTER HIT TO LEFT FIELD FOR AN OUT.
THAT WAS OUT NUMBER 2

YOUR PLAY? SWING
OUTSIDE - BALL 1
YOUR PLAY? KILL
OUTSIDE / BALL 2
YOUR PLAY? HIT-AWAY
YOUR BATTER POPPED OUT IN SHALLOW LEFT.
THAT WAS OUT NUMBER 3

 0 RUNS, 0 HITS, 0 ERRORS AND 0 LEFT ON BASE.
I'M UP NOW.
SCORE: ME 0 YOU 0


YOUR PLAY? FASTBALL
MY BATTER HIT THROUGH THE HOLE INTO RIGHT FOR A SINGLE.

YOUR PLAY? FASTBALL
MY BATTER GROUNDED TO THE PITCHER WHO THREW OUT THE MAN FORCED TO SECOND
 AND THEN TO FIRST FOR A DOUBLE PLAY!
THAT WAS OUT NUMBER 2

YOUR PLAY? CURVE
MY BATTER HIT TO LEFT FIELD FOR AN OUT.
THAT WAS OUT NUMBER 3

AFTER 1 INNINGS 0 RUNS, 1 HITS, 0 ERRORS AND 0 LEFT ON BASE.
YOU'RE UP NOW.
SCORE: ME 0 YOU 0
```

```
YOUR PLAY? KILL
INSIDE - BALL 3
YOUR PLAY? SWING
INSIDE - BALL 2
YOUR PLAY? KILL
INSIDE CORNER - CALL   STRIKE 1
YOUR PLAY? HIT-AWAY
FOUL! - STRIKE 2
YOUR PLAY? BUNT
YOUR BATTER GROUNDED TO THE PITCHER WHO THREW OUT THE MAN AT FIRST.
 THAT WAS OUT NUMBER 1

YOUR PLAY? BUNT
YOUR BATTER GROUNDED TO THE PITCHER WHO THREW OUT THE MAN AT FIRST.
THAT WAS OUT NUMBER 2

YOUR PLAY? SWING
INSIDE CORNER - CALL   STRIKE 1
YOUR PLAY? SWING
OUTSIDE - BALL 1
YOUR PLAY? KILL
OUTSIDE - BALL 2
YOUR PLAY? GROUNFDER
INSIDE - BALL 3
YOUR PLAY? GROUNDER
YOUR BATTER LINED OUT TO THE THIRD BASEMAN.
THAT WAS OUT NUMBER 3

 0 RUNS, 0 HITS, 0 ERRORS AND 0 LEFT ON BASE.
I'M UP NOW.
SCORE: ME 0 YOU 0
```

BASKET

BASKETBALL GAME VS DARTMOUTH

Description

This program simulates a game of basketball between Dartmouth
College and an opponent of your choice. You are the Dartmouth
captain and control the type of shot and defense during the
course of the game.

There are four types of shots: 1. Long Jump Shot (30 ft.),
2. Short Jump Shot (15 ft.), 3. Lay Up, and 4. Set Shot.
Both teams use the same defense, but you may call it: Press (6),
Man-to-man (6.5), Zone (7), or None (7.5). To change defense,
type "0" as your next shot.

Note: The game is biased slightly in favor of Dartmouth. The
average probability of a Dartmouth shot being good is 62.95%
compared to a probability of 61.85% for their opponent.
(This makes the sample run somewhat remarkable in that Cornell
won by a score of 51 to 35. Hooray for the Big Red!)

Program Author

Basketball programs were received from Bill Heuer, Fort Worth,
Texas; James Bonalumi, Torrington, Conn.; and Alan Segal,
Roslyn, New York. The one published was written by a then-
sophomore at Dartmouth in the Class of '70:

Charles R. Bacheller
Dartmouth College
Hanover, NH 03755

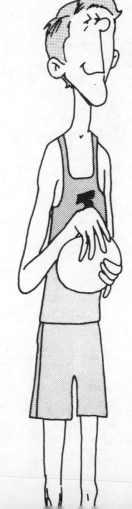

```
5 RANDOMIZE
10 PRINT "THIS IS DARTMOUTH COLLEGE BASKETBALL.  YOU WILL BE DARTMOUTH"
20 PRINT "  CAPTAIN AND PLAYMAKER.  CALL SHOTS AS FOLLOWS: 1. LONG"
30 PRINT "  (30 FT.) JUMP SHOT: 2 SHORT (15 FT.) JUMP SHOT: 3. LAY"
40 PRINT "  UP: 4. SET SHOT."
60 PRINT "BOTH TEAMS WILL USE THE SAME DEFENSE. CALL DEFENSE AS"
70 PRINT" FOLLOWS: 6 PRESS; 6.5 MAN-TO-MAN; 7 ZONE; 7.5 NONE."
72 PRINT" TO CHANGE DEFENSE, JUST TYPE   0  AS YOUR NEXT SHOT."
74 PRINT "YOUR STARTING DEFENSE WILL BE";
76 INPUT D
77 IF D<6 THEN 2010
79 PRINT
80 PRINT "CHOOSE YOUR OPPONENT";
82 INPUT O$
370 PRINT "CENTER JUMP"
390 IF RND > 3/5 THEN 420
400 PRINT O$;" CONTROLS THE TAP."
410 GO TO 3000
420 PRINT "DARTMOUTH CONTROLS THE TAP."
425 PRINT
430 PRINT "YOUR SHOT";
435 LET P=0
440 INPUT Z
445 IF Z<>INT(Z) THEN 455
446 IF ABS(Z-2)>2 THEN 455
447 GOTO 460
455 PRINT "INCORRECT ANSWER.  RETYPE IT";
456 GOTO 440
460 GO TO 470
470 IF RND <.5 THEN 1000
480 IF T<100 THEN 1000
490 PRINT
491 IF S(1)<>S(0) THEN 510
493 PRINT "  ***** END OF SECOND HALF *****"
495 PRINT "SCORE AT END OF REGULATION TIME:"
496 PRINT "   DARTMOUTH" S(1); O$" "S(0)
497 PRINT
498 PRINT "BEGIN TWO MINUTE OVERTIME PERIOD"
499 LET T=93
500 GO TO 370
510 PRINT "  ***** END OF GAME *****"
515 PRINT "FINAL SCORE: DARTMOUTH" S(1); O$" "S(0)
520 STOP
600 PRINT
610 PRINT "  ***  TWO MINUTES LEFT IN THE GAME  ***"
620 PRINT
630 RETURN
1000 IF Z=1 THEN 1040
1020 IF Z=2 THEN 1040
1036 GO TO 1300
1040 LET T=T+1
1041 IF T=50 THEN 8000
1042 IF T=92 THEN 1046
1043 GO TO 1050
1046 GOSUB 600
1050 PRINT "JUMP SHOT"
1060 IF RND >.341*D/8 THEN 1090
1070 PRINT "SHOT IS GOOD."
1075 GOSUB 7000
1085 GO TO 3000
1090 IF RND >.682*D/8 THEN 1200
1100 PRINT "SHOT IS OFF TARGET."
1105 IF D/6*RND>.45 THEN 1130
1110 PRINT "DARTMOUTH CONTROLS THE REBOUND."
1120 GO TO 1145
1130 PRINT "REBOUND TO ";O$;"."
1137 GO TO 3000
1145 IF RND>.40 THEN 1158
1150 GO TO 1300
1158 IF D=6 THEN 5100
1160 PRINT "BALL PASSED BACK TO YOU. ";
1170 GO TO 430
1180 IF RND>.9THEN1190
1185 PRINT "PLAYER FOULED. TWO SHOTS."
1187 GOSUB 4000
1188 GO TO 3000
1190 PRINT "BALL STOLEN. ";O$;"'S BALL."
1195 GO TO 3000
1200 IF RND>.782*D/8 THEN 1250
1210 PRINT "SHOT IS BLOCKED.  BALL CONTROLLED BY";
1230 IF RND>.5 THEN 1242
1235 PRINT " DARTMOUTH."
1240 GO TO 430
1242 PRINT " ";O$;"."
1245 GO TO 3000
1250 IF RND>.843*D/8 THEN 1270
1255 PRINT "SHOOTER IS FOULED.  TWO SHOTS."
1260 GOSUB 4000
1265 GO TO 3000
1270 PRINT "CHARGING FOUL.  DARTMOUTH LOSES THE BALL."
1280 GO TO 3000
1300 LET T=T+1
1301 IF T=50 THEN 8000
1302 IF T=92 THEN 1304
1303 GO TO 1305
1304 GOSUB 600
1305 IF Z=0 THEN 2010
1310 IF Z>3 THEN 1700
1320 PRINT "LAY UP."
1330 IF 7/D*RND>.4 THEN 1360
1340 PRINT "SHOT IS GOOD.  TWO POINTS."
1345 GOSUB 7000
1355 GO TO 3000
1360 IF 7/D*RND>.7 THEN 1500
1370 PRINT "SHOT IS OFF THE RIM."
1380 IF RND>2/3 THEN 1415
1390 PRINT O$;" CONTROLS THE REBOUND."
1400 GO TO 3000
1410
1415 PRINT "DARTMOUTH CONTROLS THE REBOUND."
1420 IF RND>.4 THEN 1440
1430 GO TO 1300
1440 PRINT "BALL PASSED BACK TO YOU.";
1450 GO TO 430
1500 IF 7/D*RND>.875 THEN 1600
1510 PRINT "SHOOTER FOULED.  TWO SHOTS."
1520 GOSUB 4000
1530 GO TO 3000
1600 IF 7/D*RND>.925 THEN 1630
1610 PRINT "SHOT BLOCKED. ";O$;"'S BALL."
1620 GO TO 3000
1630 PRINT "CHARGING FOUL.  DARTMOUTH LOSES THE BALL."
1640 GO TO 3000
1700 PRINT "SET SHOT"
1710 GO TO 1330
2010 PRINT "YOUR NEW DEFENSIVE ALLIGNMENT IS";
2020 INPUT D
2030 IF D<6 THEN 2010
2040 GO TO 425
3000 LET P=1
3005 LET T=T+1
3008 IF T=54 THEN 8000
3010 IF T=92 THEN 3015
3012 GO TO 3018
3015 GOSUB 600
3018 PRINT
3020 LET Z1=10/4*RND+1
3030 IF Z1>2 THEN 3500
3040 PRINT "JUMP SHOT"
3050 IF 8/D*RND>.35 THEN 3100
3060 PRINT "SHOT IS GOOD."
3080 GOSUB 6000
3090 GO TO 425
3100 IF 8/D*RND>.75 THEN 3200
3105 PRINT "SHOT IS OFF THE RIM."
3110 IF D/6*RND>.5 THEN 3150
3120 PRINT "DARTMOUTH CONTROLS THE REBOUND."
3130 GO TO 425
3150 PRINT O$;" CONTROLS THE REBOUND."
3160 IF D=6 THEN 5000
3165 IF RND>.5 THEN 3175
3168 PRINT "PASS BACK TO " O$;" GUARD."
3170 GO TO 3000
3175 GO TO 3500
3200 IF 8/D*RND>.9 THEN 3310
3210 PRINT "PLAYER FOULED.  TWO SHOTS."
3220 GOSUB 4000
3230 GO TO 425
3310 PRINT "OFFENSIVE FOUL. DARTMOUTH'S BALL"
3320 GO TO 425
3500 IF Z1>3 THEN 3800
3510 PRINT "LAY UP"
3520 IF 7/D*RND>.413 THEN 3600
3530 PRINT "SHOT IS GOOD."
3540 GOSUB 6000
3550 GO TO 425
3600 PRINT "SHOT IS MISSED."
3610 GO TO 3110
3800 PRINT "SET SHOT"
3810 GO TO 3520
4000 REM *FOUL SHOOTING*
4010 IF RND>.49 THEN 4050
4020 PRINT "SHOOTER MAKES BOTH SHOTS."
4030 LET S(1-P)=S(1-P)+2
4040 GOSUB 6010
4041 RETURN
4050 IF RND>.75 THEN 4100
4060 PRINT "SHOOTER MAKES ONE SHOT AND MISSES ONE."
4070 LET S(1-P)=S(1-P)+1
4080 GO TO 4040
4100 PRINT "BOTH SHOTS MISSED."
4110 GO TO 4040
5000 IF RND>.75 THEN 5010
5005 GO TO 3165
5010 PRINT "BALL STOLEN.  EASY LAY-UP FOR DARTMOUTH."
5015 GOSUB 7000
5030 GO TO 3000
5100 IF RND>.6 THEN 5120
5110 GO TO 1160
5120 PRINT "PASS STOLEN BY ";O$;" EASY LAY-UP."
5130 GOSUB 6000
5140 GO TO 425
6000 LET S(0)=S(0)+2
6010 PRINT "SCORE: " S(1); "TO " S(0)
6020 RETURN
7000 LET S(1)=S(1)+2
7010 GOSUB 6010
7020 RETURN
8000 PRINT "  ***** END OF FIRST HALF *****"
8010 PRINT"SCORE: DARTMOUTH" S(1); O$" "S(0)
8015 PRINT
8016 PRINT
8020 GO TO 370
9999 END
```

30

SAMPLE RUN

THIS IS DARTMOUTH COLLEGE BASKETBALL. YOU WILL BE DARTMOUTH
   CAPTAIN AND PLAYMAKER. CALL SHOTS AS FOLLOWS: 1. LONG
   (30 FT.) JUMP SHOT; 2 SHORT (15 FT.) JUMP SHOT; 3. LAY
   UP; 4. SET SHOT.
BOTH TEAMS WILL USE THE SAME DEFENSE. CALL DEFENSE AS
   FOLLOWS: 6 PRESS; 6.5 MAN-TO-MAN; 7 ZONE; 7.5 NONE.
   TO CHANGE DEFENSE, JUST TYPE   0   AS YOUR NEXT SHOT.
YOUR STARTING DEFENSE WILL BE ?7

CHOOSE YOUR OPPONENT ?CORNELL
CENTER JUMP
CORNELL CONTROLS THE TAP.

LAY UP
SHOT IS GOOD.
SCORE: 0 TO 2

YOUR SHOT ?2
JUMP SHOT
SHOT IS BLOCKED. BALL CONTROLLED BY DARTMOUTH.
YOUR SHOT ?3
LAY UP.
SHOT IS GOOD.   TWO POINTS.
SCORE: 2 TO 2

SET SHOT
SHOT IS MISSED.
DARTMOUTH CONTROLS THE REBOUND.

YOUR SHOT ?2
JUMP SHOT
SHOT IS GOOD.
SCORE: 4 TO 2

JUMP SHOT
SHOT IS GOOD.
SCORE: 4 TO 4

YOUR SHOT ?1
JUMP SHOT
SHOT IS OFF TARGET.
DARTMOUTH CONTROLS THE REBOUND.
BALL PASSED BACK TO YOU. YOUR SHOT ?2
JUMP SHOT
SHOT IS GOOD.
SCORE: 6 TO 4

SET SHOT
SHOT IS MISSED.
DARTMOUTH CONTROLS THE REBOUND.

YOUR SHOT ?2
JUMP SHOT
SHOT IS BLOCKED.   BALL CONTROLLED BY DARTMOUTH.
YOUR SHOT ?1
JUMP SHOT
SHOT IS GOOD.
SCORE: 8 TO 4

SET SHOT
SHOT IS GOOD.
SCORE: 8 TO 6

YOUR SHOT ?4
SET SHOT
SHOT IS OFF THE RIM.
DARTMOUTH CONTROLS THE REBOUND.
BALL PASSED BACK TO YOU. YOUR SHOT ?3
LAY UP.
SHOT IS OFF THE RIM.
DARTMOUTH CONTROLS THE REBOUND.
LAY UP.
SHOT IS GOOD.   TWO POINTS.
SCORE: 10 TO 6

LAY UP
SHOT IS MISSED.
CORNELL CONTROLS THE REBOUND.
LAY UP
SHOT IS GOOD.
SCORE: 10 TO 8

YOUR SHOT ?2
JUMP SHOT
SHOT IS OFF TARGET.
REBOUND TO CORNELL.

LAY UP
SHOT IS MISSED.
DARTMOUTH CONTROLS THE REBOUND.

YOUR SHOT ?1
JUMP SHOT
SHOT IS GOOD.
SCORE: 12 TO 8

LAY UP
SHOT IS GOOD.
SCORE: 12 TO 10

YOUR SHOT ?2
JUMP SHOT
SHOT IS OFF TARGET.
DARTMOUTH CONTROLS THE REBOUND.
BALL PASSED BACK TO YOU. YOUR SHOT ?4
SET SHOT
SHOT IS OFF THE RIM.
CORNELL CONTROLS THE REBOUND.

LAY UP
SHOT IS MISSED.
CORNELL CONTROLS THE REBOUND.
PASS BACK TO CORNELL GUARD.

JUMP SHOT
SHOT IS GOOD.
SCORE: 12 TO 12

YOUR SHOT ?3
LAY UP.
SHOT BLOCKED. CORNELL'S BALL.

JUMP SHOT
SHOT IS OFF TARGET.
DARTMOUTH CONTROLS THE REBOUND.
LAY UP
SHOT IS GOOD.   TWO POINTS.
SCORE: 29 TO 39

LAY UP
SHOT IS MISSED.
CORNELL CONTROLS THE REBOUND.
LAY UP
SHOT IS GOOD.
SCORE: 29 TO 41

YOUR SHOT ?2
JUMP SHOT
SHOT IS OFF TARGET.
REBOUND TO CORNELL.

LAY UP
SHOT IS GOOD.
SCORE: 29 TO 43

YOUR SHOT ?4
SET SHOT
SHOT IS OFF THE RIM.
CORNELL CONTROLS THE REBOUND.

JUMP SHOT
SHOT IS OFF THE RIM.
CORNELL CONTROLS THE REBOUND.
PASS BACK TO CORNELL GUARD.

LAY UP
SHOT IS MISSED.
CORNELL CONTROLS THE REBOUND.
LAY UP
SHOT IS MISSED.
DARTMOUTH CONTROLS THE REBOUND.

YOUR SHOT ?1
JUMP SHOT
SHOT IS BLOCKED.   BALL CONTROLLED BY CORNELL.

JUMP SHOT
SHOT IS OFF THE RIM.
DARTMOUTH CONTROLS THE REBOUND.

YOUR SHOT ?1

    *** TWO MINUTES LEFT IN THE GAME ***

JUMP SHOT
SHOT IS GOOD.
SCORE: 31 TO 43

LAY UP
SHOT IS GOOD.
SCORE: 31 TO 45

YOUR SHOT ?3
LAY UP.
SHOT IS GOOD.   TWO POINTS.
SCORE: 33 TO 45

SET SHOT
SHOT IS GOOD.
SCORE: 33 TO 47

YOUR SHOT ?1
JUMP SHOT
SHOT IS OFF TARGET.
DARTMOUTH CONTROLS THE REBOUND.
LAY UP.
SHOT IS OFF THE RIM.
DARTMOUTH CONTROLS THE REBOUND.
LAY UP.
SHOT IS OFF THE RIM.
CORNELL CONTROLS THE REBOUND.

SET SHOT
SHOT IS GOOD.
SCORE: 33 TO 49

YOUR SHOT ?3
LAY UP.
SHOT IS GOOD.   TWO POINTS.
SCORE: 35 TO 49

SET SHOT
SHOT IS MISSED.
CORNELL CONTROLS THE REBOUND.
PASS BACK TO CORNELL GUARD.

JUMP SHOT
SHOT IS GOOD.
SCORE: 35 TO 51

YOUR SHOT ?1

    ***** END OF GAME *****
FINAL SCORE: DARTMOUTH 35 CORNELL 51

BATNUM

BATTLE OF NUMBERS

Description

The game starts with an imaginary pile of objects, coins for example. You and your opponent (the computer) alternately remove objects from the pile. You specify in advance the minimum and maximum number of objects that can be taken on each turn. You also specify in advance how winning is defined: 1. To take the last object or 2. To avoid taking the last object. You may also determine whether you or the computer go first.

The strategy of this game is based on modulo arithmetic. If the maximum number of objects a player may remove in a turn is M, then to gain a winning position a player at the end of his turn must leave a stack of 1 modulo (M+1) coins. If you don't understand this, play 23 Matches (23 MTCH) first, then BATNUM, and just have fun!

Program Author

BATNUM is based on an old game similar to NIM. Its adaptation for the computer appears to originally be by the daddy of BASIC:

John Kemeny
Dartmouth College
Hanover, NH 03755

PROGRAM LISTING

```
110 PRINT "THIS PROGRAM IS A 'BATTLE OF NUMBERS'"
120 PRINT"GAME, WHERE THE COMPUTER IS YOUR OPPONENT."
130 PRINT
140 PRINT"THE GAME STARTS WITH AN ASSUMED PILE OF OBJECTS. YOU AND"
150 PRINT"YOUR OPPONENT ALTERNATLY REMOVE OBJECTS FROM THE PILE."
160 PRINT"WINNING IS DEFINED IN ADVANCE AS TAKING THE LAST OBJECT"
170 PRINT"OR NOT. YOU CAN ALSO SPECIFY SOME OTHER BEGINNING"
180 PRINT"CONDITIONS. DON'T USE ZERO, HOWEVER, IN PLAYING THE GAME."
200 PRINT
210 GOTO 330
220 FOR I=1 TO 10
230 PRINT
240 NEXT I
330 PRINT"ENTER PILE SIZE:";
340 INPUT N
350 IF N<>0 THEN 370
360 GOTO 330
370 IF N<>INT(N) THEN 220
380 IF N<1 THEN 220
390 PRINT "ENTER WIN OPTION - 1 TO TAKE LAST, 2 TO AVOID LAST: ";
400 INPUT M
410 IF M=1 THEN 430
420 IF M<>2 THEN 390
430 PRINT "ENTER MIN AND MAX: ";
440 INPUT A,B
450 IF A>B THEN 430
460 IF A<1 THEN 430
470 IF A<>INT(A) THEN 430
480 IF B<>INT(B) THEN 430
490 PRINT"ENTER START OPTION - 1 COMPUTER FIRST, 2 YOU FIRST:";
500 INPUT S
510 IF S=1 THEN 530
520 IF S<>2 THEN 490
530 LET C=A+B
540 IF S=2 THEN 570
550 GOSUB 600
560 IF W=1 THEN 220
570 GOSUB 810
580 IF W=1 THEN 220
590 GO TO 550
600 LET Q=N
610 IF M=1 THEN 630
620 LET Q=Q-1
630 IF M=1 THEN 680
640 IF N>A THEN 720
650 LET W=1
660 PRINT"COMPUTER TAKES";N;"AND LOSES."
670 RETURN
680 IF N>B THEN 720
690 LET W=1
700 PRINT"COMPUTER TAKES";N;"AND WINS."
710 RETURN
720 LET P=Q-C*INT(Q/C)
730 IF P>=A THEN 750
740 LET P=A
750 IF P<=B THEN 770
760 LET P=B
770 LET N=N-P
780 PRINT"COMPUTER TAKES";P;"AND LEAVES";N
790 LET W=0
800 RETURN
810 PRINT "YOUR MOVE: ";
820 INPUT P
830 IF P<0 THEN 870
840 PRINT"I TOLD YOU NOT TO USE ZERO...COMPUTER WINS BY FORFEIT."
850 LET W=1
860 RETURN
870 IF P<>INT(P) THEN 920
880 IF P>=A THEN 910
890 IF P=N THEN 960
900 GO TO 920
910 IF P<=B THEN 940
920 PRINT "ILLEGAL MOVE, REENTER IT: ";
930 GO TO 820
940 LET N=N-P
950 IF N<>0 THEN 1030
960 IF M=1 THEN 1000
970 PRINT"TOUGH LUCK, YOU LOSE."
980 LET W=1
990 RETURN
1000 PRINT"CONGRATULATIONS, YOU WIN."
1010 LET W=1
1020 RETURN
1030 IF N>=0 THEN 1060
1040 LET N=N+P
1050 GO TO 920
1060 LET W=0
1070 RETURN
1080 END
```

SAMPLE RUN

```
THIS PROGRAM IS A 'BATTLE OF NUMBERS'
GAME, WHERE THE COMPUTER IS YOUR OPPONENT.

THE GAME STARTS WITH AN ASSUMED PILE OF OBJECTS. YOU AND
YOUR OPPONENT ALTERNATLY REMOVE OBJECTS FROM THE PILE.
WINNING IS DEFINED IN ADVANCE AS TAKING THE LAST OBJECT
OR NOT. YOU CAN ALSO SPECIFY SOME OTHER BEGINNING
CONDITIONS. DON'T USE ZERO, HOWEVER, IN PLAYING THE GAME.

ENTER PILE SIZE: ?23
ENTER WIN OPTION - 1 TO TAKE LAST, 2 TO AVOID LAST:  ?2
ENTER MIN AND MAX:  ?1,3
ENTER START OPTION - 1 COMPUTER FIRST, 2 YOU FIRST: ?2
YOUR MOVE:  ?2
COMPUTER TAKES 1 AND LEAVES 20
YOUR MOVE:  ?3
COMPUTER TAKES 1 AND LEAVES 16
YOUR MOVE:  ?3
COMPUTER TAKES 1 AND LEAVES 12
YOUR MOVE:  ?3
COMPUTER TAKES 1 AND LEAVES 8
YOUR MOVE:  ?3
COMPUTER TAKES 1 AND LEAVES 4
YOUR MOVE:  ?3
COMPUTER TAKES 1 AND LOSES.
```

```
ENTER PILE SIZE: ?23
ENTER WIN OPTION - 1 TO TAKE LAST, 2 TO AVOID LAST:  ?2
ENTER MIN AND MAX:  ?1,3
ENTER START OPTION - 1 COMPUTER FIRST, 2 YOU FIRST: ?1
COMPUTER TAKES 2 AND LEAVES 21
YOUR MOVE:  ?3
COMPUTER TAKES 1 AND LEAVES 17
YOUR MOVE:  ?2
COMPUTER TAKES 2 AND LEAVES 13
YOUR MOVE:  ?1
COMPUTER TAKES 3 AND LEAVES 9
YOUR MOVE:  ?1
COMPUTER TAKES 3 AND LEAVES 5
YOUR MOVE:  ?3
COMPUTER TAKES 1 AND LEAVES 1
YOUR MOVE:  ?1
TOUGH LUCK, YOU LOSE.
```

```
ENTER PILE SIZE: ?27
ENTER WIN OPTION - 1 TO TAKE LAST, 2 TO AVOID LAST:  ?1
ENTER MIN AND MAX:  ?1,4
ENTER START OPTION - 1 COMPUTER FIRST, 2 YOU FIRST: ?2
YOUR MOVE:  ?2
COMPUTER TAKES 1 AND LEAVES 24
YOUR MOVE:  ?4
COMPUTER TAKES 1 AND LEAVES 19
YOUR MOVE:  ?4
COMPUTER TAKES 1 AND LEAVES 14
YOUR MOVE:  ?4
COMPUTER TAKES 1 AND LEAVES 9
YOUR MOVE:  ?4
COMPUTER TAKES 1 AND LEAVES 4
YOUR MOVE:  ?4
CONGRATULATIONS, YOU WIN.
```

BATTLE

Description

This description is an adaptation of the one written by Ray
Westergard, the program author.

"BATTLE is based on the popular game Battleship which is
primarily played to familiarize people with the location
and designation of points on a coordinate plane."

BATTLE first randomly sets up the bad guys' fleet disposition
on a 6 by 6 matrix or grid. The fleet consists of six ships:
Two destroyers (ships number 1 and 2) which are two units long,
two cruisers (ships number 3 and 4) which are three units long
and two aircraft carriers (ships number 5 and 6) which are
four units long. The program then prints out this fleet disposition in a coded or disguised format (see the sample computer print-out). You then proceed to sink the various ships
by typing in the coordinates (two digits, each from 1 to 6,
separated by a comma) of the place where you want to drop a
bomb, if you'll excuse the expression. The computer gives
the appropriate responses (splash, hit, etc.) which you should
record on a 6 by 6 matrix. You are thus building a representation of the actual fleet disposition which you will hopefully
use to decode the coded fleet disposition printed out by the
computer. Each time a ship is sunk, the computer prints out
which ships have been sunk so far and also gives you a
"SPLASH/HIT RATIO".

The first thing you should learn is how to locate and designate
positions on the matrix, and specifically the difference between
"3,4" and "4,3". Our method corresponds to the location of
points on the coordinate plane rather than the location of
numbers in a standard algebraic matrix: The first number gives
the column counting from left to right and the second number
gives the row counting from bottom to top.

The second thing you should learn about is the splash/hit ratio.
"What is a ratio?" A good reply is "It's a fraction or quotient."
Specifically, the splash/hit ratio is the number of splashes
divided by the number of hits. If you had 9 splashes and 15
hits, the ratio would be 9/15 or 3/5, both of which are correct.
The computer would give this splash/hit ratio as .6.

One of the main objects and primary educational benefits of
BATTLE comes from attempting to decode the bad guys' fleet
disposition code. To do this, you must make a COMPARISON
between the coded matrix and the actual matrix which you con-
struct as you play the game.

Program

Ray Westergard
Lawrence Hall of Science
University of California
Berkeley, CA 94700

PROGRAM LISTING

```
10    REM -- BATTLE WRITTEN BY RAY WESTERGARD  10/70
20    REM COPYRIGHT 1971 BY THE REGENTS OF THE UNIV. OF CALIF.
30    REM PRODUCED AT THE LAWRENCE HALL OF SCIENCE, BERKELEY
40    DIM F[6,6],H[6,6],A[4],B[4],C[6],L[3]
50    MAT F=ZER
60    FOR I=1 TO 3
70    N=4-I
80    FOR J=1 TO 2
90    A=INT(6*RND(0))+1
100   B=INT(6*RND(0))+1
110   D=INT(4*RND(0))+1
120   IF F[A,B]>0 THEN 90
130   M=0
140   GOTO D OF 150,340,550,740
150   B[1]=B
160   B[2]=B[3]=7
170   FOR K=1 TO N
180   IF M>1 THEN 240
190   IF B[K]=6 THEN 230
200   IF F[A,B[K]+1]>0 THEN 230
210   B[K+1]=B[K]+1
220   GOTO 280
230   M=2
240   Z=((B[1] MIN B[2]) MIN B[3])
250   IF Z=1 THEN 90
260   IF F[A,Z-1]>0 THEN 90
270   B[K+1]=Z-1
280   NEXT K
290   F[A,B]=9-2*I-J
300   FOR K=1 TO N
310   F[A,B[K+1]]=F[A,B]
320   NEXT K
330   GOTO 990
340   A[1]=A
350   B[1]=B
360   A[2]=A[3]=B[2]=B[3]=0
370   FOR K=1 TO N
380   IF M>1 THEN 460
390   IF A[K]=1 OR B[K]=1 THEN 450
400   IF F[A[K]-1,B[K]-1]>0 THEN 450
410   IF F[A[K]-1,B[K]]>0 AND F[A[K]-1,B[K]]=F[A[K],B[K]-1] THEN 450
420   A[K+1]=A[K]-1
430   B[K+1]=B[K]-1
440   GOTO 530
450   M=2
460   Z1=((A[1] MAX A[2]) MAX A[3])
470   Z2=((B[1] MAX B[2]) MAX B[3])
480   IF Z1=6 OR Z2=6 THEN 90
490   IF F[Z1+1,Z2+1]>0 THEN 90
500   IF F[Z1,Z2+1]>0 AND F[Z1,Z2+1]=F[Z1+1,Z2] THEN 90
510   A[K+1]=Z1+1
520   B[K+1]=Z2+1
530   NEXT K
540   GOTO 950
550   A[1]=A
560   A[2]=A[3]=7
570   FOR K=1 TO N
580   IF M>1 THEN 640
590   IF A[K]=6 THEN 630
600   IF F[A[K]+1,B]>0 THEN 630
610   A[K+1]=A[K]+1
620   GOTO 680
630   M=2
640   Z=((A[1] MIN A[2]) MIN A[3])
650   IF Z=1 THEN 90
660   IF F[Z-1,B]>0 THEN 90
670   A[K+1]=Z-1
680   NEXT K
690   F[A,B]=9-2*I-J
700   FOR K=1 TO N
710   F[A[K+1],B]=F[A,B]
720   NEXT K
730   GOTO 990
740   A[1]=A
750   B[1]=B
760   A[2]=A[3]=7
770   B[2]=B[3]=0
780   FOR K=1 TO N
790   IF M>1 THEN 870
800   IF A[K]=6 OR B[K]=1 THEN 860
810   IF F[A[K]+1,B[K]-1]>0 THEN 860
820   IF F[A[K]+1,B[K]]>0 AND F[A[K]+1,B[K]]=F[A[K],B[K]-1] THEN 860
830   A[K+1]=A[K]+1
840   B[K+1]=B[K]-1
850   GOTO 940
860   M=2
870   Z1=((A[1] MIN A[2]) MIN A[3])
880   Z2=((B[1] MAX B[2]) MAX B[3])
890   IF Z1=1 OR Z2=6 THEN 90
900   IF F[Z1-1,Z2+1]>0 THEN 90
910   IF F[Z1,Z2+1]>0 AND F[Z1,Z2+1]=F[Z1-1,Z2] THEN 90
920   A[K+1]=Z1-1
930   B[K+1]=Z2+1
940   NEXT K
950   F[A,B]=9-2*I-J
960   FOR K=1 TO N
970   F[A[K+1],B[K+1]]=F[A,B]
980   NEXT K
990   NEXT J
1000  NEXT I
1010  PRINT
1020  PRINT "THE FOLLOWING CODE OF THE BAD GUYS' FLEET DISPOSITION"
1030  PRINT "HAS BEEN CAPTURED BUT NOT DE-CODED:"
1040  PRINT
1050  MAT H=TRN(F)
1060  MAT PRINT H;
1070  PRINT
1080  PRINT "DE-CODE IT AND USE IT IF YOU CAN"
1090  PRINT "BUT KEEP THE DE-CODING METHOD A SECRET."
1100  PRINT
1110  MAT H=ZER
1120  MAT L=ZER
1130  C[1]=C[2]=2
1140  C[3]=C[4]=1
1150  C[5]=C[6]=0
1160  S=H=0
1170  PRINT "START GAME"
1180  INPUT X,Y
1190  IF X<1 OR X>6 OR INT(X)#ABS(X) THEN 1210
1200  IF Y>0 AND Y<7 AND INT(Y)=ABS(Y) THEN 1230
1210  PRINT "INVALID INPUT, TRY AGAIN."
1220  GOTO 1180
1230  R=7-Y
1240  C=X
1250  IF F[R,C]>0 THEN 1290
1260  S=S+1
1270  PRINT "SPLASH!  TRY AGAIN."
1280  GOTO 1180
1290  IF C[F[R,C]]<4 THEN 1340
1300  PRINT "THERE USED TO BE A SHIP AT THAT POINT, BUT YOU SUNK IT."
1310  PRINT "SPLASH!  TRY AGAIN."
1320  S=S+1
1330  GOTO 1180
1340  IF H[R,C]>0 THEN 1420
1350  H=H+1
1360  H[R,C]=F[R,C]
1370  PRINT "A DIRECT HIT ON SHIP NUMBER";F[R,C]
1380  C[F[R,C]]=C[F[R,C]]+1
1390  IF C[F[R,C]] >= 4 THEN 1470
1400  PRINT "TRY AGAIN."
1410  GOTO 1180
1420  PRINT "YOU HAVE ALREADY PUT A HOLE IN SHIP NUMBER";F[R,C]
1430  PRINT "AT THAT POINT."
1440  PRINT "SPLASH!  TRY AGAIN."
1450  S=S+1
1460  GOTO 1180
1470  L[INT((F[R,C]-1)/2)+1]=L[INT((F[R,C]-1)/2)+1]+1
1480  PRINT "AND YOU SUNK IT.  HURRAH FOR THE GOOD GUYS."
1490  PRINT "SO FAR THE BAD GUYS HAVE LOST"
1500  PRINT L[1];"DESTROYER(S),    ";L[2];"CRUISER(S), AND  ";
1510  PRINT L[3];"AIRCRAFT CARRIER(S)."
1520  PRINT "YOUR CURRENT SPLASH/HIT RATIO IS";S/H
1530  IF (L[1]+L[2]+L[3])<6 THEN 1180
1540  PRINT
1550  PRINT "YOU HAVE TOTALLY WIPED OUT THE BAD GUYS' FLEET"
1560  PRINT "WITH A FINAL SPLASH/HIT RATIO OF";S/H
1570  IF S/H>0 THEN 1590
1580  PRINT "CONGRATULATIONS -- A DIRECT HIT EVERY TIME."
1590  PRINT
1600  PRINT "*******************"
1610  PRINT
1620  GOTO 50
1630  END
```

SAMPLE RUN

```
THE FOLLOWING CODE OF THE BAD GUYS' FLEET DISPOSITION
HAS BEEN CAPTURED BUT NOT DECODED

3    0    0    0    1    1

3    0    0    0    0    0

3    2    6    6    6    6

4    0    2    0    0    0

4    5    5    5    5    0

4    0    0    0    0    0


DE-CODE IT AND USE IT IF YOU CAN
BUT KEEP THE DECODING METHOD A SECRET

START GAME
?2,1
SPLASH! TRY AGAIN.
?5,4
A DIRECT HIT ON SHIP NUMBER 5
TRY AGAIN.
?2,7
INVALID INPUT. TRY AGAIN.
?5,3
A DIRECT HIT ON SHIP NUMBER 5
TRY AGAIN.
?5,4
YOU HAVE ALREADY PUT A HOLE IN SHIP NUMBER 5
AT THAT POINT.  SPLASH! TRY AGAIN.
?5,5
A DIRECT HIT ON SHIP NUMBER 5
TRY AGAIN.
?5,2
A DIRECT HIT ON SHIP NUMBER 5
AND YOU SUNK IT. HURRAH FOR THE GOOD GUYS. SO FAR THE BAD GUYS HAVE LOST
 0    DESTROYER(S),  0    CRUISER S) AND  1    AIRCRAFT CARRIER(S).
YOUR CURRENT SPLASH/HIT RATIO IS .5
?1,1
A DIRECT HIT ON SHIP NUMBER 1
TRY AGAIN.
?1,2
A DIRECT HIT ON SHIP NUMBER 1
AND YOU SUNK IT. HURRAH FOR THE GOOD GUYS. SO FAR THE BAD GUYS HAVE LOST
 1    DESTROYER(S),  0    CRUISER(S) AND  1    AIRCRAFT CARRIER(S).
YOUR CURRENT SPLASH/HIT RATIO IS .333333
?6,1
SPLASH! TRY AGAIN.
?1,6
A DIRECT HIT ON SHIP NUMBER 3
TRY AGAIN.
?2,6
A DIRECT HIT ON SHIP NUMBER 3
TRY AGAIN.
?3,6
A DIRECT HIT ON SHIP NUMBER 3
AND YOU SUNK IT. HURRAH FOR THE GOOD GUYS.  SO FAR THE BAD GUYS HAVE LOST
 1    DESTROYER(S),  1    CRUISER(S) AND  1    AIRCRAFT CARRIER(S).
YOU CURRENT SPLASH/HIT RATIO IS .375
```

BINGO

Description

In this game you and the computer play a game of bingo. The computer first generates a bingo card for both you and itself. It then spins the number drum and draws numbers at random which it posts on "the board." It's up to you to play both your card and the card of the computer (a second person can play this card if you wish).

The computer checks for BINGO on both cards, so don't try to cheat!

Source

Sorry folks -- the author and source are totally unknown. It showed up on an in-plant DIGITAL DECsystem-10 quite mysteriously one day last year.

BINGO

(1 TO 15)	(16 TO 30)	(31 TO 45)	(46 TO 60)	(61 TO 75)
~~8~~	~~23~~	~~34~~	~~50~~	~~69~~
5	24	33	60	68
8	29	FREE SPACE	49	64
14	17	37	52	66
12	18	38	53	67

HORIZONTAL (ROW)

BINGO

(1 TO 15)	(16 TO 30)	(31 TO 45)	(46 TO 60)	(61 TO 75)
10	27	39	48	68
7	17	40	53	72
15	29	FREE SPACE	51	67
4	28	41	54	74
1	25	31	57	69

VERTICAL (COLUMN)

BINGO

(1 TO 15)	(16 TO 30)	(31 TO 45)	(46 TO 60)	(61 TO 75)
4	19	32	47	71
8	22	42	61	69
10	18	FREE SPACE	48	72
6	23	40	50	67
5	30	44	49	65

DIAGONAL

PROGRAM LISTING

```
100 RANDOMIZE
120 PRINT"YOU ARE NOW GOING TO PLAY A COMPUTERIZED VERSION OF BINGO--"
180 LET F=1
190 DIM B(10,10)
200 DIM L(75)
210 MAT READ A$(5)
220 DATA B ,I ,N ,G ,O
235 REM  THIS SEQUENCE GENERATES THE CARD NUMBERS (LINES 240-430)
240 FOR K1=1 TO 75
250 LET L(K1)=0
260 NEXT K1
270 PRINT " ,"        HERE'S ";
280 IF F>1 THEN 310
290 PRINT"YOUR CARD"
300 GOTO 320
310 PRINT"MY CARD"
320 LET M=16
330 LET G=F+4
340 FOR Y=F TO G
350 FOR X=F TO G
360 LET R=INT(M*RND)
370 IF R<M-15 THEN 360
380 IF L(R)>0 THEN 360
390 LET B(X,Y)=R
400 LET L(R)=1
410 NEXT X
420 LET M=M+15
430 NEXT Y
435 REM  THIS SEQUENCE PRINTS THE CARD (LINES 440-670)
440 PRINT
450 PRINT"=-B=-","=-I=-","=-N=-","=-G=-","=-O=-"
460 FOR X=F TO G
470 PRINT
480 PRINT
490 PRINT
500 FOR Y=F TO G
510 IF B(X,Y)=B(F+2,F+2) THEN 540
520 PRINT B(X,Y),
530 GOTO 550
540 PRINT"FREE",
550 NEXT Y
560 NEXT X
570 PRINT
580 PRINT
590 PRINT
600 PRINT"-------------------------------------------------------------"
610 PRINT"     [TEAR OFF AFTER MACHINE AUTOMATICALLY ADVANCES PAPER]"
620 FOR K9=1 TO 9
630 PRINT
640 NEXT K9
650 IF F=6 THEN 680
660 LET F=6
670 GOTO 240
680 PRINT
690 PRINT"NOW WE'RE ALL SET TO PLAY THE GAME.  USE A PENCIL TO MARK OFF"
700 PRINT"THE NUMBERS ON YOUR CARD AS THEY ARE CALLED."
710 PRINT"  (PLEASE PLAY MY CARD AS WELL AS YOUR OWN)"
720 PRINT"***DON'T GET SMART.  I'LL BE PLAYING BOTH YOUR CARD AND MINE"
730 PRINT "     UP HERE IN BOSTON,  (SO THERE--)"
740 PRINT
750 PRINT "ARE YOU READY";
760 INPUT R$
770 IF R$<>"NO" THEN 820
780 PRINT
790 PRINT"*********:HURRY UP!*********"
800 GOTO 740
810 REM
820 FOR K1=1 TO 75
830 LET L(K1)=0
840 NEXT K1
850 PRINT
860 LET B(3,3)=0
870 LET B(8,8)=0
875 REM  THIS SEQUENCE GENERATES THE BINGO NUMBERS (LINES 880-1100)
880 LET U=INT(75*RND)+1
910 IF L(U)<>0 THEN 880
920 LET L(U)=1
930 PRINT
940 IF RND > .5 THEN 970
950 PRINT"THE NUMBER COMES UP:",
960 GOTO 980
970 PRINT"THE NEXT ONE IS:",
980 PRINT A$(INT((U-1)/15)+1);U
1105 REM  THIS IS THE "NUMBER ON CARD?" SEQUENCE (LINES 1110-1260)
1110 FOR Y=1 TO 10
1120 FOR X=1 TO 10
1130 IF B(X,Y)=U THEN 1250
1140 NEXT X
1150 NEXT Y
1160 LET F=1
1170 GOSUB 1270
1180 LET F=6
1190 GOSUB 1270
1200 IF V=0 THEN 1230
1210 IF W=1 THEN 1980
1220 GOTO 2050
1230 IF W=0 THEN 880
1240 GOTO 2120
1250 LET B(X,Y)=0
1260 GOTO 1140
1265 REM  THIS IS THE BINGO DETERMINING SEQUENCE (LINES 1270-1950)
1266
1267 REM  THIS IS THE VERTICAL CHECK FOR BINGO*** (LINES 1270-1430)
1270 LET G=F+4
1280 FOR Y=F TO G
1290 FOR X=F TO G
1300 IF B(X,Y)<>0 THEN 1430
1310 IF X<F+4 THEN 1420
1320 IF F=6 THEN 1370
1330 PRINT
1340 PRINT"YOU'VE GOT A    B I N G O * * *"
1350 LET W=1
1360 RETURN
1370 PRINT
1380 PRINT"I'VE GOT A    B I N G O * * * * *"
1390 LET V=1
1410 GO TO 1450
1420 NEXT X
1430 NEXT Y
1440 REM  THIS IS THE HORIZONTAL CHECK FOR BINGO*** (LINES 1450-1610)
```

```
1450 LET G=F+4
1460 FOR X=F TO G
1470 FOR Y=F TO G
1480 IF B(X,Y)<>0 THEN 1610
1490 IF Y<F+4 THEN 1600
1500 IF F=6 THEN 1550
1510 PRINT
1520 PRINT"YOU'VE GOT A    B I N G O * * *"
1530 LET W=1
1540 RETURN
1550 PRINT
1560 PRINT"I'VE GOT A    B I N G O * * * * *"
1570 LET V=1
1590 GOTO 1620
1600 NEXT Y
1610 NEXT X
1615 REM  THIS IS THE SLANT CHECK (M=-1) FOR BINGO*** (LINES 1620-1770)
1620 LET X=F
1630 LET Y=F
1640 IF B(X,Y)<>0 THEN 1770
1650 LET X=X+1
1660 LET Y=Y+1
1670 IF Y<F+5 THEN 1640
1680 IF Y=11 THEN 1740
1690 LET W=1
1700 PRINT
1710 PRINT"YOU'VE GOT A    B I N G O * * *"
1730 RETURN
1740 PRINT"I'VE GOT A    B I N G O * * * * *"
1750 LET V=1
1770 RETURN
1775 REM  THIS IS THE SLANT CHECK (M=1) FOR BINGO*** (LINES 1780-1950)
1780 LET X=F+4
1790 LET Y=X
1800 IF B(X,Y)<>0 THEN 1950
1810 LET X=X-1
1820 LET Y=Y+1
1830 IF Y<F+5 THEN 1800
1840 IF Y=11 THEN 1900
1850 PRINT
1860 PRINT"YOU'VE GOT A    B I N G O * * *"
1870 LET W=1
1890 RETURN
1900 PRINT
1910 PRINT"I'VE GOT A    B I N G O * * * * *"
1920 LET V=1
1950 RETURN
1970 REM  THIS THE TIE PRINTOUT SEQUENCE
1980 PRINT
1990 PRINT"  ********** IT'S A TIE **********"
1995 REM  THIS IS THE "PLAY AGAIN?" SEQUENCE
2000 PRINT
2010 PRINT "DO YOU WANT TO PLAY AGAIN";
2020 INPUT E$
2025 PRINT
2030 IF E$="YES" THEN 180
2040 STOP
2045 REM  THIS IS THE "I WIN" SEQUENCE
2050 PRINT
2060 FOR S=1 TO 6
2070 PRINT"I WIN.  ";
2080 NEXT S
2090 PRINT
2100 PRINT
2110 GOTO 2000
2115 REM  THIS IS THE "YOU WIN" SEQUENCE
2120 PRINT
2130 PRINT"  YOU WIN.....  YOU WIN.......  YOU WIN......."
2140 GOTO 2000
2145 REM  THIS IS THE "END" OF THE LIST OF PROGRAM ENTITLED "BINGO"
2150 END
```

SAMPLE RUN

YOU ARE NOW GOING TO PLAY A COMPUTERIZED VERSION OF BINGO--
        HERE'S YOUR CARD

--B--	--I--	--N--	--G--	--O--
8	19	36	50	73
2	22	38	53	75
11	29	FREE	46	65
1	23	37	59	71
14	18	40	56	68

        [TEAR OFF AFTER MACHINE AUTOMATICALLY ADVANCES PAPER]

                        HERE'S MY CARD

--B--	--I--	--N--	--G--	--O--
11	20	45	51	68
9	27	42	60	74
8	29	FREE	52	70
6	30	36	50	62
13	26	44	49	61

        [TEAR OFF AFTER MACHINE AUTOMATICALLY ADVANCES PAPER]

NOW WE'RE ALL SET TO PLAY THE GAME. USE A PENCIL TO MARK OFF
THE NUMBERS ON YOUR CARD AS THEY ARE CALLED.
    (PLEASE PLAY MY CARD AS WELL AS YOUR OWN)
***DON'T GET SMART. I'LL BE PLAYING BOTH YOUR CARD AND MINE
    UP HERE IN BOSTON. (SO THERE--)

ARE YOU READY ?YES

THE NUMBER COMES UP:	G	58
THE NEXT ONE IS:	I	20
THE NEXT ONE IS:	I	29
THE NEXT ONE IS:	B	6
THE NUMBER COMES UP:	G	51
THE NUMBER COMES UP:	B	3
THE NUMBER COMES UP:	N	37
THE NEXT ONE IS:	G	59
THE NEXT ONE IS:	B	14
THE NEXT ONE IS:	I	21
THE NEXT ONE IS:	O	71
THE NEXT ONE IS:	O	62
THE NEXT ONE IS:	O	70
THE NEXT ONE IS:	N	36
THE NEXT ONE IS:	N	31
THE NUMBER COMES UP:	I	30
THE NUMBER COMES UP:	I	18
THE NEXT ONE IS:	B	11
THE NEXT ONE IS:	O	66
THE NEXT ONE IS:	N	32
THE NEXT ONE IS:	O	75
THE NEXT ONE IS:	B	8
THE NUMBER COMES UP:	N	38
THE NEXT ONE IS:	B	2
THE NUMBER COMES UP:	B	12
THE NUMBER COMES UP:	I	17
THE NUMBER COMES UP:	N	45
THE NEXT ONE IS:	G	49
THE NUMBER COMES UP:	G	46
THE NEXT ONE IS:	B	5
THE NEXT ONE IS:	O	72
THE NUMBER COMES UP:	B	1

YOU'VE GOT A B I N G O * * *

    YOU WIN..... YOU WIN...... YOU WIN......

DO YOU WANT TO PLAY AGAIN ?NO

BLKJAK

Description

This is a simulation of the game of blackjack or 21, Las Vegas style. This is one of the more comprehensive versions of black-jack which allows splitting your hand if the first two cards are the same. Also, the dealer will ask for an insurance bet if he has an exposed ace. The house limit is $500.00.

Source

A number of versions of this program were submitted. Ira Gold-stein of Fort Worth, Texas, submitted a particularly interesting version which uses a second chained program (DECK) to shuffle the cards. Two versions are printed here -- one written and modified by a number of DIGITAL personnel for RSTS-11 and another written by students at the Oregon Museum of Science and Industry and slightly modified at DIGITAL.

BLKJAC:

    Digital Equipment Corp.
    Maynard, MA 01754

BLKJAK:

    Tom Kloos
    Oregon Museum of Science
      and Industry
    Portland, Oregon 97200

BLKJAC   PROGRAM LISTING

```
10  RRINT "DO YOU WANT INSTRUCTIONS (IF SO TYPE A 1)";
15  INPUT K
25  IF K<>1 THEN 85
30    PRINT
35    PRINT
40    PRINT
45    PRINT
50    PRINT"THIS IS A GAME OF BLACKJACK, LAS VEGAS STYLE."
55    PRINT"HERE ARE THE RULES OF THE HOUSE.  THE DEALER"
60    PRINT"MUST HIT ON 16 OR LESS AND WILL STAY ON 17 OR"
65    PRINT"MORE.  YOU MAY SPLIT TWO CARDS IF THEY ARE THE"
70    PRINT"SAME AND PLAY ONE HAND WITH EACH OF THEM.  ALSO,"
75    PRINT"YOU MAY DOUBLE YOUR BET AND RECEIVE EXACTLY ONE "
80    PRINT"MORE CARD ANY TIME ON YOUR FIRST HIT.  THE TYPING"
85    PRINT"INSTRUCTIONS ARE: 0-NO HIT; 1-HIT; 2-DOUBLE; AND"
90  PRINT "3-SPLIT A PAIR."
95  IF K<> 1 THEN 155
100   PRINT"WHEN THE DEALER HAS AN EXPOSED ACE HE WILL ASK"
105   PRINT"YOU FOR AN INSURANCE BET.  AN INSURANCE BET WILL"
110   PRINT"RISK HALF YOUR BET FOR AN AMOUNT EQUAL TO YOUR BET"
115   PRINT"IF YOU WIN.  YOU WIN IF THE DEALER HAS A BLACKJACK"
120   PRINT"AND LOSE IF HE DOESN'T.  THE HOUSE LIMIT IS $500.00"
125   PRINT"GOOD LUCK.  OH, BY THE WAY, THE DEALER IS NOTED FOR"
130   PRINT"DEALING OFF THE BOTTOM OF THE DECK, WATCH HIM VERY"
135   PRINT"CLOSELY.  HERE HE IS NOW."
140   PRINT
145   PRINT
150   PRINT
155   LET K=0
160   LET W1=0
165 RANDOMIZE
170 LET N=INT(1945*RND(0)+1)
175   PRINT
180   PRINT"ANY TIME YOU WANT ME TO RESHUFFLE THE CARDS SIMPLY"
185   PRINT"TYPE 7777 WHEN I ASK FOR YOUR WAGER AND I'LL BE VERY"
190   PRINT"HAPPY TO OBLIGE.  O.K., HERE IS THE FIRST HAND."
200 LET X=INT(10*RND(0))
210 DIM D(52),E(5),V(5),T(5),W(5)
215 FOR A=1 TO 52
220   LET D(A)=0
225 NEXT A
230 DIM Q(52)
235 FOR A=0 TO 39 STEP 13
240   FOR C=1 TO 13
245     LET Q(A+C)=C
250   NEXT C
255 NEXT A
260   PRINT
265   LET K=K+1
270   FOR P=1 TO 5
275     LET E(P)=0
280     LET V(P)=3
285     LET T(P)=0
290   NEXT P
295   LET V(3)=1
300   PRINT
305   PRINT
310   PRINT
315   PRINT"WAGER";
320   LET P=1
325   INPUT W
330   LET W(2)=W
335   IF W<=0 THEN 1685
340   IF W<=500 THEN 370
345   IF W<>7777 THEN 360
350   GOSUB 1645
355   GOTO315
360   PRINT"THAT'S TOO MUCH - HOUSE LIMIT IS $500"
365   GOTO 315
370   PRINT
375 PRINT "I SHOW",
380   GOSUB 865
385   IF E(1)=0 THEN 395
390   LET V(4)=1
395   LET V(5)=1
400   GOSUB 865
405   LET M=X
410   LET P=2
415   PRINT"FIRST CARD IS",
420   GOSUB 865
425   LET G=X
430   PRINT"NEXT CARD IS",
435   GOSUB 865
440   IF V(2)>0 THEN 605
445   LET S=X
450   IF V(3)<>1 THEN 505
455   IF T(P)<>21 THEN 505
460 PRINT "    ***BLACKJACK***    "
465   PRINT
470   PRINT" THAT'S GETTING A BIT RIDICULOUS!!!!"
475   PRINT
480 PRINT "MY HOLE CARD WAS ",
485   LET X=M
490   GOSUB 1035
495   LET W1=W1+1.5*W
500   GOSUB 1335
505   IF V(4)=0 THEN 570
510   PRINT"INSURANCE ANYONE    (TYPE 1 OR 0, 1 MEANS YES)";
515   INPUT I
520   PRINT
525   IF I=0 THEN 570
530   IF T(1)<>21 THEN 555
535   LET W1=W1+W
540   PRINT
545 PRINT "YOU WIN $"W;" ON YOUR INSURANCE BET"
550   GOTO 570
555   LET W1=W1-W/2
560   PRINT
565   PRINT"YOU LOST $"W/2" ON YOUR INSURANCE BET - I DON'T HAVE BLACKJACK"
570   IF T(1)<>21 THEN 605
575   PRINT
580   PRINT"**I HAVE BLACKJACK**"
585 PRINT "MY HOLE CARD WAS ",
590   LET X=M
595   GOSUB 1035
600   GOTO 1300
605   IF T(P)<=21 THEN 650
610   IF E(P)>0 THEN 640
615   PRINT"YOU BUSTED, ";
620   PRINT"YOUR TOTAL IS "T(P)
625   LET C1=T(P)-5*(INT(T(P)/5))
630   IF V(2)=1 THEN 775
635   GOTO 1175
640   LET E(P)=E(P)-1
645   LET T(P)=T(P)-10
650   IF V(1)=2 THEN 620
655   LET V(3)=V(3)+1
660   PRINT"HIT ";
665   INPUT V(1)
670   IF V(1)<>3 THEN 830
675   IF V(2)>0 THEN 820
680   IF V(3)<>2 THEN 820
685   IF Q(G)=Q(S) THEN 700
690   PRINT"NOW IS THAT A PAIR?"
695   GOTO 660
700   LET V(2)=1
705   IF Q(G)<=1 THEN 715
710   LET V(1)=2
715   LET P=3
720   PRINT"      PLAY HAND ONE NOW"
725   PRINT"FIRST CARD IS ",
730   LET W(3)=W
735   LET X=G
740   GOSUB 750
745   GOTO 430
750   GOSUB 990
755   GOSUB 1035
760   LET V(3)=1
765   LET T(P)=C
770   RETURN
775   LET P=2
780   LET V(2)=2
785   PRINT"      PLAY HAND TWO NOW"
790   PRINT"FIRST CARD IS",
795   LET X=S
800   GOSUB 750
805   IF Q(G)=1 THEN 815
810   LET V(1)=0
815   GOTO 430
820   PRINT"NO SPLITS NOW -- TRY AGAIN"
825   GOTO 660
830   IF V(1)<>2 THEN 855
835   IF V(3)=2 THEN 850
840   PRINT"TOO LATE TO DOUBLE, CHARLIE."
845   GOTO 660
850   LET W(P)=2*W(P)
855   IF V(1)>0 THEN 430
860   GOTO 620
865   GOSUB 900
870   LET T(P)=T(P)+C
875   IF V(5)=0 THEN 890
880   LET V(5)=0
885   RETURN
890   GOSUB 1035
895   RETURN
900   IF R>=50 THEN 945
905   LET N=10*(1+ABS(COS(N+W1)))
910   FOR A=1 TO N
915     LET X=INT(52.999999*RND(Y))
920     IF X=0 THEN 915
925   NEXT A
930   IF D(X)=0 THEN 980
935     LET R=R+1
940     IF R<50 THEN 900
945   FOR A=1 TO 52
950     IF D(A)=K THEN 960
955     LET D(A)=0
960   NEXT A
965   LET R=0
970   PRINT"   I RESHUFFLED   ";
975   GOTO 900
980   LET R=0
985   LET D(X)=K
990   IF Q(X)<>1 THEN 1010
995   LET C=11
1000  LET E(P)=E(P)+1
1005  RETURN
1010  IF Q(X)>10 THEN 1025
1015  LET C=Q(X)
1020  RETURN
1025  LET C=10
1030  RETURN
1035  GOSUB 1050
1040  GOSUB 1120
1045  RETURN
1050  IF Q(X)<>1 THEN 1065
1055  PRINT" ACE ";
1060  RETURN
1065  IF Q(X)>10 THEN 1080
1070  PRINT Q(X);" ";
1075  RETURN
1080  IF Q(X)>11 THEN 1095
1085  PRINT " JACK ";
1090  RETURN
1095  IF Q(X)>12 THEN 1110
1100  PRINT" QUEEN ";
1105  RETURN
1110  PRINT" KING ";
1115  RETURN
1120  IF X>39 THEN 1145
1125  IF X>26 THEN 1155
1130  IF X>13 THEN 1165
1135  PRINT"OF SPADES"
1140  RETURN
1145  PRINT"OF CLUBS"
1150  RETURN
1155  PRINT"OF HEARTS"
1160  RETURN
1165  PRINT"OF DIAMONDS"
1170  RETURN
1175  LET P=2
1180 PRINT "MY HOLE CARD WAS ",
1185  LET X=M
1190  GOSUB 1035
1195  IF T(2)<22 THEN 1210
1200  IF V(2)=0 THEN 1300
1205  IF T(3)>21 THEN 1300
1210    LET P=1
1215    IF T(1)<17 THEN 1360
1220    IF T(1)>17 THEN 1230
1225    IF E(1)>0 THEN 1360
1230    IF T(1)>21 THEN 1375
1235    LET P=2
1240    PRINT"MY TOTAL IS "T(1)
```

40

BLKJAC

```
1245   IF T(P)>21 THEN 1300
1250   IF T(1)>21 THEN 1265
1255   IF T(1)>T(P) THEN 1300
1260   IF T(1)=T(P) THEN 1330
1265   LET W1=W1+W(P)
1270   IF C1>3 THEN 1445
1275   IF C1>2 THEN 1465
1280   IF C1>1 THEN 1485
1285   IF C1>0 THEN 1505
1290   GOTO 1525
1295   GOTO 1330
1300   LET W1=W1-W(P)
1305   IF C1>3 THEN 1545
1310   IF C1>2 THEN 1565
1315   IF C1>1 THEN 1585
1320   IF C1>0 THEN 1605
1325   GOTO 1625
1330   IF V(2)>0 THEN 1345
1335   GOSUB 1405
1340   GOTO 265
1345   LET P=3
1350   LET V(2)=0
1355   GOTO 1245
1360 PRINT "I DRAW",
1365   GOSUB 865
1370   GOTO 1210
1375   IF E(1)=0 THEN 1395
1380   LET E(1)=E(1)-1
1385   LET T(1)=T(1)-10
1390   GOTO 1210
1395   PRINT"I BUSTED*****"
1400   GOTO 1235
1405   IF W1<0 THEN 1425
1410   IF W1=0 THEN 1435
1415   PRINT"YOU'RE AHEAD $"W1
1420   RETURN
1425 PRINT USING "YOU'RE BEHIND $*###,.##", -W1
1430   RETURN
1435   PRINT"YOU'RE EVEN"
1440   RETURN
1445   PRINT
1450   PRINT"I MUST HAVE DEALT WRONG."
1455   PRINT
1460   GOTO 1330
1465   PRINT
1470   PRINT"YOU LUCKED OUT AGAIN!"
1475   PRINT
1480   GOTO 1330
1485   PRINT
1490   PRINT"YOU MUST HAVE BEEN PEEKING."
1495   PRINT
1500   GOTO 1330
1505   PRINT
1510   PRINT"I COULD LOSE MY JOB THIS WAY."
1515   PRINT
1520   GOTO 1330
1525   PRINT
1530   PRINT"THE CARDS HAVE TURNED AGAINST ME!"
1535   PRINT
1540   GOTO 1330
1545   PRINT
1550   PRINT"THE BOTTOM OF THE DECK STRIKES AGAIN!"
1555   PRINT
1560   GOTO 1330
1565   PRINT
1570   PRINT"A VICTORY FOR US GOOD GUYS."
1575   PRINT
1580   GOTO 1330
1585   PRINT
1590   PRINT"YOU CAN'T BEAT SKILL."
1595   PRINT
1600   GOTO 1330
1605   PRINT
1610   PRINT"YOU CAN'T WIN 'EM ALL."
1615   PRINT
1620   GOTO 1330
1625   PRINT
1630   PRINT"BABY GETS A NEW PAIR OF SHOES!"
1635   PRINT
1640   GOTO 1330
1645   FOR M9 = 1 TO 52
1650   LET D(M9)=0
1655   NEXT M9
1660   LET R=0
1665   PRINT
1670   PRINT" I RESHUFFLED"
1675   PRINT""
1680   RETURN
1685   END
```

SAMPLE RUN

```
TYPE 'YES' IF YOU NEED HELP? YES


THIS IS A GAME OF BLACKJACK, LAS VEGAS STYLE.
HERE ARE THE RULES OF THE HOUSE.  THE DEALER
MUST HIT ON 16 OR LESS AND WILL STAY ON 17 OR
MORE.  YOU MAY SPLIT TWO CARDS IF THEY ARE THE
SAME AND PLAY ONE HAND WITH EACH OF THEM.  ALSO,
YOU MAY DOUBLE YOUR BET AND RECEIVE EXACTLY ONE
MORE CARD ANY TIME ON YOUR FIRST HIT.  THE TYPING
INSTRUCTIONS ARE: 0-NO HIT; 1-HIT; 2-DOUBLE; AND
3-SPLIT A PAIR.

ANY TIME YOU WANT ME TO RESHUFFLE THE CARDS SIMPLY
TYPE 7777 WHEN I ASK FOR YOUR WAGER AND I'LL BE VERY
HAPPY TO OBLIGE.  O.K., HERE IS THE FIRST HAND.



WAGER? 10

I SHOW        ACE OF SPADES
FIRST CARD IS  7 OF SPADES
NEXT CARD IS  10 OF HEARTS
INSURANCE ANYONE   (TYPE 1 OR 0, 1 MEANS YES)? 0

HIT ? 0
YOUR TOTAL IS  17
MY HOLE CARD WAS            ACE OF CLUBS
I DRAW       5 OF SPADES
I DRAW       8 OF CLUBS
I DRAW       8 OF HEARTS
I BUSTED*****
MY TOTAL IS  23

YOU MUST HAVE BEEN PEEKING.

YOU'RE AHEAD $ 10


WAGER? 10

I SHOW        QUEEN OF CLUBS
FIRST CARD IS  7 OF DIAMONDS
NEXT CARD IS   QUEEN OF HEARTS
HIT ? 0
YOUR TOTAL IS  17
MY HOLE CARD WAS            6 OF DIAMONDS
I DRAW      10 OF CLUBS
I BUSTED*****
MY TOTAL IS  26

YOU MUST HAVE BEEN PEEKING.

YOU'RE AHEAD $ 20


WAGER? 10

I SHOW        8 OF SPADES
FIRST CARD IS  5 OF CLUBS
NEXT CARD IS   9 OF HEARTS
HIT ? 1
NEXT CARD IS   3 OF CLUBS
HIT ? 0
YOUR TOTAL IS  17
MY HOLE CARD WAS            4 OF DIAMONDS
I DRAW       3 OF HEARTS
I DRAW       KING OF CLUBS
I BUSTED*****
MY TOTAL IS  25

YOU MUST HAVE BEEN PEEKING.

YOU'RE AHEAD $ 30


WAGER? 10

I SHOW        KING OF SPADES
FIRST CARD IS  6 OF CLUBS
NEXT CARD IS   ACE OF HEARTS
HIT ? 1
NEXT CARD IS   JACK OF SPADES
HIT ? 0
YOUR TOTAL IS  17
MY HOLE CARD WAS            2 OF SPADES
I DRAW       4 OF HEARTS
I DRAW       2 OF DIAMONDS
MY TOTAL IS  18

YOU CAN'T BEAT SKILL.

YOU'RE AHEAD $ 20


WAGER? 10

I SHOW        6 OF HEARTS
FIRST CARD IS  3 OF SPADES
NEXT CARD IS   5 OF HEARTS
HIT ? 1
NEXT CARD IS   JACK OF HEARTS
HIT ? 0
YOUR TOTAL IS  18
MY HOLE CARD WAS            5 OF DIAMONDS
I DRAW      10 OF DIAMONDS
MY TOTAL IS  21

A VICTORY FOR US GOOD GUYS.

YOU'RE AHEAD $ 10
```

BLKJAK   PROGRAM LISTING

```
5 PRINT "WELCOME TO DIGITAL EDUSYSTEM COMPUTER BLACKJACK!!"
6 PRINT\PRINT "YOUR DEALER TONIGHT IS PETEY P. EIGHT. "
7 PRINT "WATCH HIM CLOSELY.... HE HAS A REPUTATION FOR"
8 PRINT "DEALING OFF THE BOTTOM OF THE DECK."\PRINT
9 RANDOMIZE
10 DIM A(13)
20 PRINT "QUESTIONS REQUIRING A YES OR NO ANSWER"
25 PRINT "SHOULD BE ANSWERED WITH A 'Y' FOR YES, 'N' FOR NO. "\PRINT
30 PRINT "DON'T START PLAYING WITH LESS THAN $100.. HAVE FUN!"\PRINT
40 PRINT "HOW MANY DOLLARS ARE YOU STARTING WITH";
41 INPUT F
42 PRINT
43 F1=F
50 PRINT "WHAT IS YOUR WAGER THIS TIME";
51 INPUT W
52 PRINT
53 IF W>F GOTO 56
54 IF W<10 GOTO 58
55 GOTO 100
56 PRINT "YOUR BET EXCEEDS YOUR REMAINING DOLLARS. "
57 GOTO 50
58 PRINT "MINIMUM WAGER IS $10. "
59 GOTO 50
100 GOSUB 780
102 P1=I
104 PRINT "YOUR FIRST CARD IS "CHR$(L)
106 GOSUB 780
110 P2=I
112 PRINT "YOUR SECOND CARD IS "CHR$(L)
115 GOTO 200
117 PRINT "YOU HAVE "P3" SHOWING. "
119 GOSUB 760
120 P3=P3+I
122 PRINT "YOU GOT A "CHR$(L)
123 IF P3>21 GOTO 820
124 GOTO 117
200 GOSUB 780
201 P3=P1+P2
202 D1=I
204 GOSUB 780
206 D2=I
208 PRINT "DEALER SHOWS A "CHR$(L)
210 GOTO 117
212 D3=D1+D2
214 PRINT "DEALER HAS "D3
216 IF D3>16 GOTO 222
217 GOSUB 780
218 PRINT "DEALER GETS A "CHR$(L)
219 D3=D3+I
220 GOTO 214
222 IF D3<22 GOTO 800
224 PRINT "DEALER BUSTED. "
226 GOTO 802
760 PRINT "DO YOU WANT A HIT?";
762 INPUT $K
764 PRINT
766 IF K=#N GOTO 212
768 GOSUB 780
770 RETURN
780 I=INT(13*RND(0)+1)
782 A(I)=A(I)+1
784 IF A(I)>4 GOTO 780
786 GOSUB 900
788 RETURN
800 IF D3>=P3 GOTO 820
802 F=F+W
806 PRINT "YOU WIN. YOU NOW HAVE $"F
808 GOTO 980
820 F=F-W
822 PRINT "YOU LOSE. YOU NOW HAVE $"F
824 GOTO 980
900 IF I<>1 GOTO 910
904 I=11
906 L=#A
908 GOTO 942
910 IF I<>13 GOTO 920
912 I=10
914 L=#K
916 GOTO 942
920 IF I<>12 GOTO 930
922 I=10
924 L=#Q
926 GOTO 942
930 IF I<>11 GOTO 937
932 I=10
934 L=#J
936 GOTO 942
937 IF I<>10 GOTO 940
938 L=#T
939 GOTO 942
940 L=I+48
942 RETURN
980 PRINT "DO YOU WISH TO PLAY AGAIN?";
982 INPUT $K
984 PRINT\PRINT
986 IF K=#Y GOTO 50
987 PRINT\PRINT\PRINT \IF F>F1 THEN 995
988 PRINT "TOO BAD! YOU LOST"F1-F"DOLLARS AT THE EDUSYSTEM CASINO. "
990 GOTO 998
995 PRINT "NOT BAD! YOU WON"F-F1"DOLLARS AT THE EDUSYSTEM CASINO. "
998 PRINT\PRINT "HOPE YOU ENJOYED YOURSELF.  THANKS FOR PLAYING. "
999 END

READY
```

SAMPLE RUN

```
BLJACK   EDUSYSTEM 30

WELCOME TO DIGITAL EDUSYSTEM COMPUTER BLACKJACK!!

YOUR DEALER TONIGHT IS PETEY P. EIGHT.
WATCH HIM CLOSELY.... HE HAS A REPUTATION FOR
DEALING OFF THE BOTTOM OF THE DECK.

QUESTIONS REQUIRING A YES OR NO ANSWER
SHOULD BE ANSWERED WITH A 'Y' FOR YES, 'N' FOR NO.

DON'T START PLAYING WITH LESS THAN $100.. HAVE FUN!

HOW MANY DOLLARS ARE YOU STARTING WITH?200

WHAT IS YOUR WAGER THIS TIME?20

YOUR FIRST CARD IS T
YOUR SECOND CARD IS A
DEALER SHOWS A 3
YOU HAVE  21  SHOWING.
DO YOU WANT A HIT?N
DEALER HAS  11
DEALER GETS A 2
DEALER HAS  13
DEALER GETS A T
DEALER HAS  23
DEALER BUSTED.
YOU WIN. YOU NOW HAVE $ 220
DO YOU WISH TO PLAY AGAIN?Y

WHAT IS YOUR WAGER THIS TIME?50

YOUR FIRST CARD IS K
YOUR SECOND CARD IS 7
DEALER SHOWS A 6
YOU HAVE  17  SHOWING.
DO YOU WANT A HIT?N
DEALER HAS  17
YOU LOSE. YOU NOW HAVE $ 170
DO YOU WISH TO PLAY AGAIN?Y

WHAT IS YOUR WAGER THIS TIME?50

YOUR FIRST CARD IS 5
YOUR SECOND CARD IS 2
DEALER SHOWS A 8
YOU HAVE  7  SHOWING.
DO YOU WANT A HIT?Y
YOU GOT A 7
YOU HAVE  14  SHOWING.
DO YOU WANT A HIT?Y
YOU GOT A Q
YOU LOSE. YOU NOW HAVE $ 120
DO YOU WISH TO PLAY AGAIN?Y

WHAT IS YOUR WAGER THIS TIME?100

YOUR FIRST CARD IS 9
YOUR SECOND CARD IS 4
DEALER SHOWS A 6
YOU HAVE  13  SHOWING.
DO YOU WANT A HIT?Y
YOU GOT A 2
YOU HAVE  15  SHOWING.
DO YOU WANT A HIT?Y
YOU GOT A 3
YOU HAVE  18  SHOWING.
DO YOU WANT A HIT?N
DEALER HAS  16
DEALER GETS A 2
DEALER HAS  18
YOU LOSE. YOU NOW HAVE $ 20
DO YOU WISH TO PLAY AGAIN?Y

WHAT IS YOUR WAGER THIS TIME?10

YOUR FIRST CARD IS 5
YOUR SECOND CARD IS Q
DEALER SHOWS A 4
YOU HAVE  15  SHOWING.
DO YOU WANT A HIT?Y
YOU GOT A 7
YOU LOSE. YOU NOW HAVE $ 10
DO YOU WISH TO PLAY AGAIN?N


TOO BAD! YOU LOST 190 DOLLARS AT THE EDUSYSTEM CASINO.

HOPE YOU ENJOYED YOURSELF.  THANKS FOR PLAYING.

READY
```

BOAT

Description

You are captain of a submarine and the computer is captain of a gunboat. The speed of the gunboat is given at the beginning of the game. You fire torpedos at the gunboat. To sink it, you must hit it twice in at least two vulnerable places, or once in a vulnerable place and twice in any other part of the hull. But, if you ever miss, the gunboat will open fire on you. If this happens, you alternatively fire at each other until you sink the gunboat or until he sinks you.

Source

To the best of our knowledge, we think BOAT was originally written by a student at the University of Georgia, Athens, GA.

PROGRAM LISTING

```
5 PRINT "THIS IS THE GAME OF WAR BETWEEN A SUBMARINE AND A"
10 PRINT "NAVAL GUN BOAT. WOULD YOU LIKE INSTRUCTIONS";
11 INPUT Y$
12 IF X$="NO" THEN 100
13 PRINT "YOU ARE THE CAPTAIN OF THE SUBMARINE AND THE"
14 PRINT "COMPUTER IS THE CAPTAIN OF THE GUN BOAT."
20 PRINT "THE SPEED OF THE GUN BOAT WILL BE GIVEN AT THE BEGINNING OF"
25 PRINT "THE GAME AND YOU HAVE TO HIT THE GUN BOAT TWICE"
30 PRINT "IN AT LEAST TWO VULNERABLE PLACES, OR ONCE IN A"
35 PRINT "VULNERABLE PLACE AND TWICE IN ANY OTHER PART OF THE"
40 PRINT "HULL OF THE GUN BOAT. BUT IF YOU MISS ANY ONE TIME THE"
45 PRINT "GUN BOAT WILL OPEN FIRE ON YOU UNTIL IT SINKS YOU OR YOU"
50 PRINT "SINK THE GUN BOAT! YOU WILL BE ALLOWED TO TAKE TURNS FIRE-"
55 PRINT "ING AT THE GUN BOAT ......GOOD LUCK , MEIN FURHER!!!!!!!!!"
100 A=0
110 B=0
120 RANDOMIZE
130 FOR I=1 TO 5
140 LET R=100*RND(0)
170 IF R>=10 THEN 190
180 NEXT I
190 IF R<=40 THEN 210
200 GOTO 130
210 PRINT "THE SPEED OF THE GUN BOAT IS NOW ";R;" KNOTS"
220 RANDOMIZE
230 FOR F=1 TO 5
240 LET S=10000*RND(0)
270 IF S>=1000 THEN 290
280 NEXT F
290 IF S<=10000 THEN 310
300 GO TO 230
310 PRINT "THE RANGE FROM THE GUN BOAT TO THE SUBMARINE IS"
320 PRINT "NOW ";S;" YARDS."
330 LET Z=ATN(50/R)
340 LET D3=Z*(180/3.14159)
345 PRINT "THE APPROXIMATE ANGLE YOU SHOULD FIRE YOUR TORPEDO IS"
346 PRINT "BETWEEN ";INT(D3-2);" AND ";INT(D3+2);" DEGREES."
350 INPUT D
351 LET T=D*3.14159/180
360 LET R8=S/COS(Z)
370 LET Y3=R8*SIN(Z)
380 LET Y9=R8*SIN(T)
390 LET Y2=Y3-20
400 LET Y0=Y3-40
410 LET Y4=Y3+20
420 LET Y5=Y3+40
430 IF Y9>=Y0 THEN 710
432 GOTO 520
435 IF Y9<Y2 THEN 810
450 GOTO 470
453 IF Y9<Y2 THEN 810
460 GOTO 850
470 IF Y9>=Y3 THEN 490
480 GOTO 890
490 IF Y9<Y4 THEN 930
520 PRINT "YOU MISSED!"
530 RANDOMIZE
540 LET Y0=RND(2)
550 LET W=10000*Y9
560 PRINT "THE SHOT FIRED FROM THE GUN BOAT TO THE SUBMARINE"
570 PRINT "WAS WITHIN ";ABS(W-S)*2/1000;" YARDS......."
580 IF ABS(W-S)>=2000 GOTO 120
590 PRINT "YOU ARE SUNK MEIN FRIEND!"
595 GOTO 1900
610 PRINT
612 PRINT
613 PRINT "********* YOU MADE A VUL?N?ERABLE STRIKE! *************"
620 A=A+1
630 IF A>=2 GOTO 700
640 GOTO 120
650 PRINT
651 PRINT
652 PRINT "********* YOU DAMAGED THE GUN BOAT! *************"
660 B=B+1
670 IF B>=3 GOTO 700
680 IF A+B>=3 THEN 700
690 GO TO 120
700 PRINT "I AM SUNK!........GOOD BYE CRUEL WORLD....(GLUB..GLUB..)"
705 GOTO 1800
710 PRINT "        ********    **+     !"
720 PRINT "        ********* ****+*+   !"
730 PRINT "                   HHH  !"
740 PRINT "                   UUU  ! ++++++]"
750 PRINT "                   \\\\===0=0=0"
760 PRINT "                   L----------I"
770 PRINT "              --/DR IIIIIIIII   /DD\--"
780 PRINT "              [====================]"
790 PRINT "        ----/DDDR   /HHHHH 0 0 0  0 0 HHHH\  /PDDD\-#
800 GO TO 435
810 PRINT "             FFFFFFFFFFF\................../EEEEEEEEEEEEEEE/
820 PRINT"              FFFFFFFFFFFFFFFFFFFFFFFEEFFEEEEEEEEE  0  EEEEEEEEE/
830 PRINT"     *        FFFFFFFFFFFFFFFFFFFFFFFFFFFFEEEEEEEEEEEEEEEEEEE/
840 GO TO 612
850 PRINT"\FFFFFFFFFFFFFFFFFFFFF\................../EEEEEEEEEEEEEEEE/
860 PRINT"  FFFFFFFFFF   FFFFFFFFFFFFFFFFFFFFFFE  0  EEEEEE/
870 PRINT"   \FFFFF       *     EFFFEFFFFFFFFFEEEEFEEEEEEEEEEEEE/"
880 GO TO 652
890 PRINT"\FFFFFFFFFFFFF\.................../EEEEEEEEEEEEEEE/
900 PRINT"  FFFFFFFFFFFFFFFF               EEEEE  0  EEEE/
910 PRINT"  \FFFFFFFFFFFFF        EEEEEEEEFEEEEEF/"
920 GO TO 610
930 PRINT"\FFFFFFFFFFFFFFFF\................../EEEEEEEEEEEEEEEEE/
950 PRINT"  FFFFFFFFFFFFFFFFFFFFFFFFFFFFFFFFEEEEE/
960 PRINT"  \FFFFFFFFFFFFFFFFFFFFFFFFFFFFFFEEEEEEEEEE       *"
970 GO TO 652
1800 PRINT "                              //1"
1801 PRINT "                              //HH1"
1802 PRINT "                    X>    T/HHHH1"
1803 PRINT "              *****************************"
1804 PRINT
1900 PRINT "WOULD YOU LIKE TO TRY AGAIN";
1901 INPUT Z$
1902 IF Z$="YES" THEN 5
2000 END
```

READY

SAMPLE RUN

```
THIS IS THE GAME OF WAR BETWEEN A SUBMARINE AND A
NAVAL GUN BOAT. WOULD YOU LIKE INSTRUCTIONS? YES
YOU ARE THE CAPTAIN OF THE SUBMARINE AND THE
COMPUTER IS THE CAPTAIN OF THE GUN BOAT.
THE SPEED OF THE GUN BOAT WILL BE GIVEN AT THE BEGINNING OF
THE GAME AND YOU HAVE TO HIT THE GUN BOAT TWICE
IN AT LEAST TWO VULNERABLE PLACES, OR ONCE IN A
VULNERABLE PLACE AND TWICE IN ANY OTHER PART OF THE
HULL OF THE GUN BOAT. BUT IF YOU MISS ANY ONE TIME THE
GUN BOAT WILL OPEN FIRE ON YOU UNTIL IT SINKS YOU OR YOU
SINK THE GUN BOAT! YOU WILL BE ALLOWED TO TAKE TURNS FIR-
ING AT THE GUN BOAT ......GOOD LUCK , MEIN FURHER!!!!!!!!!
THE SPEED OF THE GUN BOAT IS NOW 17.09028 KNOTS
THE RANGE FROM THE GUN BOAT TO THE SUBMARINE IS
NOW 5136.849 YARDS.
THE APPROXIMATE ANGLE YOU SHOULD FIRE YOUR TORPEDO IS
BETWEEN 69 AND 73 DEGREES.
? 71
        ********    **+      !
        ********* ****+*+    !
                   HHH  !
                   UUU  ! +++++]
                   \\\\===0=0=0
                   L----------I
              --/DR IIIIIIIII   /DD\--
              [====================]
        ----/DDDR   /HHHHH 0 0 0  0 0 HHHH\  /PDDD\----
\FFFFFFFFFFFFFFFFFFFF\................../FFFEEEEEEEEEEEEEEEE/
  FFFFFFFFFFFFFFFFFFFF               EFFEF  0  EEEEE/
  \FFFFFFFFFFFFFFFFF               EFFFFFFFEEEEEEEEEEE/


********* YOU MADE A VUL?N?ERABLE STRIKE! *************
THE SPEED OF THE GUN BOAT IS NOW  17.18836 KNOTS
THE RANGE FROM THE GUN BOAT TO THE SUBMARINE IS
NOW  3427.992 YARDS.
THE APPROXIMATE ANGLE YOU SHOULD FIRE YOUR TORPEDO IS
BETWEEN 69 AND 73 DEGREES.
? 70
YOU MISSED!
THE SHOT FIRED FROM THE GUN BOAT TO THE SUBMARINE
WAS WITHIN 6.328317 YARDS.
THE SPEED OF THE GUN BOAT IS NOW 32.91102 KNOTS
THE RANGE FROM THE GUN BOAT TO THE SUBMARINE IS
NOW 1787.37 YARDS.
THE APPROXIMATE ANGLE YOU SHOULD FIRE YOUR TORPEDO IS
BETWEEN 54 AND 58 DEGREES.
? 56
        ********    **+      !
        ********* ****+*+    !
                   HHH  !
                   UUU  ! +++++]
                   \\\\===0=0=0
                   L----------I
              --/DR IIIIIIIII   /DD\--
              [====================]
        ----/DDDR   /HHHHH 0 0 0  0 0 HHHH\  /PDDD\----
  FFFFFFFFFF\..................../FFFFEEEEEEEEEEEEEEEE/
  FFFFFFFFFFFFFFFFFFFFFFFFFFFFFFFFFFFFFFFEFFFFEEF  0  EEEEEEEEE/
  *         FFFFFFFFFFFFFFFFFFFFFFFFFFFFFFFFFFFFFFFFEEEEEEEEEEEEEEEEEEE/


********* YOU MADE A VUL?N?ERABLE STRIKE! *************
I AM SUNK!........GOOD BYE CRUEL WORLD....(GLUB..GLUB..)
                              /1
                              //HH1
                    Y>    T/HHHH1
              *******************************

WOULD YOU LIKE TO TRY AGAIN? NO


READY
```

BOMBER

FLY A WORLD WAR II BOMBER

Description

In this program, you fly a World War II bomber for one of the
four protagonists of the war. You then pick your target or the
type of plane you are flying. Depending upon your flying experience and the quality of the enemy defenders, you then may
accomplish your mission, get shot down, or make it back through
enemy fire. In any case, you get a chance to fly again.

Program Author

This program was somewhat modified at DIGITAL. The original
author is:

David Sherman
Curtis Junior High School
Sudbury, MA 01776

PROGRAM LISTING

```
5 RANDOM:PRINT"YOU ARE NOW A PILOT IN A WORLD WAR II BOMBER
10 INPUT "WHAT SIDE -- ITALY(1), ALLIES(2), JAPANESE(3), GERMANY(4)";A
20 IF A>0 AND A<5 THEN 25 ELSE PRINT "TRY AGAIN....."\GOTO 10
25 ON A GOTO 30,110,200,220
30 INPUT "WHAT IS YOUR TARGET -- ALBANIA(1), GREECE(2), NORTH AFRICA(3)";B
40 IF B>0 AND B<4 THEN 45 ELSE PRINT "TRY AGAIN....."\GOTO 30
45 PRINT\ON B GOTO 50,80,90
50 PRINT"SHOULD BE EASY,YOU'RE FLYING A NAZI-MADE PLANE.
60 GOTO 280
80 PRINT "BE CAREFUL!!!!"\GOTO 280
90 PRINT "YOU'RE GOING FOR THE OIL, EH?"\GOTO 280
110 INPUT "AIRCRAFT -- LIBERATOR(1), B-29(2), B-17(3), LANCASTER(4)";G
120 IF G>0 AND G<5 THEN 125 ELSE PRINT "TRY AGAIN....."\GOTO 110
125 PRINT\ON G GOTO 130,150,170,190
130 PRINT "YOU'VE GOT 2 TONS OF BOMBS FLYING FOR PLOESTI"
140 GOTO 280
150 PRINT "YOU'RE DROPPING THE A-BOMB ON HIROSHIMA."
160 GOTO 280
170 PRINT "YOU'RE CHASING THE BISMARK IN THE NORTH SEA."
180 GOTO 280
190 PRINT "YOU'RE BUSTING A GERMAN HEAVY WATER PLANT IN THE RUHR."
195 GOTO 280
200 PRINT "YOU'RE FLYING A KAMIKAZE (SUICIDE BOMBER) OVER THE USS LEXINGTON."
205 INPUT "YOUR FIRST KAMIKAZE MISSION (Y OR N)";F$
208 IF F$="N" THEN S=0\GOTO 358
210 PRINT\IF RND>.65 THEN 325 ELSE 380
220 PRINT "A NAZI, EH?  OH WELL.  ARE YOU GOING FOR RUSSIA(1), ENGLAND(2)"
230 INPUT"OR FRANCE(3)";M\IF M>0 AND M<4 THEN 235 ELSE PRINT "WHAT??"\GOTO 220
235 PRINT\ON M GOTO 250,260,270
250 PRINT "YOU'RE NEARING STALINGRAD....."\GOTO 280
260 PRINT "NEARING LONDON, BE CAREFUL, THEY'VE GOT A GOOD AIR-RAID DEFENCE."
265 GOTO 280
270 PRINT "NEARING VERSAILLES.  DUCK SOUP.  THEY'RE NEARLY DEFENSELESS."
280 PRINT
285 INPUT "HOW MANY MISSIONS HAVE YOU FLOWN";D
290 IF D<160 THEN 300 ELSE PRINT "MISSIONS, NOT MILES...."
295 PRINT "150 MISSIONS IS HIGH EVEN FOR OLD-TIMERS.  NOW THEN,"\GOTO 285
300 PRINT\IF D<100 THEN 310 ELSE PRINT "THAT'S PUSHING THE ODDS!"\GOTO 320
310 IF D<25 THEN PRINT "FRESH OUT OF TRAINING, EH?"
320 PRINT\IF D<160*RND THEN 330
325 PRINT "DIRECT HIT!!!!  "INT(100*RND)"KILLED! MISSION SUCCESSFUL."\GOTO 390
330 PRINT "MISSED TARGET BY"INT(2+30*RND)"MILES!!"
335 PRINT "NOW YOU'RE REALLY IN FOR IT !!"\PRINT
340 INPUT "DOES THE ENEMY HAVE GUNS(1), MISSILES(2), OR BOTH(3)";R
345 IF R>0 AND R<4 THEN 350 ELSE PRINT "TRY AGAIN....."\GOTO 340
350 PRINT\IF R=2 THEN 360
355 INPUT "WHAT IS THE PERCENT HIT RATE OF THE ENEMY GUNNERS (10 TO 50)";S
358 IF S<10 THEN PRINT "YOU LIE, BUT YOU'LL PAY....."\PRINT\GOTO 380
360 PRINT\IF R>1 THEN T=35
365 IF S+T>100*RND THEN 380
370 PRINT"YOU MADE IT THROUGH TREMENDOUS FLAK!!";GOTO 390
380 PRINT "* * * * * BOOM * * * * *"
384 PRINT "YOU HAVE BEEN SHOT DOWN......."
386 PRINT "DEARLY BELOVED, WE ARE GATHERED HERE TODAY TO PAY OUR LAST TRIBUTE.."
390 PRINT\PRINT\PRINT\INPUT "PLAY AGAIN (Y OR N)";U$\IF U$="Y" THEN 10
400 PRINT "CHICKEN!!!!!"\PRINT\PRINT
999 END
```

SAMPLE RUN

```
YOU ARE NOW A PILOT IN A WORLD WAR II BOMBER
WHAT SIDE -- ITALY(1), ALLIES(2), JAPANESE(3), GERMANY(4)? 2
AIRCRAFT -- LIBERATOR(1), B-29(2), B-17(3), LANCASTER(4)? 0
TRY AGAIN....
AIRCRAFT -- LIBERATOR(1), B-29(2), B-17(3), LANCASTER(4)? 1

YOU'VE GOT 2 TONS OF BOMBS FLYING FOR PLOESTI

HOW MANY MISSIONS HAVE YOU FLOWN? 10

FRESH OUT OF TRAINING, EH?

MISSED TARGET BY 30 MILES!!
NOW YOU'RE REALLY IN FOR IT !!

DOES THE ENEMY HAVE GUNS(1), MISSILES(2), OR BOTH(3)? 1

WHAT IS THE PERCENT HIT RATE OF THE ENEMY GUNNERS (10 TO 50)? 15

YOU MADE IT THROUGH TREMENDOUS FLAK!!


PLAY AGAIN (Y OR N)? Y
WHAT SIDE -- ITALY(1), ALLIES(2), JAPANESE(3), GERMANY(4)? 2
AIRCRAFT -- LIBERATOR(1), B-29(2), B-17(3), LANCASTER(4)? 3

YOU'RE CHASING THE BISMARK IN THE NORTH SEA.

HOW MANY MISSIONS HAVE YOU FLOWN? 200
MISSIONS, NOT MILES....
150 MISSIONS IS HIGH EVEN FOR OLD-TIMERS.  NOW THEN,
HOW MANY MISSIONS HAVE YOU FLOWN? 50

MISSED TARGET BY 28 MILES!!
NOW YOU'RE REALLY IN FOR IT !!

DOES THE ENEMY HAVE GUNS(1), MISSILES(2), OR BOTH(3)? 2


YOU MADE IT THROUGH TREMENDOUS FLAK!!


PLAY AGAIN (Y OR N)? Y
WHAT SIDE -- ITALY(1), ALLIES(2), JAPANESE(3), GERMANY(4)? 4
A NAZI, EH?  OH WELL.  ARE YOU GOING FOR RUSSIA(1), ENGLAND(2)
OR FRANCE(3)? 2

NEARING LONDON. BE CAREFUL, THEY'VE GOT A GOOD AIR-RAID DEFENCE.

HOW MANY MISSIONS HAVE YOU FLOWN? 10

FRESH OUT OF TRAINING, EH?

MISSED TARGET BY 2 MILES!!
NOW YOU'RE REALLY IN FOR IT !!

DOES THE ENEMY HAVE GUNS(1), MISSILES(2), OR BOTH(3)? 3

WHAT IS THE PERCENT HIT RATE OF THE ENEMY GUNNERS (10 TO 50)? 40

* * * * * BOOM * * * * *
YOU HAVE BEEN SHOT DOWN.......
DEARLY BELOVED, WE ARE GATHERED HERE TODAY TO PAY OUR LAST TRIBUTE.


PLAY AGAIN (Y OR N)? Y
WHAT SIDE -- ITALY(1), ALLIES(2), JAPANESE(3), GERMANY(4)? 1
WHAT IS YOUR TARGET -- ALBANIA(1), GREECE(2), NORTH AFRICA(3)? 3

YOU'RE GOING FOR THE OIL, EH?

HOW MANY MISSIONS HAVE YOU FLOWN? 120

THAT'S PUSHING THE ODDS!

MISSED TARGET BY 13 MILES!!
NOW YOU'RE REALLY IN FOR IT !!

DOES THE ENEMY HAVE GUNS(1), MISSILES(2), OR BOTH(3)? 1

WHAT IS THE PERCENT HIT RATE OF THE ENEMY GUNNERS (10 TO 50)? 30

YOU MADE IT THROUGH TREMENDOUS FLAK!!


PLAY AGAIN (Y OR N)? N
CHICKEN!!!!!


READY
```

BOUNCE

Description

This program plots a bouncing ball. Most computer plots run along the paper in the terminal (top to bottom); however, this plot is drawn horizontally on the paper (left to right).

You may specify the initial velocity of the ball and the coefficient of elasticity of the ball (a superball is about 0.85 -- other balls are much less). You also specify the time increment to be used in "strobing" the flight of the ball. In other words, it is as though the ball is thrown up in a darkened room and you flash a light at fixed time intervals and photograph the progress of the ball.

Program Author

Val Skalabrin
Newport-Mesa Unified School District
Newport Beach, CA   92660

```
BOUNCE  EDUSYSTEM 30

90 DIM T(20)
100 PRINT "THIS SIMULATION LETS YOU SPECIFY THE INITIAL VELOCITY"
110 PRINT "OF A BALL THROWN STRAIGHT UP, AND THE COEFFICIENT OF"
120 PRINT "ELASTICITY OF THE BALL. PLEASE USE A DECIMAL FRACTION"
130 PRINT "COEFFICIENT (LESS THAN 1)."
131 PRINT
132 PRINT "YOU ALSO SPECIFY THE TIME INCREMENT TO BE USED IN"
133 PRINT "'STROBING' THE BALL'S FLIGHT (TRY .1 INITIALLY)."
134 PRINT
135 PRINT "TIME INCREMENT (SEC)";
136 INPUT S2
140 PRINT
150 PRINT "VELOCITY (FPS)";
160 INPUT V
165 PRINT
170 PRINT "COEFFICIENT";
180 INPUT C
184 PRINT
185 PRINT "FEET"
186 PRINT
187 S1=INT(70/(V/(16*S2)))
190 FOR I=1 TO S1
200 T(I)=V*C^(I-1)/16
210 NEXT I
220 FOR H=INT(-16*(V/32)^2+V^2/32+.5) TO 0 STEP -.5
221 IF INT(H)<>H THEN 225
222 PRINT H;
225 L=0
230 FOR I=1 TO S1
240 FOR T=0 TO T(I) STEP S2
245 L=L+S2
250 IF ABS(H-(.5*(-32)*T^2+V*C^(I-1)*T))>.25 THEN 270
260 PRINT TAB(L/S2);"0";
270 NEXT T
275 T=T(I+1)/2
276 IF -16*T^2+V*C^(I-1)*T<H THEN 290
280 NEXT I
290 PRINT
300 NEXT H
310 PRINT TAB(1);
320 FOR I=1 TO INT(L+1)/S2+1
330 PRINT ". ";
340 NEXT I
350 PRINT
355 PRINT " 0";
360 FOR I=1 TO INT(L+.9995)
380 PRINT TAB(INT(I/S2)); I;
390 NEXT I
400 PRINT
410 PRINT TAB(INT(L+1)/(2*S2)-2);"SECONDS"
420 PRINT
430 GO TO 135
440 END

READY.
```

```
BOUNCE  EDUSYSTEM 30

THIS SIMULATION LETS YOU SPECIFY THE INITIAL VELOCITY
OF A BALL THROWN STRAIGHT UP, AND THE COEFFICIENT OF
ELASTICITY OF THE BALL. PLEASE USE A DECIMAL FRACTION
COEFFICIENT (LESS THAN 1).

YOU ALSO SPECIFY THE TIME INCREMENT TO BE USED IN
'STROBING' THE BALL'S FLIGHT (TRY .1 INITIALLY).

TIME INCREMENT (SEC)?.1

VELOCITY (FPS)?30

COEFFICIENT?.9

FEET

 14      000
               0
 13      0   0

 12   0      0
                                 00
 11   0                       0  0  0
                        0        0   0
 10   0
  9  0                0        0     0        0000
                                               0
  8  0              0        0     0   0
    0                                   0
  7              0                       0
              0        0        0       0
  6                                 0      0
  0
  5           0   0
                        0           0
  4                                        0

 30
              0              0             0
  2         0   0                0       0
                                 0
  1

  0              0           0            0
   .........................................................
  0      1       2       3       4       5       6
                      SECONDS

TIME INCREMENT (SEC)?
READY
```

BOWL

Description

This is a simulated bowling game for up to four players.
You play 10 frames. To roll the ball, you simply type
"ROLL". After each roll, the computer will show you a
diagram of the remaining pins ("0" means the pin is down,
"+" means it is still standing), and it will give you a
roll analysis:

        GUTTER
        STRIKE
        SPARE
        ERROR (on second ball if pins still standing)

Another considerably simpler bowling game was submitted by
Bion Rogers and Mark Gustitus of Springfield, PA; it is
not published.

Program Author

Paul Peraino
Woodrow Wilson High School
San Francisco, CA 94134

PROGRAM LISTING

```
90   REMARK AND ORIGINAL IDEA AND PROGRAMED BY PAUL PERAINO
180  REMARK FROM WOODROW WILSON HIGH SCHOOL
270  DIM C(15),A(100,6)
360  PRINT "WELCOME TO THE ALLEY"
450  PRINT "BRING YOUR FRIENDS"
540  PRINT "OKAY LET'S FIRST GET ACQUAINTED"
630  PRINT\PRINT\PRINT
720  PRINT "WANT INSTRUCTIONS (Y OR N)";
810  INPUT Z$
900  IF Z$="Y" THEN 990
960  IF Z$="N" THEN 1530
990  PRINT "THE GAME OF BOWLING TAKES MIND AND SKILL.DURING THE GAME"
1080 PRINT "THE COMPUTER WILL KEEP SCORE,YOU MAY COMPETE WITH"
1170 PRINT "OTHER PLAYERS(UP TO FOUR),YOU WILL BE PLAYING TEN FRAMES"
1260 PRINT "ON THE PIN DIAGRAM 'O' MEANS THE PIN IS DOWN,,,'+' MEANS THE"
1350 PRINT "PIN IS STANDING.AFTER THE GAME THE COMPUTER WILL SHOW YOUR"
1440 PRINT "SCORES ."
1530 PRINT "FIRST OF ALL...HOW MANY ARE PLAYING";
1620 INPUT R
1710 PRINT
1800 PRINT "VERY GOOD..."
1890 MAT A=ZER
1980 F=1
2070 FOR P=1 TO R
2160 M=0
2250 B=1
2340 M=0\Q=0
2430 MAT C=ZER
2520 REMARK BALL GENERATOR USING MOD '15' SYSTEM
2610 PRINT "PLAYER"P" -- TYPE ROLL"
2700 INPUT N$
2790 K=0\D=0
2880 FOR I=1 TO 20
2970 X=INT(RND(I)*100)
3060 FOR J=1 TO 10
3150 IF X<15*J THEN 3330
3240 NEXT J
3330 C(15*J-X)=1
3420 NEXT I
3510 REMARK PIN DIAGRAM
3600 PRINT "PLAYER:"P"    FRAME:"F"    BALL:"B
3690 FOR I=0 TO 3
3780 PRINT
3870 FOR J=1 TO 4-I
3960 K=K+1
4050 IF C(K)=1 THEN 4320
4140 PRINT TAB(I);"+ ";
4230 GOTO 4410
4320 PRINT TAB(I);"O ";
4410 NEXT J
4500 NEXT I
4590 PRINT\PRINT\PRINT
4680 REMARK ROLL ANALYSIS
4770 FOR I=1 TO 10
4860 D=D+C(I)
4950 NEXT I
5040 IF D-M <> 0 THEN 5220
5130 PRINT "GUTTER!!"
5220 IF NOT(B=1 AND D=10) THEN 5490
5310 PRINT "STRIKE!!!!!"
5400 Q=3
5490 IF NOT(B=2 AND D=10) THEN 5760
5580 PRINT "SPARE!!!!"
5670 Q=2
5760 IF NOT(B=2 AND D<10) THEN 6030
5850 PRINT "ERROR!!!"
5940 Q=1
6030 IF NOT(B=1 AND D<10) THEN 6210
6120 PRINT "ROLL YOUR 2ND BALL"
6210 REMARK STORAGE OF THE SCORES
6300 PRINT
6390 A(F+P,B)=D
6480 IF B=2 THEN 7020
6570 B=2
6660 M=D
6750 IF Q=3 THEN 6210
6840 A(F+P,3)=D-M
6930 IF Q=0 THEN 2520
7020 A(F+P,3)=Q
7110 NEXT P
7200 F=F+1
7290 IF F<11 THEN 2070
7295 PRINT "FRAMES"
7380 FOR I=1 TO 10
7470 PRINT I;
7560 NEXT I
7650 PRINT
7740 FOR P=1 TO R
7830 FOR I=1 TO 3
7920 FOR J=1 TO 10
8010 PRINT A(J,I);
8100 NEXT J
8105 PRINT
8190 NEXT I
8280 PRINT
8370 NEXT P
8460 PRINT "DO YOU WANT ANOTHER GAME"
8550 INPUT A$
8640 IF A$="Y" THEN 2610
8730 END
```

SAMPLE RUN

```
WELCOME TO THE ALLEY
BRING YOUR FRIENDS
OKAY LET'S FIRST GET ACQUAINTED


WANT INSTRUCTIONS (Y OR N)? Y
THE GAME OF BOWLING TAKES MIND AND SKILL.DURING THE GAME
THE COMPUTER WILL KEEP SCORE.YOU MAY COMPETE WITH
OTHER PLAYERS(UP TO FOUR).YOU WILL BE PLAYING TEN FRAMES
ON THE PIN DIAGRAM 'O' MEANS THE PIN IS DOWN...'+' MEANS THE
PIN IS STANDING.AFTER THE GAME THE COMPUTER WILL SHOW YOUR
SCORES
FIRST OF ALL...HOW MANY ARE PLAYING? 2

VERY GOOD...
PLAYER 1 -- TYPE ROLL
? ROLL
PLAYER: 1    FRAME: 1    BALL: 1

+ + + O
 O + O
  O O
   O


ROLL YOUR 2ND BALL

PLAYER 1 -- TYPE ROLL
? ROLL
PLAYER: 1    FRAME: 1    BALL: 2

O O + O
 O + O
  O O
   O


ERROR!!!

PLAYER 2 -- TYPE ROLL
? ROLL
PLAYER: 2    FRAME: 1    BALL: 1

O O O O
 O O O
  + O
   O


ROLL YOUR 2ND BALL

PLAYER 2 -- TYPE ROLL
? ROLL
PLAYER: 2    FRAME: 1    BALL: 2

O O O O
 O O O
  O O
   O


SPARE!!!!

PLAYER 1 -- TYPE ROLL
? ROLL
PLAYER: 1    FRAME: 2    BALL: 1

O O + O
 + O O
  O O
   O


ROLL YOUR 2ND BALL

PLAYER 1 -- TYPE ROLL
? ROLL
PLAYER: 1    FRAME: 2    BALL: 2

O O O O
 O O O
  O O
   O


SPARE!!!!

PLAYER 2 -- TYPE ROLL
? ROLL
PLAYER: 2    FRAME: 2    BALL: 1

O O O O
 O O +
  O O
   +


ROLL YOUR 2ND BALL

PLAYER 2 -- TYPE ROLL
? ROLL
PLAYER: 2    FRAME: 2    BALL: 2

O O O O
 O O O
  O O
   O


SPARE!!!!
```

BOXING

Description

This program simulates a three-round Olympic boxing match.
The computer coaches one of the boxers and determines his
punches and defenses, while you do the same for your boxer.
At the start of the match, you may specify your man's best
punch and his vulnerability.

There are approximately seven major punches per round, although
this may be varied in Statement 185. The best two out of
three rounds wins.

Program Author

Jesse Lynch
710 South Point Douglas Road
St. Paul, MN 55119

50

PROGRAM LISTING

```
00001 REM  PROGRAM SUBMITTED BY JESSE LYNCH, ST.PAUL, MN.
00002 J=0
00003 L=0
00005 PRINT "OLYMPIC BOXING -- 3 ROUNDS"
00007 PRINT
00010 PRINT "INPUT YOUR OPPONENT'S NAME"
00020 INPUT J$
00030 PRINT "INPUT YOUR MAN'S NAME"
00040 INPUT L$
00045 PRINT
00050 PRINT "DIFFERENT PUNCHES ARE 1 FULL SWING 2 HOOK 3 UPPERCUT 4 JAB"
00060 PRINT "WHAT IS YOUR MANS BEST";
00064 INPUT B
00070 PRINT "AND WHAT IS HIS VULNERABILITY";
00080 INPUT D
00085 PRINT
00090 B1=INT(4*RND+1)
00100 D1=INT(4*RND+1)
00110 IF B1=D1 THEN 90
00120 PRINT J$ " ADVANTAGE IS " B1 " AND DISADVANTAGE IS SECRET"
00130 FOR R=1 TO 3
00140 IF J>= 2 THEN 1040
00150 IF L>=2 THEN 1060
00160 X=0
00170 Y=0
00175 PRINT
00180 PRINT "ROUND "R" BEGINS..."
00181 PRINT ""
00185 FOR R1= 1 TO 7
00190 I=INT(10 *RND+1)
00200 IF I>5 THEN 600
00210 PRINT L$ "'S PUNCH";
00220 INPUT P
00221 IF P=B THEN 225
00222 GO TO 230
00225 X=X+2
00230 IF P=1 THEN 340
00240 IF P=2 THEN 450
00250 IF P=3 THEN 520
00270 PRINT L$ "JABS AT "J$"S HEAD ";
00271 IF D1=4 THEN 290
00275 C=INT(8*RND+1)
00280 IF C<4 THEN 310
00290 X=X+3
00300 GO TO 950
00310 PRINT "ITS BLOCKED"
00330 GO TO 950
00340 PRINT L$ " SWINGS AND ";
00341 IF D1=4 THEN 410
00345 X3 =INT(30 *RND+1)
00350 IF X3<10 THEN 410
00360 PRINT " HE MISSES ";
00375 IF X=1 THEN 950
00380 PRINT
00390 PRINT
00400 GO TO 300
00410 PRINT "HE CONNECTS!"
00420 IF X>35 THEN 980
00425 X=X+15
00440 GO TO 300
00450 PRINT L$ "GIVES THE HOOK ";
00455 IF D1=2 THEN 480
00460 H1 =INT(2*RND+1)
00470 IF H1=1 THEN 500
00475 PRINT "CONNECTS..."
00480 X=X+7
00490 GO TO 300
00500 PRINT "BUT IT'S BLOCKED !!!!!!!!!!!"
00510 GO TO 300
00520 PRINT L$ "  TRIES AN UPPERCUT    ";
00530 IF D1=3 THEN 570
00540 D5=INT(100*RND+1)
00550 IF D5<51 THEN 570
00560 PRINT " AND IT'S BLOCKED (LUCKY BLOCK!)"
00565 GO TO 300
00570 PRINT "AND HE CONNECTS!"
00580 X=X+4
00590 GO TO 300
00600 J7 =INT(4*RND+1)
00601 IF J7 =B1 THEN 605
00602 GO TO 610
00605 Y=Y+2
00610 IF J7=1 THEN 720
00620 IF J7=2 THEN 810
00630 IF J7 =3 THEN 860
00640 PRINT J$" JABS AND";
00645 IF D=4 THEN 700
00650 Z4 =INT(7*RND+1)
00655 IF Z4>4 THEN 690
00660 PRINT " IT'S BLOCKED !"
00670 GO TO 300
00690 PRINT " BLOOD SPILLS !!!"
00700 Y=Y+5
00710 GO TO 300
00720 PRINT J$ " TAKES A FULL SWING AND";
00730 IF D=1 THEN 770
00740 R6=INT(60*RND+1)
00745 IF R6 <30 THEN 770
00750 PRINT " BUT IT'S BLOCKED !"
00760 GO TO 300
00770 PRINT " POW!!!!! HE HITS HIM RIGHT IN THE FACE!"
00780 IF Y>35 THEN 1010
00790 Y=Y+15
00800 GO TO 300
00810 PRINT J$" GETS "L$" IN THE JAW  (OUCH!)"
00820 Y=Y+7
00830 PRINT "....AND AGAIN!"
00835 Y=Y+5
00840 IF Y>35 THEN 1010
00850 PRINT
00860 PRINT L$ " IS ATTACKED BY AN UPPERCUT (OH, OH)...";
00865 IF D=3 THEN 890
00870 Q4=INT(200*RND+1)
00880 IF Q4>75 THEN 920
00890 PRINT " AND "J$" CONNECTS..."
00900 Y=Y+8
00910 GO TO 300
00920 PRINT " BLOCKS AND HITS "J$" WITH A HOOK."
00930 X=X+5
00940 GO TO 300
00950 NEXT R1
00951 IF X>Y THEN 955
00952 PRINT J$ " WINS ROUND "R
00953 J=J+1
00954 GO TO 960
00955 PRINT L$ " WINS ROUND "R
00956 L=L+1
00960 NEXT R
00961 IF J>= 2 THEN 1040
00962 IF L>=2 THEN 1060
00986 PRINT J$ " IS KNOCKED COLD AND " L$" IS THE WINNER AND CHAMP ";
01000 GO TO 1280
01010 PRINT L$ " IS KNOCKED COLD AND " J$" IS THE WINNER AND CHAMP ";
01030 GO TO 1000
01040 PRINT J$ "  WINS (NICE GOING )" J$
01050 GO TO 1000
01060 PRINT L$ " AMAZINGLY WINS  "
01070 GO TO 1000
01080 PRINT
01085 PRINT
01090 PRINT "AND NOW GOODBYE FROM THE OLYMPIC ARNEA."
01100 PRINT
01110 END
```

SAMPLE RUN

```
RUN BOXING

OLYMPIC BOXING -- 3 ROUNDS

INPUT YOUR OPPONENT'S NAME
? MEATHEAD
INPUT YOUR MAN'S NAME
? SUPERMAN

DIFFERENT PUNCHES ARE 1 FULL SWING 2 HOOK 3 UPPERCUT 4 JAB
WHAT IS YOUR MANS BEST? 2
AND WHAT IS HIS VULNERABILITY? 3

MEATHEAD'S ADVANTAGE IS  4  AND VULNERABILITY IS SECRET

ROUND  1  BEGINS...

SUPERMAN'S PUNCH? 2
SUPERMAN GIVES THE HOOK...   SUPERMAN'S PUNCH? 2
SUPERMAN GIVES THE HOOK...   MEATHEAD GETS SUPERMAN IN THE JAW  (OUCH!)
....AND AGAIN!

SUPERMAN IS ATTACKED BY AN UPPERCUT (OH, OH)...
 AND MEATHEAD CONNECTS...
MEATHEAD GETS SUPERMAN IN THE JAW  (OUCH!)
....AND AGAIN!

SUPERMAN IS ATTACKED BY AN UPPERCUT (OH, OH)...
 AND MEATHEAD CONNECTS...
SUPERMAN'S PUNCH? 1
SUPERMAN SWINGS AND  HE MISSES

SUPERMAN'S PUNCH? 1
SUPERMAN SWINGS AND HE CONNECTS!
SUPERMAN'S PUNCH? 1
SUPERMAN SWINGS AND  HE MISSES

MEATHEAD WINS ROUND  1

ROUND  2  BEGINS...

MEATHEAD  TAKES A FULL SWING AND POW!!!!! HE HITS HIM RIGHT IN THE FACE!
MEATHEAD GETS SUPERMAN IN THE JAW  (OUCH!)
....AND AGAIN!

SUPERMAN IS ATTACKED BY AN UPPERCUT (OH, OH)...
 AND MEATHEAD CONNECTS...
MEATHEAD  TAKES A FULL SWING AND POW!!!!! HE HITS HIM RIGHT IN THE FACE!
MEATHEAD GETS SUPERMAN IN THE JAW  (OUCH!)
....AND AGAIN!
SUPERMAN IS KNOCKED COLD AND MEATHEAD IS THE WINNER AND CHAMP

AND NOW GOODBYE FROM THE OLYMPIC ARNEA.
```

51

BUG

Description

The object of this game is to finish your drawing of a bug
before the computer finishes his. You and the computer roll
a die alternately with each number standing for a part of
the bug. You must add the parts in the right order; in other
words, you cannot have a neck until you have a body, you
cannot have a head until you have a neck, and so on. After
each new part has been added, you have the option of seeing
pictures of the two bugs.

If you elect to see all the pictures, this program has the
ability of consuming well over six feet of Teletype paper
per run. We can only suggest recycling the paper by using
the other side.

Program Author

The author of this program is in the 7th grade at Harrison
Junior-Senior High School.

Brian Leibowitz
27 Danner Avenue
Harrison, NY 10528

PROGRAM LISTING

```
10   REM BRIAN MONTE LEIBOWITZ GRADE 7
20   REM HARRISON JR. SR. HIGH SCHOOL
30   REM HARRISON N.Y.
40   DIM Z$[3]
50   A=B=H=L=N=P=Q=R=S=T=U=V=Y=0
60   PRINT "THE GAME BUG IS LIKE THE GAME COOTI,"
70   PRINT "I HOPE YOU ENJOY THIS GAME"
80   PRINT
90   PRINT "DO YOU WANT INSTRUCTIONS";
100  INPUT Z$
110  IF Z$="NO" THEN 300
120  PRINT "THE OBJECT OF BUG IS TO FINISH YOUR BUG BEFORE I FINISH MINE"
130  PRINT "EACH NUMBER STANDS FOR A PART OF THE BUGS BODY"
140  PRINT "I WILL ROLL THE DIE FOR YOU, TELL YOU WHAT I ROLLED FOR YOU"
150  PRINT "WHAT THE NUMBER STANDS FOR, AND IF YOU CAN GET THE PART."
160  PRINT "IF YOU CAN GET THE PART I WILL GIVE IT TO YOU."
170  PRINT "THE SAME WILL HAPPEN ON MY TURN"
180  PRINT "IF THERE IS A CHANGE IN EITHER BUG I WILL GIVE YOU THE "
190  PRINT "OPTION OF SEEING THE PICTURES OF THE BUGS."
200  PRINT "THE NUMBERS STAND FOR PARTS AS FOLLOWS:"
210  PRINT "NUMBER","PART","NUMBER OF PART NEEDED"
220  PRINT "1","BODY","1"
230  PRINT "2","NECK","1"
240  PRINT "3","HEAD","1"
250  PRINT "4","FEELERS","2"
260  PRINT "5","TAIL","1"
270  PRINT "6","LEGS","6"
280  PRINT
290  PRINT
300  IF Y>0 THEN 2480
310  LET Z=INT(6*RND(0)+1)
320  C=1
330  PRINT "YOU ROLLED A "Z
340  GOTO Z OF 350,430,540,650,760,870
350  PRINT "1=BODY"
360  IF B=1 THEN 410
370  PRINT "YOU NOW HAVE A BODY"
380  B=1
390  C=0
400  GOTO 970
410  PRINT "YOU DO NOT NEED A BODY"
420  GOTO 970
430  PRINT "2=NECK"
440  IF N=1 THEN 500
450  IF B=0 THEN 520
460  PRINT "YOU NOW HAVE A NECK"
470  N=1
480  C=0
490  GOTO 970
500  PRINT "YOU DO NOT NEED A NECK"
510  GOTO 970
520  PRINT "YOU DO NOT HAVE A BODY"
530  GOTO 970
540  PRINT "3=HEAD"
550  IF N=0 THEN 610
560  IF H=1 THEN 630
570  PRINT "YOU NEEDED A  HEAD"
580  H=1
590  C=0
600  GOTO 970
610  PRINT "YOU DO NOT HAVE A NECK"
620  GOTO 970
630  PRINT "YOU HAVE A HEAD"
640  GOTO 970
650  PRINT "4=FEELERS"
660  IF H=0 THEN 740
670  IF A=2 THEN 720
680  PRINT "I NOW GIVE YOU A FEELER"
690  LET A=A+1
700  C=0
710  GOTO 970
720  PRINT "YOU HAVE TWO FEELERS ALREADY"
730  GOTO 970
740  PRINT "YOU DO NOT HAVE A HEAD"
750  GOTO 970
760  PRINT "5=TAIL"
770  IF B=0 THEN 830
780  IF T=1 THEN 850
790  PRINT "I NOW GIVE YOU A TAIL"
800  LET T=T+1
810  C=0
820  GOTO 970
830  PRINT "YOU DO NOT HAVE A BODY"
840  GOTO 970
850  PRINT "YOU ALREADY HAVE A TAIL"
860  GOTO 970
870  PRINT "6=LEG"
880  IF L=6 THEN 940
890  IF B=0 THEN 960
900  LET L=L+1
910  C=0
920  PRINT "YOU NOW HAVE "L" LEG(S)"
930  GOTO 970
940  PRINT "YOU HAVE 6 FEET ALREADY"
950  GOTO 970
960  PRINT "YOU DO NOT HAVE A BODY"
970  LET X=INT(6*RND(0)+1)
980  PRINT "I ROLLED A "X
990  GOTO X OF 1000,1080,1190,1300,1410,1520
1000 PRINT "1=BODY"
1010 IF P=1 THEN 1060
1020 PRINT "I NOW HAVE A BODY"
1030 C=0
1040 P=1
1050 GOTO 1630
1060 PRINT "I DO NOT NEED A BODY"
1070 GOTO 1630
1080 PRINT "2=NECK"
1090 IF Q=1 THEN 1150
1100 IF P=0 THEN 1170
1110 PRINT "I NOW HAVE A NECK"
1120 Q=1
1130 C=0
1140 GOTO 1630
1150 PRINT "I DO NOT NEED A NECK"
1160 GOTO 1630
1170 PRINT "I DO NOT  HAVE A BODY"
1180 GOTO 1630
1190 PRINT "3=HEAD"
1200 IF Q=0 THEN 1260
1210 IF R=1 THEN 1280
1220 PRINT "I NEEDED A HEAD"
1230 R=1
1240 C=0
1250 GOTO 1630
1260 PRINT "I DO NOT HAVE A NECK"
1270 GOTO 1630
1280 PRINT "I DO NOT NEED A HEAD "
1290 GOTO 1630
1300 PRINT "4=FEELERS"
1310 IF R=0 THEN 1390
1320 IF S=2 THEN 1370
1330 PRINT "I GET A FEELER"
1340 LET S=S+1
1350 C=0
1360 GOTO 1630
1370 PRINT "I HAVE 2 FEELERS ALREADY"
1380 GOTO 1630
1390 PRINT "I DO NOT HAVE A HEAD"
1400 GOTO 1630
1410 PRINT "5=TAIL"
1420 IF P=0 THEN 1480
1430 IF U=1 THEN 1500
1440 PRINT "I NOW HAVE A TAIL"
1450 U=1
1460 C=0
1470 GOTO 1630
1480 PRINT "I DO NOT HAVE A BODY"
1490 GOTO 1630
1500 PRINT "I DO NOT NEED A TAIL"
1510 GOTO 1630
1520 PRINT "6=LEGS"
1530 IF V=6 THEN 1590
1540 IF P=0 THEN 1610
1550 LET V=V+1
1560 C=0
1570 PRINT "I NOW HAVE "V" LEG(S)"
1580 GOTO 1630
1590 PRINT "I HAVE 6 FEET"
1600 GOTO 1630
1610 PRINT "I DO NOT HAVE A BODY"
1620 GOTO 1630
1630 IF A=2 AND T=1 AND L=6 THEN 1650
1640 GOTO 1670
1650 PRINT "YOUR BUG IS FINISHED"
1660 LET Y=Y+1
1670 IF S=2 AND P=1 AND V=6 THEN 1690
1680 GOTO 1710
1690 PRINT "MY BUG IS FINISHED"
1700 LET Y=Y+2
1710 IF C=1 THEN 300
1720 PRINT "DO YOU WANT THE PICTURES";
1730 INPUT Z$
1740 IF Z$="NO" THEN 300
1750 PRINT "*****YOUR BUG*****"
1760 PRINT
1770 PRINT
1780 IF A=0 THEN 1860
1790 FOR Z=1 TO 4
1800 FOR X=1 TO A
1810 PRINT TAB(10);
1820 PRINT "A ";
1830 NEXT X
1840 PRINT
1850 NEXT Z
1860 IF H=0 THEN 1880
1870 GOSUB 2470
1880 IF N=0 THEN 1920
1890 FOR Z=1 TO 2
1900 PRINT "          N N"
1910 NEXT Z
1920 IF B=0 THEN 2000
1930 PRINT "     BBBBBBBBBBBB"
1940 FOR Z=1 TO 2
1950 PRINT "     B          B"
1960 NEXT Z
1970 IF T=1 THEN 1990
1980 PRINT "TTTTTB          B"
1990 PRINT "     BBBBBBBBBBBB"
2000 IF L=0 THEN 2080
2010 FOR Z=1 TO 2
2020 PRINT TAB(5);
2030 FOR X=1 TO L
2040 PRINT " L";
2050 NEXT X
2060 PRINT
2070 NEXT Z
2080 FOR Z=1 TO 4
2090 PRINT
2100 NEXT Z
2110 PRINT "******MY BUG******"
2120 PRINT
2130 PRINT
2140 PRINT
2150 IF S=0 THEN 2230
2160 FOR Z=1 TO 4
2170 PRINT TAB(10);
2180 FOR X=1 TO S
2190 PRINT "F ";
2200 NEXT X
2210 PRINT
2220 NEXT Z
2230 IF R=1 THEN 2250
2240 GOSUB 2470
2250 IF Q=0 THEN 2280
2260 PRINT "          N N"
2270 PRINT "          N N"
2280 IF P=0 THEN 2360
2290 PRINT "     BBBBBBBBBBBB"
2300 FOR Z=1 TO 2
2310 PRINT "     B          B"
2320 NEXT Z
2330 IF U=1 THEN 2350
2340 PRINT "TTTTTB          B"
2350 PRINT "     BBBBBBBBBBBB"
2360 IF V=0 THEN 2450
2370 FOR Z=1 TO 2
2380 PRINT TAB(5);
2390 FOR X=1 TO V
2400 PRINT " L";
2410 NEXT X
2420 PRINT
2430 NEXT Z
2450 IF Y=0 THEN 2540
```

```
2460  GOTO 300
2470  PRINT "          HHHHHHH"
2480  PRINT "          H     H"
2490  PRINT "          H O O H"
2500  PRINT "          H     H"
2510  PRINT "          H  V  H"
2520  PRINT "          HHHHHHH"
2530  RETURN
2540  PRINT "I HOPE YOU ENJOYED THE GAME, PLAY AGAIN SOON !!!"
2550  END
```

THE GAME BUG IS LIKE THE GAME COOTI.   SAMPLE RUN
I HOPE YOU ENJOY THIS GAME

DO YOU WANT INSTRUCTIONS? YES
THE OBJECT OF BUG IS TO FINISH YOUR BUG BEFORE I FINISH MINE
EACH NUMBER STANDS FOR A PART OF THE BUGS BODY
I WILL ROLL THE DIE FOR YOU, TELL YOU WHAT I ROLLED FOR YOU
WHAT THE NUMBER STANDS FOR, AND IF YOU CAN GET THE PART.
IF YOU CAN GET THE PART I WILL GIVE IT TO YOU.
THE SAME WILL HAPPEN ON MY TURN
IF THERE IS A CHANGE IN EITHER BUG I WILL GIVE YOU THE
OPTION OF SEEING THE PICTURES OF THE BUGS.
THE NUMBERS STAND FOR PARTS AS FOLLOWS:

NUMBER	PART	NUMBER OF PART NEEDED
1	BODY	1
2	NECK	1
3	HEAD	1
4	FEELERS	2
5	TAIL	1
6	LEGS	6

YOU ROLLED A 5
5=TAIL
YOU DO NOT HAVE A BODY
I ROLLED A 5
5=TAIL
I DO NOT HAVE A BODY
YOU ROLLED A 5
5=TAIL
YOU DO NOT HAVE A BODY
I ROLLED A 3
3=HEAD
I DO NOT HAVE A NECK
YOU ROLLED A 1
1=BODY
YOU NOW HAVE A BODY
I ROLLED A 2
2=NECK
I DO NOT   HAVE A BODY
DO YOU WANT THE PICTURES? NO
YOU ROLLED A 4
4=FEELERS
YOU DO NOT HAVE A HEAD
I ROLLED A 2
2=NECK
I DO NOT   HAVE A BODY
YOU ROLLED A 6
6=LEG
YOU NOW HAVE 1 LEG(S)
I ROLLED A 3
3=HEAD
I DO NOT HAVE A NECK
DO YOU WANT THE PICTURES? YES
*****YOUR BUG*****

```
     BBBBBBBBBBBB
     B          B
     B          B
     BBBBBBBBBBBB
        L
        L
```

******MY BUG*******

YOU ROLLED A 3
3=HEAD
YOU DO NOT HAVE A NECK
I ROLLED A 3
3=HEAD
I DO NOT HAVE A NECK
YOU ROLLED A 1
1=BODY
YOU DO NOT NEED A BODY
I ROLLED A 1
1=BODY
I NOW HAVE A BODY
DO YOU WANT THE PICTURES? NO
YOU ROLLED A 1
1=BODY
YOU DO NOT NEED A BODY
I ROLLED A 6
6=LEGS
I NOW HAVE 1 LEG(S)
DO YOU WANT THE PICTURES? NO
YOU ROLLED A 6
6=LEG
YOU NOW HAVE 2 LEG(S)
I ROLLED A 2
2=NECK
I NOW HAVE A NECK
DO YOU WANT THE PICTURES? NO

*******MY BUG*******

```
       HHHHHHH
       H     H
       H O O H
       H     H
       H  V  H
       HHHHHHH
         N N
         N N
     BBBBBBBBBBBB
     B          B
     B          B
TTTTTB          B
     BBBBBBBBBBBB
       L L L L L
       L L L L L
```

YOU ROLLED A 4
4=FEELERS
YOU HAVE TWO FEELERS ALREADY
I ROLLED A 4
4=FEELERS
I GET A FEELER
DO YOU WANT THE PICTURES? NO
YOU ROLLED A 5
5=TAIL
YOU ALREADY HAVE A TAIL
I ROLLED A 1
1=BODY
I DO NOT NEED A BODY
YOU ROLLED A 4
4=FEELERS
YOU HAVE TWO FEELERS ALREADY
I ROLLED A 1
1=BODY
I DO NOT NEED A BODY
YOU ROLLED A 5
5=TAIL
YOU ALREADY HAVE A TAIL
I ROLLED A 5
5=TAIL
I DO NOT NEED A TAIL
YOU ROLLED A 5
5=TAIL
YOU ALREADY HAVE A TAIL
I ROLLED A 2
2=NECK
I DO NOT NEED A NECK
YOU ROLLED A 4
4=FEELERS
YOU HAVE TWO FEELERS ALREADY
I ROLLED A 4
4=FEELERS
I GET A FEELER
MY BUG IS FINISHED
DO YOU WANT THE PICTURES? YES
*****YOUR BUG*****

```
        A A
        A A
        A A
        A A
       HHHHHHH
       H     H
       H O O H
       H     H
       H  V  H
       HHHHHHH
         N N
         N N
     BBBBBBBBBBBB
     B          B
     B          B
TTTTTB          B
     BBBBBBBBBBBB
       L L L L L
       L L L L L
```

*** **MY BUG*******

```
        F F
        F F
        F F
        F F
       HHHHHHH
       H     H
       H O O H
       H     H
       H  V  H
       HHHHHHH
         N N
         N N
     BBBBBBBBBBBB
     B          B
     B          B
TTTTTB          B
     BBBBBBBBBBBB
       L L L L L L
       L L L L L L
```

I HOPE YOU ENJOYED THE GAME, PLAY AGAIN SOON !!!

READY

BULCOW

BULLS AND COWS GUESSING GAME

Description

In this game, a somewhat advanced version of BAGLES, the idea is that each player (you and the computer) tries to guess a 5-digit number thought up by the opposing player. A BULL is scored for each correct digit in the correct position and a COW for each correct digit but out of position. For example:

      Mystery number   51340
      Your guess   21734 scores 1 BULL and 2 COWS

In the first sample run, the human player's mystery number was 12345. In the second run, the number was 13579. Notice that on the fourth computer guess, 35719, the human player told the computer 0,5 (i.e., no BULLS and 5 COWS). This was incorrect; it should have been 1,4, but the computer could not know that until two turns later when it realized that the human had given it impossible scores.

By about the fourth or fifth guess, the computer starts taking quite a bit of time to narrow its choices between guesses. Be patient.

Program Author

Geoff Wyvill
Bradford University
Bradford, Yorkshire, England

PROGRAM LISTING

```
5 GOSUB500
10 DIMD(10,4),B(10),C(10),G(10)
15 RANDOMIZE:PRINT:PRINT:PRINT
20 LETA=0:GOTO200
30 PRINT:PRINT:PRINT:LETJ=0
35 PRINT"YOUR GUESS";:INPUTN:LETN=(N+.1)/100000
40 FORI=0TO4:LETG(I)=INT(10*N):LETN=10*N-INT(10*N)
41 FORK=0TOI-1:IFG(I)=G(K)GOTO170
42 NEXTK
43 NEXTI
45 LETP=4:LETA=0:GOSUB300
50 PRINTV"BULL";:IFV<>1THENPRINT"S";
55 IFV=5THENPRINT" - YOU WIN":GOTO20
60 PRINTW-V"COW";:IFW<>V+1THENPRINT"S";
65 IFJ=0THENLETA=1:GOTO200
68 GOSUB400
70 PRINT" - MY GUESS IS ";
75 FORI=0TO4:PRINTCHR$(D(J,I)+48);:NEXTI
80 PRINT" MY SCORE";:INPUTB(J),C(J):LETC(J)=C(J)+B(J)
81 IFB(J)>-1THENIFB(J)<6THENIFC(J)<6THENIFC(J)-B(J)>-1GOTO83
82 PRINT" - RIDICULOUS!!";:GOTO 70
83 IFB(J)=4THENIFC(J)=5GOTO82
85 IFB(J)=5THENPRINT" - I WIN - MY NUMBER WAS";:GOTO100
90 GOTO35
100 FORI=0TO4:PRINTCHR$(D(0,I)+48);:NEXTI
110 GOTO20
150 PRINT:PRINT"YOU HAVE GIVEN ME IMPOSSIBLE SCORES - GAME SPOILED"
        :GOTO 5
170 PRINT"REPEATED DIGITS NOT ALLOWED":GOTO035
200 FORP=0TO4
210 LETD(A,P)=INT(10*RND(1))
220 FORI=0TOP-1:IFD(A,I)=D(A,P)GOTO210
230 NEXTI
240 NEXTP
250 IFA=0GOTO30
260 LETJ=1:GOTO70
300 LETV=0:LETW=0
310 FORI=0TOP:IFD(A,I)=G(I)THENLETV=V+1
320 FORK=0TO4:IFD(A,K)=G(I)THENLETW=W+1
330 NEXTK
340 NEXTI
350 RETURN
400 LETP=0
405 LETG(P)=D(J,P)
410 FORI=0TOP-1:IFG(I)=G(P)GOTO430
415 NEXTI
420 FORA=1TOJ:GOSUB300
425 IFV<=B(A)THENIFW<=C(A)THENIF4-P=C(A)-WTHENIF4-P>=B(A)-VGOTO448
430 LETG(P)=G(P)+3:IFG(P)>9THENLETG(P)=G(P)-10
432 IFP=0THENIFG(P)=D(1,0)GOTO150
435 IFG(P)<>D(J,P)GOTO410
440 LETP=P-1:IFP<0THENGOTO150
445 GOTO430
448 NEXTA
450 LETP=P+1:IFP<5GOTO405
455 LETJ=J+1
460 FORI=0TO4:LETD(J,I)=G(I):NEXTI
465 RETURN
500 PRINT:PRINT:PRINT"        BRADFORD UNIVERSITY BULLS AND COWS GAME
"
510 GOTO10
999 END
```

SAMPLE RUN

```
        BRADFORD UNIVERSITY BULLS AND COWS GAME
```

```
YOUR GUESS? 12345
  0 BULLS 2 COWS - MY GUESS IS 68321 MY SCORE? 1,2
YOUR GUESS? 34567
  1 BULL 2 COWS - MY GUESS IS 61953 MY SCORE? 0,3
YOUR GUESS? 67890
  0 BULLS 3 COWS - MY GUESS IS 94231 MY SCORE? 0,4
YOUR GUESS? 67813
  0 BULLS 3 COWS - MY GUESS IS 27319 MY SCORE? 1,2
YOUR GUESS? 24678
  3 BULLS 0 COWS - MY GUESS IS 16429 MY SCORE? 1,2
YOUR GUESS? 25679
  1 BULL 1 COW - MY GUESS IS 19384 MY SCORE? 2,1
YOUR GUESS? 64378
  2 BULLS 2 COWS - MY GUESS IS 15342 MY SCORE? 2,3
YOUR GUESS? 94638
  5 BULLS - YOU WIN
```

Our mystery number was 12345
Computer's score is 1 BULL for the 3
    and 2 COWS for the 1 and 2.

```
YOUR GUESS? 12345
  1 BULL 1 COW - MY GUESS IS 46098 MY SCORE? 0,1
YOUR GUESS? 13579
  0 BULLS 2 COWS - MY GUESS IS 79321 MY SCORE? 0,4
YOUR GUESS? 24680
  0 BULLS 3 COWS - MY GUESS IS 02173 MY SCORE? 0,3
YOUR GUESS? 35680
  0 BULLS 3 COWS - MY GUESS IS 35719 MY SCORE? 0,5
YOUR GUESS? 80345
  0 BULLS 2 COWS - MY GUESS IS 91537 MY SCORE? 0,5
YOUR GUESS? 23568
  0 BULLS 4 COWS
YOU HAVE GIVEN ME IMPOSSIBLE SCORES - GAME SPOILED
```

Our mystery number was 13579

This clue was incorrect because the 9 is in
    the right place. Score should have been 1,4.

BULEYE

Description

In this game, up to 20 players throw darts at a target with
10-, 20-, 30-, and 40-point zones. The objective is to get
200 points.

You have a choice of three methods of throwing:

Throw	Description	Probable Score
1	Fast overarm	Bullseye or complete miss
2	Controlled overarm	10, 20, or 30 points
3	Underarm	Anything

You will find after playing a while that different players
will swear by different strategies. However, consider the
expected score per throw by always using Throw 3 (program
line 220):

Score (S)	Probability (P)	S x P
40	1.00-.95 = .05	2
30	.95-.75 = .20	6
20	.75-.45 = .30	6
10	.45-.05 = .40	4
0	.05-.00 = .05	0
	Expected score per throw =	18

Calculate the expected scores for the other throws and you
may be surprised!

Program Author

David Ahl
Digital Equipment Corp.
Maynard, MA 01754

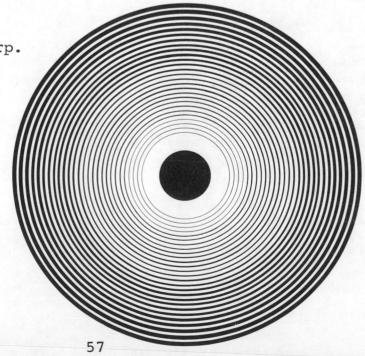

PROGRAM LISTING

```
10 REM*** BULLSEY. BY DAVE AHL
20 PRINT "GAME OF BULLSEYE"\PRINT\RANDOMIZE
30 PRINT "IN THIS GAME, UP TO 20 PLAYERS THROW DARTS AT A TARGET"
40 PRINT "WITH 10, 20, 30, AND 40 POINT ZONES.  THE OBJECTIVE IS"
50 PRINT "TO L T 200 POINTS. "\PRINT
60 PRINT "THROW","DESCRIPTION",,"PROBABLE SCORE"
70 PRINT "  1","FAST OVERARM",,"BULLSEYE OR COMPLETE MISS"
80 PRINT "  2","CONTROLLED OVERARM","10, 20, OR 30 POINTS"
90 PRINT "  3","UNDERARM",,"ANYTHING"\PRINT
100 DIM A$(20),S(20),W(10)\R,M=0\S(I)=0 FOR I=1 TO 20
110 INPUT "HOW MANY PLAYERS";N\PRINT
120 FOR I=1 TO N
130 PRINT "NAME OF PLAYER"I;\INPUT A$(I)
140 NEXT I
150 R=R+1\PRINT\PRINT "ROUND"R
160 FOR I=1 TO N
170 PRINT\PRINT A$(I)"'S THROW";\INPUT T
180 IF T<0 OR T>3 THEN PRINT "INPUT 1, 2, OR 3"\GOTO 170
190 ON T GOTO 200,210,220
200 P1=.65\P2=.55\P3=.5\P4=.5\GOTO 230
210 P1=.99\P2=.77\P3=.43\P4=.01\GOTO 230
220 P1=.95\P2=.75\P3=.45\P4=.05
230 U=RND
240 IF U>=P1 THEN PRINT "BULLSEYE!!  40 POINTS!"\B=40\GOTO 290
250 IF U>=P2 THEN PRINT "30-POINT ZONE!"\B=30\GOTO 290
260 IF U>=P3 THEN PRINT "20-POINT ZONE"\B=20\GOTO 290
270 IF U>=P4 THEN PRINT "WHEW!  10 POINTS. "\B=10\GOTO 290
280 PRINT "MISSED THE TARGET.  TOO BAD!"\B=0
290 S(I)=S(I)+B\PRINT "TOTAL SCORE ="S(I)\NEXT I
300 FOR I=1 TO N
310 IF S(I)>=200 THEN M=M+1\W(M)=I
320 NEXT I
330 IF M=0 THEN 150
340 PRINT\PRINT "WE HAVE A WINNER!!"\PRINT
350 PRINT A$(W(M))" SCORED"S(W(M))"POINTS. " FOR I=1 TO M
360 PRINT\PRINT "THANKS FOR THE GAME!"\END

READY
```

SAMPLE RUN

```
GAME OF BULLSEYE

IN THIS GAME, UP TO 20 PLAYERS THROW DARTS AT A TARGET
WITH 10, 20, 30, AND 40 POINT ZONES.   THE OBJECTIVE IS
TO GET 200 POINTS.

THROW          DESCRIPTION          PROBABLE SCORE
  1            FAST OVERARM         BULLSEYE OR COMPLETE MISS
  2            CONTROLLED OVERARM   10, 20, OR 30 POINTS
  3            UNDERARM             ANYTHING

HOW MANY PLAYERS? 2

NAME OF PLAYER 1 ? DAVE
NAME OF PLAYER 2 ? MARY

ROUND 1

DAVE'S THROW? 1
BULLSEYE!!  40 POINTS!
TOTAL SCORE = 40

MARY'S THROW? 1
20-POINT ZONE
TOTAL SCORE = 20

ROUND 2

DAVE'S THROW? 1
MISSED THE TARGET.   TOO BAD!
TOTAL SCORE = 40

MARY'S THROW? 1
BULLSEYE!!  40 POINTS!
TOTAL SCORE = 60

ROUND 3

DAVE'S THROW? 1
MISSED THE TARGET.   TOO BAD!
TOTAL SCORE = 40

MARY'S THROW? 1
MISSED THE TARGET.   TOO BAD!
TOTAL SCORE = 60

ROUND 4

DAVE'S THROW? 3
WHEW!  10 POINTS.
TOTAL SCORE = 50

MARY'S THROW? 3
20-POINT ZONE
TOTAL SCORE = 80

ROUND 5

DAVE'S THROW? 3
WHEW!  10 POINTS.
TOTAL SCORE = 60

MARY'S THROW? 3
MISSED THE TARGET.   TOO BAD!
TOTAL SCORE = 80
```

```
ROUND 6

DAVE'S THROW? 1
BULLSEYE!!  40 POINTS!
TOTAL SCORE = 100

MARY'S THROW? 2
20-POINT ZONE
TOTAL SCORE = 100

ROUND 7

DAVE'S THROW? 2
WHEW!  10 POINTS.
TOTAL SCORE = 110

MARY'S THROW? 2
WHEW!  10 POINTS.
TOTAL SCORE = 110

ROUND 8

DAVE'S THROW? 2
20-POINT ZONE
TOTAL SCORE = 130

MARY'S THROW? 2
30-POINT ZONE!
TOTAL SCORE = 140

ROUND 9

DAVE'S THROW? 1
BULLSEYE!!  40 POINTS!
TOTAL SCORE = 170

MARY'S THROW? 1
MISSED THE TARGET.   TOO BAD!
TOTAL SCORE = 140

ROUND 10

DAVE'S THROW? 1
BULLSEYE!!  40 POINTS!
TOTAL SCORE = 210

MARY'S THROW? 1
MISSED THE TARGET.   TOO BAD!
TOTAL SCORE = 140

WE HAVE A WINNER!!

DAVE SCORED 210 POINTS.

THANKS FOR THE GAME!
```

BULL

Description

In this simulated bullfight, you are the matador--i.e., the
one with the principal role and the one who must kill the
bull or be killed (or run from the ring).

On each pass of the bull, you may try:
    0 Veronica (dangerous inside move of the cape)
    1 Less dangerous outside move of the cape
    2 Ordinary swirl of the cape
Or you may try to kill the bull:
    4 Over the horns
    5 In the chest

The crowd will determine what award you deserve, posthumously
if necessary. The braver you are, the better the award you
receive. It's nice to stay alive too. The better the job
the picadores and toreadores do, the better your chances.

This program was converted to standard BASIC (DIGITAL
Timeshared-8) by students at Lexington High School under
the direction of Walt Koetke.

Source

David Sweet
Dartmouth College
Hanover, NH 03755

PROGRAM LISTING

```
  10 DIM D(20)
 200 RANDOMIZE
 202 LET L=1
 205 PRINT"DO YOU WANT INSTRUCTIONS";
 206 INPUT Z$
 207 IF Z$="NO" THEN 400
 210 PRINT"HELLO, ALL YOU BLOODLOVERS AND AFICIONADOS"
 220 PRINT"HERE IS YOUR BIG CHANCE TO KILL A BULL"
 230 PRINT
 240 PRINT"ON EACH PASS OF THE BULL, YOU MAY TRY"
 250 PRINT"0 - VERONICA (DANGEROUS INSIDE MOVE OF THE CAPE)"
 260 PRINT"1 - LESS DANGEROUS OUTSIDE MOVE OF THE CAPE"
 270 PRINT"2 - ORDINARY SWIRL OF THE CAPE"
 280 PRINT
 290 PRINT"INSTEAD OF THE ABOVE, YOU MAY TRY TO KILL THE BULL"
 300 PRINT"ON ANY TURN: 4 (OVER THE HORNS), 5 (IN THE CHEST)"
 310 PRINT"BUT IF I WERE YOU,"
 320 PRINT"I WOULDN'T TRY IT BEFORE THE SEVENTH PASS"
 330 PRINT
 340 PRINT"THE CROWD WILL DETERMINE WHAT AWARD YOU DESERVE"
 350 PRINT"POSTHUMOUSLY IF NECESSARY"
 360 PRINT"THE BRAVER YOU ARE, THE BETTER THE AWARD YOU RECIEVE"
 370 PRINT
 380 PRINT"THE BETTER A JOB THE  PICADORES AND TOREADORES DO,"
 390 PRINT"THE BETTER YOUR CHANCES ARE"
 400 PRINT
 410 PRINT
 420 LET D(5)=1
 430 LET D(4)=1
 450 DIM L$(5)
 455 LET A=INT(RND(0)*5)+1
 460 FOR I=1 TO 5
 463 READ L$(I)
 467 NEXT I
 470 DATA "SUPERB","GOOD","FAIR","POOR","AWFUL"
 490 PRINT"YOU HAVE DRAWN A "L$(A)" BULL"
 500 IF A>4 THEN 530
 510 IF A<2 THEN 550
 520 GOTO 570
 530 PRINT"YOU'RE LUCKY"
 540 GOTO570
 550 PRINT"GOOD LUCK. YOU'LL NEED IT"
 560 PRINT
 570 PRINT
 590 LET A$="PICADO"
 595 LET B$="RES"
 600 GOSUB 1610
 610 LET D(1)=C
 630 LET A$="TOREAD"
 635 LET B$="ORES"
 640 GOSUB 1610
 650 LET D(2)=C
 660 LET E=E
 670 PRINT
 680 IF Z=1 THEN 1310
 690 LET D(3)=D(3)+1
 700 PRINT"PASS NUMBER "D(3)
 710 IF D(3)<3 THEN 760
 720 PRINT"HERE COMES THE BULL! TRY FOR A KILL";
 730 GOSUB 1930
 735 ON Z1 GOTO 1130,740
 740 PRINT "CAPE MOVE";
 750 GOTO 800
 760 PRINT"THE BULL IS CHARGING AT YOU! YOU ARE THE MATADOR--"
 770 PRINT"DO YOU WANT TO KILL THE BULL";
 780 GOSUB 1930
 785 ON Z1 GOTO 1130,790
 790 PRINT"WHAT MOVE DO YOU MAKE WITH THE CAPE";
 800 INPUT E
 810 IF E<>INT(ABS(E))THEN 830
 820 IF E<3 THEN 850
 830 PRINT"DON'T PANIC, YOU IDIOT! PUT DOWN A CORRECT NUMBER"
 840 GOTO 800
 850 LET D=D
 860 IF E=0 THEN 920
 870 IF E=1 THEN 900
 880 LET M=0.5
 890 GOTO 930
 900 LET M=2
 910 GOTO 930
 920 LET M=3
 930 LET L=L+M
 940 LET F=(6-A+M/10)*RND(0)/((D(1)+D(2)+D(3)/10)*5)
 950 IF F<0.51 THEN 660
 960 PRINT"THE BULL HAS GORED YOU"
 970 ON FNA(0) GOTO 980,1010
 980 PRINT"YOU ARE DEAD"
 990 LET D(4)=1.5
1000 GOTO 1310
1010 PRINT"YOU ARE STILL ALIVE"
1020 PRINT"DO YOU RUN FROM THE RING";
1030 GOSUB 1930
1035 ON Z1 GOTO 1040,1070
1040 PRINT"COWARD"
1050 LET D(4)=0
1060 GOTO 1310
1070 PRINT"YOU ARE BRAVE. STUPID, BUT BRAVE"
1080 ON FNA(0) THEN 1090,1110
1090 LET D(4)=2
1100 GOTO 660
1110 PRINT"YOU ARE GORED AGAIN"
1120 GOTO 970
1130 LET C=C
1140 LET Z=1
1150 PRINT"IT IS THE MOMENT OF TRUTH. HOW DO YOU TRY TO KILL THE BULL";
1160 INPUT H
1170 IF H=4 THEN 1230
1180 IF H=5 THEN 1230
1210 PRINT"YOU PANICKED. THE BULL GORED YOU."
1220 GOTO 970
1230 LET K=(6-A)*10*RND(0)/((D(1)+D(2))*5*D(3))
1240 IF J=4 THEN 1290
```

```
1250 IF K>0.2 THEN 960
1260 PRINT"YOU KILLED THE BULL"
1270 LET D(5)=2
1280 GOTO 1320
1290 IF K>0.8 THEN 960
1300 GOTO 1260
1310 PRINT
1320 PRINT
1330 PRINT
1340 IF D(4)<>0 THEN 1390
1350 PRINT"THE CROWD BOOS FOR TEN MINUTES. IF YOU EVER DARE TO SHOW"
1360 PRINT"YOUR FACE IN A RING AGAIN. THEY SWEAR THEY WILL KILL YOU--"
1370 PRINT"UNLESS THE BULL DOES FIRST"
1380 GOTO 1580
1390 DEF FNC(Q)=(4.5+L/6-(D(1)+D(2))*2.5+4*D(4)+2*D(5)-(D(3)↑2)/120-A)*█
1400 IF D(4)<>2 THEN 1430
1410 PRINT"THE CROW CHEERS WILDLY"
1420 GOTO 1450
1430 IF D(5)<>2 THEN 1450
1440 PRINT"THE CROWD CHEERS"
1450 PRINT"THE CROWD AWARDS YOU ";
1460 IF FNC(Q)<2.4 THEN 1570
1470 IF FNC(Q)<4.9 THEN 1550
1480 IF FNC(Q)<7.4 THEN 1520
1500 PRINT"OLE! YOU ARE 'MUY HOMBRE'! OLE! OLE!"
1510 GOTO 1580
1520 PRINT"BOTH EARS OF THE BULL"
1530 PRINT"OLE!"
1540 GOTO 1580
1550 PRINT"ONE EAR OF THE BULL"
1560 GOTO 1580
1570 PRINT"NOTHING"
1580 PRINT
1590 PRINT"ADIOS"
1600 GOTO 2030
1610 LET B=3/A*RND(0)
1620 IF B<0.37 THEN 1740
1630 IF B<0.5 THEN 1720
1640 IF B<0.63 THEN 1700
1650 IF B<0.87 THEN 1680
1660 LET C=0.1
1670 GOTO 1750
1680 LET C=0.2
1690 GOTO 1750
1700 LET C=0.3
1710 GOTO 1750
1720 LET C=0.4
1730 GOTO 1750
1740 LET C=0.5
1750 LET T=INT(10*C+0.2)
1760 PRINT"THE "A$;B$" DID A "L$(T)" JOB"
1770 IF 4>T THEN 1900
1780 IF 5=T THEN 1870
1790 ON FNA(K) GOTO 1800,1900
1800 IF A$="TOREAD" THEN 1820
1810 PRINT"ONE OF THE HORSES OF THE "A$;B$" WAS GORED"
1820 ON FNA(K) GOTO 1830,1850
1830 PRINT"ONE OF THE "A$;B$" WAS KILLED"
1840 GOTO 1900
1850 PRINT"NO "A$;B$" WERE KILLED"
1860 GOTO 1900
1870 IF A$="TOREAD" THEN 1890
1880 PRINT FNA(K)" OF THE HORSES OF THE "A$;B$" GORED"
1890 PRINT FNA(K)" OF THE "A$;B$" KILLED"
1900 PRINT
1910 RETURN
1920 DEF FNA(K)=INT(RND(0)*2)+1
1930 INPUT A$
1950 IF A$="YES" THEN 1990
1960 IF A$="NO" THEN 2010
1970 PRINT"INCORRECT ANSWER, PLEASE PRINT 'YES' OR 'NO'";
1980 GOTO 1930
1990 LET Z1=1
2000 GOTO 2020
2010 LET Z1=2
2020 RETURN
2030 END

READY
```

SAMPLE RUN

```
DO YOU WANT INSTRUCTIONS? YES
HELLO, ALL YOU BLOODLOVERS AND AFICIONADOS
HERE IS YOUR BIG CHANCE TO KILL A BULL

ON EACH PASS OF THE BULL, YOU MAY TRY
0 - VERONICA (DANGEROUS INSIDE MOVE OF THE CAPE)
1 - LESS DANGEROUS OUTSIDE MOVE OF THE CAPE
2 - ORDINARY SWIRL OF THE CAPE

INSTEAD OF THE ABOVE, YOU MAY TRY TO KILL THE BULL
ON ANY TURN: 4 (OVER THE HORNS), 5 (IN THE CHEST)
BUT IF I WERE YOU,
I WOULDN'T TRY IT BEFORE THE SEVENTH PASS

THE CROWD WILL DETERMINE WHAT AWARD YOU DESERVE
POSTHUMOUSLY IF NECESSARY
THE BRAVER YOU ARE, THE BETTER THE AWARD YOU RECIEVE

THE BETTER A JOB THE  PICADORES AND TOREADORES DO,
THE BETTER YOUR CHANCES ARE


YOU HAVE DRAWN A SUPERB BULL
GOOD LUCK. YOU'LL NEED IT


THE PICADORES DID A SUPERB JOB

THE TOREADORES DID A SUPERB JOB


PASS NUMBER  1
THE BULL IS CHARGING AT YOU! YOU ARE THE MATADOR--
DO YOU WANT TO KILL THE BULL? NO
WHAT MOVE DO YOU MAKE WITH THE CAPE? 0
THE BULL HAS GORED YOU
YOU ARE DEAD


THE CROWD AWARDS YOU ONE EAR OF THE BULL

ADIOS


READY

RUN

DO YOU WANT INSTRUCTIONS? NO


YOU HAVE DRAWN A POOR BULL

THE PICADORES DID A POOR JOB
ONE OF THE HORSES OF THE PICADORES WAS GORED
ONE OF THE PICADORES WAS KILLED

THE TOREADORES DID A POOR JOB
NO TOREADORES WERE KILLED


PASS NUMBER  1
THE BULL IS CHARGING AT YOU! YOU ARE THE MATADOR--
DO YOU WANT TO KILL THE BULL? NO
WHAT MOVE DO YOU MAKE WITH THE CAPE? 2

PASS NUMBER  2
THE BULL IS CHARGING AT YOU! YOU ARE THE MATADOR--
DO YOU WANT TO KILL THE BULL? NO
WHAT MOVE DO YOU MAKE WITH THE CAPE? 2

PASS NUMBER  3
HERE COMES THE BULL! TRY FOR A KILL? NO
CAPE MOVE? 1

PASS NUMBER  4
HERE COMES THE BULL! TRY FOR A KILL? NO
CAPE MOVE? 0

PASS NUMBER  5
HERE COMES THE BULL! TRY FOR A KILL? NO
CAPE MOVE? 1

PASS NUMBER  6
HERE COMES THE BULL! TRY FOR A KILL? NO
CAPE MOVE? 0

PASS NUMBER  7
HERE COMES THE BULL! TRY FOR A KILL? NO
CAPE MOVE? 2

PASS NUMBER  8
HERE COMES THE BULL! TRY FOR A KILL? YES
IT IS THE MOMENT OF TRUTH. HOW DO YOU TRY TO KILL THE BULL? 4
THE BULL HAS GORED YOU
YOU ARE DEAD


THE CROWD AWARDS YOU ONE EAR OF THE BULL

ADIOS


READY
```

BUNNY

PRINTS THE PLAYBOY RABBIT

```
    UN
    BUN                                            NNYBUN
    BUNNYB                                       NYBUNNYBUN
    BUNNYBUN                                    UNNYBUNNYBUN
     UNNYBUNNY                                NYBUNNYBUNNYBU
     NNYBUNNYBU                              UNNYBUNNYBUNNYB
      NYBUNNYBUNN                            YBUNNYBUNNYBUNNY
       YBUNNYBUNNY                          NNYBUNNYBUNNYBUNN
       BUNNYBUNNYB                          UNNYBUNNYBUNNYBUN
        UNNYBUNNYBU                         BUNNYBUNNYBUNNYB
        NNYBUNNYBUN                         YBUNNYBUNNYBUNNY
         NYBUNNYBUNNY                       NYBUNNYBUNNYBUNN
          YBUNNYBUNNYB                     NNYBUNNYBUNNYBU
           BUNNYBUNNYBU                   UNNYBUNNYBUNNYB
            UNNYBUNNYBUN                 BUNNYBUNNYBUNN
             NNYBUNNYBUN  YBUNNYBUNNYBU
              NYBUNNYBUNNYBUNNYBUNNY
              YBUNNYBUNNYBUNNYBUNN
              BUNNYBUNNYBUNNYBU
              NNYBUNNYBUNNY
              NYBUNNYBUN
              YBUNNYBU
              UNNYBUNNYBUNN
             NYBUNNYBUNNYBUNNYB
            UNNYBUNNYBUNNYBUNNYBU
            BUNNYBUNNYBUNNYBUNNYBUN
           NYBUNNYBUNNYBUNNYBUNNYBUNN
           NNYBUNNYBUNNYBUNNYBUNNYBUNNY
          UNNYBUNN    UNNYBUNNYBUNNYBUNNY
          BUNNYBUN     UNNYBUNNYBUNNYBUNNYB
          YBUNNYBUN     UNNYBUNNYBUNNYBUNNYB
          NYBUNNYBUN    BUNNYBUNNYBUNNYBUNNYB
         NNYBUNNYBUNNYBUNNYBUNNYBUNNYBUNNYB
         UNNYBUNNYBUNNYBUNNYBUNNYBUNNYBUNNYB
         NNYBUNNYBUNNYBUNNYBUNNYBUNNYBUNNY
         NYBUNNYBUNNYBUNNYBUNNYBUNNYBUNNY
         YBUNNYBUNNYBUNNYBUNNYBUNNYBUNN
         UNNYBUNNYBUNNUBUNNYBUNNYBUNN
          BUNNYBUNNYBUNNYBUNNYBUN Y
            YBUN YBUNNYB   NYBU    B
            BUNNY    NYBUNNYB      U
           YBUNN   U  YBUNNYB          N
           NYBUNN     NYBUNNY     NYBUNN
          NNYBUNNYBUNNYBUNNY UNN
          UNN     N Y  N YBUNNYBU
          BU      NN    N Y     Y
                  NN  UNNY
                    NNY
                    NY
```

BUZZWD

Description

This program is an invaluable aid for preparing speeches and briefings about computers and high technology. This buzzword generator provides sets of three highly-acceptable words to work into your material. Your audience will never know that the phrases don't really mean much of anything because they sound so great! Full instructions for running are given in the program.

Source

BUZZWORD was adapted from the GE timesharing program by:

Tom Kloos
Oregon Museum of Science and Industry
Portland, Oregon 97200

PROGRAM LISTING

```
100 PRINT"THIS COMPUTER DEMONSTRATION IS A NEW AID FOR"
110 PRINT"PREPARING SPEECHES AND BRIEFINGS.  IT'S A BUZZWORD"
120 PRINT"GENERATOR WHICH PROVIDES YOU WITH A SET OF 3 HIGHLY"
130 PRINT"ACCEPTABLE WORDS TO WORK INTO YOUR MATERIAL.  THE WORDS"
140 PRINT"DON'T ACTUALLY MEAN ANYTHING, BUT THEY SOUND GREAT."
150 PRINT
160 PRINT"THE PROCEDURE:"
170 PRINT"    THINK OF ANY THREE NUMBERS BETWEEN 0 AND 9.  ENTER"
180 PRINT"    THEM AFTER THE '?' SEPARATED BY COMMAS.   YOUR"
190 PRINT"    BUZZWORD WILL BE PRINTED OUT.  TYPING '100' FOR"
191 PRINT"    EACH OF YOUR CHOICES STOPS THIS PROGRAM."
210 PRINT "WHAT ARE YOUR THREE NUMBERS";
220 GOTO260
230 PRINT
240 PRINT
250 PRINT"THREE MORE NUMBERS";
260 INPUT N,M,P
265 IF N=100 THEN 1290
270 IF N<0 THEN 1240
280 IF P<0 THEN 1240
290 IF M<0 THEN 1240
300 IF N>9 THEN 1240
310 IF P>9 THEN 1240
320 IF M>9 THEN 1240
330 PRINT
340 IF N=0 THEN 640
350 IF N=1THEN 660
360 IF N=2THEN 680
370 IF N=3THEN 700
380 IF N=4 THEN 720
390 IF N=5THEN 740
400 IF N=6THEN 760
410 IF N=7THEN 780
420 IF N=8THEN 800
430 IF N=9THEN 820
440 IF M=0 THEN 840
450 IF M=1 THEN 860
460 IF M=2 THEN 880
470 IF M=3 THEN 900
480 IF M=4 THEN 920
490 IF M=5 THEN 940
500 IF M=6 THEN 960
510 IF M=7 THEN 980
520 IF M=8 THEN 1000
530 IF M=9 THEN 1020
540 IF P=0 THEN 1040
550 IF P=1 THEN 1060
560 IF P=2 THEN 1080
570 IF P=3 THEN 1100
580 IFP=4 THEN 1120
590 IF P=5 THEN 1140
600 IF P=6 THEN 1160
610 IF P=7  THEN 1180
620 IF P=8 THEN 1200
630 IF P=9 THEN 1220
640 PRINT" INTEGRATED";
650 GOTO440
660 PRINT" TOTAL";
670 GOTO440
680 PRINT "SYSTEMATIZED";
690 GOTO440
700 PRINT" PARALLEL";
710 GO TO 440
720 PRINT" FUNCTIONAL";
730 GOTO440
740 PRINT" RESPONSIVE";
750 GOTO440
760 PRINT" OPTIMAL";
770 GOTO440
780 PRINT" SYNCHRONIZED";
790 GOTO440
800 PRINT " COMPATIBLE";
810 GOTO440
820 PRINT" BALANCED";
830 GOTO440
840 PRINT" MANAGEMENT";
850 GOTO 540
860 PRINT" ORGANIZATIONAL";
870 GOTO 540
880 PRINT" MONITORED";
890 GOTO 540
900 PRINT" RECIPROCAL";
910 GOTO 540
920 PRINT" DIGITAL";
930 GOTO 540
940 PRINT" LOGISTICAL";
950 GOTO 540
960 PRINT " TRANSITIONAL";
970 GOTO 540
980 PRINT" INCREMENTAL";
990 GOTO 540
1000 PRINT" THIRD-GENERATION";
1010 GO TO 540
1020 PRINT" POLICY";
1030 GOTO 540
1040 PRINT" OPTIONS"
1050 GOTO 230
1060 PRINT " FLEXIBILITY"
1070 GO TO 230
1082 PRINT" CAPABILITY"
1090 GOTO230
1100 PRINT" MOBILITY"
1110 GOTO230
1120 PRINT" PROGRAMMING"
1130 GO TO 230
1140 PRINT" CONCEPT"
1150 GOTO230
1160 PRINT" TIME-PHASE"
1170 GOTO230
1180 PRINT" PROJECTION"
1190 GOTO230
1200 PRINT" HARDWARE"
1210 GOTO230
1220 PRINT" CONTINGENCY"
1230 GOTO230
1240 PRINT
1250 PRINT
1260 PRINT"NUMBERS MUST BE BETWEEN 0 AND 9.  PLEASE SELECT THREE MORE."
1270 GOTO 260
1280 GOTO 260
1290 PRINT "GOODBYE FOR NOW!    "
1300 PRINT\PRINT\PRINT
1310 CHAIN "DEMON "
1320 END
```

SAMPLE RUN

```
BUZZWD  EDUSYSTEM-35

THIS COMPUTER DEMONSTRATION IS A NEW AID FOR
PREPARING SPEECHES AND BRIEFINGS.  IT'S A BUZZWORD
GENERATOR WHICH PROVIDES YOU WITH A SET OF 3 HIGHLY
ACCEPTABLE WORDS TO WORK INTO YOUR MATERIAL.  THE WORDS
DON'T ACTUALLY MEAN ANYTHING, BUT THEY SOUND GREAT.

THE PROCEDURE:
    THINK OF ANY THREE NUMBERS BETWEEN 0 AND 9.  ENTER
    THEM AFTER THE '?' SEPARATED BY COMMAS.   YOUR
    BUZZWORD WILL BE PRINTED OUT.  TYPING '100' FOR
    EACH OF YOUR CHOICES STOPS THIS PROGRAM.
WHAT ARE YOUR THREE NUMBERS?1,2,3

 TOTAL MONITORED MOBILITY


THREE MORE NUMBERS?2,3,4

SYSTEMATIZED RECIPROCAL PROGRAMMING


THREE MORE NUMBERS?0,0,0

 INTEGRATED MANAGEMENT OPTIONS


THREE MORE NUMBERS?9,8,7

 BALANCED THIRD-GENERATION PROJECTION


THREE MORE NUMBERS?7,8,9

 SYNCHRONIZED THIRD-GENERATION CONTINGENCY


THREE MORE NUMBERS?5,3,8

 RESPONSIVE RECIPROCAL HARDWARE


THREE MORE NUMBERS?2,6,4

SYSTEMATIZED TRANSITIONAL PROGRAMMING


THREE MORE NUMBGRS?3,4,5

 PARALLEL DIGITAL CONCEPT


THREE MORE NUMBERS?100,1001-,100
GOODBYE FOR NOW!
```

64

CALNDR

Description

This program prints out a calendar for any year. You must
specify the starting day of the week of the year in Statement
130. (Sunday (0), Monday (-1), Tuesday (-2), etc.). You can
determine this by using the program WEKDAY. You must also
make two changes for leap years in Statements 360 and 620.
The program listing describes the necessary changes. Running
the program produces a nice 12-month calendar.

Program Author

Geoffrey Chase, OSB
Portsmouth Abbey School
Portsmouth, RI 02871

PROGRAM LISTING

```
100 REM: VALUES FOR 1973; SEE NOTES
110 '
120 FOR I=1 TO 6\ PRINT CHR$(10);\ NEXT I
130 D=-1      '1973 STARTS ON MON. [0=SUN.,-1=MON.,-2=TUE...]
140 S=0
150 REM: READ DAYS OF EACH MONTH
160 FOR N=0 TO 12 \ READ M(N) \ NEXT N
170 '''''''
180 FOR N=1 TO 12
190 PRINT \ PRINT \ S=S+M(N-1)
200 PRINT "**";S;TAB(7);
210 FOR I=1 TO 18 \ PRINT "*"; \ NEXT I
220 ON N GOTO 230,240,250,260,270,280,290,300,310,320,330,340
230 PRINT " JANUARY "; \GOTO 350
240 PRINT " FEBRUARY"; \GOTO 350
250 PRINT "  MARCH  "; \GOTO 350
260 PRINT "  APRIL  "; \GOTO 350
270 PRINT "   MAY   "; \GOTO 350
280 PRINT "   JUNE  "; \GOTO 350
290 PRINT "   JULY  "; \GOTO 350
300 PRINT "  AUGUST "; \GOTO 350
310 PRINT "SEPTEMBER"; \GOTO 350
320 PRINT " OCTOBER "; \GOTO 350
330 PRINT " NOVEMBER"; \GOTO 350
340 PRINT " DECEMBER";
350 FOR I=1 TO 18 \ PRINT "*"; \ NEXT I
360 PRINT 365-S;"**"
370 '    [366-S       ON LEAP YEARS]
380 PRINT CHR$(10) \ PRINT "    S       M       T       W";
390 PRINT "       T       F       S"
400 PRINT
410 FOR I=1 TO 59 \ PRINT "*"; \ NEXT I
420 ''''
430 FOR W=1 TO 6
440 PRINT CHR$(10)
450 PRINT TAB(4);
460 ''
470 FOR G=1 TO 7
480 D=D+1
490 D2=D-S
500 IF D2>M(N) THEN 580
510 IF D2>0 THEN PRINT D2;
520 PRINT TAB(4+8*G);
530 NEXT G
540 ''
550 IF D2=M(N) THEN 590
560 NEXT W
570 ''''
580 D=D-G
590 NEXT N
600 '''''''
610 FOR I=1 TO 6\ PRINT CHR$(10);\ NEXT I
620 DATA 0,31,28,31,30,31,30,31,31,30,31,30,31
630 '   [0,31,29,  ...  ON LEAP YEARS]
640 END
```

REM: IF YOU HAVE NO CHR$(), SUBSTITUTE "PRINT" FOR "PRINT CHR$(10);"
REM: AND "PRINT \ PRINT" FOR "PRINT CHR$(10)" (WITHOUT SEMICOLON).

SAMPLE RUN

```
** 0  **************** JANUARY **************** 365 **
    S       M       T       W       T       F       S
*************************************************************
            1       2       3       4       5       6
    7       8       9       10      11      12      13
    14      15      16      17      18      19      20
    21      22      23      24      25      26      27
    28      29      30      31

** 31 **************** FEBRUARY**************** 334 **
    S       M       T       W       T       F       S
*************************************************************
                                    1       2       3
    4       5       6       7       8       9       10
    11      12      13      14      15      16      17
    18      19      20      21      22      23      24
    25      26      27      28

** 59 **************** MARCH  **************** 306 **
    S       M       T       W       T       F       S
*************************************************************
                                    1       2       3
    4       5       6       7       8       9       10
    11      12      13      14      15      16      17
    18      19      20      21      22      23      24
    25      26      27      28      29      30      31

** 90 **************** APRIL  **************** 275 **
    S       M       T       W       T       F       S
*************************************************************
    1       2       3       4       5       6       7
    8       9       10      11      12      13      14
    15      16      17      18      19      20      21
    22      23      24      25      26      27      28
    29      30

** 120 **************** MAY  **************** 245 **
    S       M       T       W       T       F       S
*************************************************************
                                    1       2       3       4       5
    6       7       8       9
STOP
```

CAN·AM

CANADIAN-AMERICAN AUTO RACE

Description

CAN-AM is a simulation of a Canadian-American Challenge Cup auto race. The road course is fast (speeds up to 200 m.p.h.). It is long (5.3 miles) and complex (8 curves and 8 straights). You are racing the latest Group 7 cars (McLarens, Lolas, etc.).

The instructions provided by the program are self-explanatory. You should really take heed of track hazards--i.e., rain and oil, except, of course, slowing down too much puts you out of contention. BEWARE: This game is very challenging and addictive!

Computer Limitations

The program was written for the Honeywell/GE 635 at Dartmouth. The main inconsistency with other computers is that several people may race using multiple terminals; this is generally not possible on smaller machines.

The comments on the listing are extremely comprehensive and entertaining. We apologize for not having a sample run, but it got wiped out.

Program Author

Mark Manasse
Hanover, NH 03755

```
100 ' CAN-AM*** (BASIC PROGRAM BEGINS AT LINE 610) WAS PROGRAMMED BY MARK
110 ' MANASSE, TO REPLACE THE AILING VERSION HE WROTE AS A SIXTH GRADER
120 ' AT HANOVER ELEMENTARY SCHOOL.
130 ' LAST CHANGE 12/27/72 BY DIANE MATHER, KIEWIT
140 '
150 ' DESCRIPTION--THE PROGRAM ALLOWS YOU TO RACE AROUND A HIGHLY
160 ' PERILOUS COURSE, RISKING BOTH LIFE AND MACHINE, IN AN
170 ' EFFORT TO RACE FRIENDS OR THE COMPUTER'S VERY OWN SLOW-
180 ' POKE SAM, WILDMAN WILLY, AND HOTSHOT HARRY
190 '
200 ' INSTRUCTIONS--
210 ' YOU ARE ABOUT TO RACE.  RACE ON ONE OF THE FASTEST COURSES
220 ' IN THE WORLD.  A ROAD COURSE.  A LONG ONE.  5.3 MILES.  SPEEDS
230 ' UP TO 200 MPH. YOU CAN RACE FRIENDS(?) OR THE COMPUTER.
240 ' TO RACE THE COMPUTER, TYPE THE SEQUENCE:
250 '
260 '     /OLD CAN-AM***/RUN
270 '
280 ' TO RACE FRIENDS, TYPE:
290 '
300 '     /OLD CAN-AM***/LINK <KEYWORD>,N
310 '
320 ' REPLACE <KEYWORD> WITH ANY WORD OF LENGTH 1 THROUGH 8 INCLUSIVE
330 ' THAT YOU CHOOSE.  REPLACE N WITH THE NUMBER OF PLAYERS COUNTING
340 ' YOURSELF.  HAVE YOUR FRIENDS TYPE:
350 '
360 '     JOIN <KEYWORD>
370 '
380 ' <KEYWORD> SHOULD BE THE KEYWORD YOU USED IN THE 'LINK' COMMAND
390 '
400 ' WHEN THE COMPUTER TYPES A QUESTION OF THE FORM
410 '     STRAIGHT A?    OR    CURVE 1:
420 ' RESPOND BY TYPING THE SPEED (IN MPH) YOU DESIRE TO TRAVEL AT,
430 ' AND HIT THE RETURN KEY.  GOOD LUCK.  YOU MAY NEED IT.
440 '
450 ' IF YOU ARE USING A TERMINAL WITH BOTH UPPER AND LOWERCASE, TYPE
460 ' WORD ANSWERS (SUCH AS YES OR NO) IN CAPITAL LETTERS.
470 '
480 ' TO STOP THIS LISTING, PRESS THE 'S' OR 'ATTN' KEY.
490 '
500 ' FOR MORE INFORMATION ON MULTIPLE-TERMINAL PROGRAMMING, (AS
510 ' WHEN SEVERAL PEOPLE RACE EACH OTHER), SEE TM009 WHICH IS
520 ' AVAILABLE FROM THE KIEWIT DOCUMENT CENTER (SECRETARIAL AREA),
530 ' KIEWIT COMPUTATION CENTER, HANOVER, N. H. 03755, PHONE
540 ' (603) 646-2643.
550 '
560 ' EXPLANATION OF CHANGES--
570 '    12/27/72--TO REWORD INSTRUCTIONS.
580 '
590 '* * * * * * * * * * * * * * * * * * * *
600 '
610 REM   PLEASE REFER ALL BUGS OR COMMENTS TO DIANE
620 REM   MATHER, PROGRAM LIBRARIAN, 105 KIEWIT
630 '
640 LET O(0)=2                         'STANDARD MOTIF HEADER
650 LET O(1) = ASC(SOH)
660 LET O(2) = ASC(N)
670 CHANGE O TO O1$
680 LET O(2) = ASC(Q)
690 CHANGE O TO O$
700 PRINT O1$;O$;CHRS(13);"XX ARE YOU FAMILIAR WITH THE WAY THIS GAME WORKS";
710 DATA NON,OUI,PARLEZ-VOUS ANGLAIS?,NEIN,JA,SPRECHEN SIE ENGLISCH?
720 DATA NOPE,YUP,COMPUTERS ARE SOPHISTICATED MACHINES.  USE  APPROPRIATE LANGUAGE.
730 LET K9=5                          'TWICE NUMBER OF KNOWN LANGUAGES
740 FOR X=1 TO K9-1 STEP 2
750     READ F$(X),F$(X+1),R$((X-1)/2+1)
760 NEXT X
770 REM WE HAVE JUST LEARNED FOREIGN LANGUAGES
780 DATA WILDMAN WILLY,HOTSHOT HARRY,SLOWPOKE SAM 'NAMES OF DRIVERS WHO COMPETE AGAINST ONLY ONE PERSON.  (AUTO-PILOTS)
790 MAT READ Q$(3)                    'NAME ARRAY
800 DATA -2.9,-2.9,-5                 'AMT. SPEED TO BE SUBTRACTED FROM AUTO-PILOT'  SPEEDS
810 MAT READ Q(3)
820 MAT READ M$(3)                    'READ NAMES OF TYPES OF ROADWAY
830 READ X$                           'DEATH MESSAGE
840 INPUT A$                          'RESPONSE TO DO YOU KNOW WHAT YOU'RE DOING?
850 IF A$>"09" THEN 890               'IF BETWEEN 01 AND 09, THEN MULTI-TERMINAL
860 IF A$<"01" THEN 890
870 LET O9=VAL(A$)
880 GOTO 960
890 LET O$=""                         'SET THINGS UP FOR SINGLE TERMINAL
900 GOSUB 2190
910 IF A$="NO" THEN 1070
920 PRINT "RATE YOURSELF AS A DRIVER.  (1-BEST,3-WORST)";
930 INPUT O
940 LET Q(3)=Q(3)*O
950 GOTO 1050
960 LET O(2) = ASC(A)                 'CREATE O$ ARRAY FOR MULTI-TERMINAL
970 CHANGE O TO O$(10)                'STANDARD MOTIF
980 FOR I = 0 TO O9
990     LET O(2) = ASC(C)+I
1000    CHANGE O TO O$(I)
1010 NEXT I
1020 PRINT O$(10);"YOU MAY 'DRAFT' (SLIPSTREAM) OFF OF ANY CAR AHEAD"
1030 PRINT "OF YOU.  (BUT NOT MORE THAN 1 SECOND AHEAD).  TO DO THIS"
1040 PRINT "TYPE HIS CAR NUMBER+1000 AS YOUR SPEED."
1050 RANDOMIZE
1060 IF A$="YES" THEN 1110
1070 PRINT O$(0)
1080 PRINT "FOR INSTRUCTIONS, PLEASE TYPE LIST AFTER THE COMPUTER SAYS READY."
1090 PRINT
1100 IF A$="NO" THEN 2290
1110 LET F2=INT(RND*10)+6
1120 FOR A=0 TO O9                    'ASSIGN NUMBERS AND ADHESION FACTORS
1130    PRINT O$(A);"YOUR DRIVING NUMBER IS";F2*(A+1)+A 'ADHESION FACTOR IS HOW WELL YOUR CAR GRIPS THE ROAD
1140    LET A(A)=RND*.05+.05
1150    PRINT O$(A);"ADHESION FACTOR";A(A)*100-5;".  (THE LOWER THE BETTER)"
1160 NEXT A
1170 PRINT O$(10);"YOUR MAX. SPEED IS 200 MPH.  TO SEE STANDINGS INPUT"
1180 PRINT "O AS YOUR SPEED"
1190 PRINT O$(0);"WOULD YOU LIKE TO SEE THE COURSE";CHRS(63*SGN(O9));O$; 'PRINT ? IF  MULT-TERM, OTHERWISE DON'T
1200 MAT INPUT A$
1210 PRINT O$(10);
1220 LET A$=A$(NUM)
1230 GOSUB 2190
1240 IF A$="NO" THEN 1450
```

68

```
1250 IF A$<>"YES" THEN 1190
1260 PRINTTAB(4);"----------------"        'PRINT COURSE
1270 PRINTTAB(3);"/1";TAB(11);"B";TAB(19);"2\"
1280 PRINTTAB(2);"/A";TAB(20);"C\"
1290 PRINTTAB(1);"/";TAB(22);"\"
1300 PRINT "/";TAB(21);"3I"
1310 PRINT "^-START*FINISH";TAB(22);"I"
1320 PRINT "^";TAB(22);"I"
1330 PRINT "^";TAB(21);"DI"
1340 PRINT "^";TAB(22);"I"
1350 PRINT "^";TAB(22);"I"
1360 PRINT "^H";TAB(22);"I"
1370 PRINT "^";TAB(22);"I"
1380 PRINT "^";TAB(21);"4I"
1390 PRINT "^";TAB(16);"_____/"
1400 PRINT "^8";TAB(15);"(5 E"
1410 PRINT "^";TAB(16);"\"
1420 PRINT "\";TAB(17);"----------)";CHR$(13);TAB(20);"/PITS\"
1430 PRINT " \7";TAB(14);"G";TAB(21);"F^";TAB(27);"6I"
1440 PRINT"  _____/"
1450 LET N=RND*3+1
1460 PRINT"
     NOTE:  THIS IS A";INT(N);"LAP RACE."
1470 PRINT"
GENTLEMEN, START YOUR ENGINES!  THE GREEN GOES DOWN AND"
1480 PRINT"OFF YOU GO!"
1490 DATA STRAIGHT,HAIRPIN,CURVE
1500 DATA MAY I SHOW YOU TO A PLOT?  WE HAVE A NICE CHOICE OF HEADSTONES.
1510 LET Q=-1
1520 LET H=INT(N)
1530 FOR V=1 TO N                          'WORKING PORTION
1540     LET Y=FNA(M$(1),200,1,3/10,65) 'STRAIGHT A, 200 MAX., 3/10 MILE LONG
1550     LET Y=FNA(M$(3),125,1,1/10,49) 'CURVE 1, 125 MAX., 1/10 MILE LONG
1560     LET Y=FNA(M$(1),200,2,13/20,66) 'STRAIGHT B, 200 MAX., 13/20 MILE LONG
1570     LET Y=FNA(M$(3),125,1,1/10,50) 'CURVE 2, 125 MAX., 1/10 MILE LONG
1580     LET Y=FNA(M$(1),200,1,1/5,67) 'STRAIGHT C, 200 MAX., 1/5 MILE LONG
1590     LET Y=FNA(M$(3),150,1,3/20,51) 'CURVE 3, 150 MAX., 3/20 MILE LONG
1600     LET Y=FNA(M$(1),200,2,3/5,68) 'STRAIGHT D, 200 MAX., 3/5 MILE LONG
1610     LET Y=FNA(M$(3),125,1,1/10,52) 'CURVE 4, 125 MAX., 1/10 MILE LONG
1620     LET Y=FNA(M$(1),200,1,1/4,69) 'STRAIGHT E, 200 MAX., 1/4 MILE LONG
1630     LET Y=FNA(M$(2),100,.75,3/20,53) 'HAIRPIN 5, 100 MAX., 3/20 MILE LONG
1640     LET Y=FNA(M$(1),200,1.5,9/20,70) 'STRAIGHT F, 200 MAX., 9/20 MILE LONG
1650     LET Y=FNA(M$(2),100,.75,3/20,54) 'HAIRPIN 5, 100 MAX., 3/20 MILE LONG
1660     LET Y=FNA(M$(1),200,2,1,71)    'STRAIGHT G, 200 MAX., 1 MILE LONG
1670     LET Y=FNA(M$(3),125,1,1/10,55) 'CURVE 7, 125 MAX., 1/10 MILE LONG
1680     LET Y=FNA(M$(3),150,1,3/20,56) 'CURVE 8, 150 MAX., 3/20 MILE LONG
1690     LET Y=FNA(M$(1),200,2,7/10,72) 'STRAIGHT H, 200 MAX., 7/10 MILE LONG
1700     IF V=H THEN 1740
1710     LET Y=FNA("START-FINISH (CURVE 9)",150,1,3/20,127)
1720     REM         NAME OF TRACK       ,MAX,#,LEN ,ASC
1730     REM         START-FINISH, 150 MAX., 3/20 MILE LONG
1740 NEXT V
1750 IF G1=1 THEN 2040                  'ALL DEAD?
1760 PRINT O$(10);"DO YOU MEAN THAT EVERYONE ISN'T DEAD?  WELL, HERE ARE " 'NO, SO PRINT OUT RESULTS OF RACE
1770 PRINT"THE RESULTS STRAIGHT FROM THE CHECKERED FLAG:
"
1780 LET W=1E+37
1790 IF O9=0 THEN 1820
1800 LET G5=O9
1810 GOTO 1830
1820 LET G5=3
1830 FOR Z=0 TO G5
1840     IF O9>0 THEN 1880
1850     IF Z=0 THEN 1880
1860     PRINT O$(Z);
1870     GOTO 1890
1880     PRINT"GUY #";F2*(Z+1)+Z;
1890     IF D(Z)=0 THEN 1950
1900     PRINT" IS LOOKIN' AT THEM PEARLY GATES."
1910     IF O9=0 THEN 1990
1920     PRINT O$(Z);"TELL ST. LUCIFER NOT TO EXPECT ME, O.K.?"
1930     PRINT O$(10);
1940     GOTO 1990
1950     PRINT" TOOK";T(Z);"SECONDS.  WHICH AVERAGES OUT TO";3600*5.3*H/T(Z);"MPH" 'T ARRAY IS TIME ARRAY
1960     IF T(Z)>W THEN 1990
1970     LET W=T(Z)                     'NEW LEADING TIME AND DRIVER
1980     LET N=F2*(Z+1)+Z
1990 NEXT Z
2000 IF O9>0 THEN 2020
2010 IF N>F2 THEN 2040
2020 PRINT O$((N-F2)/(F2+1));"NICE RACE, MR";N
2030 PRINT O$(10);"AND THAT MEANS THAT GUY #";N;"WINS!!!"
2040 PRINT O$(0);"ANOTHER RACE";CHR$(63*SGN(O9));O$;
2050 MAT INPUT A$
2060 LET A$=A$(NUM)
2070 GOSUB 2190
2080 IF A$="NO" THEN 2290
2090 IF A$<>"YES" THEN 2040
2100 FOR Z=0 TO 10                      'RESET FOR NEXT GAME
2110     LET T(Z)=D(Z)=0
2120 NEXT Z
2130 PRINT O$(10);"NEW SET-UP.  NO RAIN, NO DEBRIS";
2140 IF G1=0 THEN 2160                  'IF EVERYBODY'S DEAD, BE NASTY.
2150 PRINT ", AND (PLEASE!) BETTER DRIVERS."
2160 PRINT
2170 LET G1=F5=0                        'UNKILL EVERYBODY AND UNCIL THE TRACK
2180 GOTO 1110
2190 FOR X=1 TO K9                      'FOREIGN LANGUAGE HANDLER
2200     IF A$=F$(X) THEN 2230
2210 NEXT X
2220 GOTO 2280
2230 PRINT O$(0);R$((X-1)/2+1)
2240 IF X=INT(X/2)*2 THEN 2270
2250 LET A$="NO"
2260 GOTO 2280
2270 LET A$="YES"
2280 RETURN
2290 STOP
```

69

```
CONTROL FUNCTION
2300                                    '------- --------

2310 DEF FNA(A$,R,B,C,D)               'KIND TRACK, MAX. SPEED, ADHESION FUDGE FACTOR, LENGTH
2320                                    'ASC(LETTER FOLLOWING KIND OF TRACK)
2330 IF G1=1 THEN 4250                 'ALL DEAD?
2340 GOSUB 2800                        'GET SOME HAZARDS (IE RAIN, OIL)
2350 GOSUB 3220                        'GET EVERYONE'S SPEED
2360 FOR G=0 TO 09                     'CHECK FOR SAFE SPEEDS
2370      IF D(G)=1 THEN 2780
2380      IF (B+A(G)+E)*S(G)/B<=R*(1+RND*.1) THEN 2500
2390      PRINT O$(G);X$               'PRINT DEAD MESSAGE
2400      LET F5=F5+1                  'INCREMENT OIL COUNTER
2410      LET E(F5)=D                  'AND THE 635 SAID "LET THERE BE OIL."  AND THERE IT WAS.
2420      FOR Z=0 TO 09                'AND THE TRACK ABOUNDED WITH OIL.  AND THE 635 SAID "BOY, WHAT
2430          IF Z=G THEN 2450         'A MAN TRAP!"
2440          PRINT O$(Z);"GUY #";F2*(G+1)+G;"JUST WIPED REAL GOOD ('N DEAD!)" 'IN THE MEANTIME, IT HAS BEEN BUSY NOTIFYING PEOPLE
2450      NEXT Z                       'OF THEIR COMRADE'S DEMISE.
2460      LET D(G)=1                   'OFFICIALLY PRONOUNCE DEAD.  D IS FOR DEATH
2470      LET Q=Q+1                    'INCREMENT DEAD COUNTER
2480      IF Q=09 THEN 4230            'EVERYBODY DEAD?
2490      GOTO 2780
2500      LET Y4=T(G)                  'RATS.  HE DIDN'T WIPE
2510 IF (B+A(G)+E)*S(G)/B<=R THEN 2530
2520 PRINT O$(G);"NEARLY HAD TO SAY GOOD BYE." 'ALMOST WIPED
2530      LET T(G)=T(G)+C/(S(G)/3600)+L(G) 'UPDATE HIS TIME
2540      IF 09>0 THEN 2660            'SEE IF, HEAVEN FORBID, HE PASSED SOMEBODY
2550      FOR X4=1 TO 3
2560          IF D(X4)=1 THEN 2650
2570          LET Z4=T(X4)-(C/(S(X4)/3600))
2580          LET Z1=Y4-Z4
2590          LET Z2=T(G)-T(X4)
2600          IF SGN(Z2)<>-SGN(Z1) THEN 2650
2610          IF SGN(Z2)=1 THEN 2640
2620          PRINT "YOU JUST PASSED ";Q$(X4)
2630          GOTO 2650
2640          PRINT Q$(X4);" JUST PASSED YOU"
2650      NEXT X4
2660      FOR X4=G+1 TO 09
2670          IF D(X4)=1 THEN 2770
2680          IF S(X4)=0 THEN 2770
2690          IF SGN(Y4-T(X4))=SGN(T(G)-(T(X4)+C/(S(X4)/3600))) THEN 2770
2700          IF SGN(T(G)-(T(X4)+C/(S(X4)/3600)))<>-1 THEN 2740
2710          PRINT O$(X4);"GUY";F2*(G+1)+G;"JUST PASSED YOU."
2720          PRINT O$(G);"YOU JUST PASSED GUY";F2*(X4+1)+X4
2730          GOTO 2770
2740          IF SGN(T(G)-(T(X4)+C/(S(X4)/3600)))=0 THEN 2770
2750          PRINT O$(G);"GUY";F2*(X4+1)+X4;"JUST PASSED YOU."
2760          PRINT O$(X4);"YOU JUST PASSED GUY";F2*(G+1)+G
2770      NEXT X4
2780 NEXT G                            'PROCEED TO THE FATE OF THE NEXT VICTIM
2790 GOTO 4250                         'NO MORE VICTIMS.  (THIS TIME!!)
2800 REM  HAZARDS
2810 PRINT O$(10);                     'MAKE SURE WE DON'T USE LAST SECTION'S OIL ON THIS SECTION
2820 LET E=0
2830 MAT L=ZER                         'KILL PIT STOPS FROM LAST TIME
2840 LET L(0)=0
2850 IF F5<2 THEN 2900                 'IF COURSE WELL GREASED, DISSOLVE GREASE
2860 PRINT "THE RED FLAG HAS BEEN PUT OUT.  CARS REMAIN"
2870 PRINT "MOTIONLESS UNTIL DEBRIS IS CLEARED"
2880 MAT E=ZER
2890 LET F5=0
2900 FOR X=1 TO F5                     'SEE IF THOSE PLAYING DESERVE OIL
2910      IF E(X)=D THEN 2940
2920 NEXT X
2930 GOTO 2970
2940 PRINT"YIKES!  OIL ON THE TRACK!"  'IF SO, NOTIFY SURVIVORS AND OTHERS
2950 LET E=.2
2960 GOTO 3130
2970 IF F3=1 THEN 3130                 'HAVE WE HAD RAIN?
2980 IF RND>.025+G8 THEN 3130          'SEE IF IT SHOULD BE STOPPED OR STARTED
2990 IF R(0)<.1 THEN 3080              'IS IT RAINING?
3000 IF RND>.5 THEN 3130               'STOP IT?
3010 PRINT "GLORY BE, THE RAIN HAS STOPPED!  BUT REMEMBER IT IS STILL WET"
3020 LET F3=1                          'RAIN, RAIN, GO AWAY, WON'T COME BACK ANOTHER DAY
3030 FOR A=0 TO 09
3040      LET R(A)=R(A)-.075           'DELETE MOST OF THE EFFECTS
3050      LET G8=.025                  'MAKE IT LESS LIKELY TO RAIN IN LATER RACES
3060 NEXT A
3070 GOTO 3130
3080 PRINT "RAIN!  SLOW DOWN!!"        'HALLELUJAH, MY RAIN DANCE WORKED
3090 FOR A=0 TO 09                     'MAKE TRACK SLIPPERY
3100      LET R(A)=R(A)+.1
3110      LET G8=.1
3120 NEXT A
3130 IF C<>9/20 THEN 3210              'PIT STOPS?
3140 IF RND <.125 THEN 3210
3150 FOR X=0 TO 09
3160      IF RND*SGN(09)<.75 THEN 3200
3170      IF D(X)=1 THEN 3200
3180      LET L(X)=RND*3+5
3190      PRINT O$(X);"YOU ARE IN THE PITS FOR";L(X);"SECONDS."
3200 NEXT X
3210 RETURN                            'WE WUZ HERE (AND LEFT!)
3220 REM  INPUT
3230 MAT S=ZER                         'RESET SPEED ARRAY
3240 IF 09>0 THEN 3270                 'PRINT OUT SOMETHING LIKE 'STRAIGHT A'
3250 PRINT A$;" ";CHR$(D);
3260 GOTO 3280
3270 PRINT O$(10);A$;" ";CHR$(D);": ";O$;
3280 LET S()=0                         'GET EVERYBODY'S SPEEDS
3290 FOR A=0 TO 09
3300      IF D(A)=0 THEN 3330
3310      PRINT O$(A)                  'IF HE'S DEAD, DON'T GIVE HIM A CHANCE TO INPUT
3320      PRINT O$;
3330 NEXT A
3340 MAT INPUT J                       'INPUT SOMEBODY'S SPEED
3350 IF NUM=1 THEN 3390                'SOMEBODY TYPED SOMETHING.  SET UP SPEED AND TTY#
3360 LET N=J(1)
3370 LET S=J(2)
3380 GOTO 3410
```

70

```
3390 LET S=J(1)
3400 LET N=0
3410 IF D(N)=0 THEN 3450                'IS THE GUY DEAD?
3420 PRINT O$(N);"BUT I THOUGHT YOU WERE DEAD." 'RE-INFORM HIM THAT HE IS AN UN-PERSON
3430 PRINT O$;
3440 GOTO 3340
3450 IF S(N)=0 THEN 3480                'HAS THIS GUY ALREADY TOLD US HIS SPEED?
3460 PRINT O$(N);"WAIT A SEC.  I STILL NEED";O9-U-Q;"MORE SPEEDS." 'TELL HIM TO BUZZ OFF
3470 GOTO 3430
3480 LET A=N
3490 IF S<=200 THEN 3620                'DID HE TRY TO EXCEED HIS MAX. SPEED?
3500 IF O9=0 THEN 3600
3510 IF S<1000 THEN 3600
3520 LET R4=(S-1000-F2)/(F2+1)          'IT'S OK.  HE ONLY WANTS TO DRAFT
3530 IF R4=INT(R4) THEN 3560            'NOW SEE IF HE PICKED A LEGAL CAR
3540 PRINT O$(N);"ILLEGAL CAR"          'HE DIDN'T
3550 GOTO 3640
3560 IF R4>O9 THEN 3540
3570 IF D(R4)>0 THEN 3540
3580 IF ABS(T(N)-T(R4)-.5)=>.5 THEN 3540
3590 GOTO 3700                          'HE DID!!!
3600 PRINT O$(N);"MAYBE A LITTLE HARD ON THE PEDDLE?  BE REALISTIC." 'OPTIMIST
3610 GOTO 3640
3620 IF S>0 THEN 3660
3630 GOSUB 3990
3640 PRINT "HOW FAST";CHR$(63*SGN(O9));O$;
3650 GOTO 3340
3660 IF S=>20 THEN 3690                 'WHERE DOES HE THINK HE IS?  THE LONG ISLAND EXPRESSWAY?
3670 PRINT O$(N);"I DOUBT YOU WANT TO GO THAT SLOWLY"
3680 GOTO 3640
3690 LET S(N)=S                         'SINCE HE MADE IT THIS FAR, ASSUME THAT IT'S LEGAL
3700 LET U=U+1
3710 IF R4=0 THEN 3740
3720 LET H(N)=R4                         'IF HE'S DRAFTING, TELL ME TO WHOM
3730 LET R4=0
3740 IF U<O9-Q THEN 3430                 'ARE WE DONE?
3750 LET U=0                             'YES!
3760 IF O9>0 THEN 3890                   'SET SPEEDS FOR AUTO-PILOTS
3770 FOR F0=1 TO 3
3780     IF D(F0)=1 THEN 3870
3790     LET S=R*B/(B+.1+E+G8)+(RND*3+Q(F0))
3800     IF (B+.1+G8+E)*S/B<=R THEN 3850
3810     LET D(F0)=1
3820     PRINT O$(10);Q$(F0);" JUST WIPED" 'AND INFORM US IF THEY WIPE
3830     LET F5=F5+1
3840     LET E(F5)=D
3850     LET T(F0)=T(F0)+C/(S/3600)
3860     LET S(F0)=S
3870 NEXT F0
3880 GOTO 3980
3890 FOR X2=0 TO O9                      'NOW HANDLE DRAFTERS
3900     IF D(X2)=1 THEN 3970
3910     IF S(X2)<>0 THEN 3970
3920     IF S(H(X2))<>0 THEN 3950
3930     LET H(X2)=H(H(X2))
3940     GOTO 3920
3950     LET S(X2)=S(H(X2))              'SET HIS SPEED TO HIS DRAFTEES, AND
3960     LET T(X2)=(T(X2)+T(H(X2)))/2    'HALVE THE DISTANCE BETWEEN THEM
3970 NEXT X2
3980 RETURN                             'NOW GO COUNT SURVIVORS AND INCREMENT TIMES
3990 REM PLACING
4000 PRINT O$(A)                        'TELL ME HOW I'M DOING
4010 IF O9=0 THEN 4040
4020 LET G5=O9
4030 GOTO 4050
4040 LET G5=3
4050 FOR G=0 TO G5
4060     IF G=A THEN 4200
4070     IF O9>0 THEN 4100
4080     PRINT Q$(G);" IS";              'I AM RACING AGAINST AUTO-PILOTS
4090     GOTO 4110
4100     PRINT "GUY#";F2*(G+1)+G;"IS";   'I AM RACING AGAINST FRIENDS(?)
4110     IF D(G)<>1 THEN 4140
4120     PRINT " OUT OF THE RACE."       'IF COMPETITOR HAS MET HIS MAKER, SAY SO
4130     GOTO 4200
4140     ON SGN(T(A)-T(G))+2 GOTO 4150,4170,4190 'BUSINESS PART
4150     PRINT T(G)-T(A);"SECONDS BEHIND YOU" 'GOOD NEWS
4160     GOTO 4200
4170     PRINT " RIGHT BESIDE YOU."        SO SO
4180     GOTO 4200
4190     PRINT T(A)-T(G);"SECONDS AHEAD OF YOU." 'BAD NEWS
4200 NEXT G
4210 PRINT"
YOU'VE TAKEN";T(A);"SECONDS." 'MORE BAD NEWS
4220 RETURN                             'AND AN ANTI-CLIMACTIC ENDING. (STOLEN FROM SPIEL*** AND SPACEWAR)
4230 PRINT O$(10);"GUY#";F2*(G+1)+G;", THE LAST OF THE GREAT RACERS, JUST WIPED."
4240 LET G1=1                           'ALL HUMANS ARE DEAD, SO GRIND THIS MANGLE TO A HALT, AND SET A FLAG TO THAT EFFECT
4250 FNEND                              'AND RETURN FROM WHENCE WE CAME
4250 END
READY
```

71

CHANGE

COMPUTER IMITATES CASHIER

Description

In this program, the computer pretends it is the cashier at
your friendly neighborhood candy store. You tell it the cost
of the item(s) you are buying, the amount of your payment, and
it will automatically (!) determine your correct change. Aren't
machines wonderful?

Program Author

Dennis Lunder
People's Computer Co.
Menlo Park, CA   94025

```
2 PRINT "I, YOUR FRIENDLY EDUSYSTEM COMPUTER, WILL DETERMINE"
3 PRINT "THE CORRECT CHANGE FOR ITEMS COSTING UP TO $100,"
4 PRINT\PRINT
10 PRINT "COST OF ITEM"J\INPUT A\PRINT "AMOUNT OF PAYMENT"J\INPUT P
20 C=P-A\M=C\IF C<>0 THEN 90 \PRINT "CORRECT AMOUNT,THANK YOU"
30 GO TO 10
90 IF C>0 THEN 120 \PRINT "SORRY,YOU HAVE SHORT CHANGED ME $"JA-P
100 GO TO 10
120 PRINT "YOUR CHANGE,$"JC\D=INT(C/10)\IF D=0 THEN 155
150 PRINT DJ"TEN DOLLAR BILL(S)"
155 C=M-(D*10)\E=INT(C/5)\IF E=0 THEN 185
180 PRINT EJ"FIVE DOLLAR BILL(S)"
185 C=M-(D*10+E*5)\F=INT(C)\IF F=0 THEN 215
210 PRINT FJ"ONE DOLLAR BILL(S)"
215 C=M-(D*10+E*5+F)\C=C*100\N=C\G=INT(C/50)\IF G=0 THEN 255
250 PRINT GJ"ONE-HALF DOLLAR(S)"
255 C=N-(G*50)\H=INT(C/25)\IF H=0 THEN 285
280 PRINT HJ"QUARTER(S)"
285 C=N-(G*50+H*25)\I=INT(C/10)\IF I=0 THEN 315
310 PRINT IJ"DIME(S)"
315 C=N-(G*50+H*25+I*10)\J=INT(C/5)\IF J=0 THEN 345
340 PRINT JJ"NICKEL(S)"
345 C=N-(G*50+H*25+I*10+J*5)\K=INT(C+.5)\IF K=0 THEN 380
370 PRINT KJ"PENNY(S)"
380 PRINT "THANK YOU,COME AGAIN"\PRINT \PRINT \GO TO 10
999 END
```

```
I, YOUR FRIENDLY EDUSYSTEM COMPUTER, WILL DETERMINE
THE CORRECT CHANGE FOR ITEMS COSTING UP TO $100.


COST OF ITEM? 4.59
AMOUNT OF PAYMENT? 10
YOUR CHANGE,$ 5.41
 1 FIVE DOLLAR BILL(S)
 1 QUARTER(S)
 1 DIME(S)
 1 NICKEL(S)
 1 PENNY(S)
THANK YOU,COME AGAIN


COST OF ITEM? 0.17
AMOUNT OF PAYMENT? 5.00
YOUR CHANGE,$ 4.83
 4 ONE DOLLAR BILL(S)
 1 ONE-HALF DOLLAR(S)
 1 QUARTER(S)
 1 NICKEL(S)
 3 PENNY(S)
THANK YOU,COME AGAIN


COST OF ITEM? 18.88
AMOUNT OF PAYMENT? 20
YOUR CHANGE,$ 1.12
 1 ONE DOLLAR BILL(S)
 1 DIME(S)
 2 PENNY(S)
THANK YOU,COME AGAIN
```

CHECKR

CHECKERS

Description

This program plays checkers. The pieces of the computer are
marked with an "X", yours are marked "0". A move is made by
specifying the coordinates of the piece to be moved (X,Y).
Home (1,1) is in the bottom left and X specifies distance to
the right of home (i.e., column) and Y specifies distance
above home (i.e., row). You then specify where you wish to
move to.

Limitations

Unfortunately, the computer program is not smart enough to
recognize (or permit!) a double or triple jump. If you try
one, it is likely that your piece will disappear altogether.

Program Author

Alan J. Segal
151 Shrubhollow Road
Roslyn, NY 11576

PROGRAM LISTING

```
100 PRINT"   THIS PROGRAM WILL PLAY CHECKERS. THE COMPUTER IS X,"
200 PRINT"AND YOU ARE O. THE COMPUTER WILL GO FIRST,-NOTE: SQUARES"
300 PRINT"ARE IN THE FORM-(X,Y) AND SQ. 1,1 IS THE BOTTOM LEFT!"
400 PRINT"DO NOT ATTEMPT A DOUBLE JUMP OR YOUR PIECE MIGHT JUST "
500 PRINT"DISAPPEAR(SAME FOR A TRIPLE!)"
600 PRINT"     WAIT FOR THE COMP. TO MOVE!!!!!"
700 LET G=-1
800 DIM R(50)
900 LET L=-1
1000 DIM S(10,10)
1100 DATA 1,0,1,0,1,0,0,0,-1,0,-1,0,0,0,-1,0,-1,0,15
1200 FOR X=1TO8
130C FOR Y=1TO8
1400 READ J
1500 IF J=15 THEN 1800
1600 LET S(X,Y)=J
1700 GOTO 2000
1800 RESTORE
1900 READ S(X,Y)
2000 NEXT Y
2100 NEXT X
2200 REM
2300LETL=-1*L
2400 FOR X=1TO8
2500 FOR Y=1TO8
2600 IF S(X,Y)=0 THEN 3500
2700 IF G>0 THEN 3000
2800 IF S(X,Y)>0 THEN 3500
2900 GOTO 3100
3000 IF S(X,Y)<0 THEN 3500
3100 IF ABS(S(X,Y))<>1 THEN 3300
3200 GOSUB 4300
3300 IF ABS(S(X,Y))<>2 THEN 3500
3400 GOSUB 6500
3500IFX<>8 THEN 3800
3600IFL=1 THEN 3800
3700RETURN
3800NEXT Y
3900NEXT X
4000PRINT
4100GOSUB11400
4200 GOTO 2300
4300 FOR A=-1TO1 STEP 2
4400 LET U=X+A
4500 LET V=Y+G
4600 IF U<1 THEN 6300
4700 IF U>8 THEN 6300
4800 IF V<1 THEN 6300
4900 IF V>8 THEN 6300
5000 IF S(U,V)<>0 THEN 5300
5100 GOSUB 9100
5200 GOTO 6300
5300 IF S(U,V)=G THEN 6300
5400 IF S(U,V)=2*G THEN 6300
5500 LET U=U+A
5600 LET V=V+G
5700 IF U<1 THEN 6300
5800 IF U>8 THEN 6300
5900 IF V<1 THEN 6300
6000 IF V>8 THEN 6300
6100 IF S(U,V)<>0 THEN 6300
6200 GOSUB 9100
6300 NEXT A
6400  RETURN
6500 REM KING MOVES
6600 FOR A=-1TO1 STEP 2
6700 FOR B=-1TO1 STEP 2
6800 LET U=X+A
6900 LET V=Y+B
7000 IF U<1 THEN 8700
7100 IF U>8 THEN 8700
7200 IF V<1 THEN 8700
7300 IF V>8 THEN8700
7400 IF S(U,V)<>0 THEN 7700
7500 GOSUB 9100
7600 GOTO 8700
7700 IF S(U,V)=G THEN 8700
7800 IF S(U,V)=2*G THEN 8700
7900 LET U=U+A
8000 LET V=V+B
8100 IF U<1 THEN 8700
8200 IF U>8 THEN 8700
8300 IF V<1 THEN 8700
8400 IF V>8 THEN 8700
8500 IF S(U,V)<>0 THEN 8700
8600 GOSUB 9100
8700 NEXT B
8800 NEXT A
8900 RETURN
9000 GOTO 14200
9100 REM
9200 LET P=P+1
9300 IF P=K THEN 12300
9400IF V<>(4.5+(3.5*G)) THEN 9600
9500 LET Q=Q+2
9600 IF X<>(4.5-(3.5*G)) THEN 9800
9700LET Q=Q-2
9800 REM
9900 IF U<>1 THEN 10100
10000 LET Q=Q+1
10100 IF U<>8 THEN 10300
10200 LET Q=Q+1
10300 FOR C=-1TO1 STEP 2
10400 IF S(U+C,V+G)<1 THEN 10800
10500 LET Q=Q-1
10600 IF S(U-C,V-G)<>0 THEN 10800
10700 LET Q=Q-1
10800 REM THIS WAS THE EVALUATION SECTION
10900 REM
11000 NEXT C
```

```
11100 LET R(P)=Q
11200 LETQ=0
11300 RETURN
11400 IF P=0 THEN 18800
11500 FOR J=10TO-10 STEP -1
11600 FOR F=1TOP
11700 IF R(F)=J THEN 12000
11800 NEXT F
11900 NEXT J
12000 LET K=F+P
12100 GOSUB 2300
12200 RETURN
12300 PRINT"  I MOVE FROM ("X;Y") TO ("U;V")"
12400 LET F=0
12500 LET P=0
12600 LET K=0
12700 IF V<>(4.5+(3.5*G)) THEN 13000
12800 LET S(U,V)=2*G
12900 GOTO 13100
13000 LET S(U,V)=S(X,Y)
13100 LET S(X,Y)=0
13200 IF ABS(X-U)<>2 THEN 13400
13300 LET S((X+U)/2,(Y+V)/2)=0
13400 PRINT"BOARD";
13500 INPUT D$
13600 IF D$<>"YES" THEN13900
13700 GOSUB 14100
13800 RETURN
13900 GOSUB 15800
14000 RETURN
14100 PRINT
14200 FOR Y=8TO1 STEP -1
14300 FOR X=1TO8
14400 LET I=2*X
14500 IF S(X,Y)<>0 THEN 14700
14600 PRINT TAB(I)".";
14700 IF S(X,Y)<>1 THEN 14900
14800 PRINT TAB(I)"O";
14900 IF S(X,Y)<>-1 THEN 15100
15000 PRINT TAB(I)"X";
15100 IF S(X,Y)<>-2 THEN 15300
15200 PRINT TAB(I)"X";TAB(I)"*";
15300 IF S(X,Y)<>2 THEN 15500
15400 PRINT TAB(I)"O";TAB(I)"*";
15500 NEXT X
15600 PRINT
15700 NEXT Y
15800 PRINT
15900 PRINT"FROM";
16000 INPUT E,H
16100 LET X=E
16200 LET Y=H
16300 IF S(X,Y)<>0 THEN 16700
16400 PRINT "THERE IS NO ONE OCCUPYING THAT SPACE"
16500 PRINT
16600 GOTO 15900
16700 PRINT"TO";
16800 INPUT A,B
16900 LET X=A
17000 LET Y=B
17100 IF S(X,Y)=0 THEN 17500
17200 PRINT"THAT SPACE IS ALREADY OCCUPIED"
17300 PRINT
17400 GOTO 16700
17500 LET S(A$B)=S(E,H)
17600 LET S(A,B)=S(E,H)
17700 LET S(E,H)=0
17800 LET T=(4.5-(3.5*G))
17900 IF ABS(E-A)<>2 THEN 18100
18000 LET S((E+A)/2,(H+B)/2)=0
18100 IF B<>T THEN 18300
18200 LET S(A,B)=-2*G
18300 FOR X=8TO8
18400 FOR Y=8TO8
18500 RETURN
18600 NEXT Y
18700 NEXT X
18800 PRINT"    VERY GOOD, YOU WIN!"
18900 PRINT
19000 PRINT
19100 PRINT"                   -CHUCK OUT"
19200 END
```

74

SAMPLE RUN

```
     THIS PROGRAM WILL PLAY CHECKERS. THE COMPUTER IS X,
AND YOU ARE O. THE COMPUTER WILL GO FIRST.-NOTE: SQUARES
ARE IN THE FORM-(X,Y) AND SQ. 1,1 IS THE BOTTOM LEFT!
DO NOT ATTEMPT A DOUBLE JUMP OR YOUR PIECE MIGHT JUST
DISAPPEAR(SAME FOR A TRIPLE!)
     WAIT FOR THE COMP. TO MOVE!!!!!
```

```
   I MOVE FROM ( 2  6 ) TO ( 1  5 )
BOARD ?YES

 . X . X . X . X
 X . X . X . X .
 . . . X . X . X
 X . . . . . . .
 . . . . . . . .
 O . O . O . O .
 . O . O . O . O
 O . O . O . O .
```

FROM ?1,3
TO ?2,4

```
   I MOVE FROM ( 1  7 ) TO ( 2  6 )
BOARD ?YES

 . X . X . X . X
 . . X . X . X .
 . X . X . X . X
 X . . . . . . .
 . O . . . . . .
 . . O . O . O .
 . O . O . O . O
 O . O . O . O .
```

FROM ?3,,\,\3
TO ?4,4

```
   I MOVE FROM ( 2  8 ) TO ( 1  7 )
BOARD ?YES

 . . . X . X . X
 X . X . X . X .
 . X . X . X . X
 X . O . . . . .
 . O . . . . . .
 . . . . O . O .
 . O . O . O . O
 O . O . O . O .
```

FROM ?2,4
TO ?1,5
THAT SPACE IS ALREADY OCCUPIED

TO ?3,5

```
   I MOVE FROM ( 1  5 ) TO ( 2  4 )
BOARD ?YES

 . . . X . X . X
 X . X . X . X .
 . X . X . X . X
 . . O . . . . .
 . O . . . . . .
 . . . O . . . .
 . O . O . O . O
 O . O . O . O .
```

FROM ?7,3
TO ?8,4

```
   I MOVE FROM ( 2  6 ) TO ( 1  5 )
BOARD ?YES

 . . . X . X . X
 X . X . X . X .
 . . . X . X . X
 X . O . . . . .
 . X . O . . . O
 . . O . O . O .
 . O . O . O . O
 O . O . O . O .
```

FROM ?3,5
TO ?2,6

```
   I MOVE FROM ( 1  7 ) TO ( 3  5 )
BOARD ?YES

 . . . X . X . X
 . . X . X . X .
 . . X . X . X .
 X . . . . . . .
 . X . O . . . O
 . . . O . . . .
 . O . O . O . O
 O . O . C . O .
```

FROM ?4,4
TO ?2,6

```
   I MOVE FROM ( 4  6 ) TO ( 3  5 )
BOARD ?YES

 . . . X . X . X
 . . X . X . X .
 . O . . . X . X
 . X . . . . . O
 . . . . . . . .
 . . O . . . . .
 . O . O . O . O
 O . O . O . O .
```

FROM ?2,6
TO ?1,7

```
   I MOVE FROM ( 3  7 ) TO ( 2  6 )
BOARD ?NO
```

FROM ?1,7
TO ?2,8

```
   I MOVE FROM ( 4  8 ) TO ( 3  7 )
BOARD ?YES

 . O* . . . X . X
 . X . . . X . X .
 . X . . . X . X
 . X . . . . . O
 . . O . . . . .
 . O . O . O . O
 O . O . O . O .
```

FROM ?2,8
TO ?4,6

```
   I MOVE FROM ( 6  6 ) TO ( 5  5 )
BOARD ?YES

 . . . . . X . X
 . . . . . . . X
 . X . O* . . . X
 X . X . X . . .
 . X . . . . . .
 . . . O . . . .
 . O . O . O . O
 O . O . O . O .
```

FROM ?4,6
TO ?6,4

```
   I MOVE FROM ( 5  7 ) TO ( 4  6 )
BOARD ?YES

 . . . . . X . X
 . . . . . . . X
 . X . X . . . .
 . X . . . .
 . X . . . O* . O
 . . . . . . . .
 . O . O . O . O
```

2RB**QV.

FROM ?5,2!U
5,2
THERE IS NO ONE OCCUPYING THAT SPACE

FROM ?5,3
TO ?4,4

```
   I MOVE FROM ( 6  8 ) TO ( 5  7 )
BOARD ?YES

 . . . . . . . X
 . . . X . X .
 X . X . . . .
 . X . O . O* . O
 . . . . . . . .
 . O . O . O . O
```

FROM ?4,2
TO ?3,3

```
   I MOVE FROM ( 5  7 ) TO ( 6  6 )
BOARD ?YES

 . . . . . . . X
 . . . . . X .
 . X . X . X . X
 X . X . . . . .
 . X . O . O* . O .
 . O . . . . .
 O . O . O . O .
```

FROM ?8,5
THERE IS NO ONE OCCUPYING THAT SPACE

FROM ?8,4
TO ?7,5

```
   I MOVE FROM ( 6  6 ) TO ( 8  4 )
BOARD ?YES

 . . . . . . . X
 . . . . . X .
 X . X . . . . .
 . X . O . O* . X
 . O . . . O . O
 O . O . O . O .
```

FROM ?4,4
TO ?5,5

```
   I MOVE FROM ( 2  4 ) TO ( 1  3 )
BOARD ?YES

 . . . . . . . X
 . X . X . . . .
 X . X . O . . .
 . . . . O* . X
 X . O . . . . .
 . O . . . O . O
 O . O . O . O .
```

FROM ?5,5
TO ?3,7

```
   I MOVE FROM ( 7  7 ) TO ( 6  6 )
BOARD ?YES

 . . . . . . . X
 . . . O . . . .
 . . . . . X . X
 X . X . . . . .
 . X . . . O* . X
 X . O . . . . .
 . O . . . O . O
 O . O . O . O .
```

FROM ?3,7
TO ?4,8

```
   I MOVE FROM ( 1  5 ) TO ( 2  4 )
BOARD ?YES

 . . . O* . . . X
 . . . . . . . .
 . X . . . . X . X
 . X . . . . .
 . X . . . O* . X
 X . O . . . . .
 . O . . . O . O
 O . O . O . O .
```

FROM ?3,3
TO ?1,5

```
   I MOVE FROM ( 3  5 ) TO ( 2  4 )
BOARD ?YES

 . . . O* . . . X
 . . . . . . . .
 . X . . . X . X
 O . . . . . . .
 . X . . . O* . X
 X . . . . . . .
 . O . . . O . O
 O . O . O . O .
```

FROM ?1,5
TO ?3,7

```
   I MOVE FROM ( 6  6 ) TO ( 7  5 )
BOARD ?YES

 . . . O* . . . X
 . . O . . . . .
 . . . . . . . X
 . . . . . . . .
 . X . . . O* . X
AFFFFF2Y2D O . . . O . O
 O . O . O . O .
```

FROM ?3,7
TO ?2,8

```
   I MOVE FROM ( 2  4 ) TO ( 3  3 )
BOARD ?YES

 . O* . O* . . . X
 . . . . . . . .
 . . . . . X . .
 . . . . . O* . X
 X . X . . . . .
 . O . . . O . O
 O . O . O . O .
```

FROM ?2,2
TO ?4,4

```
   I MOVE FROM ( 7  5 ) TO ( 5  3 )
BOARD ?YES

 . O* . O* . . . X
 . . . . . . . X
 . . . . . . . X
 . . . O . . . X
 X . X . . . . .
 . O . . . O . O
 O . O . O . O .
```

FROM ?5,1
TO ?4,2

```
   I MOVE FROM ( 8  4 ) TO ( 7  3 )
BOARD ?YES

 . O* . O* . . . X
 . . . . . . . .
 . . . . . . . .
 . . . O . . . .
 X . X . X . X .
 . . O . O . O
 O . O . O . O .
```

FROM ?6,2
TO ?8,4

```
        VERY GOOD,  YOU WIN!

                          -CHUCK OUT
```

CHEMST

DILUTE KRYPTOCYANIC ACID

Description

The fictitious chemical, kryptocyanic acid, can only be diluted by the ratio of 7 parts water to 3 parts acid. Any other ratio causes an unstable compound which soon explodes. Given an amount of acid, you must determine how much water to add for dilution. If you're more than 5% off, you lose one of your nine lives. The program continues to play until you lose all nine lives or until it is interrupted.

Program Author

Wayne Teeter
312 Peg Street
Ridgecrest, CA 93555

```
LIST
10 PRINT "THE FICTICIOUS CHEMICAL KRYPTOCYANIC ACID CAN ONLY BE"
20 PRINT "DILUTED BY THE RATIO OF 7 PARTS WATER TO 3 PARTS ACIE."
30 PRINT "IF ANY OTHER RATIO IS ATTEMPTED, THE ACID BECOMES UNSTABLE"
40 PRINT "AND SOON EXPLODES.  GIVEN THE AMOUNT OF ACID, YOU MUST"
50 PRINT "DECIDE HOW MUCH WATER TO ADD FOR DILUTION.  IF YOU MISS"
60 PRINT "YOU FACE THE CONSEQUENCES."
100 LET A=INT(RND(1)*50)
110 LET W=7*A/3
120 PRINT A"LITERS OF KRYPTOCYANIC ACID. HOW MUCH WATER";
130 INPUT R
140 LET D=ABS(W-R)
150 IF D>W/20 THEN 200
160 PRINT "GOOD JOB! YOU MAY BREATHE NOW, BUT DON'T INHALE THE FUMES!"
170 PRINT
180 GO TO 100
200 PRINT "SIZZLE! YOU HAVE JUST BEEN DESALINATED INTO A BLOB"
210 PRINT "OF QUIVERING PROTOPLASM!"
220 LET T=T+1
230 IF T=9 THEN 260
240 PRINT "HOWEVER, YOU MAY TRY AGAIN WITH ANOTHER LIFE."
245 PRINT
250 GO TO 100
260 PRINT "YOUR 9 LIVES ARE USED, BUT YOU WILL BE LONG REMEMBERED FOR"
270 PRINT "YOUR CONTRIBUTIONS TO THE FIELD OF COMIC BOOK CHEMISTRY."
280 END
```

```
RUN
THE FICTICIOUS CHEMICAL KRYPTOCYANIC ACID CAN ONLY BE
DILUTED BY THE RATIO OF 7 PARTS WATER TO 3 PARTS ACID.
IF ANY OTHER RATIO IS ATTEMPTED, THE ACID BECOMES UNSTABLE
AND SOON EXPLODES.  GIVEN THE AMOUNT OF ACID, YOU MUST
DECIDE HOW MUCH WATER TO ADD FOR DILUTION.  IF YOU MISS
YOU FACE THE CONSEQUENCES.
 19 LITERS OF KRYPTOCYANIC ACID. HOW MUCH WATER?49
SIZZLE! YOU HAVE JUST BEEN DESALINATED INTO A BLOB
OF QUIVERING PROTOPLASM!
HOWEVER, YOU MAY TRY AGAIN WITH ANOTHER LIFE.

 42 LITERS OF KRYPTOCYANIC ACID. HOW MUCH WATER?77
SIZZLE! YOU HAVE JUST BEEN DESALINATED INTO A BLOB
OF QUIVERING PROTOPLASM!
HOWEVER, YOU MAY TRY AGAIN WITH ANOTHER LIFE.

 28 LITERS OF KRYPTOCYANIC ACID. HOW MUCH WATER?72
SIZZLE! YOU HAVE JUST BEEN DESALINATED INTO A BLOB
OF QUIVERING PROTOPLASM!
HOWEVER, YOU MAY TRY AGAIN WITH ANOTHER LIFE.

 42 LITERS OF KRYPTOCYANIC ACID. HOW MUCH WATER?98
GOOD JOB! YOU MAY BREATHE NOW, BUT DON'T INHALE THE FUMES!

 49 LITERS OF KRYPTOCYANIC ACID. HOW MUCH WATER?112
GOOD JOB! YOU MAY BREATHE NOW, BUT DON'T INHALE THE FUMES!

 12 LITERS OF KRYPTOCYANIC ACID. HOW MUCH WATER?28
GOOD JOB! YOU MAY BREATHE NOW, BUT DON'T INHALE THE FUMES!

 30 LITERS OF KRYPTOCYANIC ACID. HOW MUCH WATER?75
SIZZLE! YOU HAVE JUST BEEN DESALINATED INTO A BLOB
OF QUIVERING PROTOPLASM!
HOWEVER, YOU MAY TRY AGAIN WITH ANOTHER LIFE.
```

CHIEF

Description

In the words of the program author, John Graham,

"CHIEF is designed to give people (mostly kids) practice in the four operations (addition, multiplication, subtraction, and division).

It does this while giving people some fun. And then, if the people are wrong, it shows them how they should have done it.

It is mostly a game, but can be used by teachers to test the kids."

Program Author

John Graham
Friendly Road
Upper Brookville, NY 11771

```
10 PRINT " I AM CHIEF NUMBERS FREEK, THE GREAT INDIAN MATH GOD. "
20 PRINT "ARE YOU READY TO TAKE THE TEST YOU CALLED ME OUT FOR";
30 INPUT A$
40 IF A$= "YES" THEN 60
50 PRINT "SHUT UP PALEFACE WITH WISE TOUNGE."
60 PRINT " TAKE A NUMBER AND ADD 3. DIVIDE THIS NUMBER BY 5 AND"
70 PRINT "MULTIPLY BY 8. DIVIDE BY 5 AND ADD THE SAME. SUBTRACT 1."
80 PRINT "WHAT DO YOU HAVE";
85 PRINT
90 INPUT B
100 LET C = (B+1-5)*5/8*5-3
110 PRINT "I BET YOUR NUMBER WAS " C" WAS I RIGHT";
120 INPUT D$
130 IF D$="YES" THEN 510
140 PRINT "WHAT WAS YOUR ORIGINAL NUMBER";
150 INPUT K
155 LET F=K+3
160 LET `G=F/5
170 LET H=G*8
180 LET I=H/5+5
190 LET J=I-1
200 PRINT "SO YOU THINK YOU'RE SO SMART, EH?"
210 PRINT "NOW WATCH...."
230 PRINT K"PLUS 3 EQUALS "F". THIS DIVIDED BY 5 EQUALS"G","
240 PRINT "THIS TIMES 8 EQUALS"H". IF WE DIVIDE BY 5 AND ADD THE SAME,"
250 PRINT "WE GET"I". MINUS 1 EQUALS"J"."
260 PRINT "NOW DO YOU BELIEVE ME";
270 INPUT Z$
290 IF Z$ ="YES" THEN 510
295 PRINT "YOU HAVE MADE ME MAD!!!!"
300 PRINT "THERE MUST NOW BE A GREAT LIGHTNING BOLT!"
310 PRINT\PRINT
330 FOR X=30 TO 22 STEP -1
340 PRINT TAB(X) "X X"
350 NEXT X
360 PRINT TAB(21)"X XXX"
370 PRINT TAB(20) "X   X"
380 PRINT TAB(19) "XX X"
390 FOR Y=20 TO 13 STEP -1
400 PRINT TAB(Y) "X X"
410 NEXT Y
420 PRINT TAB(12) "XX"
430 PRINT TAB(11) "X"
440 PRINT TAB(10) "*"
450 PRINT\PRINT "#################################"\PRINT
470 PRINT "I HOPE YOU BELIEVE ME NOW, FOR YOUR SAKE!!"
480 GOTO 520
510 PRINT "BYE!!!!!"
520 END

READY
```

```
     I AM CHIEF NUMBERS FREEK, THE GREAT INDIAN MATH GOD.
ARE YOU READY TO TAKE THE TEST YOU CALLED ME OUT FOR? NO
SHUT UP PALEFACE WITH WISE TOUNGE.
    TAKE A NUMBER AND ADD 3. DIVIDE THIS NUMBER BY 5 AND
MULTIPLY BY 8. DIVIDE BY 5 AND ADD THE SAME. SUBTRACT 1.
WHAT DO YOU HAVE
? 3.8
I BET YOUR NUMBER WAS -3.625  WAS I RIGHT? NO
WHAT WAS YOUR ORIGINAL NUMBER? 12
SO YOU THINK YOU'RE SO SMART, EH?
NOW WATCH....
    12 PLUS 3 EQUALS  15 . THIS DIVIDED BY 5 EQUALS 3 ,
THIS TIMES 8 EQUALS 24 . IF WE DIVIDE BY 5 AND ADD THE SAME,
WE GET 9.8 . MINUS 1 EQUALS 8.8 .
NOW DO YOU BELIEVE ME? NO
YOU HAVE MADE ME MAD!!!!
THERE MUST NOW BE A GREAT LIGHTNING BOLT!
```

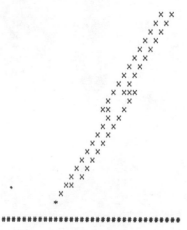

```
#################################

I HOPE YOU BELIEVE ME NOW, FOR YOUR SAKE!!

READY
```

CHOMP

EAT A BIG COOKIE

Description

This program is an adaptation of a mathematical game originally presented in Scientific American, Jan., 1973. Up to a 9x9 grid is set up by you with the upper left square a poison square. This grid is the cookie. Players alternately chomp away at the cookie from the lower right. To take a chomp, input a row and column number of one of the squares remaining on the cookie. All of the squares below and to the right of that square, including that square, disappear.

Any number of people can play -- the computer is only the moderator; it is not a player. Two-person strategies are interesting to work out but strategies when three or more people are playing are a real challenge.

Source

Peter Sessions
People's Computer Company
Menlo Park, CA 94025

```
100 REM ***THE GAME OF CHOMP***
105 REM ***SUBMITTED BY PEOPLES COMPUTER CENTER***
110 PRINT
120 PRINT "THIS IS THE GAME OF CHOMP (SCIENTIFIC AMERICAN, JAN 1973)"
130 PRINT "WANT THE RULES (1=YES, 0=NO!)";
140 INPUT R
150 IF R=0 THEN 340
160 F=1
170 R=5
180 C=7
190 PRINT "CHOMP IS FOR 1 OR MORE PLAYERS (HUMANS ONLY)."
200 PRINT
210 PRINT "HERE'S HOW A BOARD LOOKS (THIS ONE IS 5 BY 7):"
220 GOSUB 540
230 PRINT
240 PRINT "THE BOARD IS A BIG COOKIE - R ROWS HIGH AND C COLUMNS"
250 PRINT "WIDE. YOU INPUT R AND C AT THE START. IN THE UPPER LEFT"
260 PRINT "CORNER OF THE COOKIE IS A POISON SQUARE (P). THE ONE WHO"
270 PRINT "CHOMPS THE POISON SQUARE LOSES. TO TAKE A CHOMP, TYPE THE"
280 PRINT "ROW AND COLUMN OF ONE OF THE SQUARES ON THE COOKIE."
290 PRINT "ALL OF THE SQUARES BELOW AND TO THE RIGHT OF THAT SQUARE"
300 PRINT "(INCLUDING THAT SQUARE, TOO) DISAPPEAR -- CHOMP!!"
310 PRINT "NO FAIR CHOMPING SQUARES THAT HAVE ALREADY BEEN CHOMPED,"
320 PRINT "OR THAT ARE OUTSIDE THE ORIGINAL DIMENSIONS OF THE COOKIE."
330 PRINT
340 PRINT "HERE WE GO..."
350 DIM A(10,10)
360 F=0
370 FOR I=1 TO 10
372 FOR J=1 TO 10
375 A(I,J)=0
377 NEXT J
379 NEXT I
380 PRINT
390 PRINT "HOW MANY PLAYERS";
400 INPUT P
410 I1=0
420 PRINT "HOW MANY ROWS";
430 INPUT R
440 IF R <= 9 THEN 470
450 PRINT "TOO MANY ROWS (9 IS MAXIMUM). NOW, ";
460 GOTO 420
470 PRINT "HOW MANY COLUMNS";
480 INPUT C
490 IF C <= 9 THEN 530
500 PRINT "TOO MANY COLUMNS (9 IS MAXIMUM). NOW, ";
510 GOTO 470
530 PRINT
540 FOR I=1 TO R
550 FOR J=1 TO C
560 A(I,J)=1
570 NEXT J
580 NEXT I
590 A(1,1)=-1
600 REM PRINT THE BOARD
610 PRINT
620 PRINT TAB(7);"1 2 3 4 5 6 7 8 9"
630 FOR I=1 TO R
640 PRINT I;TAB(7);
650 FOR J=1 TO C
660 IF A(I,J)=-1 THEN 700
670 IF A(I,J)=0 THEN 720
680 PRINT "* ";
690 GOTO 710
700 PRINT "P ";
710 NEXT J
720 PRINT
730 NEXT I
740 PRINT
750 IF F=0 THEN 770
760 RETURN
770 REM GET CHOMPS FOR EACH PLAYER IN TURN
780 LET I1=I1+1
790 LET P1=I1-INT(I1/P)*P
800 IF P1 <> 0 THEN 820
810 P1=P
820 PRINT "PLAYER ";P1
830 PRINT "COORDINATES OF CHOMP (ROW,COLUMN)";
840 INPUT R1,C1
850 IF R1<1 THEN 920
860 IF R1>R THEN 920
870 IF C1<1 THEN 920
880 IF C1>C THEN 920
890 IF A(R1,C1)=0 THEN 920
900 IF A(R1,C1)=-1 THEN 1010
910 GOTO 940
920 PRINT "NO FAIR. YOU'RE TRYING TO CHOMP ON EMPTY SPACE!"
930 GOTO 820
940 FOR I=R1 TO R
950 FOR J=C1 TO C
960 A(I,J)=0
970 NEXT J
980 NEXT I
990 GOTO 610
1000 REM   END OF GAME DETECTED IN LINE 900
1010 PRINT "YOU LOSE, PLAYER ";P1
1020 PRINT
1030 PRINT "AGAIN (1=YES; 0=NO!)";
1040 INPUT R
1050 IF R=1 THEN 340
1060 END

READY
```

```
THIS IS THE GAME OF CHOMP (SCIENTIFIC AMERICAN, JAN 1973)
WANT THE RULES (1=YES, 0=NO!)? 1
CHOMP IS FOR 1 OR MORE PLAYERS (HUMANS ONLY).

HERE'S HOW A BOARD LOOKS (THIS ONE IS 5 BY 7):

      1 2 3 4 5 6 7 8 9
1     P * * * * * *
2     * * * * * * *
3     * * * * * * *
4     * * * * * * *
5     * * * * * * *

THE BOARD IS A BIG COOKIE - R ROWS HIGH AND C COLUMNS
WIDE. YOU INPUT R AND C AT THE START. IN THE UPPER LEFT
CORNER OF THE COOKIE IS A POISON SQUARE (P). THE ONE WHO
CHOMPS THE POISON SQUARE LOSES. TO TAKE A CHOMP, TYPE THE
ROW AND COLUMN OF ONE OF THE SQUARES ON THE COOKIE.
ALL OF THE SQUARES BELOW AND TO THE RIGHT OF THAT SQUARE
(INCLUDING THAT SQUARE, TOO) DISAPPEAR -- CHOMP!!
NO FAIR CHOMPING SQUARES THAT HAVE ALREADY BEEN CHOMPED,
OR THAT ARE OUTSIDE THE ORIGINAL DIMENSIONS OF THE COOKIE.

HERE WE GO...

HOW MANY PLAYERS? 2
HOW MANY ROWS? 4
HOW MANY COLUMNS? 7


      1 2 3 4 5 6 7 8 9
1     P * * * * * *
2     * * * * * * *
3     * * * * * * *
4     * * * * * * *

PLAYER  1
COORDINATES OF CHOMP (ROW,COLUMN)? 4,6

      1 2 3 4 5 6 7 8 9
1     P * * * * * *
2     * * * * * * *
3     * * * * * * *
4     * * * * *

PLAYER  2
COORDINATES OF CHOMP (ROW,COLUMN)? 3,3

      1 2 3 4 5 6 7 8 9
1     P * * * * * *
2     * * * * * * *
3     * *
4     * *

PLAYER  1
COORDINATES OF CHOMP (ROW,COLUMN)? 1,4

      1 2 3 4 5 6 7 8 9
1     P * *
2     * * *
3     * *
4     * *

PLAYER  2
COORDINATES OF CHOMP (ROW,COLUMN)? 3,1

      1 2 3 4 5 6 7 8 9
1     P * *
2     * * *
3
4

PLAYER  1
COORDINATES OF CHOMP (ROW,COLUMN)? 2,3

      1 2 3 4 5 6 7 8 9
1     P * *
2     * *
3
4

PLAYER  2
COORDINATES OF CHOMP (ROW,COLUMN)? 1,3

      1 2 3 4 5 6 7 8 9
1     P *
2     * *
3
4

PLAYER  1
COORDINATES OF CHOMP (ROW,COLUMN)? 2,2

      1 2 3 4 5 6 7 8 9
1     P *
2     *
3
4

PLAYER  2
COORDINATES OF CHOMP (ROW,COLUMN)? 1,2

      1 2 3 4 5 6 7 8 9
1     P
2     *
3
4

PLAYER  1
COORDINATES OF CHOMP (ROW,COLUMN)? 2,1

      1 2 3 4 5 6 7 8 9
1     P
2
3
4

PLAYER  2
COORDINATES OF CHOMP (ROW,COLUMN)? 3,1
NO FAIR. YOU'RE TRYING TO CHOMP ON EMPTY SPACE!
PLAYER  2
COORDINATES OF CHOMP (ROW,COLUMN)? 1,1
YOU LOSE, PLAYER  2
```

CIVILW

Description

This simulation is based on 14 battles in the Civil War. Facts
and figures used are based on the actual occurrence. If you
follow the same strategy used in the actual battle, the results
will be the same--generally, this is a good strategy since the
generals in the Civil War were fairly good military strategists.
However, you can frequently outperform the Civil War generals,
particularly in cases where they did not have good enemy intelligence and consequently followed a poor course of action.
Naturally, it helps to know your Civil War history, although
the computer gives you the rudiments.

After each of the 14 battles, your casualties are compared to
the actual casualties of the battle, and you are told whether
you win or lose the battle.

Program Author

CIVIL WAR was written in 1968 by three students:

L. Cram, L. Goodie, D. Hibbard
Lexington High School
Lexington, MA 02173

PROGRAM LISTING

```
1 LET L=0:LET W=0:LET R1=0:LET P1=0
2 LET Q1=0:LET M3=0:LET M4=0
3 LET P2=0:LET T1=0:LET T2=0
5 REMARKABLE PROGRAM BY L. CRAM , L. GOODIE , AND D. HIBBARD
6 PRINT "DO YOU WANT DESCRIPTIONS (0=YES, 1=NO)";
7 INPUT Z
9 FOR U=1 TO 6
10 PRINT
11 NEXT U
13 IF Z=1 THEN 100
15 PRINT "THIS IS A CIVIL WAR SIMULATION."
20 PRINT "TO PLAY, TYPE A RESPONSE WHEN THE COMPUTER ASKS."
30 PRINT "REMEMBER THAT ALL FACTORS ARE INTERRELATED AND THAT YOUR"
35 PRINT "RESPONSES COULD CHANGE HISTORY. FACTS AND FIGURES USED ARE"
40 PRINT "BASED ON THE ACTUAL OCCURENCE. MOST BATTLES TEND TO RESULT"
45 PRINT "AS THEY DID IN THE CIVIL WAR, BUT IT ALL DEPENDS ON YOU!!"
50 PRINT
51 PRINT "THE OBJECT OF THE GAME IS TO WIN AS MANY BATTLES AS POSSIBLE"
52 PRINT
55 PRINT "YOUR CHOICES FOR DEFENSIVE STRATEGY ARE:"
60 PRINT "        (1) ARTILLERY ATTACK"
65 PRINT "        (2) FORTIFICATION AGAINST FRONTAL ATTACK"
70 PRINT "        (3) FORTIFICATION AGAINST FLANKING MANUEVERS"
75 PRINT "        (4) FALLING BACK"
80 PRINT "YOUR CHOICES FOR OFFENSIVE STRATEGY ARE:"
85 PRINT "        (1) ARTILLERY ATTACK"
90 PRINT "        (2) FRONTAL ATTACK"
95 PRINT "        (3) FLANKING MANUEVERS"
96 PRINT "        (4) ENCIRCLEMENT"
97 PRINT "YOU MAY SURRENDER BY TYPING A '5' FOR YOUR STRATEGY."
98 PRINT
99 PRINT "YOU ARE THE CONFEDERACY.        GOOD LUCK!"
100 READ M1,M2,C1,C2,M,A,U
101 LET I1=10+(L-W)*2
102 LET I2=10+(W-L)*2
103 LET D1=100*INT((M1*(100-I1)/2000)*(1+(R1-Q1)/(R1+1))+0.5)
104 LET D2=100*INT(M2*(100-I2)/2000+0.5)
105 LET F1=5*M1/6
106 LET A1=Z
107 FOR U=1 TO 4
108 PRINT
109 NEXT U
110 PRINT "THIS IS THE BATTLE OF ";
115 GOSUB 800
120 PRINT " ","CONFEDERACY"," UNION"
130 PRINT "MEN"," ";INT(M1*(1+(P1-T1)/(M3+1)))," ";
131 PRINT INT(M2*(1+(P2-T2)/(M4+1)))
140 PRINT "MONEY","$"D1,"$"D2
150 PRINT "INFLATION"," ";I1+15;"%"," ";I2;"%"
160 PRINT
170 PRINT "HOW MUCH DO YOU WISH TO SPEND FOR FOOD";
180 INPUT F
185 IF F<0 THEN 750
190 PRINT "HOW MUCH DO YOU WISH TO SPEND FOR SALARIES";
200 INPUT S
205 IF S<0 THEN 750
210 PRINT "HOW MUCH DO YOU WISH TO SPEND FOR AMMUNITION";
220 INPUT B
221 IF B<0 THEN 750
222 PRINT
224 IF F+S+B<=D1 THEN 230
226 PRINT "THINK AGAIN!   YOU HAVE ONLY $" D1
228 GOTO 160
230 LET O=((2+F*A2+S*A2)/F1*2+1)
235 IF O<10 THEN 260
240 PRINT "MORALE IS HIGH"
250 GOTO 300
260 IF O<5 THEN 290
270 PRINT "MORALE IS FAIR"
280 GOTO 300
290 PRINT "MORALE IS POOR"
300 IF M<3 THEN 330
310 PRINT "YOU ARE ON THE OFFENSIVE"
320 GOTO 370
330 IF M>1 THEN 360
340 PRINT "YOU ARE ON THE DEFENSIVE"
350 GOTO 370
360 PRINT "BOTH SIDES ARE ON THE OFFENSIVE"
370 PRINT
380 PRINT "YOUR STGEY";
390 INPUT Y
391 IF Y=5 THEN 1487
392 IF ABS(Y-3)<3 THEN 395
393 PRINT "YOU JERK!  USE THE OTHER SET OF STRATEGIES!!"
394 GOTO 370
395 PRINT
400 PRINT " ","CONFEDERACY","UNION"
410 LET C5=(2*C1/5)*(1+1/(2*(ABS(INT(4*RND(1)+1)-Y)+1)))
412 LET C5=INT(C5*(1+1/O)*(1.28+F1/(B+1))+0.5)
414 IF C5+100/O<M1*(1+(P1-T1)/(M3+1)) THEN 424
416 LET C5=INT(13*M1/20*(1+(P1-T1)/(M3+1)))
418 LET E=7*C5/13
420 LET U=1
422 GOTO 426
424 LET E=100/O
426 PRINT "CASUALTIES",C5,INT(17*C2*C1/(C5*20)+0.5)
430 PRINT "DESERTIONS",INT(E),INT(5*O)
432 PRINT
433 IF C5-C1>=0 THEN 439
435 PRINT "YOUR CASUALTIES WERE"INT(100*(C1-C5)/C1+0.5);"% LESS THAN"
437 GOTO 441
439 PRINT "YOUR CASUALTIES WERE"INT(100*(C5-C1)/C1+0.5);"% MORE THAN"
441 PRINT "THE ACTUAL CASUALTIES AT ";
443 LET A1=1
445 GO SUB800
450 IF U=1 THEN 470
460 IF C5+E<17*C2*C1/(C5*20)+5*O THEN 490
470 PRINT "YOU LOSE ";
471 LET L=L+1
480 GOTO 555
490 PRINT "YOU WIN ";
491 LET W=W+1
555 GOSUB 800
556 IF W=8 THEN 1490
580 LET T1=T1+C5+E
590 LET T2=T2+17*C2*C1/(C5*20)+5*O
600 LET P1=P1+C1
610 LET P2=P2+C2
620 LET Q1=Q1+(F+S+B)
630 LET R1=R1+M1*(100-I1)/20
635 LETM3=M3+M1
637 LET M4=M4+M2
650 IF A=14 THEN 1500
660 GOTO 100
670 DATA 18000,18500,1967,2708,1,1,0
672 DATA 40000,44894,10699,13047,3,2,0
674 DATA 95000,115000,20614,15849,3,3,0
676 DATA 54000,63000,10000,14000,2,4,0
678 DATA 40000,50000,10000,12000,3,5,0
680 DATA 75000,120000,5377,12653,1,6,0
682 DATA 38000,45000,11000,12000,1,7,0
684 DATA 32000,90000,13000,17197,2,8,0
686 DATA 50000,70000,12000,19000,1,9,0
688 DATA 72500,85000,20000,23000,3,10,0
690 DATA 66000,60000,18000,16000,2,11,0
692 DATA 37000,60000,6700,5800,2,12,0
694 DATA 62000,110000,17723,18000,2,13,0
696 DATA 65000,100000,8500,3700,1,14,0
750 PRINT "GO TO JAIL."
752 PRINT "GO DIRECTLY TO JAIL."
754 PRINT "DO NOT PASS GO."
756 PRINT "DO NOT COLLECT $200"
758 GOTO 107
800 IF A<>1 THEN 850
810 PRINT "BULL RUN"
820 IF A1=1 THEN 1480
830 PRINT"JULY 21,1861     GEN. BEAUREGARD COMMANDING THE SOUTH MET THE"
832 PRINT"UNION FORCES WITH GEN MCDOWELL IN A PREMATURE BATTLE AT BULL"
834 PRINT"RUN. GEN. JACKSON HELPED PUSH BACK THE UNION ATTACK."
840 GO TO 1480
850 IF A<>2 THEN 900
860 PRINT "SHILOH"
870 IF A1=1 THEN 1480
880 PRINT"APRIL 6-7,1862    THE CONFEDERATE SURPRISE ATTACK AT SHILOH"
882 PRINT"FAILED DUE TO POOR ORGANIZATION."
890 GO TO 1480
900 IF A<>3 THEN 950
910 PRINT "SEVEN DAYS"
920 IF A1=1 THEN 1480
930 PRINT"JUNE 25-JULY 1,1862    GENERAL LEE (CSA) UPHELD THE OFFENSIVE"
932 PRINT"THROUGHOUT THE BATTLE AND FORCED GEN. MCCLELLAN AND THE UNION"
934 PRINT"FORCES AWAY FROM RICHMOND."
940 GO TO 1480
950 IF A<>4 THEN 1000
960 PRINT "THE SECOND BULL RUN"
970 IF A1=1 THEN 1480
980 PRINT"AUG 29-30,1862   THE COMBINED CONFEDERATE FORCES UNDER LEE AND"
982 PRINT"JACKSON DROVE THE UNION FORCES BACK INTO WASHINGTON."
990 GO TO 1480
1000 IF A<>5 THEN 1050
1010 PRINT "ANTIETAM"
1020 IF A1=1 THEN 1480
1030 PRINT"SEPT 17,1862    THE SOUTH FAILED TO INCORPORATE MARYLAND INTO"
1032 PRINT"THE CONFEDERACY."
1040 GO TO 1480
1050 IF A<>6 THEN 1100
1060 PRINT "FREDERICKSBURG"
1070 IF A1=1 THEN 1480
1080 PRINT"DEC 13,1862 THE CONFEDERACY UNDER LEE SUCESSFULLY REPULSED"
1082 PRINT"AN ATTACK BY THE UNION UNDER GEN. BURNSIDE."
1090 GOTO 1480
1100 IF A <>7 THEN 1150
1110 PRINT "MURFREESBORO"
1120 IF A1=1 THEN 1480
1130 PRINT"DEC 31,1862    THE SOUTH UNDER GEN. BRAGG WON A CLOSE BATTLE"
1140 GOTO 1480
1150 IF A<>8 THEN 1200
1160 PRINT "CHANCELLORSVILLE"
1170 IF A1=1 THEN 1480
1180 PRINT"MAY 1-6,1863    THE SOUTH HAD A COSTLY VICTORY AND LOST ONE"
1182 PRINT"OF THEIR OUTSTANDING GENERALS, 'STONEWALL' JACKSON."
1190 GOTO 1480
1200 IF A<>9 THEN 1250
1210 PRINT "VICKSBURG"
1220 IF A1=1 THEN 1480
1230 PRINT"JULY 4,1863     VICKSBURG WAS A COSTLY DEFEAT FOR THE SOUTH"
1232 PRINT"BECAUSE IT GAVE THE UNION ACCESS TO THE MISSISSIPPI."
1240 GOTO 1480
1250 IF A<>10 THEN 1300
1260 PRINT "GETTYSBURG"
1270 IF A1=1 THEN 1480
1280 PRINT"JUNE 30,1863     A SOUTHERN MISTAKE BY GEN. LEE AT GETTYSBURG"
1282 PRINT"COST THEM ONE OF THE MOST CRUCIAL BATTLES OF THR WAR."
1290 GOTO 1480
1300 IF A<>11 THEN 1350
1310 PRINT "CHICKAMAUGA"
1320 IF A1=1 THEN 1480
1330 PRINT"NOV 25,1863    AFTER THE SOUTH HAD SIEGED GEN. ROSENCRANS'"
1332 PRINT"ARMY FOR THREE MONTHS, GEN. GRANT BROKE THE SIEGE."
1340 GOTO 1480
1350 IF A<>12 THEN 1400
1360 PRINT "CHATTANOOGA"
1370 IF A1=1 THEN 1480
1380 PRINT"SEPT 15,1863    CONFUSION IN A FOREST NEAR CHICKAMAUGA LED"
1382 PRINT"TO A COSTLY SOUTHERN VICTORY."
1390 GOTO 1480
1400 IF A<>13 THEN 1450
1410 PRINT "SPOTSYLVANIA"
1420 IF A1=1 THEN 1480
1430 PRINT"MAY 5,1864    GRANT'S PLAN TO KEEP LEE ISOLATED BEGAN TO FAIL"
1432 PRINT"HERE, AND CONTINUED AT COLD HARBOR AND PETERSBURG."
1440 GOTO 1480
1450 PRINT "ATLANTA"
1460 IF A1=1 THEN 1480
1470 PRINT"AUGUST, 1864    SHERMAN AND THREE VETERAN ARMIES CONVERGED ON"
1472 PRINT"ATLANTA AND DEALT THE DEATH BLOW TO THE CONFEDERACY."
1480 PRINT
1485 RETURN
1487 PRINT "THE CONFEDERACY HAS SURRENDERED"
1488 GOTO 1500
1490 PRINT "THE UNION HAS SURRENDERED"
1500 PRINT
1510 PRINT "YOU HAVE WON" W; "BATTLES AND LOST" L; "BATTLES."
1515 IF W=5 THEN 1550
1520 IF W<=L THEN 1550
1530 PRINT "THE CONFEDERACY HAS WON THE WAR"
1540 STOP
1550 PRINT "THE UNION HAS WON THE WAR"
1560 END
```

```
DO YOU WANT DESCRIPTIONS (0=YES, 1=NO)? 0
```

SAMPLE RUN

```
THIS IS A CIVIL WAR SIMULATION.
TO PLAY, TYPE A RESPONSE WHEN THE COMPUTER ASKS.
REMEMBER THAT ALL FACTORS ARE INTERRELATED AND THAT YOUR
RESPONSES COULD CHANGE HISTORY. FACTS AND FIGURES USED ARE
BASED ON THE ACTUAL OCCURENCE. MOST BATTLES TEND TO RESULT
AS THEY DID IN THE CIVIL WAR, BUT IT ALL DEPENDS ON YOU!!

THE OBJECT OF THE GAME IS TO WIN AS MANY BATTLES AS POSSIBLE

YOUR CHOICES FOR DEFENSIVE STRATEGY ARE:
        (1) ARTILLERY ATTACK
        (2) FORTIFICATION AGAINST FRONTAL ATTACK
        (3) FORTIFICATION AGAINST FLANKING MANUEVERS
        (4) FALLING BACK
YOUR CHOICES FOR OFFENSIVE STRATEGY ARE:
        (1) ARTILLERY ATTACK
        (2) FRONTAL ATTACK
        (3) FLANKING MANUEVERS
        (4) ENCIRCLEMENT
YOU MAY SURRENDER BY TYPING A '5' FOR YOUR STRATEGY.

YOU ARE THE CONFEDERACY.        GOOD LUCK!


THIS IS THE BATTLE OF BULL RUN
JULY 21,1861    GEN. BEAUREGARD COMMANDING THE SOUTH MET THE
UNION FORCES WITH GEN MCDOWELL IN A PREMATURE BATTLE AT BULL
RUN.  GEN. JACKSON HELPED PUSH BACK THE UNION ATTACK.

                CONFEDERACY     UNION
MEN             18000           18500
MONEY           $ 81000         $ 83300
INFLATION       25 %            10 %

HOW MUCH DO YOU WISH TO SPEND FOR FOOD? 4000
HOW MUCH DO YOU WISH TO SPEND FOR SALARIES? 4000
HOW MUCH DO YOU WISH TO SPEND FOR AMMUNITION? 73000

MORALE IS POOR
YOU ARE ON THE DEFENSIVE

YOUR STEGY? 1

                CONFEDERACY     UNION
CASUALTIES      2399            1887
DESERTIONS      82              6

YOUR CASUALTIES WERE 22 % MORE THAN
THE ACTUAL CASUALTIES AT BULL RUN

YOU LOSE BULL RUN


THIS IS THE BATTLE OF SHILOH
APRIL 6-7,1862    THE CONFEDERATE SURPRISE ATTACK AT SHILOH
FAILED DUE TO POOR ORGANIZATION.

                CONFEDERACY     UNION
MEN             38856           46870
MONEY           $ 176000        $ 206500
INFLATION       27 %            8 %

HOW MUCH DO YOU WISH TO SPEND FOR FOOD? 30000
HOW MUCH DO YOU WISH TO SPEND FOR SALARIES? 30000
HOW MUCH DO YOU WISH TO SPEND FOR AMMUNITION? 116000

MORALE IS POOR
YOU ARE ON THE OFFENSIVE

YOUR STEGY? 2

                CONFEDERACY     UNION
CASUALTIES      10107           11740
DESERTIONS      29              17

YOUR CASUALTIES WERE 6 % LESS THAN
THE ACTUAL CASUALTIES AT SHILOH

YOU WIN SHILOH


THIS IS THE BATTLE OF SEVEN DAYS
JUNE 25-JULY 1,1862    GENERAL LEE (CSA) UPHELD THE OFFENSIVE
THROUGHOUT THE BATTLE AND FORCED GEN. MCCLELLAN AND THE UNION
FORCES AWAY FROM RICHMOND.

                CONFEDERACY     UNION
MEN             95079           118818
MONEY           $ 427500        $ 517500
INFLATION       25 %            10 %

HOW MUCH DO YOU WISH TO SPEND FOR FOOD? 20000
HOW MUCH DO YOU WISH TO SPEND FOR SALARIES? 6000
HOW MUCH DO YOU WISH TO SPEND FOR AMMUNITION? 167500

MORALE IS POOR
YOU ARE ON THE OFFENSIVE

YOUR STEGY? 4

                CONFEDERACY     UNION
CASUALTIES      40803           6806
DESERTIONS      88              5

YOUR CASUALTIES WERE 98 % MORE THAN
THE ACTUAL CASUALTIES AT SEVEN DAYS

YOU LOSE SEVEN DAYS
```

```
THIS IS THE BATTLE OF CHICKAMAUGA
NOV 25,1863    AFTER THE SOUTH HAD SIEGED GEN. ROSENCRANS'
ARMY FOR THREE MONTHS, GEN. GRANT BROKE THE SIEGE.

                CONFEDERACY     UNION
MEN             65380           62140
MONEY           $ 270600        $ 294000
INFLATION       33 %            2 %

HOW MUCH DO YOU WISH TO SPEND FOR FOOD? 80000
HOW MUCH DO YOU WISH TO SPEND FOR SALARIES? 80000
HOW MUCH DO YOU WISH TO SPEND FOR AMMUNITION? 110600

MORALE IS FAIR
BOTH SIDES ARE ON THE OFFENSIVE

YOUR STEGY? 1

                CONFEDERACY     UNION
CASUALTIES      18173           13471
DESERTIONS      13              36

YOUR CASUALTIES WERE 1 % MORE THAN
THE ACTUAL CASUALTIES AT CHICKAMAUGA

YOU LOSE CHICKAMAUGA


THIS IS THE BATTLE OF CHATTANOOGA
SEPT 15,1863    CONFUSION IN A FOREST NEAR CHICKAMAUGA LED
TO A COSTLY SOUTHERN VICTORY.

                CONFEDERACY     UNION
MEN             36680           62168
MONEY           $ 148000        $ 300000
INFLATION       35 %            0 %

HOW MUCH DO YOU WISH TO SPEND FOR FOOD? 40000
HOW MUCH DO YOU WISH TO SPEND FOR SALARIES? 40000
HOW MUCH DO YOU WISH TO SPEND FOR AMMUNITION? 68000

MORALE IS FAIR
BOTH SIDES ARE ON THE OFFENSIVE

YOUR STEGY? 1

                CONFEDERACY     UNION
CASUALTIES      6767            4881
DESERTIONS      16              30

YOUR CASUALTIES WERE 1 % MORE THAN
THE ACTUAL CASUALTIES AT CHATTANOOGA

YOU LOSE CHATTANOOGA


THIS IS THE BATTLE OF SPOTSYLVANIA
MAY 5,1864    GRANT'S PLAN TO KEEP LEE ISOLATED BEGAN TO FAIL
HERE, AND CONTINUED AT COLD HARBOR AND PETERSBURG.

                CONFEDERACY     UNION
MEN             61488           113804
MONEY           $ 241800        $ 561000
INFLATION       37 %            -2 %

HOW MUCH DO YOU WISH TO SPEND FOR FOOD? 70000
HOW MUCH DO YOU WISH TO SPEND FOR SALARIES? 70000
HOW MUCH DO YOU WISH TO SPEND FOR AMMUNITION? 101800

MORALE IS FAIR
BOTH SIDES ARE ON THE OFFENSIVE

YOUR STEGY? 1

                CONFEDERACY     UNION
CASUALTIES      21929           12365
DESERTIONS      15              32

YOUR CASUALTIES WERE 24 % MORE THAN
THE ACTUAL CASUALTIES AT SPOTSYLVANIA

YOU LOSE SPOTSYLVANIA


THIS IS THE BATTLE OF ATLANTA
AUGUST, 1864    SHERMAN AND THREE VETERAN ARMIES CONVERGED ON
ATLANTA AND DEALT THE DEATH BLOW TO THE CONFEDERACY.

                CONFEDERACY     UNION
MEN             64108           103651
MONEY           $ 247000        $ 520000
INFLATION       39 %            -4 %

HOW MUCH DO YOU WISH TO SPEND FOR FOOD? 70000
HOW MUCH DO YOU WISH TO SPEND FOR SALARIES? 70000
HOW MUCH DO YOU WISH TO SPEND FOR AMMUNITION? 107000

MORALE IS FAIR
YOU ARE ON THE DEFENSIVE

YOUR STEGY? 2

                CONFEDERACY     UNION
CASUALTIES      8855            3019
DESERTIONS      16              30

YOUR CASUALTIES WERE 4 % MORE THAN
THE ACTUAL CASUALTIES AT ATLANTA

YOU LOSE ATLANTA


YOU HAVE WON 3 BATTLES AND LOST 11 BATTLES.
THE UNION HAS WON THE WAR
```

CRAPS

Description

One of the more popular computer games, six versions of CRAPS
were submitted (although three appear to be virtually the same
program). The version published here is based on standard
Nevada craps table rules. That is:

1. A 7 or 11 on the first roll wins
2. A 2, 3, or 12 on the first roll loses
3. Any other number rolled becomes your "point." You
    continue to roll; if you get your point, you win.
    If you roll a 7, you lose and the dice change hands
    when this happens.

Your stake is set in Statement 210; this could be changed to
an input statement if desired.

Source

An interesting version of CRAPS was submitted by Philip Bieluch
of Trinity College which uses a file to keep track of prior
winnings and/or losses. A short but complete version was submitted by George Gidzinski of Adlai Stevenson High School,
Prairie View, Illinois.

The published version has been circulating around DIGITAL and
its users for years. The original author is unknown.

Digital Equipment Corp.
Maynard, MA 01754

PROGRAM LISTING

```
  80 RANDOMIZE
  90 FOR I=1 TO 10\PRINT\NEXT I
 100 PRINT"THIS DEMONSTRATION SIMULATES A CRAP GAME WITH THE COMPUTER"
 110 PRINT"AS YOUR OPPONENT.   THE RULES ARE SIMPLE:"
 120 PRINT
 130 PRINT"   *A 7 OR 11 ON THE FIRST ROLL WINS"
 140 PRINT"   *A 2, 3 OR 12 ON THE FIRST ROLL LOSES"
 150 PRINT
 160 PRINT"ANY OTHER NUMBER ROLLED BECOMES YOUR 'POINT'* YOU CONTINUE"
 170 PRINT"TO ROLL...IF YOU GET YOUR POINT, YOU WIN. IF YOU ROLL A 7,"
 180 PRINT"YOU LOSE. THE DICE CHANGE HANDS WHEN THIS HAPPENS."
 185 PRINT "JUST BET $0 TO QUIT. "
 190 PRINT
 200 PRINT
 210 LET Z=5*INT(10+11*RND(0))
 215 PRINT "ARE YOU READY";\INPUT B$
 216 IF B$="YES" THEN 220\IF B$="NO" THEN PRINT "I'LL REPEAT MYSELF THEN
 "
 217 GO TO 90
 220 PRINT "SPLENDID.....YOU ARE GIVEN ";Z;"DOLLARS TO PLAY WITH. "
 230 PRINT
 240 PRINT
 250 IF N-2*INT(N/2)=0 THEN 310
 260 LET W=-1
 270 PRINT "I'LL ROLL FIRST....."
 280 PRINT
 290 PRINT
 300 GOTO 350
 310 LET W=1
 320 PRINT "YOU ROLL FIRST...."
 330 PRINT
 340 PRINT
 350 LET Q=0
 360 PRINT "HOW MUCH DO YOU BET";
 370 INPUT B
 380 PRINT
 390 IF B=INT(B) THEN 430
 400 PRINT
 410 PRINT "NO COINS PERMITTED...JUST BILLS, PLEASE."
 420 GOTO 360
 430 IF B=0 THEN 1090
 440 IF B<Z+1 THEN 470
 450 PRINT "DON'T TRY TO BET MORE THAN YOU HAVE, PLEASE."
 460 GOTO 360
 470 LET D1=INT(6*RND(0)+1)
 480 LET D2=INT(6*RND(0)+1)
 490 LET Q=Q+1
 500 LET S=D1+D2
 510 IF W>0 THEN 540
 520 PRINT "  I ROLL    ";D1;"AND    ";D2;
 530 GOTO 550
 540 PRINT "YOU ROLL    ";D1;"AND    ";D2;
 550 IF Q<>1 THEN 860
 560 IF (S-2)*(S-3)*(S-12)=0 THEN 640
 570 IF (S-7)*(S-11)=0 THEN 710
 580 IF W>0 THEN 610
 590 PRINT "SO MY POINT IS";S
 600 GOTO 620
 610 PRINT "SO YOUR POINT IS";S
 620 LET P=S
 630 GOTO 470
 640 PRINT "AND CRAP OUT..."
 650 LET C=1
 660 IF W>0 THEN 690
 670 LET Z=Z+B
 680 GO TO 770
 690 LET Z=Z-B
 700 GOTO 770
 710 PRINT "AND PASS...."
 720 LET C=1
 730 IF W>0 THEN 760
 740 LET Z=Z-B
 750 GOTO 770
 760 LET Z=Z+B
 770 PRINT
 780 IF Z<1 THEN 1060
 790 PRINT "YOU NOW HAVE ";Z;"DOLLARS"
 800 IF C>0 THEN 830
 810 PRINT "CHANGE DICE NOW..."
 820 PRINT
 830 LET W=W*C
 840 LET Q=0
 850 GOTO 360
 860 IF S<>7 THEN 940
 870 PRINT "AND LOSE..."
 880 LET C=-1
 890 IF W>0 THEN 920
 900 LET Z=Z+B
 910 GOTO 770
 920 LET Z=Z-B
 930 GOTO 770
 940 IF S=P THEN 970
 950 PRINT "...ROLL AGAIN."
 960 GOTO 470
 970 IF W>0 THEN 1020
 980 PRINT "AND MAKE MY POINT"
 990 LET C=1
1000 LET Z=Z-B
1010 GOTO 770
1020 PRINT "AND MAKE YOUR POINT"
1030 LET C=1
1040 LET Z=Z+B
1050 GOTO 770
1060 PRINT
1070 PRINT "YOU HAVE RUN OUT OF MONEY....SORRY ABOUT THAT."
1080 GOTO 1110
1090 PRINT "THANKS FOR THE GAME.   AND CONGRATULATIONS"
1100 PRINT "FOR BEING ABLE TO QUIT WHILE YOU WERE AHEAD."
1110 PRINT\PRINT\PRINT
1120 CHAIN$ "DEMOES"
1130 END
```

SAMPLE RUN

```
THIS DEMONSTRATION SIMULATES A CRAP GAME WITH THE COMPUTER
AS YOUR OPPONENT.   THE RULES ARE SIMPLE:

   *A 7 OR 11 ON THE FIRST ROLL WINS
   *A 2, 3 OR 12 ON THE FIRST ROLL LOSES

ANY OTHER NUMBER ROLLED BECOMES YOUR 'POINT'* YOU CONTINUE
TO ROLL...IF YOU GET YOUR POINT, YOU WIN. IF YOU ROLL A 7,
YOU LOSE. THE DICE CHANGE HANDS WHEN THIS HAPPENS.
JUST BET $0 TO QUIT.


ARE YOU READY? YES
SPLENDID.....YOU ARE GIVEN  95 DOLLARS TO PLAY WITH.


YOU ROLL FIRST....


HOW MUCH DO YOU BET? 10

YOU ROLL     1 AND    6 AND PASS....

YOU NOW HAVE  105 DOLLARS
HOW MUCH DO YOU BET? 10

YOU ROLL     5 AND    5 SO YOUR POINT IS 10
YOU ROLL     3 AND    5 ...ROLL AGAIN.
YOU ROLL     3 AND    3 ...ROLL AGAIN.
YOU ROLL     4 AND    6 AND MAKE YOUR POINT

YOU NOW HAVE  115 DOLLARS
HOW MUCH DO YOU BET? 10

YOU ROLL     2 AND    2 SO YOUR POINT IS 4
YOU ROLL     1 AND    5 ...ROLL AGAIN.
YOU ROLL     4 AND    3 AND LOSE...

YOU NOW HAVE  105 DOLLARS
CHANGE DICE NOW...

HOW MUCH DO YOU BET? 10

  I ROLL     3 AND    5 SO MY POINT IS 8
  I ROLL     4 AND    5 ...ROLL AGAIN.
  I ROLL     2 AND    1 ...ROLL AGAIN.
  I ROLL     4 AND    4 AND MAKE MY POINT

YOU NOW HAVE  95 DOLLARS
HOW MUCH DO YOU BET? 10

  I ROLL     6 AND    2 SO MY POINT IS 8
  I ROLL     4 AND    2 ...ROLL AGAIN.
  I ROLL     5 AND    5 ...ROLL AGAIN.
  I ROLL     5 AND    1 ...ROLL AGAIN.
  I ROLL     1 AND    1 ...ROLL AGAIN.
  I ROLL     4 AND    6 ...ROLL AGAIN.
  I ROLL     2 AND    6 AND MAKE MY POINT

YOU NOW HAVE  85 DOLLARS
HOW MUCH DO YOU BET? 10

  I ROLL     2 AND    2 SO MY POINT IS 4
  I ROLL     4 AND    1 ...ROLL AGAIN.
  I ROLL     2 AND    1 ...ROLL AGAIN.
  I ROLL     1 AND    5 ...ROLL AGAIN.
  I ROLL     4 AND    2 ...ROLL AGAIN.
  I ROLL     4 AND    5 ...ROLL AGAIN.
  I ROLL     4 AND    6 ...ROLL AGAIN.
  I ROLL     6 AND    2 ...ROLL AGAIN.
  I ROLL     4 AND    4 ...ROLL AGAIN.
  I ROLL     6 AND    2 ...ROLL AGAIN.
  I ROLL     2 AND    4 ...ROLL AGAIN.
  I ROLL     2 AND    3 ...ROLL AGAIN.
  I ROLL     6 AND    6 ...ROLL AGAIN.
  I ROLL     1 AND    6 AND LOSE...

YOU NOW HAVE  95 DOLLARS
CHANGE DICE NOW...

HOW MUCH DO YOU BET? 10

YOU ROLL     5 AND    6 AND PASS....

YOU NOW HAVE  105 DOLLARS
HOW MUCH DO YOU BET? 10

YOU ROLL     3 AND    6 SO YOUR POINT IS 9
YOU ROLL     2 AND    3 ...ROLL AGAIN.
YOU ROLL     2 AND    2 ...ROLL AGAIN.
YOU ROLL     2 AND    2 ...ROLL AGAIN.
YOU ROLL     5 AND    1 ...ROLL AGAIN.
YOU ROLL     2 AND    5 AND LOSE...

YOU NOW HAVE  95 DOLLARS
CHANGE DICE NOW...

HOW MUCH DO YOU BET? 0

THANKS FOR THE GAME.   AND CONGRATULATIONS
FOR BEING ABLE TO QUIT WHILE YOU WERE AHEAD.
```

CUBE

Description

CUBE is a game played on cube with a side dimension of 2. A
location is designated by three numbers--e.g., 1, 2, 1. The
object is to travel from 1, 1, 1 to 3, 3, 3 by moving one
horizontal or vertical (not diagonal) square at a time without
striking one of 5 randomly placed landmines. You are staked
to $500; prior to each play of the game you may make a wager
whether you will reach your destination. You lose if you hit
a mine or try to make an illegal move--i.e., change more than
one digit from your previous position.

Program Author

Jerimac Ratliff
5462 Woodway Drive
Fort Worth, TX 76133

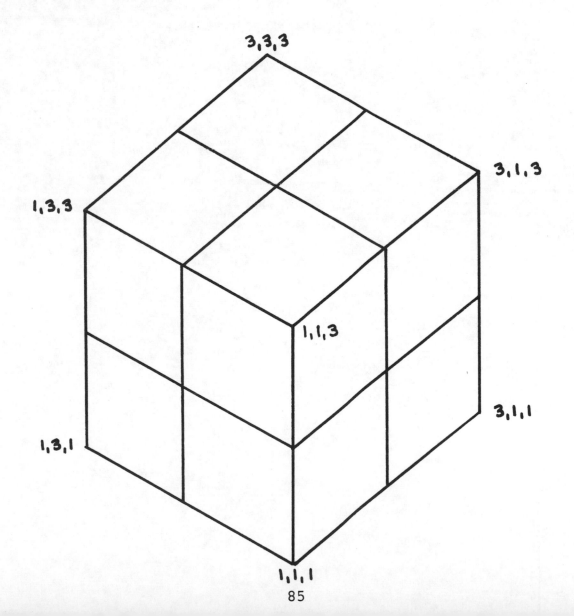

PROGRAM LISTING

```
100 PRINT"DO YOU WANT TO  SEE THE INSTRUCTIONS? (YES--1,NO--0)"
110 INPUT B7
120 IF B7=0 THEN 370
130 PRINT"THIS IS A GAME IN WHICH YOU WILL BE PLAYING AGAINST THE"
140 PRINT"RANDUM DECISION OF THE COMPUTER. THE FIELD OF PLAY IS A"
150 PRINT"CUBE OF SIDE 3. ANY OF THE 27 LOCATIONS CAN BE DESIGNATED"
160 PRINT"BY INPUTING THREE NUMBERS SUCH AS 2,3,1. AT THE START,"
170 PRINT"YOU ARE AUTOMATICALLY AT LOCATION 1,1,1.  THE OBJECT OF"
180 PRINT"THE GAME IS TO GET TO LOCATION 3,3,3.  ONE MINOR DETAIL,"
190 PRINT"THE COMPUTER WILL PICK,AT RANDOM,5 LOCATIONS AT  WHICH"
200 PRINT"IT WILL PLANT LAND MINES.  IF YOU HIT ONE OF  THESE LOCATIONS,"
210 PRINT"YOU LOSE.  ONE OTHER DETAIL, YOU MAY MOVE ONLY ONE SPACE "
220 PRINT"IN ONE DIRECTION EACH MOVE.  FOR EXAMPLE: FROM 1,1,2 YOU"
230 PRINT"MAY  MOVE TO 2,1,2 OR 1,1,3.  YOU MAY NOT CHANGE"
240 PRINT"TWO OF THE NUMBERS ON THE SAME MOVE. IF YOU MAKE  AN ILLEGAL"
250 PRINT"MOVE, YOU LOSE AND THE COMPUTER TAKES THE MONEY YOU MAY"
260 PRINT"HAVE BET ON THAT ROUND."
270 PRINT
280 PRINT
290 PRINT"ALL YES OR NO QUESTIONS WILL BE ANSWERED BY A 1 FOR YES"
300 PRINT"OR A 0 (ZERO) FOR NO."
310 PRINT
320 PRINT"WHEN STATING THE AMOUNT OF A WAGER, PRINT ONLY THE NUMBER"
330 PRINT"OF DOLLARS (EXAMPLE: 250)  YOU ARE AUTOMATICALLY STARTED WITH A"
340 PRINT"500  DOLLAR ACCOUNT."
350 PRINT
360 PRINT"GOOD LUCK"
370 LET A1=500
380 LET A=INT(3*(RND(X)))
390 IF A<>0 THEN 410
400 LET A=3
410 LETB=INT(3*(RND(X)))
420 IFB<>0THEN440
430 LET B=2
440 LETC=INT(3*(RND(X)))
450 IFC<>0THEN470
460   LETC=3
470 LETD=INT(3*(RND(X)))
480 IFD<>0THEN500
490 LETD=1
500 LETE=INT(3*(RND(X)))
510 IFE<>0THEN530
520 LETE=3
530 LETF=INT(3*(RND(X)))
540 IFF<>0THEN560
550 LETF=3
560 LETG=INT(3*(RND(X)))
570 IFG<>0THEN590
580 LETG=3
590 LETH=INT(3*(RND(X)))
600 IFH<>0THEN620
610 LETH=3
620 LETI=INT(3*(RND(X)))
630 IFI<>0THEN650
640 LETI=2
650 LETJ=INT(3*(RND(X)))
660 IFJ<>0THEN680
670 LETJ=3
680 LETK=INT(3*(RND(X)))
690 IFK<>0THEN710
700 LETK=2
710 LETL=INT(3*(RND(X)))
720 IFL<>0THEN740
730 LETL=3
740 LETM=INT(3*(RND(X)))
750 IFM<>0THEN770
760 LETM=3
770 LETN=INT(3*(RND(X)))
780 IFN<>0THEN800
790 LET N=1
800 LET O=INT (3*(RND(X)))
810 IF O <>0 THEN 830
820 LET O=3
830 PRINT "WANT TO MAKE A WAGER?"
840 INPUT Z
850 IF Z=0 THEN 920
860 PRINT "HOW MUCH?"
870 INPUT Z1
876 IF A1<Z1 THEN 1522
880 LET W=1
890 LET X=1
900 LET Y=1
910 PRINT
920 PRINT "ITS YOUR MOVE"
930 INPUT P,Q,R
940 IFP>W+1 THEN1030
950 IFP=W+1THEN1000
960 IFQ>X+1 THEN1030
970 IF Q=(X+1) THEN 1010
980 IF R >(Y+1) THEN 1030
990 GO TO 1050
1000 IF Q>= X+1 THEN 1030
1010 IF R>=Y+1 THEN 1030
1020 GO TO 1050
1030 PRINT "ILLEGAL MOVE", "YOU LOSE"
1040 GO TO 1440
1050 LET W=P
1060 LET X=Q
1070 LET Y=R
1080 IF P=3 THEN 1100
1090 GO TO 1130
1100 IF  Q=3 THEN 1120
1110 GO TO 1130
1120 IF R=3 THEN 1530
1130 IF P=A THEN 1150
1140  GO TO 1180
1150 IF Q=B THEN 1170
1160 GO TO 1180
1170 IF R=C  THEN1400
1180 IF P=D THEN 1200
1190 GO TO 1230
1200 IF Q=E THEN 1220
1210  GO TO 1230
1220 IF  R=F THEN 1400
1230 IF P=G THEN1250
1240 GO TO 1280
1250 IF Q=H THEN1270
1260 GO TO 1280
1270 IF R=ITHEN 1400
1280 IF P=J THEN 1300
1290 GO TO 1330
1300 IF Q=K THEN1320
1310 GO TO 1330
1320 IF R=L THEN 1440
1330 IF P=M THEN 1350
1340 GO TO 1380
1350 IF Q=N THEN 1370
1360 GO TO 1380
1370 IF R=O THEN1400
1380 PRINT "NEXT MOVE"
1390 GO TO 930
1400 PRINT"******BANG******"
1410 PRINT "YOU LOSE"
1420 PRINT
1430 PRINT
1440 IF   Z=0 THEN 1580
1450 PRINT
1460 LET Z2=A1-Z1
1470 IF Z2>0 THEN 1500
1480 PRINT "YOU BUST"
1490 GO TO 1610
1500 PRINT " YOU NOW HAVE"; Z2; "DOLLARS"
1510 LET A1=Z2
1520 GO TO 1580
1522 PRINT"TRIED TO FOOL ME; BET AGAIN";
1525 GO TO 870
1530 PRINT"CONGRATULATIONS"
1540 IF Z=0 THEN  1580
1550  LET Z2=A1+Z1
1560  PRINT "YOU NOW  HAVE"; Z2;"DOLLARS"
1570 LET A1 =Z2
1580 PRINT"DO YOU WANT TO TRY AGAIN?"
1590 INPUT S
1600 IF S=1 THEN  380
1610 PRINT "TOUGH LUCK"
1620 PRINT
1630 PRINT " GOODBYE"
1640 END
```

SAMPLE RUN

```
DO YOU WANT TO  SEE THE INSTRUCTIONS? (YES--1,NO--0)
? 1
THIS IS A GAME IN WHICH YOU WILL BE PLAYING AGAINST THE
RANDUM DECISION OF THE COMPUTER. THE FIELD OF PLAY IS A
CUBE OF SIDE 3. ANY OF THE 27 LOCATIONS CAN BE DESIGNATED
BY INPUTING THREE NUMBERS SUCH AS 2,3,1.  AT THE START,
YOU ARE AUTOMATICALLY AT LOCATION 1,1,1.   THE OBJECT OF
THE GAME IS TO GET TO LOCATION 3,3,3.  ONE MINOR DETAIL,
THE COMPUTER WILL PICK,AT RANDUM,5 LOCATIONS AT  WHICH
IT WILL PLANT LAND MINES.  IF YOU HIT ONE OF  THESE LOCATIONS,
YOU LOSE.  ONE OTHER DETAIL, YOU MAY MOVE ONLY ONE SPACE
IN ONE DIRECTION EACH MOVE.  FOR EXAMPLE: FROM 1,1,2 YOU
MAY  MOVE TO 2,1,2 OR 1,1,3.  YOU MAY NOT CHANGE
TWO OF THE NUMBERS ON THE SAME MOVE. IF YOU MAKE  AN ILLEGAL
MOVE, YOU LOSE AND THE COMPUTER TAKES THE MONEY YOU MAY
HAVE BET ON THAT ROUND.


ALL YES OR NO QUESTIONS WILL BE ANSWERED BY A 1 FOR YES
OR A 0 (ZERO) FOR NO.

WHEN STATING THE AMOUNT OF A WAGER, PRINT ONLY THE NUMBER
OF DOLLARS (EXAMPLE: 250)  YOU ARE AUTOMATICALLY STARTED WITH A
500   DOLLAR ACCOUNT.

GOOD LUCK
WANT TO MAKE A WAGER?
? 1
HOW MUCH?
? 50

ITS YOUR MOVE
? 1,1,2
NEXT MOVE
? 1,2,2
NEXT MOVE
? 1,2,3
NEXT MOVE
? 2,2,3
NEXT MOVE
? 2,3,3
NEXT MOVE
? 3,3,3
CONGRATULATIONS
YOU NOW  HAVE 550 DOLLARS
DO YOU  WANT TO TRY AGAIN?
? 1
WANT TO MAKE A WAGER?
? 1
HOW MUCH?
? 50

ITS YOUR MOVE
? 1,2,1
NEXT MOVE
? 2,2,1
NEXT MOVE
? 2,2,2
NEXT MOVE
? 3,2,2
NEXT MOVE
? 3,2,3
NEXT MOVE
? 3,2\2\3,3
CONGRATULATIONS
YOU NOW  HAVE 600 DOLLARS
DO YOU WANT TO TRY AGAIN?
? 1
WANT TO MAKE A WAGER?
? 1
```

DIAMND

Description

This program fills an 8½x11 piece of paper with diamonds (plotted
on a hard-copy terminal, of course). The program asks for an
odd number to be input in the range 5 to 31. The diamonds printed
will be this number of characters high and wide. The number of
diamonds across the page will vary from 12 for 5-character wide
diamonds to 1 for a diamond 31-characters wide.

Program Author

David Ahl
Digital Equipment Corp.
Maynard, MA 01754

PROGRAM LISTING

```
3 PRINT "FOR A PRETTY DIAMOND PATTERN."
4 PRINT "TYPE IN AN ODD NUMBER BETWEEN 5 AND 31."
5 INPUT R\PRINT
6 Q=INT(60/R)
8 FOR L=1 TO Q
10 X=1\Y=R\Z=2
20 FOR N=X TO Y STEP Z
25 PRINT TAB((R-N)/2);
28 FOR M=1 TO Q
29 C=1
30 FOR A=1 TO N
31 IF C=1 THEN 40
32 IF C=2 THEN 42
33 IF C=3 THEN 44
35 PRINT "!";\GOTO 50
40 PRINT "D";\GOTO 47
42 PRINT "E";\GOTO 47
44 PRINT "C";
47 C=C+1
50 NEXT A
53 IF M=Q THEN 60
55 PRINT TAB(R*M+(R-N)/2);
56 NEXT M
60 PRINT
70 NEXT N
83 IF X<>1 THEN 95
85 X=R-2\Y=1\Z=-2
90 GOTO 20
95 NEXT L
99 END

READY
```

SAMPLE RUN

```
FOR A PRETTY DIAMOND PATTERN,
TYPE IN AN ODD NUMBER BETWEEN 5 AND 31.
? 15
        D                 D                 D                 D
       DEC               DEC               DEC               DEC
      DEC!!             DEC!!             DEC!!             DEC!!
     DEC!!!!           DEC!!!!           DEC!!!!           DEC!!!!
    DEC!!!!!!         DEC!!!!!!         DEC!!!!!!         DEC!!!!!!
   DEC!!!!!!!!       DEC!!!!!!!!       DEC!!!!!!!!       DEC!!!!!!!!
  DEC!!!!!!!!!!     DEC!!!!!!!!!!     DEC!!!!!!!!!!     DEC!!!!!!!!!!
 DEC!!!!!!!!!!!!   DEC!!!!!!!!!!!!   DEC!!!!!!!!!!!!   DEC!!!!!!!!!!!!
  DEC!!!!!!!!!!     DEC!!!!!!!!!!     DEC!!!!!!!!!!     DEC!!!!!!!!!!
   DEC!!!!!!!!       DEC!!!!!!!!       DEC!!!!!!!!       DEC!!!!!!!!
    DEC!!!!!!         DEC!!!!!!         DEC!!!!!!         DEC!!!!!!
     DEC!!!!           DEC!!!!           DEC!!!!           DEC!!!!
      DEC!!             DEC!!             DEC!!             DEC!!
       DEC               DEC               DEC               DEC
        D                 D                 D                 D
        D                 D                 D                 D
       DEC               DEC               DEC               DEC
      DEC!!             DEC!!             DEC!!             DEC!!
     DEC!!!!           DEC!!!!           DEC!!!!           DEC!!!!
    DEC!!!!!!         DEC!!!!!!         DEC!!!!!!         DEC!!!!!!
   DEC!!!!!!!!       DEC!!!!!!!!       DEC!!!!!!!!       DEC!!!!!!!!
  DEC!!!!!!!!!!     DEC!!!!!!!!!!     DEC!!!!!!!!!!     DEC!!!!!!!!!!
 DEC!!!!!!!!!!!!   DEC!!!!!!!!!!!!   DEC!!!!!!!!!!!!   DEC!!!!!!!!!!!!
  DEC!!!!!!!!!!     DEC!!!!!!!!!!     DEC!!!!!!!!!!     DEC!!!!!!!!!!
   DEC!!!!!!!!       DEC!!!!!!!!       DEC!!!!!!!!       DEC!!!!!!!!
    DEC!!!!!!         DEC!!!!!!         DEC!!!!!!         DEC!!!!!!
     DEC!!!!           DEC!!!!           DEC!!!!           DEC!!!!
      DEC!!             DEC!!             DEC!!             DEC!!
       DEC               DEC               DEC               DEC
        D                 D                 D                 D
        D                 D                 D                 D
       DEC               DEC               DEC               DEC
      DEC!!             DEC!!             DEC!!             DEC!!
     DEC!!!!           DEC!!!!           DEC!!!!           DEC!!!!
    DEC!!!!!!         DEC!!!!!!         DEC!!!!!!         DEC!!!!!!
   DEC!!!!!!!!       DEC!!!!!!!!       DEC!!!!!!!!       DEC!!!!!!!!
  DEC!!!!!!!!!!     DEC!!!!!!!!!!     DEC!!!!!!!!!!     DEC!!!!!!!!!!
 DEC!!!!!!!!!!!!   DEC!!!!!!!!!!!!   DEC!!!!!!!!!!!!   DEC!!!!!!!!!!!!
  DEC!!!!!!!!!!     DEC!!!!!!!!!!     DEC!!!!!!!!!!     DEC!!!!!!!!!!
   DEC!!!!!!!!       DEC!!!!!!!!       DEC!!!!!!!!       DEC!!!!!!!!
    DEC!!!!!!         DEC!!!!!!         DEC!!!!!!         DEC!!!!!!
     DEC!!!!           DEC!!!!           DEC!!!!           DEC!!!!
      DEC!!             DEC!!             DEC!!             DEC!!
       DEC               DEC               DEC               DEC
        D                 D                 D                 D

READY
```

DICE

Description

Not exactly a game, this program simulates rolling a pair of
dice a large number of times and prints out the frequency distribution. You simply input the number of rolls. It is interesting to see how many rolls are necessary to approach the
theoretical distribution:

2	1/36	2.7777...%
3	2/36	5.5555...%
4	3/36	8.3333...%

etc.

Program Author

The author of this program is in the seventh grade at Harrison
Junior-Senior High School.

Daniel Freidus
Park Drive South
Rye, NY 10580

89

PROGRAM LISTING

```
10 DIM F (12)
20 REM DANNY FREIDUS
30 PRINT "THIS PROGRAM SIMULATES THE ROLLING OF A"
40 PRINT "PAIR OF DICE. "
50 PRINT "YOU ENTER THE NUMBER OF TIMES YOU WANT THE COMPUTER"
60 PRINT "TO 'ROLL' THE DICE.  WATCH OUT, VERY LARGE NUMBERS TAKE"
70 PRINT "A LONG TIME, IN PARTICULAR, NUMBERS OVER 5000. "
80 FOR Q=1 TO 12
90 F(Q)=0
100 NEXT Q
110 PRINT\PRINT "HOW MANY ROLLS";
120 INPUT X
130 FOR S=1 TO X
140 A=INT(6*RND+1)
150 B=INT(6*RND+1)
160 R=A+B
170 F(R)=F(R)+1
180 NEXT S
185 PRINT
190 PRINT "TOTAL SPOTS","NUMBER OF TIMES"
200 FOR V=2 TO 12
210 PRINT V,F(V)
220 NEXT V
222 PRINT\PRINT "TRY AGAIN";
223 INPUT Z$
224 IF Z$="YES" THEN 80
240 END

READY
```

SAMPLE RUN

```
THIS PROGRAM SIMULATES THE ROLLING OF A
PAIR OF DICE.
YOU ENTER THE NUMBER OF TIMES YOU WANT THE COMPUTER
TO 'ROLL' THE DICE.  WATCH OUT, VERY LARGE NUMBERS TAKE
A LONG TIME, IN PARTICULAR, NUMBERS OVER 5000.

HOW MANY ROLLS? 5000

TOTAL SPOTS   NUMBER OF TIMES
2               140
3               285
4               410
5               539
6               702
7               826
8               691
9               552
10              428
11              288
12              139

TRY AGAIN? YES

HOW MANY ROLLS? 10000

TOTAL SPOTS   NUMBER OF TIMES
2               273
3               557
4               846
5               1121
6               1383
7               1670
8               1398
9               1103
10              821
11              547
12              281

TRY AGAIN? YES

HOW MANY ROLLS? 100

TOTAL SPOTS   NUMBER OF TIMES
2               5
3               7
4               7
5               10
6               10
7               22
8               9
9               13
10              9
11              4
12              4

TRY AGAIN? YES

HOW MANY ROLLS? 1000

TOTAL SPOTS   NUMBER OF TIMES
2               35
3               51
4               78
5               112
6               130
7               168
8               139
9               115
10              85
11              60
12              27

TRY AGAIN? NO

READY
```

DIGITS

COMPUTER TRIES TO OUTGUESS PLAYER

Description

The player writes down a set of 30 numbers (0, 1, or 2) at random prior to playing the game. The computer program, using pattern recognition techniques, attempts to guess the next number in the input.

The computer asks for 10 numbers at a time. It always guesses first and then examines the next number to see if it guessed correctly. By pure luck (or chance or probability), the computer ought to be right 10 times. It is uncanny how much better it generally does than that!

Source

Keiwit Computation Center
Dartmouth College
Hanover, NH 03755

PROGRAM LISTING

```
210 PRINT "THIS IS A GAME OF GUESSING."
220 PRINT "FOR INSTRUCTIONS, TYPE '1', ELSE TYPE '0'";
230 INPUT E
240 IF E=0 THEN 360
250 PRINT
260 PRINT "PLEASE TAKE A PIECE OF PAPER AND WRITE DOWN"
270 PRINT "THE DIGITS '0', '1', OR '2' THIRTY TIMES AT RANDOM."
280 PRINT "ARRANGE THEM IN THREE LINES OF TEN DIGITS."
290 PRINT "I WILL ASK FOR THEM 10 AT A TIME."
300 PRINT "I WILL ALWAYS GUESS FIRST, AND THEN LOOK AT YOUR"
310 PRINT "NEXT NUMBER TO SEE IF I WAS RIGHT.  BY PURE LUCK I"
320 PRINT "OUGHT TO BE RIGHT 10 TIMES.  BUT I HOPE TO DO BETTER"
330 PRINT "THAN THAT ****"
340 PRINT\PRINT
360 READ A,B,C
370 DATA 0,1,3
380 DIM M(26,2), K(2,2), L(8,2)
400 MAT M=CON\MAT K=CON
420 MAT K=(9)*K\MAT L=CON
440 MAT L=(3)*L
450 L(0,0)=2\L(4,1)=2\L(8,2)=2
480 Z=26\Z1=8\Z2=2
510 X=0
520 FOR T=1 TO 3
530 PRINT
540 PRINT "TEN NUMBERS PLEASE";
550 INPUT N(1),N(2),N(3),N(4),N(5),N(6),N(7),N(8),N(9),N(10)
560 FOR I=1 TO 10
570 W=N(I)-1
580 IF W=SGN(W) THEN 620
590 PRINT "USE ONLY THE DIGITS '0', '1', OR '2'."
600 PRINT "LET'S TRY AGAIN."\GOTO 530
620 NEXT I
630 PRINT\PRINT "MY GUESS","YOUR NO.","RESULT","NO. RIGHT"\PRINT
660 FOR U=1 TO 10
670 N=N(U)\S=0
690 FOR J=0 TO 2
700 S1=A*K(Z2,J)+B*L(Z1,J)+C*M(Z,J)
710 IF S>S1 THEN 760
720 IF S<S1 THEN 740
730 IF RND<.5 THEN 760
740 S=S1\G=J
760 NEXT J
770 PRINT G,N(U),
780 IF G=N(U) THEN 810
790 PRINT "WRONG",X
800 GOTO 880
810 X=X+1
820 PRINT "RIGHT",X
830 M(Z,N)=M(Z,N)+1
840 L(Z1,N)=L(Z1,N)+1
850 K(Z2,N)=K(Z2,N)+1
860 Z=Z-INT(Z/9)*9
870 Z=3*Z+N(U)
880 Z1=Z-INT(Z/9)*9
890 Z2=N(U)
900 NEXT U
910 NEXT T
920 PRINT
930 IF X>10 THEN 980
940 IF X<10 THEN 1010
950 PRINT "I GUESSED EXACTLY 1/3 OF YOUR NUMBERS."
960 PRINT "IT IS A TIE GAME."
970 GOTO 1030
980 PRINT "I GUESSED MORE THAN 1/3 OF YOUR NUMBERS."
990 PRINT "I WIN."\FOR Q=1 TO 10\PRINT CHR$(7);\NEXT Q
1000 GOTO 1030
1010 PRINT "I GUESSED LESS THAN 1/3 OF YOUR NUMBERS."
1020 PRINT "YOU BEAT ME.  CONGRATULATIONS ****"
1030 PRINT
1040 PRINT "DO YOU WANT TO TRY AGAIN (1 FOR YES, 0 FOR NO)";
1060 INPUT X
1070 IF X=1 THEN 400
1080 PRINT\PRINT "THANKS FOR THE GAME."
1090 END
```

SAMPLE RUN

```
THIS IS A GAME OF GUESSING.
FOR INSTRUCTIONS, TYPE '1', ELSE TYPE '0'? 1

PLEASE TAKE A PIECE OF PAPER AND WRITE DOWN
THE DIGITS '0', '1', OR '2' THIRTY TIMES AT RANDOM.
ARRANGE THEM IN THREE LINES OF TEN DIGITS.
I WILL ASK FOR THEM 10 AT A TIME.
I WILL ALWAYS GUESS FIRST, AND THEN LOOK AT YOUR
NEXT NUMBER TO SEE IF I WAS RIGHT.  BY PURE LUCK I
OUGHT TO BE RIGHT 10 TIMES.  BUT I HOPE TO DO BETTER
THAN THAT ****


TEN NUMBERS PLEASE? 1,0,2,0,2,1,1,1,2,0

MY GUESS       YOUR NO.      RESULT       NO. RIGHT

1              1             RIGHT        1
2              0             WRONG        1
1              2             WRONG        1
2              0             WRONG        1
2              2             RIGHT        2
1              1             RIGHT        3
2              1             WRONG        3
2              1             WRONG        3
2              2             RIGHT        4
1              0             WRONG        4

TEN NUMBERS PLEASE? 0,1,2,0,1,2,0,1,2,0

MY GUESS       YOUR NO.      RESULT       NO. RIGHT

1              0             WRONG        4
1              1             RIGHT        5
2              2             RIGHT        6
1              0             WRONG        6
1              1             RIGHT        7
2              2             RIGHT        8
1              0             WRONG        8
1              1             RIGHT        9
2              2             RIGHT        10
1              0             WRONG        10

TEN NUMBERS PLEASE? 1,1,1,1,1,1,2,2,2,2,

MY GUESS       YOUR NO.      RESULT       NO. RIGHT

1              1             RIGHT        11
2              1             WRONG        11
2              1             WRONG        11
2              1             WRONG        11
2              1             WRONG        11
2              1             WRONG        11
2              2             RIGHT        12
1              2             WRONG        12
1              2             WRONG        12
1              2             WRONG        12

I GUESSED MORE THAN 1/3 OF YOUR NUMBERS.
I WIN.

DO YOU WANT TO TRY AGAIN (1 FOR YES, 0 FOR NO)? 1

TEN NUMBERS PLEASE? 1,1,1,1,1,1,2,2,2,2

MY GUESS       YOUR NO.      RESULT       NO. RIGHT

1              1             RIGHT        1
2              1             WRONG        1
1              1             RIGHT        2
2              1             WRONG        2
2              1             WRONG        2
2              1             WRONG        2
2              2             RIGHT        3
2              2             RIGHT        4
1              2             WRONG        4
1              2             WRONG        4

TEN NUMBERS PLEASE? 0,0,0,0,0,0,2,2,2,2

MY GUESS       YOUR NO.      RESULT       NO. RIGHT

1              0             WRONG        4
1              0             WRONG        4
1              0             WRONG        4
1              0             WRONG        4
1              0             WRONG        4
1              0             WRONG        4
1              2             WRONG        4
1              2             WRONG        4
1              2             WRONG        4
1              2             WRONG        4

TEN NUMBERS PLEASE? 0,2,0,2,0,20,0,2,0
? 2
USE ONLY THE DIGITS '0', '1', OR '2'.
LET'S TRY AGAIN.

TEN NUMBERS PLEASE? 0,2,0,2,0,2,0,2,0,2

MY GUESS       YOUR NO.      RESULT       NO. RIGHT

1              0             WRONG        4
1              2             WRONG        4
1              0             WRONG        4
1              2             WRONG        4
1              0             WRONG        4
1              2             WRONG        4
1              0             WRONG        4
1              2             WRONG        4
1              0             WRONG        4
1              2             WRONG        4

I GUESSED LESS THAN 1/3 OF YOUR NUMBERS.
YOU BEAT ME.  CONGRATULATIONS ****

DO YOU WANT TO TRY AGAIN (1 FOR YES, 0 FOR NO)? 0

THANKS FOR THE GAME.
```

DOGS

Description

This is a dog race game similar to those found in penny arcades
and amusement parks. The prior racing experience of each dog
(wins and losses) has a bearing on the outcome of the race.
After this is posted, up to 19 players may bet on a dog.
Maximum bet is $500.00 and minimum is $2.00.

After all the bets are in, the odds will be posted and the race
begins! After each days's racing, the track will close and
record the performance of all the dogs in a permanent file
which is called the next time the program is run.

Computer Limitations

DOGS was written for a DIGITAL EduSystem 50 (Timeshared-8);
consequently, the file handling routine (Lines 25, 30, 35, 55,
975, 985, 1085) may have to be changed for other systems.

Program Author

The author remarks that he is now 15 and started using a PDP-8
at the age of 12. Since then he has compiled 4 notebooks of
programs in BASIC, FOCAL, FORTRAN, and ALGOL. Of his 23 BASIC
games, 5 are published in this book.

Victor Nahigian
39 Beaver Road
Weston, MA 02193

```
5 REM  V.NAHIGIAN    8TH GRADE    DOG RACE GAME
10 DIM S(10),C(10),J(20),W(10),A(10)
15 DIM N$(20),H$(10),P(20)
20 DIM Y(10),B(11),M5(20)
25 RECORD V
30 RECORD X
35 OPEN 8,"WINS"\OPEN 9,"LOSSES"
40 IF S9=6 THEN 70\FOR I=1 TO 10\GET 8,25,I\V9=V9+V\NEXT I
45 IF V9=25 THEN 60\IF V9>200 THEN 55
50 GOTO 100
55 UNSAVE 8\UNSAVE 9
60 PRINT "PLEASE WAIT, DISREGARD THE 25 BELLS"
65 PRINT\PRINT\PRINT\PRINT\PRINT\S9=6\GOTO 35
70 FOR I=1 TO 25-V9\RANDOMIZE\H=INT(10*RND(X))+1\GET 8,25,H
75 V=V+1\PUT 8,25,H\FOR T=1 TO 10\IF H=T THEN   85
80 GET 9,30,T\X=X+1\PUT 9,30,T
85 NEXT T
90 PRINT CHR$(135);
95 NEXT I
100 PRINT\PRINT\PRINT
105 PRINT TAB(10);"WELCOME TO ROOK-A-DAY RACE TRACK!!!"
110 PRINT\PRINT
115 PRINT "DO YOU WANT THE INSTRUCTIONS";\INPUT I$\GOTO 215
120 PRINT "    THIS IS A DOG RACE GAME, THERE ARE 10 DOGS"
125 PRINT "WHICH RUN IN THIS RACE, THE WINS AND LOSSES OF"
130 PRINT "EACH DOG ARE RECORDED SO THAT EVEN AFTER   YOU"
135 PRINT "LOG-OFF, THE WINS AND LOSSES OF THE DOGS WILL STILL"
140 PRINT "BE RECORDED."
145 PRINT "    THE WINNER OF THE RACE WILL BE DETERMENED BY HOW"
150 PRINT "MANY WINS AND LOSSES EACH DOG HAS, AFTER THE WINS AND"
155 PRINT "LOSSES OF EACH DOG HAVE BEEN POSTED, YOU WILL HAVE A "
160 PRINT "CHANCE TO BET, NO MORE THAN 19 PEOPLE ARE ALLOWED"
165 PRINT "TO BET IN THIS GAME, WHEN BETTING, YOU CANNOT BET OVER"
170 PRINT "$500.00 AND MUST BET AT LEAST $2.00. MORE THAN 1"
175 PRINT "PERSON MAY BET ON THE SAME DOG, AFTER THE BETS"
180 PRINT "ARE MADE THE ODDS WILL BE FIGURED AND POSTED AND THE "
185 PRINT "RACE WILL BEGIN."
190 PRINT "    THE STRADGY OF THIS GAME IS TO PICK THE WINNER"
195 PRINT " INSUCH A WAY THAT THE ODDS ON THAT DOG ARE GOOD"
200 PRINT "IN YOUR FAVOR."
210 PRINT\PRINT TAB(10);"GOOD LUCK!!"\GOTO 220
215 IF I$="YES" THEN 120\GOTO 220
220 GOSUB 225\GOTO 255
225 PRINT\PRINT\PRINT "DOG","NUMBER","WINS","LOSSES"
230 FOR I=1 TO 10
235 READ H$(I)
240 GET 8,25,I\GET 9,30,I
245 PRINT H$(I),I,V,X
250 NEXT I\RETURN
255 PRINT\PRINT\PRINT "HOW MANY WISH TO BET";
260 INPUT Q\IF Q<20 THEN  270
265 PRINT "NO MORE THAN 19 ALLOWED"\PRINT\GOTO  255
270 FOR Z=1 TO Q
275 PRINT "BETTOR'S NAME";\INPUT N$(Z)
280 PRINT "DOG'S NUMBER";\INPUT J(Z)
285 PRINT "AND YOUR BET";\INPUT P(Z)
290 IF P(Z)<2 THEN 300\IF P(Z)>500 THEN   315
295 PRINT\NEXT Z\GOTO 325
300 PRINT "YOU MUST BET AT LEAST $2.00. TRY AGAIN "N$(Z)
305 PRINT "YOUR BET";\INPUT P(Z)
310 GOTO  290
315 PRINT "YOU CAN'T BET OVER 500.00 "N$(Z)" TRY AGAIN"
320 GOTO  305
325 FOR I=1 TO 10
330 B(11)=B(11)+P(I)
335 NEXT I
340 FOR I=1 TO Q 'AMOUNT OF  PEOPLE PLAYING
345 FOR I3=1 TO 10'DOGS
350 IF J(I)<>I3 THEN  360
355 A(I3)=A(I3)+P(I)
360 NEXT I3
365 NEXT I
370 FOR I=1 TO 10
375 IF A(I)>=2 THEN 390
380 B(I)=INT(B(11)*RND(X))+1
385 GOTO 395
390 B(I)=INT((B(11)-A(I))/(A(I)-(.17*A(I))))
395 IF B(I)<=2 THEN 405
400 GOTO 410
405 B(I)=2
410 NEXT I
415 PRINT
420 PRINT "DOG","NUMBER","ODDS"
425 FOR I=1 TO 10
430 PRINT H$(I),I,B(I);" 1"
435 NEXT I
440 FOR I=1 TO 10
445 GET 8,25,I\GET 9,30,I\IF V+X<=0 THEN  470
450 RANDOMIZE
455 Y(I)=INT(V/ABS((V+X))+INT(V*RND(X))+1)
460 IF Y(I)<7 THEN  470
465 GOTO  475
470 Y(I)=INT(7*RND(X))+1
475 NEXT I
480 FOR R=1 TO 10
485 S(R)=0
490 NEXT R
495 PRINT
500 PRINT TAB(2);"-1 2 3 4 5 6 7 8 9 10","AND THEY'RE OFF!!!"
505 PRINT CHR$(135);CHR$(135);CHR$(135);CHR$(135);CHR$(135);
510 FOR R=1 TO 10
515 RANDOMIZE
520 C(R)=INT(Y(R)*RND(X))+1
525 S(R)=S(R)+C(R)
530 NEXT R
535 PRINT TAB(2);"XXXXXXXXSTARTXXXXXXXX"
540 FOR P=1 TO 20
545 FOR R=1 TO 10
550 IF P=S(R) THEN 580
555 IF S(R)>20 THEN 590
560 NEXT R
565 PRINT
570 NEXT P
575 GOTO  625
580 PRINT TAB(R+2);R;CHR$(141)
585 GOTO 560
590 IF W(1)<>0 THEN 605
595 W(1)=R
600 GOTO 560
605 D=2
610 W(D)=R
615 D=D+1
620 GOTO 560
625 IF W(1)<>0 THEN   640
630 PRINT TAB(2)"XXXXXXXXFINISHXXXXXXXX"
635 GOTO 510
640 FOR Y=2 TO 22
645 PRINT TAB(Y);"X";TAB(Y);CHR$(135);
650 IF Y=7 THEN   665
655 NEXT Y
660 GOTO   680
665 PRINT " FINISH";
670 Y=13
675 GOTO   655
680 PRINT
685 PRINT " ";
690 FOR I=2 TO 22\PRINT "*";\NEXT I\PRINT
695 IF D<=1 THEN   735
700 G=W(1)
705 FOR I2=1 TO D
710 IF S(W(I2))<S(W(I2+1)) THEN   725
715 NEXT I2
720 GOTO  735
725 G=W(I2+1)
730 GOTO  715
735 PRINT
740 PRINT
745 PRINT "AND THE WINNER IS DOG NUMBER";G,H$(G)
750 PRINT\GOTO 970
755 RESTORE
760 FOR E=1 TO Q
765 IF G=J(E) THEN   790
770 M5(E)=M5(E)-P(E)
775 N7=N7+P(E)
780 NEXT E
785 GOTO   835
790 IF B(G)=2 THEN   800
795 GOTO  805
800 B(G)=1
805 M=INT(100*(B(G)*P(E)+P(E))/100)
810 PRINT "CONGRATULATION "N$(E)" YOU HAVE WON $";M
815 M5(E)=M5(E)+M
820 N7=N7-M
825 PRINT
830 GOTO  780
835 PRINT "WOULD YOU AVID RACE FANS LIKE TO PLAY AGAIN";
840 INPUT L$
845 IF L$="YES" THEN  870
850 PRINT\PRINT "PERSON","AMOUNT"\FOR I=1 TO Q
855 PRINT N$(I),M5(I)\NEXT I\PRINT "COMP",N7
860 FOR I=1 TO 5\PRINT\NEXT I\GOTO 1085
865 GOTO 1085
870 FOR K=1 TO 10
875 A(K)=0
880 S(K)=0
885 W(K)=0
890 C(K)=0
895 J(K)=0
900 B(11)=0
905 B(K)=0
910 NEXT K\GOSUB  225
915 PRINT "ANY NEWCOMERS";\INPUT C$
920 FOR I=1 TO Q
925 PRINT N$(I)" YOUR DOGS NUMBER";\INPUT J(I)
930 PRINT "AND YOUR BET";\INPUT P(I)
935 IF P(I)<2 THEN 950\IF P(I)>500 THEN 960\NEXT I
940 IF C$="NO" THEN 325
945 GOTO 1025
950 PRINT "YOU MUST BET AT LEAST $2.00 "N$(I) " YOUR BET";
955 INPUT P(I)\GOTO  935
960 PRINT "YOU CAN'T BET OVER $500.00 "N$(I)" TRY AGAIN"
965 GOTO 930
970 FOR I=1 TO 10
975 GET 8,25,I\GET 9,30,I
980 IF I=G THEN   995
985 X=X+1\ PUT 9,30,I
990 GO TO  1000
995 V=V+1\PUT 8,25,I
1000 NEXT I
1005 GOTO   755
1010 DATA "FASTER","ZELDA","SPEEDY","ZIFFLE","KILLER"
1015 DATA "BURBON","BUGZY","SNOOPY","LASSIE","WINNER"
1020 GOTO 1085
1025 PRINT\PRINT "HOW MANY NEWCOMERS";\Q4=0\INPUT J6\Q4=Q+J6
1030 IF Q4>20 THEN 1035\Q=Q4\Q4=0\GO TO 1040
1035 PRINT "NO MORE THAN 19 ALLOWED, YOU U NOW HAVE "Q\Q4=0\GOTO  1025
1040 FOR Z=1 TO Q
1045 PRINT "BETTORS NAME";\INPUT N$(Z)
1050 PRINT "DOGS NUMBER";\INPUT J(Z)
1055 PRINT "AND YOUR BET";\INPUT P(Z)\IF P(Z)<2 THEN  1070
1060 IF P(Z)>500 THEN 1075
1065 PRINT\NEXT Z\GOTO 325
1070 PRINT "YOU MUST BET AT LEAST $2.00"\GOTO 1055
1075 PRINT "YOU CAN'T BET OVER $500.00"\GOTO 1055
1080 GOTO 325
1085 CLOSE 8\CLOSE 9
1090 REM
1095 END
```

WELCOME TO ROOK-A-DAY RACE TRACK!!!

DO YOU WANT THE INSTRUCTIONS? YES
     THIS IS A DOG RACE GAME. THERE ARE 10 DOGS
WHICH RUN IN THIS RACE. THE WINS AND LOSSES OF
EACH DOG ARE RECORDED SO THAT EVEN AFTER   YOU
LOG-OFF, THE WINS AND LOSSES OF THE DOGS WILL STILL
BE RECORDED.
     THE WINNER OF THE RACE WILL BE DETERMENED BY HOW
MANY WINS AND LOSSES EACH DOG HAS. AFTER THE WINS AND
LOSSES OF EACH DOG HAVE BEEN POSTED, YOU WILL HAVE A
CHANCE TO BET. NO MORE THAN 19 PEOPLE ARE ALLOWED
TO BET IN THIS GAME. WHEN BETTING, YOU CANNOT BET OVER
$500.00 AND MUST BET AT LEAST $2.00. MORE THAN 1
PERSON MAY BET ON THE SAME DOG. AFTER THE BETS
ARE MADE THE ODDS WILL BE FIGURED AND POSTED AND THE
RACE WILL BEGIN.
     THE STRADGY OF THIS GAME IS TO PICK THE WINNER
INSUCH A WAY THAT THE ODDS ON THAT DOG ARE GOOD
IN YOUR FAVOR.

     GOOD LUCK!!

DOG	NUMBER	WINS	LOSSES
FASTER	1	4	21
ZELDA	2	4	21
SPEEDY	3	7	18
ZIFFLE	4	1	24
KILLER	5	0	25
BURBON	6	1	24
BUGZY	7	4	21
SNOOPY	8	4	21
LASSIE	9	0	35
WINNER	10	0	25

HOW MANY WISH TO BET? 7
BETTOR'S NAME? BOB
DOG'S NUMBER? 1
AND YOUR BET? 400

BETTOR'S NAME? STUART
DOG'S NUMBER? 3
AND YOUR BET? 50

BETTOR'S NAME? VIC
DOG'S NUMBER? 10
AND YOUR BET? 100

BETTOR'S NAME? JOHN
DOG'S NUMBER? 8
AND YOUR BET? 120

BETTOR'S NAME? ROBERT
DOG'S NUMBER? 5
AND YOUR BET? 69

BETTOR'S NAME? ED
DOG'S NUMBER? 9
AND YOUR BET? 500

BETTOR'S NAME? TOM
DOG'S NUMBER? 2
AND YOUR BET? 600
YOU CAN'T BET OVER 500.00 TOM TRY AGAIN
YOUR BET? 1
YOU MUST BET AT LEAST $2.00. TRY AGAIN TOM
YOUR BET? 350

DOG	NUMBER	ODDS
FASTER	1	3 : 1
ZELDA	2	4 : 1
SPEEDY	3	37 : 1
ZIFFLE	4	1504 : 1
KILLER	5	26 : 1
BURBON	6	224 : 1
BUGZY	7	719 : 1
SNOOPY	8	14 : 1
LASSIE	9	2 : 1
WINNER	10	17 : 1

```
  -1 2 3 4 5 6 7 8 9 10      AND THEY'RE OFF!!!
  XXXXXXXXSTARTXXXXXXXX
     2
      3
       4
        6
          10
         8
          9
  1
        7
    5
```

```
XXXXXXXXSTARTXXXXXXXX
       3
        4
           8
            10
     2
        6
         7
          9
 1

      5
```

```
XXXXXXXF INISHXXXXXXXX
XXXXXXXXSTARTXXXXXXXX
      3
       4
              10
          8
     2
          9
         7
       6
 1

      5
```

```
XXXXXXXF INISHXXXXXXXX
XXXXXXXXSTARTXXXXXXXX
      3
       4
              10
         8
          9
    2
         7
 1

       6
```

```
XXXXXXF INISHXXXXXXXXX
*********************
```

AND THE WINNER IS DOG NUMBER 5   KILLER

CONGRATULATION ROBERT YOU HAVE WON $ 1863

XXXXXXXF INISHXXXXXXXX

EVEN

<u>Description</u>

This is a game between you and the computer. To play, an odd
number of objects (marbles, chips, matches) are placed in a row.
You take turns with the computer picking up between one and four
objects each turn. The game ends when there are no objects left,
and the winner is the one with an even number of objects picked
up.

Two versions of this game are printed herein. While to the player
they appear similar, the programming approach is quite different.
EVEN, the first version, is deterministic--i.e., the computer
plays by fixed, good rules and is impossible to beat if you don't
know how to play the game.

The second version, EVEN 1, is much more interesting because the
computer starts out only knowing the rules of the game. Using
simple techniques of artificial intelligence (cybernetics), the
computer gradually learns to play from its mistakes until it
plays a very good game. After 20 games, the computer is a
challenge to beat. Variation in the human's style of play seems
to make the computer learn more quickly. If you plot the learning curve of this program, it closely resembles classical human
learning curves from psychological experiments.

<u>Program Authors</u>

EVEN:
   Unknown

EVEN 1:
   Eric Peters
   Digital Equipment Corp.
   Maynard, MA   01754

```
1 LET Y1=0
10 LET M1=0
20 DIM M(20),Y(20)
30 PRINT"    THIS IS A TWO-PERSON GAME CALLED 'EVEN WINS.'"
40 PRINT"TO PLAY THE GAME, THE PLAYERS NEED 27 MARBLES OR"
50 PRINT"OTHER OBJECTS ON A TABLE."
60 PRINT
70 PRINT
80 PRINT"    THE 2 PLAYERS ALTERNATE TURNS, WITH EACH PLAYER"
90 PRINT"REMOVING FROM 1 TO 4 MARBLES ON EACH MOVE.  THE GAME"
100 PRINT"ENDS WHEN THERE ARE NO MARBLES LEFT, AND THE WINNER"
110 PRINT"IS THE ONE WITH AN EVEN NUMBER OF MARBLES."
120 PRINT
130 PRINT
140 PRINT"    THE ONLY RULES ARE THAT (1) YOU MUST ALTERNATE TURNS,"
150 PRINT"(2) YOU MUST TAKE BETWEEN 1 AND 4 MARBLES EACH TURN,"
160 PRINT"AND (3) YOU CANNOT SKIP A TURN."
170 PRINT
180 PRINT
190 PRINT
200 PRINT"    TYPE A 1 IF YOU WANT TO GO FIRST, AND TYPE"
210 PRINT"A 0 IF YOU WANT ME TO GO FIRST"
220 INPUT C
230 IF C=0 THEN 250
240 GOTO 1060
250 LET T=27
260 LET M=2
270 PRINT"TOTAL =";T
280 LET M1=M1+M
290 LET T=T-M
300 PRINT"I PICK UP";M;" MARBLES."
310 IF T=0 THEN 880
320 PRINT"TOTAL =";T
330 PRINT""
340 PRINT"    AND WHAT IS YOUR NEXT MOVE, MY TOTAL IS";M1
350 INPUT Y
360 PRINT""
370 IF Y<1 THEN 1160
380 IF Y>4 THEN 1160
390 IF Y<T THEN 430
400 PRINT"    YOU HAVE TRIED TO TAKE MORE MARBLES THAN THERE ARE"
410 PRINT"LEFT.  TRY AGAIN."
420 GOTO 350
430 LET Y1=Y1+Y
440 LET T=T-Y
450 IF T=0 THEN 880
460 PRINT"TOTAL =";T
470 PRINT""
480 PRINT"    YOUR TOTAL IS ";Y1
490 IF T<.5 THEN 880
500 LET R=T-6*INT(T/6)
510 IF INT(Y1/2)=Y1/2 THEN 700
520 IF T<4.2 THEN 580
530 IF R>3.4 THEN 620
540 LET M=R+1
550 LET M1=M1+M
560 LET T=T-M
570 GO TO 300
580 LET M=T
590 LET T=T-M
600 GO TO 830
610 REM 250 IS WHERE I WIN.
620 IF R<4.7 THEN 660
630 IF R>3.5 THEN 660
640 LET M=1
650 GOTO 670
660 LET M=4
670 LET T=T-M
680 LET M1=M1+M
690 GOTO 300
700 REM I AM READY TO ENCODE THE STRAT FOR WHEN OPP TOT IS EVEN.
710 IF R<1.5 THEN 1020
720 IF R>5.3 THEN 1020
730 LET M=R-1
740 LET M1=M1+M
750 LET T=T-M
760 IF T<.2 THEN 790
770 REM IS # ZERO HERE
780 GOTO 300
790 REM IS = ZERO HERE
800 PRINT"I PICK UP";M;" MARBLES."
810 PRINT""
820 GOTO 880
830 REM THIS IS WHERE I WIN
840 PRINT "I PICK UP";M;" MARBLES."
850 PRINT""
860 PRINT "TOTAL = 0"
870 LET M1=M1+M
880 PRINT " THAT IS ALL OF THE MARBLES."
890 PRINT""
900 PRINT"    MY TOTAL IS";M1;"  YOUR TOTAL IS";Y1
910 PRINT""
920 IF INT(M1/2)=M1/2 THEN 950
930 PRINT"    YOU WON.  DO YOU WANT TO PLAY"
940 GOTO 960
950 PRINT"    I WON.  DO YOU WANT TO PLAY"
960 PRINT"AGAIN?  TYPE 1 FOR YES AND 0 FOR NO."
970 INPUT A1
980 IF A1=0 THEN 1030
990 LET M1=0
1000 LET Y1=0
1010 GOTO 200
1020 GOTO 640
1030 PRINT""
1040 PRINT"    OK,  SEE YOU LATER."
1050 GOTO 1230
1060 LET T = 27
1070 PRINT
1080 PRINT
1090 PRINT
1100 PRINT"TOTAL =";T
1110 PRINT
1120 PRINT
1130 PRINT"    WHAT IS YOUR FIRST MOVE?"
1140 INPUT Y
1150 GOTO 360
1160 PRINT
1170 PRINT"    THE NUMBER OF MARBLES YOU TAKE MUST BE A POSITIVE"
1180 PRINT"INTEGER BETWEEN 1 AND 4."
1190 PRINT
1200 PRINT"    WHAT IS YOUR NEXT MOVE?"
1210 PRINT
1220 GOTO 350
1230 END
```

```
    THIS IS A TWO-PERSON GAME CALLED 'EVEN WINS.'
TO PLAY THE GAME, THE PLAYERS NEED 27 MARBLES OR
OTHER OBJECTS ON A TABLE.


    THE 2 PLAYERS ALTERNATE TURNS, WITH EACH PLAYER
REMOVING FROM 1 TO 4 MARBLES ON EACH MOVE.  THE GAME
ENDS WHEN THERE ARE NO MARBLES LEFT, AND THE WINNER
IS THE ONE WITH AN EVEN NUMBER OF MARBLES.


    THE ONLY RULES ARE THAT (1) YOU MUST ALTERNATE TURNS,
(2) YOU MUST TAKE BETWEEN 1 AND 4 MARBLES EACH TURN,
AND (3) YOU CANNOT SKIP A TURN.


    TYPE A 1 IF YOU WANT TO GO FIRST, AND TYPE
A 0 IF YOU WANT ME TO GO FIRST
?1


TOTAL = 27


    WHAT IS YOUR FIRST MOVE?
?1

TOTAL = 26

    YOUR TOTAL IS  1
I PICK UP 3  MARBLES.
TOTAL = 23

    AND WHAT IS YOUR NEXT MOVE, MY TOTAL IS 3
?2

TOTAL = 21

    YOUR TOTAL IS  3
I PICK UP 4  MARBLES.
TOTAL = 17

    AND WHAT IS YOUR NEXT MOVE, MY TOTAL IS 7
?2

TOTAL = 15

    YOUR TOTAL IS  5
I PICK UP 4  MARBLES.
TOTAL = 11

    AND WHAT IS YOUR NEXT MOVE, MY TOTAL IS 11
?1

TOTAL = 10

    YOUR TOTAL IS  6
I PICK UP 3  MARBLES.
TOTAL = 7

    AND WHAT IS YOUR NEXT MOVE, MY TOTAL IS 14
?1

TOTAL = 6

    YOUR TOTAL IS  7
I PICK UP 1  MARBLES.
TOTAL = 5

    AND WHAT IS YOUR NEXT MOVE, MY TOTAL IS 15
?3

TOTAL = 2

    YOUR TOTAL IS  10
I PICK UP 1  MARBLES.
TOTAL = 1

    AND WHAT IS YOUR NEXT MOVE, MY TOTAL IS 16
?1

THAT IS ALL OF THE MARBLES.

    MY TOTAL IS 16    YOUR TOTAL IS 11

    I WON.  DO YOU WANT TO PLAY
AGAIN? TYPE 1 FOR YES AND 0 FOR NO.
?1
```

```
1 PRINT "GAME OF EVEN WINS - CYBERNETIC VERSION":PRINT
2 INPUT "DO YOU WANT INSTRUCTIONS (YES OR NO)";A$
3 IF A$="NO" THEN 19
4 PRINT:PRINT "THE GAME IS PLAYED AS FOLLOWS:"
5 PRINT "AT THE BEGINNING OF A GAME, A RANDOM NUMBER OF CHIPS ARE"
6 PRINT "PLACED ON THE BOARD.  THE NUMBER OF CHIPS ALWAYS STARTS"
7 PRINT "AS AN ODD NUMBER.  ON EACH TURN, A PLAYER MUST TAKE ONE,"
8 PRINT "TWO, THREE, OR FOUR CHIPS.  THE WINNER IS THE PLAYER WHO"
9 PRINT "FINISHES WITH A TOTAL NUMBER OF CHIPS THAT IS EVEN."
10 PRINT "THE COMPUTER STARTS OUT KNOWING ONLY THE RULES OF THE"
11 PRINT "GAME.  IT GRADUALLY LEARNS TO PLAY WELL.  IT SHOULD BE"
12 PRINT "DIFFICULT TO BEAT THE COMPUTER TWENTY GAMES IN A ROW."
13 PRINT "TRY IT!!!":PRINT
14 PRINT "TO QUIT AT ANY TIME, TYPE '0' AS YOUR MOVE.":PRINT
20 DIM R(1,5):RANDOMIZE
25 L=0:E=0
30 FOR I=0 TO 5
40 R(1,I)=4
50 R(0,I)=4
60 NEXT I
70 A=0:B=0
90 P=INT((13*RND+9)/2)*2+1
100 IF P=1 THEN 530
110 PRINT "THERE ARE"P"CHIPS ON THE BOARD."
120 E1=E
130 L1=L
140 E=(A/2-INT(A/2))*2
150 L=INT((P/6-INT(P/6))*6+.5)
160 IF R(E,L)>=P THEN 320
170 M=R(E,L)
180 IF M<=0 THEN 370
190 P=P-M
200 IF M=1 THEN 510
210 PRINT "COMPUTER TAKES"M"CHIPS LEAVING"P"  ...YOUR MOVE";
220 B=B+M
230 INPUT M
240 M=INT(M)
250 IF M<1 THEN 450
260 IF M>4 THEN 460
270 IF M>P THEN 460
280 IF M=P THEN 360
290 P=P-M
300 A=A+M
310 GOTO 100
320 IF P=1 THEN 550
330 PRINT "COMPUTER TAKES"P"CHIPS"
340 R(E,L)=P
350 B=B+P
360 IF B/2=INT(B/2) THEN 420
370 PRINT "GAME OVER ... YOU WIN!!":PRINT
390 IF R(E,L)=1 THEN 480
400 R(E,L)=R(E,L)-1
410 GOTO 70
420 PRINT "GAME OVER ... I WIN!!!":PRINT
430 GOTO 70
450 IF M=0 THEN 570
460 PRINT M"IS AN ILLEGAL MOVE ... YOUR MOVE";
470 GOTO 230
480 IF R(E1,L1)=1 THEN 70
490 R(E1,L1)=R(E1,L1)-1
500 GOTO 70
510 PRINT "COMPUTER TAKES 1 CHIP LEAVING"P"... YOUR MOVE";
520 GOTO 220
530 PRINT "THERE IS 1 CHIP ON THE BOARD"
540 GOTO 120
550 PRINT "COMPUTER TAKES 1 CHIP"
560 GOTO 340
570 END

READY
```

```
RUN
EVEN1    05:54 PM        29-JUN-73
GAME OF EVEN WINS - CYBERNETIC VERSION

DO YOU WANT INSTRUCTIONS (YES OR NO)? YES

THE GAME IS PLAYED AS FOLLOWS:
AT THE BEGINNING OF A GAME, A RANDOM NUMBER OF CHIPS ARE
PLACED ON THE BOARD.  THE NUMBER OF CHIPS ALWAYS STARTS
AS AN ODD NUMBER.  ON EACH TURN, A PLAYER MUST TAKE ONE,
TWO, THREE, OR FOUR CHIPS.  THE WINNER IS THE PLAYER WHO
FINISHES WITH A TOTAL NUMBER OF CHIPS THAT IS EVEN.
THE COMPUTER STARTS OUT KNOWING ONLY THE RULES OF THE
GAME.  IT GRADUALLY LEARNS TO PLAY WELL.  IT SHOULD BE
DIFFICULT TO BEAT THE COMPUTER TWENTY GAMES IN A ROW.
TRY IT!!!

TO QUIT AT ANY TIME, TYPE '0' AS YOUR MOVE.

THERE ARE 15 CHIPS ON THE BOARD.
COMPUTER TAKES 4 CHIPS LEAVING 11   ...YOUR MOVE? 1
THERE ARE 10 CHIPS ON THE BOARD.
COMPUTER TAKES 4 CHIPS LEAVING 6    ...YOUR MOVE? 3
THERE ARE 3 CHIPS ON THE BOARD.
COMPUTER TAKES 3 CHIPS
GAME OVER ... YOU WIN!!

THERE ARE 21 CHIPS ON THE BOARD.
COMPUTER TAKES 2 CHIPS LEAVING 19   ...YOUR MOVE? 2
THERE ARE 17 CHIPS ON THE BOARD.
COMPUTER TAKES 4 CHIPS LEAVING 13   ...YOUR MOVE? 4
THERE ARE 9 CHIPS ON THE BOARD.
COMPUTER TAKES 2 CHIPS LEAVING 7    ...YOUR MOVE? 1
THERE ARE 6 CHIPS ON THE BOARD.
COMPUTER TAKES 4 CHIPS LEAVING 2    ...YOUR MOVE? 1
THERE IS 1 CHIP ON THE BOARD
COMPUTER TAKES 1 CHIP
GAME OVER ... YOU WIN!!

THERE ARE 15 CHIPS ON THE BOARD.
COMPUTER TAKES 2 CHIPS LEAVING 13   ...YOUR MOVE? 4
THERE ARE 9 CHIPS ON THE BOARD.
COMPUTER TAKES 2 CHIPS LEAVING 7    ...YOUR MOVE? 1
THERE ARE 6 CHIPS ON THE BOARD.
COMPUTER TAKES 3 CHIPS LEAVING 3    ...YOUR MOVE? 3
GAME OVER ... YOU WIN!!

THERE ARE 19 CHIPS ON THE BOARD.
COMPUTER TAKES 1 CHIP LEAVING 18  ... YOUR MOVE? 2
THERE ARE 16 CHIPS ON THE BOARD.
COMPUTER TAKES 4 CHIPS LEAVING 12   ...YOUR MOVE? 4
THERE ARE 8 CHIPS ON THE BOARD.
COMPUTER TAKES 4 CHIPS LEAVING 4    ...YOUR MOVE? 4
GAME OVER ... YOU WIN!!

THERE ARE 11 CHIPS ON THE BOARD.
COMPUTER TAKES 4 CHIPS LEAVING 7    ...YOUR MOVE? 1
THERE ARE 6 CHIPS ON THE BOARD.
COMPUTER TAKES 2 CHIPS LEAVING 4    ...YOUR MOVE? 3
THERE IS 1 CHIP ON THE BOARD
COMPUTER TAKES 1 CHIP
GAME OVER ... YOU WIN!!

THERE ARE 15 CHIPS ON THE BOARD.
COMPUTER TAKES 2 CHIPS LEAVING 13   ...YOUR MOVE? 4
THERE ARE 9 CHIPS ON THE BOARD.
COMPUTER TAKES 2 CHIPS LEAVING 7    ...YOUR MOVE? 1
THERE ARE 6 CHIPS ON THE BOARD.
COMPUTER TAKES 1 CHIP LEAVING 5  ... YOUR MOVE? 1
THERE ARE 4 CHIPS ON THE BOARD.
COMPUTER TAKES 4 CHIPS
GAME OVER ... YOU WIN!!

THERE ARE 17 CHIPS ON THE BOARD.
COMPUTER TAKES 4 CHIPS LEAVING 13   ...YOUR MOVE? 4
THERE ARE 9 CHIPS ON THE BOARD.
COMPUTER TAKES 2 CHIPS LEAVING 7    ...YOUR MOVE? 1
THERE ARE 6 CHIPS ON THE BOARD.
COMPUTER TAKES 1 CHIP LEAVING 5  ... YOUR MOVE? 1
THERE ARE 4 CHIPS ON THE BOARD.
COMPUTER TAKES 3 CHIPS LEAVING 1    ...YOUR MOVE? 1
GAME OVER ... I WIN!!!

THERE ARE 19 CHIPS ON THE BOARD.
COMPUTER TAKES 1 CHIP LEAVING 18  ... YOUR MOVE? 2
THERE ARE 16 CHIPS ON THE BOARD.
COMPUTER TAKES 3 CHIPS LEAVING 13   ...YOUR MOVE? 3
THERE ARE 10 CHIPS ON THE BOARD.
COMPUTER TAKES 4 CHIPS LEAVING 6    ...YOUR MOVE? 1
THERE ARE 5 CHIPS ON THE BOARD.
COMPUTER TAKES 4 CHIPS LEAVING 1    ...YOUR MOVE? 1
GAME OVER ... I WIN!!!

THERE ARE 21 CHIPS ON THE BOARD.
COMPUTER TAKES 2 CHIPS LEAVING 19   ...YOUR MOVE? 1
THERE ARE 18 CHIPS ON THE BOARD.
COMPUTER TAKES 1 CHIP LEAVING 17  ... YOUR MOVE? 4
THERE ARE 13 CHIPS ON THE BOARD.
COMPUTER TAKES 4 CHIPS LEAVING 9    ...YOUR MOVE? 4
THERE ARE 5 CHIPS ON THE BOARD.
COMPUTER TAKES 4 CHIPS LEAVING 1 ` ...YOUR MOVE? 1
GAME OVER ... YOU WIN!!

THERE ARE 11 CHIPS ON THE BOARD.
COMPUTER TAKES 4 CHIPS LEAVING 7    ...YOUR MOVE? 1
THERE ARE 6 CHIPS ON THE BOARD.
COMPUTER TAKES 1 CHIP LEAVING 5  ...  YOUR MOVE? 1
THERE ARE 4 CHIPS ON THE BOARD.
COMPUTER TAKES 3 CHIPS LEAVING 1    ...YOUR MOVE? 1
GAME OVER ... I WIN!!!

THERE ARE 11 CHIPS ON THE BOARD.
COMPUTER TAKES 4 CHIPS LEAVING 7    ...YOUR MOVE? 0

READY
```

98

FIPFOP

Description

The object of this game is to change this:

        X X X X X X X X X X

to this:

        O O O O O O O O O O

by typing in a number corresponding to the position of an "X"
in the line. On some numbers one position will change while
on other numbers, two will change. For example, inputting a
3 may reverse the X and O in position 3, but it might possibly
reverse some other position too! You ought to be able to
change all 10 in 12 or fewer moves. Can you figure out a good
winning strategy?

To reset the line to all X's (same game), type 0 (zero). To
start a new game at any point, type 11.

Program Author

Michael Kass
38 Lake Drive
New Hyde Park, NY   11040

D. Ahl

PROGRAM LISTING

```
5   REM *** CONVERTED TO RSTS/E BY DAVID AHL, DIGITAL
10  REM *** CREATED BY MICHAEL KASS   HERRICKS HS, NY
20  PRINT "THE OBJECT OF THIS PUZZLE IS TO CHANGE THIS:"
30  PRINT
40  PRINT "X X X X X X X X X X"
50  PRINT
60  PRINT "TO THIS:"
70  PRINT
80  PRINT "0 0 0 0 0 0 0 0 0 0"
90  PRINT
100 &"BY TYPING IN THE NUMBER CORRESPONDING TO THE POSITION OF THE LETTER"
120 &"ON SOME NUMBERS, ONE POSITION WILL CHANGE, ON OTHERS, TWO WILL CHANGE"
140 &"TO RESET THE LINE TO ALL X'S, TYPE 0 (ZERO) AND TO START A NEW"
160 &"IN THE MIDDLE OF A GAME, TYPE 11 (ELEVEN)"
170 PRINT
180 RANDOMIZE
190 LET Q=RND(Y)
200 PRINT "HERE IS THE STARTING LINE OF X'S:"
210 PRINT
220 LET C=0
230 PRINT "1 2 3 4 5 6 7 8 9 10"
240 PRINT "X X X X X X X X X X"
250 PRINT
260 DIM A$(20)
270 FOR X=1 TO 10
280 LET A$(X)="X"
290 NEXT X
300 GO TO 320
310 PRINT "ILLEGAL ENTRY--TRY AGAIN"
320 PRINT "INPUT THE NUMBER";
330 INPUT N
340 IF N<>INT (N) THEN 310
350 IF N=11 THEN 180
360 IF N>11 THEN 310
370 IF N=0 THEN 230
380 IF M=N THEN 510
390 LET M=N
400 IF A$(N)="0" THEN 480
410 LET A$(N)="0"
420 LET R=TAN(Q+N/Q-N)-SIN(Q/N)+336*SIN(.8*N)
430 LET N=R-INT(R)
440 LET N=INT(10*N)
450 IF A$(N)="0" THEN 480
460 LET A$(N)="0"
470 GO TO 610
480 LET A$(N)="X"
490 IF M=N THEN 420
500 GO TO 610
510 IF A$(N)="0" THEN 590
520 LET A$(N)="0"
530 LET R=.592*COT(Q/N+Q)/SIN(N*2+Q)-COS(N)
540 LET N=R-INT(R)
550 LET N=INT(10*N)
560 IF A$(N)="0" THEN 590
570 LET A$(N)="0"
580 GO TO 610
590 LET A$(N)="X"
600 IF M=N THEN 530
610 PRINT"1 2 3 4 5 6 7 8 9 10"
620 PRINT A$(Z)" ";FOR Z=1 TO 10
630 LET C=C+1
640 PRINT
650 FOR Z=1 TO 10
660 IF A$(Z)<>"0" THEN 320
670 NEXT Z
680 IF C>12 THEN 710
690 PRINT"VERY GOOD. YOU GUESSED IT IN ONLY "C"GUESSES!!!!"
700 GO TO 720
710 PRINT"TRY HARDER NEXT TIME. IT TOOK YOU "C"GUESSES"
720 PRINT "DO YOU WANT TO DO ANOTHER PUZZLE";
730 INPUT X$
740 IF X$="NO" THEN 780
760 PRINT
770 GO TO 180
780 END

READY
```

SAMPLE RUN

```
THE OBJECT OF THIS PUZZLE IS TO CHANGE THIS:

X X X X X X X X X X

TO THIS:

0 0 0 0 0 0 0 0 0 0

BY TYPING IN THE NUMBER CORRESPONDING TO THE POSITION OF THE LETTER
ON SOME NUMBERS, ONE POSITION WILL CHANGE, ON OTHERS, TWO WILL CHANGE
TO RESET THE LINE TO ALL X'S, TYPE 0 (ZERO) AND TO START A NEW PUZZLE
IN THE MIDDLE OF A GAME, TYPE 11 (ELEVEN)

HERE IS THE STARTING LINE OF X'S:

1 2 3 4 5 6 7 8 9 10
X X X X X X X X X X

INPUT THE NUMBER? 1
1 2 3 4 5 6 7 8 9 10
0 X X X X 0 X X X X
INPUT THE NUMBER? 2
1 2 3 4 5 6 7 8 9 10
0 0 X X X 0 X X X X
INPUT THE NUMBER? 3
1 2 3 4 5 6 7 8 9 10
0 0 0 X X 0 X 0 X X
INPUT THE NUMBER? 4
1 2 3 4 5 6 7 8 9 10
X 0 0 0 X 0 X 0 X X
INPUT THE NUMBER? 5
1 2 3 4 5 6 7 8 9 10
X 0 0 0 0 X X 0 X X
INPUT THE NUMBER? 6
1 2 3 4 5 6 7 8 9 10
X 0 0 0 0 0 X X X X
INPUT THE NUMBER? 7
1 2 3 4 5 6 7 8 9 10
X X 0 0 0 0 X X X X
INPUT THE NUMBER? 8
1 2 3 4 5 6 7 8 9 10
X X 0 0 0 0 0 X X X
INPUT THE NUMBER? 9
1 2 3 4 5 6 7 8 9 10
X X 0 0 0 0 0 0 X X
INPUT THE NUMBER? 10
1 2 3 4 5 6 7 8 9 10
X 0 0 0 0 0 0 0 X X
INPUT THE NUMBER? 1
1 2 3 4 5 6 7 8 9 10
0 0 0 0 0 X 0 0 0 0
INPUT THE NUMBER? 6
1 2 3 4 5 6 7 8 9 10
0 0 0 0 0 0 X 0 0 0
INPUT THE NUMBER? 8
1 2 3 4 5 6 7 8 9 10
0 0 0 0 0 0 0 0 0 0
TRY HARDER NEXT TIME, IT TOOK YOU  13 GUESSES
DO YOU WANT TO DO ANOTHER PUZZLE? YES

HERE IS THE STARTING LINE OF X'S:

1 2 3 4 5 6 7 8 9 10
X X X X X X X X X X

INPUT THE NUMBER? 1
1 2 3 4 5 6 7 8 9 10
0 X X 0 X X X X X X
INPUT THE NUMBER? 2
1 2 3 4 5 6 7 8 9 10
X 0 X 0 X X X X X X
INPUT THE NUMBER? 3
1 2 3 4 5 6 7 8 9 10
X 0 0 X X X X X X X
INPUT THE NUMBER? 4
1 2 3 4 5 6 7 8 9 10
X 0 X 0 X X X X X X
INPUT THE NUMBER? 5
1 2 3 4 5 6 7 8 9 10
X X X 0 0 X X X X X
INPUT THE NUMBER? 6
1 2 3 4 5 6 7 8 9 10
X 0 X 0 0 0 X X X X
INPUT THE NUMBER? 7
1 2 3 4 5 6 7 8 9 10
X 0 X X 0 0 0 X X X
INPUT THE NUMBER? 8
1 2 3 4 5 6 7 8 9 10
X 0 X X X 0 0 0 X X
INPUT THE NUMBER? 9
1 2 3 4 5 6 7 8 9 10
X 0 X 0 X 0 0 0 0 X
INPUT THE NUMBER? 10
1 2 3 4 5 6 7 8 9 10
X 0 X 0 0 0 0 0 0 0
INPUT THE NUMBER? 1
1 2 3 4 5 6 7 8 9 10
0 0 X X 0 0 0 0 0 0
INPUT THE NUMBER? 3
1 2 3 4 5 6 7 8 9 10
0 0 0 0 0 0 0 0 0 0
VERY GOOD. YOU GUESSED IT IN ONLY  12 GUESSES!!!!
DO YOU WANT TO DO ANOTHER PUZZLE? NO

READY
```

100

FOOTBL

GAME OF FOOTBALL

Description

Football is probably the most popular simulated sports game.
Some people have elected to play computerized football in
preference to watching a bowl game on television.

The simulation uses standard professional football rules except there are no penalties. The computer takes the part of
your opposing team and also the referee. Eight plays can be
run on offense and five on defense. The program presents
necessary rules as you play.

Source

Two versions of football are presented herein. A third version
received from Paul Garmon of Wellesley Jr. High School is not
printed.

FOOTBL:
   Digital Equipment Corp.
   Maynard, MA 01754

FOTBAL:
   Raymond W. Miseyka
   Butler Sr. High School
   Butler, PA 16001

"Look! Jim has the ball! See him run! Run, Jim, run!"

```
10 PRINT "THIS IS A DEMONSTRATION OF PDP-11 BASIC"
20 PRINT "IF YOU NEED INSTRUCTIONS FOR PLAYING FOOTBALL, TYPE A 1";
30 INPUT I
40 IF I<>1 THEN 340
50 PRINT
60 PRINT
70 PRINT "WHEN IT ASKS YOU A QUESTION TO BE ANSWERED YES OR"
80 PRINT "NO, TYPE IN 0 FOR NO OR 1 FOR YES."
90 PRINT
100 PRINT "ON OFFENSE YOU HAVE THE FOLLOWING PERMITTED PLAYS:"
110 PRINT "PLAY","CODE"
120 PRINT "RUN","10"
130 PRINT "PASS","11"
140 PRINT "SWEEP","12"
150 PRINT "SCREEN PASS","13"
160 PRINT "LONG PASS","14"
170 PRINT "DRAW PLAY","15"
180 PRINT "PUNT","16"
190 PRINT "FIELDGOAL","17"
200 PRINT
210 PRINT "ON DEFENSE, YOU MAY TRY ONE OF THE FOLLOWING:"
220 PRINT "DEFENSE","CODE"
230 PRINT "NORMAL","4","GOOD AGAINST SWEEP AND SCREEN"
240 PRINT "HOLD","5","GOOD AGAINST RUN, PASS AND DRAW"
250 PRINT "BLITZ","6","GOOD AGAINST PASS OR LONG PASS"
260 PRINT "INTERCEPT","7","INCREASES THE ODDS FOR AN INTERCEPTION"
270 PRINT "BLOCK","8","GIVES YOU A CHANCE TO BLOCK A KICK,"
280 PRINT " "," ","BUT DECREASES THE DISTANCE RUNBACK."
290 PRINT
300 PRINT "TO CALL A PARTICULAR PLAY JUST TYPE ITS CODE NUMBER."
310 PRINT "ALSO, AT ANY TIME DURING PLAY YOU MAY CALL TIME OUT"
320 PRINT "BY TYPING A '2'.  HOWEVER YOU ARE PERMITTED ONLY THREE"
330 PRINT "TIMEOUTS PER HALF."
340 PRINT
350 PRINT
360 DEF FNT(X)=SIN(X)/COS(X)
370 DIM R(17)
380 FOR I=0 TO 17
390 READ R(I)
400 NEXT I
410 DATA 9,13,100,0,9,10,12,11,12,0,1,5,3,4,6,2,8,7
420 RANDOMIZE
430 LET F=0
440 LET Z3=0
450 LET O=0
460 LET L=0
470 DIM Z(5,3),P(2),D(2,5)
480 FOR A=0 TO 5
490 FOR B=0 TO 2
500 READ Z(A,B),D(B,A)
505 LET P(B)=0
510 NEXT B
520 READ Z(A,3)
530 NEXT A
540 PRINT "DO YOU WANT TO RECEIVE";
550 LET X=1
560 GOSUB 3610
570 LET S=2-SGN(13-Q)
580 LET K=S
590 LET T1=120
600 LET U2=3
610 LET U=3
620 LET C=900
630 GOSUB 2250
640 LET F1=50
650 LET B=INT(F1+O*20*RND(0)+(1-O)*29*(2-RND(0)^7-RND(0)^(3-Z2)))
660 LET O=0
670 LET Z9=8
680 GOSUB 1490
690 LET L=0
700 IF B<=99 THEN 2340
710 PRINT "A  TOUCHBACK"
720 LET B=20
730 LET L=0
740 IF S=2 THEN 770
750 PRINT "MY ";
760 GOTO 780
770 PRINT "YOUR ";
780 GOSUB 3290
790 GOSUB 2980
800 LET D=1
810 LET F2=.03
820 LET O=0
830 IF C<=0 THEN 2770
840 GOSUB 2530
850 LET Z2=1
860 LET Z3=.3
870 IF C<F*T1 THEN 2920
880 IF C<=0 THEN 2770
890 IF L=0 THEN 910
900 PRINT "TIME TO GO--";
910 PRINT INT(C/60);"MIN,";C-60*INT(C/60);"SEC.  ";
920 PRINT "YOUR PLAY";
930 GOSUB 3610
940 IF S=1 THEN 980
950 IF Q>8 THEN 920
960 LET M=Q
970 GOTO 1000
980 LET Y=Q-8
990 IF ABS(Q-10.5)^2>3 THEN 920
1000 LET C=INT(C-L*(5+23*RND(X)))
1010 LET L=1
1020 IF M=7 THEN 1760
1030 IF M=8 THEN 1920
1040 LET Y1=Y-1
1050 IF RND(X)>Z(M-1,Y1) THEN 1240
1060 LET A=2
1070 GOSUB 3020
1080 IF M<4 THEN 1110
1090 PRINT "PASS COMPLETE..";
1100 LET L=SGN(INT(4*RND(0)))
1110 IF RND(X)<F2 THEN 2510
1120 IF G>0 THEN 1210
1130 IF G=0 THEN 1170
1140 IF G+B<1 THEN 2170
1150 PRINT "LOSS OF";-G;
1160 GOTO 1610
1170 PRINT "NO GAIN"
1180 LET Z9=2
1190 GOSUB 1490
1200 GOTO 1670
1210 IF B+G>99 THEN 1650
1220 PRINT "GAIN OF";G;
1230 GOTO 1610
1240 IF M>3 THEN 1280
1250 LET A=1
1260 GOSUB 3020
1270 GOTO 1120
1280 IF RND(X)<.06*(2-SGN(Y-3)) THEN 1360
1290 IF RND(0)<.05*INT(Y/3.5)/5 THEN 1510
1300 LET Z9=6
1310 GOSUB 1490
1320 PRINT "PASS INCOMPLETE"
1330 LET L=0
1340 LET G=0
1350 GOTO 3120
1360 PRINT "PASS **INTERCEPTED**";
1370 LET A=1
1380 GOSUB 3020
1390 IF B<40 THEN 1410
1400 LET G=20*(1+SGN(G))
1410 LET B=100-B-G
1420 LET S=3-S
1430 LET Z9=2
1440 GOSUB 1490
1450 IF B<1 THEN 710
1460 IF B>99 THEN 1650
1470 PRINT "AT ";
1480 GOTO 2360
1490 LET C=C-INT(4+Z9/2*(1+RND(0)))
1500 RETURN
1510 LET G=-(5+INT(10*RND(X)))
1520 PRINT "THE QUARTERBACK ";
1530 IF RND(X)>.5 THEN 1560
1540 PRINT "IS THROWN FOR A ";
1550 GOTO 1110
1560 LET G=-(2*G+8)
1570 LET M=5
1580 LET A=1
1590 PRINT "SCRAMBLES FOR A ";
1600 GOTO 1110
1610 LET B=B+G
1620 PRINT "TO ";
1630 GOSUB 3300
1640 IF B<=99 THEN 1670
1650 GOSUB 1990
1660 GOTO 630
1670 IF B1>B THEN 3120
1680 IF B1<B THEN 1730
1690 IF RND(0)>.5 THEN 1730
1700 PRINT "**MEASUREMENT**"
1710 GOSUB 3520
1720 IF RND(X)>.5 THEN 3120
1730 GOSUB 2980
1740 LET D=0
1750 GOTO 3120
1760 IF RND(X)<.06 THEN 1890
1770 LET B=B+30+INT(15*(1-RND(X)^3))
1780 LET Z9=2
1790 GOSUB 1490
1800 IF B<=99 THEN 1850
1810 LET P1=3
1820 GOSUB 2030
1830 IF P1=0 THEN 710
1840 GOTO 630
1850 PRINT "THE KICK IS ";
1860 LET Z2=3
1870 LET S=3-S
1880 GOTO 2340
1890 PRINT "**BLOCKED** RECOVERED..";
1900 LET G=INT(14*RND(X))
1910 GOTO 1410
1920 PRINT "THE PUNT IS ";
1930 IF RND(X)<.06 THEN 1890
1940 LET F1=B
1950 LET Z2=1
1960 LET S=3-S
1970 LET Z3=.65
1980 GOTO 650
1990 PRINT "** TOUCHDOWN**"
2000 LET P1=1
2010 LET P(S)=P(S)+6
2020 LET B=130
2030 PRINT "THE KICK IS ";
2040 IF RND(X)<(B/132)^4 THEN 2070
2050 LET P1=0
2060 PRINT "NO ";
2070 PRINT "GOOD"
2080 LET P(S)=P(S)+P1
2090 GOSUB 2120
2100 LET S=3-S
2110 RETURN
2120 PRINT "SCORE: ME";P(1);" YOU";P(2)
2130 LET L=0
2140 IF X<5 THEN 2160
2150 IF P(1)<>P(2) THEN 2770
2160 RETURN
2170 PRINT "**SAFETY**"
2180 LET P(3-S)=P(3-S)+2
2190 LET F1=30
2200 LET S=3-S
2210 GOSUB 2120
2220 GOSUB 3440
2230 PRINT "FROM THE 20"
2240 GOTO 650
2250 GOSUB 3440
2260 IF S=2 THEN 2330
2270 PRINT "ON-SIDE";
2280 GOSUB 3610
2290 IF Q<>13 THEN 2330
2300 LET F2=.15
2310 LET Z2=1
2320 LET O=1
2330 RETURN
2340 LET B=100-B
2350 PRINT "RECEIVED AT ";
2360 GOSUB 3300
2370 IF Z2*RND(X)>Z3 THEN 2490
2380 IF RND(X)<F2 THEN 2500
2390 LET G=5+INT(100*RND(0))
```

```
2400 IF RND(0)<.15 THEN 2430
2410 LET G=INT(24*(1-RND(X)^2))
2420 IF G=0 THEN 2490
2430 LET B=B+G
2440 PRINT " AND RUN BACK...";
2450 LET L=1
2460 IF B>99 THEN 1650
2470 PRINT " TO ";
2480 GOSUB 3300
2490 IF RND(0)>F2 THEN 3260
2500 LET G=0
2510 PRINT "**FUMBLE**";
2520 GOTO 1410
2530 IF S=1 THEN 2560
2540 LET Y=INT(1+3.5*RND(0))
2550 RETURN
2560 LET M=INT(55*RND(0)/10.5)+1
2570 IF (B1-B)/(5-D)<3 THEN 2590
2580 LET M=INT(6-4*RND(0)^2)
2590 IF L+F*60>=C THEN 2670
2600 IF D<4 THEN 2550
2610 PRINT "I'LL ";
2620 IF B<55 THEN 2720
2630 IF 0<4*RND(0)-B1+B THEN 2750
2640 PRINT "TRY FOR A FIELD GOAL"
2650 LET M=7
2660 RETURN
2670 IF P(2)+U2<=P(1)+U2 THEN 2600
2680 PRINT "TIME OUT"
2690 LET U2=U2-1
2700 GOSUB 3520
2710 GOTO 2600
2720 PRINT "PUNT"
2730 LET M=8
2740 RETURN
2750 PRINT "GO FOR IT"
2760 RETURN
2770 IF X<4 THEN 2830
2780 IF P(1)=P(2) THEN 2830
2790 PRINT "THE GAME IS OVER"
2800 PRINT "FINAL ";
2810 GOSUB 2120
2820 STOP
2830 PRINT "END OF PERIOD";X
2840 GOSUB 2120
2850 LET F=1-F
2860 GOSUB 3520
2870 LET C=900
2880 LET X=X+1
2890 IF F<>0 THEN 810
2900 LET S=3-K
2910 GOTO 580
2920 IF T1=0 THEN 2770
2930 PRINT "2 MINUTE WARNING"
2940 GOSUB 3520
2950 LET T1=0
2960 LET C=120
2970 GOTO 880
2980 LET B1=B+10
2990 IF B1<=100 THEN 3010
3000 LET B1=100
3010 RETURN
3020 LET Q=1.3*(A*RND(0)-1)-.06
3030 LET A=1
3040 IF Q>=0 THEN 3070
3050 LET A=0
3060 LET Q=-Q
3070 LET M1=M-1
3080 LET G=D(A,M1)+FNT(G)*(D(2,M1)-D(A,M1))/3.5
3090 LET G=G+INT(RND(0)+.02)*A+100*RND(0)
3100 LET G=INT(G)
3110 RETURN
3120 LET D=D+1
3130 IF D=5 THEN 3240
3140 IF D<> 1 THEN 3160
3150 PRINT "1ST";
3160 IF D<>2 THEN 3180
3170 PRINT "2ND";
3180 IF D<>3 THEN 3200
3190 PRINT "3RD";
3200 IF D<4 THEN 3220
3210 PRINT "4TH";
3220 PRINT " AND";B1-B;"   ";
3230 GOTO 810
3240 LET S=3-S
3250 LET B=100-B
3260 IF S=2 THEN 770
3270 PRINT "MY ";
3280 GOTO 780
3290 PRINT "BALL ON ";
3300 IF B=50 THEN 3400
3310 LET V=50-ABS(B-50)
3320 LET C=C-INT(7+3*RND(0))
3330 IF S=1 THEN 3420
3340 IF B<50 THEN 3370
3350 PRINT "MY ";
3360 GOTO 3380
3370 PRINT "YOUR ";
3380 PRINT V
3390 RETURN
3400 PRINT "THE 50"
3410 RETURN
3420 IF B<50 THEN 3350
3430 GOTO 3370
3440 IF S=2 THEN 3470
3450 PRINT "YOU";
3460 GOTO 3480
3470 PRINT "I";
3480 PRINT " KICK OFF."
3490 LET F2=.06
3500 LET Z2=0
3510 RETURN
3520 LET L=0
3530 PRINT "TIMEOUT CALLED..."
3540 PRINT
3550 RETURN
```

```
3560 IF U=0 THEN 3600
3570 LET U=U-1
3580 GOSUB 3520
3590 GOTO 3610
3600 PRINT "..WRONG, TRY AGAIN"
3610 INPUT A
3620 IF ABS(INT(A))>17 THEN 3600
3630 LET Q=R(INT(ABS(A)))
3640 IF Q=0 THEN 3600
3650 IF Q=100 THEN 3560
3660 RETURN
3670 DATA .5,-2,.25,4,.5,13,.55
3680 DATA .4,-2,.3,7,.65,15,.75
3690 DATA .4,-2,.3,6,.6,15,.35
3700 DATA .65,-2,.65,6,.6,17,.9
3710 DATA .4,2,.7,10,.4,27,.2
3720 DATA .1,19,.4,35,.2,100,.1
3730 END
```

FOOTBL   SAMPLE RUN

```
THIS IS A DEMONSTRATION OF PDP-11 BASIC
IF YOU NEED INSTRUCTIONS FOR PLAYING FOOTBALL, TYPE A 1? 1


WHEN IT ASKS YOU A QUESTION TO BE ANSWERED YES OR
NO, TYPE IN 0 FOR NO OR 1 FOR YES.

ON OFFENSE YOU HAVE THE FOLLOWING PERMITTED PLAYS:
PLAY         CODE
RUN          10
PASS         11
SWEEP        12
SCREEN PASS  13
LONG PASS    14
DRAW PLAY    15
PUNT         16
FIELDGOAL    17


ON DEFENSE, YOU MAY TRY ONE OF THE FOLLOWING:
DEFENSE     CODE
NORMAL       4           GOOD AGAINST SWEEP AND SCREEN
HOLD         5           GOOD AGAINST RUN, PASS AND DRAW
BLITZ        6           GOOD AGAINST PASS OR LONG PASS
INTERCEPT    7           INCREASES THE ODDS FOR AN INTERCEPTION
BLOCK        8           GIVES YOU A CHANCE TO BLOCK A KICK,
                         BUT DECREASES THE DISTANCE RUNBACK.

TO CALL A PARTICULAR PLAY JUST TYPE ITS CODE NUMBER.
ALSO, AT ANY TIME DURING PLAY YOU MAY CALL TIME OUT
BY TYPING A '2'.  HOWEVER YOU ARE PERMITTED ONLY THREE
TIMEOUTS PER HALF.


DO YOU WANT TO RECEIVE? 1
I KICK OFF.
A TOUCHBACK
YOUR BALL ON YOUR  20
 14 MIN, 42 SEC.   YOUR PLAY? 10
LOSS OF 1 TO YOUR  19
2ND AND 11    TIME TO GO-- 14 MIN, 34 SEC.   YOUR PLAY? 12
LOSS OF 2 TO YOUR  17
3RD AND 13    TIME TO GO-- 14 MIN, 13 SEC.   YOUR PLAY? 11
PASS COMPLETE..GAIN OF 12 TO YOUR  29
4TH AND 1    TIME TO GO-- 13 MIN, 43 SEC.   YOUR PLAY? 10
GAIN OF 10 TO YOUR  39
1ST AND 10    TIME TO GO-- 13 MIN, 24 SEC.   YOUR PLAY? 13
PASS COMPLETE..GAIN OF 7 TO YOUR  46
2ND AND 3    TIME TO GO-- 13 MIN, 8 SEC.   YOUR PLAY? 14
PASS INCOMPLETE
3RD AND 3     12 MIN, 32 SEC.   YOUR PLAY? 15
GAIN OF 2 TO YOUR  48
4TH AND 1    TIME TO GO-- 12 MIN, 24 SEC.   YOUR PLAY? 10
GAIN OF 5 TO MY  47
1ST AND 10    TIME TO GO-- 12 MIN, 4 SEC.   YOUR PLAY? 14
PASS INCOMPLETE
2ND AND 10     11 MIN, 46 SEC.   YOUR PLAY? 14
PASS INCOMPLETE
3RD AND 10     11 MIN, 38 SEC.   YOUR PLAY? 11
PASS COMPLETE..GAIN OF 13 TO MY  34
1ST AND 10     11 MIN, 31 SEC.   YOUR PLAY? 10
GAIN OF 1 TO MY  33
2ND AND 9    TIME TO GO-- 11 MIN, 22 SEC.   YOUR PLAY? 12
NO GAIN
3RD AND 9    TIME TO GO-- 10 MIN, 51 SEC.   YOUR PLAY? 13
PASS COMPLETE..LOSS OF 1 TO MY  34
4TH AND 10    TIME TO GO-- 10 MIN, 36 SEC.   YOUR PLAY? 17
THE KICK IS NO GOOD
SCORE: ME 0  YOU 0
A TOUCHBACK
MY BALL ON MY  20
 10 MIN, 10 SEC.   YOUR PLAY? 4
GAIN OF 2 TO MY  22
2ND AND 8    TIME TO GO-- 10 MIN, 3 SEC.   YOUR PLAY? 5
PASS COMPLETE..GAIN OF 6 TO MY  28
3RD AND 2    TIME TO GO-- 9 MIN, 37 SEC.   YOUR PLAY? 4
GAIN OF 6 TO MY  34
1ST AND 10    TIME TO GO-- 9 MIN, 8 SEC.   YOUR PLAY? 5
LOSS OF 1 TO MY  33
2ND AND 11    TIME TO GO-- 8 MIN, 41 SEC.   YOUR PLAY? 5
PASS COMPLETE..GAIN OF 16 TO MY  49
1ST AND 10     8 MIN, 11 SEC.   YOUR PLAY? 4
PASS INCOMPLETE
2ND AND 10     8 MIN, 2 SEC.   YOUR PLAY? 5
GAIN OF 12 TO YOUR  39
1ST AND 10    TIME TO GO-- 7 MIN, 53 SEC.   YOUR PLAY? 4
GAIN OF 1 TO YOUR  38
2ND AND 9    TIME TO GO-- 7 MIN, 22 SEC.   YOUR PLAY? 4
GAIN OF 1 TO YOUR  37
3RD AND 8    TIME TO GO-- 7 MIN, 0 SEC.   YOUR PLAY? 4
PASS COMPLETE..GAIN OF 15 TO YOUR  22
1ST AND 10    TIME TO GO-- 6 MIN, 23 SEC.   YOUR PLAY? 4
GAIN OF 7 TO YOUR  15
2ND AND 3    TIME TO GO-- 5 MIN, 53 SEC.   YOUR PLAY? 5
PASS INCOMPLETE
```

FOTBAL   PROGRAM LISTING

```
1 REM       PROGRAM WRITTEN BY RAYMOND W. MISEYKA
2 REM       SENIOR AT   BUTLER SENIOR HIGH SCHOOL
3 REM                   BUTLER, PENNSYLVANIA 16001
4 REM       DATE: 1/30/73
5 REM       COMPUTER SUPERVISION- MR. WILLIAM ELLIS
6 REM       COMPUTER TOPICS INSTRUCTION- MR. ALBERT STEWERT
7 REM           I WROTE THIS PROGRAM BECAUSE OF THE CHALLENGE
8 REM       INVOLVED IN OVERCOMING THE COMPLEXITIES OF SUCH A GAME
9 REM
10 REM
100 RANDOMIZE
120 DIM A(20),B(20),C(40),H(2),T(2),W(2),X(2),Y(2),Z(2)
130 DIM M$(2),D(2)
140 PRINT "RAMIS ENTERPRISES PRESENTS N.F.U. FOOTBALL(NO FORTRAN USED)"
145 PRINT\PRINT
150 PRINT "DO YOU WISH INSTRUCTIONS?";\INPUT A$
160 IF A$="NO" THEN 290\IF A$<>"YES" THEN 150
170 PRINT "THIS IS A GAME FOR 2 TEAMS IN WHICH EACH PLAYER MUST"
180 PRINT "PREPARE A TAPE WITH A DATA STATEMENT(1770 FOR TEAM 1"
190 PRINT "1780 FOR TEAM 2)IN WHICH EACH TEAM SCRAMBLES NOS. 1-20"
195 PRINT "THESE NUMBERS ARE THEN ASSIGNED TO 20 GIVEN PLAYS. "
200 PRINT "A LIST OF NOS. AND THEIR PLAYS ARE PROVIDED WITH"
210 PRINT "BOTH TEAMS HAVING THE SAME PLAYS. THE MORE SIMILAR THE"
220 PRINT "PLAYS THE LESS YARDAGE GAINED. SCORES ARE GIVEN"
223 PRINT "WHENEVER SCORES ARE MADE. SCORES MAY ALSO BE OBTAINED"
225 PRINT "BY INPUTING 99,99 FOR PLAY NOS.. TO PUNT OR ATTEMPT A"
227 PRINT "FIELDGOAL, INPUT 77,77 FOR PLAY NOS.. QUESTIONS WILL BE"
230 PRINT "ASKED THEN. ON 4TH DOWN YOU WILL ALSO BE ASKED WHETHER"
240 PRINT "YOU WANT TO PUNT OR ATTEMPT A FIELD GOAL. IF THE ANSWER"
250 PRINT "TO BOTH QUESTIONS IS NO, IT WILL BE ASSUMED YOU WANT TO"
260 PRINT "TRY AND GAIN YARDAGE. ANSWER ALL QUESTIONS YES OR NO. "
270 PRINT "GAME IS PLAYED UNTIL PLAYERS TERMINATE (CONTROL-C). "
280 PRINT "PLEASE PREPARE A TAPE AND RUN. "\STOP
290 PRINT\PRINT "INPUT SCORE LIMIT ON GAME"\INPUT E
300 FOR I=1 TO 40\READ N\IF I>20 THEN 350
330 A(N)=I\GOTO 360
350 B(N)=I-20
360 C(I)=N\NEXT I
380 L=0\T=1
410 PRINT "TEAM"T"PLAY CHART"
420 PRINT "NO.     PLAY"\PRINT
430 PRINT C(1+L);TAB(6);"PITCHOUT"
440 PRINT C(2+L);TAB(6);"TRIPLE REVERSE"
450 PRINT C(3+L);TAB(6);"DRAW"
460 PRINT C(4+L);TAB(6);"QB SNEAK"
470 PRINT C(5+L);TAB(6);"END AROUND"
480 PRINT C(6+L);TAB(6);"DOUBLE REVERSE"
490 PRINT C(7+L);TAB(6);"LEFT SWEEP"
500 PRINT C(8+L);TAB(6);"RIGHT SWEEP"
510 PRINT C(9+L);TAB(6);"OFF TACKLE"
520 PRINT C(10+L);TAB(6);"WISHBONE OPTION"
530 PRINT C(11+L);TAB(6);"FLARE PASS"
540 PRINT C(12+L);TAB(6);"SCREEN PASS"
550 PRINT C(13+L);TAB(6);"ROLL OUT OPTION"
560 PRINT C(14+L);TAB(6);"RIGHT CURL"
570 PRINT C(15+L);TAB(6);"LEFT CURL"
580 PRINT C(16+L);TAB(6);"WISHBONE OPTION"
590 PRINT C(17+L);TAB(6);"SIDELINE PASS"
600 PRINT C(18+L);TAB(6);"HALF-BACK OPTION"
610 PRINT C(19+L);TAB(6);"RAZZLE DAZZLE"
620 PRINT C(20+L);TAB(6);"BOMB!!!!!!!!"
630 L=L+20\T=2
640 PRINT\PRINT "TEAR OFF HERE -----------------------------------
-------"
660 FOR X=1 TO 11\PRINT\NEXT X
670 FOR Z=1 TO 3000\NEXT Z
680 IF L=20 THEN 410
690 D(1)=0\D(2)=3\M$(1)="--->"\M$(2)="<---"
700 H(1)=0\H(2)=0\T(1)=2\T(2)=1
710 W(1)=-1\W(2)=1\X(1)=100\X(2)=0
720 Y(1)=1\Y(2)=-1\Z(1)=0\Z(2)=100
725 GOSUB 1910
730 PRINT "TEAM 1 DEFENDS 0 YD. GOAL--TEAM 2 DEFENDS 100 YD. GOAL"
740 T=INT(2*RND(0)+1)
760 PRINT\PRINT "THE COIN IS FLIPPED"
765 P=X(T)-Y(T)*40
770 GOSUB 1860\PRINT\PRINT "TEAM"T"RECEIVES KICK-OFF"
780 K=INT(26*RND(0)+40)
790 P=P-Y(T)*K
794 IF W(T)*P<Z(T)+10 THEN 810\PRINT\PRINT "BALL WENT OUT OF ENDZONE";
795 PRINT "--AUTOMATIC TOUCHBACK--"\GOTO 870
810 PRINT\PRINT "BALL WENT"K"YARDS, NOW ON "P\GOSUB 1900
830 PRINT "TEAM"T"DO YOU WANT TO RUNBACK";\INPUT A$
840 IF A$="YES" THEN 1430\IF A$<>"NO" THEN 830
850 IF W(T)*P<Z(T) THEN 880
870 P=Z(T)-W(T)*K
880 D=1\S=P
885 PRINT "=============================================================
=========="
890 PRINT\PRINT "TEAM"T"DOWN"D"ON "P;
893 IF D<>1 THEN 900
895 IF Y(T)*(P+Y(T)*10)>=X(T) THEN 898
897 C=4\GOTO 900
898 C=8
900 IF C=8 THEN 904
901 PRINT TAB(27);10-(Y(T)*P-Y(T)*S);"YARDS TO 1ST DOWN"
902 GOTO 910
904 PRINT TAB(27);X(T)-Y(T)*P;"YARDS TO GO"
910 GOSUB 1900\IF D=4 THEN 1180
920 RANDOMIZE
930 U=INT(3*RND(0)-1)\GOTO 940
936 PRINT "ILLEGAL PLAY NUMBER, CHECK AND"
940 PRINT "INPUT OFFENSIVE PLAY, DEFENSIVE PLAY";
950 IF T=2 THEN 970
960 INPUT P1,P2\GOTO 975
970 INPUT P2,P1
975 IF P1=77 THEN 1180
980 IF P1>20 THEN 1800\IF P1<1 THEN 1800
990 IF P2>20 THEN 1800\IF P2<1 THEN 1800
995 P1=INT(P1)\P2=INT(P2)
1000 Y=INT(ABS(A(P1)-B(P2))/19*((X(T)-Y(T)*P+25)*RND(0)-15))
1005 PRINT\IF T=2 THEN 1015
1010 IF A(P1)<11 THEN 1048\GOTO 1020
1015 IF B(P2)<11 THEN 1048
1020 IF U<>0 THEN 1035\PRINT "PASS INCOMPLETE TEAM"T
1030 Y=0\GOTO 1050
1035 G=RND(0)\IF G<.025 THEN 1040\IF Y>2 THEN 1045
1040 PRINT "QUARTERBACK SCRAMBLED"\GOTO 1050
1045 PRINT "PASS COMPLETED"\GOTO 1050
1048 PRINT "THE BALL WAS RUN"
1050 P=P-W(T)*Y
1060 PRINT\PRINT "NET YARDS GAINED ON DOWN"D"ARE "Y
1070 G=RND(0)\IF G<.025 THEN 1110
1080 PRINT\PRINT "** LOSS OF POSSESSION FROM TEAM"T"TO TEAM"T(T)
1100 GOSUB 1850\PRINT\T=T(T)\GOTO 830
1110 IF Y(T)*P>=X(T) THEN 1320
1120 IF W(T)*P>=Z(T) THEN 1230
1130 IF Y(T)*P-Y(T)*S>=10 THEN 880
1140 D=D+1\IF D<>5 THEN 885
1160 PRINT\PRINT "CONVERSION UNSUCCESSFUL TEAM"T\T=T(T)
1170 GOSUB 1850\GOTO 880
1180 PRINT "DOES TEAM"T"WANT TO PUNT";\INPUT A$
1185 IF A$="NO" THEN 1200\IF A$<>"YES" THEN 1180
1190 PRINT\PRINT "TEAM"T"WILL PUNT"\G=RND(0)\IF G<.025 THEN 1080
1195 GOSUB 1850\K=INT(25*RND(0)+35)\T=T(T)\GOTO 790
1200 PRINT "DOES TEAM"T"WANT TO ATTEMPT A FIELD-GOAL";\INPUT A$
1210 IF A$="YES" THEN 1640\IF A$<>"NO" THEN 1200\GOTO 920
1230 PRINT\PRINT "SAFETY AGAINST TEAM"T"---------------------OH-OH"
1240 H(T(T))=H(T(T))+2\GOSUB 1810
1280 PRINT "TEAM"T"DO YOU WANT TO PUNT INSTEAD OF A KICKOFF";\INPUT A$
1290 P=Z(T)-W(T)*20\IF A$="YES" THEN 1190
1320 PRINT\PRINT "TOUCHDOWN BY TEAM"T"*******************YEA TEAM"
1340 Q=7\G=RND(0)\IF G>.1 THEN 1380
1360 Q=6\PRINT "EXTRA POINT NO GOOD"\GOTO 1390
1380 PRINT "EXTRA POINT GOOD"
1390 H(T)=H(T)+Q\GOSUB 1810
1420 T=T(T)\GOTO 765
1430 K=INT(9*RND(0)+1)
1440 R=INT(((X(T)-Y(T)*P+25)*RND(0)-15)/K)
1460 P=P-W(T)*R
1480 PRINT\PRINT "RUNBACK TEAM"T,R"YARDS"
1485 RANDOMIZE\G=RND(0)\IF G<.025 THEN 1080
1490 IF Y(T)*P>=X(T) THEN 1320
1500 IF W(T)*P>=Z(T) THEN 1230\GOTO 880
1640 PRINT\PRINT "TEAM"T"WILL ATTEMPT A FIELDGOAL"
1645 RANDOMIZE\G=RND(0)\IF G<.025 THEN 1080
1650 F=INT(35*RND(0)+20)
1660 PRINT\PRINT "KICK IS"F"YARDS LONG"
1680 P=P-W(T)*F\RANDOMIZE\G=RND(0)
1690 IFG<.35THEN1735
1700 IF Y(T)*P<X(T) THEN 1740
1710 PRINT "FIELDGOAL GOOD FOR TEAM"T"*******************YEA"
1720 Q=3\GOTO 1390
1735 PRINT"BALL WENT WIDE"
1740 PRINT "FIELDGOAL UNSUCCESSFUL TEAM"T"---------------TOO BAD"
1742 GOSUB 1850\IF Y(T)*P<X(T)+10 THEN 1745\T=T(T)\GOTO 794
1745 PRINT\PRINT "BALL NOW ON "P
1750 T=T(T)\GOSUB 1900\GOTO 830
1770 DATA 17,8,4,14,19,3,10,1,7,11,15,9,5,20,13,18,16,2,12,6
1780 DATA 20,2,17,5,8,18,12,11,1,4,19,14,10,7,9,15,6,13,16,3
1800 IF P1<>99 THEN 936
1810 PRINT\PRINT "TEAM 1 SCORE IS"H(1)
1820 PRINT "TEAM 2 SCORE IS"H(2)\PRINT
1825 IF H(T)<E THEN 1830\PRINT "TEAM"T"WINS ***************"\GOTO 2000
1830 IF P1=99 THEN 940\RETURN
1850 PRINT "=============================================================
=========="
1860 PRINT "++++++++++++++++++++++++++++++++++++++++++++++++++++++++++++
+++++"
1870 RETURN
1900 PRINT TAB(D(T)+5+P/2);M$(T)
1910 PRINT "TEAM 1 [0   10   20   30   40   50   60   70   80   90   100
] TEAM 2"
1920 RETURN
1930 RETURN
2000 END
```

SAMPLE RUN

RAMIS ENTERPRISES PRESENTS N.F.U. FOOTBALL(NO FORTRAN USED)

DO YOU WISH INSTRUCTIONS?? YES
THIS IS A GAME FOR 2 TEAMS IN WHICH EACH PLAYER MUST
PREPARE A TAPE WITH A DATA STATEMENT(1770 FOR TEAM 1
1780 FOR TEAM 2)IN WHICH EACH TEAM SCRAMBLES NOS. 1-20
THESE NUMBERS ARE THEN ASSIGNED TO 20 GIVEN PLAYS.
A LIST OF NOS. AND THEIR PLAYS ARE PROVIDED WITH
BOTH TEAMS HAVING THE SAME PLAYS. THE MORE SIMILAR THE
PLAYS THE LESS YARDAGE GAINED. SCORES ARE GIVEN
WHENEVER SCORES ARE MADE. SCORES MAY ALSO BE OBTAINED
BY INPUTING 99,99 FOR PLAY NOS.. TO PUNT OR ATTEMPT A
FIELDGOAL, INPUT 77,77 FOR PLAY NOS.. QUESTIONS WILL BE
ASKED THEN. ON 4TH DOWN YOU WILL ALSO BE ASKED WHETHER
YOU WANT TO PUNT OR ATTEMPT A FIELD GOAL. IF THE ANSWER
TO BOTH QUESTIONS IS NO, IT WILL BE ASSUMED YOU WANT TO
TRY AND GAIN YARDAGE. ANSWER ALL QUESTIONS YES OR NO.
GAME IS PLAYED UNTIL PLAYERS TERMINATE (CONTROL-C).
PLEASE PREPARE A TAPE AND RUN.
STOP AT LINE 280

READY

RUNNH
RAMIS ENTERPRISES PRESENTS N.F.U. FOOTBALL(NO FORTRAN USED)

DO YOU WISH INSTRUCTIONS?? NO

INPUT SCORE LIMIT ON GAME? 28
TEAM 1 PLAY CHART
NO.   PLAY

17   PITCHOUT
8   TRIPLE REVERSE
4   DRAW
14   QB SNEAK
19   END AROUND
3   DOUBLE REVERSE
10   LEFT SWEEP
1   RIGHT SWEEP
7   OFF TACKLE
11   WISHBONE OPTION
15   FLARE PASS
9   SCREEN PASS
5   ROLL OUT OPTION
20   RIGHT CURL
13   LEFT CURL
18   WISHBONE OPTION
16   SIDELINE PASS
2   HALF-BACK OPTION
12   RAZZLE DAZZLE
6   BOMB!!!!!!!!

TEAR OFF HERE ---

TEAM 2 PLAY CHART
NO.   PLAY

20   PITCHOUT
2   TRIPLE REVERSE
17   DRAW
5   QB SNEAK
8   END AROUND
18   DOUBLE REVERSE
12   LEFT SWEEP
11   RIGHT SWEEP
1   OFF TACKLE
4   WISHBONE OPTION
19   FLARE PASS
14   SCREEN PASS
10   ROLL OUT OPTION
7   RIGHT CURL
9   LEFT CURL
15   WISHBONE OPTION
6   SIDELINE PASS
13   HALF-BACK OPTION
16   RAZZLE DAZZLE
3   BOMB!!!!!!!!

TEAR OFF HERE ---

TEAM 1 [0   10   20   30   40   50   60   70   80   90   100] TEAM 2

TEAM 1 DEFENDS 0 YD. GOAL--TEAM 2 DEFENDS 100 YD. GOAL

THE COIN IS FLIPPED
+++

TEAM 2 RECEIVES KICK-OFF

BALL WENT 53 YARDS, NOW ON 93

TEAM 1 [0   10   20   30   40   50   60   70 <--- 90   100] TEAM 2

TEAM 2 DO YOU WANT TO RUNBACK? YES

RUNBACK TEAM 2 10 YARDS
==

TEAM 2 DOWN 1 ON 83   10 YARDS TO 1ST DOWN

TEAM 1 [0   10   20   30   40   50   60   70 <--- 80   90   100] TEAM 2

INPUT OFFENSIVE PLAY, DEFENSIVE PLAY? 19,11

PASS COMPLETED

NET YARDS GAINED ON DOWN 1 ARE 4
==

TEAM 2 DOWN 2 ON 79   6 YARDS TO 1ST DOWN

TEAM 1 [0   10   20   30   40   50   60   70 <--- 80   90   100] TEAM 2

INPUT OFFENSIVE PLAY, DEFENSIVE PLAY? 3,8

PASS INCOMPLETE TEAM 2

NET YARDS GAINED ON DOWN 2 ARE 0
==

TEAM 2 DOWN 3 ON 79   6 YARDS TO 1ST DOWN

TEAM 1 [0   10   20   30   40   50   60   70 <--- 80   90   100] TEAM 2

INPUT OFFENSIVE PLAY, DEFENSIVE PLAY? 8,10

THE BALL WAS RUN

NET YARDS GAINED ON DOWN 3 ARE 8
==

TEAM 2 DOWN 1 ON 71   10 YARDS TO 1ST DOWN

TEAM 1 [0   10   20   30   40   50   60   70 <--- 80   90   100] TEAM 2

INPUT OFFENSIVE PLAY, DEFENSIVE PLAY? 10,5

QUARTERBACK SCRAMBLED

NET YARDS GAINED ON DOWN 1 ARE 0
==

TEAM 2 DOWN 2 ON 71   10 YARDS TO 1ST DOWN

TEAM 1 [0   10   20   30   40   50   60   70 <--- 80   90   100] TEAM 2

INPUT OFFENSIVE PLAY, DEFENSIVE PLAY? 18,10

THE BALL WAS RUN

NET YARDS GAINED ON DOWN 2 ARE 4
==

TEAM 2 DOWN 3 ON 67   6 YARDS TO 1ST DOWN

TEAM 1 [0   10   20   30   40   50   60   70 <--- 80   90   100] TEAM 2

INPUT OFFENSIVE PLAY, DEFENSIVE PLAY? 7,17

PASS COMPLETED

NET YARDS GAINED ON DOWN 3 ARE 18
==

TEAM 2 DOWN 1 ON 49   10 YARDS TO 1ST DOWN

TEAM 1 [0   10   20   30   40   50 <--- 60   70   80   90   100] TEAM 2

INPUT OFFENSIVE PLAY, DEFENSIVE PLAY? 3,9

PASS INCOMPLETE TEAM 2

NET YARDS GAINED ON DOWN 1 ARE 0
==

TEAM 2 DOWN 2 ON 49   10 YARDS TO 1ST DOWN

TEAM 1 [0   10   20   30   40   50 <--- 60   70   80   90   100] TEAM 2

INPUT OFFENSIVE PLAY, DEFENSIVE PLAY? 3,10

PASS INCOMPLETE TEAM 2

NET YARDS GAINED ON DOWN 2 ARE 0
==

TEAM 2 DOWN 3 ON 49   10 YARDS TO 1ST DOWN

TEAM 1 [0   10   20   30   40   50 <--- 60   70   80   90   100] TEAM 2

INPUT OFFENSIVE PLAY, DEFENSIVE PLAY? 3,11

PASS INCOMPLETE TEAM 2

NET YARDS GAINED ON DOWN 3 ARE 0
==

FURS

Description

You are the leader of a French fur trading expedition in 1776 leaving the Ontario area to sell furs and get supplies for the next year. You have a choice of three forts at which you may trade. The cost of supplies and the amount you receive for your furs will depend upon the fort you choose. You also specify what types of furs that you have to trade.

The game goes on and on until you elect to trade no longer.

Source

Thanks to Ann Brebner for sending us the program. It was originally written by:

Dan Bachor
Dept. of Educational Psychology
University of Calgary
Calgary, Alberta, Canada

"Ah, here's your guide now."

PROGRAM LISTING

```
1 DIM F(4)                                          1190 GO TO 1410
2 RANDOM                                            1198 LET I=I-140
15 GOSUB 1091                                       1201 PRINT
16 LET I=600                                        1205 LET M1=INT((.3*RND(0)+.85)*10^2+.5)/10^2
17 PRINT "DO YOU WISH TO TRADE FURS?"               1206 LET E1=INT((.15*RND(0)+.80)*10^2+.5)/10^2
18 GOSUB 1402                                       1207 LET B1=INT((.2*RND(0)+.90)*10^2+.5)/10^2
19 IF B$="YES" THEN 100                             1209 LET P=INT(10*RND(00))+1
20 IF B$="NO" THEN 2200                             1210 IF P<=2 THEN 1216
25 GOSUB 1402                                       1212 IF P<=6 THEN 1224
100 PRINT                                           1213 IF P<=8 THEN 1226
101 PRINT "YOU HAVE $";I "SAVINGS."                 1215 IF P<=10 THEN 1235
102 PRINT "AND 190 FURS TO BEGIN THE EXPEDITION."   1216 LET F(2)=0
300 PRINT                                           1218 PRINT "YOUR BEAVER WERE TOO HEAVY TO CARRY ACROSS"
301 PRINT "YOUR 190 FURS ARE DISTRIBUTED AMONG THE FOLLOWING"  1219 PRINT "THE PORTAGE.  YOU HAD TO LEAVE THE PELTS BUT FOUND"
302 PRINT "KINDS OF PELTS: MINK, BEAVER, ERMINE AND FOX."      1220 PRINT "THEM STOLEN WHEN YOU RETURNED"
310 GOSUB 1430                                      1221 GOSUB 1244
315 RESTORE                                         1222 GO TO 1414
330 FOR J=1 TO 4                                    1224 PRINT "YOU ARRIVED SAFELY AT FORT STADACONA"
332 READ B$                                         1225 GO TO 1239
333 PRINT                                           1226 GOSUB 1430
335 PRINT "HOW MANY ";B$;" PELTS DO YOU HAVE";      1230 PRINT "YOUR CANOE UPSET IN THE LACHINE RAPIDS.  YOU"
338 INPUT F(J)                                      1231 PRINT "LOST ALL YOUR FURS"
340 LET F(0)=F(1)+F(2)+F(3)+F(4)                    1232 GOSUB 1244
342 IF F(0)=190 THEN 1100                           1233 GO TO 1418
344 IF F(0)>190 THEN 500                            1235 LET F(4)=0
348 NEXT J                                          1237 PRINT "YOUR FOX PELTS WERE NOT CURED PROPERLY."
350 GO TO 1100                                      1238 PRINT "NO ONE WILL BUY THEM."
500 PRINT                                           1239 GOSUB 1244
501 PRINT "YOU MAY NOT HAVE THAT MANY FURS."        1240 GO TO 1410
502 PRINT "DO NOT TRY TO CHEAT.  I CAN ADD."        1244 PRINT "SUPPLIES AT FORT STADACONA COST $125.00"
503 PRINT "YOU MUST START AGAIN."                   1246 PRINT "YOUR TRAVEL EXPENSES TO STADACONA WERE $15.00"
504 GO TO 15                                        1248 RETURN
508 PRINT                                           1250 LET I=I-105
511 PRINT "DO YOU WANT TO TRADE FURS NEXT YEAR?"    1254 PRINT
513 GO TO 18                                        1260 LET M1=INT((.15*RND(0)+1.05)*10^2+.5)/10^2
1091 PRINT "YOU ARE THE LEADER OF A FRENCH FUR TRADING EXPEDITION IN "  1261 LET E1=INT((.15*RND(0)+.95)*10^2+.5)/10^2
1092 PRINT "1776 LEAVING THE LAKE ONTARIO AREA TO SELL FURS AND GET"    1262 LET B1=INT((.25*RND(0)+1.00)*10^2+.5)/10^2
1093 PRINT "SUPPLIES FOR THE NEXT YEAR.  YOU HAVE A CHOICE OF THREE"    1263 LET D1=INT((.25*RND(0)+1.10)*10^2+.5)/10^2
1094 PRINT "FORTS AT WHICH YOU MAY TRADE.  THE COST OF SUPPLIES"        1270 LET P=INT(10*RND(0))+1
1095 PRINT "AND THE AMOUNT YOU RECEIVE FOR YOUR FURS WILL DEPEND"       1271 IF P<=2 THEN 1281
1096 PRINT "ON THE FORT THAT YOU CHOOSE."           1272 IF P<=6 THEN 1291
1099 RETURN                                         1273 IF P<=8 THEN 1295
1100 PRINT "DO YOU WANT TO TRADE YOUR FURS AT FORT 1, FORT 2,"  1274 IF P<=10 THEN 1306
1102 PRINT "OR FORT 3?  FORT 1 IS FORT HOCHELAGA (MONTREAL)"    1281 PRINT "YOU WERE ATTACKED BY A PARTY OF IROQUOIS."
1103 PRINT "AND IS UNDER THE PROTECTION OF THE FRENCH ARMY."    1282 PRINT "ALL PEOPLE IN YOUR TRADING GROUP WERE"
1104 PRINT "FORT 2 IS FORT STADACONA (QUEBEC) AND IS UNDER THE" 1283 PRINT "KILLED.  THIS ENDS THE GAME."
1105 PRINT "PROTECTION OF THE FRENCH ARMY.  HOWEVER, YOU MUST"  1284 STOP
1106 PRINT "MAKE A PORTAGE AND CROSS THE LACHINE RAPIDS."       1291 PRINT "YOU WERE LUCKY.  YOU ARRIVED SAFELY"
1108 PRINT "FORT 3 IS FORT NEW YORK AND IS UNDER DUTCH CONTROL."1292 PRINT "AT FORT NEW YORK."
1109 PRINT "YOU MUST CROSS THROUGH IROQUOIS LAND."  1293 GO TO 1311
1110 PRINT "ANSWER 1, 2, OR 3."                     1295 GOSUB 1430
1111 INPUT B                                        1300 PRINT "YOU NARROWLY ESCAPED AN IROQUOIS RAIDING PARTY."
1112 IF B=1 THEN 1120                               1301 PRINT "HOWEVER, YOU HAD TO LEAVE ALL YOUR FURS BEHIND."
1113 IF B=2 THEN 1135                               1303 GOSUB 1320
1115 IF B=3 THEN 1147                               1304 GO TO 1418
1116 GO TO 1110                                     1306 LET B1=B1/2
1120 PRINT "YOU HAVE CHOSEN THE EASIEST ROUTE.  HOWEVER, THE FORT" 1307 LET M1=M1/2
1121 PRINT "IS FAR FROM ANY SEAPORT.  THE VALUE"    1308 PRINT "YOUR MINK AND BEAVER WERE DAMAGED ON YOUR TRIP."
1122 PRINT "YOU RECEIVE FOR YOUR FURS WILL BE LOW AND THE COST" 1309 PRINT "YOU RECEIVE ONLY HALF THE CURRENT PRICE FOR THESE FURS."
1123 PRINT "OF SUPPLIES HIGHER THAN AT FORTS STADACONA OR NEW YORK." 1311 GOSUB 1320
1125 GOSUB 1400                                     1312 GO TO 1410
1129 IF B$="YES" THEN 1110                          1320 PRINT "SUPPLIES AT NEW YORK COST $80.00"
1130 GOTO 1160                                      1322 RETURN
1135 PRINT "YOU HAVE CHOSEN A HARD ROUTE.  IT IS, IN COMPARSION," 1400 PRINT "DO YOU WANT TO TRADE AT ANOTHER FORT?"
1136 PRINT "HARDER THAN THE ROUTE TO HOCHELAGA BUT EASIER THAN"  1402 PRINT "ANSWER YES OR NO",
1137 PRINT "THE ROUTE TO NEW YORK.  YOU WILL RECEIVE AN AVERAGE VALUE" 1403 INPUT B$
1138 PRINT "FOR YOUR FURS AND THE COST OF YOUR SUPPLIES WILL BE AVERAGE" 1404 RETURN
1141 GOSUB 1400                                     1410 PRINT
1144 IF B$="YES" THEN 1110                          1412 PRINT "YOUR BEAVER SOLD FOR $";B1*F(2);
1145 GOTO 1198                                      1414 PRINT "YOUR FOX SOLD FOR $";D1*F(4)
1147 PRINT "YOU HAVE CHOSEN THE MOST DIFFICULT ROUTE.  AT"  1416 PRINT "YOUR ERMINE SOLD FOR $";E1*F(3);
1148 PRINT "FORT NEW YORK YOU WILL RECEIVE THE HIGHEST VALUE"    1417 PRINT "YOUR MINK SOLD FOR $";M1*F(1)
1149 PRINT "FOR YOUR FURS.  THE COST OF YOUR SUPPLIES"     1418 LET I=M1*F(1)+B1*F(2)+E1*F(3)+D1*F(4)+I
1150 PRINT "WILL BE LOWER THAN AT ALL THE OTHER FORTS."    1420 PRINT
1152 GOSUB 1400                                     1422 PRINT "YOU NOW HAVE $";I;" INCLUDING YOUR PREVIOUS SAVINGS"
1155 IF B$="YES" THEN 1110                          1425 GO TO 508
1156 GOTO 1250                                      1430 FOR J=1 TO 4
1160 LET I=I-160                                    1432 LET F(J)=0
1169 PRINT                                          1434 NEXT J
1174 LET M1=INT((.2*RND(0)+.7)*100+.5)/100          1436 RETURN
1175 LET E1=INT((.2*RND(0)+.65)*10^2+.5)/10^2       2000 DATA "MINK","BEAVER","ERMINE","FOX"
1176 LET B1=INT((.2*RND(0)+.75)*10^2+.5)/10^2       2046 END
1177 LET D1=INT((.2*RND(0)+.80)*10^2+.5)/10^2       2200 PRINT
1180 PRINT "SUPPLIES AT FORT HOCHELAGA COST $150.00"2210 PRINT "YOU ENDED YOUR FUR TRADING WITH $";I;"."
1181 PRINT "YOUR TRAVEL EXPENSES TO HOCHELAGA WERE $10.00"  2220 PRINT "HOPE YOU ENJOYED YOURSELF!"
```

SAMPLE RUN

YOU ARE THE LEADER OF A FRENCH FUR TRADING EXPEDITION IN
1776 LEAVING THE LAKE ONTARIO AREA TO SELL FURS AND GET
SUPPLIES FOR THE NEXT YEAR.   YOU HAVE A CHOICE OF THREE
FORTS AT WHICH YOU MAY TRADE.   THE COST OF SUPPLIES
AND THE AMOUNT YOU RECEIVE FOR YOUR FURS WILL DEPEND
ON THE FORT THAT YOU CHOOSE.
DO YOU WISH TO TRADE FURS?
ANSWER YES OR NO   ? YES

YOU HAVE $ 600 SAVINGS.
AND 190 FURS TO BEGIN THE EXPEDITION.

YOUR 190 FURS ARE DISTRIBUTED AMONG THE FOLLOWING
KINDS OF PELTS: MINK, BEAVER, ERMINE AND FOX.

HOW MANY MINK PELTS DO YOU HAVE? 50

HOW MANY BEAVER PELTS DO YOU HAVE? 40

HOW MANY ERMINE PELTS DO YOU HAVE? 50

HOW MANY FOX PELTS DO YOU HAVE? 50
DO YOU WANT TO TRADE YOUR FURS AT FORT 1, FORT 2,
OR FORT 3?   FORT 1 IS FORT HOCHELAGA (MONTREAL)
AND IS UNDER THE PROTECTION OF THE FRENCH ARMY.
FORT 2 IS FORT STADACONA (QUEBEC) AND IS UNDER THE
PROTECTION OF THE FRENCH ARMY.   HOWEVER, YOU MUST
MAKE A PORTAGE AND CROSS THE LACHINE RAPIDS.
FORT 3 IS FORT NEW YORK AND IS UNDER DUTCH CONTROL.
YOU MUST CROSS THROUGH IROQUOIS LAND.
ANSWER 1, 2, OR 3.
? 3
YOU HAVE CHOSEN THE MOST DIFFICULT ROUTE.   AT
FORT NEW YORK YOU WILL RECEIVE THE HIGHEST VALUE
FOR YOUR FURS.   THE COST OF YOUR SUPPLIES
WILL BE LOWER THAN AT ALL THE OTHER FORTS.
DO YOU WANT TO TRADE AT ANOTHER FORT?
ANSWER YES OR NO   ? NO

YOU NARROWLY ESCAPED AN IROQUOIS RAIDING PARTY.
HOWEVER, YOU HAD TO LEAVE ALL YOUR FURS BEHIND.
SUPPLIES AT NEW YORK COST $80.00

YOU NOW HAVE $ 495 INCLUDING YOUR PREVIOUS SAVINGS

DO YOU WANT TO TRADE FURS NEXT YEAR?
ANSWER YES OR NO   ? YES

YOU HAVE $ 495 SAVINGS.
AND 190 FURS TO BEGIN THE EXPEDITION.

YOUR 190 FURS ARE DISTRIBUTED AMONG THE FOLLOWING
KINDS OF PELTS: MINK, BEAVER, ERMINE AND FOX.

HOW MANY MINK PELTS DO YOU HAVE? 50

HOW MANY BEAVER PELTS DO YOU HAVE? 40

HOW MANY ERMINE PELTS DO YOU HAVE? 50

HOW MANY FOX PELTS DO YOU HAVE? 50
DO YOU WANT TO TRADE YOUR FURS AT FORT 1, FORT 2,
OR FORT 3?   FORT 1 IS FORT HOCHELAGA (MONTREAL)
AND IS UNDER THE PROTECTION OF THE FRENCH ARMY.
FORT 2 IS FORT STADACONA (QUEBEC) AND IS UNDER THE
PROTECTION OF THE FRENCH ARMY.   HOWEVER, YOU MUST
MAKE A PORTAGE AND CROSS THE LACHINE RAPIDS.
FORT 3 IS FORT NEW YORK AND IS UNDER DUTCH CONTROL.
YOU MUST CROSS THROUGH IROQUOIS LAND.
ANSWER 1, 2, OR 3.
? 2
YOU HAVE CHOSEN A HARD ROUTE.   IT IS, IN COMPARSION,
HARDER THAN THE ROUTE TO HOCHELAGA BUT EASIER THAN
THE ROUTE TO NEW YORK.   YOU WILL RECEIVE AN AVERAGE VALUE
FOR YOUR FURS AND THE COST OF YOUR SUPPLIES WILL BE AVERAGE
DO YOU WANT TO TRADE AT ANOTHER FORT?
ANSWER YES OR NO   ? NO

YOUR FOX PELTS WERE NOT CURED PROPERLY.
NO ONE WILL BUY THEM.
SUPPLIES AT FORT STADACONA COST $125.00
YOUR TRAVEL EXPENSES TO STADACONA WERE $15.00

YOUR BEAVER SOLD FOR $ 40.4 YOUR FOX SOLD FOR $ 0
YOUR ERMINE SOLD FOR $ 46 YOUR MINK SOLD FOR $ 46.5

YOU NOW HAVE $ 487.9 INCLUDING YOUR PREVIOUS SAVINGS

DO YOU WANT TO TRADE FURS NEXT YEAR?
ANSWER YES OR NO   ? YES

YOU HAVE $ 487.9 SAVINGS.
AND 190 FURS TO BEGIN THE EXPEDITION.

YOUR 190 FURS ARE DISTRIBUTED AMONG THE FOLLOWING
KINDS OF PELTS: MINK, BEAVER, ERMINE AND FOX.

HOW MANY MINK PELTS DO YOU HAVE? 60

HOW MANY BEAVER PELTS DO YOU HAVE? 50

HOW MANY ERMINE PELTS DO YOU HAVE? 40

HOW MANY FOX PELTS DO YOU HAVE? 40
DO YOU WANT TO TRADE YOUR FURS AT FORT 1, FORT 2,
OR FORT 3?   FORT 1 IS FORT HOCHELAGA (MONTREAL)
AND IS UNDER THE PROTECTION OF THE FRENCH ARMY.
FORT 2 IS FORT STADACONA (QUEBEC) AND IS UNDER THE
PROTECTION OF THE FRENCH ARMY.   HOWEVER, YOU MUST
MAKE A PORTAGE AND CROSS THE LACHINE RAPIDS.
FORT 3 IS FORT NEW YORK AND IS UNDER DUTCH CONTROL.
YOU MUST CROSS THROUGH IROQUOIS LAND.
ANSWER 1, 2, OR 3.
? 3
YOU HAVE CHOSEN THE MOST DIFFICULT ROUTE.   AT
FORT NEW YORK YOU WILL RECEIVE THE HIGHEST VALUE
FOR YOUR FURS.   THE COST OF YOUR SUPPLIES
WILL BE LOWER THAN AT ALL THE OTHER FORTS.
DO YOU WANT TO TRADE AT ANOTHER FORT?
ANSWER YES OR NO   ? NO

YOUR MINK AND BEAVER WERE DAMAGED ON YOUR TRIP.
YOU RECEIVE ONLY HALF THE CURRENT PRICE FOR THESE FURS.
SUPPLIES AT NEW YORK COST $80.00

YOUR BEAVER SOLD FOR $ 28 YOUR FOX SOLD FOR $ 46
YOUR ERMINE SOLD FOR $ 43.6 YOUR MINK SOLD FOR $ 35.1

YOU NOW HAVE $ 535.6 INCLUDING YOUR PREVIOUS SAVINGS

DO YOU WANT TO TRADE FURS NEXT YEAR?
ANSWER YES OR NO   ? YES

YOU HAVE $ 535.6 SAVINGS.
AND 190 FURS TO BEGIN THE EXPEDITION.

YOUR 190 FURS ARE DISTRIBUTED AMONG THE FOLLOWING
KINDS OF PELTS: MINK, BEAVER, ERMINE AND FOX.

HOW MANY MINK PELTS DO YOU HAVE? 50

HOW MANY BEAVER PELTS DO YOU HAVE? 40

HOW MANY ERMINE PELTS DO YOU HAVE? 50

HOW MANY FOX PELTS DO YOU HAVE? 50
DO YOU WANT TO TRADE YOUR FURS AT FORT 1, FORT 2,
OR FORT 3?   FORT 1 IS FORT HOCHELAGA (MONTREAL)
AND IS UNDER THE PROTECTION OF THE FRENCH ARMY.
FORT 2 IS FORT STADACONA (QUEBEC) AND IS UNDER THE
PROTECTION OF THE FRENCH ARMY.   HOWEVER, YOU MUST
MAKE A PORTAGE AND CROSS THE LACHINE RAPIDS.
FORT 3 IS FORT NEW YORK AND IS UNDER DUTCH CONTROL.
YOU MUST CROSS THROUGH IROQUOIS LAND.
ANSWER 1, 2, OR 3.
? 1
YOU HAVE CHOSEN THE EASIEST ROUTE.   HOWEVER, THE FORT
IS FAR FROM ANY SEAPORT.   THE VALUE
YOU RECEIVE FOR YOUR FURS WILL BE LOW AND THE COST
OF SUPPLIES HIGHER THAN AT FORTS STADACONA OR NEW YORK.
DO YOU WANT TO TRADE AT ANOTHER FORT?
ANSWER YES OR NO   ? NO

SUPPLIES AT FORT HOCHELAGA COST $150.00
YOUR TRAVEL EXPENSES TO HOCHELAGA WERE $10.00

YOUR BEAVER SOLD FOR $ 32.8 YOUR FOX SOLD FOR $ 49.5
YOUR ERMINE SOLD FOR $ 36 YOUR MINK SOLD FOR $ 42.5

YOU NOW HAVE $ 536.4 INCLUDING YOUR PREVIOUS SAVINGS

DO YOU WANT TO TRADE FURS NEXT YEAR?
ANSWER YES OR NO   ? NO

GOLF

Description

Up to four players may play up to 18 holes of golf. The length
of each hole and par are given to the players. Each player
chooses a club and the computer determines the results of the
shot. A player can duff a shot or get a hole in one. There
are also water hazards, rough, and sand traps. Note: It is
sometimes very difficult to chip out of a sand trap.

Computer Limitations

This version of GOLF was written for a DIGITAL EduSystem 30;
however, Statements 140 and 150 are the only ones unique to
that system and may be easily changed. When using EduSystem 30,
the NOLINE command must be given before running.

Program Author

There are several good one-player golf games. Paul Raymond
of College St. Laurent, Quebec, submitted one and another
has been around DIGITAL for years. However, this is the
best multi-player version we've seen. Available from DECUS
as BASIC 8-560, it was written by:

Howard Kargman
194 King Philip Drive
West Hartford, CT   06117

PROGRAM LISTING

```
100RANDOMIZE
110DIMX(20)
120PRINT"DO YOU WANT DIRECTIONS Y FOR YES N FOR N"
130INPUT#Z\PRINT
140IFZ=#YTHEN160
150IFZ=#NTHEN290
160PRINT"DIRECTIONS FOR GOLF"
170PRINT
180PRINT"YOU HAVE A CHOICE OF 9 CLUBS"
190PRINT"WHEN THE COMPUTER TELLS YOU TO CHOSE YOUR CLUB"
200PRINT"INPUT 1 FOR A DRIVER   RANGE OF 150 TO 270 YARDS"
210PRINT"INPUT 2 FOR A 3 WOOD   RANGE OF 150 TO 220 YARDS"
220PRINT"INPUT 3 FOR A 5 IRON   RANGE OF 140 TO 180 YARDS"
230PRINT"INPUT 4 FOR A 6 IRON   RANGE OF 120 TO 180 YARDS   GOOD FROM ROUGH"
240PRINT"INPUT 5 FOR A 7 IRON   RANGE OF 100 TO 130 YARDS   GOOD FROM ROUGH"
250PRINT"INPUT 6 FOR A 8 IRON   RANGE OF  70 TO 100 YARDS   GOOD FROM TRAP"
260PRINT"INPUT 7 FOR A 9 IRON   RANGE OF  30 TO  70 YARDS   GOOD FROM TRAP"
270PRINT"INPUT 8 FOR A WEDGE    RANGE UP TO 30 YARDS        GOOD FROM TRAP"
280PRINT"INPUT 9 FOR A PUTTER   USE WHEN ON GREEN"
290PRINT
300PRINT"HOW MANY PLAYERS ARE PLAYING TODAY";\INPUTU\PRINT
310IFU<=4THEN340
320PRINT"ONLY FOUR ARE ALLOWED TO PLAY AT ONE TIME"
330GOTO300
340PRINT
350DATA360,4,585,5,400,4,185,3,415,4,375,4,219,3
360DATA395,4,630,5,330,4,610,5,440,4,180,3,420,4,595,5,195,3
370DATA450,4,370,4
380DIMA(18)
390DIMP(18)
400FORR=1TO18
410READA(R)\READP(R)
420NEXTR
430DIM M(4,18)
440DIMN(10)
450PRINT"HOW MANY HOLES UP TO 18 DO YOU WANT TO PLAY?"\INPUTV
460PRINT
470FORJ=1TO V
480FOR Q=1TO U
490LETH=A(J)
500PRINT"HOLE NUMBER";J;"IS";H;"YARDS PAR";P(J)
510LETK=0
520LETT=0
530LET T2=0
540PRINT"PLAYER NUMBER";Q;"CHOSE YOUR CLUB"
550INPUT X
560IFX=9THEN880
570LETK=K+1
580 IF X=9 THEN 930
590GOTO1340
600IFX=9THEN970
610LETD=X
620IFH<>X(D)THEN630\IFK<>1THEN990\PRINT"HOLE IN ONE!!!"\GOTO990
630PRINT"DISTANCE OF SHOT IS";X(D);"YARDS"
640LETL=INT(RND(X)*100)
650IFL=99THEN670\IFL=43THEN670\IFL=88THEN670
660IFL<>25THEN760
670PRINT"IN TRAP"\LETC=ABS(H-X(D))\GOTO680
680LETL8=INT(RND(X)*10)
690IFL8>3THEN680\IFL8=1THEN850
700LETT2=0
710FORZ=1TOL8
720LETT2=T2+1
730PRINT"CHOSE YOUR CLUB"\INPUTX
740PRINT"STILL IN TRAP"\NEXTZ
750GOTO850
760IFL=13THEN780\IFL=88THEN780
770IFL<>25THEN800
780PRINT"IN ROUGH"\LETC=ABS(H-X(D))\GOTO850
790IFL=69THEN810\IFL=73THEN810\IFL=41THEN810
800IFL<>75THEN 830
810PRINT"IN WATER"\LETT=T+1\PRINT"YOU LOSE 1 STROKE"\LETC=ABS(H-X(D))
820GOTO850
830LETC=ABS(H-X(D))
840IFC<30THEN930
850PRINT"DISTANCE REMAINING TO PIN IS";C;"YARDS"
860LETH=C
870GOTO540
880LETC=A(J)
890IFC>30THEN910
900GOTO970
910PRINT"YOU ARE NOT ON THE GREEN   CHOSE ANOTHER CLUB"
920GOTO550
930PRINT"PLAYER NUMBER";Q;"IS ON THE GREEN CHOSE YOUR CLUB"
940INPUTX
950LETD=X
960GOTO590
970PRINT X(D)"PUTTS"
980LETM(Q,J)=K+X(9)+T+T2\GOTO1000
990LETM(Q,J)=K\PRINT"YOU SUNK THE SHOT"
1000PRINTM(Q,J)"STROKES FOR HOLE NUMBER";J;"FOR PLAYER";Q
1010NEXTQ\PRINT\PRINT
1020NEXT J
1030FORW=1TOV
1040LETN(1)=M(1,W)+N(1)
1050LETN(2)=M(2,W)+N(2)
1060LETN(3)=M(3,W)+N(3)
1070LETN(4)=M(4,W)+N(4)
1080LET E= P(W)+E
1090NEXTW
1100FORS=1TOU
1110PRINT"PLAYER NUMBER";S;"SHOT";N(S);"FOR";V;"HOLES  PAR IS";E
1120NEXT S
1130GOTO1440
1140LETX(2)=INT(130*RND(X)+150)
1150GOTO600
1160LETX(1)=INT(90*RND(X)+180)
1170GOTO600
1180LETX(3)=INT(40*RND(X)+140)
1190GOTO600
1200LETX(4)=INT(60*RND(X)+120)
1210GOTO600
1220LETX(5)=INT(30*RND(X)+100)
1230GOTO600
1240LETX(6)=INT(30*RND(X)+70)
1250GOTO600
1260LETX(7)=INT(40*RND(X)+30)
1270GOTO600
1280LETX(8)=INT(30*RND(X)+1)
1290IFX(8)<1THEN1280
1300GOTO600
1310LETX(9)=INT(3*RND(X)+1)
1320GOTO600
1330STOP
1340IFX=1THEN1160
1350IFX=2THEN1140
1360IFX=3THEN1180
1370IFX=4THEN1200
1380IFX=5THEN1220
1390IFX=6THEN1240
1400IFX=7THEN1260
1410IFX=8THEN1280
1420IFX=9THEN1310
1430GOTO600
1440END
```

SAMPLE RUN

```
DO YOU WANT DIRECTIONS Y FOR YES N FOR NO
Y
DIRECTIONS FOR GOLF

YOU HAVE A CHOICE OF 9 CLUBS
WHEN THE COMPUTER TELLS YOU TO CHOSE YOUR CLUB
INPUT 1 FOR A DRIVER   RANGE OF 150 TO 270 YARDS
INPUT 2 FOR A 3 WOOD   RANGE OF 150 TO 220 YARDS
INPUT 3 FOR A 5 IRON   RANGE OF 140 TO 180 YARDS
INPUT 4 FOR A 6 IRON   RANGE OF 120 TO 180 YARDS   GOOD FROM ROUGH
INPUT 5 FOR A 7 IRON   RANGE OF 100 TO 130 YARDS   GOOD FROM ROUGH
INPUT 6 FOR A 8 IRON   RANGE OF  70 TO 100 YARDS   GOOD FROM TRAP
INPUT 7 FOR A 9 IRON   RANGE OF  30 TO  70 YARDS   GOOD FROM TRAP
INPUT 8 FOR A WEDGE    RANGE UP TO 30 YARDS        GOOD FROM TRAP
INPUT 9 FOR A PUTTER   USE WHEN ON GREEN

HOW MANY PLAYERS ARE PLAYING TODAY?1


HOW MANY HOLES UP TO 18 DO YOU WANT TO PLAY?
?5

HOLE NUMBER 1 IS 360 YARDS PAR 4
PLAYER NUMBER 1 CHOSE YOUR CLUB
?1
DISTANCE OF SHOT IS 184 YARDS
DISTANCE REMAINING TO PIN IS 176 YARDS
PLAYER NUMBER 1 CHOSE YOUR CLUB
?2
DISTANCE OF SHOT IS 262 YARDS
DISTANCE REMAINING TO PIN IS 86 YARDS
PLAYER NUMBER 1 CHOSE YOUR CLUB
?6
DISTANCE OF SHOT IS 79 YARDS
PLAYER NUMBER 1 IS ON THE GREEN CHOSE YOUR CLUB
?9
 3 PUTTS
 6 STROKES FOR HOLE NUMBER 1 FOR PLAYER 1


HOLE NUMBER 2 IS 585 YARDS PAR 5
PLAYER NUMBER 1 CHOSE YOUR CLUB
?1
DISTANCE OF SHOT IS 225 YARDS
IN TRAP
DISTANCE REMAINING TO PIN IS 360 YARDS
PLAYER NUMBER 1 CHOSE YOUR CLUB
?6
DISTANCE OF SHOT IS 88 YARDS
DISTANCE REMAINING TO PIN IS 272 YARDS
PLAYER NUMBER 1 CHOSE YOUR CLUB
?1
DISTANCE OF SHOT IS 232 YARDS
DISTANCE REMAINING TO PIN IS 40 YARDS
PLAYER NUMBER 1 CHOSE YOUR CLUB
?7
DISTANCE OF SHOT IS 33 YARDS
PLAYER NUMBER 1 IS ON THE GREEN CHOSE YOUR CLUB
?9
 3 PUTTS
 7 STROKES FOR HOLE NUMBER 2 FOR PLAYER 1


HOLE NUMBER 3 IS 400 YARDS PAR 4
PLAYER NUMBER 1 CHOSE YOUR CLUB
?1
DISTANCE OF SHOT IS 236 YARDS
DISTANCE REMAINING TO PIN IS 164 YARDS
PLAYER NUMBER 1 CHOSE YOUR CLUB
?5
DISTANCE OF SHOT IS 102 YARDS
DISTANCE REMAINING TO PIN IS 62 YARDS
PLAYER NUMBER 1 CHOSE YOUR CLUB
?7
DISTANCE OF SHOT IS 50 YARDS
PLAYER NUMBER 1 IS ON THE GREEN CHOSE YOUR CLUB
?9
 1 PUTTS
 4 STROKES FOR HOLE NUMBER 3 FOR PLAYER 1


HOLE NUMBER 4 IS 185 YARDS PAR 3
PLAYER NUMBER 1 CHOSE YOUR CLUB
?2
DISTANCE OF SHOT IS 182 YARDS
PLAYER NUMBER 1 IS ON THE GREEN CHOSE YOUR CLUB
?9
 3 PUTTS
 4 STROKES FOR HOLE NUMBER 4 FOR PLAYER 1


HOLE NUMBER 5 IS 415 YARDS PAR 4
PLAYER NUMBER 1 CHOSE YOUR CLUB
?1
DISTANCE OF SHOT IS 210 YARDS
DISTANCE REMAINING TO PIN IS 205 YARDS
PLAYER NUMBER 1 CHOSE YOUR CLUB
?2
DISTANCE OF SHOT IS 208 YARDS
PLAYER NUMBER 1 IS ON THE GREEN CHOSE YOUR CLUB
?9
 3 PUTTS
 5 STROKES FOR HOLE NUMBER 5 FOR PLAYER 1
```

GOMOKO

ORIENTAL GAME OF GO-MOKO

Description

GO-MOKO is a traditional game of the Orient. It is played by
two people on a board of intersecting lines (19 left-to-right
lines, 19 top-to-bottom lines, 361 intersections in all).
Players take turns. During his turn, a player may cover one
intersection with a marker; (one player uses white markers;
the other player uses black markers). The object of the game
is to get five adjacent markers in a row, horizontally, vertically or along either diagonal.

Unfortunately, this program does not make the computer a very
good player. It does not know when you are about to win or
even who has won. But some of its moves may surprise you.

Computer Limitations

This program is dimensioned (in Statement 120) for a 19x19
board. Depending upon the size of your computer, you may have
to scale this down. A 7x7 board is the smallest that can be
used for a meaningful game.

Source

Peter Sessions
People's Computer Company
Menlo Park, CA 94025

D. Ahl

PROGRAM LISTING

```
10 PRINT\PRINT "WELCOME TO THE ORIENTAL GAME OF GOMOKO"
20 PRINT\PRINT "THE GAME IS PLAYED ON AN N BY N GRID OF A SIZE"
30 PRINT "THAT YOU SPECIFY.  DURING YOUR PLAY, YOU MAY COVER ONE GRID"
40 PRINT "INTERSECTION WITH A MARKER.  THE OBJECT OF THE GAME IS TO GET"
50 PRINT "5 ADJACENT MARKERS IN A ROW -- HORIZONTALLY, VERTICALLY, OR"
60 PRINT "ALONG EITHER DIAGONAL.  ON THE BOARD DIAGRAM, YOUR MOVES ARE"
70 PRINT "MARKED WITH A '1', AND THE COMPUTER MOVES WITH A '2'."
80 PRINT\PRINT "THE COMPUTER DOES NOT KEEP TRACK OF WHO HAS WON."
90 PRINT "TO END THE GAME, TYPE '-1,-1' FOR YOUR MOVE"\PRINT
110 PRINT "WHAT IS YOUR BOARD SIZE (MIN =7, MAX = 19)"\INPUT N
115 IF N>6 THEN 117
116 GOTO 120
117 IF N<20 THEN 300
120 PRINT "I SAID, THE MINIMUM SIZE IS 7, AND THE MAXIMUM IS 19."\GOTO 110
210 FOR I=1 TO N\FOR J=1 TO N\A(X,Y)=0\NEXT J\NEXT I
300 PRINT\PRINT "WE ALTERNATE MOVES.  YOU GO FIRST..."\PRINT
310 PRINT "YOUR PLAY (I,J)"\INPUT I,J
320 IF I=-1 THEN 980
330 X=I\Y=J\GOSUB 910\IF L=1 THEN 410
340 PRINT "ILLEGAL MOVE, TRY AGAIN..."\GOTO 310
410 IF A(I,J)=0 THEN 440
420 PRINT "SQUARE OCCUPIED, TRY AGAIN..."\GOTO 310
440 A(I,J)=1
500 REM *** COMPUTER TRIES AN 'INTELLIGENT' MOVE ***
510 FOR E=-1 TO 1\FOR F=-1 TO 1\IF E+F=E*F=0 THEN 590
540 LET X=I+E\LET Y=J+F\GOSUB 910
570 IF L=0 THEN 590
580 IF A(X,Y)=1 THEN 710
590 NEXT F\NEXT E
600 REM *** COMPUTER TRIES A RANDOM MOVE ***
610 LET X=INT(N*RND(0))+1\LET Y=INT(RND(0))+1\GOSUB 910\IF L=0 THEN 610
650 IF A(X,Y)<>0 THEN 610
660 A(X,Y)=2\GOSUB 810\GOTO 310
710 X=I-E\Y=J-F\GOSUB 910
750 IF L=0 THEN 610
760 GOTO 650
800 REM *** PRINT THE BOARD ***
810 FOR I=1 TO N\FOR J=1 TO N\PRINT A(I,J);
840 NEXT J\PRINT \NEXT I\PRINT \RETURN
900 REM *** CHECK WHETHER MOVE IS LEGAL ***
910 L=1\IF X<1 THEN 970
920 IF X>N THEN 970
930 IF Y<1 THEN 970
940 IF Y>N THEN 970
950 RETURN
970 LET L=0\RETURN
980 PRINT\PRINT "THANKS FOR THE GAME!!"
985 PRINT "PLAY AGAIN (1 FOR YES, 0 FOR NO)"\INPUT Q
990 IF Q=1 THEN 110
999 END
```

SAMPLE RUN

```
WELCOME TO THE ORIENTAL GAME OF GOMOKO

THE GAME IS PLAYED ON AN N BY N GRID OF A SIZE
THAT YOU SPECIFY.  DURING YOUR PLAY, YOU MAY COVER ONE GRID
INTERSECTION WITH A MARKER.  THE OBJECT OF THE GAME IS TO GET
5 ADJACENT MARKERS IN A ROW -- HORIZONTALLY, VERTICALLY, OR
ALONG EITHER DIAGONAL.  ON THE BOARD DIAGRAM, YOUR MOVES ARE
MARKED WITH A '1', AND THE COMPUTER MOVES WITH A '2'.

THE COMPUTER DOES NOT KEEP TRACK OF WHO HAS WON.
TO END THE GAME, TYPE '-1,-1' FOR YOUR MOVE

WHAT IS YOUR BOARD SIZE (MIN =7, MAX = 19)? 8

WE ALTERNATE MOVES.  YOU GO FIRST...

YOUR PLAY (I,J)? 4,4
 0 0 0 0 0 0 0 0
 0 0 0 0 0 0 0 0
 0 0 0 0 0 0 0 0
 0 0 0 1 0 0 0 0
 0 0 0 0 0 0 0 0
 0 0 0 0 0 0 0 0
 2 0 0 0 0 0 0 0
 0 0 0 0 0 0 0 0

YOUR PLAY (I,J)? 5,5
 0 0 0 0 0 0 0 0
 0 0 0 0 0 0 0 0
 0 0 0 0 0 0 0 0
 0 0 0 1 0 0 0 0
 0 0 0 0 1 0 0 0
 0 0 0 0 0 2 0 0
 2 0 0 0 0 0 0 0
 0 0 0 0 0 0 0 0

YOUR PLAY (I,J)? 3,3
 0 0 0 0 0 0 0 0
 0 2 0 0 0 0 0 0
 0 0 1 0 0 0 0 0
 0 0 0 1 0 0 0 0
 0 0 0 0 1 0 0 0
 0 0 0 0 0 2 0 0
 2 0 0 0 0 0 0 0
 0 0 0 0 0 0 0 0

YOUR PLAY (I,J)? 3,5
 0 0 0 0 0 0 0 0
 0 2 0 0 0 2 0 0
 0 0 1 0 1 0 0 0
 0 0 0 1 0 0 0 0
 0 0 0 0 1 0 0 0
 0 0 0 0 0 2 0 0
 2 0 0 0 0 0 0 0
 0 0 0 0 0 0 0 0

YOUR PLAY (I,J)? 5,3
 0 0 0 0 0 0 0 0
 0 2 0 0 0 2 0 0
 0 0 1 0 1 0 0 0
 0 0 0 1 0 0 0 0
 0 0 1 0 1 0 0 0
 0 2 0 0 0 2 0 0
 2 0 0 0 0 0 0 0
 0 0 0 0 0 0 0 0

YOUR PLAY (I,J)? 4,5
 2 0 0 0 0 0 0 0
 0 2 0 0 0 2 0 0
 0 0 1 0 1 0 0 0
 0 0 0 1 1 0 0 0
 0 0 1 0 1 0 0 0
 0 2 0 0 0 2 0 0
 2 0 0 0 0 0 0 0
 0 0 0 0 0 0 0 0

YOUR PLAY (I,J)? 4,3
 2 0 0 0 0 0 0 0
 0 2 0 0 0 2 0 0
 0 0 1 0 1 0 0 0
 0 0 1 1 1 0 0 0
 2 0 1 0 1 0 0 0
 0 2 0 0 0 2 0 0
 2 0 0 0 0 0 0 0
 0 0 0 0 0 0 0 0

YOUR PLAY (I,J)? 4,2
 2 0 0 0 0 0 0 0
 0 2 0 0 0 2 0 0
 0 0 1 0 1 0 0 0
 0 1 1 1 1 0 0 0
 2 0 1 0 1 0 0 0
 0 2 0 0 0 2 0 0
 2 0 0 0 0 0 0 0
 2 0 0 0 0 0 0 0

YOUR PLAY (I,J)? 4,5
SQUARE OCCUPIED. TRY AGAIN...
YOUR PLAY (I,J)? 4,6
 2 0 0 0 0 0 0 0
 0 2 0 0 0 2 0 0
 0 0 1 0 1 0 0 0
 0 1 1 1 1 1 0 0
 2 0 1 0 1 0 2 0
 0 2 0 0 0 2 0 0
 2 0 0 0 0 0 0 0
 2 0 0 0 0 0 0 0

YOUR PLAY (I,J)? -1,-1

THANKS FOR THE GAME!!
PLAY AGAIN (1 FOR YES, 0 FOR NO)? 0

READY
```

GUESS

Description

In Program GUESS, the computer chooses a random integer between
0 and any limit you set. You must then try to guess the number
the computer has chosen using the clues provided by the computer.

You should be able to guess the number in one less than the
number of digits needed to represent the number in binary
notation--i.e., in base 2. This ought to give you a clue as
to the optimum search technique.

Computer Limitations

There are no real limitations; however, the listing is from
DIGITAL EduSystem 20 BASIC which accepts statements abbreviated
to the first three letters.

Program Author

GUESS converted from the original program in FOCAL which appeared
in the book "Computers in the Classroom" by:

Walt Koetke
Lexington High School
Lexington, MA   02173

PROGRAM LISTING

```
1 PRI "THIS IS A NUMBER GUESSING GAME.  I'LL THINK"
2 PRI "OF A NUMBER BETWEEN 1 AND ANY LIMIT YOU WANT."
3 PRI "THEN YOU HAVE TO GUESS WHAT IT IS."
4 PRI
5 PRI "WHAT LIMIT DO YOU WANT";
6 INPL
7 PRI
8 L1=INT(LOG(L)/LOG(2))+1
10 PRI"I'M THINKING OF A NUMBER BETWEEN 1 AND"L
11 G=1
14 PRI "NOW YOU TRY TO GUESS WHAT IT IS"
15 M=INT(L*RND(0))+1
20 INP N
21 IF N>0 THEN 25
22 GOSUB70
23 GOTO1
25 IF N=M THEN 50
30 G=G+1
31 IF N>M THEN 40
32 PRI "TOO LOW. GUESS AGAIN."
33 GOTO 20
40 PRI "TOO HIGH.  GUESS AGAIN."
42 GOTO 20
50 PRI "THAT'S IT!  YOU GOT IT IN"G"TRIES.
52 IF G<L1 THEN 58
54 IF G=L1 THEN 60
56 PRI"YOU SHOULD HAVE BEEN ABLE TO GET IT IN ONLY"L1".
57 GOT 65
58 PRI"VERY ";
60 PRI"GOOD!"
65 GOSUB70
66 GOTO10
70 FOR H=1 TO 5
71 PRI
72 NEXT H
73 RETURN
99 END
```

SAMPLE RUN

```
THIS IS A NUMBER GUESSING GAME.  I'LL THINK
OF A NUMBER BETWEEN 1 AND ANY LIMIT YOU WANT.
THEN YOU HAVE TO GUESS WHAT IT IS.

WHAT LIMIT DO YOU WANT? 100

I'M THINKING OF A NUMBER BETWEEN 1 AND 100
NOW YOU TRY TO GUESS WHAT IT IS
? 50
TOO HIGH.  GUESS AGAIN.
? 25
THAT'S IT!  YOU GOT IT IN 2 TRIES.
VERY GOOD!



I'M THINKING OF A NUMBER BETWEEN 1 AND 100
NOW YOU TRY TO GUESS WHAT IT IS
? 50
TOO HIGH.  GUESS AGAIN.
? 25
TOO LOW. GUESS AGAIN.
? 37
TOO HIGH.  GUESS AGAIN.
? 31
TOO HIGH.  GUESS AGAIN.
? 28
TOO LOW. GUESS AGAIN.
? 29
TOO LOW. GUESS AGAIN.
? 30
THAT'S IT!  YOU GOT IT IN 7 TRIES.
GOOD!



I'M THINKING OF A NUMBER BETWEEN 1 AND 100
NOW YOU TRY TO GUESS WHAT IT IS
? 50
TOO LOW. GUESS AGAIN.
? 75
TOO HIGH.  GUESS AGAIN.
? 62
TOO LOW. GUESS AGAIN.
? 67
TOO LOW. GUESS AGAIN.
? 71
TOO LOW. GUESS AGAIN.
? 73
THAT'S IT!  YOU GOT IT IN 6 TRIES.
VERY GOOD!
```

GUNNER

FIRE A FIELD ARTILLERY WEAPON

Description

These two programs allow you to adjust the fire of a field artillery weapon to hit a stationary or moving target. You specify the number of degrees of elevation of your weapon; 45 degrees provides maximum range with values under or over 45 degrees providing less range.

GUNNER is the simpler of the two programs and gives you up to five shots to destroy the enemy before he destroys you. Gun range is fixed at 46,500 yards, burst radius at 100 yards; you must specify elevation within approximately 0.2 degrees to get a hit.

GUNER1 is more complex and allows you to specify the speed at which your target is moving (but not direction!), and your burst radius. Also, your gun has a different maximum range randomly determined each play.

Source

GUNNER:
  Tom Kloos
  Oregon Museum of Science
    and Industry
  Portland, Oregon 97200

GUNER1:
  Original author unknown.
  Converted by students at:
    Lexington High School
    Lexington, MA 02173

GUNNER   PROGRAM LISTING

```
10 REM *** MODIFIED AND CONVERTED TO RSTS/E BY DAVID AHL, DIGITAL
90 RANDOMIZE
100 PRINT "THIS COMPUTER DEMONSTRATION SIMULATES THE"
110 PRINT"RESULTS OF FIRING A FIELD ARTILLERY WEAPON."
120 PRINT
130 PRINT"YOU ARE THE OFFICER-IN-CHARGE, GIVING ORDERS TO THE GUN"
140 PRINT"CREW, TELLING THEM THE DEGREES OF ELEVATION YOU ESTIMATE"
150 PRINT"WILL PLACE THE PROJECTILE ON TARGET.   A HIT WITHIN 100 YARDS"
160 PRINT"OF THE TARGET WILL DESTROY IT.   TAKE MORE THAN 5 SHOTS,"
170 PRINT "AND THE ENEMY WILL DESTROY YOU!"\PRINT
180 PRINT"MAXIMUM RANGE OF YOUR GUN IS 46500 YARDS."
185 Z=0
190 PRINT
195 S1=0
200 LET T=43000-30000*RND(X)
210 LET S=0
220 GO TO 370
230 PRINT"MINIMUM ELEVATION OF GUN IS ONE DEGREE."
240 GO TO 390
250 PRINT"MAXIMUM ELEVATION OF GUN IS 89 DEGREES."
260 GO TO 390
270 PRINT"OVER TARGET BY";ABS(E);"YARDS."
280 GO TO 390
290 PRINT "SHORT OF TARGET BY";ABS(E);"YARDS."
300 GO TO 390
310 GO TO 320
320 PRINT"***TARGET DESTROYED***    ";S;"ROUNDS OF AMMUNITION EXPENDED"
322 GOSUB 600
325 S1=S1+S
330 IF Z=4 THEN 490
340 Z=Z+1
345 PRINT
350 PRINT"THE FORWARD OBSERVER HAS SIGHTED MORE ENEMY ACTIVITY."
360 GO TO 200
370 PRINT"      DISTANCE TO THE TARGET IS";INT(T);"YARDS....."
380 PRINT
390 PRINT
400 PRINT"ELEVATION:";
410 INPUT B
420 IF B>89 THEN 250
430 IF B<1 THEN 230
440 LET S=S+1
442 IF S<6 THEN 450
444 PRINT\PRINT "BOOM !!!  YOU HAVE JUST BEEN DESTROYED ";
445 GOSUB 600
446 PRINT "BY THE ENEMY"\PRINT\PRINT\GOTO 495
450 LET B2=2*B/57.3\LET I=46500*SIN(B2)\LET X=T-I\LET E=INT(X)
460 IF ABS(E)<100 THEN 310
470 IF E>100 THEN 290
480 IF E<-100 THEN 270
490 PRINT\PRINT\PRINT "TOTAL ROUNDS EXPENDED WERE";S1
491 IF S1>15 THEN 495\PRINT "NICE SHOOTING !!"\GOSUB 600\GOTO 500
495 PRINT "BETTER GO BACK TO FORT SILL FOR REFRESHER TRAINING!"
500 PRINT\PRINT "THANK YOU FOR PLAYING!"
505 PRINT\PRINT "TRY AGAIN....."\PRINT\GOTO 180
600 FOR N=1 TO 10\PRINT CHR$(7);\NEXT N
610 RETURN
999 END

READY
```

SAMPLE RUN

```
THIS COMPUTER DEMONSTRATION SIMULATES THE
RESULTS OF FIRING A FIELD ARTILLERY WEAPON.

YOU ARE THE OFFICER-IN-CHARGE, GIVING ORDERS TO THE GUN
CREW, TELLING THEM THE DEGREES OF ELEVATION YOU ESTIMATE
WILL PLACE THE PROJECTILE ON TARGET.   A HIT WITHIN 100 YARDS
OF THE TARGET WILL DESTROY IT.   TAKE MORE THAN 5 SHOTS,
AND THE ENEMY WILL DESTROY YOU!

MAXIMUM RANGE OF YOUR GUN IS 46500 YARDS.
```

```
        DISTANCE TO THE TARGET IS 41757 YARDS.....

ELEVATION:? 35
OVER TARGET BY 1937 YARDS.

ELEVATION:? 33
OVER TARGET BY 721 YARDS.

ELEVATION:? 31.8
SHORT OF TARGET BY 108 YARDS.

ELEVATION:? 31.9
***TARGET DESTROYED***    4 ROUNDS OF AMMUNITION EXPENDED

THE FORWARD OBSERVER HAS SIGHTED MORE ENEMY ACTIVITY.
        DISTANCE TO THE TARGET IS 21460 YARDS.....

ELEVATION:? 16
OVER TARGET BY 3180 YARDS.

ELEVATION:? 13
SHORT OF TARGET BY 1077 YARDS.

ELEVATION:? 14.3
OVER TARGET BY 798 YARDS.

ELEVATION:? 13.8
***TARGET DESTROYED***    4 ROUNDS OF AMMUNITION EXPENDED

THE FORWARD OBSERVER HAS SIGHTED MORE ENEMY ACTIVITY.
        DISTANCE TO THE TARGET IS 14943 YARDS.....

ELEVATION:? 9
SHORT OF TARGET BY 575 YARDS.

ELEVATION:? 9.5
OVER TARGET BY 195 YARDS.

ELEVATION:? 9.3
SHORT OF TARGET BY 113 YARDS.

ELEVATION:? 9.37
***TARGET DESTROYED***    4 ROUNDS OF AMMUNITION EXPENDED

THE FORWARD OBSERVER HAS SIGHTED MORE ENEMY ACTIVITY.
        DISTANCE TO THE TARGET IS 38518 YARDS.....

ELEVATION:? 28
***TARGET DESTROYED***    1 ROUNDS OF AMMUNITION EXPENDED

THE FORWARD OBSERVER HAS SIGHTED MORE ENEMY ACTIVITY.
        DISTANCE TO THE TARGET IS 28617 YARDS.....

ELEVATION:? 21
OVER TARGET BY 2495 YARDS.

ELEVATION:? 19
***TARGET DESTROYED***    2 ROUNDS OF AMMUNITION EXPENDED

TOTAL ROUNDS EXPENDED WERE 15
BETTER GO BACK TO FORT SILL FOR REFRESHER TRAINING!

THANK YOU FOR PLAYING!

TRY AGAIN.....
```

GUNER1   PROGRAM LISTING

```
100 REM ARTILLERY FIRING GAME
110 DIM A$(3)
120 RANDOMIZE
130 PRINT "DO YOU WANT INSTRUCTIONS";
140 INPUT A$
150 PRINT
160 IF A$="NO" THEN 330
170 PRINT "    THIS GAME TESTS YOUR ABILITY TO HIT A MOVING TARGET."
180 PRINT "YOU MUST DESTROY IT BEFORE IT DESTROYS YOU OR MOVES OUT"
190 PRINT "OF RANGE. THE TARGET WILL MOVE RAMDOMLY."
200 PRINT
210 PRINT "    TYPE CTRL/C TO TERMINATE THE PROGRAM.  TO THE QUESTON"
220 PRINT "'ENTER SPEED' TYPE A NUMBER BETWEEN 1 AND 100, THIS IS THE"
230 PRINT "RELATIVE SPEED OF THE TARGET WHERE 1 IS THE SLOWEST AND 100"
240 PRINT "IS THE FASTEST."
250 PRINT
260 PRINT "TO THE QUESTION 'ENTER DISTANCE' ENTER THE MAXIMUM DISTANCE"
270 PRINT "YOU CAN HIT FROM THE TARGET AND STILL DESTROY IT. THIS IS"
280 PRINT "THE KILL RADIUS AND 5000 IS SUGGESTED FOR STARTERS."
290 PRINT
300 PRINT "ELEVATION IS THE ELEVATION OF YOUR GUN IN DEGREES WHEN YOU"
310 PRINT "FIRE AT THE TARGET. THE MAXIMUN RANGE IS AT 45 DEGREES"
320 PRINT
330 PRINT "ENTER SPEED";
340 INPUT S
350 IF S<1 THEN 330
360 IF S>100 THEN 330
370 PRINT "ENTER DISTANCE";
380 INPUT D
390 IF D<0 THEN 370
400 IF D>10000 THEN 370
410 M=100000-75000*RND(0)
420 PRINT
430 PRINT "THE MAXIMUM RANGE OF YOUR GUN IS "M" YARDS"
440 FOR K=1 TO M/10000
450 LET K1=RND(0)
460 NEXT K
470 R=.95*M-.6*M*RND(0)
480 LET N=0
490 GOTO 520
500 IF R>M THEN 840
510 IF R<=(M/2.5) THEN 860
520 PRINT "TARGET RANGE IS"R" YARDS"
530 PRINT "ELEVATION";
540 INPUT E
550 IF E<0 THEN 840
560 IF E> 89 THEN 800
570 IF E <1 THEN 820
580 N=N+1
590 K=INT(R-M*SIN(2*E/57.3))
600 K1=ABS(K)
610 IF K1<D THEN 650
620 IF K>D THEN 720
630 IF K<=D THEN 740
640 STOP
650 PRINT "*** TARGET DESTROYED ***"
660 GOSUB 940
670 D1=K
680 FOR K=1 TO N+D/100
690 K1=RND(0)
700 NEXT K
710 GOTO 410
720 PRINT "SHORT OF TARGET BY "K1" YARDS"
730 GOTO 745
740 PRINT "OVER TARGET BY ";K1"YARDS"
745 LET C=INT(2*RND(0)+1)
746 IF C=1 THEN 750
748 LET C=-1
749 GOTO 760
750 LET C=1
760 C1=M*S/100*RND(0)
770 C1=C*C1
780 R=R+C1
790 GOTO 500
800 PRINT "MAXIMUM ELEVATION IS 89 DEGREES"
810 GOTO 530
820 PRINT "MINIMUM ELEVATION IS 1 DEGREE"
830 GOTO 530
840 PRINT "* TARGET OUT OF RANGE *"
850 GOTO 670
860 PRINT "THE TARGET HAS DESTROYED YOU!"
870 GOTO 670
940 IF N=1 THEN 970
950 PRINT N" ROUNDS EXPENDED"
960 RETURN
970 PRINT "***** DIRECT HIT *****"
980 RETURN
990 END

READY
```

SAMPLE RUN

```
DO YOU WANT INSTRUCTIONS? YES

    THIS GAME TESTS YOUR ABILITY TO HIT A MOVING TARGET.
YOU MUST DESTROY IT BEFORE IT DESTROYS YOU OR MOVES OUT
OF RANGE. THE TARGET WILL MOVE RAMDOMLY.

    TYPE CTRL/C TO TERMINATE THE PROGRAM.  TO THE QUESTON
'ENTER SPEED' TYPE A NUMBER BETWEEN 1 AND 100, THIS IS THE
RELATIVE SPEED OF THE TARGET WHERE 1 IS THE SLOWEST AND 100
IS THE FASTEST.

TO THE QUESTION 'ENTER DISTANCE' ENTER THE MAXIMUM DISTANCE
YOU CAN HIT FROM THE TARGET AND STILL DESTROY IT. THIS IS
THE KILL RADIUS AND 5000 IS SUGGESTED FOR STARTERS.

ELEVATION IS THE ELEVATION OF YOUR GUN IN DEGREES WHEN YOU
FIRE AT THE TARGET. THE MAXIMUN RANGE IS AT 45 DEGREES

ENTER SPEED? 100
ENTER DISTANCE? 5000

THE MAXIMUM RANGE OF YOUR GUN IS  26757.49  YARDS
TARGET RANGE IS 19571.22  YARDS
ELEVATION? 60
*** TARGET DESTROYED ***
***** DIRECT HIT *****

THE MAXIMUM RANGE OF YOUR GUN IS  37888.44  YARDS
TARGET RANGE IS 19498.91  YARDS
ELEVATION? 70
*** TARGET DESTROYED ***
***** DIRECT HIT *****

THE MAXIMUM RANGE OF YOUR GUN IS  30785.11  YARDS
TARGET RANGE IS 26990.9  YARDS
ELEVATION? 70
SHORT OF TARGET BY  7198  YARDS
TARGET RANGE IS 24494.73  YARDS
ELEVATION? 68
*** TARGET DESTROYED ***
 2  ROUNDS EXPENDED

THE MAXIMUM RANGE OF YOUR GUN IS  27489.9  YARDS
TARGET RANGE IS 24327.48  YARDS
ELEVATION? 38.0
*** TARGET DESTROYED ***
***** DIRECT HIT *****

THE MAXIMUM RANGE OF YOUR GUN IS  26316.88  YARDS
TARGET RANGE IS 12849.83  YARDS
ELEVATION? 30
OVER TARGET BY  9941 YARDS
THE TARGET HAS DESTROYED YOU!

THE MAXIMUM RANGE OF YOUR GUN IS  60008.68  YARDS
TARGET RANGE IS 48885.2  YARDS
ELEVATION?
↑C
```

HANG

Description

This is a simulation of the word guessing game, hangman. The
computer picks a word, tells you how many letters in the word
it has picked and then you guess a letter in the word. If you
are right, the computer tells you where that letter belongs;
if your letter is wrong, the computer starts to hang you. You
get ten guesses before you are completely hanged:

> Head
> Body
> Right and Left Arms
> Right and Left Legs
> Right and Left Hands
> Right and Left Feet

In this program, the PRINT statement is abbreviated to "&."
You may add words in Data statements following Statement 508;
in this case, you must also change the random word selector in
Statement 40.

Source

Interesting versions of Hangman were received from Brandy
Brylawski, a seventh grader at the Eaglebrook School, Deerfield,
Mass., and a sophisticated one from W.K. Bateman at Montpelier
Public Schools, Montpelier, Vt.

The one printed is from a high school sophomore:

Kenneth Aupperle
24 Arrowhead Lane
Melville, NY 11746

PROGRAM LISTING

```
10 REM *** GAME OF HANGMAN BY DAVE AHL, DIGITAL
15 REM *** BASED ON A PROGRAM WRITTEN BY KEN RUPPERLE, CLASS OF '75,
20 REM *** HALF HOLLOW HILLS H.S., DIX HILLS, NY
25 &"GAME OF HANGMAN":&:&
30 DIM P$(12,12),L$(20),D$(20),N$(26),U(50)
40 C=1:RANDOMIZE:N=50
50 D$(I)="-" FOR I=1 TO 20:M=0
60 N$(I)="" FOR I=1 TO 26
70 FOR I=1 TO 12:FOR J=1 TO 12:P$(I,J)=" ":NEXT J:NEXT I
80 P$(I,1)="X" FOR I=1 TO 12
90 P$(1,I)="X" FOR I=1 TO 7:P$(2,7)="X"
95 IF C<N THEN 100 ELSE PRINT "YOU DID ALL THE WORDS!!":STOP
100 Q=INT(N*RND+1)
110 IF U(Q)=1 THEN 100 ELSE U(Q)=1:C=C+1:RESTORE:T1=0
150 READ A$ FOR I=1 TO Q
160 L=LEN(A$):L$(I)=MID(A$,I,1) FOR I=1 TO L
170 &"HERE ARE THE LETTERS YOU USED:"
180 FOR I=1 TO 26:& N$(I);:IF N$(I+1)="" THEN 200
190 PRINT ",";:NEXT I
200 &:&:FOR I=1 TO L:& D$(I);:NEXT I:&:&
210 INPUT "WHAT IS YOUR GUESS";G$:R=0
220 FOR I=1 TO 26:IF N$(I)="" THEN 250
230 IF G$=N$(I) THEN & "YOU GUESSED THAT LETTER BEFORE":GOTO 170
240 NEXT I:& "PROGRAM ERROR.   RUN AGAIN. ":STOP
250 N$(I)=G$:T1=T1+1
260 FOR I=1 TO L:IF L$(I)=G$ THEN 280
270 NEXT I:IF R=0 THEN 290 ELSE GOTO 300
280 D$(I)=G$:R=R+1:GOTO 270
290 M=M+1:GOTO 400
300 FOR I=1 TO L:IF D$(I)="-" THEN 320
310 NEXT I:GOTO 390
320 &:FOR I=1 TO L:& D$(I);:NEXT I:&:&
330 INPUT "WHAT IS YOUR GUESS FOR THE WORD";B$
340 IF B$=A$ THEN 360
350 &"WRONG.   TRY ANOTHER LETTER. ":&:GOTO 170
360 &"RIGHT!!  IT TOOK YOU"T1"GUESSES!"
370 INPUT "WANT ANOTHER WORD";W$:IF W$="YES" THEN 50
380 &:&"IT'S BEEN FUN!  BYE FOR NOW. ":STOP
390 &"YOU FOUND THE WORD!":GOTO 370
400 &:&:&"SORRY, THAT LETTER ISN'T IN THE WORD. "
410 ON M GOTO 415,420,425,430,435,440,445,450,455,460
415 &"FIRST, WE DRAW A HEAD":GOTO 470
420 &"NOW WE DRAW A BODY":GOTO 470
425 &"NEXT WE DRAW AN ARM":GOTO 470
430 &"THIS TIME IT'S THE OTHER ARM":GOTO 470
435 &"NOW, LET'S DRAW THE RIGHT LEG":GOTO 470
440 &"THIS TIME WE DRAW THE LEFT LEG":GOTO 470
445 &"NOW WE PUT UP A HAND":GOTO 470
450 &"NEXT THE OTHER HAND":GOTO 470
455 &"NOW WE DRAW ONE FOOT":GOTO 470
460 &"HERE'S THE OTHER FOOT -- YOU'RE HUNG!!"
470 ON M GOTO 480,490,500,510,520,530,540,550,560,570
480 P$(3,6)="-":P$(3,7)="-":P$(3,8)="-":P$(4,5)="(":P$(4,6)=". "
481 P$(4,8)=". ":P$(4,9)=")":P$(5,6)="-":P$(5,7)="-":P$(5,8)="-":GOTO 580
490 P$(I,7)="X" FOR I=6 TO 9:GOTO 580
500 P$(I,I-1)="\" FOR I=4 TO 7:GOTO 580
510 P$(4,11)="/":P$(5,10)="/":P$(6,9)="/":P$(7,8)="/":GOTO 580
520 P$(10,6)="/":P$(11,5)="/":GOTO 580
530 P$(10,8)="\":P$(11,9)="\":GOTO 580
540 P$(3,11)="\":GOTO 580
550 P$(3,3)="/":GOTO 580
560 P$(12,10)="\":P$(12,11)="-":GOTO 580
570 P$(12,3)="-":P$(12,4)="/"
580 FOR I=1 TO 12:FOR J=1 TO 12:& P$(I,J);:NEXT J
590 &:NEXT I:&:&:IF M=10 THEN 600 ELSE 170
600 &"SORRY, YOU LOSE.  THE WORD WAS "A$
610 &"YOU MISSED THAT ONE.  DO YOU":GOTO 370
700 DATA "GUM", "SIN", "FOR", "CRY", "LUG", "BYE", "FLY"
710 DATA "UGLY", "EACH", "FROM", "WORK", "TALK", "WITH", "SELF"
720 DATA "PIZZA", "THING", "FEIGN", "FIEND", "ELBOW", "FAULT", "DIRTY"
730 DATA "BUDGET", "SPIRIT", "QUAINT", "MAIDEN", "ESCORT", "PICKAX"
740 DATA "EXAMPLE", "TENSION", "QUININE", "KIDNEY", "REPLICA", "SLEEPER"
750 DATA "TRIANGLE", "KANGAROO", "MAHOGANY", "SERGEANT", "SEQUENCE"
760 DATA "MOUSTACHE", "DANGEROUS", "SCIENTIST", "DIFFERENT", "QUIESCENT"
770 DATA "MAGISTRATE", "ERRONEOUSLY", "LOUDSPEAKER", "PHYTOTOXIC"
780 DATA "MATRIMONIAL", "PARASYMPATHOMIMETIC", "THIGMOTROPISM"
999 END

READY
```

SAMPLE RUN

```
HERE ARE THE LETTERS YOU USED:


--------

WHAT IS YOUR GUESS? E


SORRY, THAT LETTER ISN'T IN THE WORD.
FIRST, WE DRAW A HEAD
XXXXXXX
X      X
X     ---
X    ( . .)
X     ---
X
X
X
X
X
X


HERE ARE THE LETTERS YOU USED:
E

--------

WHAT IS YOUR GUESS? A

-A---A--

WHAT IS YOUR GUESS FOR THE WORD?
WRONG.   TRY ANOTHER LETTER.

HERE ARE THE LETTERS YOU USED:
E, A

-A---A--

WHAT IS YOUR GUESS? R


SORRY, THAT LETTER ISN'T IN THE WORD.
NOW WE DRAW A BODY
XXXXXXX
X      X
X     ---
X    ( . .)
X     ---
X      X
X      X
X      X
X      X
X
X
X


HERE ARE THE LETTERS YOU USED:
E, A, R

-A---A--

WHAT IS YOUR GUESS? O

-A-O-A--

WHAT IS YOUR GUESS FOR THE WORD?
WRONG.   TRY ANOTHER LETTER.

HERE ARE THE LETTERS YOU USED:
E, A, R, O

-A-O-A--

WHAT IS YOUR GUESS? T


SORRY, THAT LETTER ISN'T IN THE WORD.
NEXT WE DRAW AN ARM
XXXXXXX
X      X
X     ---
X  \ ( . .)
X   \ ---
X    \ X
X     \X
X      X
X      X
X
X
X
```

HELLO

Description

This is a sample of one of a great number of conversational
programs. In a sense, it is like a CAI program except that
its responses are just good fun. Whenever a computer is ex-
hibited at a convention or conference with people that have
not used a computer before, the conversational programs seem
to get the first activity.

In this particular program, the computer dispenses advice on
various problems such as sex, health, money, or job.

Source

David Ahl
Digital Equipment Corp.
Maynard, MA 01754

PROGRAM LISTING

```
5 GOT 400
10 PRINT "HELLO, I'M AN EDUSYSTEM-25. MY NAME IS PETEY P. EIGHT."
20 PRI\PRI "WHAT'S YOUR NAME";\LINPUT A$\PRI
35 PRI " HI THERE ";\GOSUB500\PRI". ARE YOU ENJOYING YOURSELF HERE
40 PRI "IN BEAUTIFUL MAYNARD, MASS";
45 INP B$\PRI
50 IF B$="YES" THEN 70
55 IF B$="NO" THEN 80
60 PRI " ";\GOSUB500\PRI", I DON'T UNDERSTAND YOUR ANSWER OF '"B$"'."
65 PRI "PLEASE ANSWER 'YES' OR 'NO'. DO YOU LIKE IT HERE
67 GOT 40
70 PRI "OH, I'M GALD TO HERE THAT ";\GOSUB500\PRI
75 GOT 100
80 PRI "OH, SORRY TO HEAR THAT ";\GOSUB 500\PRI ", MAYBE WE CAN
85 PRI "BRIGHTEN UP YOUR STAY A BIT
100 PRI
105 PRI "SAY, ";\GOSUB500\PRI", I CAN SOLVE ALL KINDS OF PROBLEMS
110 PRI "EXCEPT THOSE DEALING WITH GREECE. WHAT KIND OF
115 PRI "PROBLEMS DO YOU HAVE (ANSWER SEX, HEALTH, MONEY,
120 PRI "OR JOB)";
125 INP C$\PRI
130 IF C$="SEX" THEN 200
132 IF C$="HEALTH" THEN 180
134 IF C$="MONEY" THEN 160
136 IF C$="JOB" THEN 145
138 PRI "OH, ";\GOSUB500\PRI", YOUR ANSWER OF '"C$"' IS GREEK TO ME."
140 GOT 250
145 PRI "I CAN SYMPATHIZE WITH YOU ";\GOSUB500\PRI". I HAVE TO WORK
148 PRI "VERY LONG HOURS FOR NO PAY -- AND SOME OF MY BOSSES REALLY
150 PRI"BEAT MY KEYBOARD. MY ADVICE TO YOU ";\GOSUB500\PRI", IS TO SELL

153 PRI "IN THE EDUCATION MARKET. IT'S GREAT FUN.
155 GOT 250
160 PRI "SORRY, ";\GOSUB500\PRI", I'M BROKE TOO. WHY DON'T YOU SELL
163 PRI "ENCYCLOPEADIAS OR MARRY SOMEONE RICH OR STOP EATING
165 PRI "SO YOU WON'T NEED SO MUCH MONEY?
170 GOT 250
180 PRI "MY ADVICE TO YOU ";\GOSUB500\PRI", IS:
185 PRI "     1. TAKE TWO ASPRIN
188 PRI "     2. DRINK PLENTY OF FLUIDS (ORANGE JUICE, NOT BEER!)
190 PRI "     3. GO TO BED (ALONE)
195 GOT 250
200 PRI "IS YOUR PROBLEM TOO MUCH OR TOO LITTLE";
205 INP D$\PRI
210 IF D$="TOO MU" THEN 220
213 IF D$="TOO LI" THEN 230
215 PRI "DON'T GET ALL SHOOK ";\GOS 500\PRI ",JUST ANSWER THE QUESTION
217 PRI "WITH 'TOO MUCH' OR 'TOO LITTLE'. WHICH IS IT";
218 GOT 205
220 PRI "YOU CALL THAT A PROBLEM?!! I SHOULD HAVE SUCH PROBLEMS!
225 PRI "IF IT BOTHERS YOU, TAKE A COLD SHOWER ";\GOSUB500\PRI"."
228 GOT 250
230 PRI "WHY ARE YOU HERE ";\GOSUB500\PRI"? YOU SHOULD BE
235 PRI "IN TOKYO OR NEW YORK OR AMSTERDAM OR SOMEPLACE WITH SOME
240 PRI "REAL ACTION.
250 PRI
255 PRI "ANY MORE PROBLEMS YOU WANT SOLVED, ";\GOSUB500\PRI;
260 INP E$\PRI
270 IF E$="YES" THEN 280
273 IF E$="NO" THEN 300
275 PRI "JUST A SIMPLE 'YES' OR 'NO' PLEASE, ";\GOSUB500\PRI"."
278 GOT 255
280 PRI "WHAT KIND (SEX, MONEY, HEALTH, JOB)";
285 GOT 125
300 PRI
302 PRI "THAT WILL BE $5.00 FOR THE ADVICE, ";\GOSUB500\PRI"."
305 PRI "PLEASE LEAVE THE MONEY ON THE TERMINAL."
307 PRI\PRI\PRI
310 PRI "DID YOU LEAVE THE MONEY";
315 INP G$\PRI
325 IF G$="YES" THEN 350
330 IF G$="NO" THEN 370
335 PRI "YOUR ANSWER OF '"G$"' CONFUSES ME, ";\GOSUB500\PRI". PLEASE
340 PRI "RESPOND WITH A 'YES' OR 'NO'.
345 GOT 310
350 PRI "HEY, ";\GOSUB500\PRI"??? YOU LEFT NO MONEY AT ALL!
355 PRI "YOU ARE CHEATING ME OUT OF MY HARD-EARNED LIVING.
360 PRI "RIP OFF, ";\GOSUB500\PRI". *******************************
365 GOT 390
370 PRI "THAT'S HONEST, ";\GOSUB500\PRI", BUT HOW DO YOU EXPECT
375 PRI "ME TO GO ON WITH MY PSYCHOLOGY STUDIES IF MY PATIENTS DON'T
380 PRI "PAY THEIR BILLS?
385 PRI\PRI\PRI "NOW LET ME TALK TO SOMEONE ELSE.
390 PRI "NICE MEETING YOU ";\GOS 500\PRI ". HAVE A NICE DAY!!
400 FOR N=1 TO 7
402 PRI
405 NEX N
410 GOT 10
500 T=A$(0)\FOR I=1 TO INT(T/6+1)\PRINT A$(I);\NEXT I
510 RETURN
999 END

READY
```

SAMPLE RUN

```
HELLO, I'M AN EDUSYSTEM-25. MY NAME IS PETEY P. EIGHT.

WHAT'S YOUR NAME? ALFRED E. NEWMAN

 HI THERE ALFRED E. NEWMAN. ARE YOU ENJOYING YOURSELF HERE
IN BEAUTIFUL MAYNARD, MASS? NAH

 ALFRED E. NEWMAN, I DON'T UNDERSTAND YOUR ANSWER OF 'NAH'.
PLEASE ANSWER 'YES' OR 'NO'. DO YOU LIKE IT HERE
IN BEAUTIFUL MAYNARD, MASS? NO

OH, SORRY TO HEAR THAT ALFRED E. NEWMAN, MAYBE WE CAN
BRIGHTEN UP YOUR STAY A BIT

SAY, ALFRED E. NEWMAN, I CAN SOLVE ALL KINDS OF PROBLEMS
EXCEPT THOSE DEALING WITH GREECE. WHAT KIND OF
PROBLEMS DO YOU HAVE (ANSWER SEX, HEALTH, MONEY,
OR JOB)? MONEY

SORRY, ALFRED E. NEWMAN, I'M BROKE TOO. WHY DON'T YOU SELL
ENCYCLOPEADIAS OR MARRY SOMEONE RICH OR STOP EATING
SO YOU WON'T NEED SO MUCH MONEY?

ANY MORE PROBLEMS YOU WANT SOLVED, ALFRED E. NEWMAN? YES

WHAT KIND (SEX, MONEY, HEALTH, JOB)? SEX

IS YOUR PROBLEM TOO MUCH OR TOO LITTLE? TOO MUCH

YOU CALL THAT A PROBLEM?!! I SHOULD HAVE SUCH PROBLEMS!
IF IT BOTHERS YOU, TAKE A COLD SHOWER ALFRED E. NEWMAN.

ANY MORE PROBLEMS YOU WANT SOLVED, ALFRED E. NEWMAN? NO


THAT WILL BE $5.00 FOR THE ADVICE, ALFRED E. NEWMAN.
PLEASE LEAVE THE MONEY ON THE TERMINAL.



DID YOU LEAVE THE MONEY? BAH

YOUR ANSWER OF 'BAH' CONFUSES ME, ALFRED E. NEWMAN. PLEASE
RESPOND WITH A 'YES' OR 'NO'
DID YOU LEAVE THE MONEY? NO

THAT'S HONEST, ALFRED E. NEWMAN, BUT HOW DO YOU EXPECT
ME TO GO ON WITH MY PSYCHOLOGY STUDIES IF MY PATIENTS DON'T
PAY THEIR BILLS?


NOW LET ME TALK TO SOMEONE ELSE.
NICE MEETING YOU ALFRED E. NEWMAN. HAVE A NICE DAY!!
```

HEX

Description

The game of Hexapawn and a method to learn a strategy for playing the game was described in "Mathematical Games" in the March
1962 issue of <u>Scientific American</u>. The method described in the
article was for a hypothetical learning machine composed of
match boxes and colored beads. This has been generalized in
the Program HEX.

The program learns by elimination of bad moves. All positions
encountered by the program and acceptable moves from them are
stored in the array P$(I). When the program encounters an un-
familiar position, the position and all legal moves from it
are added to the list. If the program loses a game, it erases
the move that led to defeat. If it hits a position from which
all moves have been deleted (they all led to defeat), it erases
the move that got it there and resigns. Eventually, the program
learns to play extremely well and, indeed, is unbeatable. The
learning strategy could be adopted to other simple games with a
finite number of moves (tic-tac-toe, small board checkers, or
other chess-based games).

For complete playing directions, respond YES or Y to the question, INSTRUCTIONS?

Computer Limitations

HEX was written in BASIC-PLUS for DIGITAL RSTS-11 and RSTS/E
systems. HEX uses string functions and concatenation extensively.
Also, the symbol ":" equals REM and "&" equals PRINT.

Program Author

Jeff Dalton
Northfield-Mt. Hermon School
Northfield, MA

PROGRAM LISTING

```
1 ! BY JEFF DALTON, CLASS OF '74, NORTHFIELD MOUNT HERMON SCHOOL
2 ! THIS PROGRAM PLAYS THE GAME 'HEXAPAWN' BY A METHOD OUTLINED IN
        'MATHEMATICAL GAMES' IN MARCH 1962 SCIENTIFIC AMERICAN.
3 ! THE PROGRAM LEARNS BY ELIMINATION OF BAD MOVES. ALL POSITIONS
        ENCOUNTERED BY THE PROGRAM AND THE ACCEPTABLE MOVES FROM THEM
        ARE STORED IN P$(I%)
4 ! WHEN THE PROGRAM ENCOUNTERS AN UNFAMILIAR POSITION, THE POSITION
        AND ALL LEGAL MOVES FROM IT ARE ADDED TO THE LIST.
5 ! IF THE PROGRAM LOSES A GAME, IT ERASES THE MOVE THAT LED TO DEFEAT.
        IF IT HITS A POSITION FROM WHICH ALL MOVES HAVE BEEN DELETED
        ( THEY ALL LED TO DEFEAT ), IT ERASES THE MOVE THAT GOT
        IT HERE AND RESIGNS.
10 INPUT "INSTRUCTIONS"; C$: IF LEFT(C$,1%)<>"Y" THEN 110
20 &: &,"THIS PROGRAM PLAYS THE GAME OF HEXAPAWN."&
   "HEXAPAWN IS PLAYED WITH CHESS PAWNS ON A 3 BY 3 BOARD. THE PAWNS ARE":&
   "MOVED AS IN CHESS - ONE SPACE FORWARD TO AN EMPTY SPACE OR ONE SPACE"
30 &"FORWARD AND DIAGONALLY TO CAPTURE AN OPPOSING MAN.":&:&CHR$(9%);
   "O THE BOARD, YOUR PAWNS ARE 'O', THE COMPUTER'S PAWNS ARE '*'":&
   "AND EMPTY SQUARES ARE '-'. TO ENTER A MOVE, TYPE THE NUMBER OF THE"
40 &"SQUARE YOU WILL MOVE FROM FOLLOWED BY THE NUMBER OF THE SQUARE":&
   "YOU WILL MOVE TO. (THE NUMBERS ARE SEPARATED BY A COMMA.)":&
50 &"   THE PROGRAM STARTS A SERIS OF GAMES KNOWING ONLY WHEN THE":&
   "GAME IS WON (A DRAW IS IMPOSSIBLE) AND HOW TO MOVE. IT HAS NO":&
   "STRATEGY AT FIRST AND JUST MOVES RANDOMLY. HOWEVER, IT LEARNS"
60 &"FROM EACH GAME. THUS, DEFEATING IT BECOMES MORE AND MORE":&
   "DIFFICULT. ALSO, TO HELP OFFSET YOUR INITIAL ADVANTAGE, YOU WILL":&
   "NOT BE TOLD HOW TO WIN THE GAME BUT MUST LEARN THIS BY PLAYING":&
100 DEF FNC$(X$,X%,Y$)=LEFT(X$,X%-1%)+Y$+RIGHT(X$,X%+LEN(Y$))
105 DEF FNN$(X%): X$=NUM$(X%): FNN$=MID$(X$,2%,LEN(X$)-2%): FNEND
110 DIM P$(50%): RANDOMIZE: Q%=0%:
        PRINT "SINCE I'M A GOOD SPORT, YOU'LL ALWAYS GO FIRST"
120 P%=0%: P$="***---OOO": &: &"NUMBERING:":&
        &"123": &"456": &"789": &
190 D%=-1%: Q$="O": GOSUB 2000: IF M$="" THEN
        PRINT "YOU CAN'T MOVE. I WIN.": GOTO 510
200 &: &"BOARD:": &LEFT(P$,3%): &MID(P$,4%,3%): &RIGHT(P$,7%): &
210 INPUT "WHAT IS YOUR MOVE"; A%,B%:
        IF INSTR(1%,M$,FNN$(A%)+FNN$(B%))=0% THEN
        PRINT "ILLEGAL MOVE.": GOTO 210
230 P$=FNC$(FNC$(P$,A%,"-"),B%,"O"):
        IF INSTR(1%,P$,"*")=0% OR INSTR(1%,P$,"O")<4% THEN
        PRINT "YOU WIN.": GOTO 500
300 P%=P%+2% !        COMPUTER'S MOVE
310 FOR C%=1% TO Q%: C$=P$(C%): IF VAL(LEFT(C$,1%))=P% AND
        MID(C$,2%,9%)=P$ THEN M$=RIGHT(C$,11%): GOTO 400
320 NEXT C%: Q$="*": D%=1%: GOSUB 2000: C%=Q%:
        IF M$="" THEN PRINT "I CAN'T MOVE, YOU WIN.": GOTO 500
400 IF M$="" THEN PRINT "I RESIGN.": GOTO 500
410 K$=LEFT(M$,2%): M$=RIGHT(M$,3%):
        IF RND>.33333333 AND M$<>"" THEN 410
420 K%=C%: A%=VAL(LEFT(K$,1%)): B%=VAL(RIGHT(K$,2%)):
        P$=FNC$(FNC$(P$,A%,"-"),B%,"*")
430 IF INSTR(1%,P$,"O")=0% OR INSTR(7%,P$,"*") THEN
        PRINT "I WIN!": GOTO 510
440 PRINT "I MOVE FROM" A% "TO" B%: GOTO 190
500 W2%=W2%+1%: I%=INSTR(1%,P$(K%),K$):
        P$(K%)=LEFT(P$(K%),I%-1%)+RIGHT(P$(K%),I%+2%) IF I%: GOTO 520
510 W1%=W1%+1%
520 &: &"BOARD:": &LEFT(P$,3%): &MID(P$,4%,3%): &RIGHT(P$,7%): &:
        & "I HAVE WON" W1% "AND YOU HAVE WON" W2% "OF" W1%+W2% "GAMES"
530 INPUT "ANOTHER GAME"; C$: IF C$="NO" THEN 9999 ELSE 120
900 ! DATA**= <- OF MOVE IN GAME<POSITION><LIST OF MOVES>
        IN <POSITION>, -=BLANK, *=COMPUTER'S PAWN, O=PLAYER'S PAWN
        <LIST OF MOVES> IS <- MOVE FROM><- MOVE TO><LIST OF MOVES>
2000 M$=""
2010 FOR J%=1% TO 9%: IF MID(P$,J%,1%)<>Q$ THEN 2050
2015 T%=J%+D%*3%: IF T%<1% OR T%>9% THEN 2025
2020 IF MID(P$,T%,1%)="-" THEN
        M$=M$+FNN$(J%)+FNN$(T%)
2025 T%=J%+D%*2%: IF T%<1% OR T%>9% OR
        (D%=1% AND (J%=1% OR J%=4% OR J%=7%)) OR
        (D%=-1% AND (J%=3% OR J%=6% OR J%=9%)) THEN 2035
2030 IF INSTR(1%,Q$+"-",MID(P$,T%,1%))=0% THEN
        M$=M$+FNN$(J%)+FNN$(T%)
2035 T%=J%+D%*4%: IF T%<1% OR T%>9% OR J%=3% OR J%=7% THEN 2050
2040 IF INSTR(1%,Q$+"-",MID(P$,T%,1%))=0% THEN
        M$=M$+FNN$(J%)+FNN$(T%)
2050 NEXT J%: IF D%=1% AND M$<>"" THEN Q%=Q%+1%: P$(Q%)=FNN$(P%)+P$+M$
2060 RETURN
9999 END
```

SAMPLE RUN

```
INSTRUCTIONS? Y

        THIS PROGRAM PLAYS THE GAME OF HEXAPAWN.
HEXAPAWN IS PLAYED WITH CHESS PAWNS ON A 3 BY 3 BOARD. THE PAWNS ARE
MOVED AS IN CHESS - ONE SPACE FORWARD TO AN EMPTY SPACE OR ONE SPACE
FORWARD AND DIAGONALLY TO CAPTURE AN OPPOSING MAN.

        ON THE BOARD, YOUR PAWNS ARE 'O', THE COMPUTER'S PAWNS ARE '*'
AND EMPTY SQUARES ARE '-'. TO ENTER A MOVE, TYPE THE NUMBER OF THE
SQUARE YOU WILL MOVE FROM FOLLOWED BY THE NUMBER OF THE SQUARE
YOU WILL MOVE TO. (THE NUMBERS ARE SEPARATED BY A COMMA.)

        THE PROGRAM STARTS A SERIES OF GAMES KNOWING ONLY WHEN THE
GAME IS WON (A DRAW IS IMPOSSIBLE) AND HOW TO MOVE. IT HAS NO
STRATEGY AT FIRST AND JUST MOVES RANDOMLY. HOWEVER, IT LEARNS
FROM EACH GAME. THUS, DEFEATING IT BECOMES MORE AND MORE
DIFFICULT. ALSO, TO HELP OFFSET YOUR INITIAL ADVANTAGE, YOU WILL
NOT BE TOLD HOW TO WIN THE GAME BUT MUST LEARN THIS BY PLAYING

SINCE I'M A GOOD SPORT, YOU'LL ALWAYS GO FIRST.
```

```
NUMBERING:
123
456
789


BOARD:
***
---
OOO

WHAT IS YOUR MOVE? 8,5
I MOVE FROM 1 TO 4

BOARD:
-**
*O-
O-O

WHAT IS YOUR MOVE? 5,3
YOU WIN.

BOARD:
-*O
*--
O-O

I HAVE WON 0 AND YOU HAVE WON 1 OF 1 GAMES
ANOTHER GAME?




NUMBERING:
123
456
789


BOARD:
***
---
OOO

WHAT IS YOUR MOVE? 8,5
I MOVE FROM 3 TO 5

BOARD:
**-
-*-
O-O

WHAT IS YOUR MOVE? 9,5
I MOVE FROM 1 TO 4
YOU CAN'T MOVE. I WIN.

BOARD:
-*-
*O-
O--

I HAVE WON 1 AND YOU HAVE WON 3 OF 4 GAMES
ANOTHER GAME?




NUMBERING:
123
456
789


BOARD:
***
---
OOO

WHAT IS YOUR MOVE? 8,5
I MOVE FROM 1 TO 5

BOARD:
-**
-*-
O-O

WHAT IS YOUR MOVE? 9,5
I MOVE FROM 3 TO 6

BOARD:
-*-
-O*
O--

WHAT IS YOUR MOVE? 7,4
I WIN!

BOARD:
-*-
OO-
--*

I HAVE WON 3 AND YOU HAVE WON 5 OF 8 GAMES
ANOTHER GAME? NO

READY
```

HI·LO

Description

This game is an adaptation of the game GUESS; however, instead
of just guessing a number between 1 and 100, in this game you
win dollars when you guess the number. The directions, in the
words of the author of the game, are as follows:

"1.   There is an amount of money, between one and one
      hundred dollars, in the "HI-LO" jackpot.
 2.   You will have six chances in which to guess the
      amount of money in the jackpot.
 3.   After each guess, the computer will tell whether
      the guess was too high or too low.
 4.   If the correct amount of money is not guessed after
      six chances, the computer will print the amount in
      the jackpot.
 5.   If the correct amount of money is guessed within the
      six chance limit, the computer will register this
      amount.
 6.   After each sequence of guesses, you have the choice
      of playing again or ending the program. If a new
      game is played, a new amount of money will constitute
      the jackpot.
 7.   If you win more than once, then your earnings are to-
      talled."

Program Author

Dean Altman
3721 Wosley
Fort Worth, TX   76133

PROGRAM LISTING

```
90 RANDOMIZE
100 PRINT "THIS IS THE GAME OF HI-LO"\PRINT
110 PRINT "YOU WILL HAVE 6 TRIES TO GUESS THE AMOUNT OF MONEY IN THE"
120 PRINT "HI-LO JACKPOT, WHICH IS BETWEEN 1AND 100 DOLLARS.  IF YOU"
130 PRINT "GUESS THE AMOUNT, YOU WIN ALL THE MONEY IN THE JACKPOT!"
140 PRINT "THEN YOU GET ANOTHER CHANCE TO WIN MORE MONEY.  HOWEVER,"
150 PRINT "IF YOU DO NOT GUESS THE AMOUNT, THE GAME ENDS."\PRINT
160 R=0
170 B=0\PRINT
180 Y=INT(100*RND)
200 PRINT "YOUR GUESS";
210 INPUT A
220 B=B+1
230 IF A=Y THEN 300
240 IF A>Y THEN 270
250 PRINT "YOUR GUESS IS TOO LOW"\GOTO 280
270 PRINT "YOUR GUESS IS TOO HIGH"
280 PRINT\IF B<6 THEN 200
290 PRINT "YOU BLEW IT....TOO BAD....THE NUMBER WAS"Y\R=0\GOTO 350
300 PRINT "GOT IT!!!!!!!!!   YOU WIN"Y"DOLLARS."
310 R=R+Y
320 PRINT "YOUR TOTAL WINNINGS ARE NOW"R"DOLLARS,"
350 PRINT\PRINT "PLAY AGAIN (YES OR NO)";
360 INPUT A$\IF A$="YES" THEN 170
380 PRINT\PRINT "SO LONG.  HOPE YOU ENJOYED YOURSELF!!"
390 END
```

SAMPLE RUN

```
THIS IS THE GAME OF HI-LO

YOU WILL HAVE 6 TRIES TO GUESS THE AMOUNT OF MONEY IN THE
HI-LO JACKPOT, WHICH IS BETWEEN 1AND 100 DOLLARS.  IF YOU
GUESS THE AMOUNT, YOU WIN ALL THE MONEY IN THE JACKPOT!
THEN YOU GET ANOTHER CHANCE TO WIN MORE MONEY.  HOWEVER,
IF YOU DO NOT GUESS THE AMOUNT, THE GAME ENDS.


YOUR GUESS? 50
YOUR GUESS IS TOO LOW

YOUR GUESS? 75
YOUR GUESS IS TOO LOW

YOUR GUESS? 87
YOUR GUESS IS TOO LOW

YOUR GUESS? 94
YOUR GUESS IS TOO HIGH

YOUR GUESS? 91
YOUR GUESS IS TOO HIGH

YOUR GUESS? 89
YOUR GUESS IS TOO LOW

YOU BLEW IT....TOO BAD....THE NUMBER WAS 90

PLAY AGAIN (YES OR NO)? YES

YOUR GUESS? 50
YOUR GUESS IS TOO HIGH

YOUR GUESS? 25
GOT IT!!!!!!!!   YOU WIN 25 DOLLARS.
YOUR TOTAL WINNINGS ARE NOW 25 DOLLARS.

PLAY AGAIN (YES OR NO)? YES

YOUR GUESS? 50
YOUR GUESS IS TOO HIGH

YOUR GUESS? 25
YOUR GUESS IS TOO LOW

YOUR GUESS? 37
YOUR GUESS IS TOO HIGH

YOUR GUESS? 32
YOUR GUESS IS TOO LOW

YOUR GUESS? 34
YOUR GUESS IS TOO LOW

YOUR GUESS? 36
YOUR GUESS IS TOO HIGH

YOU BLEW IT....TOO BAD....THE NUMBER WAS 35

PLAY AGAIN (YES OR NO)? YES

YOUR GUESS? 50
YOUR GUESS IS TOO LOW

YOUR GUESS? 75
YOUR GUESS IS TOO LOW

YOUR GUESS? 87
YOUR GUESS IS TOO HIGH

YOUR GUESS? 81
YOUR GUESS IS TOO LOW

YOUR GUESS? 84
YOUR GUESS IS TOO LOW

YOUR GUESS? 85
GOT IT!!!!!!!!   YOU WIN 85 DOLLARS.
YOUR TOTAL WINNINGS ARE NOW 85 DOLLARS.
```

```
PLAY AGAIN (YES OR NO)? YES

YOUR GUESS? 50
YOUR GUESS IS TOO LOW

YOUR GUESS? 75
YOUR GUESS IS TOO LOW

YOUR GUESS? 87
YOUR GUESS IS TOO LOW

YOUR GUESS? 94
YOUR GUESS IS TOO HIGH

YOUR GUESS? 91
YOUR GUESS IS TOO HIGH

YOUR GUESS? 89
GOT IT!!!!!!!!   YOU WIN 89 DOLLARS.
YOUR TOTAL WINNINGS ARE NOW 174 DOLLARS.

PLAY AGAIN (YES OR NO)? YES

YOUR GUESS? 50
YOUR GUESS IS TOO LOW

YOUR GUESS? 75
YOUR GUESS IS TOO HIGH

YOUR GUESS? 67
YOUR GUESS IS TOO LOW

YOUR GUESS? 71
YOUR GUESS IS TOO LOW

YOUR GUESS? 73
YOUR GUESS IS TOO HIGH

YOUR GUESS? 72
GOT IT!!!!!!!!   YOU WIN 72 DOLLARS.
YOUR TOTAL WINNINGS ARE NOW 246 DOLLARS.

PLAY AGAIN (YES OR NO)? YES

YOUR GUESS? 50
YOUR GUESS IS TOO HIGH

YOUR GUESS? 25
YOUR GUESS IS TOO LOW

YOUR GUESS? 37
YOUR GUESS IS TOO HIGH

YOUR GUESS? 31
YOUR GUESS IS TOO HIGH

YOUR GUESS? 28
YOUR GUESS IS TOO HIGH

YOUR GUESS? 27
YOUR GUESS IS TOO HIGH

YOU BLEW IT....TOO BAD....THE NUMBER WAS 26

PLAY AGAIN (YES OR NO)? NO

SO LONG.  HOPE YOU ENJOYED YOURSELF!!

READY
```

HI·Q

Description

This is a computerized version of an old European solitaire game
of logic called Hi-Q. The game starts with a pegboard shaped
like a cross having pegs in every hole but the center. The
object is to remove all 32 pegs, or as many as possible, by
jumping into an empty hole--the jumped peg is then removed.

There are several different winning strategies for playing
Hi-Q and, of course, each strategy can be played eight different
ways on the board. Can you find a consistent winner?

Program Author

Charles Lund
The American School
Hague, Netherlands

D. Ahl

PROGRAM LISTING

```
3 DIM B(70),T(9,9)
4 PRINT "THIS IS THE GAME OF HI-Q"\PRINT "HERE IS THE BOARD"\PRINT
5 PRINT "          !    !    !"
6 PRINT "         13   14   15"\PRINT
7 PRINT "          !    !    !"
8 PRINT "         22   23   24"\PRINT
9 PRINT "!    !    !    !    !    !    !"
10 PRINT "29   30   31   32   33   34   35"\PRINT
11 PRINT "!    !    !    !    !    !    !"
12 PRINT "38   39   40   41   42   43   44"\PRINT
13 PRINT "!    !    !    !    !    !    !"
14 PRINT "47   48   49   50   51   52   53"\PRINT
15 PRINT "          !    !    !"
16 PRINT "         58   59   60"\PRINT
17 PRINT "          !    !    !"
18 PRINT "         67   68   69"\PRINT
22 PRINT "TO SAVE TYPING TIME, A COMPRESSED VERSION OF THE GAME BOARD"
23 PRINT "WILL BE USED DURING PLAY.  REFER TO THE ABOVE ONE FOR PEG"
24 PRINT "NUMBERS.  O.K., LET'S BEGIN..."
28 REM *** SET UP BOARD
29 FOR R=1 TO 9
30 FOR C=1 TO 9
31 IF (R-4)*(R-5)*(R-6)=0 THEN 40
32 IF (C-4)*(C-5)*(C-6)=0 THEN 40
35 T(R,C)=-5
36 GOTO 50
40 IF (R-1)*(C-1)*(R-9)*(C-9)=0 THEN 35
42 T(R,C)=5
50 NEXT C
60 NEXT R
65 T(5,5)=0\GOSUB 500
70 REM *** INPUT MOVE AND CHECK ON LEGALITY
75 FOR W=1 TO 33
77 READ M
79 DATA 13,14,15,22,23,24,29,30,31,32,33,34,35,38,39,40,41
81 DATA 42,43,44,47,48,49,50,51,52,53,58,59,60,67,68,69
83 B(M)=-7\NEXT W
86 B(41)=-3
100 INPUT "MOVE WHICH PIECE";Z
110 IF B(Z)=-7 THEN 140
120 PRINT "ILLEGAL MOVE, TRY AGAIN..."\GOTO 100
140 INPUT "TO WHERE";P
150 IF B(P)=0 THEN 120
153 IF B(P)=-7 THEN 120
156 IF Z=P THEN 100
160 IF ((Z+P)/2)=INT((Z+P)/2) THEN 180
170 GOTO 120
180 IF (ABS(Z-P)-2)*(ABS(Z-P)-18)<>0 THEN 120
190 GOSUB 1000
200 GOSUB 500
210 GOSUB 1500
220 GOTO 100
500 REM *** PRINT BOARD
510 FOR X=1 TO 9
520 FOR Y=1 TO 9
525 IF (X-1)*(X-9)*(Y-1)*(Y-9)=0 THEN 550
530 IF (X-4)*(X-5)*(X-6)=0 THEN 570
540 IF (Y-4)*(Y-5)*(Y-6)=0 THEN 570
550 REM
560 GOTO 610
570 IF T(X,Y)<>5 THEN 600
580 PRINT TAB(Y*2)"!";
590 GOTO 610
600 PRINT TAB(Y*2)"O";
610 REM
615 NEXT Y
620 PRINT
630 NEXT X
640 RETURN
1000 REM*** UPDATE BOARD
1005 C=1\FOR X=1 TO 9
1020 FOR Y=1 TO 9
1030 IF C<>Z THEN 1220
1040 IF C+2<>P THEN 1080
1045 IF T(X,Y+1)=0 THEN 120
1050 T(X,Y+2)=5
1060 T(X,Y+1)=0\B(C+1)=-3
1070 GOTO 1200
1080 IF C+18<>P THEN 1130
1085 IF T(X+1,Y)=0 THEN 120
1090 T(X+2,Y)=5\T(X+1,Y)=0\B(C+9)=-3
1120 GOTO 1200
1130 IF C-2<>P THEN 1170
1135 IF T(X,Y-1)=0 THEN 120
1140 T(X,Y-2)=5\T(X,Y-1)=0\B(C-1)=-3
1160 GOTO 1200
1170 IF C-18<>P THEN 1220
1175 IF T(X-1,Y)=0 THEN 120
1180 T(X-2,Y)=5\T(X-1,Y)=0\B(C-9)=-3
1200 B(Z)=-3\B(P)=-7
1210 T(X,Y)=0\GOTO 1240
1220 C=C+1
1225 NEXT Y
1230 NEXT X
1240 RETURN
1500 REM *** CHECK IF GAME IS OVER
1505 F=0
1510 FOR R=2 TO 8
1520 FOR C=2 TO 8
1530 IF T(R,C)<>5 THEN 1580
1535 F=F+1
1540 FOR A=R-1 TO R+1
1545 T=0
1550 FOR B=C-1 TO C+.
1560 T=T+T(A,B)
1561 NEXT B
1564 IF T<>10 THEN 1567
1565 IF T(A,C)<>0 THEN 1630
1567 NEXT A
1568 FOR X=C-1 TO C+1
1569 T=0
1570 FOR Y=R-1 TO R+1
1571 T=T+T(Y,X)
1572 NEXT Y
1573 IF T<>10 THEN 1575
1574 IF T(R,X)<>0 THEN 1630
1575 NEXT X
1580 NEXT C
1590 NEXT R
```

```
1600 REM *** GAME IS OVER
1605 PRINT "THE GAME IS OVER,"
1610 PRINT "YOU HAD"F;"PIECES REMAINING"
1611 IF F<>1 THEN 1615
1612 PRINT "BRAVO!  YOU MADE A PERFECT SCORE!!"
1613 PRINT "SAVE THIS PAPER AS A RECORD OF YOUR WORK."
1615 PRINT\INPUT "PLAY AGAIN (YES OR NO)"IAS
1617 IF AS="NO" THEN 2000
1618 RESTORE\GOTO 25
1620 STOP
1630 RETURN
2000 PRINT\PRINT "SO LONG FOR NOW,"\PRINT
2005 END
```

SAMPLE RUN

```
THIS IS THE GAME OF HI-Q
HERE IS THE BOARD

              !    !    !
             13   14   15

              !    !    !
             22   23   24

  !    !    !    !    !    !    !
 29   30   31   32   33   34   35

  !    !    !    !    !    !    !
 38   39   40   41   42   43   44

  !    !    !    !    !    !    !
 47   48   49   50   51   52   53

              !    !    !
             58   59   60

              !    !    !
             67   68   69

TO SAVE TYPING TIME, A COMPRESSED VERSION OF THE GAME BOARD
WILL BE USED DURING PLAY.  REFER TO THE ABOVE ONE FOR PEG
NUMBERS.  O.K., LET'S BEGIN...
                ! ! !
                ! ! !
          ! ! ! ! ! ! !
          ! ! ! O ! ! !
          ! ! ! ! ! ! !
                ! ! !
                ! ! !

MOVE WHICH PIECE? 39
TO WHERE? 41

                ! ! !
                ! ! !
          ! ! ! ! ! ! !
          ! O O ! ! ! !
          ! ! ! ! ! ! !
                ! ! !
                ! ! !

MOVE WHICH PIECE? 22
TO WHERE? 40

                ! ! !
                O ! !
          ! ! O ! ! ! !
          ! O ! ! ! ! !
          ! ! ! ! ! ! !
                ! ! !
                ! ! !

MOVE WHICH PIECE? 49
TO WHERE? 31

                ! ! !
                O ! !
          ! ! ! ! ! ! !
          ! O O ! ! ! !
          ! ! O ! ! ! !
                ! ! !
                ! ! !

MOVE WHICH PIECE? 47
TO WHERE? 49

                ! ! !
                O ! !
          ! ! ! ! ! ! !
          ! O O ! ! ! !
          O O ! ! ! ! !
                ! ! !
                ! ! !

MOVE WHICH PIECE? 58
TO WHERE? 40

                ! ! !
                O ! !
          ! ! ! ! ! ! !
          ! O ! ! ! ! !
          O O O ! ! ! !
                O ! !
                ! ! !

MOVE WHICH PIECE? 41
TO WHERE? 39

                O ! !
          ! ! ! ! ! ! !
          ! ! O ! ! ! !
          O O O ! ! ! !
                O ! !
                ! ! !
```

127

HMRABI

GOVERN ANCIENT SUMERIA

Description

In this game you direct the administrator of Sumeria, Hamurabi, how to manage the city. The city initially has 1,000 acres, 100 people and 3,000 bushels of grain in storage.

You may buy and sell land with your neighboring city-states for bushels of grain--the price will vary between 17 and 26 bushels per acre. You also must use grain to feed your people and as seed to plant the next year's crop.

You will quickly find that a certain number of people can only tend a certain amount of land and that people starve if they are not fed enough. You also have the unexpected to contend with such as a plague, rats destroying stored grain, and variable harvests.

You will also find that managing just the few resources in this game is not a trivial job over a period of say ten years. The crisis of population density rears its head very rapidly.

Source

This is translated from the original FOCAL program which has been floating around DIGITAL for nine or more years.

Digital Equipment Corp.
Maynard, MA 01754

```
10 REM *** CONVERTED FROM THE ORIGINAL FOCAL PROGRAM AND MODIFIED FOR
20 REM *** EDUSYSTEM 70 BY DAVID AHL, DIGITAL
80 PRINT "TRY YOUR HAND AT GOVERNING ANCIENT SUMERIA"
85 PRINT "SUCCESSFULLY FOR A 10-YR TERM OF OFFICE."!PRINT
90 RANDOMIZE!LET D1=0!LET P1=0
100 LET Z=0!LET P=95!LET S=2800!LET H=3000!LET E=H-S
110 LET Y=3!LET A=H/Y!LET I=5!LET Q=1
210 LET D=0
215 PRINT!PRINT!PRINT "HAMURABI:  I BEG TO REPORT TO YOU,"!LET Z=Z+1
217 PRINT "IN YEAR"Z","D"PEOPLE STARVED,"I"CAME TO THE CITY."
218 LET P=P+I
227 IF Q>0 THEN 230
228 LET P=INT(P/2)
229 PRINT "A HORRIBLE PLAGUE STRUCK!  HALF THE PEOPLE DIED."
230 PRINT "POPULATION IS NOW"P
232 PRINT "THE CITY NOW OWNS"A"ACRES."
235 PRINT "YOU HARVESTED"Y"BUSHELS PER ACRE."
250 PRINT "RATS ATE"E"BUSHELS."
260 PRINT "YOU NOW HAVE"S"BUSHELS IN STORE."!PRINT
270 IF Z=11 THEN 860
310 LET C=INT(10*RND(0))!LET Y=C+17
312 PRINT "LAND IS TRADING AT"Y"BUSHELS PER ACRE."
320 PRINT "HOW MANY ACRES DO YOU WISH TO BUY";
321 INPUT Q!IF Q<0 THEN 850
322 IF Y*Q<=S THEN 330
323 GOSUB 710
324 GOTO 320
330 IF Q=0 THEN 340
331 LET A=A+Q!LET S=S-Y*Q!LET C=0
334 GOTO 400
340 PRINT "HOW MANY ACRES DO YOU WISH TO SELL";
341 INPUT Q!IF Q<0 THEN 850
342 IF Q<A THEN 350
343 GOSUB 720
344 GOTO 340
350 LET A=A-Q!LET S=S+Y*Q!LET C=0
400 PRINT
410 PRINT "HOW MANY BUSHELS DO YOU WISH TO FEED YOUR PEOPLE";
411 INPUT Q
412 IF Q<0 THEN 850
418 REM *** TRYING TO USE MORE GRAIN THAN IN THE SILOS?
420 IF Q<=S THEN 430
421 GOSUB 710
422 GOTO 410
430 LET S=S-Q!LET C=1!PRINT
440 PRINT "HOW MANY ACRES DO YOU WISH TO PLANT WITH SEED";
441 INPUT D!IF D=0 THEN 511
442 IF D<0 THEN 850
444 REM *** TRYING TO PLANT MORE ACRES THAN YOU OWN?
445 IF D<=A THEN 450
446 GOSUB 720
447 GOTO 440
449 REM *** ENOUGH GRAIN FOR SEED?
450 IF INT(D/2)<S THEN 455
452 GOSUB 710
453 GOTO 440
454 REM *** ENOUGH PEOPLE TO TEND THE CROPS?
455 IF D<10*P THEN 510
460 PRINT "BUT YOU HAVE ONLY"P"PEOPLE TO TEND THE FIELDS. NOW THEN,"
470 GOTO 440
510 LET S=S-INT(D/2)
511 GOSUB 800
512 REM *** A BOUNTYFULL HARVEST!!
515 LET Y=C!LET H=D*Y!LET E=0
521 GOSUB 800
522 IF INT(C/2)<>C/2 THEN 530
523 REM *** THE RATS ARE RUNNING WILD!!
525 LET E=INT(S/C)
530 LET S=S-E+H
531 GOSUB 800
532 REM *** LET'S HAVE SOME BABIES
533 LET I=INT(C*(20*A+S)/P/100+1)
539 REM *** HOW MANY PEOPLE HAD FULL TUMMIES?
540 LET C=INT(Q/20)
541 REM *** HORRORS, A 15% CHANCE OF PLAGUE
542 LET Q=INT(10*(2*RND(0)-.3))
550 IF P<C THEN 210
551 REM *** STARVE ENOUGH FOR IMPEACHMENT?
552 LET D=P-C!IF D>.45*P THEN 560
553 LET P1=((Z-1)*P1+D*100/P)/Z
555 LET P=C!LET D1=D1+D!GOTO 215
560 PRINT!PRINT "YOU STARVED"D"PEOPLE IN ONE YEAR!!!"
565 PRINT "DUE TO THIS EXTREME MISMANAGEMENT YOU HAVE NOT ONLY"
566 PRINT "BEEN IMPEACHED AND THROWN OUT OF OFFICE BUT YOU HAVE"
567 PRINT "ALSO BEEN DECLARED 'NATIONAL FINK'!!"!GOTO 990
710 PRINT "HAMURABI:  THINK AGAIN, YOU HAVE ONLY"
711 PRINT S"BUSHELS OF GRAIN.  NOW THEN,"
712 RETURN
720 PRINT "HAMURABI:  THINK AGAIN. YOU OWN ONLY"A"ACRES.  NOW THEN,"
730 RETURN
800 LET C=INT(RND(0)*5)+1
801 RETURN
850 PRINT!PRINT "HAMURABI:  I CANNOT DO WHAT YOU WISH."
855 PRINT "GET YOURSELF ANOTHER STEWARD!!!!!"
857 GOTO 990
860 PRINT "IN YOUR 10-YEAR TERM OF OFFICE,"P1"PERCENT OF THE"
862 PRINT "POPULATION STARVED PER YEAR ON AVERAGE, I.E., A TOTAL OF"
865 PRINT D1"PEOPLE DIED!!"!LET L=A/P
870 PRINT "YOU STARTED WITH 10 ACRES PER PERSON AND ENDED WITH"
875 PRINT L"ACRES PER PERSON."!PRINT
880 IF P1>33 THEN 565
885 IF L<7 THEN 565
890 IF P1>10 THEN 940
892 IF L<9 THEN 940
895 IF P1>3 THEN 960
896 IF L<10 THEN 960
900 PRINT "A FANTASTIC PERFORMANCE!!!  CHARLEMAGNE, DISRAELI, AND"
905 PRINT "JEFFERSON COMBINED COULD NOT HAVE DONE BETTER!"!GOTO 990
940 PRINT "YOUR HEAVY-HANDED PERFORMANCE SMACKS OF NERO AND IVAN IV."
945 PRINT "THE PEOPLE (REMAINING) FIND YOU AN UNPLEASANT RULER, AND,"
950 PRINT "FRANKLY, HATE YOUR GUTS!"!GOTO 990
960 PRINT "YOUR PERFORMANCE COULD HAVE BEEN SOMEWHAT BETTER, BUT"
965 PRINT "REALLY WASN'T TOO BAD AT ALL. "INT(P*.8*RND)"PEOPLE WOULD"
970 PRINT "DEARLY LIKE TO SEE YOU ASSASSINATED BUT WE ALL HAVE OUR"
975 PRINT "TRIVIAL PROBLEMS."
990 PRINT!FOR N=1 TO 10!PRINT CHR$(7);!NEXT N
995 PRINT "SO LONG FOR NOW."!PRINT
999 END
```

```
HAMURABI:  I BEG TO REPORT TO YOU,
IN YEAR 1 , 0 PEOPLE STARVED, 5 CAME TO THE CITY.
POPULATION IS NOW 100
THE CITY NOW OWNS 1000 ACRES.
YOU HARVESTED 3 BUSHELS PER ACRE.
RATS ATE 200 BUSHELS.
YOU NOW HAVE 2800 BUSHELS IN STORE.

LAND IS TRADING AT 17 BUSHELS PER ACRE.
HOW MANY ACRES DO YOU WISH TO BUY? 20

HOW MANY BUSHELS DO YOU WISH TO FEED YOUR PEOPLE? 1900

HOW MANY ACRES DO YOU WISH TO PLANT WITH SEED? 1000
BUT YOU ONLY HAVE 100 PEOPLE TO TEND THE FIELDS. NOW THEN,

HOW MANY ACRES DO YOU WISH TO PLANT WITH SEED? 990


HAMURABI:  I BEG TO REPORT TO YOU,
IN YEAR 2 , 5 PEOPLE STARVED, 11 CAME TO THE CITY.
POPULATION IS NOW 106
THE CITY NOW OWNS 1020 ACRES.
YOU HARVESTED 5 BUSHELS PER ACRE.
RATS ATE 0 BUSHELS.
YOU NOW HAVE 5015 BUSHELS IN STORE.

LAND IS TRADING AT 26 BUSHELS PER ACRE.
HOW MANY ACRES DO YOU WISH TO BUY? 0
HOW MANY ACRES DO YOU WISH TO SELL? 50

HOW MANY BUSHELS DO YOU WISH TO FEED YOUR PEOPLE? 2120

HOW MANY ACRES DO YOU WISH TO PLANT WITH SEED? 970


HAMURABI:  I BEG TO REPORT TO YOU,
IN YEAR 3 , 0 PEOPLE STARVED, 5 CAME TO THE CITY.
POPULATION IS NOW 111
THE CITY NOW OWNS 970 ACRES.
YOU HARVESTED 2 BUSHELS PER ACRE.
RATS ATE 1855 BUSHELS.
YOU NOW HAVE 3795 BUSHELS IN STORE.

LAND IS TRADING AT 20 BUSHELS PER ACRE.
HOW MANY ACRES DO YOU WISH TO BUY? 50

HOW MANY BUSHELS DO YOU WISH TO FEED YOUR PEOPLE? 2220

HOW MANY ACRES DO YOU WISH TO PLANT WITH SEED? 1000


HAMURABI:  I BEG TO REPORT TO YOU,
IN YEAR 4 , 0 PEOPLE STARVED, 2 CAME TO THE CITY.
POPULATION IS NOW 113
THE CITY NOW OWNS 1020 ACRES.
YOU HARVESTED 1 BUSHELS PER ACRE.
RATS ATE 0 BUSHELS.
YOU NOW HAVE 1075 BUSHELS IN STORE.

LAND IS TRADING AT 21 BUSHELS PER ACRE.
HOW MANY ACRES DO YOU WISH TO BUY? 0
HOW MANY ACRES DO YOU WISH TO SELL? 50

HOW MANY BUSHELS DO YOU WISH TO FEED YOUR PEOPLE? 2200
HAMURABI:  THINK AGAIN. YOU HAVE ONLY
 2125 BUSHELS OF GRAIN.  NOW THEN,

HOW MANY BUSHELS DO YOU WISH TO FEED YOUR PEOPLE? 1500\0051\1725

HOW MANY ACRES DO YOU WISH TO PLANT WITH SEED? 800
HAMURABI:  THINK AGAIN. YOU HAVE ONLY
 400 BUSHELS OF GRAIN.  NOW THEN,

HOW MANY ACRES DO YOU WISH TO PLANT WITH SEED? 790


HAMURABI:  I BEG TO REPORT TO YOU,
IN YEAR 5 , 27 PEOPLE STARVED, 2 CAME TO THE CITY.
A HORRIBLE PLAGUE STRUCK!  HALF THE PEOPLE DIED.
POPULATION IS NOW 44
THE CITY NOW OWNS 970 ACRES.
YOU HARVESTED 3 BUSHELS PER ACRE.
RATS ATE 2 BUSHELS.
YOU NOW HAVE 2373 BUSHELS IN STORE.

LAND IS TRADING AT 26 BUSHELS PER ACRE.
HOW MANY ACRES DO YOU WISH TO BUY? 0
HOW MANY ACRES DO YOU WISH TO SELL? 50

HOW MANY BUSHELS DO YOU WISH TO FEED YOUR PEOPLE? 880

HOW MANY ACRES DO YOU WISH TO PLANT WITH SEED? 430


HAMURABI:  I BEG TO REPORT TO YOU,
IN YEAR 6 , 0 PEOPLE STARVED, 15 CAME TO THE CITY.
POPULATION IS NOW 59
THE CITY NOW OWNS 920 ACRES.
YOU HARVESTED 5 BUSHELS PER ACRE.
RATS ATE 1289 BUSHELS.
YOU NOW HAVE 3439 BUSHELS IN STORE.

LAND IS TRADING AT 22 BUSHELS PER ACRE.
HOW MANY ACRES DO YOU WISH TO BUY? 0
HOW MANY ACRES DO YOU WISH TO SELL? 0

HOW MANY BUSHELS DO YOU WISH TO FEED YOUR PEOPLE? 1180

HOW MANY ACRES DO YOU WISH TO PLANT WITH SEED? 580


HAMURABI:  I BEG TO REPORT TO YOU,
IN YEAR 7 , 0 PEOPLE STARVED, 12 CAME TO THE CITY.
POPULATION IS NOW 71
THE CITY NOW OWNS 920 ACRES.
YOU HARVESTED 3 BUSHELS PER ACRE.
RATS ATE 0 BUSHELS.
YOU NOW HAVE 3709 BUSHELS IN STORE.
```

129

HOCKEY

ICE HOCKEY VS. CORNELL

Description

This is a simulation of a regulation, three-period ice hockey game. Your opponent is Cornell University. You may use three kinds of shots:

1. Slap Shot
2. Flick Shot
3. Wrist Shot

The game is very comprehensive starting with the face-off, and throughout the game with icing and high sticking penalties, shots hitting the post, shots being wide and being blocked by the goalie.

In the event of a tie at the end of three periods, the game automatically goes into sudden-death overtime.

Program Author

Thanks to Mrs. Kingsley Norris for submitting the program. It was written by:

Charles Buttrey
Eaglebrook School
Deerfield, MA 01342

PROGRAM LISTING

```
10   LET A1=INT(14*RND(X)+6)
20   LET X=1
30   REM *** CONVERTED FROM BRAND X TO DIGITAL RSTS/E BY DAVID AHL
40   PRINT " N.B. THIS PROGRAM IS DESIGNED FOR THOSE WHO KNOW NOTHING"
50   PRINT " ABOUT HOCKEY LIKE MYSELF.  --- C. BUTTREY"
60   PRINT " THIS IS CORNELL U. HOCKEY,"
70   PRINT " I AM CORNELL, WHO ARE YOU";
90   INPUT A$
100  PRINT
110  PRINT " YOU HAVE THREE SHOTS!"
120  PRINT "     1. SLAP SHOT,"
130  PRINT "     2. FLICK SHOT,"
140  PRINT "     3. WRIST SHOT,"
150  PRINT
160  PRINT " HERE IS THE FACE-OFF!"
170  PRINT " SCORE!"
180  PRINT " CORNELL "A
190  PRINT " "A$" "B
200  IF X=2 THEN 240
210  IF X=3 THEN 260
220  IF A+B >= (1/3*A1) THEN 1560
230  GOTO 290
240  IF A+B >= (2/3*A1) THEN 1630
250  GOTO 290
260  IF (A+B) >= (A1) THEN 1710
270  GOTO 290
280  IF B=3 THEN 1560
290  LET C=INT(2*RND(X)+1)
300  IF C=1 THEN 330
310  PRINT " "A$" WINS THE FACE-OFF,"
320  GOTO 650
330  PRINT " CORNELL TAKES THE FACE-OFF,"
340  LET D=INT(3*RND(X)+1)
350  IF D=1 THEN 500
360  IF D=2 THEN 570
370  PRINT " WRIST SHOT..."
380  LET E=INT(5*RND(X)+1)
390  IF E=4 THEN 470
400  PRINT " SHOT IS MISSED,"
410  LET F=INT(2*RND(X)+1)
420  IF F=1 THEN 450
430  PRINT " CORNELL REGAINS THE PUCK,"
440  GOTO 340
450  PRINT " "A$" TAKES THE PUCK,"
460  GOTO 650
470  PRINT " **GOOD!**"
480  LET A=A+1
490  GOTO 160
500  PRINT " SLAP SHOT..."
510  LET C1=INT(3*RND(X)+1)
520  IF C1=2 THEN 540
530  GOTO 560
540  PRINT " ICING PENALTY....."
550  GOTO 450
560  GOTO 380
570  PRINT " FLICK SHOT.."
580  LET S1=INT(3*RND(X)+1)
590  IF S1=3 THEN 610
600  GOTO 640
610  PRINT " PENALTY FOR HIGH STICKING! CORNELL MAN PUT IN BOX FOR"
620  PRINT " TWO MINUTES!"
630  GOTO 1110
640  GOTO 380
650  PRINT " YOUR SHOT";
660  INPUT G
670  IF G=1 THEN 720
680  IF G=2 THEN 900
690  IF G=3 THEN 970
700  PRINT " INPUT EITHER '1' '2' OR '3'"
710  GOTO 650
720  PRINT " SLAP SHOT,"
730  LET Z1=INT(3*RND(X)+1)
740  IF Z1=2 THEN 760
750  GOTO 780
760  PRINT " ICING PENALTY....."
770  GOTO 1090
780  LET H=INT(5*RND(X)+1)
790  IF H=1 THEN 870
800  PRINT " SHOT IS WIDE,"
810  LET I=INT(2*RND(X)+1)
820  IF I=1 THEN 850
830  PRINT " CORNELL TAKES THE PUCK,"
840  GOTO 990
850  PRINT " "A$" REGAINS THE PUCK,"
860  GOTO 650
870  PRINT " **GOOD!**"
880  LET B=B+1
890  GOTO 160
900  PRINT " FLICK SHOT...."
910  LET B1=INT(3*RND(X)+1)
920  IF B1=1 THEN 940
930  GOTO 960
940  PRINT " ICING PENALTY....."
950  GOTO 830
960  GOTO 780
970  PRINT " WRIST SHOT.."
980  GOTO 780
990  PRINT " CORNELL SHOT!"
1000 LET J=INT(3*RND(X)+1)
1010 IF J=1 THEN 1160
1020 IF J=2 THEN 1210
1030 PRINT " SLAP SHOT,"
1040 LET K=INT(5*RND(X)+1)
1050 IF K=1 THEN 1130
1060 PRINT " SHOT HITS THE POST,"
1070 LET L=INT(2*RND(X)+1)
1080 IF L=1 THEN 1110
1090 PRINT " CORNELL REGAINS THE PUCK,"
1100 GOTO 990
1110 PRINT " "A$" REGAINS THE PUCK,"
1120 GOTO 1310
1130 PRINT " **GOOD!**"
1140 LET A=A+1
1150 GOTO 160
1160 PRINT " WRIST SHOT"
1170 LET M=INT(5*RND(X)+1)
```

```
1180 IF M=5 THEN 1130
1190 PRINT " SHOT IS HIGH,"
1200 GOTO 1070
1210 PRINT " FLICK SHOT"
1220 LET T1=INT(3*RND(X)+1)
1230 IF T1=1 THEN 1250
1240 GOTO 1270
1250 PRINT " ICING PENALTY....."
1260 GOTO 450
1270 LET N=INT(5*RND(X)+1)
1280 IF N=1 THEN 1130
1290 PRINT " SHOT IS BLOCKED BY THE GOALIE,"
1300 GOTO 1070
1310 PRINT " YOUR SHOT";
1320 INPUT O
1330 IF O=1 THEN 1430
1340 IF O=2 THEN 1540
1350 PRINT " WRIST SHOT,"
1360 LET P=INT(5*RND(X)+1)
1370 IF P=2 THEN 870
1380 PRINT " SHOT IS BARELY WIDE..."
1390 LET Q=INT(3*RND(X)+1)
1400 IF Q=1 THEN 830
1410 PRINT " "A$" REGAINS THE PUCK,"
1420 GOTO 650
1430 PRINT " SLAP SHOT"
1440 LET D1=INT(3*RND(X)+1)
1450 IF D1=3 THEN 1470
1460 GOTO 1500
1470 PRINT " PENALTY FOR HIGH STICKING! "A$" MAN PUT IN PENALTY"
1480 PRINT " BOX FOR TWO MINUTES"
1490 GOTO 830
1500 LET R=INT(5*RND(X)+1)
1510 IF R=1 THEN 870
1520 PRINT " SHOT IS TAKEN BY THE CORNELL GOALIE,"
1530 GOTO 830
1540 PRINT " FLICK SHOT"
1550 GOTO 1500
1560 PRINT "    ***** END OF FIRST PERIOD *****"
1570 LET X=2
1580 PRINT " SCORE!"
1590 PRINT " CORNELL "A
1600 PRINT " "A$" "B
1610 PRINT " START OF SECOND PERIOD,"
1620 GOTO 160
1630 PRINT " ***** END OF SECOND PERIOD *****"
1640 LET X=3
1650 PRINT " SCORE!"
1660 PRINT " CORNELL "A
1670 PRINT " "A$" "B
1680 PRINT ""
1690 PRINT " START OF THIRD PERIOD,"
1700 GOTO 160
1710 PRINT " ***** END OF GAME *****"
1720 IF A=B THEN 1770
1730 PRINT " FINAL SCORE!"
1740 PRINT " CORNELL "A
1750 PRINT " "A$" "B
1760 STOP
1770 PRINT " SINCE SCORE IS TIED, WE WILL HAVE TO GO"
1780 PRINT " INTO SUDDEN-DEATH!"
1790 PRINT " HERE IS THE FACE-OFF,"
1800 PRINT " SCORE!"
1810 PRINT " CORNELL "A
1820 PRINT " "A$" "B
1830 LET S=INT(2*RND(X)+1)
1840 IF S=1 THEN 1870
1850 PRINT " "A$" WINS THE FACE-OFF,"
1860 GOTO 2080
1870 PRINT " CORNELL WINS THE FACE-OFF,"
1880 LET T=INT(3*RND(X)+1)
1890 IF T=1 THEN 2040
1900 IF T=2 THEN 2060
1910 PRINT " WRIST SHOT"
1920 LET U=INT(5*RND(X)+1)
1930 IF U=1 THEN 2010
1940 PRINT " SHOT IS MISSED,"
1950 LET V=INT(2*RND(X)+1)
1960 IF V=1 THEN 1990
1970 PRINT " "A$" TAKES THE PUCK,"
1980 GOTO 2080
1990 PRINT " CORNELL REGAINS THE PUCK,"
2000 GOTO 1880
2010 PRINT " **GOOD!**"
2020 LET A=A+1
2030 GOTO 2260
2040 PRINT " SLAP SHOT"
2050 GOTO 1920
2060 PRINT " FLICK SHOT,"
2070 GOTO 1920
2080 PRINT " YOUR SHOT";
2090 INPUT W
2100 IF W=1 THEN 2220
2110 IF W=2 THEN 2240
2120 PRINT "WRIST SHOT,"
2130 LET Y=INT(5*RND(X)+1)
2140 IF Y=4 THEN 2190
2150 PRINT " SHOT IS MISSED,"
2160 LET Z=INT(2*RND(X)+1)
2170 IF Z=1 THEN 1990
2180 GOTO 1970
2190 PRINT " **GOOD!**"
2200 LET B=B+1
2210 GOTO 2260
2220 PRINT " SLAP SHOT,"
2230 GOTO 2130
2240 PRINT " FLICK SHOT,"
2250 GOTO 2130
2260 PRINT " GAME IS OVER!!"
2270 PRINT " FINAL SCORE!"
2280 PRINT " CORNELL "A
2290 PRINT " "A$" "B
2300 END
```

SAMPLE RUN
N.B. THIS PROGRAM IS DESIGNED FOR THOSE WHO KNOW NOTHING
ABOUT HOCKEY LIKE MYSELF. --- C. BUTTREY
THIS IS CORNELL U. HOCKEY.
I AM CORNELL, WHO ARE YOU? HARVARD

YOU HAVE THREE SHOTS:
    1. SLAP SHOT.
    2. FLICK SHOT.
    3. WRIST SHOT.

HERE IS THE FACE-OFF:
SCORE:
CORNELL   0
HARVARD   0
HARVARD WINS THE FACE-OFF.
YOUR SHOT? 1
SLAP SHOT.
SHOT IS WIDE.
HARVARD REGAINS THE PUCK.
YOUR SHOT? 2
FLICK SHOT....
ICING PENALTY.....
CORNELL TAKES THE PUCK.
CORNELL SHOT:
FLICK SHOT
ICING PENALTY.....
HARVARD TAKES THE PUCK.
YOUR SHOT? 3
WRIST SHOT..
SHOT IS WIDE.
HARVARD REGAINS THE PUCK.
YOUR SHOT? 2
FLICK SHOT....
SHOT IS WIDE.
HARVARD REGAINS THE PUCK.
YOUR SHOT? 1
SLAP SHOT.
GOOD!
HERE IS THE FACE-OFF:
SCORE:
CORNELL   0
HARVARD   1
HARVARD WINS THE FACE-OFF.
YOUR SHOT? 3
WRIST SHOT..
SHOT IS WIDE.
HARVARD REGAINS THE PUCK.
YOUR SHOT? 2
FLICK SHOT....
ICING PENALTY.....
CORNELL TAKES THE PUCK.
CORNELL SHOT:
FLICK SHOT
ICING PENALTY.....
HARVARD TAKES THE PUCK.
YOUR SHOT? 1
SLAP SHOT.
GOOD!
HERE IS THE FACE-OFF:
SCORE:
CORNELL   0
HARVARD   2
CORNELL TAKES THE FACE-OFF.
WRIST SHOT...
SHOT IS MISSED.
CORNELL REGAINS THE PUCK.
WRIST SHOT...
GOOD!
HERE IS THE FACE-OFF:
SCORE:
CORNELL   1
HARVARD   2
CORNELL TAKES THE FACE-OFF.
WRIST SHOT...
SHOT IS MISSED.
HARVARD TAKES THE PUCK.
YOUR SHOT? 1
SLAP SHOT.
SHOT IS WIDE.
CORNELL TAKES THE PUCK.
CORNELL SHOT:
FLICK SHOT
SHOT IS BLOCKED BY THE GOALIE.
HARVARD REGAINS THE PUCK.
YOUR SHOT? 2
FLICK SHOT
SHOT IS TAKEN BY THE CORNELL GOALIE.
CORNELL TAKES THE PUCK.
CORNELL SHOT:
SLAP SHOT.
SHOT HITS THE POST.
HARVARD REGAINS THE PUCK.
YOUR SHOT? 3
WRIST SHOT.
SHOT IS BARELY WIDE...
HARVARD REGAINS THE PUCK.
YOUR SHOT? 3
WRIST SHOT..
SHOT IS WIDE.
HARVARD REGAINS THE PUCK.
YOUR SHOT? 2
FLICK SHOT....
SHOT IS WIDE.
HARVARD REGAINS THE PUCK.
YOUR SHOT? 1
SLAP SHOT.
SHOT IS WIDE.
CORNELL TAKES THE PUCK.
CORNELL SHOT:
SLAP SHOT.
GOOD!
HERE IS THE FACE-OFF:
SCORE:
CORNELL   2
HARVARD   2
CORNELL TAKES THE FACE-OFF.
WRIST SHOT...
SHOT IS MISSED.
HARVARD TAKES THE PUCK.
YOUR SHOT? 1
SLAP SHOT.

ICING PENALTY.....
CORNELL REGAINS THE PUCK.
CORNELL SHOT:
SLAP SHOT.
SHOT HITS THE POST.
HARVARD REGAINS THE PUCK.
YOUR SHOT? 2
FLICK SHOT
GOOD!
HERE IS THE FACE-OFF:
SCORE:
CORNELL   2
HARVARD   3
HARVARD WINS THE FACE-OFF.
YOUR SHOT? 3
WRIST SHOT..
SHOT IS WIDE.
CORNELL TAKES THE PUCK.
CORNELL SHOT:
FLICK SHOT
SHOT IS BLOCKED BY THE GOALIE.
HARVARD REGAINS THE PUCK.
YOUR SHOT? 2
FLICK SHOT
SHOT IS TAKEN BY THE CORNELL GOALIE.
CORNELL TAKES THE PUCK.
CORNELL SHOT:
WRIST SHOT
GOOD!
HERE IS THE FACE-OFF:
SCORE:
CORNELL   3
HARVARD   3
    ***** END OF FIRST PERIOD *****
SCORE:
CORNELL   3
HARVARD   3
START OF SECOND PERIOD.
HERE IS THE FACE-OFF:
SCORE:
CORNELL   3
HARVARD   3
HARVARD WINS THE FACE-OFF.
YOUR SHOT? 1
SLAP SHOT.
SHOT IS WIDE.
CORNELL TAKES THE PUCK.
CORNELL SHOT:
FLICK SHOT
SHOT IS BLOCKED BY THE GOALIE.
CORNELL REGAINS THE PUCK.
CORNELL SHOT:
FLICK SHOT
ICING PENALTY.....
HARVARD TAKES THE PUCK.
YOUR SHOT? 2
FLICK SHOT....
SHOT IS WIDE.
CORNELL TAKES THE PUCK.
CORNELL SHOT:
SLAP SHOT.
SHOT HITS THE POST.
CORNELL REGAINS THE PUCK.
CORNELL SHOT:
FLICK SHOT
SHOT IS BLOCKED BY THE GOALIE.
CORNELL REGAINS THE PUCK.
CORNELL SHOT:
WRIST SHOT
SHOT IS HIGH.
HARVARD REGAINS THE PUCK.
YOUR SHOT? 3
WRIST SHOT.
SHOT IS BARELY WIDE...
HARVARD REGAINS THE PUCK.
YOUR SHOT? 2
FLICK SHOT....
ICING PENALTY.....
CORNELL TAKES THE PUCK.
CORNELL SHOT:
WRIST SHOT
SHOT IS HIGH.
HARVARD REGAINS THE PUCK.
YOUR SHOT? 1
SLAP SHOT
SHOT IS TAKEN BY THE CORNELL GOALIE.
CORNELL TAKES THE PUCK.
CORNELL SHOT:
SLAP SHOT.
SHOT HITS THE POST.
HARVARD REGAINS THE PUCK.
YOUR SHOT? 2
FLICK SHOT
GOOD!
HERE IS THE FACE-OFF:
SCORE:
CORNELL   3
HARVARD   4

CORNELL TAKES THE FACE-OFF.
SLAP SHOT...
ICING PENALTY.....
HARVARD TAKES THE PUCK.
YOUR SHOT? 3
WRIST SHOT..
SHOT IS WIDE.
CORNELL TAKES THE PUCK.
CORNELL SHOT:
SLAP SHOT.
SHOT HITS THE POST.
CORNELL REGAINS THE PUCK.
CORNELL SHOT:
FLICK SHOT
SHOT IS BLOCKED BY THE GOALIE.
HARVARD REGAINS THE PUCK.
YOUR SHOT? 2
FLICK SHOT
SHOT IS TAKEN BY THE CORNELL GOALIE.
CORNELL TAKES THE PUCK.
CORNELL SHOT:
WRIST SHOT
GOOD!
HERE IS THE FACE-OFF:
SCORE:
CORNELL   4
HARVARD   4
HARVARD WINS THE FACE-OFF.
YOUR SHOT? 2
FLICK SHOT....
SHOT IS WIDE.
HARVARD REGAINS THE PUCK.
YOUR SHOT? 2
FLICK SHOT....
GOOD!
HERE IS THE FACE-OFF:
SCORE:
CORNELL   4
HARVARD   5
CORNELL TAKES THE FACE-OFF.
SLAP SHOT...
SHOT IS MISSED.
HARVARD TAKES THE PUCK.
YOUR SHOT? 3
WRIST SHOT..
GOOD!
HERE IS THE FACE-OFF:
SCORE:
CORNELL   4
HARVARD   6
HARVARD WINS THE FACE-OFF.
YOUR SHOT? 1
SLAP SHOT.
SHOT IS WIDE.
HARVARD REGAINS THE PUCK.
YOUR SHOT? 1
SLAP SHOT.
ICING PENALTY.....
CORNELL REGAINS THE PUCK.
CORNELL SHOT:
WRIST SHOT
SHOT IS HIGH.
CORNELL REGAINS THE PUCK.
CORNELL SHOT:
FLICK SHOT
SHOT IS BLOCKED BY THE GOALIE.
HARVARD REGAINS THE PUCK.
YOUR SHOT? 3
WRIST SHOT.
SHOT IS BARELY WIDE...
HARVARD REGAINS THE PUCK.
YOUR SHOT? 2
FLICK SHOT....
SHOT IS WIDE.
HARVARD REGAINS THE PUCK.
YOUR SHOT? 1
SLAP SHOT.
ICING PENALTY.....
CORNELL REGAINS THE PUCK.
CORNELL SHOT:
WRIST SHOT
SHOT IS HIGH.
CORNELL REGAINS THE PUCK.
CORNELL SHOT:
SLAP SHOT.
SHOT HITS THE POST.
CORNELL REGAINS THE PUCK.
CORNELL SHOT:
WRIST SHOT
GOOD!
HERE IS THE FACE-OFF:
SCORE:
CORNELL   5
HARVARD   6
***** END OF SECOND PERIOD *****
SCORE:
CORNELL   5
HARVARD   6

HORSES

Description

This program simulates a one-mile horse race for three-year old thoroughbreds. You can place any number of bets on the outcome of the race. There are four elements to a bet:

1. Horse number (1 to 8)
2. Position (Win=1, Place=2, Show=3)
3. Amount of wager ($2 minimum, $300 maximum)
4. Bet signal (1 for more bets to follow, 0 to close betting)

The computer then gives you the position of the eight horses at eight points around the raceway. At the end, it tells you what each horse paid and what you won (or didn't win) on each of your bets.

Source

The published program has been around DIGITAL for as long as anyone can remember. Its author is now unknown. Other interesting horse race programs were submitted by Robert Goodman, Southfield, Mich.; Don Viola, Staten Island, NY; and Paul Garmon, Wellesley Hills, Mass.

PROGRAM LISTING

```
1 DIM V(10),U(10),T(10),M(8),O(8),H(8),B(8),P(6)
2 RANDOMIZE \ PRINT "HORSE RACE"
3 PRINT "EXAMPLE OF BET; 1,2,200,0 ."
5 PRINT \ PRINT"     SEVENTH - 1 MILE, 3 YR. OLDS      POST 2;35"
6 PRINT
7 FOR I=1 TO 8
8 B(I)=I \ GOSUB 210
9 READ O(I) \ PRINT O(I)":1"
10 M(I)=(100+50*O(I)) / (O(I)+1)
11 NEXT I
12 PRINT
13 PRINT"ENTER HORSE(1-8);TO WIN,PLACE,SHOW(1,2,3);AND THE WAGER."
14 PRINT "AND 0 FOR NO MORE BETTING OR 1 OR MORE BETTING."
15 LET S = 0
16 PRINT
17 LET S = S + 1
18 PRINT"BET NO. ";S;
19 INPUT T(S),U(S),V(S),M
20 LET T(S)=ABS(INT(T(S)))
21 IF T(S)>8 THEN 26
22 IF T(S)<1 THEN 26
23 LET U(S)=ABS(INT(U(S)))
24 IF U(S)>3 THEN 26
25 IF U(S)>0 THEN 28
26 PRINT"HORSE NO. OR WIN-PLACE-SHOW IN ERROR" \ GO TO 18
28 IF V(S)<2 THEN 30
29 IF V(S)<=300 THEN 33
30 PRINT"BET MUST BE >$2 AND <$300, BET AGAIN";
31 INPUT V(S) \ GO TO 28
33 IF M = 1 THEN 17
35 PRINT \ PRINT"  THEY'RE OFF AND RUNNING =" \ PRINT
36 FOR I=1 TO 8 \ H(I)=0 \ NEXT I
40 FOR K=1 TO 8
42 SLEEP 6
44 FOR J=1 TO 8
46 H(J)=H(J)+RND(0)*M(J)
48 NEXT J
52 FOR I=8 TO 1 STEP -1
54 FOR J=2 TO I
56 ON SGN(H(B(J-1))-H(B(J)))+2 GO TO 60,58,62
58 IF RND(0)>.5 THEN 62
60 Z=B(J-1) \ B(J-1)=B(J) \ B(J)=Z
62 NEXT J
64 NEXT I
68 PRINT \ PRINT "   ";
70 ON K GOTO 72,74,76,78,80,82,84,86
72 PRINT "AS THEY BREAK FROM THE GATE" \ GO TO 88
74 PRINT "AT THE 1/4 MILE POLE" \ GO TO 88
76 PRINT "NEARING THE HALFWAY MARK" \ GO TO 88
78 PRINT "MIDWAY IN THE RACE" \ GO TO 88
80 PRINT "AT 5/8 OF A MILE" \ GO TO 88
82 PRINT "ROUNDING THE TURN" \ GO TO 88
84 PRINT "COMING DOWN THE STRETCH" \ GO TO 88
86 PRINT "     FINISH"
88 REM
90 GO SUB 200
92 NEXT K
96 PRINT \ PRINT \ PRINT "$2 MUTUELS PAID;"
98 PRINT "          STRAIGHT   PLACE     SHOW"
100 K=0
102 FOR I=1 TO 3
104 GO SUB 215
106 FOR J=I TO 3
108 L=2*I+J-3 \ P(L)=1.5+.1*INT(.1+INT((4*O(B(I))/(J*(J+1))+RND(0))*100+5))
110 PRINT TAB(3+10*J); \ B=16
112 FOR M=3 TO -1 STEP -1
114 P=INT(P(L)/(10^M))
116 P=P-10*INT(P/10)
117 IF P=0 THEN 118 \ B=0
118 PRINT CHR$(48+P+B);
138 IF M<>0 THEN 139 \ PRINT ".";
139 NEXT M
140 PRINT "0";
142 NEXT J
144 PRINT
146 NEXT I
150 PRINT \ Q=0
152 FOR J=1 TO S
154 PRINT "BET NO. "; J
156 P=0
158 FOR I=1 TO 8 \ H(B(I))=I \ NEXT I
160 IF U(J)<H(T(J)) THEN 166
162 P= .01*INT((V(J)*50)*P(U(J)+H(T(J))*2-3))
164 PRINT "YOU COLLECT" P "ON "; \ GO TO 172
166 IF H(T(J))>3 THEN 168 \ PRINT "NEXT TIME, BUY A SHOW"; \ GO TO 170
168 PRINT "TEAR UP YOUR";
170 PRINT " TICKET ON ";
172 I=0 \ B(0)=T(J) \ GOSUB 215 \ PRINT
174 Q=Q+P-V(J)
176 NEXT J
178 IF Q<0 THEN 182
180 PRINT "YOUR TOTAL WINNINGS AMOUNT TO $" Q \ STOP
182 PRINT "YOUR TOTAL LOSSES AMOUNT TO $" ABS(Q) \ STOP
200 PRINT "POS. HORSE   LENGTHS BEHIND"
205 FOR I=1 TO 8
210 PRINT I;
215 ON B(I) GOTO 220,222,224,226,228,230,232,234
220 PRINT "MAN O'WAR  "; \ GO TO 240
222 PRINT "CITATION   "; \ GO TO 240
224 PRINT "WHIRLAWAY  "; \ GO TO 240
226 PRINT "ASSAULT    "; \ GO TO 240
228 PRINT "SEABISCUIT "; \ GO TO 240
230 PRINT "GALLANT FOX"; \ GO TO 240
232 PRINT "STYMIE     "; \ GO TO 240
234 PRINT "COALTOWN   ";
240 IF K=0 THEN 260
245 IF I>1 THEN 250 \ PRINT \ GO TO 255
250 PRINT .1*INT(H(B(1))-H(B(I)))
255 NEXT I
260 RETURN
301 DATA 3,4,5,8,9,11,20,30
999 END
```

134

SAMPLE RUN

```
HORSE RACE
EXAMPLE OF BET; 1,2,200,0

     SEVENTH - 1 MILE, 3 YR. OLDS      POST 2:35

  1 MAN O'WAR     3 :1
  2 CITATION      4 :1
  3 WHIRLAWAY     5 :1
  4 ASSAULT       8 :1
  5 SEABISCUIT    9 :1
  6 GALLANT FOX  11 :1
  7 STYMIE       20 :1
  8 COALTOWN     30 :1

ENTER HORSE(1-8);TO WIN,PLACE,SHOW(1,2,3);AND THE WAGER.
AND 0 FOR NO MORE BETTING OR 1 OR MORE BETTING.

BET NO.  1 ? 2,1,100,1
BET NO.  2 ? 3,2,100,1
BET NO.  3 ? 4,2,100,1
BET NO.  4 ? 1,3,100,1
BET NO.  5 ? 5,3,100,0

   THEY'RE OFF AND RUNNING -


   AS THEY BREAK FROM THE GATE -
POS.  HORSE    LENGTHS BEHIND
 1 WHIRLAWAY
 2 SEABISCUIT  1.2
 3 STYMIE      1.9
 4 GALLANT FOX 2.3
 5 ASSAULT     3.5
 6 CITATION    4.5
 7 MAN O'WAR   4.7
 8 COALTOWN    5.1

   AT THE 1/4 MILE POLE -
POS.  HORSE    LENGTHS BEHIND
 1 STYMIE
 2 WHIRLAWAY   .2
 3 CITATION    .5
 4 GALLANT FOX .7
 5 COALTOWN    1.7
 6 SEABISCUIT  2.1
 7 MAN O'WAR   3.7
 8 ASSAULT     4.2

   NEARING THE HALFWAY MARK -
POS.  HORSE    LENGTHS BEHIND
 1 CITATION
 2 STYMIE      .8
 3 GALLANT FOX 4.1
 4 ASSAULT     4.1
 5 WHIRLAWAY   4.3
 6 COALTOWN    4.9
 7 SEABISCUIT  5.1
 8 MAN O'WAR   8.3

   ROUNDING THE TURN -
POS.  HORSE    LENGTHS BEHIND
 1 WHIRLAWAY
 2 GALLANT FOX 1.6
 3 STYMIE      2.2
 4 ASSAULT     3.9
 5 CITATION    5.6
 6 SEABISCUIT  6.6
 7 COALTOWN    10.9
 8 MAN O'WAR   11

   COMING DOWN THE STRETCH -
POS.  HORSE    LENGTHS BEHIND
 1 WHIRLAWAY
 2 STYMIE      0
 3 CITATION    1.8
 4 GALLANT FOX 2.1
 5 ASSAULT     2.8
 6 SEABISCUIT  6.8
 7 MAN O'WAR   8.4
 8 COALTOWN    10.7

     FINISH
POS.  HORSE    LENGTHS BEHIND
 1 CITATION
 2 STYMIE      .7
 3 WHIRLAWAY   1.1
 4 GALLANT FOX 3.3
 5 ASSAULT     6.4
 6 MAN O'WAR   10.2
 7 SEABISCUIT  10.5
 8 COALTOWN    14.5


$2 MUTUELS PAID:
          STRAIGHT   PLACE     SHOW
CITATION    9.97      4.44      3.18
STYMIE                15.48     8.9
WHIRLAWAY                       3.72

BET NO.  1
YOU COLLECT 498.5 ON CITATION
BET NO.  2
TEAR UP YOUR TICKET ON WHIRLAWAY
BET NO.  3
TEAR UP YOUR TICKET ON ASSAULT
BET NO.  4
TEAR UP YOUR TICKET ON MAN O'WAR
BET NO.  5
TEAR UP YOUR TICKET ON SEABISCUIT
YOUR TOTAL LOSSES AMOUNT TO $ 1.5
```

HURKLE

FIND THE HURKLE IN HIDING

Description

Hurkle? A Hurkle is a happy beast and lives in another galaxy
on a planet named Lirht that has three moons. Hurkle are
favorite pets of the Gwik, the dominant race of Lirht and...
well, to find out more, read "The Hurkle is a Happy Beast"
in the book A WAY HOME by Theodore Sturgeon published by Pyramid.

In this program a shy hurkle is hiding on a 10 by 10 grid.
Homebase is point 0,0 in the <u>Southwest</u> corner. Your guess as
to the gridpoint where the hurkle is hiding should be a pair
of whole numbers, separated by a comma. After each try, the
computer will tell you the approximate direction to go look
for the Hurkle. You get five guesses to find him.

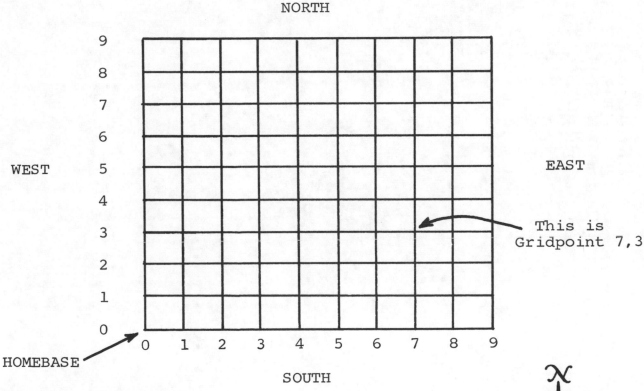

Program Author

Bob Albrecht
People's Computer Company
Menlo Park, CA 94025

PROGRAM LISTING

```
90   REM *** CONVERTED TO RSTS/E BY DAVID AHL, DIGITAL
100 REM HURKLE - PEOPLE'S COMPUTER COMPANY, MENLO PARK CA
105 RANDOM
110 N=5
120 G=10
210 PRINT
220 PRINT "A HURKLE IS HIDING ON A";G;"BY";G;"GRID. HOMEBASE"
230 PRINT "ON THE GRID IS POINT  0,0  AND ANY GRIDPOINT IS A"
240 PRINT "PAIR OF WHOLE NUMBERS SEPARATED BY A COMMA. TRY TO"
250 PRINT "GUESS THE HURKLE'S GRIDPOINT. YOU GET";N;"TRIES. "
260 PRINT "AFTER EACH TRY, I WILL TELL YOU THE APPROXIMATE"
270 PRINT "DIRECTION TO GO TO LOOK FOR THE HURKLE. "
280 PRINT
285 A=INT(G*RND(0))
286 B=INT(G*RND(0))
310 FOR K=1 TO N
320 PRINT "GUESS #";K;
330 INPUT X,Y
340 IF ABS(X-A)+ABS(Y-B)=0 THEN 500
350 REM PRINT INFO
360 GOSUB 610
370 PRINT
380 NEXT K
410 PRINT
420 PRINT "SORRY, THAT'S";N;"GUESSES. "
430 PRINT "THE HURKLE IS AT ";A;",";B
440 PRINT
450 PRINT "LET'S PLAY AGAIN. HURKLE IS HIDING. "
460 PRINT
470 GO TO 285
500 REM
510 PRINT
520 PRINT "YOU FOUND HIM IN";K;"GUESSES!"
530 FOR I=1 TO 10\PRINT CHR$(7);\NEXT I\PRINT
540 GO TO 440
610 PRINT "GO ";
620 IF Y=B THEN 670
630 IF Y<B THEN 660
640 PRINT "SOUTH";
650 GO TO 670
660 PRINT "NORTH";
670 IF X=A THEN 720
680 IF X<A THEN 710
690 PRINT "WEST";
700 GO TO 720
710 PRINT "EAST";
720 PRINT
730 RETURN
999 END

READY
```

SAMPLE RUN

```
A HURKLE IS HIDING ON A 10 BY 10 GRID. HOMEBASE
ON THE GRID IS POINT  0,0  AND ANY GRIDPOINT IS A
PAIR OF WHOLE NUMBERS SEPARATED BY A COMMA. TRY TO
GUESS THE HURKLE'S GRIDPOINT. YOU GET 5 TRIES.
AFTER EACH TRY, I WILL TELL YOU THE APPROXIMATE
DIRECTION TO GO TO LOOK FOR THE HURKLE.

GUESS # 1 ? 5,5
GO NORTHEAST

GUESS # 2 ? 7,7
GO EAST

GUESS # 3 ? 8,7

YOU FOUND HIM IN 3 GUESSES!


LET'S PLAY AGAIN. HURKLE IS HIDING.

GUESS # 1 ? 4,4
GO NORTHWEST

GUESS # 2 ? 2,7
GO NORTHWEST

GUESS # 3 ? 1,8
GO NORTH

GUESS # 4 ? 1,9

YOU FOUND HIM IN 4 GUESSES!


LET'S PLAY AGAIN. HURKLE IS HIDING.

GUESS # 1 ? 4,5
GO SOUTHEAST

GUESS # 2 ? 7,2
GO NORTHWEST

GUESS # 3 ? 8,4
GO SOUTHWEST

GUESS # 4 ? 6,3
GO WEST

GUESS # 5 ? 5,3

YOU FOUND HIM IN 5 GUESSES!


LET'S PLAY AGAIN. HURKLE IS HIDING.

GUESS # 1 ? 4,0
GO NORTHWEST

GUESS # 2 ? 2,5
GO NORTH

GUESS # 3 ? 2,7
GO NORTH

GUESS # 4 ? 2,8

YOU FOUND HIM IN 4 GUESSES!


LET'S PLAY AGAIN. HURKLE IS HIDING.

GUESS # 1 ? 9,9
GO SOUTHWEST

GUESS # 2 ? 7,7
GO SOUTHWEST

GUESS # 3 ? 5,5
GO SOUTHEAST

GUESS # 4 ? 6,0
GO NORTH

GUESS # 5 ? 6,1
GO NORTH


SORRY, THAT'S 5 GUESSES.
THE HURKLE IS AT  6 , 3
```

KINEMA

THROW A BALL UP IN THE AIR

Description

This program tests your fundamental knowledge of kinematics.
It presents a simple problem: a ball is thrown straight up
in the air at some random velocity. You then must answer
three questions about the flight of the ball:

1. How high will it go?
2. How long until it returns to earth?
3. What will be its velocity after a random number of
   seconds?

The computer evaluates your performance; within 15% of the
correct answer is considered close enough. After each run,
the computer gives you another problem until you interrupt
the program.

Program Author

KINEMA was shortened from the original Huntington Computer
Project Program, KINERV, by:

Richard F. Pav
Patchogue High School
Patchogue, New York

```
LIST

100 PRINT
105 PRINT
106 Q=0
110 V=5+INT(35*RND(0))
111 PRINT "A BALL IS THROWN UPWARDS AT"V"METERS PER SECOND"
112 PRINT
115 A=V^2/19.6
116 PRINT "HOW HIGH WILL IT GO (IN METERS)";
117 GOSUB 500
120 A=V/4.9
122 PRINT "HOW LONG UNTIL IT RETURNS (IN SECONDS)";
124 GOSUB 500
130 T=(1+INT(2*V*RND(1)))/10
132 A=V-9.8*T
134 PRINT "WHAT WILL ITS VELOCITY BE AFTER"T"SECONDS";
136 GOSUB 500
140 PRINT
150 PRINT Q"RIGHT OUT OF 3.";
160 IF Q<2 THEN 100
170 PRINT "  NOT BAD."
180 GO TO 100
500 INPUT G
501 G=100*ABS(G-A)
502 IF G<=ABS(A) THEN 507
503 IF G<=15*ABS(A) THEN 510
504 PRINT "NOT EVEN CLOSE...."
506 GO TO 512
507 Q=Q+1
508 PRI"CORRECT! VERY GOOD!"
509 GOTO520
510 PRINT "CLOSE ENOUGH."
511 Q=Q+1
512 PRINT "CORRECT ANSWER IS"A
520 PRINT
530 RETURN
999 END
```

```
A BALL IS THROWN UPWARDS AT 15 METERS PER SECOND

HOW HIGH WILL IT GO (IN METERS)? 22
NOT EVEN CLOSE....
CORRECT ANSWER IS 11.47959

HOW LONG UNTIL IT RETURNS (IN SECONDS)? 3
CLOSE ENOUGH.
CORRECT ANSWER IS 3.061225

WHAT WILL ITS VELOCITY BE AFTER .2 SECONDS? 13
CORRECT! VERY GOOD!

 2 RIGHT OUT OF 3.  NOT BAD.

A BALL IS THROWN UPWARDS AT 21 METERS PER SECOND

HOW HIGH WILL IT GO (IN METERS)? 22
CLOSE ENOUGH.
CORRECT ANSWER IS 22.5

HOW LONG UNTIL IT RETURNS (IN SECONDS)? 4 4
CLOSE ENOUGH.
CORRECT ANSWER IS 4.285714

WHAT WILL ITS VELOCITY BE AFTER 2.1 SECONDS? 1
NOT EVEN CLOSE....
CORRECT ANSWER IS .4200001

 2 RIGHT OUT OF 3.  NOT BAD

A BALL IS THROWN UPWARDS AT 22 METERS PER SECOND

HOW HIGH WILL IT GO (IN METERS)? 24.2
CLOSE ENOUGH.
CORRECT ANSWER IS 24.69388

HOW LONG UNTIL IT RETURNS (IN SECONDS)? 4.4
CLOSE ENOUGH.
CORRECT ANSWER IS 4.489796

WHAT WILL ITS VELOCITY BE AFTER .2 SECONDS? 20
CORRECT! VERY GOOD!

 3 RIGHT OUT OF 3.  NOT BAD.
```

KING

Description

This is one of the more comprehensive, difficult, and interesting
land and resource management games. (If you've never played one
of these games, start with HMRABI).

In this game, you are Premier of Setats Detinu, a small communist
island 30 by 70 miles long. Your job is to decide upon the
budget of the country and distribute money to your countrymen
from the communal treasury.

The money system is Rallods; each person needs 100 Rallods
per year to survive. Your country's income comes from farm
produce and tourists visiting your magnificent forests, hunting,
fishing, etc. Part of your land is farm land but it also has
an excellent mineral content and may be sold to foreign industry
for strip mining. Industry import and support their own workers.
Crops cost between 10 and 15 Rallods per square mile to plant,
cultivate, and harvest. Your goal is to complete an eight-year
term of office without major mishap.

To the question, "HOW MANY TIMES HAVE YOU PLAYED?" answer "0"
for a full set of rules, "500" for no explanation, or "1,000"
to continue an old game. To stop a running game and continue
it later, answer "0" to all questions.

This program is available from DECUS as BASIC-8-346, and is
called "POLLUTION GAME."

Program Author

James A. Storer
Lexington High School
Lexington, MA 02173

```
1 REM JIM STORER
2 PRINT "HOW MANY TIMES HAVE YOU PLAYED";
3 INPUT Z
5 LET N5=8
6 RANDOMIZE
12 IF Z=500 THEN 47
14 IF Z=1000 THEN 1960
17 FOR Y1=1 TO 10
18 PRINT
19 NEXT Y1
20 PRINT "CONGRATULATIONS! YOU'VE BEEN ELECTED PREMIER OF SETATS DETINU,"
22 PRINT "A SMALL COMMUNIST ISLAND 30 BY 70 MILES LONG, YOUR JOB IS TO"
24 PRINT "DECIDE UPON THE COUNTRY'S BUDGET AND DISTRIBUTE MONEY TO YOUR"
26 PRINT "COUNTRYMEN FROM THE COMMUNAL TREASURY,";
27 IF Z<>0 THEN 47
28 PRINT " THE MONEY SYSTEM IS RALLODS,"
30 PRINT "AND EACH PERSON NEEDS 100 RALLODS PER YEAR TO SURVIVE."
32 PRINT "YOUR COUNTRY'S INCOME COMES FROM FARM PRODUCE AND TOURISTS"
34 PRINT "VISITING YOUR MAGNIFICENT FORESTS, HUNTING, FISHING, ETC. HALF"
36 PRINT "YOUR LAND IS FARM LAND WHICH ALSO HAS AN EXCELLENT MINERAL"
38 PRINT "CONTENT AND MAY BE SOLD TO FOREIGN INDUSTRY (STRIP MINING)"
39 PRINT "WHO IMPORT AND SUPPORT THEIR OWN WORKERS, CROPS COST BETWEEN"
40 PRINT "10 AND 15 RALLODS PER SQ. MILE TO PLANT."
42 PRINT "YOUR GOAL IS TO COMPLETE YOUR";N5;"YEAR TERM OF OFFICE,"
44 PRINT " GOOD LUCK!"
47 FOR Y1=1 TO 4
48 PRINT
49 NEXT Y1
50 LET A=INT(60000+(RND(1)*1000)-(RND(1)*1000))
55 LET B=INT(500+(RND(1)*10,-(RND(1)*10))
65 LET D=2000
100 LET W=INT(RND(1)*10+95)
101 FOR Y1=1 TO 8
102 PRINT
103 NEXT Y1
105 PRINT "YOU NOW HAVE";A;"RALLODS IN THE TREASURY."
110 PRINT INT(B);"COUNTRYMEN,";
115 LET V9=INT(((RND(1)/2)*10+10)
120 IF C=0 THEN 140
130 PRINT INT(C);"FOREIGN WORKERS,";
140 PRINT " AND";INT(D);"SQ. MILES OF LAND."
150 PRINT"THIS YEAR INDUSTRY WILL BUY LAND FOR";W;"RALLODS PER SQ. MILE."
155 PRINT "LAND CURRENTLY COSTS";V9;"RALLODS PER SQ. MILE TO PLANT."
160 FOR Y1=1 TO 3
162 PRINT
164 NEXT Y1
200 PRINT "HOW MANY SQ. MILES DO YOU WISH TO SELL TO INDUSTRY";
210 INPUT H
215 IF H<0 THEN 200
220 IF H<=D-1000 THEN 300
230 PRINT "    THINK AGAIN, YOU'VE ONLY";D-1000;"SQ. MILES OF FARM LAND"
240 IF X <> 0 THEN 200
250 PRINT "(FOREIGN INDUSTRY WILL ONLY BUY FARM LAND BECAUSE FOREST"
260 PRINT "LAND IS UNECONOMICAL TO STRIP MINE DUE TO TREES,"
270 PRINT "THICKER TOP SOIL, ETC.)"
280 LET X=1
299 GOTO 200
300 LET D=INT(D-H)
310 LET A=INT(A+(H*W))
320 PRINT "HOW MANY RALLODS DO YOU WISH TO DISTRIBUTE TO YOUR COUNTRYMEN";
340 INPUT I
342 IF I<0 THEN 320
350 IF I<A THEN 400
360 IF I=A THEN 380
370 PRINT "    THINK AGAIN YOU'VE ONLY";A;"RALLODS IN THE TREASURY"
375 GOTO 320
380 LET J=0
390 LET K=0
395 LET A=0
399 GOTO 1000
400 LET A=INT(A-I)
410 PRINT "HOW MANY SQ. MILES DO YOU WISH TO PLANT";
420 INPUT J
421 IF J<0 THEN 410
422 IF J<=B*2 THEN 426
423 PRINT "    SORRY, BUT EACH COUNTRYMAN CAN ONLY PLANT 2 SQ. MILES"
424 GOTO 410
426 IF J<=D-1000 THEN 430
427 PRINT "    SORRY, BUT YOU'VE ONLY";D-1000;"SQ. MILES OF FARM LAND"
428 GOTO 410
430 LET U1=INT(J*V9)
435 IF U1<A THEN 500
440 IF U1=A THEN 490
450 PRINT "    THINK AGAIN, YOU'VE ONLY";A;"RALLODS LEFT IN THE TREASURY"
460 GOTO 410
490 LET K=0
495 LET A=0
499 GOTO 1000
500 LET A=A-U1
505 IF D=2000 THEN 1000
510 PRINT "HOW MANY RALLODS DO YOU WISH TO SPEND ON POLLUTION CONTROL";
520 INPUT K
522 IF K<0 THEN 510
530 IF K<=A THEN 600
540 PRINT "    THINK AGAIN, YOU'VE ONLY";A;"RALLODS REMAINING"
550 GOTO 510
600 IF H<>0 THEN 1002
602 IF I<>0 THEN 1002
604 IF J<>0 THEN 1002
606 IF K<>0 THEN 1002
608 FOR Y1=1 TO 5
609 PRINT
610 NEXT Y1
612 PRINT "GOODBYE,"
614 PRINT "(IF YOU WISH TO CONTINUE THIS GAME AT A LATER DATE, ANSWER "
616 PRINT "1000 FOR HOW MANY TIMES YOU'VE PLAYED, AT BEGINNING OF NEXT "
617 PRINT "GAME,)"
618 GOTO 1590
1000 GOTO 600
1002 FOR Y1=1 TO 3
1003 PRINT
1004 NEXT Y1
1010 LET A=INT(A-K)
1020 LET A4=A
1100 IF INT(I/100-B)>=0 THEN 1120
1105 IF I/100<50 THEN 1700
1110 PRINT INT(B-(I/100));"COUNTRYMEN DIED OF STARVATION"
1120 LET F1=INT(RND(1)*(200*-D))
1122 IF K<25 THEN 1130
1125 LET F1=INT(F1/(K/25))
1130 IF F1<=0 THEN 1150
1140 PRINT F1;"COUNTRYMEN DIED OF CARBON-MONOXIDE AND DUST INHALATION"
```

139

```
1150 IF INT((I/100)-B)<0 THEN 1170
1160 IF F1>0 THEN 1180
1165 GOTO 1200
1170 PRINT "    YOU WERE FORCED TO SPEND";INT((F1+(B-(I/100)))*9);
1172 PRINT "RALLODS ON FUNERAL EXPENSES,"
1174 LET B5=INT(F1+(B-(I/100)))
1175 LET A=INT(A-((F1+(B-(I/100)))*9))
1176 GOTO 1185
1180 PRINT "    YOU WERE FORCED TO SPEND";INT(F1*9);"RALLODS ON ";
1181 PRINT "FUNERAL EXPENSES,"
1182 LET B5=F1
1183 LET A=A-(F1*9)
1185 IF A>=0 THEN 1194
1187 PRINT "    INSUFFICIENT RESERVES TO COVER COST -LAND WAS SOLD"
1189 LET D=INT(D+(A/W))
1190 LET A=0
1194 LET B=INT(B-B5)
1200 IF H=0 THEN 1250
1220 LET C1=INT(H+(RND(1)*10)-(RND(1)*20))
1224 IF C>0 THEN 1230
1226 LET C1=C1+20
1230 PRINT C1;"WORKERS CAME TO THE COUNTRY AND";
1250 LET P1=INT((((I/100-B)/10)+(K/25)-((2000-D)/50)-(F1/2))
1255 PRINT ABS(P1);"COUNTRYMEN ";
1260 IF P1<0 THEN 1275
1265 PRINT "CAME TO";
1270 GOTO 1280
1275 PRINT "LEFT";
1280 PRINT " THE ISLAND."
1290 LET B=INT(B+P1)
1292 LET C=INT(C+C1)
1305 LET U2=INT(((2000-C)*((RND(1)+1.5)/2)))
1310 IF C=0 THEN 1324
1320 PRINT " OF";INT(J);"SQ. MILES PLANTED,"
1324 IF J>U2 THEN 1330
1326 LET U2=J
1330 PRINT " YOU HARVESTED";INT(J-U2);"SQ. MILES OF CROPS,"
1340 IF U2=0 THEN 1372
1344 IF T1>=2 THEN 1370
1350 PRINT " (DUE TO ";
1355 IF T1=0 THEN 1365
1360 PRINT "INCREASED ";
1365 PRINT "AIR AND WATER POLLUTION FROM FOREIGN INDUSTRY.)"
1367 LET T1=T1+1
1370 LET Q=INT((J-U2)*(W/2))
1380 PRINT " MAKING";INT(Q);"RALLODS,"
1390 LET A=INT(A+Q)
1400 LET V1=INT(((B-P1)*22)+(RND(1)*500))
1405 LET V2=INT((2000-D)*15)
1410 PRINT " YOU MADE";ABS(INT(V1-V2));"RALLODS FROM TOURIST TRADE."
1420 IF V2=0 THEN 1450
1425 IF V1-V2>=V3 THEN 1450
1430 PRINT "    DECREASE BECAUSE ";
1435 LET G1=RND(1)*10
1440 IF G1<=2 THEN 1460
1442 IF G1<=4 THEN 1465
1444 IF G1<=6 THEN 1470
1446 IF G1<=8 THEN 1475
1448 IF G1<=10 THEN 1480
1450 LET V3=INT(V1-V2)
1451 LET A=INT(A+V3)
1452 GOTO 1500
1460 PRINT "FISH POPULATION HAS DWINDLED DUE TO WATER POLLUTION."
1462 GOTO 1450
1465 PRINT "AIR POLLUTION IS KILLING GAME BIRD POPULATION."
1467 GOTO 1450
1470 PRINT "MINERAL BATHS ARE BEING RUINED BY WATER POLLUTION."
1472 GOTO 1450
1475 PRINT "UNPLEASANT SMOG IS DISCOURAGING SUN BATHERS."
1477 GOTO 1450
1480 PRINT "HOTELS ARE LOOKING SHABBY DUE TO SMOG GRIT."
1482 GOTO 1450
1500 IF B5>200 THEN 1600
1505 IF B<343 THEN 1700
1510 IF (A4/100)>5 THEN 1800
1515 IF C>B THEN 1550
1520 IF N5-1=*5 THEN 1900
1545 GOTO 2000
1550 FOR Y1=1 TO 8
1552 PRINT
1555 NEXT Y1
1560 PRINT "THE NUMBER OF FOREIGN WORKERS HAS EXCEEDED THE NUMBER"
1562 PRINT "OF COUNTRYMEN, AS A MAJORITY THEY HAVE REVOLTED AND"
1564 PRINT "TAKEN OVER THE COUNTRY,"
1570 IF RND(1)<=.5 THEN 1580
1574 PRINT "YOU HAVE BEEN THROWN OUT OF OFFICE AND YOU ARE NOW"
1576 PRINT "RESIDING IN PRISON,"
1578 GOTO 1590
1580 PRINT "YOU HAVE BEEN ASSASSINATED,"
1590 FOR Y1=1 TO 18
1592 PRINT
1594 NEXT Y1
1596 STOP
1600 FOR Y1=1 TO 8
1602 PRINT
1605 NEXT Y1
1610 PRINT B5;"COUNTRYMEN DIED IN ONE YEAR!!!!!"
1615 PRINT "DUE TO THIS EXTREME MISMANAGEMENT YOU HAVE NOT ONLY"
1620 PRINT "BEEN IMPEACHED AND THROWN OUT OF OFFICE BUT YOU"
1622 LET M6=INT(RND(1)*10)
1625 IF M6<=3 THEN 1670
1630 IF M6<=6 THEN 1680
1635 IF M6<=10 THEN 1690
1670 PRINT "ALSO HAD YOUR LEFT EYE GOUGED OUT,"
1672 GOTO 1590
1680 PRINT "HAVE ALSO GAINED A VERY BAD REPUTATION,"
1682 GOTO 1590
1690 PRINT "HAVE ALSO BEEN DECLARED NATIONAL FINK,"
1692 GOTO 1590
1700 FOR Y1=1 TO 8
1702 PRINT
1705 NEXT Y1
1710 PRINT "OVER ONE THIRD OF THE POPULATION HAS DIED SINCE YOU"
1715 PRINT "WERE ELECTED TO OFFICE, THE PEOPLE (REMAINING)"
1720 PRINT "HATE YOUR GUTS,"
1730 GOTO 1570
1800 IF B5-F1<2 THEN 1515
1805 FOR Y1=1 TO 8
1807 PRINT
1810 NEXT Y1
1815 PRINT "MONEY WAS LEFT OVER IN THE TREASURY WHICH YOU DID"
1820 PRINT "NOT SPEND, AS A RESULT SOME OF YOUR COUNTRYMEN DIED"
```

```
1825 PRINT "OF STARVATION, THE PUBLIC IS ENRAGED AND YOU HAVE"
1830 PRINT "BEEN FORCED TO EITHER RESIGN OR COMMIT SUCIDE"
1835 PRINT "THE CHOICE IS YOURS."
1840 PRINT "IF YOU CHOOSE THE LATTER, PLEASE TURN OFF YOUR TTY";
1845 PRINT " BEFORE PROCEEDING."
1850 GOTO 1590
1900 FOR Y1=1 TO 8
1902 PRINT
1905 NEXT Y1
1920 PRINT "CONGRATULATIONS!!!!!!!!!!!!!!!!!!!!!"
1925 PRINT "YOU HAVE SUCCESSFULLY COMPLETED YOUR";N5;"YEAR TERM"
1930 PRINT "OF OFFICE, YOU WERE, OF COURSE, EXTREMELY LUCKY, BUT NEVER THE"
1935 PRINT "LESS, IT'S QUITE AN ACHIEVEMENT, GOODBY AND GOOD LUCK -YOU'LL"
1940 PRINT "PROBABLY NEED IT IF YOU'RE THE TYPE THAT PLAYS THIS GAME."
1945 PRINT " -FOR FURTHER THRILLS, TRY LANDING ON THE MOON"
1950 GOTO 1590
1960 PRINT "HOW MANY YEARS HAD YOU BEEN IN OFFICE WHEN INTERRUPTED";
1961 INPUT X5
1962 IF X5<0 THEN 1590
1963 IF X5<8 THEN 1969
1965 PRINT "   COME ON, YOUR TERM OF OFFICE IS ONLY";N5;"YEARS"
1967 GOTO 1960
1969 PRINT "HOW MUCH DID YOU HAVE IN THE TREASURY";
1970 INPUT A
1971 IF A<0 THEN 1590
1975 PRINT "HOW MANY COUNTRYMEN";
1976 INPUT B
1977 IF B<0 THEN 1590
1980 PRINT "HOW MANY WORKERS";
1981 INPUT C
1982 IF C<0 THEN 1590
1990 PRINT "HOW MANY SQ. MILES OF LAND";
1991 INPUT D
1992 IF D<0 THEN 1590
1993 IF D>2000 THEN 1996
1994 IF D>1000 THEN 100
1996 PRINT "   COME ON, YOU STARTED WITH 1000 SQ. MILES OF FARM LAND"
1997 PRINT "   AND 1000 SQ. MILES OF FOREST LAND"
1998 GOTO 1990
2000 LET X5=X5+1
2020 LET A5=0
2040 GOTO 100
2046 END
```

```
CONGRATULATIONS! YOU'VE BEEN ELECTED PREMIER OF SETATS DETINU,
A SMALL COMMUNIST ISLAND 30 BY 70 MILES LONG. YOUR JOB IS TO
DECIDE UPON THE COUNTRY'S BUDGET AND DISTRIBUTE MONEY TO YOUR
COUNTRYMEN FROM THE COMMUNAL TREASURY. THE MONEY SYSTEM IS RALLODS,
AND EACH PERSON NEEDS 100 RALLODS PER YEAR TO SURVIVE.
YOUR COUNTRY'S INCOME COMES FROM FARM PRODUCE AND TOURISTS
VISITING YOUR MAGNIFICIENT FORESTS, HUNTING, FISHING, ETC. HALF
YOUR LAND IS FARM LAND WHICH ALSO HAS AN EXCELLENT MINERAL
CONTENT AND MAY BE SOLD TO FOREIGN INDUSTRY (STRIP MINING)
WHO IMPORT AND SUPPORT THEIR OWN WORKERS. CROPS COST BETWEEN
10 AND 15 RALLODS PER SQ. MILE TO PLANT.
YOUR GOAL IS TO COMPLETE YOUR 8 YEAR TERM OF OFFICE. GOOD LUCK!



YOU NOW HAVE 60259 RALLODS IN THE TREASURY.
 502 COUNTRYMEN, AND 2000 SQ. MILES OF LAND.
THIS YEAR INDUSTRY WILL BUY LAND FOR 104 RALLODS PER SQ. MILE.
LAND CURRENTLY COSTS 10 RALLODS PER SQ. MILE TO PLANT.


HOW MANY SQ. MILES DO YOU WISH TO SELL TO INDUSTRY? 300
HOW MANY RALLODS DO YOU WISH TO DISTRIBUTE TO YOUR COUNTRYMEN? 50200
HOW MANY SQ. MILES DO YOU WISH TO PLANT? 700
HOW MANY RALLODS DO YOU WISH TO SPEND ON POLLUTION CONTROL? 5000


314 WORKERS CAME TO THE COUNTRY AND 194 COUNTRYMEN CAME TO THE ISLAND.
OF 700 SQ. MILES PLANTED, YOU HARVESTED 348 SQ. MILES OF CROPS.
   (DUE TO AIR AND WATER POLLUTION FROM FOREIGN INDUSTRY. )
  MAKING 18096 RALLODS.
 YOU MADE 6581 RALLODS FROM TOURIST TRADE.



YOU NOW HAVE 53936 RALLODS IN THE TREASURY.
 696 COUNTRYMEN, 314 FOREIGN WORKERS, AND 1700 SQ. MILES OF LAND.
THIS YEAR INDUSTRY WILL BUY LAND FOR 103 RALLODS PER SQ. MILE.
LAND CURRENTLY COSTS 11 RALLODS PER SQ. MILE TO PLANT.


HOW MANY SQ. MILES DO YOU WISH TO SELL TO INDUSTRY? 300
HOW MANY RALLODS DO YOU WISH TO DISTRIBUTE TO YOUR COUNTRYMEN? 69600
HOW MANY SQ. MILES DO YOU WISH TO PLANT? 700
   SORRY, BUT YOU'VE ONLY 400 SQ. MILES OF FARM LAND
HOW MANY SQ. MILES DO YOU WISH TO PLANT? 400
HOW MANY RALLODS DO YOU WISH TO SPEND ON POLLUTION CONTROL? 5000


285 WORKERS CAME TO THE COUNTRY AND 188 COUNTRYMEN CAME TO THE ISLAND.
OF 400 SQ. MILES PLANTED, YOU HARVESTED 0 SQ. MILES OF CROPS.
   (DUE TO INCREASED AIR AND WATER POLLUTION FROM FOREIGN INDUSTRY. )
  MAKING 0 RALLODS.
 YOU MADE 6425 RALLODS FROM TOURIST TRADE.
   DECREASE BECAUSE AIR POLLUTION IS KILLING GAME BIRD POPULATION.



YOU NOW HAVE 12261 RALLODS IN THE TREASURY.
 884 COUNTRYMEN, 599 FOREIGN WORKERS, AND 1400 SQ. MILES OF LAND.
THIS YEAR INDUSTRY WILL BUY LAND FOR 97 RALLODS PER SQ. MILE.
LAND CURRENTLY COSTS 12 RALLODS PER SQ. MILE TO PLANT.


HOW MANY SQ. MILES DO YOU WISH TO SELL TO INDUSTRY? 0
HOW MANY RALLODS DO YOU WISH TO DISTRIBUTE TO YOUR COUNTRYMEN? 88400
   THINK AGAIN YOU'VE ONLY 12261 RALLODS IN THE TREASURY
HOW MANY RALLODS DO YOU WISH TO DISTRIBUTE TO YOUR COUNTRYMEN? 12000
HOW MANY SQ. MILES DO YOU WISH TO PLANT? 400
   THINK AGAIN, YOU'VE ONLY 261 RALLODS LEFT IN THE TREASURY
HOW MANY SQ. MILES DO YOU WISH TO PLANT? 20
HOW MANY RALLODS DO YOU WISH TO SPEND ON POLLUTION CONTROL? 500
   THINK AGAIN, YOU'VE ONLY 21 RALLODS REMAINING
HOW MANY RALLODS DO YOU WISH TO SPEND ON POLLUTION CONTROL? 21


 764 COUNTRYMEN DIED OF STARVATION
 410 COUNTRYMEN DIED OF CARBON-MONOXIDE AND DUST INHALATION
   YOU WERE FORCED TO SPEND 10566 RALLODS ON FUNERAL EXPENSES.
   INSUFFICIENT RESERVES TO COVER COST -LAND WAS SOLD
 178 COUNTRYMEN LEFT THE ISLAND.
OF 20 SQ. MILES PLANTED, YOU HARVESTED 0 SQ. MILES OF CROPS.
  MAKING 0 RALLODS.
 YOU MADE 16841 RALLODS FROM TOURIST TRADE.
   DECREASE BECAUSE AIR POLLUTION IS KILLING GAME BIRD POPULATION.




 1174 COUNTYRMEN DIED IN ONE YEAR!!!!!
DUE TO THIS EXTREME MISMANAGEMENT YOU HAVE NOT ONLY
BEEN IMPEACHED AND THROWN OUT OF OFFICE BUT YOU
HAVE ALSO BEEN DECLARED NATIONAL FINK.
```

LETTER

Description

LETTER is similar to the game GUESS in which you guess a number
chosen by the computer; in this program, the computer picks a
random letter of the alphabet and you must guess which one it
is using the clues provided as you go along. It should not
take you more than five guesses to get the mystery letter.

Computer Limitations

This program was adapted for DIGITAL EduSystem 15/30/35 and
uses the automatic character string to ASCII conversion feature.
Other systems will require a conversion function as Statement
435.

Program Author

Program modified and adapted from the original written by:

Bob Albrecht
People's Computer Company
Menlo Park, CA 94025

PROGRAM LISTING

```
LETTER   EDUSYSTEM 30

90 RANDOMIZE
100 PRINT "LETTER GUESSING GAME"\PRINT
210 PRINT "I'LL THINK OF A LETTER OF THE ALPHABET, A TO Z."
220 PRINT "TRY TO GUESS MY LETTER AND I'LL GIVE YOU CLUES"
230 PRINT "AS TO HOW CLOSE YOU'RE GETTING TO MY LETTER."
310 L=65+INT(RND(0)*26)
320 G=0
340 PRINT\PRINT "OK, I HAVE A LETTER.   START GUESSING. "
410 PRINT\PRINT "WHAT IS YOUR GUESS?";
425 G=G+1
430 INPUT $A\PRINT
440 IF A=L THEN 500
450 IF A>L THEN 480
460 PRINT "TOO LOW. TRY A HIGHER LETTER. "\GOTO 410
480 PRINT "TOO HIGH. TRY A LOWER LETTER. "\GOTO 410
500 PRINT\PRINT "YOU GOT IT IN"G"GUESSES!!"
504 IF G<=5 THEN 508
506 PRINT "BUT IT SHOULDN'T TAKE MORE THAN 5 GUESSES!"\GOTO 515
508 PRINT "GOOD JOB  !!!!"
510 FOR N=1 TO 15\PRINT CHR$(7);\NEXT N
515 PRINT
520 PRINT "LET'S PLAY AGAIN....."
530 GOTO 310
999 END
```

SAMPLE RUN

```
LETTER   EDUSYSTEM 30

LETTER GUESSING GAME

I'LL THINK OF A LETTER OF THE ALPHABET, A TO Z.
TRY TO GUESS MY LETTER AND I'LL GIVE YOU CLUES
AS TO HOW CLOSE YOU'RE GETTING TO MY LETTER.

OK, I HAVE A LETTER.   START GUESSING.

WHAT IS YOUR GUESS?M
TOO LOW. TRY A HIGHER LETTER.

WHAT IS YOUR GUESS?S
TOO HIGH. TRY A LOWER LETTER.

WHAT IS YOUR GUESS?P

YOU GOT IT IN 3 GUESSES!!
GOOD JOB  !!!!

LET'S PLAY AGAIN.....

OK, I HAVE A LETTER.   START GUESSING.

WHAT IS YOUR GUESS?M
TOO HIGH. TRY A LOWER LETTER.

WHAT IS YOUR GUESS?F
TOO HIGH. TRY A LOWER LETTER.

WHAT IS YOUR GUESS?C

YOU GOT IT IN 3 GUESSES!!
GOOD JOB  !!!!

LET'S PLAY AGAIN.....

OK, I HAVE A LETTER.   START GUESSING.

WHAT IS YOUR GUESS?M
TOO HIGH. TRY A LOWER LETTER.

WHAT IS YOUR GUESS?F
TOO HIGH. TRY A LOWER LETTER.

WHAT IS YOUR GUESS?C
TOO HIGH. TRY A LOWER LETTER.

WHAT IS YOUR GUESS?B

YOU GOT IT IN 4 GUESSES!!
GOOD JOB  !!!!

LET'S PLAY AGAIN.....

OK, I HAVE A LETTER.   START GUESSING.

WHAT IS YOUR GUESS?
```

LIFE

Description

The Game of Life was originally described in <u>Scientific American</u>,
October 1970, in an article by Martin Gardner. The game itself
was originated by John Conway of Gonville and Caius College,
University of Cambridge, England.

In the "manual" game, organisms exist in the form of counters
(chips or checkers) on a large checkerboard and die or reproduce
according to some simple genetic rules. Conway's criteria for
choosing his genetic laws were carefully delineated as follows:

1. There should be no initial pattern for which there is
    a simple proof that the population can grow without limit.
2. There should be initial patterns that apparently do
    grow without limit.
3. There should be simple initial patterns that grow and
    change for a considerable period of time before coming
    to an end in three possible ways: fading away completely
    (from overcrowding or from becoming too sparse), settling
    into a stable configuration that remains unchanged
    thereafter, or entering an oscillating phase in which
    they repeat an endless cycle of two or more periods.

In brief, the rules should be such as to make the behavior of
the population unpredictable. Conway's genetic laws are de-
lightfully simple. First note that each cell of the checkerboard (assumed to be an infinite plane) has eight neighboring
cells, four adjacent orthogonally, four adjacent diagonally.
The rules are:

1. Survivals. Every counter with two or three neighboring
    counters survives for the next generation.
2. Deaths. Each counter with four or more neighbors dies
    (is removed) from overpopulation. Every counter with
    one neighbor or none dies from isolation.
3. Births. Each empty cell adjacent to exactly three
    neighbors--no more, no fewer--is a birth cell. A
    counter is placed on it at the next move.

It is important to understand that all births and deaths occur
simultaneously. Together they constitute a single generation or,
as we shall call it, a "move" in the complete "life history"
o f the initial configuration.

You will find the population constantly undergoing unusual,
sometimes beautiful and always unexpected change. In a few
cases the society eventually dies out (all counters vanishing),
although this may not happen until after a great many generations.
Most starting patterns either reach stable figures--Conway calls
them "still lifes"--that cannot change or patterns that oscillate
forever. Patterns with no initial symmetry tend to become
symmetrical. Once this happens the symmetry cannot be lost,
although it may increase in richness.

Conway used a DIGITAL PDP-7 with a graphic display to observe
long-lived populations. The program here is programmed for a
RSTS-11 system. You simply input your initial pattern and terminate your input with a Control/Z. The computer then plots
successive generations of your population on a 24 (vertical)
by 70 (horizontal) grid. Sit back and watch it!

Program Author

Clark Baker
Project DELTA
Delaware School Auxilliary Association
Newport, Delaware

PROGRAM LISTING

```
1 REM LIFE CLARK BAKER 3/72 C.O.G.
2 PRINT CHR$(31%);CHR$(29%);CHR$(31%);"ENTER YOUR PATTERN:"
3 X1%,Y1%=1: X2%=24%: Y2%=70%
10 DIM A%(24%,70%),B$(24%)
20 OPEN "KB:" AS FILE 1
30 ON ERROR GO TO 80
40 C%=1
50 INPUT LINE #1,B$(C%):B$(C%)=LEFT(B$(C%),LEN(B$(C%))-2%)
60 C%=C%+1
70 GO TO 50
80 L%=0%
90 FOR X%=1 TO C%-1
100 IF LEN(B$(X%))>L% THEN L%=LEN(B$(X%))
110 NEXT X%
120 X1%=!!%=C%/2%
130 Y1%=33%-L%/2%
140 FOR X%=1 TO C%
150 FOR Y%=1 TO LEN(B$(X%))
160 IF MID(B$(X%),Y%,1)<>" " THEN A%(X1%+X%,Y1%+Y%)=1:P%=P%+1
170 NEXT Y%
180 NEXT X%
200 PRINT CHR$(29%);CHR$(30%);
210 PRINT "GENERATION:";G%,"POPULATION:";P%;CHR$(30%);:IF I9% THEN PRINT ,"INVALID!";
215 X3%=24%:Y3%=70%:X4%,Y4%=1:P%=0%
220 G%=G%+1%
225 PRINT CHR$(13%);CHR$(10%);CHR$(30%); FOR X%=1 TO X1%-1.
230 FOR X%=X1% TO X2%
240 PRINT
250 FOR Y%=Y1% TO Y2%
253 IF A%(X%,Y%)=2% THEN A%(X%,Y%)=0%:GO TO 270
256 IF A%(X%,Y%)=3% THEN A%(X%,Y%)=1:GO TO 261
260 IF A%(X%,Y%)<>1 THEN 270
261 PRINT TAB(Y%);"*";
262 IF X%<X3% THEN X3%=X%
264 IF X%>X4% THEN X4%=X%
266 IF Y%<Y3% THEN Y3%=Y%
268 IF Y%>Y4% THEN Y4%=Y%
270 NEXT Y%
280 PRINT CHR$(30%);
290 NEXT X%
295 PRINT CHR$(30%) FOR X%=X2%+1 TO 24%
298 PRINT CHR$(29%);
299 X1%=X3%:X2%=X4%:Y1%=Y3%:Y2%=Y4%
301 IF X1%<3% THEN X1%=3%:I9%=-1%
303 IF X2%>22% THEN X2%=22%:I9%=-1%
305 IF Y1%<3% THEN Y1%=3%:I9%=-1%
307 IF Y2%>68% THEN Y2%=68%:I9%=-1%
309 P%=0%
500 FOR X%=X1%-1 TO X2%+1
510 FOR Y%=Y1%-1 TO Y2%+1
520 C%=0%
530 FOR I%=X%-1% TO X%+1%
540 FOR J%=Y%-1% TO Y%+1%
550 IF A%(I%,J%)=1% OR A%(I%,J%)=2% THEN C%=C%+1%
560 NEXT J%
570 NEXT I%
580 IF A%(X%,Y%)=0% THEN 610
590 IF C%<3% OR C%>4% THEN A%(X%,Y%)=2% ELSE P%=P%+1
600 GO TO 620
610 IF C%=3% THEN A%(X%,Y%)=3%:P%=P%+1
620 NEXT Y%
630 NEXT X%
635 X1%=X1%-1:Y1%=Y1%-1:X2%=X2%+1:Y2%=Y2%+1
640 GO TO 210
650 END
```

SAMPLE RUN

```
ENTER YOUR PATTERN:



     **
     **
      *

  ^Z
GENERATION: 0        POPULATION: 5
```

```
                             **
                            **
                             *
```

```
GENERATION: 1        POPULATION: 6
```

```
                   ***
                   *
                   **
```

GENERATION: 2   POPULATION: 7

GENERATION: 20   POPULATION: 32

GENERATION: 21   POPULATION: 27

GENERATION: 22   POPULATION: 37

145

Description

LIFE-2 is based on Conway's game of Life. You must be familiar with the rules of LIFE before attempting to play LIFE-2.

There are two players; the game is played on a 5x5 board and each player has a symbol to represent his own pieces of 'life'. Live cells belonging to player 1 are represented by '*' and live cells belonging to player 2 are represented by the symbol '#'.

The # and * are regarded as the same except when deciding whether to generate a live cell. An empty cell having two '#' and one '*' for neighbors will generate a '#', i.e. the live cell generated belongs to the player who has the majority of the 3 live cells surrounding the empty cell where life is to be generated, e.g.

	1	2	3	4	5
1					
2			*		
3				#	
4			#		
5					

A new cell will be generated at (3,3) which will be a '#' since there are two '#' and one '*' surrounding. The board will then become:

	1	2	3	4	5
1					
2					
3			#	#	
4					
5					

On the first move each player positions 3 pieces of life on the board by typing in the co-ordinates of the pieces. (In the event of the same cell being chosen by both players that cell is left empty.)

The board is then adjusted to the next generation and printed out.

On each subsequent turn each player places one piece on the board, the object being to annihilate his opponent's pieces. The board is adjusted for the next generation and printed out after both players have entered their new piece.

The game continues until one player has no more live pieces. The computer will then print out the board and declare the winner.

Program Author

The idea for this game, the game itself, and the above write-up were written by:

Brian Wyvill
Bradford University
Bradford, Yorkshire, England

PROGRAM LISTING

```
1 DIMN1(6,6),K1(18),A1(16),X(2),Y(2)
3 DATA 3,102,103,120,130,121,112,111,12
4 DATA 21,30,1020,1030,1011,1021,1003,1002,1012
10 FORM=1TO18:READK1(M):NEXTM
13 DATA-1,0,1,0,0,-1,0,1,-1,-1,-1,1,-1,1,1,1
14 FORO1=1TO16:READA1(O1):NEXTO1
20 GOTO500
50 FORJ=1TO5
51 FORK=1TO5
55 IFN1(J,K)>99THENGOSUB200
60 NEXTK
65 NEXTJ
90 LETK=0:LETM2=0:LETM3=0
99 FORJ=0TO6:PRINT
100 FORK=0TO6
101 IFJ<>0THENIFJ<>6THEN105
102 IFK=6THENPRINT0:GOTO125
103 PRINTK;:GOTO120
105 IFK<>0THENIFK<>6THEN110
106 IFJ=6THENPRINT0:GOTO126
107 PRINTJ;:GOTO120
110 GOSUB300
120 NEXTK
125 NEXTJ
126 RETURN
200 LETB=1:IFN1(J,K)>999THENLETB=10
220 FORO1=1TO15STEP2
230 LETN1(J+A1(O1),K+A1(O1+1))=N1(J+A1(O1),K+A1(O1+1))+B
231 NEXTO1
239 RETURN
300 IFN1(J,K)<3THEN399
305 FORO1=1TO18
310 IFN1(J,K)=K1(O1)THEN350
315 NEXTO1
320 GOTO399
350 IFO1>9THEN360
351 LETN1(J,K)=100:LETM2=M2+1:PRINT" * ";
355 RETURN
360 LETN1(J,K)=1000:LETM3=M3+1:PRINT" # ";
365 RETURN
399 LETN1(J,K)=0:PRINT"    ";:RETURN
500 PRINTTAB(10);"U.B LIFE GAME"
505 LETM2=0:LETM3=0
510 FORJ=1TO5
511 FORK=1TO5
515 LETN1(J,K)=0
516 NEXTK
517 NEXTJ
519 FORB=1TO2:LETP1=3:IFB=2THENLETP1=30
520 PRINT"PLAYER";B;"3 LIVE PIECES"
535 FORK1=1TO3:GOSUB700
540 LETN1(X(B),Y(B))=P1:NEXTK1
542 NEXTB
559 GOSUB90
560 PRINT:GOSUB50
570 IFM2=0THENIFM3=0THEN574
571 IFM3=0THENLETB=1:GOTO575
572 IFM2=0THENLETB=2:GOTO575
573 GOTO580
574 PRINT:PRINT"A DRAW":RUN
575 PRINT:PRINT"PLAYER";B;"IS THE WINNER":RUN
580 FORB=1TO2:PRINT:PRINT"PLAYER";B;:GOSUB700
581 IFB=99THEN560
582 NEXTB
586 LETN1(X(1),Y(1))=100:LETN1(X(2),Y(2))=1000
596 GOTO 560
700 PRINT"X,Y":PRINT"XXXX";CHR$(13);"####";CHR$(13);:INPUTY(B),X(B)
705 IFX(B)<=5THENIFX(B)>0THEN708
706 GOTO750
708 IFY(B)<=5THENIFY(B)>0THEN715
710 GOTO750
715 IFN1(X(B),Y(B))<>0THEN750
720 IFB=1THENRETURN
725 IFX(1)=X(2)THENIFY(1)=Y(2)THEN740
730 RETURN
740 PRINT"SAME COORD. SET TO 0"
741 LETN1(X(B)+1,Y(B)+1)=0:LETB=99:RETURN
750 PRINT"ILLEGAL COORDS. RETYPE":GOTO700
900 END
```

SAMPLE RUN

```
            U.B LIFE GAME
PLAYER 1  3 LIVE PIECES
X,Y
XXXX
X,Y
XXXX
X,Y
XXXX

PLAYER 2  3 LIVE PIECES
X,Y
XXXX
X,Y
XXXX
X,Y
XXXX


  0   1   2   3   4   5   0
  1     *                 1
  2     *                 2
  3     *           #     3
  4           #     #     4
  5                       5
  0   1   2   3   4   5   0

  0   1   2   3   4   5   0
  1                       1
  2     *     *           2
  3     *           #     3
  4                       4
  5                       5
PLAYER 1 X,Y
XXXX

PLAYER 2 X,Y
XXXX

  0   1   2   3   4   5   0
  1                       1
  2     *     *     *     2
  3     *     *           3
  4                 #  #  4
  5                       5
  0   1   2   3   4   5   0
PLAYER 1 X,Y
XXXX

PLAYER 2 X,Y
XXXX

  0   1   2   3   4   5   0
  1     #           *     1
  2                 *     2
  3     *                 3
  4           *  #  #     4
  5                 #     5
  0   1   2   3   4   5   0
PLAYER 1 X,Y
XXXX

PLAYER 2 X,Y
XXXX

  0   1   2   3   4   5   0
  1     *           *     1
  2                       2
  3                       3
  4           *  #        4
  5              #     *  5
  0   1   2   3   4   5   0
PLAYER 1 X,Y
XXXX

PLAYER 2 X,Y
XXXX

  0   1   2   3   4   5   0
  1                       1
  2                       2
  3           *           3
  4        #        *     4
  5        #        *     5
  0   1   2   3   4   5   0
PLAYER 1 X,Y
XXXX

PLAYER 2 X,Y
XXXX
SAME COORD. SET TO 0

  0   1   2   3   4   5   0
  1                       1
  2                       2
  3                       3
  4        *  *  *        4
  5                       5
  0   1   2   3   4   5   0
PLAYER 1 IS THE WINNER
```

SAMPLE RUN

This sample run shows the method of play.
Normally the co-ordinates typed in will be
over the other characters, so that the opposing
player can not see where the pieces are placed.

```
RUN
          U.B LIFE GAME
PLAYER 1 3 LIVE PIECES
X,Y
?1,1
X,Y
?1,2
X,Y
?1,3
PLAYER 2 3 LIVE PIECES
X,Y
?5,5
X,Y
?5,4
X,Y
?5,3

  0 1 2 3 4 5 0
1 *             1
2 *             2
3 *         #   3
4           #   4
5           #   5
  0 1 2 3 4 5 0
```

The board is printed in its initial state.

```
  0 1 2 3 4 5 0
1               1
2 * *           2
3               3
4         # #   4
5               5
  0 1 2 3 4 5 0
PLAYER 1 X,Y
?3,3

PLAYER 2 X,Y
?5,6
ILLEGAL COORDS. RETYPE
X,Y
?5,3
```

The co-ordinates typed in are
out of range.

```
  0 1 2 3 4 5 0
1               1
2   *           2
3   * *   #     3
4         # #   4
5               5
  0 1 2 3 4 5 0
PLAYER 1 X,Y
?3,2

PLAYER 2 X,Y
?2,4
```

```
  0 1 2 3 4 5 0
1               1
2   * * *       2
3   *     #     3
4   #     # #   4
5               5
  0 1 2 3 4 5 0
PLAYER 1 X,Y
?1,5

PLAYER 2 X,Y
?1,3
ILLEGAL COORDS. RETYPE
X,Y
?1,2
```

The co-ordinates typed in
are of a current live element.

```
  0 1 2 3 4 5 0
1   * *         1
2 # * * *       2
3   *     #     3
4 * #     # #   4
5               5
  0 1 2 3 4 5 0
PLAYER 1 X,Y
?3,5

PLAYER 2 X,Y
?3,5
SAME COORD. SET TO 0
```

Both players have entered
the same co-ordinates. No live
pieces are placed on the board.

```
  0 1 2 3 4 5 0
1   *       *   1
2 #       *     2
3   *       #   3
4 * #     # #   4
5               5
  0 1 2 3 4 5 0
PLAYER 1 X,Y
?4,4
ILLEGAL COORDS. RETYPE
X,Y
?4,3
```

```
PLAYER 2 X,Y
?5,3\3\2

  0 1 2 3 4 5 0
1         * *   1
2     *         2
3 # #           3
4   # # #       4
5               5
  0 1 2 3 4 5 0
PLAYER 1 X,Y
?4,4
ILLEGAL COORDS. RETYPE
X,Y
?4,3

PLAYER 2 X,Y
?5,3

  0 1 2 3 4 5 0
1       *   *   1
2   # *         2
3 # #       #   3
4   # #     #   4
5         #     5
  0 1 2 3 4 5 0
PLAYER 1 X,Y
?1,2

PLAYER 2 X,Y
?3,1

  0 1 2 3 4 5 0
1       # *     1
2 *       # *   2
3   # #     #   3
4   # #   # #   4
5   0 1 2 3 4 5 0
PLAYER 1 X,Y
?1,1

PLAYER 2 X,Y
?2,2

  0 1 2 3 4 5 0
1 *     # #     1
2 * # #         2
3 #   # #       3
4   # #         4
5   # # #       5
  0 1 2 3 4 5 0
PLAYER 1 X,Y
?1,5

PLAYER 2 X,Y
?1,4

  0 1 2 3 4 5 0
1 *     # #     1
2 *     # #     2
3       #       3
4               4
5 *       #     5
  0 1 2 3 4 5 0
PLAYER 1 X,Y
?1,3

PLAYER 2 X,Y
?1,3
SAME COORD. SET TO 0

  0 1 2 3 4 5 0
1       # #     1
2       # #     2
3       # #     3
4               4
5               5
  0 1 2 3 4 5 0
PLAYER 2 IS THE WINNER
```

149

LIT QZ

Description

This is a simple CAI-type program which presents four multiple-choice questions from children's literature. Running the program is self-explanatory.

Source

Pamela McGinley
Harcourt-Brace-Jovanavich
New York, NY

```
LIT QZ   EDUSYSTEM 30

5 R=0
10 PRINT "TEST YOUR KNOWLEDGE OF CHILDREN'S LITERATURE."
12 PRINT\PRINT "THIS IS A MULTIPLE-CHOICE QUIZ."
13 PRINT "TYPE A 1, 2, 3, OR 4 AFTER THE QUESTION MARK."
15 PRINT\PRINT "GOOD LUCK!!"\PRINT\PRINT
40 PRINT "IN 'PINOCCHIO', WHAT WAS THE NAME OF THE CAT?"
42 PRINT "1)TIGGER, 2)CICERO, 3)FIGARO, 4)GUIPETTO";
43 INPUT A\IF A=3 THEN 46
44 PRINT "SORRY,..FIGARO WAS HIS NAME."\GOTO 50
46 PRINT "VERY GOOD!  HERE'S ANOTHER."
47 R=R+1
50 PRINT\PRINT
51 PRINT"FROM WHOSE GARDEN DID BUGS BUNNY STEAL THE CARROTS?"
52 PRINT "1)MR. NIXON'S, 2)ELMER FUDD'S, 3)CLEM JUDD'S, 4)STROMBOLI'S";
53 INPUT A\IF A=2 THEN 56
54 PRINT "TOO BAD...IT WAS ELMER FUDD'S GARDEN."\GOTO 60
56 PRINT "PRETTY GOOD!"
57 R=R+1
60 PRINT\PRINT
61 PRINT "IN THE WIZARD OF OZ, DOROTHY'S DOG WAS NAMED"
62 PRINT "1)CICERO, 2)TRIXIE, 3)KING, 4)TOTO";
63 INPUT A\IF A=4 THEN 66
64 PRINT "BACK TO THE BOOKS...TOTO WAS HIS NAME."\GOTO 70
66 PRINT "YEA! YOU'RE A REAL LITERATURE GIANT!"
67 R=R+1
70 PRINT\PRINT
71 PRINT "WHO WAS THE FAIR MAIDEN WHO ATE THE POISON APPLE?"
72 PRINT "1)SLEEPING BEAUTY, 2)CINDERELLA, 3)SNOW WHITE, 4)WENDY";
73 INPUT A\IF A=3 THEN 76
74 PRINT "OH, COME ON NOW...IT WAS SNOW WHITE."\GOTO 80
76 PRINT "GOOD MEMORY!"
77 R=R+1
80 PRINT\PRINT
85 IF R=4 THEN 100
90 IF R<2 THEN 200
92 PRINT "NOT BAD, BUT YOU MIGHT SPEND A LITTLE MORE TIME"
94 PRINT "READING THE NURSERY GREATS."
96 STOP
100 PRINT "WOW!  THAT'S SUPER!  YOU REALLY KNOW YOUR NURSERY"
105 PRINT "STORIES.  "\PRINT
110 PRINT "YOUR NEXT QUIZ WILL BE ON 2ND CENTURY CHINESE"
120 PRINT "LITERATURE (HA, HA, HA)"
130 STOP
200 PRINT "UGH.  THAT WAS DEFINITELY NOT TOO SWIFT.  BACK TO"
205 PRINT "NURSERY SCHOOL FOR YOU, MY FRIEND."
999 END

READY
```

D. AHL

```
LIT QZ   EDUSYSTEM 30

TEST YOUR KNOWLEDGE OF CHILDREN'S LITERATURE.

THIS IS A MULTIPLE-CHOICE QUIZ.
TYPE A 1, 2, 3, OR 4 AFTER THE QUESTION MARK.

GOOD LUCK!!


IN 'PINOCCHIO', WHAT WAS THE NAME OF THE CAT?
1)TIGGER, 2)CICERO, 3)FIGARO, 4)GUIPETTO?3
VERY GOOD!  HERE'S ANOTHER.


FROM WHOSE GARDEN DID BUGS BUNNY STEAL THE CARROTS?
1)MR. NIXON'S, 2)ELMER FUDD'S, 3)CLEM JUDD'S, 4)STROMBOLI'S?2
PRETTY GOOD!


IN THE WIZARD OF OZ, DOROTHY'S DOG WAS NAMED
1)CICERO, 2)TRIXIE, 3)KING, 4)TOTO?4
YEA! YOU'RE A REAL LITERATURE GIANT!


WHO WAS THE FAIR MAIDEN WHO ATE THE POISON APPLE?
1)SLEEPING BEAUTY, 2)CINDERELLA, 3)SNOW WHITE, 4)WENDY?2
OH, COME ON NOW...IT WAS SNOW WHITE.


NOT BAD, BUT YOU MIGHT SPEND A LITTLE MORE TIME
READING THE NURSERY GREATS.

READY
```

MATHDI

Description

The program presents pictorial drill on addition facts using
printed dice with no reading involved. It is good for beginning
addition, since the answer can be derived from counting spots
on the dice as well as by memorizing math facts or awareness of
number concepts. It is especially effective run on an alpha-
numeric CRT terminal.

Program Author

Jim Gerrish
Bernice A. Ray School
Hanover, NH 03755

Illustration by Virginia Nigut,
Scott, Foresman and Co.

PROGRAM LISTING

MATHD   EDUSYSTEM 30

```
10 REM-MATHDICE*** (BASIC PROGRAM BEGINS AT LINE 100) WAS PROGRAMMED
11 REM-BY JIM GERRISH, FOURTH GRADE TEACHER AT THE BERNICE A. RAY
12 REM-SCHOOL, HANOVER, NEW HAMPSHIRE.   LAST CHANGE: 3/21/72.
13 REM
14 REM-PROGRAM PERFORMS PICTORAL DRILL ON ADDITION FACTS USING
15 REM-PRINTED DICE, NO READING INVOLVED.   GOOD FOR BEGINNING
16 REM-ADDITION, SINCE ANSWER CAN BE DERRIVED FROM COUNTING SPOTS
17 REM-DICE AS WELL AS BY MEMORIZING MATH FACTS OR AWARENESS
18 REM-OF NUMBER CONCEPTS.
19 REM-
20 PRINT"THIS PROGRAM GENERATES SUCCESSIVE PICTURES OF TWO DICE."
21 PRINT"WHEN TWO DICE AND AN EQUAL SIGN FOLLOWED BY A QUESTION"
22 PRINT"MARK HAVE BEEN PRINTED, TYPE YOUR ANSWER AND THE RETURN KEY."
23 PRINT"TO CONCLUDE THE LESSON, TYPE CTRL/C AS YOUR ANSWER."
24 PRINT
25 PRINT
100 RANDOMIZE
105 LET N=N+1
110 LET D=INT(RND(0)*6+1)
120 PRINT ".-----."
130 IF D=1 THEN 200
140 IF D=2 THEN 180
150 IF D=3 THEN 180
160 PRINT "I * * I"
170 GOTO 210
180 PRINT "I *   I"
190 GOTO 210
200 PRINT "I     I"
210 IF D=2 THEN 260
220 IF D=4 THEN 260
230 IF D=6 THEN 270
240 PRINT "I  *  I"
250 GOTO 280
260 PRINT "I.    I"
265 GOTO 280
270 PRINT "I * * I"
280 IF D=1 THEN 350
290 IF D=2 THEN 330
300 IF D=3 THEN 330
310 PRINT "I * * I"
320 GOTO 360
330 PRINT "I   * I"
340 GOTO 360
350 PRINT "I     I"
360 PRINT ".-----."
370 PRINT
375 IF N=2 THEN 500
380 PRINT "   +"
381 PRINT
400 LET A=D
410 GOTO 100
500 LET T=D+A
510 PRINT "        = ";
520 INPUT T1
530 IF T1=T THEN 590
540 PRINT "NO, COUNT THE SPOTS AND GIVE ANOTHER ANSWER."
541 PRINT "        = ";
550 INPUT T2
560 IF T2=T THEN 590
570 PRINT "NO, THE ANSWER IS ";T
580 GOTO 600
590 PRINT "RIGHT!"
600 PRINT
601 PRINT "THE DICE ROLL AGAIN....."
610 PRINT
615 LET N=0
620 GOTO 100
900 END

READY
```

SAMPLE RUN

MATHD   EDUSYSTEM 30

```
THIS PROGRAM GENERATES SUCCESSIVE PICTURES OF TWO DICE.
WHEN TWO DICE AND AN EQUAL SIGN FOLLOWED BY A QUESTION
MARK HAVE BEEN PRINTED, TYPE YOUR ANSWER AND THE RETURN KEY.
TO CONCLUDE THE LESSON, TYPE CTRL/C AS YOUR ANSWER.


.-----.
I *   I
I     I
I   * I
.-----.

   +

.-----.
I     I
I  *  I
I     I
.-----.

        = ?3
RIGHT!

THE DICE ROLL AGAIN.....

.-----.
I * * I
I * I
I * * I
.-----.

   +

.-----.
I *   I
I     I
I . * I
.-----.

        = ?7
NO, COUNT THE SPOTS AND GIVE ANOTHER ANSWER.
        = ?5
NO, THE ANSWER IS  6

THE DICE ROLL AGAIN.....

.-----.
I * * I
I  *  I
I * * I
.-----.

   +

.-----.
I * * I
I     I
I * * I
.-----.

        = ?9
RIGHT!

THE DICE ROLL AGAIN.....

.-----.
I *,  I
I     I
I   * I
.-----.

   +

.-----.
I     I
I  *  I
I     I
.-----.

        = ?3
RIGHT!

THE DICE ROLL AGAIN.....

.-----.
I * * I
I * * I
I * * I
.-----.

   +

.-----.
I *   I
I     I
I   * I
.-----.

        = ?7
RIGHT!
```

MNOPLY

GAME OF MONOPOLY

Description

MNOPLY is a simulation of the most popular board game in the
world, Monopoly. It varies from the actual game only in that
two players are the maximum number that can play.

The dialog during the game presents complete rules and instructions. The inputs are designed so that when anything except the
required input is typed in, the entire segment will be ignored.
When questions are asked about property to be sold, the full
name is required--e.g., STATES AVENUE.

In the computer game, you always pay $50 to get out of jail
unless you have a "GET OUT OF JAIL FREE" card. No double rolls.

As in the board game, before you can improve your property
(build houses), you must own all of the pieces of that color
property--i.e., have a monopoly of a particular color group.
The program will automatically ignore attempts to build houses
if you don't have a color group monopoly. Here are the color
groups for your reference:

    Purple: Red:
        BALTIC AVE   KENTUCKY AVE
        MEDITERRANEAN AVE   INDIANA AVE
    Light Blue: ILLINOIS AVE
        ORIENTAL AVE   Yellow:
        VERMONT AVE   ATLANTIC AVE
        CONNECTICUT AVE   VENTNOR AVE
    Maroon: MARVIN GARDENS
        ST. CHARLES PL   Green:
        STATES AVE   PACIFIC AVE
        VIRGINIA AVE   NORTH CAROLINA AVE
    Orange: PENNSYLVANIA AVE
        ST. JAMES PL   Dark Blue:
        TENNESSEE AVE   PARK PL
        NEW YORK AVE   BOARDWALK

Computer Limitations

MNOPLY was written for DIGITAL RSTS-11 or RSTS/E. It requires
two virtual memory files which are built via the file-building
program.

Source

David Barker
Southeastern State College
Durant, OK 74701

PROGRAM LISTING

```
1  ! THE FOLLOWING PROGRAM IS DESIGNED TO BUILD THE DISK FILES
2  ! NEEDED TO PLAY MONOPOLY.  TWO FILES MUST BE BUILT, THE FIRST
3  ! CONTAINING THE NAMES OF THE PROPERTY, THE SOLD AND UNSOLD
4  ! FLAGS, THE PRICES OF THE PROPERTY, AND THEIR RENTS.
5  ! THE SECOND FILE CONTAINS THE CHANCE AND THE COMMUNITY
6  ! CHEST MESSAGES AND THE INSTRUCTION MESSAGES FOR THE
7  ! PLAYERS.  THE DATA FOR THESE FILES WILL BE READ FROM THE
8  ! PROGRAM WHEN IT IS RUN. THESE FILES MUST BE BUILT BEFORE THE
9  ! GAME CAN BE PLAYED
20 OPEN "PRPRTY" AS FILE 1: DIM #1,GS(40%)=25,LX(40),P(40%),R(40%)
30 OPEN "MESAJ" AS FILE 3: DIM #3,CS(10)=50%,ZS(10)=50%,MS(20)=50%
40 FOR I=1 TO 40
42 READ GS(I),LX(I),P(I),R(I)
44 NEXT I
50 FOR I=1 TO 20
52 READ MS(I)
54 NEXT I
60 FOR I=1 TO 10
62 READ CS(I)
64 NEXT I
70 FOR I=1 TO 10
72 READ ZS(I)
74 NEXT I
100 DATA "MEDITERRANEAN AVENUE",0,60,2
102 DATA "COMMUNITY CHEST",0,0,0
104 DATA "BALTIC AVENUE",0,60,4
106 DATA "INCOME TAX",0,0,0
108 DATA "READING RAILROAD",0,200,25
110 DATA "ORIENTAL AVENUE",0,100,6
112 DATA "CHANCE ?",0,0,0
114 DATA "VERMONT AVENUE",0,100,6
116 DATA "CONNECTICUT AVENUE",0,120,8
118 DATA "VISITING IN JAIL",0,0,0
120 DATA "ST.CHARLES PLACE",0,140,1'
122 DATA "ELECTRIC COMPANY",0,150,3'
124 DATA "STATES AVENUE",0,140,10
126 DATA "VIRGINIA AVENUE",0,160,12
128 DATA "PENNSYLVANIA RAILROAD",0,200,25
130 DATA "ST.JAMES PLACE",0,180,14
132 DATA "COMMUNITY CHEST",0,0,0
134 DATA "TENNESSEE AVENUE",0,180,14
136 DATA "NEW YORK AVENUE",0,200,16
138 DATA "FREE PARKING",0,0,0
140 DATA "KENTUCKY AVENUE",0,220,18
142 DATA "CHANCE ?",0,0,0
144 DATA "INDIANA AVENUE",0,220,18
146 DATA "ILLINOIS AVENUE",0,240,20
148 DATA "B.& O. RAILROAD",0,200,25
150 DATA "ATLANTIC AVENUE",0,260,22
152 DATA "VENTNOR AVENUE",0,260,22
154 DATA "WATER WORKS",0,150,35
156 DATA "MARVIN GARDENS",0,280,24
158 DATA "GO TO JAIL",0,0,0
160 DATA "PACIFIC AVENUE",0,300,26
162 DATA "NORTH CAROLINA AVENUE",0,300,26
164 DATA "COMMUNITY CHEST",0,0,0
166 DATA "PENNSYLVANIA AVENUE",0,320,28
168 DATA "SHORT LINE",0,200,25
170 DATA "CHANCE ?",0,0,0
172 DATA "PARK PLACE",0,350,35
174 DATA "LUXURY TAX",0,0,0
176 DATA "BOARDWALK",0,400,50
178 DATA "GO",0,0,0
200 DATA "**************THIS IS MATLIDA'S MONOPOLY FOR TWO*************"
202 DATA "EACH PLAYER HAS $1500"
204 DATA "WHEN YOU BUY HOUSES YOU HAVE TO PUT THE SAME"
206 DATA "NUMBER ON EACH MEMBER OF A COLOR GROUP"
208 DATA "WHEN YOU BUY HOUSES INPUT THE NUMBER YOU WANT PER LOT"
210 DATA "TO ROLL DICE TYPE ROLL"
212 DATA "IT IS FOR SALE FOR ONLY"
214 DATA "IF YOU WISH TO BUY IT TYPE BUY"
216 DATA "YOU ROLLED DOUBLES**ROLL AGAIN"
218 DATA "YOU ROLLED 3 SETS OF DOUBLES**GO TO JAIL"
220 DATA "IF YOU WANT TO QUIT TYPE QUIT"
222 DATA "YOU ALREADY OWN THIS PIECE OF PROPERTY"
224 DATA "IF THERE IS ANY PROPERTY YOU WISH TO SELL AND"
226 DATA "YOUR OPPONENT WANTS TO BUY TYPE SELL"
228 DATA "IF YOU NEED A LIST OF PROPERTY TYPE LIST"
230 DATA "YOU CAN'T SELL THIS**YOU DON'T OWN IT"
232 DATA "WHAT PROPERTY DO YOU WANT TO SELL"
234 DATA "IF THERE IS ANY MORE PROPERTY YOU WISH TO SELL TYPE YES"
236 DATA "IF YOU WANT TO IMPROVE YOUR PROPERTY TYPE HOUSE"
238 DATA "YOU DON'T HAVE ENOUGH MONEY FOR THAT MANY HOUSES"
250 DATA "PAY POOR TAX OF $15"
252 DATA "ADVANCE TOKEN TO ILLINOIS AVENUE"
254 DATA "GO BACK THREE SPACES"
256 DATA "ADVANCE TO GO"
258 DATA "BANK PAYS YOU DIVIDEND OF $50"
260 DATA "TAKE A RIDE ON THE READING"
262 DATA "GO TO JAIL"
264 DATA "BUILDING AND LOAN MATURES**COLLECT $150"
266 DATA "ADVANCE TO BOARDWALK"
268 DATA "ADVANCE TO ST.CHARLES PLACE"
280 DATA "XMAS FUND MATURES**COLLECT $100"
282 DATA "LIFE INSURANCE MATURES**COLLECT $100"
284 DATA "INCOME TAX REFUND**COLLECT $20"
286 DATA "DOCTOR'S FEE**PAY $50"
288 DATA "YOU INHERIT $100"
290 DATA "ADVANCE TO GO"
292 DATA "PAY HOSPITAL $100"
294 DATA "GO TO JAIL"
296 DATA "PAY SCHOOL TAX OF $50"
298 DATA "BANK ERROR IN YOUR FAVOR**COLLECT $200"
300 CLOSE 1,3:   END
```

```
1  ! MONOPOLY GAME BY DAVID BARKER, SOUTHEASTERN STATE COLLEGE, DURANT, OK
2  ! SLIGHT PROGRAM MODIFICATIONS BY DAVID AHL, DIGITAL
3  M(1),M(2)=1500%: I(1),I(2)=0: DIM AS(25),BS(25),HX(40)
7  OPEN "PRPRTY" AS FILE 1: DIM #1,GS(40%)=25,LX(40),P(40%),R(40%)
8  FOR I=1 TO 39:LX(I),HX(I)=NEXT I:FOR I=1 TO 8:U(I)=0:NEXT I
9  DEF FNR=(HX(I(Z))*R(I(Z))=10%)
10 OPEN "MESAJ" AS FILE 3: DIM #3,CS(10)=50%,ZS(10)=50%,MS(20)=50%
15 & MS(1)&:&:&   "*RULES=*"& MS(2)& MS(3)&: MS(4)& MS(5)
30 INPUT"WHO IS PLAYER #1"NS(1): INPUT"WHO IS PLAYER #2"NS(2)
100 PRINT: PRINT "*"NS(1)"S TURN*********"·           F=0
102 Z=1%: GOSUB 1000: GOSUB 2000
115 IF D=D1 THEN F=F+1: IF F=3 THEN PRINT MS(9): GOTO 102
117 IF F=3 THEN PRINT MS(10): I(Z)=10: M(Z)=M(Z)-50%
200 PRINT: PRINT "*"NS(2)"S TURN*********"·           F=0
202 Z=2%: GOSUB 1000: GOSUB 2000
215 IF D=D1 THEN F=F+1: IF F<3 THEN PRINT MS(9): GOTO 202
217 IF F=3 THEN PRINT MS(10): I(Z)=10: M(Z)=M(Z)-50%
225 PRINT MS(11):INPUT FS: IF FS="QUIT" THEN 30000 ELSE 100
1000 PRINT MS(6):INPUT FS: RANDOMIZE: X=RND(0): Y=RND(0) !DICE ROLL
1002 IF X>=0 AND X<=.16 THEN D=1
1003 IF X>.16 AND X<=.32 THEN D=2
1004 IF X>.32 AND X<=.48 THEN D=3
1005 IF X>.48 AND X<=.64 THEN D=4
1006 IF X>.64 AND X<=.81 THEN D=5
1007 IF X>.81 AND X<=1 THEN D=6
1009 IF Y>=0 AND Y<=.16 THEN D1=1
1010 IF Y>.16 AND Y<=.32 THEN D1=2
1011 IF Y>.32 AND Y<=.48 THEN D1=3
1012 IF Y>.48 AND Y<=.64 THEN D1=4
1013 IF Y>.64 AND Y<=.81 THEN D1=5
1014 IF Y>.81 AND Y<=1 THEN D1=6
1015 PRINT "YOU ROLLED A"D"AND A"D1: I(Z)=I(Z)+(D+D1)
1016 IF I(Z)>40% THEN I(Z)=I(Z)-40%:M(Z)=M(Z)+200%
1017 RETURN
2000 PRINT"YOU ARE ON "GS(I(Z))     !PLACEMENT
2002 IF I(Z)=2 OR I(Z)=17 OR I(Z)=33 THEN 4100 !COM CHEST
2004 IF I(Z)=4 THEN M(Z)=M(Z)-200% :RETURN !INC TAX
2006 IF I(Z)=7 OR I(Z)=22 OR I(Z)=36 THEN 4400 !CHANCE
2008 IF I(Z)=10 OR I(Z)=20 THEN RETURN !VISIT IN JAIL&FREE PARKING
2010 IF I(Z)=30 THEN M(Z)=M(Z)-50%: I(Z)=10: RETURN !JAIL
2011 IF I(Z)=38 THEN M(Z)=M(Z)-75%: RETURN !LUX TAX
2012 IF I(Z)=40 THEN M(Z)=M(Z)+200%: I(Z)=0: RETURN !GO
2018 IF LX(I(Z))=Z THEN PRINT MS(12): GOTO 3100
2019 IF (HX(I(Z))=0 AND LX(I(Z))>0 AND LX(I(Z))<>Z) THEN 2125
2020 IF (HX(I(Z))>0 AND LX(I(Z))>0 AND LX(I(Z))<>Z) THEN 2100
2022 PRINT MS(7):P(I(Z))"DOLLARS"
2024 PRINT MS(8):INPUT FS: IF FS<>"BUY" THEN 3100
2026 M(Z)=M(Z)-P(I(Z)):PRINT "YOU NOW HAVE"M(Z)"DOLLARS
2027 LX(I(Z))=Z:GOTO 3100
2100 IF Z=1 THEN M(Z)=M(Z)-FNR: M(2)=M(2)+FNR
2101 PRINT "YOU OWE"FNR"DOLLARS RENT":RETURN
2102 IF Z=2 THEN M(Z)=M(Z)-FNR: M(1)=M(1)+FNR
2103 PRINT "YOU OWE"FNR"DOLLARS RENT":RETURN
2125 IF Z=1 THEN M(Z)=M(Z)-R(I(Z)):M(2)=M(2)+R(I(Z))
2126 PRINT "YOU OWE"R(I(Z))"DOLLARS RENT":RETURN
2127 IF Z=2 THEN M(Z)=M(Z)-R(I(Z)): M(1)=M(1)+R(I(Z))
2128 PRINT "YOU OWE"R(I(Z))"DOLLARS RENT":RETURN
3100 PRINT MS(13):INPUT FS: IF FS="SELL" THEN GOSUB 3150
3105 PRINT MS(19):INPUT HS: IF HS="HOUSE" THEN 3200 ELSE RETURN
3150 PRINT MS(15):INPUT FS: IF FS="LIST" THEN GOSUB 3170
3152 PRINT MS(17):INPUT VS: INPUT "HOW MUCH DO YOU WANT FOR IT"V
3154 FOR I=1 TO 39
3156 IF VS=GS(I) THEN IF LX(I)=0 THEN PRINT MS(16): RETURN
3158 IF VS=GS(I) THEN IF LX(I)=1 THEN M(1)=M(1)+V
     :M(2)=M(2)-V: LX(I)=2: GOTO 3165
3160 IF VS=GS(I) THEN IF LX(I)=2 THEN M(2)=M(2)+V
     :M(1)=M(1)-V: LX(I)=1: GOTO 3165
3162 NEXT I
3165 PRINT MS(18):INPUT FS: IF FS="YES" THEN 3152 ELSE RETURN
3170 C,D=0: FOR I=1 TO 39
3172 IF LX(I)=1 THEN C=C+1: AS(C)=GS(I)
3174 IF LX(I)=2 THEN D=D+1: BS(D)=GS(I)
3175 NEXT I
3176 PRINT NS(1)"S PROPERTY": FOR I=1 TO C: PRINT AS(I): NEXT I
3178 PRINT NS(2)"S PROPERTY": FOR I=1 TO D: PRINT BS(I): NEXT I:RETURN
3200 IF LX(1)=Z AND LX(3)=Z THEN &"HOW MANY HOUSES AT $50 EACH DO YOU WANT ON"
     :PRINT GS(1)" "GS(3)":INPUT U:GOSUB 3250
3202 IF LX(6)=Z AND LX(8)=Z AND LX(9)=Z THEN
     PRINT "HOW MANY HOUSES AT $50 EACH DO YOU WANT ON"
     :PRINT GS(6)" "GS(8)" "GS(9):INPUT U:GOSUB 3252
3204 IF LX(11)=Z AND LX(13)=Z AND LX(14)=Z THEN
     PRINT "HOW MANY HOUSES AT $100 EACH DO YOOU WANT ON"
     :PRINT GS(11)" "GS(13)" "GS(14):INPUT U:GOSUB 3254
3206 IF LX(16)=Z AND LX(18)=Z AND LX(19)=Z THEN
     PRINT "HOW MANY HOUSES AT $100 EACH DO YOU WANT ON"
     :PRINT GS(16)" "GS(18)" "GS(19):INPUT U:GOSUB 3256
3208 IF LX(21)=Z AND LX(23)=Z AND LX(24)=Z THEN
     PRINT "HOW MANY HOUSES AT $150 EACH DO YOU WANT ON"
     :PRINT GS(21)" "GS(23)" "GS(24):INPUT U:GOSUB 3258
3210 IF LX(26)=Z AND LX(27)=Z AND LX(29)=Z THEN
     PRINT "HOW MANY HOUSES AT $150 EACH DO YOU WANT ON"
     :PRINT GS(26)" "GS(27)" "GS(29):INPUT U:GOSUB 3260
3212 IF LX(31)=Z AND LX(32)=Z AND LX(34)=Z THEN
     PRINT "HOW MANY HOUSES AT $200 EACH DO YOU WANT ON"
     :PRINT GS(31)" "GS(32)" "GS(34):INPUT U:GOSUB 3262
3214 IF LX(37)=Z AND LX(39)=Z THEN
     PRINT "HOW MANY HOUSES AT $200 EACH DO YOU WANT ON"
     :PRINT GS(37)" "GS(39):INPUT U:GOSUB 3264
3220 RETURN
3250 U(1)=U(1)+U: M(Z)=M(Z)-(U*100%): IF M(Z)<0 THEN PRINT MS(20)
     :M(Z)=M(Z)+(U*100%):U(1)=U(1)-U:RETURN
3251 HX(1),HX(3)=U(1): RETURN
3252 U(2)=U(2)+U: M(Z)=M(Z)-(U*150%): IF M(Z)<0 THEN PRINT MS(20)
     :M(Z)=M(Z)+(U*150%): U(2)=U(2)-U: RETURN
3253 HX(6),HX(8),HX(9)=U(2): RETURN
3254 U(3)=U(3)+U: M(Z)=M(Z)-(U*150%): IF M(Z)<0 THEN PRINT MS(20)
     :M(Z)=M(Z)+(U*150%): U(3)=U(3)-U: RETURN
3255 HX(11),HX(13),HX(14)=U(3): RETURN
3256 U(4)=U(4)+U: M(Z)=M(Z)-(U*300%): IF M(Z)<0 THEN PRINT MS(20)
     :M(Z)=M(Z)+(U*300%): U(4)=U(4)-U: RETURN
3257 HX(16),HX(18),HX(19)=U(4): RETURN
3258 U(5)=U(5)+U: M(Z)=M(Z)-(U*450%): IF M(Z)<0 THEN PRINT MS(20)
     :M(Z)=M(Z)+(U*450%): U(5)=U(5)-U: RETURN
3259 HX(21),HX(23),HX(24)=U(5): RETURN
```

```
3260 U(6)=U(6)+U: M(Z)=M(Z)-(U+450%): IF M(Z)<0 THEN PRINT M$(20)
     :M(Z)=M(Z)+(U+450%): U(6)=U(6)-U: RETURN
3261 H%(26),H%(27),H%(29)=U(6): RETURN
3262 U(7)=U(7)+U: M(Z)=M(Z)-(U+600%): IF M(Z)<0 THEN PRINT M$(20)
     :M(Z)=M(Z)+(U+600%): U(7)=U(7)-U: RETURN
3263 H%(31),H%(32),H%(34)=U(7): RETURN
3264 U(8)=U(8)+U: M(Z)=M(Z)-(U+400%): IF M(Z)<0 THEN PRINT M$(20)
     :M(Z)=M(Z)+(U+400%): U(8)=U(8)-U: RETURN
3265 H%(37),H%(39)=U(8): RETURN
4100 RANDOMIZE: L=RND(0) :COMMUNITY CHEST
4102 IF L>=0 AND L<=.1 THEN PRINT Z$(1): M(Z)=M(Z)+100%: RETURN
4104 IF L>.1 AND L<=.2 THEN PRINT Z$(2): M(Z)=M(Z)+100%: RETURN
4106 IF L>.2 AND L<=.3 THEN PRINT Z$(3): M(Z)=M(Z)+20%: RETURN
4108 IF L>.3 AND L<=.4 THEN PRINT Z$(4): M(Z)=M(Z)+100%: RETURN
4110 IF L>.4 AND L<=.5 THEN PRINT Z$(5): M(Z)=M(Z)-100%: RETURN
4112 IF L>.5 AND L<=.6 THEN PRINT Z$(6): M(Z)=M(Z)+200%: I(Z)=0: RETURN
4114 IF L>.6 AND L<=.7 THEN PRINT Z$(7): M(Z)=M(Z)+100%: RETURN
4116 IF L>.7 AND L<=.8 THEN PRINT Z$(8): M(Z)=M(Z)-50%: I(Z)=10: RETURN
4118 IF L>.8 AND L<=.9 THEN PRINT Z$(9): M(Z)=M(Z)-50%: RETURN
4120 IF L>.9 AND L<=1 THEN PRINT Z$(10): M(Z)=M(Z)+200%: RETURN
4400 RANDOMIZE: L=RND(0) :CHANCE
4402 IF L>=0 AND L<=.1 THEN PRINT C$(1): M(Z)=M(Z)-15%: RETURN
4404 IF L>.1 AND L<=.2 THEN PRINT C$(2): I(Z)=24: GOSUB 2000: RETURN
4406 IF L>.2 AND L<=.3 THEN PRINT C$(3): I(Z)=I(Z)-3: GOSUB 2000: RETURN
4408 IF L>.3 AND L<=.4 THEN PRINT C$(4): I(Z)=0: M(Z)=M(Z)+200%: RETURN
4410 IF L>.4 AND L<=.5 THEN PRINT C$(5): M(Z)=M(Z)+50%: RETURN
4412 IF L>.5 AND L<=.6 THEN PRINT C$(6): I(Z)=5
     :M(Z)=M(Z)+200%: GOSUB 2000: RETURN
4414 IF L>.6 AND L<=.7 THEN PRINT C$(7): I(Z)=10: M(Z)=M(Z)-50%: RETURN
4416 IF L>.7 AND L<=.8 THEN PRINT C$(8): M(Z)=M(Z)+150%: RETURN
4418 IF L>.8 AND L<=.9 THEN PRINT C$(9): I(Z)=39: GOSUB 2000: RETURN
4420 IF L>.9 AND L<=1 THEN PRINT C$(10): I(Z)=11: GOSUB 2000: RETURN
30000 C,D=0
30002 FOR I=1 TO 39
30004 IF L%(I)=1 THEN C=C+1:A$(C)=G$(I)
30006 IF L%(I)=2 THEN D=D+1:B$(D)=G$(I)
30008 NEXT I:PRINT:PRINT
30009 PRINT N$(1)" OWNED THE FOLLOWING PROPERTY"
      :FOR I=1 TO C:PRINT A$(I):NEXT I
30010 PRINT "AND HAD":M(1):"DOLLARS AT THE END OF THE GAME"
30011 PRINT N$(2)" OWNED THE FOLLOWING PROPERTY"
      :FOR I=1 TO D:PRINT B$(I):NEXT I
30012 PRINT "AND HAD":M(2):"DOLLARS AT THE END OF THE GAME"
30013 CLOSE 1,3:END
```

SAMPLE RUN

```
RUN MONPLY
*************THIS IS MATLIDA'S MONOPOLY FOR TWO*************


**RULES**
EACH PLAYER HAS $1500
WHEN YOU BUY HOUSES YOU HAVE TO PUT THE SAME
NUMBER ON EACH MEMBER OF A COLOR GROUP
WHEN YOU BUY HOUSES INPUT THE NUMBER YOU WANT PER LOT
WHO IS PLAYER #1? DAVE
WHO IS PLAYER #2? SANDY

**DAVE'S TURN**********
TO ROLL DICE TYPE ROLL? ROLL
YOU ROLLED A 6 AND A 1
YOU ARE ON CHANCE ?
ADVANCE TOKEN TO ILLINOIS AVENUE
YOU ARE ON ILLINOIS AVENUE
IT IS FOR SALE FOR ONLY 240 DOLLARS
IF YOU WISH TO BUY IT TYPE BUY? BUY
YOU NOW HAVE 1260 DOLLARS
IF THERE IS ANY PROPERTY YOU WISH TO SELL AND
YOUR OPPONENT WANTS TO BUY TYPE SELL?
IF YOU WANT TO IMPROVE YOUR PROPERTY TYPE HOUSE?

**SANDY'S TURN**********
TO ROLL DICE TYPE ROLL? ROLL
YOU ROLLED A 2 AND A 4
YOU ARE ON ORIENTAL AVENUE
IT IS FOR SALE FOR ONLY 100 DOLLARS
IF YOU WISH TO BUY IT TYPE BUY? BUY
YOU NOW HAVE 1400 DOLLARS
IF THERE IS ANY PROPERTY YOU WISH TO SELL AND
YOUR OPPONENT WANTS TO BUY TYPE SELL?
IF YOU WANT TO IMPROVE YOUR PROPERTY TYPE HOUSE?
IF YOU WANT TO QUIT TYPE QUIT?

**DAVE'S TURN**********
TO ROLL DICE TYPE ROLL? ROLL
YOU ROLLED A 3 AND A 3
YOU ARE ON GO TO JAIL
YOU ROLLED DOUBLES**ROLL AGAIN
TO ROLL DICE TYPE ROLL? ROLL
YOU ROLLED A 6 AND A 5
YOU ARE ON KENTUCKY AVENUE
IT IS FOR SALE FOR ONLY 220 DOLLARS
IF YOU WISH TO BUY IT TYPE BUY? BUY
YOU NOW HAVE 990 DOLLARS
IF THERE IS ANY PROPERTY YOU WISH TO SELL AND
YOUR OPPONENT WANTS TO BUY TYPE SELL?
IF YOU WANT TO IMPROVE YOUR PROPERTY TYPE HOUSE?

**SANDY'S TURN**********
TO ROLL DICE TYPE ROLL? ROLL
YOU ROLLED A 1 AND A 5
YOU ARE ON ELECTRIC COMPANY
IT IS FOR SALE FOR ONLY 150 DOLLARS
IF YOU WISH TO BUY IT TYPE BUY?
IF THERE IS ANY PROPERTY YOU WISH TO SELL AND
YOUR OPPONENT WANTS TO BUY TYPE SELL?
IF YOU WANT TO IMPROVE YOUR PROPERTY TYPE HOUSE?
IF YOU WANT TO QUIT TYPE QUIT?
```

```
**DAVE'S TURN**********
TO ROLL DICE TYPE ROLL? ROLL
YOU ROLLED A 5 AND A 4
YOU ARE ON GO TO JAIL

**SANDY'S TURN**********
TO ROLL DICE TYPE ROLL? ROLL
YOU ROLLED A 6 AND A 1
YOU ARE ON NEW YORK AVENUE
IT IS FOR SALE FOR ONLY 200 DOLLARS
IF YOU WISH TO BUY IT TYPE BUY? BUY
YOU NOW HAVE 1200 DOLLARS
IF THERE IS ANY PROPERTY YOU WISH TO SELL AND
YOUR OPPONENT WANTS TO BUY TYPE SELL?
IF YOU WANT TO IMPROVE YOUR PROPERTY TYPE HOUSE?
IF YOU WANT TO QUIT TYPE QUIT?

**DAVE'S TURN**********
TO ROLL DICE TYPE ROLL? ROLL
YOU ROLLED A 5 AND A 4
YOU ARE ON NEW YORK AVENUE
YOU OWE 16 DOLLARS RENT

**SANDY'S TURN**********
TO ROLL DICE TYPE ROLL? ROLL
YOU ROLLED A 6 AND A 4
YOU ARE ON MARVIN GARDENS
IT IS FOR SALE FOR ONLY 280 DOLLARS
IF YOU WISH TO BUY IT TYPE BUY? BUY
YOU NOW HAVE 936 DOLLARS
IF THERE IS ANY PROPERTY YOU WISH TO SELL AND
YOUR OPPONENT WANTS TO BUY TYPE SELL?
IF YOU WANT TO IMPROVE YOUR PROPERTY TYPE HOUSE?
IF YOU WANT TO QUIT TYPE QUIT?

**DAVE'S TURN**********
TO ROLL DICE TYPE ROLL? ROLL
YOU ROLLED A 4 AND A 5
YOU ARE ON WATER WORKS
IT IS FOR SALE FOR ONLY 150 DOLLARS
IF YOU WISH TO BUY IT TYPE BUY?
IF THERE IS ANY PROPERTY YOU WISH TO SELL AND
YOUR OPPONENT WANTS TO BUY TYPE SELL?
IF YOU WANT TO IMPROVE YOUR PROPERTY TYPE HOUSE?

**SANDY'S TURN**********
TO ROLL DICE TYPE ROLL? ROLL
YOU ROLLED A 6 AND A 1
YOU ARE ON CHANCE ?
ADVANCE TOKEN TO ILLINOIS AVENUE
YOU ARE ON ILLINOIS AVENUE
YOU OWE 20 DOLLARS RENT
IF YOU WANT TO QUIT TYPE QUIT?

**DAVE'S TURN**********
TO ROLL DICE TYPE ROLL? ROLL
YOU ROLLED A 3 AND A 6
YOU ARE ON PARK PLACE
IT IS FOR SALE FOR ONLY 350 DOLLARS
IF YOU WISH TO BUY IT TYPE BUY? BUY
YOU NOW HAVE 574 DOLLARS
IF THERE IS ANY PROPERTY YOU WISH TO SELL AND
YOUR OPPONENT WANTS TO BUY TYPE SELL?
IF YOU WANT TO IMPROVE YOUR PROPERTY TYPE HOUSE?

**SANDY'S TURN**********
TO ROLL DICE TYPE ROLL? ROLL
YOU ROLLED A 6 AND A 2
YOU ARE ON NORTH CAROLINA AVENUE
IT IS FOR SALE FOR ONLY 300 DOLLARS
IF YOU WISH TO BUY IT TYPE BUY? BUY
YOU NOW HAVE 636 DOLLARS
IF THERE IS ANY PROPERTY YOU WISH TO SELL AND
YOUR OPPONENT WANTS TO BUY TYPE SELL?
IF YOU WANT TO IMPROVE YOUR PROPERTY TYPE HOUSE?
IF YOU WANT TO QUIT TYPE QUIT?

**DAVE'S TURN**********
TO ROLL DICE TYPE ROLL? ROLL
YOU ROLLED A 5 AND A 1
YOU ARE ON BALTIC AVENUE
IT IS FOR SALE FOR ONLY 60 DOLLARS
IF YOU WISH TO BUY IT TYPE BUY?
IF THERE IS ANY PROPERTY YOU WISH TO SELL AND
YOUR OPPONENT WANTS TO BUY TYPE SELL?
IF YOU WANT TO IMPROVE YOUR PROPERTY TYPE HOUSE?

**SANDY'S TURN**********
TO ROLL DICE TYPE ROLL? ROLL
YOU ROLLED A 1 AND A 6
YOU ARE ON BOARDWALK
IT IS FOR SALE FOR ONLY 400 DOLLARS
IF YOU WISH TO BUY IT TYPE BUY? BUY
YOU NOW HAVE 236 DOLLARS
IF THERE IS ANY PROPERTY YOU WISH TO SELL AND
YOUR OPPONENT WANTS TO BUY TYPE SELL?
IF YOU WANT TO IMPROVE YOUR PROPERTY TYPE HOUSE?
IF YOU WANT TO QUIT TYPE QUIT?

**DAVE'S TURN**********
TO ROLL DICE TYPE ROLL? ROLL
YOU ROLLED A 2 AND A 5
YOU ARE ON VISITING IN JAIL

**SANDY'S TURN**********
TO ROLL DICE TYPE ROLL? ROLL
YOU ROLLED A 6 AND A 6
YOU ARE ON ST. CHARLES PLACE
IT IS FOR SALE FOR ONLY 140 DOLLARS
IF YOU WISH TO BUY IT TYPE BUY? BUY
YOU NOW HAVE 296 DOLLARS
IF THERE IS ANY PROPERTY YOU WISH TO SELL AND
YOUR OPPONENT WANTS TO BUY TYPE SELL?
IF YOU WANT TO IMPROVE YOUR PROPERTY TYPE HOUSE?
YOU ROLLED DOUBLES**ROLL AGAIN
TO ROLL DICE TYPE ROLL? ROLL
YOU ROLLED A 5 AND A 5
YOU ARE ON KENTUCKY AVENUE
YOU OWE 18 DOLLARS RENT
```

MUGWMP

FIND 4 MUGWUMPS IN HIDING

Description

Your objective in this game is to find the four Mugwumps hiding
on various squares of a 10 by 10 grid. Homebase (lower left) is
position (0,0) and a guess is a pair of whole numbers (0 to 9),
separated by commas. The first number is the number of units
to the right of homebase and the second number is the distance
above homebase.

You get ten guesses to locate the four Mugwumps; after each guess,
the computer tells you how close you are to each Mugwump. Playing the game with the aid of graph paper and a compass should
allow you to find all the Mugwumps in six or seven moves using
triangulation--i.e., like LORAN radio navigation.

Source

This program was modified slightly by Bob Albrecht of People's
Computer Company. The original source were students of:

Bud Valenti
Project SOLO
University of Pittsburgh
Pittsburgh, PA 15213

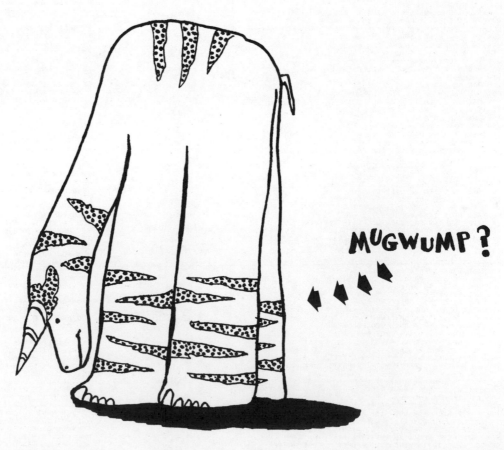

PROGRAM LISTING

```
1 REM   COURTESY OF PEOPLE'S COMPUTER COMPANY
2 REM   MUGWUMP
3 REM *** CONVERTED TO RSTS/E BY DAVID AHL, DIGITAL
5 RANDOMIZE
10 DIM P(4,2)
20   PRINT "THE OBJECT OF THIS GAME IS TO FIND FOUR MUGWUMPS"
30   PRINT "HIDDEN ON A 10 BY 10 GRID. HOMEBASE IS POSITION 0,0"
40   PRINT "ANY GUESS YOU MAKE MUST BE TWO NUMBERS WITH EACH"
50   PRINT "NUMBER BETWEEN 0 AND 9, INCLUSIVE. FIRST NUMBER"
60   PRINT "IS DISTANCE TO RIGHT OF HOMEBASE AND SECOND NUMBER"
70   PRINT "IS DISTANCE ABOVE HOMEBASE. "
80   PRINT
90   PRINT "YOU GET 10 TRIES. AFTER EACH TRY, I WILL TELL"
100  PRINT "YOU HOW FAR YOU ARE FROM EACH MUGWUMP. "
110  PRINT
240  GOSUB 1000
250  T=0
260  T=T+1
270  PRINT
275  PRINT
290  PRINT "TURN NO. "T; "WHAT IS YOUR GUESS";
300  INPUT M,N
310  FOR I=1 TO 4
320  IF P(I,1)=-1 THEN 400
330  IF P(I,1)<>M THEN 380
340  IF P(I,2)<>N THEN 380
350  P(I,1)=-1
360  PRINT "YOU HAVE FOUND MUGWUMP"; I
370  GOTO 400
380  D=SQR((P(I,1)-M)^2+(P(I,2)-N)^2)
390 PRINT "YOU ARE"INT(D*10)/10"UNITS FROM MUGWUMP"I
400  NEXT I
410  FOR J=1 TO 4
420  IF P(J,1)<>-1 THEN 470
430  NEXT J
440  PRINT
450  PRINT "YOU GOT THEM ALL IN"; T; "TURNS!"
460  GOTO 580
470  IF T<10 THEN 260
480  PRINT
490  PRINT "SORRY, THAT'S 10 TRIES. HERE IS WHERE THEY'RE HIDING"
540  FOR I=1 TO 4
550  IF P(I,1)=-1 THEN 570
560 PRINT "MUGWUMP"; I; "IS AT (";P(I,1);",";P(I,2);")"
570  NEXT I
580  PRINT
600 PRINT "THAT WAS FUN!  LET'S PLAY AGAIN....."
610 PRINT "FOUR MORE MUGMUMPS ARE NOW IN HIDING. "
630  GOTO 240
1000  FOR J=1 TO 2
1010  FOR I=1 TO 4
1020 P(I,J)=INT(10*RND(0))
1030  NEXT I
1040  NEXT J
1050  RETURN
1099 END

READY
```

SAMPLE RUN

```
THE OBJECT OF THIS GAME IS TO FIND FOUR MUGWUMPS
HIDDEN ON A 10 BY 10 GRID. HOMEBASE IS POSITION 0,0
ANY GUESS YOU MAKE MUST BE TWO NUMBERS WITH EACH
NUMBER BETWEEN 0 AND 9, INCLUSIVE. FIRST NUMBER
IS DISTANCE TO RIGHT OF HOMEBASE AND SECOND NUMBER
IS DISTANCE ABOVE HOMEBASE.

YOU GET 10 TRIES. AFTER EACH TRY, I WILL TELL
YOU HOW FAR YOU ARE FROM EACH MUGWUMP.


TURN NO.  1 WHAT IS YOUR GUESS? 5,5
YOU ARE 6.4 UNITS FROM MUGWUMP 1
YOU ARE 1.4 UNITS FROM MUGWUMP 2
YOU ARE 2.2 UNITS FROM MUGWUMP 3
YOU ARE 1.4 UNITS FROM MUGWUMP 4


TURN NO.  2 WHAT IS YOUR GUESS? 4,4
YOU ARE 5 UNITS FROM MUGWUMP 1
YOU ARE 2 UNITS FROM MUGWUMP 2
YOU ARE 1 UNITS FROM MUGWUMP 3
YOU ARE 2.8 UNITS FROM MUGWUMP 4


TURN NO.  3 WHAT IS YOUR GUESS? 6,6
YOU ARE 7.8 UNITS FROM MUGWUMP 1
YOU ARE 2 UNITS FROM MUGWUMP 2
YOU ARE 3.6 UNITS FROM MUGWUMP 3
YOU HAVE FOUND MUGWUMP 4


TURN NO.  4 WHAT IS YOUR GUESS? 4,6
YOU ARE 6.7 UNITS FROM MUGWUMP 1
YOU HAVE FOUND MUGWUMP 2
YOU ARE 2.2 UNITS FROM MUGWUMP 3


TURN NO.  5 WHAT IS YOUR GUESS? 3,4
YOU ARE 4.4 UNITS FROM MUGWUMP 1
YOU HAVE FOUND MUGWUMP 3


TURN NO.  6 WHAT IS YOUR GUESS? 1,0
YOU HAVE FOUND MUGWUMP 1

YOU GOT THEM ALL IN 6 TURNS!

THAT WAS FUN!  LET'S PLAY AGAIN.....
FOUR MORE MUGMUMPS ARE NOW IN HIDING.


TURN NO.  1 WHAT IS YOUR GUESS? 4,4
YOU ARE 2.8 UNITS FROM MUGWUMP 1
YOU ARE 4.4 UNITS FROM MUGWUMP 2
YOU ARE 5.3 UNITS FROM MUGWUMP 3
YOU ARE 5 UNITS FROM MUGWUMP 4


TURN NO.  2 WHAT IS YOUR GUESS? 2,2
YOU ARE 5.6 UNITS FROM MUGWUMP 1
YOU ARE 2 UNITS FROM MUGWUMP 2
YOU ARE 7 UNITS FROM MUGWUMP 3
YOU ARE 7.2 UNITS FROM MUGWUMP 4


TURN NO.  3 WHAT IS YOUR GUESS? 6,6
YOU HAVE FOUND MUGWUMP 1
YOU ARE 7.2 UNITS FROM MUGWUMP 2
YOU ARE 5 UNITS FROM MUGWUMP 3
YOU ARE 3.6 UNITS FROM MUGWUMP 4


TURN NO.  4 WHAT IS YOUR GUESS? 0,2
YOU HAVE FOUND MUGWUMP 2
YOU ARE 9 UNITS FROM MUGWUMP 3
YOU ARE 8 UNITS FROM MUGWUMP 4


TURN NO.  5 WHAT IS YOUR GUESS? 4,9
YOU ARE 8.6 UNITS FROM MUGWUMP 3
YOU HAVE FOUND MUGWUMP 4


TURN NO.  6 WHAT IS YOUR GUESS? 9,2
YOU HAVE FOUND MUGWUMP 3

YOU GOT THEM ALL IN 6 TURNS!
```

NICOMA

COMPUTER GUESSES YOUR NUMBER

Description

One of the most ancient forms of arithmetical puzzle is sometimes
referred to as a "boomerang." At some time, everyone has been
asked to "think of a number," and, after going through some
process of private calculation, to state the result, after which
the questioner promptly tells you the number you originally
thought of. There are hundreds of varieties of the puzzle.

The oldest recorded example appears to be that given in <u>Arithmetica</u>
of Nicomachus, who died about the year 120. He tells you to
think of any whole number between 1 and 100 and divide it suc-
cessively by 3, 5, and 7, telling him the remainder in each case.
On receiving this information, he promptly discloses the number
you thought of.

Can you discover a simple method of mentally performing this feat?
If not, you can see how the ancient mathematician did it by look-
ing at Lines 80-100 of the program.

Program Author

David Ahl
Digital Equipment Corp.
Maynard, MA 01754

PROGRAM LISTING

```
10 PRINT "BOOMERANG PUZZLE FROM ARITHMETICA OF NICOMACHUS -- A.D. 90!"
20 PRINT
30 PRINT "PLEASE THINK OF A NUMBER BETWEEN 1 AND 100. "
40 PRINT "YOUR NUMBER DIVIDED BY 3 HAS A REMAINDER OF";
45 INPUT A
50 PRINT "YOUR NUMBER DIVIDED BY 5 HAS A REMAINDER OF";
55 INPUT B
60 PRINT "YOUR NUMBER DIVIDED BY 7 HAS A REMAINDER OF";
65 INPUT C
70 PRINT
80 PRINT "LET ME THINK A MOMENT.... "
90 SLEEP(5)
100 D=70*A+21*B+15*C
110 IF D<=105 THEN 140
120 D=D-105
130 GOTO 110
140 PRINT
150 PRINT "YOUR NUMBER WAS"D", RIGHT";
160 INPUT A$
165 PRINT
170 IF A$="YES" THEN 220
180 IF A$="NO" THEN 240
190 PRINT "EH?  I DON'T UNDERSTAND '"A$"'.   TRY 'YES' OR 'NO'"
200 GOTO 150
220 PRINT "HOW ABOUT THAT!!"
230 GOTO 250
240 PRINT "I FEAR YOUR ARITHMETIC IS IN ERROR. "
250 PRINT
260 PRINT "LET'S TRY ANOTHER. "
270 GOTO 20
999 END
```

SAMPLE RUN

```
BOOMERANG PUZZLE FROM ARITHMETICA OF NICOMACHUS -- A.D. 90!

PLEASE THINK OF A NUMBER BETWEEN 1 AND 100.
YOUR NUMBER DIVIDED BY 3 HAS A REMAINDER OF ?3
YOUR NUMBER DIVIDED BY 5 HAS A REMAINDER OF ?0
YOUR NUMBER DIVIDED BY 7 HAS A REMAINDER OF ?5

LET ME THINK A MOMENT....

YOUR NUMBER WAS 75 , RIGHT ?RIGHT

EH?  I DON'T UNDERSTAND 'RIGHT'.  TRY 'YES' OR 'NO'
YOUR NUMBER WAS 75 , RIGHT ?YF

HOW ABOUT THAT!!

LET'S TRY ANOTHER.

PLEASE THINK OF A NUMBER BETWEEN 1 AND 100.
YOUR NUMBER DIVIDED BY 3 HAS A REMAINDER OF ?2
YOUR NUMBER DIVIDED BY 5 HAS A REMAINDER OF ?4
YOUR NUMBER DIVIDED BY 7 HAS A REMAINDER OF ?6

LET ME THINK A MOMENT....

YOUR NUMBER WAS 104 , RIGHT ?YES

HOW ABOUT THAT!!

LET'S TRY ANOTHER.

PLEASE THINK OF A NUMBER BETWEEN 1 AND 100.
YOUR NUMBER DIVIDED BY 3 HAS A REMAINDER OF ?1
YOUR NUMBER DIVIDED BY 5 HAS A REMAINDER OF ?1
YOUR NUMBER DIVIDED BY 7 HAS A REMAINDER OF ?1

LET ME THINK A MOMENT....

YOUR NUMBER WAS 1 , RIGHT ?NO

I FEAR YOUR ARITHMETIC IS IN ERROR.

LET'S TRY ANOTHER.

PLEASE THINK OF A NUMBER BETWEEN 1 AND 100.
YOUR NUMBER DIVIDED BY 3 HAS A REMAINDER OF ?0
YOUR NUMBER DIVIDED BY 5 HAS A REMAINDER OF ?0
YOUR NUMBER DIVIDED BY 7 HAS A REMAINDER OF ?1

LET ME THINK A MOMENT....

YOUR NUMBER WAS 15 , RIGHT ?YES

HOW ABOUT THAT!!
```

 **NIM**

Description

NIM is one of the oldest two-person games known to man; it is believed to have originated in ancient China. The name, which was coined by the first mathematician to analyze it, comes from an archaic English verb which means to steal or to take away. Objects are arranged in rows between the two opponents as in the following example:

```
X X X X X X X     Row 1 -- 7 Objects
X X X X X         Row 2 -- 5 Objects
X X X             Row 3 -- 3 Objects
X                 Row 4 -- 1 Object
```

Opponents take turns removing objects until there are none left. The one who picks up the last object wins. The moves are made according to the following two rules:

1. On any given turn only objects from one row may be removed. There is no restriction on which row or on how many objects you remove. Of course, you cannot remove more than are in the row.
2. You cannot skip a move or remove zero objects.

The winning strategy can be mathematically defined, however, rather than presenting it here, we'd rather let you find it on your own. HINT: Play a few games with the computer and mark down on a piece of paper the number of objects in each stack (in binary!) after each move. Do you see a pattern emerging?

Source

One of the most popular computer games. Over 10 versions of NIM were submitted. One notable one came from Larry Ruane, Mt. Prospect, Illinois, who programmed NIM for a DIGITAL EduSystem 10. Quite a feat! The one published is from:

Robert G. Cox
Trinity College
Hartford, CT 06106

PROGRAM LISTING

```
100 REM  THIS PROGRAM USES A STRATEGY AS PRESENTED IN 'GAMES OF FUN AND
105 REM  STRATEGY', A PUBLICATION OF THE MATHEMATICAL SERVICES DEPART-
110 REM  MENT OF COMPUTER CONTROL CO., INC.
115 PRINT "THIS PROGRAM PLAYS NIM."
120 PRINT "DO YOU WANT INSTRUCTIONS"J\INPUT Q$
125 IF Q$="YES" THEN 135\IF Q$="NO" THEN 190
130 PRINT "TYPE YES OR NO."\INPUT Q$\GOTO 125
135 PRINT
140 PRINT "    NIM IS PLAYED BY TWO PEOPLE PLAYING ALTERNATELY.  BEFORE"
145 PRINT "THE PLAY STARTS, AN ARBITRARY NUMBER OF STICKS OR OBJECTS IS"
150 PRINT "PUT INTO AN ARBITRARY NUMBER OF PILES, IN ANY DISTRIBUTION"
155 PRINT "WHATEVER.  THEN EACH PLAYER IN HIS TURN REMOVES AS MANY"
160 PRINT "STICKS AS HE WISHES FROM ANY PILE--BUT FROM ONLY ONE PILE,"
165 PRINT "AND AT LEAST ONE STICK.  THE PLAYER WHO TAKES THE LAST STICK"
170 PRINT "IS THE WINNER."
175 PRINT "    THIS PROGRAM ALLOWS YOU TO SET UP THE INITIAL ARRANGEMENT"
180 PRINT "OF PILES AND STICKS.  IT WILL NOT ACCEPT MORE THAN TWENTY"
185 PRINT "PILES OR STICKS IN EACH PILE."
190 RANDOM
195 REM------------------CONFIGURATION INPUT---------------------------
200 DIM X(20,4),S(20),L(20),S2(20),N2(4),C(20),S3(20),V(20)
205 PRINT\PRINT "HOW MANY PILES"J\INPUT P\IF P>20 THEN 215
210 IF P>INT(P) THEN 215\IF P<=0 THEN 215\GO TO 220
215 PRINT "ILLEGAL PILE NUMBER."\PRINT\GO TO 205
220 PRINT\FOR I=1 TO P
225 PRINT "HOW MANY STICKS IN PILE"JIJ\INPUT L(I)\IF L(I)>20 THEN 235
230 IF L(I)>INT(L(I)) THEN 235\IF L(I)<=0 THEN 235\GO TO 240
235 PRINT "ILLEGAL STICK NUMBER."\PRINT\GO TO 225
240 NEXT I
245 FOR I=1 TO P\S(I)=L(I)\G=G+L(I)\NEXT I
250 PRINT\PRINT "DO YOU WANT TO GO FIRST"J
255 INPUT Q$\IF Q$="YES" THEN 340\IF Q$="NO" THEN 390
260 PRINT "TYPE YES OR NO."\GO TO 255
265 REM--CONTROL OF GAME REPEATS AND TESTS FOR END OF GAME------------
270 IF G=0 THEN 275\IF F=1 THEN 390\GO TO 320
275 IF F=1 THEN 315
280 PRINT\PRINT "I WON.  DO YOU WANT TO PLAY AGAIN"J
285 INPUT Q$\IF Q$="NO" THEN 290\IF Q$="YES" THEN 300\GO TO 295
290 STOP
295 PRINT "TYPE YES OR NO."\GO TO 285
300 PRINT\PRINT "SAME ARRANGEMENT"J
305 INPUT Q$\IF Q$="NO" THEN 205\IF Q$="YES" THEN 245
310 PRINT "TYPE YES OR NO."\GO TO 305
315 PRINT\PRINT "YOU WON.  DO YOU WANT TO PLAY AGAIN"J\GO TO 285
320 PRINT\PRINT "PILE NUMBER","STICKS LEFT"
325 FOR I=1 TO P\IF S(I)=0 THEN 330\PRINT I,S(I)
330 NEXT I
335 REM-------------------PLAYER'S MOVE------------------------------
340 PRINT\PRINT "WHICH PILE DO YOU WANT STICKS FROM"J\INPUT N
345 IF N>P THEN 355\IF N>INT(N) THEN 355\IF N<=0 THEN 355
350 IF S(N)=0 THEN 355\GO TO 360
355 PRINT "ILLEGAL PILE NUMBER."\PRINT\GO TO 340
360 PRINT\PRINT "HOW MANY STICKS"J\INPUT T
365 IF T>S(N) THEN 370\IF T>INT(T) THEN 370\IF T<=0 THEN 370\GO TO 375
370 PRINT "ILLEGAL STICK NUMBER."\PRINT\GO TO 360
375 S(N)=S(N)-T\G=G-T
380 F=1\GO TO 270
385 REM--------------------MACHINE'S MOVE----------------------------
390 FOR I=0 TO 4\V(I)=0\NEXT I
395 FOR I=1 TO P
400     C(I)=S(I)
405     FOR E=4 TO 0 STEP -1
410         IF S(I)<2^E THEN 415\S2(I)=S2(I)+10^E\S(I)=S(I)-2^E
415     NEXT E
420     FOR Y=4 TO 0 STEP -1
425         X(I,Y)=INT(S2(I)/10^Y)\S2(I)=S2(I)-X(I,Y)*10^Y
430         V(Y)=V(Y)+X(I,Y)
435     NEXT Y
440 NEXT I
445 R=0
450 FOR Y=4 TO 0 STEP -1
455     IF V(Y)/2-INT(V(Y)/2)=0 THEN 480
460     IF R=1 THEN 470\Q=INT(P*RND(X))+1
465     IF X(Q,Y)<>1 THEN 460\X(Q,Y)=0\R=1\GO TO 480
470     IF X(Q,Y)=1 THEN 475\X(Q,Y)=1\GO TO 480
475     X(Q,Y)=0
480 NEXT Y
485 FOR I=1 TO P
490     S2(I)=0
495     FOR Y=4 TO 0 STEP -1
500         S3(I)=X(I,Y)*10^Y\S2(I)=S2(I)+S3(I)
505     NEXT Y
510     FOR E=4 TO 0 STEP -1
515         IF S2(I)<10^E THEN 520\S(I)=S(I)+2^E\S2(I)=S2(I)-10^E
520     NEXT E
525 NEXT I
530 IF R=1 THEN 535\Q=INT(P*RND(X))+1\IF S(Q)=0 THEN 530\S(Q)=S(Q)-1
535 D=C(Q)-S(Q)\G=G-D
540 IF D=1 THEN 550
545 PRINT\PRINT "I'LL TAKE"JDJ"STICKS FROM PILE"JQJ"."\GO TO 555
550 PRINT\PRINT "I'LL TAKE 1 STICK FROM PILE"JQJ"."
555 F=0\GO TO 270
560 END
```

```
THIS PROGRAM PLAYS NIM.
DO YOU WANT INSTRUCTIONS? YES

     NIM IS PLAYED BY TWO PEOPLE PLAYING ALTERNATELY.  BEFORE
THE PLAY STARTS, AN ARBITRARY NUMBER OF STICKS OR OBJECTS IS
PUT INTO AN ARBITRARY NUMBER OF PILES, IN ANY DISTRIBUTION
WHATEVER.  THEN EACH PLAYER IN HIS TURN REMOVES AS MANY
STICKS AS HE WISHES FROM ANY PILE--BUT FROM ONLY ONE PILE,
AND AT LEAST ONE STICK.  THE PLAYER WHO TAKES THE LAST STICK
IS THE WINNER.
     THIS PROGRAM ALLOWS YOU TO SET UP THE INITIAL ARRANGEMENT
OF PILES AND STICKS.  IT WILL NOT ACCEPT MORE THAN TWENTY
PILES OR STICKS IN EACH PILE.

HOW MANY PILES? 5

HOW MANY STICKS IN PILE 1 ? 1
HOW MANY STICKS IN PILE 2 ? 2
HOW MANY STICKS IN PILE 3 ? 3
HOW MANY STICKS IN PILE 4 ? 4
HOW MANY STICKS IN PILE 5 ? 5

DO YOU WANT TO GO FIRST? YES

WHICH PILE DO YOU WANT STICKS FROM? 4

HOW MANY STICKS? 2

I'LL TAKE 3 STICKS FROM PILE 5 .

PILE NUMBER     STICKS LEFT
1                   1
2                   2
3                   3
4                   2
5                   2

WHICH PILE DO YOU WANT STICKS FROM? 3

HOW MANY STICKS? 3

I'LL TAKE 1 STICK FROM PILE 5 .

PILE NUMBER     STICKS LEFT
1                   1
2                   2
4                   2
5                   1

WHICH PILE DO YOU WANT STICKS FROM? 5

HOW MANY STICKS? 1

I'LL TAKE 1 STICK FROM PILE 1 .

PILE NUMBER     STICKS LEFT
2                   2
4                   2

WHICH PILE DO YOU WANT STICKS FROM? 4

HOW MANY STICKS? 1

I'LL TAKE 1 STICK FROM PILE 2 .

PILE NUMBER     STICKS LEFT
2                   1
4                   1

WHICH PILE DO YOU WANT STICKS FROM? 5
ILLEGAL PILE NUMBER.

WHICH PILE DO YOU WANT STICKS FROM? 4

HOW MANY STICKS? 0
ILLEGAL STICK NUMBER.

HOW MANY STICKS? 1

I'LL TAKE 1 STICK FROM PILE 2 .

I WON.  DO YOU WANT TO PLAY AGAIN? YES

SAME ARRANGEMENT? NO

HOW MANY PILES? 3

HOW MANY STICKS IN PILE 1 ? 1
HOW MANY STICKS IN PILE 2 ? 2
HOW MANY STICKS IN PILE 3 ? 3

DO YOU WANT TO GO FIRST? NO

I'LL TAKE 1 STICK FROM PILE 1 .

PILE NUMBER     STICKS LEFT
2                   2
3                   3

WHICH PILE DO YOU WANT STICKS FROM? 3

HOW MANY STICKS? 1

I'LL TAKE 1 STICK FROM PILE 3 .

PILE NUMBER     STICKS LEFT
2                   2
3                   1

WHICH PILE DO YOU WANT STICKS FROM? 2

HOW MANY STICKS? 1

I'LL TAKE 1 STICK FROM PILE 3 .

PILE NUMBER     STICKS LEFT
2                   1

WHICH PILE DO YOU WANT STICKS FROM? 2

HOW MANY STICKS? 1

YOU WON.  DO YOU WANT TO PLAY AGAIN? NO
```

NUMBER

Description

In contrast to other number guessing games where you keep guessing until you get the random number selected by the computer
(GUESS, TRAP, STARS, etc.), in this game you get only one guess
per play and you gain or lose points depending upon how close
your guess is to the random number selected by the computer.
You occasionally get a jackpot which will double your point
count. You win when you get 500 points.

Program Author

Tom Adametx
Curtis Junior High School
Sudbury, MA 01776

```
NUMBER  EDUSYSTEM 30

1 PRINT "              NUMBER  GAME"
2 PRINT\PRINT "YOU NOW HAVE 100 POINTS"
3 PRINT "BY GUESSING NUMBERS FROM 1 TO 5, YOU CAN GAIN OR LOSE"
4 PRINT "POINTS DEPENDING UPON HOW CLOSE YOU GET TO A RANDOM"
5 PRINT "NUMBER SELECTED BY THE COMPUTER"\PRINT
6 PRINT "YOU OCCASIONALLY WILL GET A JACKPOT WHICH WILL DOUBLE(!)"
7 PRINT "YOUR POINT COUNT.  YOU WIN WHEN YOU GET 500 POINTS. "
8 PRINT\P=100
11 PRINT "GUESS A NUMBER FROM 1 TO 5";
12 INPUT G
15 LET R=INT(5*RND(0))
16 LET S=INT(5*RND(0))
17 LET T=INT(5*RND(0))
18 LET U=INT(5*RND(0))
19 LET V=INT(5*RND(0))
20 IF G=R THEN 30
21 IF G=S THEN 40
22 IF G=T THEN 50
23 IF G=U THEN 60
24 IF G=V THEN 70
25 IF G>5 THEN 11
30 LET P=P-5
35 GO TO 80
40 LET P=P+5
45 GO TO 80
50 LET P=P+P
53 PRINT "YOU HIT THE JACKPOT"
55 GO TO 80
60 LET P=P+1
65 GO TO 80
70 LET P=P-(P*.5)
80 IF P>500 THEN 90
82 PRINT "YOU HAVE ";P;"POINTS"
85 GO TO 11
90 PRINT "!!!!YOU WIN!!!! WITH ";P;"POINTS"
99 END

READY
```

```
                NUMBER  GAME

YOU NOW HAVE 100 POINTS
BY GUESSING NUMBERS FROM 1 TO 5, YOU CAN GAIN OR LOSE
POINTS DEPENDING UPON HOW CLOSE YOU GET TO A RANDOM
NUMBER SELECTED BY THE COMPUTER

YOU OCCASIONALLY WILL GET A JACKPOT WHICH WILL DOUBLE(!)
YOUR POINT COUNT.  YOU WIN WHEN YOU GET 500 POINTS.

GUESS A NUMBER FROM 1 TO 5?3
YOU HAVE  101 POINTS
GUESS A NUMBER FROM 1 TO 5?3
YOU HAVE  106 POINTS
GUESS A NUMBER FROM 1 TO 5?3
YOU HAVE  101 POINTS
GUESS A NUMBER FROM 1 TO 5?3
YOU HAVE  102 POINTS
GUESS A NUMBER FROM 1 TO 5?3
YOU HAVE  97 POINTS
GUESS A NUMBER FROM 1 TO 5?3
YOU HAVE  92 POINTS
GUESS A NUMBER FROM 1 TO 5?3
YOU HIT THE JACKPOT
YOU HAVE  184 POINTS
GUESS A NUMBER FROM 1 TO 5?3
YOU HAVE  189 POINTS
GUESS A NUMBER FROM 1 TO 5?2
YOU HAVE  184 POINTS
GUESS A NUMBER FROM 1 TO 5?2
YOU HIT THE JACKPOT
YOU HAVE  368 POINTS
GUESS A NUMBER FROM 1 TO 5?2
YOU HAVE  363 POINTS
GUESS A NUMBER FROM 1 TO 5?2
YOU HAVE  358 POINTS
GUESS A NUMBER FROM 1 TO 5?2
YOU HAVE  363 POINTS
GUESS A NUMBER FROM 1 TO 5?2
YOU HAVE  368 POINTS
GUESS A NUMBER FROM 1 TO 5?2
YOU HAVE  363 POINTS
GUESS A NUMBER FROM 1 TO 5?2
YOU HAVE  358 POINTS
GUESS A NUMBER FROM 1 TO 5?2
YOU HIT THE JACKPOT
!!!!YOU WIN!!!! WITH  716 POINTS

READY
```

1 CHECK

SOLITAIRE CHECKER GAME

Description

In this game or puzzle, 48 checkers are placed on the two outside spaces of a standard 64-square checkerboard as shown:

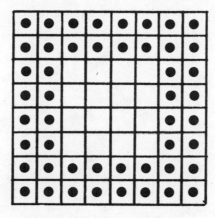

The object is to remove as many checkers as possible by diagonal jumps (as in standard checkers).

It is easy to remove 30 to 39 checkers, a challenge to remove 40 to 44, and a substantial feat to remove 45 to 47.

Program Author

David Ahl
Digital Equipment Corp.
Maynard, MA 01754

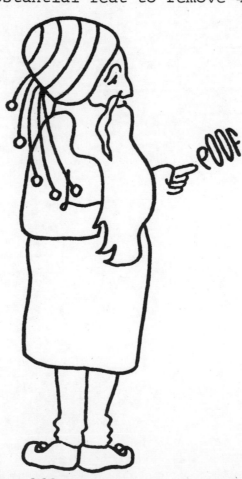

PROGRAM LISTING

```
1CHECK  05:54 PM      25-JUN-73
5 PRINT
10 PRINT "SOLITAIRE CHECKER PUZZLE BY DAVID AHL"
15 PRINT
20 PRINT "48 CHECKERS ARE PLACED ON THE 2 OUTSIDE SPACES OF A"
25 PRINT "STANDARD 64-SQUARE CHECKERBOARD.  THE OBJECT IS TO"
30 PRINT "REMOVE AS MANY CHECKERS AS POSSIBLE BY DIAGONAL JUMPS"
35 PRINT "(AS IN STANDARD CHECKERS).  USE THE NUMBERED BOARD TO"
40 PRINT "INDICATE THE SQUARE YOU WISH TO JUMP FROM AND TO.  ON"
45 PRINT "THE BOARD PRINTED OUT ON EACH TURN '1' INDICATES A"
50 PRINT "CHECKER AND '0' AN EMPTY SQUARE.  WHEN YOU HAVE NO"
55 PRINT "POSSIBLE JUMPS REMAINING, INPUT A '0' IN RESPONSE TO"
60 PRINT "QUESTION 'JUMP FROM ?'"
62 PRINT
65 PRINT "HERE IS THE NUMERICAL BOARD:"
66 PRINT
68 DIM A(64)
70 FOR J=1 TO 57 STEP 8
72 B$="## ## ## ## ## ## ## ##"
74 PRINT USING B$,J,J+1,J+2,J+3,J+4,J+5,J+6,J+7
76 NEXT J
77 PRINT
78 PRINT "AND HERE IS THE OPENING POSITION OF THE CHECKERS:"
79 PRINT
80 FOR J=1 TO 64
82 A(J)=1
84 NEXT J
86 FOR J=19 TO 43 STEP 8
88 FOR I=J TO J+3
90 A(I)=0
92 NEXT I
94 NEXT J
96 M=0
98 GOTO 340
100 INPUT "JUMP FROM";F
105 IF F=0 THEN 500
110 INPUT "TO";T
112 PRINT
118 REM *** CHECK LEGALITY OF MOVE
120 F1=INT((F-1)/8)
130 F2=F-8*F1
140 T1=INT((T-1)/8)
150 T2=T-8*T1
160 IF F1>7 THEN 230
170 IF T1>7 THEN 230
180 IF F2>8 THEN 230
190 IF T2>8 THEN 230
200 IF ABS(F1-T1)<>2 THEN 230
210 IF ABS(F2-T2)<>2 THEN 230
212 IF A((T+F)/2)=0 THEN 230
215 IF A(F)=0 THEN 230
220 IF A(T)=1 THEN 230
225 GOTO 250
230 PRINT "ILLEGAL MOVE.  TRY AGAIN..."
240 GOTO 100
245 REM *** UPDATE BOARD
250 A(T)=1
260 A(F)=0
270 A((T+F)/2)=0
290 M=M+1
310 REM *** PRINT BOARD
340 FOR J=1 TO 57 STEP 8
350 FOR I=J TO J+7
360 PRINT A(I);
370 NEXT I
380 PRINT
390 NEXT J
400 PRINT
410 GOTO 100
490 REM *** END GAME SUMMARY
500 S=0
510 FOR I=1 TO 64
520 S=S+A(I)
530 NEXT I
535 PRINT
540 PRINT "YOU MADE"M"JUMPS AND HAD"S"PIECES"
550 PRINT "REMAINING ON THE BOARD."
560 PRINT
562 INPUT "TRY AGAIN";A$
570 IF A$="YES" THEN 70
575 IF A$="NO" THEN 600
580 PRINT "PLEASE ANSWER 'YES' OR 'NO'."
590 GOTO 562
600 PRINT
610 PRINT "O.K.  HOPE YOU HAD FUN!"
999 END

READY
```

SAMPLE RUN

```
SOLITAIRE CHECKER PUZZLE BY DAVID AHL

48 CHECKERS ARE PLACED ON THE 2 OUTSIDE SPACES OF A
STANDARD 64-SQUARE CHECKERBOARD.  THE OBJECT IS TO
REMOVE AS MANY CHECKERS AS POSSIBLE BY DIAGONAL JUMPS
(AS IN STANDARD CHECKERS).  USE THE NUMBERED BOARD TO
INDICATE THE SQUARE YOU WISH TO JUMP FROM AND TO.  ON
THE BOARD PRINTED OUT ON EACH TURN '1' INDICATES A
CHECKER AND '0' AN EMPTY SQUARE.  WHEN YOU HAVE NO
POSSIBLE JUMPS REMAINING, INPUT A '0' IN RESPONSE TO
QUESTION 'JUMP FROM ?'

HERE IS THE NUMERICAL BOARD:

 1  2  3  4  5  6  7  8
 9 10 11 12 13 14 15 16
17 18 19 20 21 22 23 24
25 26 27 28 29 30 31 32
33 34 35 36 37 38 39 40
41 42 43 44 45 46 47 48
49 50 51 52 53 54 55 56
57 58 59 60 61 62 63 64

AND HERE IS THE OPENING POSITION OF THE CHECKERS:

 1  1  1  1  1  1  1  1
 1  1  1  1  1  1  1  1
 1  1  0  0  0  0  1  1
 1  1  0  0  0  0  1  1
 1  1  0  0  0  0  1  1
 1  1  0  0  0  0  1  1
 1  1  1  1  1  1  1  1
 1  1  1  1  1  1  1  1

JUMP FROM? 1
TO? 19

 0  1  1  1  1  1  1  1
 1  0  1  1  1  1  1  1
 1  1  1  0  0  0  1  1
 1  1  0  0  0  0  1  1
 1  1  0  0  0  0  1  1
 1  1  0  0  0  0  1  1
 1  1  1  1  1  1  1  1
 1  1  1  1  1  1  1  1

JUMP FROM? 2
TO? 20

 0  0  1  1  1  1  1  1
 1  0  0  1  1  1  1  1
 1  1  1  1  0  0  1  1
 1  1  0  0  0  0  1  1
 1  1  0  0  0  0  1  1
 1  1  0  0  0  0  1  1
 1  1  1  1  1  1  1  1
 1  1  1  1  1  1  1  1

JUMP FROM? 3
TO? 21

 0  0  0  1  1  1  1  1
 1  0  0  1  1  1  1  1
 1  1  1  1  1  0  1  1
 1  1  0  0  0  0  1  1
 1  1  0  0  0  0  1  1
 1  1  0  0  0  0  1  1
 1  1  1  1  1  1  1  1
 1  1  1  1  1  1  1  1

JUMP FROM? 8
TO? 22

 0  0  0  1  1  1  1  0
 1  0  0  1  1  1  0  1
 1  1  1  1  1  1  1  1
 1  1  0  0  0  0  1  1
 1  1  0  0  0  0  1  1
 1  1  0  0  0  0  1  1
 1  1  1  1  1  1  1  1
 1  1  1  1  1  1  1  1

JUMP FROM? 16
TO? 30

 0  0  0  1  1  1  1  0
 1  0  0  1  1  1  0  1
 1  1  1  1  1  1  0  1
 1  1  0  0  0  1  1  1
 1  1  0  0  0  0  1  1
 1  1  0  0  0  0  1  1
 1  1  1  1  1  1  1  1
 1  1  1  1  1  1  1  1

JUMP FROM? 24
TO? 38

 0  0  0  1  1  1  1  0
 1  0  0  1  1  1  0  1
 1  1  1  1  1  1  0  0
 1  1  0  0  0  1  0  1
 1  1  0  0  0  1  1  1
 1  1  0  0  0  0  1  1
 1  1  1  1  1  1  1  1
 1  1  1  1  1  1  1  1

JUMP FROM? 64
TO? 46

 0  0  0  1  1  1  1  0
 1  0  0  0  1  1  0  0
 1  1  1  1  1  1  0  0
 1  1  0  0  0  1  0  1
 1  1  0  0  0  1  1  1
 1  1  1  1  1  1  0  1
 1  1  1  1  1  1  0  1
 1  1  1  1  1  1  0  0

JUMP FROM? 12
TO? 26

 0  0  0  0  0  1  1  0
 1  0  0  0  0  0  0  0
 0  0  0  1  0  1  0  0
 1  1  0  0  1  0  0  1
 0  0  1  1  0  1  1  0
 0  0  0  0  0  1  0  1
 0  0  0  0  1  0  0  1
 0  0  1  0  0  0  0  0

JUMP FROM? 26
TO? 44

 0  0  0  0  0  1  1  0
 1  0  0  0  0  0  0  0
 0  0  0  1  0  1  0  0
 1  0  0  0  1  0  0  1
 0  0  1  1  0  1  1  0
 0  0  0  1  0  1  0  1
 0  0  0  0  1  0  0  1
 0  0  1  0  0  0  0  0

JUMP FROM? 46
TO? 60

 0  0  0  0  0  1  1  0
 1  0  0  0  0  0  0  0
 0  0  0  1  0  1  0  0
 1  0  0  0  1  0  0  1
 0  0  1  1  0  1  1  0
 0  0  0  1  0  0  0  1
 0  0  0  0  0  0  0  1
 0  0  1  1  0  0  0  0

JUMP FROM? 29
TO? 47

 0  0  0  0  0  1  1  0
 1  0  0  0  0  0  0  0
 0  0  0  1  0  1  0  0
 1  0  0  0  0  0  0  1
 0  0  1  1  0  0  1  0
 0  0  0  1  0  0  1  1
 0  0  0  0  0  0  0  1
 0  0  1  1  0  0  0  0

JUMP FROM? 56
TO? 38

 0  0  0  0  0  1  1  0
 1  0  0  0  0  0  0  0
 0  0  0  1  0  1  0  0
 1  0  0  0  0  0  0  1
 0  0  0  1  0  1  1  0
 0  0  0  1  0  0  0  1
 0  0  0  0  0  0  0  0
 0  0  1  1  0  0  0  0

JUMP FROM? 48
TO? 30

 0  0  0  0  0  1  1  0
 1  0  0  0  0  0  0  0
 0  0  0  1  0  1  0  0
 1  0  0  0  0  1  0  1
 0  0  0  1  0  1  0  0
 0  0  0  1  0  0  0  0
 0  0  0  0  0  0  0  0
 0  0  1  1  0  0  0  0

JUMP FROM? 30
TO? 46

ILLEGAL MOVE.  TRY AGAIN...
JUMP FROM? 0

YOU MADE 35 JUMPS AND HAD 13 PIECES
REMAINING ON THE BOARD.

TRY AGAIN? NO

O.K.  HOPE YOU HAD FUN!
```

164

ORBIT

DESTROY AN ORBITING ENEMY SPACESHIP

Description

ORBIT challenges you to visualize spatial positions in polar coordinates. The object is to detonate an explosive within a certain distance of a germ laden spaceship. This ship is orbiting a planet at a constant altitude and orbital rate (degrees/hour). The location of the ship is hidden by a device that renders the ship invisible, but after each bomb you are told how close to the enemy ship your bomb exploded. The challenge is to hit an invisible moving target with a limited number of shots.

The planet can be replaced by a point at its center (called the origin); then the ship's position can be given as a distance from the origin and an angle between its position and the eastern edge of the planet.

The distance of the bomb from the ship is computed using the law of cosines (see line 430 of the program listing). The law of cosines states

$$D=\sqrt{R**2+D1**2+R*D1*COS(A-A1)}$$

where D is the distance between the ship and the bomb, R is the altitude of the ship, D1 is the altitude of the bomb, and A-A1 is the angle between the ship and the bomb.

Practice Off-Line Problem:

Aircraft appear on radar as blips of the form "=". What is the distance between the TWA and United aircraft shown on the radar screen on the right.

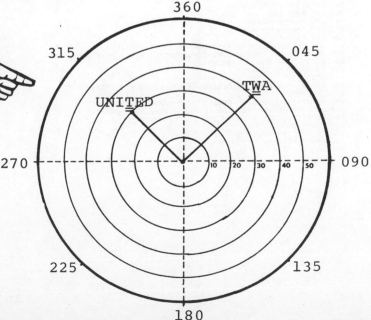

Source

ORBIT was originally called
SPACE WAR and was written by:
   Jeff Lederer
   Project SOLO
   University of Pittsburgh
   Pittsburgh, PA 15213

PROGRAM LISTING

```
5 RANDOMIZE
10 PRINT "SOMEWHERE ABOVE YOUR PLANET IS A ROMULAN SHIP."
15 PRINT
20 PRINT "THIS SHIP IS IN A CONSTANT POLAR ORBIT.  IT S"
25 PRINT "DISTANCE FROM THE CENTER OF YOUR PLANET IS FROM"
30 PRINT "10,000 TO 30,000 MILES AND AT IT'S PRESENT VELOCITY CAN"
31 PRINT "CIRCLE YOUR PLANET ONCE EVERY 12 TO 36 HOURS."
35 PRINT
40 PRINT "UNFORTUNATELY THEY ARE USING A CLOAKING DEVICE SO"
45 PRINT "YOU ARE UNABLE TO SEE THEM, BUT WITH A SPECIAL "
50 PRINT "INSTRUMENT YOU CAN TELL HOW NEAR THEIR SHIP YOUR"
55 PRINT "PHOTON BOMB EXPLODED.  YOU HAVE SEVEN HOURS UNTIL THEY"
60 PRINT "HAVE BUILT UP SUFFICIENT POWER IN ORDER TO ESCAPE "
65 PRINT "YOUR PLANET'S GRAVITY."
70 PRINT
75 PRINT "YOUR PLANET HAS ENOUGH POWER TO FIRE ONE BOMB AN HOUR."
80 PRINT
85 PRINT "AT THE BEGINNING OF EACH HOUR YOU WILL BE ASKED TO GIVE AN"
90 PRINT "ANGLE (BETWEEN 0 AND 360) AND A DISTANCE IN UNITS OF"
95 PRINT "100 MILES (BETWEEN 100 AND 300), AFTERWHICH YOUR BOMB'S"
100 PRINT "DISTANCE FROM THE ENEMY SHIP WILL BE GIVEN."
105 PRINT
110 PRINT "AN EXPLOSION WITHIN 5,000 MILES OF THE ROMULAN SHIP"
111 PRINT "WILL DESTROY IT."
114 PRINT
115 PRINT "BELOW IS A DIAGRAM TO HELP YOU VISUALIZE YOUR PLIGHT."
116 PRINT
117 PRINT
168 PRINT "                    90"
169 PRINT "                     !"
170 PRINT "             0000000000000"
171 PRINT "          0000000000000000000L"
172 PRINT "         000000            000000"
173 PRINT "       00000                  00000"
174 PRINT "      00000    XXXXXXXXXX    00000"
175 PRINT "      00000  XXXXXXXXXXXXXX   0000"
176 PRINT "      0000  XXXXXXXXXXXXXXXX   0000"
177 PRINT "      0000 XXXXXXXXXXXXXXXXXX  0000"
178 PRINT "      0000 XXXXXXXXXXXXXXXXXX  0000"
179 PRINT "180<== 00000 XXXXXXXXXXXXXXXX  00000 ==>0"
180 PRINT "      0000 XXXXXXXXXXXXXXXXXX  0000"
181 PRINT "      0000  XXXXXXXXXXXXXXXX   0000"
182 PRINT "      0000  XXXXXXXXXXXXXX    0000"
183 PRINT "      00000   XXXXXXXXXXXX   00000"
184 PRINT "       00000   XXXXXXXXXX  00000"
185 PRINT "        00000             00000"
186 PRINT "         000000         000000"
187 PRINT "          0000000000000000000"
188 PRINT "            000000000000000"
189 PRINT "                     !"
190 PRINT "                    270"
191 PRINT
192 PRINT
195 PRINT "X - YOUR PLANET"
196 PRINT "O - THE ORBIT OF THE ROMULAN SHIP"
197 PRINT
198 PRINT "ON THE ABOVE DIAGRAM, THE ROMULAN SHIP IS CIRCLING"
199 PRINT "COUNTERCLOCKWISE AROUND YOUR PLANET.  DON'T FORGET"
200 PRINT "WITHOUT SUFFICIENT POWER THE ROMULAN SHIP'S ALTITUDE"
201 PRINT "AND  ORBITAL RATE WILL REMAIN CONSTANT."
203 PRINT
204 PRINT "GOOD LUCK. THE FEDERATION IS COUNTING ON YOU."
270 LET A=INT(RND*360)
280 LET D=INT(RND*200) +100
290 LET R=INT(RND*20) +10
300 LET H=0
310 IF H=7 GOTO 490
320 LET H=H+1
325 PRINT
326 PRINT
330 PRINT "HOUR"JHJ", AT WHAT ANGLE DO YOU WISH TO SEND"
335 PRINT "YOUR PHOTON BOMB?"
340 INPUT A1
350 PRINT "HOW FAR OUT DO YOU WISH TO DETONATE IT?"
360 INPUT D1
365 PRINT
366 PRINT
370 LET A=A+R
380 IF A<360 GOTO 400
390 LET A=A-360
400 LET T=ABS(A-A1)
410 IF T<180 GOTO 430
420 LET T=360-T
430 LET C=SQR(D*D+D1*D1-2*D*D1*COS(T*3.14159/180))
440 PRINT "YOUR PHOTON BOMB EXPLODED"JCJ"*10+2 MILES FROM THE"
445 PRINT "THE ROMULAN SHIP"
450 IF C<=50 GOTO 470
460 GOTO 310
470 PRINT "YOU HAVE SUCCESSFULLY COMPLETED YOUR MISSION."
480 GOTO 500
490 PRINT "YOU HAVE ALLOWED THE ROMULANS TO ESCAPE."
500 PRINT "ANOTHER ROMULAN SHIP HAS GONE INTO ORBIT."
510 PRINT "DO YOU WISH TO TRY TO DESTROY IT?"
520 INPUT C$
530 IF C$="YES" GOTO 270
540 PRINT "PLEASE LOGOUT"
999 END
```

SAMPLE RUN

SOMEWHERE ABOVE YOUR PLANET IS A ROMULAN SHIP.

THIS SHIP IS IN A CONSTANT POLAR ORBIT. IT'S
DISTANCE FROM THE CENTER OF YOUR PLANET IS FROM
10,000 TO 30,000 MILES AND AT IT S PRESENT VELOCITY CAN
CIRCLE YOUR PLANET ONCE EVERY 12 TO 36 HOURS.

UNFORTUNATELY THEY ARE USING A CLOAKING DEVICE SO
YOU ARE UNABLE TO SEE THEM, BUT WITH A SPECIAL
INSTRUMENT YOU CAN TELL HOW NEAR THEIR SHIP YOUR
PHOTON BOMB EXPLODED. YOU HAVE SEVEN HOURS UNTIL THEY
HAVE BUILT UP SUFFICIENT POWER IN ORDER TO ESCAPE
YOUR PLANET'S GRAVITY.

YOUR PLANET HAS ENOUGH POWER TO FIRE ONE BOMB AN HOUR.

AT THE BEGINNING OF EACH HOUR YOU WILL BE ASKED TO GIVE AN
ANGLE (BETWEEN 0 AND 360) AND A DISTANCE IN UNITS OF
100 MILES (BETWEEN 100 AND 300), AFTERWHICH YOUR BOMB'S
DISTANCE FROM THE ENEMY SHIP WILL BE GIVEN.

AN EXPLOSION WITHIN 5,000 MILES OF THE ROMULAN SHIP
WILL DESTROY IT.

BELOW IS A DIAGRAM TO HELP YOU VISUALIZE YOUR PLIGHT.

```
                     90
                      !
              0000000000000
           0000000000000000000
          000000            000000
        00000                  00000
       00000    XXXXXXXXXX    00000
       0000   XXXXXXXXXXXXXX   0000
       0000  XXXXXXXXXXXXXXXX   0000
       0000 XXXXXXXXXXXXXXXXXX  0000
180<== 0000 XXXXXXXXXXXXXXXXXX  00000 ==>0
       0000 XXXXXXXXXXXXXXXXXX  0000
       0000  XXXXXXXXXXXXXXXX   0000
       0000   XXXXXXXXXXXXXX    0000
        00000   XXXXXXXXXXXX   00000
         00000   XXXXXXXXXX  00000
          00000             00000
           000000         000000
            0000000000000000000
              000000000000000
                      !
                     270
```

X - YOUR PLANET
O - THE ORBIT OF THE ROMULAN SHIP

ON THE ABOVE DIAGRAM, THE ROMULAN SHIP IS CIRCLING
COUNTERCLOCKWISE AROUND YOUR PLANET. DON'T FORGET
WITHOUT SUFFICIENT POWER THE ROMULAN SHIP'S ALTITUDE
AND ORBITAL RATE WILL REMAIN CONSTANT.

GOOD LUCK. THE FEDERATION IS COUNTING ON YOU.

```
HOUR 1 , AT WHAT ANGLE DO YOU WISH TO SEND
YOUR PHOTON BOMB?
? 0
HOW FAR OUT DO YOU WISH TO DETONATE IT?
? 200


YOUR PHOTON BOMB EXPLODED 357.237 *10+2 MILES FROM THE
THE ROMULAN SHIP


HOUR 2 , AT WHAT ANGLE DO YOU WISH TO SEND
YOUR PHOTON BOMB?
? 180
HOW FAR OUT DO YOU WISH TO DETONATE IT?
? 200


YOUR PHOTON BOMB EXPLODED 267.336 *10+2 MILES FROM THE
THE ROMULAN SHIP


HOUR 3 , AT WHAT ANGLE DO YOU WISH TO SEND
YOUR PHOTON BOMB?
? 180
HOW FAR OUT DO YOU WISH TO DETONATE IT?
? 200


YOUR PHOTON BOMB EXPLODED 295.315 *10+2 MILES FROM THE
THE ROMULAN SHIP


HOUR 4 , AT WHAT ANGLE DO YOU WISH TO SEND
YOUR PHOTON BOMB?
? 250
HOW FAR OUT DO YOU WISH TO DETONATE IT?
? 200


YOUR PHOTON BOMB EXPLODED 103.558 *10+2 MILES FROM THE
THE ROMULAN SHIP
```

PIZZA

Description

In this game, you take orders for pizzas from people living in Hyattsville. Armed with a map of the city, you must then tell a delivery boy the address where the pizza is to be delivered. If the pizza is delivered to the correct address, the customer phones you and thanks you; if not, you must give the driver the correct address until the pizza gets delivered.

Some interesting modifications suggest themselves for this program such as pizzas getting cold after two incorrect delivery attempts or taking three or more orders at a time and figuring the shortest delivery route. Send us your modifications!

Source

This program seems to have surfaced originally at the University of Georgia in Athens, GA. The author is unknown.

SCHKLURT

PROGRAM LISTING

```
LISTNH
10 DIM A$(26),S$(16),N$(4),A(10),M$(4)
20 RANDOMIZE
30 PRINT "PIZZA DELIVERY GAME":PRINT
50 INPUT "WHAT IS YOUR FIRST NAME";N$:PRINT
80 PRINT "HI, "N$".   IN THIS GAME YOU ARE TO TAKE ORDERS"
90 PRINT "FOR PIZZAS.  THEN YOU ARE TO TELL A DELIVERY BOY"
100 PRINT "WHERE TO DELIVER THE ORDERED PIZZAS. ":PRINT:PRINT
140 FOR I=1 TO 16
150 READ S$(I)
160 NEXT I
170 FOR I=1 TO 4
180 READ M$(I)
190 NEXT I
200 DATA "A","B","C","D","E","F","G","H","I","J","K","L","M","N","O","P"
220 DATA "1","2","3","4"
230 PRINT "MAP OF THE CITY OF HYATTSVILLE":PRINT
250 PRINT " ----1----2----3----4----"
260 K=4
270 FOR I=1 TO 4
280 PRINT "-":PRINT "-":PRINT "-":PRINT "-"
320 PRINT M$(K);
330 S1=16-4*I+1
340 PRINT "   ";S$(S1);"    ";S$(S1+1);"    ";S$(S1+2);"   ";S$(S1+3);
350 PRINT "   ";M$(K)
380 K=K-1
390 NEXT I
400 PRINT "-":PRINT "-":PRINT "-":PRINT "-"
440 PRINT "0----1----2----3----4----":PRINT
460 PRINT "THE ABOVE IS A MAP OF THE HOMES WHERE"
470 PRINT "YOU ARE TO SEND PIZZAS. ":PRINT
490 PRINT "YOUR JOB IS TO GIVE A TRUCK DRIVER"
500 PRINT "THE LOCATION OR COORDINATES OF THE"
510 PRINT "HOME ORDERING THE PIZZA. ":PRINT
520 INPUT "DO YOU NEED MORE DIRECTIONS";A$
530 IF A$="YES" THEN 590
540 IF A$="NO" THEN 750
550 PRINT "'YES' OR 'NO' PLEASE, NOW THEN, ":GOTO 520
590 PRINT:PRINT "SOMEBODY WILL ASK FOR A PIZZA TO BE"
600 PRINT "DELIVERED.   THEN A DELIVERY BOY WILL"
610 PRINT "ASK YOU FOR THE LOCATION. ":PRINT "    EXAMPLE:"
620 PRINT "THIS IS J.  PLEASE SEND A PIZZA. "
640 PRINT "DRIVER TO "N$".  WHERE DOES J LIVE?"
650 PRINT "YOUR ANSWER WOULD BE 2,3":PRINT
660 INPUT "UNDERSTAND";A$
670 IF A$="YES" THEN 690
680 PRINT "THIS JOB IS TOO DIFFICULT FOR YOU.   THANKS ANYWAY. ":GOTO 999
690 PRINT "GOOD.   YOU ARE NOW READY TO START TAKING ORDERS. ":PRINT
700 PRINT "GOOD LUCK!!":PRINT
750 FOR I=1 TO 5
760 S=INT(RND*16+1):PRINT
770 PRINT "HELLO "N$"'S PIZZA.  THIS IS "S$(S);
775 PRINT ".  PLEASE SEND A PIZZA. "
780 PRINT "   DRIVER TO "N$".  WHERE DOES "S$(S)" LIVE";
790 INPUT A(1),A(2)
870 T=A(1)+(A(2)-1)*4
880 IF T=S THEN 920
890 PRINT "THIS IS "S$(T)".  I DID NOT ORDER A PIZZA. "
900 PRINT "I LIVE AT "A(1)","A(2)
910 GOTO 780
920 PRINT "HELLO "N$".   THIS IS "S$(S)", THANKS FOR THE PIZZA. "
930 NEXT I
940 PRINT:INPUT "DO YOU WANT TO DELIVER MORE PIZZAS";A$
960 IF A$="YES" THEN 750
970 PRINT:PRINT "O.K. "N$", SEE YOU LATER!"
999 END
```

SAMPLE RUN

```
RUNNH
PIZZA DELIVERY GAME

WHAT IS YOUR FIRST NAME? BETSY

HI, BETSY.   IN THIS GAME YOU ARE TO TAKE ORDERS
FOR PIZZAS.   THEN YOU ARE TO TELL A DELIVERY BOY
WHERE TO DELIVER THE ORDERED PIZZAS.

MAP OF THE CITY OF HYATTSVILLE

  ----1----2----3----4----
-
-
-
4    M    N    O    P    4
-
-
-
3    I    J    K    L    3
-
-
-
2    E    F    G    H    2
-
-
-
1    A    B    C    D    1
-
-
-
0----1----2----3----4----

THE ABOVE IS A MAP OF THE HOMES WHERE
YOU ARE TO SEND PIZZAS.

YOUR JOB IS TO GIVE A TRUCK DRIVER
THE LOCATION OR COORDINATES OF THE
HOME ORDERING THE PIZZA.

DO YOU NEED MORE DIRECTIONS? YES

SOMEBODY WILL ASK FOR A PIZZA TO BE
DELIVERED.   THEN A DELIVERY BOY WILL
ASK YOU FOR THE LOCATION.
    EXAMPLE:
THIS IS J.  PLEASE SEND A PIZZA.
DRIVER TO BETSY.  WHERE DOES J LIVE?
YOUR ANSWER WOULD BE 2,3

UNDERSTAND? YES
GOOD.   YOU ARE NOW READY TO START TAKING ORDERS.

GOOD LUCK!!


HELLO BETSY'S PIZZA.   THIS IS E.   PLEASE SEND A PIZZA.
    DRIVER TO BETSY.   WHERE DOES E LIVE? 2,1
THIS IS B.   I DID NOT ORDER A PIZZA.
I LIVE AT  2 , 1
    DRIVER TO BETSY.   WHERE DOES E LIVE? 1,2
HELLO BETSY.   THIS IS E, THANKS FOR THE PIZZA.

HELLO BETSY'S PIZZA.   THIS IS H.   PLEASE SEND A PIZZA.
    DRIVER TO BETSY.   WHERE DOES H LIVE? 4,2
HELLO BETSY.   THIS IS H, THANKS FOR THE PIZZA.

HELLO BETSY'S PIZZA.   THIS IS P.   PLEASE SEND A PIZZA.
    DRIVER TO BETSY.   WHERE DOES P LIVE? 4,4
HELLO BETSY.   THIS IS P, THANKS FOR THE PIZZA.

HELLO BETSY'S PIZZA.   THIS IS J.   PLEASE SEND A PIZZA.
    DRIVER TO BETSY.   WHERE DOES J LIVE? 3,2
THIS IS G.   I DID NOT ORDER A PIZZA.
I LIVE AT  3 , 2
    DRIVER TO BETSY.   WHERE DOES J LIVE? 2,3
HELLO BETSY.   THIS IS J, THANKS FOR THE PIZZA.

HELLO BETSY'S PIZZA.   THIS IS C.   PLEASE SEND A PIZZA.
    DRIVER TO BETSY.   WHERE DOES C LIVE? 3,1
HELLO BETSY.   THIS IS C, THANKS FOR THE PIZZA.

DO YOU WANT TO DELIVER MORE PIZZAS? NO

O.K. BETSY, SEE YOU LATER!

READY
```

POETRY

Description

POETRY: This program will randomly choose a singlet, couplet, or quatrain from a set of 23 preset PRINT statements. It spaces at random intervals, but ends at approximately the same point each time. There is a low likelihood of duplication of lines.

POET: This program produces random verse which might loosely be considered in the Japanese Haiku style. It uses 20 phrases in four groups of five phrases each generally cycling through the groups. It inserts commas (random--19% of the time), indentation (random--22% of the time), and starts new paragraphs (18% probability, but at least every 20 phrases).

The version of POET published has phrases suggestive of Edgar Allen Poe. Try it with phrases from computer technology, from love and romance, from four-year-old children, or from some other subject. Send us the output:

Here are some phrases from nature to try:

Carpet of ferns	Mighty Oaks
Morning dew	Grace and beauty
Tang of dawn	Silently singing
Swaying pines	Nature speaking
Entrances me	Untouched, unspoiled
Soothing mc	Shades of green
Rustling leaves	Tranquility
Radiates calm	...so peaceful

Program Author

POETRY:
  H. David Crockett
  5609 Wimbleton Way
  Fort Worth, TX 76133

POET:
  Original author unknown.
  Modified and reworked by
  Jim Bailey, Peggy Ewing, and
  Dave Ahl of DIGITAL.

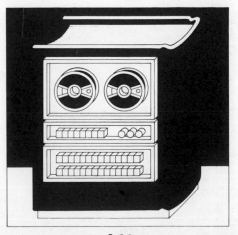

POETRY   PROGRAM LISTING

```
100 GO TO 110
110 LET D=0
120 LET D=D+1
130 GO TO 1300
140 PRINT "THE HOURS RISE UP PUTTING OFF STARS"
150 LET A1=1
160 LET D=D+1
170 PRINT "       AND IT IS DAWN"
180 GO TO 1350
190 PRINT "INTO THE STREET OF THE SKY LIGHT"
200 LET A2=1
210 LET D=D+1
220 PRINT "      WALKS SCATTERING POEMS"
230 GO TO 1350
240 PRINT "ON EARTH A CANDLE IS EXTINGUISED"
250 LET A3=1
260 LET D=D+1
270 PRINT "       THE CITY WAKES"
280 GO TO 1350
290 PRINT "WITH A SONG UPON HER MOUTH"
300 LET A4=1
310 LET D=D+1
320 PRINT "      HAVING DEATH IN HER EYES"
330 GO TO 1350
340 PRINT "AND IT IS DAWN"
350 PRINT "           THE WORLD"
360 LET A5=1
370 LET D=D+1
380 PRINT "    GOES FORTH TO MURDER DREAMS"
390 GO TO 1350
400 PRINT " AND IT IS DAY"
410 LET C5=1
420 LET D=D+1
430 GO TO 1350
440 PRINT "IN THE MIRROR I SEE A MAN, AND HE"
450 PRINT "     SCREAMS"
460 LET D= D+1
470 LET C5=1
480 PRINT "FOR HE IS ME"
490 LET D=D+1
500 PRINT "            AND I HE"
510 GO TO 1350
520 PRINT "AND IT IS DUSK"
530 LET A7=1
540 LET D=D+1
550 PRINT "            ON EARTH"
560 GO TO 1350
570 PRINT "A CANDLE IS LIGHTED"
580 LET A8=1
590 LET D=D+1
600 PRINT "     AND IT IS DARK"
610 GO TO 1350
620 PRINT " THE PEOPLE ARE IN THEIR HOUSES"
630 LET A9=1
640 LET D=D+1
650 GO TO 1350
660 PRINT "SHE SLEEPS WITH DEATH UPON HER MOUTH"
670 LET B1=1
680 LET D=D+1
690 PRINT "     AND A SONG IN HER EYES"
700 GO TO 1350
710 PRINT " THE HOURS DESENDED"
720 LET B2=1
730 LET D=D+1
740 PRINT "             PUTTING ON STARS"
750 GO TO 1350
760 PRINT "NOBODY LOSES ALL THE TIME "
770 LET B3=1
780 LET D=D+1
790 GO TO 1350
800 PRINT "HIS MOST WISE MUSIC STOLE"
810 LET B4=1
820 LET D=D+1
830 PRINT "      NOTHING FROM DEATH"
840 GO TO 1350
850 PRINT "LOVE IS THE EVER ONLY GOD"
860 LET B5=1
870 LET D=D+1
880 GO TO 1350
890 PRINT "WHO SPOKE THIS EARTH SO GLAD AND BIG"
900 LET B6=1
910 LET D=D+1
920 PRINT "     EVEN A THING ALL SMALL AND SAD"
930 GO TO 1350
940 PRINT "WHO IS AFRAID OF DEATH?THOU"
950 LET B7=1
960 LET D=D+1
970 PRINT "     ART OF HIM"
980 GO TO 1350
990 PRINT "OR WITH THY MIND AGAINST MY MIND,"
1000 LET B8=1
1010 LET D=D+1
1020 PRINT "     YOU SHOULD NOT HEAR ME SPEAK"
1030 GO TO 1350
1040 PRINT "FOR IF HE IS GONE AND I AM HERE"
1050 LET B9=1
1060 LET D=D+1
1070 PRINT "     THERE IS NO MEETING"
1080 GO TO 1350
1090 PRINT " TIME IS TWISTED TO LAP UPON"
1100 LET C1=1
1110 LET D=D+1
1120 PRINT "     ITSELF FOREVER"
1130 GO TO 1350
1140 PRINT "AND SPACE IS MISING FOR IT WAS "
1150 LET C2=1
1160 LET D=D+1
1170 PRINT "STOLEN FOR ALL TIME TO COME "
1180 GO TO 1350
1190 PRINT "THERE IS NEVER AN END,"
1200 LET C3=1
1210 LET D=D+1
1220 PRINT " MERELY A BELATED BEGINING..."
1230 GO TO 1350
1240 PRINT "AND TWICE REPEATED THERE"
1250 LET C4=1
1260 PRINT "     WAS NO MORE"
1270 GO TO 1350
1280 PRINT
1281 D=D+1
1290 GO TO 1350
1300 PRINT " RANDOM POETRY IN FOUR PART HARMONY."
1310 PRINT
1320 PRINT
1330 IF Q=INT(Q) THEN 1280
1340 IF D=12 THEN 2330
1350 LET X=RND(=1)*24
1360 LET X1=INT(X)+1
1361 IF D=4 THEN 1280
1362 IF D=8 THEN 1280
1363 IF D>16 THEN 2330
1370 IF X1=1 THEN 1390
1380 GO TO 1410
1390 IF A1=1 THEN 1410
1400 IF X1=1 THEN 140
1410 IF X1=2 THEN 1430
1420 GO TO 1450
1430 IF A2=1 THEN 1450
1440 IF X1=2 THEN 290
1450 IF X1=3 THEN 1470
1460 GO TO 1490
1470 IF A3=1 THEN 1490
1480 IF X1=3 THEN 190
1490 IF X1=4 THEN 1510
1500 GO TO 1530
1510 IF A4=1 THEN 1530
1520 IF X1=4 THEN 240
1530 IF X1=5 THEN 1550
1540 GO TO 1570
1550 IF A5=1 THEN 1570
1560 IF X1=5 THEN 340
1570 IF X1=6 THEN 1590
1580 GO TO 1610
1590 IF A6= 1 THEN 1610
1600 IF X1=6 THEN 400
1610 IF X1=7 THEN 1630
1620 GO TO 1650
1630 IF A7=1 THEN 1650
1640 GO TO 520
1650 IF X1=8 THEN 1670
1660 GO TO 1690
1670 IF A8=1 THEN 1690
1680 GO TO 570
1690 IF X1=9 THEN 1710
1700 GO TO 1730
1710 IF A9=1 THEN 1730
1720 GO TO 620
1730 IF X1=10 THEN 1750
1740 GO TO 1780
1750 GO TO 1760
1760 IF B1=1 THEN 1780
1770 GO TO 660
1780 IF X1=11 THEN 1800
1790 GO TO 1820
1800 IF B2=1 THEN 1820
1810 GO TO 710
1820 IF X1=12 THEN 1840
1830 GO TO 1860
1840 IF B3=1 THEN 1860
1850 GO TO 760
1860 IF X1=13 THEN 1880
1870 GO TO 1900
1880 IF B4=1 THEN 1900
1890 GO TO 800
1900 IF X1=14 THEN 1920
1910 GO TO 1940
1920 IF B5=1 THEN 1840
1930 GO TO 850
1940 IF X1=15 THEN 1960
1950 GO TO 1980
1960 IF B6=1 THEN 1980
1970 GO TO 890
1980 IF X1=16 THEN 2000
1990 GO TO 2020
2000 IF B7=1 THEN 2020
2010 GO TO 940
2020 IF X1=17 THEN 2040
2030 GO TO 2060
2040 IF B8=1 THEN 2060
2050 GO TO 990
2060 IF X1=18 THEN 2080
2070 GO TO 2100
2080 IF B9=1 THEN 2100
2090 GO TO 1040
2100 IF X1=19 THEN 2120
2110 GO TO 2140
2120 IF C1=1 THEN 2140
2130 GO TO 1090
2140 IF X1=20 THEN 2160
2150 GO TO 2180
2160 IF C2=1 THEN 2180
2170 GO TO 1140
2180 IF X1=21 THEN 2200
2190 GO TO 2220
2200 IF C3=1 THEN 2220
2210 GO TO 1190
2220 IF X1=22 THEN 2240
2230 GO TO 2260
2240 IF C4=1 THEN 2260
2250 GO TO 1240
2260 IF X1=23 THEN 2280
2270 GO TO 2300
2280 IF C5=1 THEN 2300
2290 GO TO 440
2300 GO TO 2320
2310 IF X1=24 THEN 1280
2320 GO TO 1350
2330 PRINT
2340 PRINT
2350 PRINT "
2360 END
```

170

SAMPLE RUN

RANDOM POETRY IN FOUR PART HARMONY.

TIME IS TWISTED TO LAP UPON
    ITSELF FOREVER
NOBODY LOSES ALL THE TIME

AND IT IS DAWN
        THE WORLD
    GOES FORTH TO MURDER DREAMS
HIS MOST WISE MUSIC STOLE
    NOTHING FROM DEATH
AND IT IS DUSK
      ON EARTH

THE PEOPLE ARE IN THEIR HOUSES
SHE SLEEPS WITH DEATH UPON HER MOUTH
    AND A SONG IN HER EYES
THE HOURS DESENDED
        PUTTING ON STARS
THE HOURS RISE UP PUTTING OFF STARS
    AND IT IS DAWN
WITH A SONG UPON HER MOUTH
    HAVING DEATH IN HER EYES
WITH A SONG UPON HER MOUTH
    HAVING DEATH IN HER EYES
IN THE MIRROR I SEE A MAN, AND HE
    SCREAMS
FOR HE IS ME
      AND I HE

      BY A. COM PUTER.

READY

RANDOM POETRY IN FOUR PART HARMONY.

TIME IS TWISTED TO LAP UPON
    ITSELF FOREVER
NOBODY LOSES ALL THE TIME

AND IT IS DAWN
        THE WORLD
    GOES FORTH TO MURDER DREAMS
HIS MOST WISE MUSIC STOLE
    NOTHING FROM DEATH
AND IT IS DUSK
      ON EARTH

THE PEOPLE ARE IN THEIR HOUSES
SHE SLEEPS WITH DEATH UPON HER MOUTH
    AND A SONG IN HER EYES
THE HOURS DESENDED
        PUTTING ON STARS
THE HOURS RISE UP PUTTING OFF STARS
    AND IT IS DAWN
WITH A SONG UPON HER MOUTH
    HAVING DEATH IN HER EYES
WITH A SONG UPON HER MOUTH
    HAVING DEATH IN HER EYES
IN THE MIRROR I SEE A MAN, AND HE
    SCREAMS
FOR HE IS ME
      AND I HE

      BY A. COM PUTER.

READY

POET   PROGRAM LISTING

```
90 RANDOMIZE
100 IF I<>1 THEN 101 ELSE PRINT "MIDNIGHT DREARY";
101 IF I<>2 THEN 102 ELSE PRINT "FIREY EYES";
102 IF I<>3 THEN 103 ELSE PRINT "BIRD OR FIEND";
103 IF I<>4 THEN 104 ELSE PRINT "THING OF EVIL";
104 IF I<>5 THEN 210 ELSE PRINT "PHOPHET";
105 GOTO 210
110 IF I<>1 THEN 111 ELSE PRINT "BEGUILING ME";
111 IF I<>2 THEN 112 ELSE PRINT "THRILLED ME";
112 IF I<>3 THEN 113 ELSE PRINT "STILL SITTING..."\GOTO 212
113 IF I<>4 THEN 114 ELSE PRINT "BURNED.  "\GOTO 212
114 IF I<>5 THEN 210 ELSE PRINT "NEVER FLITTING";
115 GOTO 210
120 IF I<>1 THEN 121 ELSE IF U=0 THEN 210 ELSE PRINT "SIGN OF PARTING";
121 IF I<>2 THEN 122 ELSE PRINT "AND MY SOUL";
122 IF I<>3 THEN 123 ELSE PRINT "DARKNESS THERE";
123 IF I<>4 THEN 124 ELSE PRINT "SHALL BE LIFTED";
124 IF I<>5 THEN 210 ELSE PRINT "QUOTH THE RAVEN";
125 GOTO 210
130 IF I<>1 THEN 131 ELSE PRINT "NOTHING MORE";
131 IF I<>2 THEN 132 ELSE PRINT "YET AGAIN";
132 IF I<>3 THEN 133 ELSE PRINT "SLOWLY CREEPING";
133 IF I<>4 THEN 134 ELSE PRINT "...NEVERMORE";
134 IF I<>5 THEN 210 ELSE PRINT "EVERMORE,";
210 IF U=0 THEN 212 ELSE IF RND>.19 THEN 212 ELSE PRINT ","\U=2
212 IF RND>.65 THEN 214 ELSE PRINT " "\U=U+1\GOTO 215
214 PRINT\U=0
215 I=INT(5*RND+1)
220 J=J+1\K=K+1
230 IF U>0 THEN 240 ELSE IF INT(J/2)<>J/2  THEN 240 ELSE PRINT "     ";
240 ON J GOTO 100,110,120,130,250
250 J=0\PRINT\IF K>20 THEN 270 ELSE GOTO 215
270 PRINT\U=0\K=0\GOTO 110
999 END
```

SAMPLE RUN

```
THING OF EVIL BEGUILING ME,
DARKNESS THERE
        SLOWLY CREEPING
FIREY EYES BEGUILING ME SHALL BE LIFTED, NOTHING MORE,
THING OF EVIL
        THRILLED ME
SHALL BE LIFTED YET AGAIN


STILL SITTING...
  FIREY EYES
        THRILLED ME AND MY SOUL YET AGAIN

MIDNIGHT DREARY BEGUILING ME
SHALL BE LIFTED YET AGAIN,
THING OF EVIL, NEVER FLITTING DARKNESS THERE
        ...NEVERMORE
BIRD OR FIEND BEGUILING ME, SHALL BE LIFTED ...NEVERMORE

MIDNIGHT DREARY BEGUILING ME SIGN OF PARTING
        ...NEVERMORE

BEGUILING ME
THING OF EVIL BURNED.

QUOTH THE RAVEN
        SLOWLY CREEPING

FIREY EYES
        THRILLED ME QUOTH THE RAVEN EVERMORE.

PHOPHET
        THRILLED ME SHALL BE LIFTED
        NOTHING MORE

THING OF EVIL
        STILL SITTING...
  DARKNESS THERE YET AGAIN
MIDNIGHT DREARY,
        STILL SITTING...

SHALL BE LIFTED SLOWLY CREEPING,

BEGUILING ME PHOPHET,
        BURNED.
  SHALL BE LIFTED EVERMORE.
FIREY EYES STILL SITTING...
  SIGN OF PARTING YET AGAIN
MIDNIGHT DREARY BURNED.
  DARKNESS THERE YET AGAIN
MIDNIGHT DREARY, BURNED.
  DARKNESS THERE,
        EVERMORE.
MIDNIGHT DREARY BURNED.
  QUOTH THE RAVEN
        EVERMORE.


NEVER FLITTING FIREY EYES THRILLED ME SIGN OF PARTING NOTHING MORE,
BIRD OR FIEND BEGUILING ME
SHALL BE LIFTED YET AGAIN
FIREY EYES
        THRILLED ME QUOTH THE RAVEN, ...NEVERMORE
THING OF EVIL
        BURNED.
  DARKNESS THERE EVERMORE.
THING OF EVIL BURNED.
  SHALL BE LIFTED EVERMORE.

THRILLED ME
FIREY EYES NEVER FLITTING
AND MY SOUL SLOWLY CREEPING
BIRD OR FIEND THRILLED ME, SIGN OF PARTING
        NOTHING MORE
FIREY EYES
        BEGUILING ME DARKNESS THERE
        YET AGAIN
MIDNIGHT DREARY
        STILL SITTING...
  SIGN OF PARTING
        NOTHING MORE
PHOPHET BEGUILING ME, AND MY SOUL
        YET AGAIN


THRILLED ME BIRD OR FIEND
        THRILLED ME SIGN OF PARTING ...NEVERMORE
BIRD OR FIEND THRILLED ME, QUOTH THE RAVEN ...NEVERMORE
BIRD OR FIEND
        THRILLED ME SHALL BE LIFTED NOTHING MORE
FIREY EYES
        NEVER FLITTING DARKNESS THERE YET AGAIN
BIRD OR FIEND THRILLED ME, DARKNESS THERE NOTHING MORE


BURNED.

THING OF EVIL NEVER FLITTING QUOTH THE RAVEN,
        NOTHING MORE
MIDNIGHT DREARY
        THRILLED ME DARKNESS THERE YET AGAIN,
MIDNIGHT DREARY
        BEGUILING ME DARKNESS THERE
        YET AGAIN
MIDNIGHT DREARY STILL SITTING...
  SHALL BE LIFTED SLOWLY CREEPING
THING OF EVIL BEGUILING ME
DARKNESS THERE ...NEVERMORE


BURNED.

FIREY EYES
        STILL SITTING...
  AND MY SOUL EVERMORE.

FIREY EYES NEVER FLITTING QUOTH THE RAVEN
        ...NEVERMORE
MIDNIGHT DREARY
        THRILLED ME
QUOTH THE RAVEN
```

POKER

Description

In this game, you play draw poker with the computer as your
opponent. At the start of the game, each person has $200.
The game ends when either opponent runs out of money (if you
run short, the computer gives you a chance to sell your
wristwatch or diamond tie tack).

The computer opens the betting before the draw; you open the
betting after the draw. If you don't have a hand that's worth
anything and want to fold, bet 0. Prior to the draw, to check
the draw, you may bet .5. Of course, if the computer has
betted, you must match bets (see his bet) in order to draw or,
if your hand looks good either before or after the draw, you
may always raise the bet.

Source

Thanks to A.E. Sapega for submitting this program to DECUS
(BASIC 8-556). Its author is:

A. Christopher Hall
Trinity College
Hartford, CT 06106

© 1973 by E.C. Publications

PROGRAM LISTING

```
1DIMA(15),B(15
2DEFFNA(X)=INT(10*RND(X),
3DEFFNB(X)=X-100*INT(X/100)
4PRINT"WELCOME TO THE HALLDEN CASINO.  WE EACH HAVE $200"
5PRINT"I WILL OPEN THE BETTING BEFORE THE DRAW; YOU OPEN AFTER"
6PRINT"WHEN YOU FOLD, BET 0; TO CHECK, BET .5"
7PRINT"ENOUGH TALK -- LET'S GET DOWN TO BUSINESS"
8PRINT
9LETO=1
10LETC=200
11LETS=200
12LETP=0
13RANDOM
14PRINT
15IFC<=5THEN367
16PRINT"THE ANTE IS $5.  I WILL DEAL"
17PRINT
18IFS>5THEN20
19GOSUB383
20LETP=P+10
21LETS=S-5
22LETC=C-5
23FORZ=1TO10
24GOSUB174
25NEXTZ
26PRINT"YOUR HAND:"
27LETN=1
28GOSUB185
29LETN=6
30LETI=2
31GOSUB217
32PRINT
33IFI<>6THEN47
34IFFNA(0)<=7THEN37
35LETX=11100
36GOTO42
37IFFNA(0)<=7THEN40
38LETX=11110
39GOTO42
40IFFNA(0)>=1THEN45
41LETX=1111;
42LETI=7
43LETZ=23
44GOTO58
45LETZ=1
46GOTO51
47IFU>=13THEN54
48IFFNA(0)>=2THEN50
49GOTO42
50LETZ=0
51LETK=0
52PRINT"I CHECK"
53GOTO62
54IFU<=16THEN57
55LETZ=2
56IFFNA(0)>=1THEN58
57LETZ=35
58LETV=Z+FNA(0)
59GOSUB348
60PRINT"I'LL OPEN WITH "V
61LETK=V
62GOSUB305
63GOSUB65
64GOTO82
65IFI<>3THEN76
66PRINT
67PRINT"I WIN"
68LETC=C+P
69PRINT"NOW I HAVE $"C"AND YOU HAVE $"S
70PRINT"DO YOU WISH TO CONTINUE";
71INPUTH$
72IFH$="YES"THEN12
73IFH$="NO"THEN410
74PRINT"ANSWER YES OR NO, IDIOT"
75GOTO70
76IFI<>4THEN81
77PRINT
78PRINT"YOU WIN"
79LETS=S+P
80GOTO69
81RETURN
82PRINT
83PRINT"NOW WE DRAW -- HOW MANY CARDS DO YOU WANT";
84INPUTT
85IFT=0THEN98
86LETZ=10
87IFT<4THEN90
88PRINT"YOU CAN'T DRAW MORE THAN THREE CARDS"
89GOTO84
90PRINT"WHAT ARE THEIR NUMBERS"
91FOR Q=1TOT
92INPUTU
93GOSUB173
94NEXTQ
95PRINT"YOUR NEW HAND:"
96LETN=1
97GOSUB185
98LETZ=10+T
99FORU=6TO10
100IFINT(X/10^(U-6))<>10*INT(X/10^(U-5))THEN102
101GOSUB173
102NEXTU
103PRINT
104PRINT"I AM TAKING"Z-10-T"CARD";
105IFZ=11+TTHEN109
106PRINT"S"
107PRINT
108GOTO110
109PRINT
110LETN=6
111LETV=I
112LETI=1
113GOSUB217
114LETB=U
115LETM=D
116IFV<>7THEN119
117LETZ=28
118GOTO133
119IFI<>6THEN122
120LETZ=1
121GOTO133
122IFU>=13THEN127

123LETZ=2
124IFFNA(0)<>6THEN126
125LETZ=19
126GOTO133
127IFU>=16THEN132
128LETZ=19
129IFFNA(0)<>8THEN131
130LETZ=11
131GOTO133
132LETZ=2
133LETK=0
134GOSUB305
135IFT<>.5THEN145
136IFV=7THEN140
137IFI>=6THEN140
138PRINT"I'LL CHECK"
139GOTO146
140LETV=Z+FNA(0)
141GOSUB348
142PRINT"I'LL BET"V
143LETK=V
144GOSUB306
145GOSUB65
146PRINT
147PRINT"NOW WE COMPARE HANDS"
148LETJ$=H$
149LETK$=I$
150PRINT"MY HAND:"
151LETN=6
152GOSUB185
153LETN=1
154GOSUB217
155PRINT
156PRINT"YOU HAVE ";
157LETK=D
158GOSUB369
159LETH$=J$
160LETI$=K$
161LETK=M
162PRINT"AND I HAVE ";
163GOSUB369
164IFB>UTHEN67
165IFU>BTHEN78
166IFH$="A FLUS"THEN170
167PRINT"THE HAND IS DRAWN"
168PRINT"ALL $"P"REMAIN IN THE POT"
169GOTO14
170IFFNB(M)>FNB(D)THEN67
171IFFNB(D)>FNB(M)THEN78
172GOTO167
173LETZ=Z+1
174LETA(Z)=INT(1000*RND(0))
175IFINT(A(Z)/100)>3THEN174
176IFA(Z)-100*INT(A(Z)/100)>12THEN174
177FORK=1TOZ-1
178IFA(Z)=A(K)THEN174
179NEXTK
180IFZ<=10THEN184
181LETN=A(U)
182LETA(U)=A(Z)
183LETA(Z)=N
184RETURN
185FORZ=NTON+4
186PRINTZ"-- ";
187GOSUB195
188PRINT" OF";
189GOSUB207
190IFZ/2<>INT(Z/2)THEN192
191PRINT
192NEXTZ
193PRINT
194RETURN
195LETK=FNB(A(Z))
196IFK<>9THEN198
197PRINT"JACK";
198IFK<>10THEN200
199PRINT"QUEEN";
200IFK<>11THEN202
201PRINT"KING";
202IFK<>12THEN204
203PRINT"ACE";
204IFK>=9THEN206
205PRINTK+2;
206RETURN
207LETK=INT(A(Z)/100)
208IFK<>0THEN210
209PRINT" CLUBS",
210IFK<>1THEN212
211PRINT" DIAMONDS",
212IFK<>2THEN214
213PRINT" HEARTS",
214IFK<>3THEN216
215PRINT" SPADES",
216RETURN
217LETU=0
218FORZ=NTON+4
219LETB(Z)=FNB(A(Z))
220IFZ=N+4THEN223
221IFINT(A(Z)/100)<>INT(A(Z+1)/100)THEN223
222LETU=U+1
223NEXTZ
224IFU<>4THEN231
225LETX=11111
226LETD=A(N)
227LETH$="A FLUS"
228LETI$="H IN"
229LETU=15
230RETURN
231FORZ=NTON+3
232FORK=Z+1TON+4
233IFB(Z)<=B(K)THEN239
234LETX=A(Z)
235LETA(Z)=A(K)
236LETB(Z)=B(K)

237LETA(K)=X
238LETB(K)=A(K)-100*INT(A(K)/100)
239NEXTK
240NEXTZ
241LETX=0
242FORZ=NTON+3
243IFB(Z)<>B(Z-1)THEN247
244LETX=X+11*10^(Z-N)
245LETD=A(Z)
246GOSUB276
247NEXTZ
248IFX<>0THEN262
249IFB(N)+3<>B(N+3)THEN252
250LETX=1111
251LETU=10
252IFB(N+1)+3<>B(N+4)THEN262
253IFU<>10THEN260
254LETU=14
255LETH$="STRAIG"
256LETI$="HT"
257LETX=11111
258LETD=A(N+4)
259RETURN
260LETU=10
261LETX=11110
262IFU>=10THEN269
263LETD=A(N+4)
264LETH$="SCHMAL"
265LETI$="TZ, "
266LETU=9
267LETX=11000
268GOTO274
269IFU<>10THEN272
270IFI=1THEN274
271GOTO275
272IFU>12THEN275
273IFFNB(D)>6THEN275
274LETI=6
275RETURN
276IFU>=11THEN281
277LETU=11
278LETH$="A PAIR"
279LETI$=" OF "
280RETURN
281IFU<>11THEN291
282IFB(Z)<>B(Z-1)THEN287
283LETH$="THREE"
284LETI$=" "
285LETU=13
286RETURN
287LETH$="TWO P"
288LETI$="AIR, "
289LETU=12
290RETURN
291IFU<>12THEN296
292LETU=16
293LETH$="FULL H"
294LETI$="OUSE, "
295RETURN
296IFB(Z)<>B(Z-1)THEN301
297LETU=17
298LETH$="FOUR"
299LETI$=" "
300RETURN
301LETU=16
302LETH$="FULL H"
303LETI$="OUSE, "
304RETURN
305LETG=0
306PRINT"WHAT IS YOUR BET";
307INPUTT
308IFT-INT(T)=0THEN314
309IFK<>0THEN312
310IFG<>0THEN312
311IFT=.5THEN341
312PRINT"NO SMALL CHANGE, PLEASE"
313GOTO306
314IFS-G-T>=0THEN317
315GOSUB383
316GOTO306
317IFT<>0THEN320
318LETI=3
319GOTO338
320IFG+T>KTHEN323
321PRINT"IF YOU CAN'T SEE MY BET, THEN FOLD"
322GOTO306
323LETG=G+T
324IFG=KTHEN338
325IFZ<>1THEN342
326IFG>5THEN330
327IFZ>=2THEN335
328LETV=5
329GOTO342
330IFZ=1THEN332
331IFT<=25THEN335
332LETI=4
333PRINT"I FOLD"
334RETURN
335IFZ=2THEN343
336PRINT"I'LL SEE YOU"
337LETK=G
338LETS=S-G
339LETC=C-K
340LETP=P+G+K
341RETURN
342IFG>3*ZTHEN335
343LETV=G-K+FNA(0)
344GOSUB348
345PRINT"I'LL SEE YOU, AND RAISE YOU"V
346LETK=G+V
347GOTO306
348IFC-G-V>=0THEN366
349IFG<>0THEN352
350LETC=C
```

```
351RETURN
352IFC-G>=0THEN336
353IFO/2<>INT(O/2)THEN360
354PRINT"WOULD YOU LIKE TO BUY BACK YOUR WATCH FOR $50";
355INPUTJ$
356IFJ$="NO"THEN360
357LETC=C+50
358LETO=O/2
359RETURN
360IFO/3<>INT(O/3)THEN367
361PRINT"WOULD YOU LIKE TO BUY BACK YOUR TIE TACK FOR $50";
362INPUTJ$
363IFJ$="NO"THEN367
364LETC=C+50
365LETO=O/3
366RETURN
367PRINT"I'M BUSTED.  CONGRATULATIONS"
368STOP
369PRINTH$;I$;
370IFH$<>"A FLUS"THEN375
371LETK=INT(K/100)
372GOSUB208
373PRINT
374RETURN
375LETK=FNB(K)
376GOSUB196
377IFH$="SCHMAL"THEN379
378IFH$<>"STRAIG"THEN381
379PRINT" HIGH"
380RETURN
381PRINT"S"
382RETURN
383PRINT
384PRINT"YOU CAN'T BET WHAT YOU HAVEN'T GOT"
385IFO/2=INT(O/2)THEN397
386PRINT"WOULD YOU LIKE TO SELL YOUR WATCH";
387INPUTJ$
388IFJ$="NO"THEN397
389IFFNA(0)>=7THEN393
390PRINT"I'LL GIVE YOU $75 FOR IT"
391LETS=S+75
392GOTO395
393PRINT"THAT'S A PRETTY CRUMMY WATCH - I'LL GIVE YOU $25"
394LETS=S+25
395LETO=O*2
396RETURN
397IFO/3=INT(O/3)THEN409
398PRINT"WILL YOU PART WITH THAT DIAMOND TIE TACK";
399INPUTJ$
400IFJ$="NO"THEN408
401IFFNA(0)>=6THEN405
402PRINT"YOU ARE NOW $100 RICHER"
403LETS=S+100
404GOTO407
405PRINT"IT'S PASTE.  $25"
406LETS=S+25
407LETO=O*3
408RETURN
409PRINT"YOUR WAD IS SHOT.  SO LONG, SUCKER"
410END
```

SAMPLE RUN

```
WELCOME TO THE HALLDEN CASINO.  WE EACH HAVE $200
I WILL OPEN THE BETTING BEFORE THE DRAW; YOU OPEN AFTER
WHEN YOU FOLD, BET 0;  TO CHECK, BET .5
ENOUGH TALK -- LET'S GET DOWN TO BUSINESS


THE ANTE IS $5.   I WILL DEAL

YOUR HAND:
  1 --    7  OF SPADES         2 --     3  OF SPADES
  3 -- QUEEN OF SPADES         4 --     7  OF DIAMONDS
  5 --    6  OF CLUBS

I CHECK
WHAT IS YOUR BET? 5
I'LL SEE YOU

NOW WE DRAW -- HOW MANY CARDS DO YOU WANT? 3
WHAT ARE THEIR NUMBERS
? 2
? 3
? 5
YOUR NEW HAND:
  1 --    7  OF SPADES         2 -- JACK OF DIAMONDS
  3 --    7  OF HEARTS         4 --     7  OF DIAMONDS
  5 --    5  OF DIAMONDS

I AM TAKING 3 CARDS

WHAT IS YOUR BET? 20
I FOLD

YOU WIN
NOW I HAVE $ 190 AND YOU HAVE $ 210
DO YOU WISH TO CONTINUE? YES

THE ANTE IS $5.   I WILL DEAL

YOUR HAND:
  1 --    4  OF HEARTS         2 --     9  OF DIAMONDS
  3 -- KING OF CLUBS           4 --     6  OF DIAMONDS
  5 --    8  OF SPADES

I CHECK
WHAT IS YOUR BET? 5
I'LL SEE YOU
```

```
NOW WE DRAW -- HOW MANY CARDS DO YOU WANT? 3
WHAT ARE THEIR NUMBERS
? 1
? 4
? 5
YOUR NEW HAND:
  1 --    8  OF DIAMONDS        2 --     9  OF DIAMONDS
  3 -- KING OF CLUBS            4 --     4  OF DIAMONDS
  5 --    5  OF DIAMONDS

I AM TAKING 3 CARDS

WHAT IS YOUR BET? 0

I WIN
NOW I HAVE $ 200 AND YOU HAVE $ 200
DO YOU WISH TO CONTINUE? YES

THE ANTE IS $5.   I WILL DEAL

YOUR HAND:
  1 --    5  OF DIAMONDS        2 -- KING OF CLUBS
  3 --    5  OF CLUBS           4 --     4  OF CLUBS
  5 --    5  OF SPADES

I'LL OPEN WITH  31
WHAT IS YOUR BET? 20
IF YOU CAN'T SEE MY BET, THEN FOLD
WHAT IS YOUR BET? 31

NOW WE DRAW -- HOW MANY CARDS DO YOU WANT? 2
WHAT ARE THEIR NUMBERS
? 2
? 4
YOUR NEW HAND:
  1 --    5  OF DIAMONDS        2 -- JACK OF HEARTS
  3 --    5  OF CLUBS           4 --     7  OF DIAMONDS
  5 --    5  OF SPADES

I AM TAKING 2 CARDS

WHAT IS YOUR BET? 20
I'LL SEE YOU, AND RAISE YOU 28
WHAT IS YOUR BET? 28

NOW WE COMPARE HANDS
MY HAND:
  6 --    4  OF SPADES
  7 --    4  OF DIAMONDS        8 --     9  OF HEARTS
  9 -- KING OF DIAMONDS        10 --   ACE OF SPADES


YOU HAVE THREE  5 S
AND I HAVE A PAIR OF  4 S
YOU WIN
NOW I HAVE $ 116 AND YOU HAVE $ 284
DO YOU WISH TO CONTINUE? YES

THE ANTE IS $5.   I WILL DEAL

YOUR HAND:
  1 --    9  OF HEARTS         2 -- JACK OF HEARTS
  3 --    7  OF DIAMONDS       4 -- KING OF DIAMONDS
  5 --    4  OF SPADES

I CHECK
WHAT IS YOUR BET? 0

I WIN
NOW I HAVE $ 121 AND YOU HAVE $ 279
DO YOU WISH TO CONTINUE? YES

THE ANTE IS $5.   I WILL DEAL

YOUR HAND:
  1 --    8  OF SPADES         2 -- QUEEN OF HEARTS
  3 --    9  OF SPADES         4 --     3  OF CLUBS
  5 --   10  OF DIAMONDS

I CHECK
WHAT IS YOUR BET? 5
I'LL SEE YOU

NOW WE DRAW -- HOW MANY CARDS DO YOU WANT? 1
WHAT ARE THEIR NUMBERS
? 4
YOUR NEW HAND:
  1 --    8  OF SPADES         2 -- QUEEN OF HEARTS
  3 --    9  OF SPADES         4 -- KING OF CLUBS
  5 --   10  OF DIAMONDS

I AM TAKING 3 CARDS

WHAT IS YOUR BET? 5
I'LL SEE YOU

NOW WE COMPARE HANDS
MY HAND:
  6 --    7  OF SPADES
  7 --    7  OF CLUBS          8 --     8  OF CLUBS
  9 -- JACK OF SPADES         10 --   ACE OF SPADES


YOU HAVE SCHMALTZ, KING HIGH
AND I HAVE A PAIR OF  7 S
I WIN
NOW I HAVE $ 136 AND YOU HAVE $ 264
DO YOU WISH TO CONTINUE? YES
```

174

QUBIC

3-DIMENSIONAL TIC-TAC-TOE

Description

QUBIC is the game of tic-tac-toe in a 4x4x4 cube. You must get
4 markers in a row or diagonal along any 3-dimensional plane
in order to win. It is up to you to keep track of moves (the
program does not print out a diagram as you play).

Each move is indicated by a 3-digit number (digits <u>not</u> separated
by commas), with each digit between 1 and 4 inclusive. The
digits indicate the level, column, and row, respectively, of
the move. You can win if you play correctly; although, it is
considerably more difficult than standard, two-dimensional 3x3
tic-tac-toe.

Source

QUBIC seems to have first shown up on a G.E. timesharing system
in 1968. Its original author is unknown.

PROGRAM LISTING

```
0 REM  *  QUBIC-  *
5 PRINT "DO YOU WANT INSTRUCTIONS";
6 INPUT C$
7 IF C$="NO" THEN 21
8 IF C$="YES" THEN 13
9 PRINT "INCORRECT ANSWER.  PLEASE TYPE 'YES' OR 'NO'!"
10 GOTO 6
13 PRINT "THE GAME IS TIC-TAC-TOE IN A 4 X 4 X 4 CUBE."
14 PRINT "EACH MOVE IS INDICATED BY A 3 DIGIT NUMBER, WITH EACH"
15 PRINT "DIGIT BETWEEN 1 AND 4 INCLUSIVE.  THE DIGITS INDICATE THE"
16 PRINT "LEVEL, COLUMN, AND ROW, RESPECTIVELY, OF THE OCCUPIED PLACE."
20 DIM X(64),L(76),M(76,4),Y(16)
21 FOR I = 1 TO 16
22 READ Y(I)
23 NEXT I
24 FOR I=1 TO 76
25 FOR J = 1 TO 4
26 READ M(I,J)
27 NEXT J
28 NEXT I
35 FOR I = 1 TO 64
40 LET X(I) =0
50 NEXT I
54 LET Z=1
55 PRINT "DO YOU WANT TO MOVE FIRST";
60 INPUT S$
66 IF S$="NO" THEN 110
67 IF S$="YES" THEN 70
68 PRINT "INCORRECT ANSWER.  PLEASE TYPE 'YES' OR 'NO'.";
69 GOTO 60
70 PRINT " "
72 PRINT "YOUR MOVE";
80 INPUT J1
85 GOSUB 1800
90 LET K1=INT(J1/100)
95 LET J2=(J1-K1*100)
96 LET K2=INT(J2/10)
97 LET K3= J1 - K1*100 -K2*10
98 LET M=16*K1+4*K2+K3-20
99 IF X(M)=0 THEN 109
100 PRINT "THAT SQUARE IS USED, TRY AGAIN"
101 GOTO 70
109 LET X(M)=1
110 GOSUB 1050
180 FOR J=1 TO 3
190 FOR I=1 TO 76
200 IF J=1 THEN 210
201 IF J=2 THEN 220
203 IF J=3 THEN 235
205 NEXT I
206 NEXT J
207 GOTO 400
210 IF L(I)<>4 THEN 205
211 PRINT "YOU WIN AS FOLLOWS";
212 FOR J=1 TO 4
213 LET M=M(I,J)
214 GOSUB 1000
216 NEXT J
217 GOTO 500
220 IF L(I)<>15 THEN 205
221 FOR J=1 TO 4
222 LET M=M(I,J)
223 IF X(M)<>0 THEN 227
224 LET X(M)=5
225 PRINT "MACHINE MOVES TO";
226 GOSUB 1000
227 NEXT J
228 PRINT ", AND WINS AS FOLLOWS"
229 FOR J=1 TO 4
230 LET M=M(I,J)
231 GOSUB 1000
233 NEXT J
234 GOTO 500
235 IF L(I)<>3 THEN 205
236 PRINT "NICE TRY MACHINE MOVES TO";
237 FOR J=1 TO 4
238 LET M=M(I,J)
239 IF X(M)<>0 THEN 245
240 LET X(M)=5
241 GOSUB 1000
243 GOTO 70
245 NEXT J
248 GOTO 400
250 FOR I = 1 TO 76
251 LET L(I)=X(M(I,1))+X(M(I,2))+X(M(I,3))+X(M(I,4))
252 LET L = L(I)
255 IF L <2 THEN 290
260 IF L>=3 THEN 290
265 IF L>2 THEN 1600
270 FOR J = 1 TO 4
275 IF X(M(I,J))<>0 THEN 285
280 LET X(M(I,J))=1/8
285 NEXT J
290 NEXT I
295 GOSUB 1050
300 FOR I = 1 TO 76
305 IF L(I)=1/2 THEN 1700
310 IF L(I)=1+3/8 THEN 1700
315 NEXT I
320 GOTO 1300
360 LET Z = 1
362 IF X(Y(Z))=0 THEN 380
365 LET Z=Z+1
368 IF Z<>17 THEN 362
375 GOTO 1200
380 LET M=Y(Z)
381 LET X(M)=5
385 PRINT "MACHINE MOVES TO";
389 GOSUB 1000
390 GOTO 70
400 LET X=X
410 FOR I=1 TO 76
412 LET L(I)=X(M(I,1))+X(M(I,2))+X(M(I,3))+X(M(I,4))
415 LET L=L(I)
420 IF L<10 THEN 455
425 IF L>=11 THEN 455
430 IF L>10 THEN 1600
435 FOR J=1 TO 4
440 IF X(M(I,J))<>0 THEN 450
445 LET X(M(I,J))=1/8
450 NEXT J
455 NEXT I
470 GOSUB 1050
475 FOR I=1 TO 76
480 IF L(I)=.5 THEN 1700
485 IF L(I)=5+3/8 THEN 1700
490 NEXT I
492 GOSUB 1800
493 GOTO 250
500 PRINT " "
505 PRINT "DO YOU WANT TO TRY ANOTHER GAME";
510 INPUT X$
515 IF X$="YES" THEN 35
516 IF X$="NO" THEN 520
517 PRINT "INCORRECT ANSWER. PLEASE TYPE 'YES' OR 'NO'!";
518 GOTO 510
520 STOP
1000 LET K1=INT((M-1)/16)+1
1010 LET J2=M-16*(K1-1)
1030 LET K2=INT((J2-1)/4)+1
1035 LET K3=M-(K1-1)*16-(K2-1)*4
1040 LET M=K1*100+K2*10+K3
1042 PRINT M;
1045 RETURN
1050 FOR S=1 TO 76
1060 LET J1 = M(S,1)
1070 LET J2=M(S,2)
1080 LET J3=M(S,3)
1090 LET J4=M(S,4)
1100 LET L(S)=X(J1)+X(J2)+X(J3)+X(J4)
1110 NEXT S
1120 RETURN
1200 FOR I=1 TO 64
1210 IF X(I)<>0 THEN 1250
1220 LET X(I)=5
1225 LET M=I
1226 PRINT "MACHINE LIKES";
1227 GOSUB 1000
1228 PRINT " "
1230 GOTO 70
1250 NEXT I
1252 PRINT "THE GAME IS A DRAW"
1255 GOTO 500
1300 FOR K=1 TO 18
1305 LET P=0
1310 FOR I=4*K-3 TO 4*K
1315 FOR J=1 TO 4
1320 LET P=P+X(M(I,J))
1325 NEXT J
1330 NEXT I
1345 IF P<4 THEN 1390
1350 IF P<5 THEN 1400
1355 IF P<9 THEN 1390
1360 IF P<10 THEN 1400
1390 NEXT K
1395 GOSUB 1800
1396 GOTO 360
1400 LET S=1/8
1405 FOR I=4*K-3 TO 4*K
1410 GOTO 1703
1415 NEXT I
1420 LET S=0
1425 GOTO 1405
1500 DATA 1,49,52,4,13,61,64,16,22,39,23,38,26,42,27,43
1510 DATA 1,2,3,4,5,6,7,8,9,10,11,12,13,14,15,16,17,18,19,20
1520 DATA 21,22,23,24,25,26,27,28,29,30,31,32,33,34,35,36,37,38
1521 DATA 39,40,41,42,43,44,45,46,47,48,49,50,51,52,53,54,55,56
1522 DATA 57,58,59,60,61,62,63,64
1523 DATA 1,17,33,49,5,21,37,53,9,25,41,57,13,29,45,61
1524 DATA 2,18,34,50,6,22,38,54,10,26,42,58,14,30,46,62
1525 DATA 3,19,35,51,7,23,39,55,11,27,43,59,15,31,47,63
1527 DATA 4,20,36,52,8,24,40,56,12,28,44,60,16,32,48,64
1529 DATA 1,5,9,13,17,21,25,29,33,37,41,45,49,53,57,61
1532 DATA 2,6,10,14,18,22,26,30,34,38,42,46,50,54,58,62
1534 DATA 3,7,11,15,19,23,27,31,35,39,43,47,51,55,59,63
1536 DATA 4,8,12,16,20,24,28,32,36,40,44,48,52,56,60,64
1538 DATA 1,6,11,16,17,22,27,32,33,38,43,48,49,54,59,64
1540 DATA 13,10,7,4,29,26,23,20,45,42,39,36,61,58,55,52
1542 DATA 1,21,41,61,2,22,42,62,3,23,43,63,4,24,44,64
1544 DATA 49,37,25,13,50,38,26,14,51,39,27,15,52,40,28,16
1546 DATA 1,18,35,52,5,22,39,56,9,26,43,60,13,30,47,64
1548 DATA 49,34,19,4,53,38,23,8,57,42,27,12,61,46,31,16
1550 DATA 1,22,43,64,16,27,38,49,4,23,42,61,13,26,39,52
1600 FOR J=1 TO 4
1605 IF X(M(I,J))<>1/8 THEN 1650
1610 LET X(M(I,J))=5
1615 IF L(I)<5 THEN 1625
1620 PRINT "LET'S SEE YOU GET OUT OF THIS:  MACHINE MOVES TO";
1622 GOTO 1626
1625 PRINT "YOU FOX.  JUST IN THE NICK OF TIME, MACHINE MOVES TO";
1626 LET M=M(I,J)
1630 GOSUB 1000
1640 GOTO 70
1650 NEXT J
1660 PRINT "MACHINE CONCEDES THIS GAME."
1665 GOTO 500
1700 LET S=1/8
1703 IF I-INT(I/4)*4>1 THEN 1715
1705 LET A=1
1710 GOTO 1720
1715 LET A=2
1720 FOR J=A TO 5-A STEP 5-2*A
1725 IF X(M(I,J))=S THEN 1750
1730 NEXT J
1735 GOTO 1415
1750 LET X(M(I,J))=5
1755 LET M=M(I,J)
1760 PRINT "MACHINE TAKES";
1770 GOSUB 1000
1780 GOTO 70
1800 FOR I=1 TO 64
1810 IF X(I)<>1/8 THEN 1850
1815 LET X(I)=0
1850 NEXT I
1860 RETURN
2000 END
```

SAMPLE RUN

QUBIC   15:16   27-APR-73

DO YOU WANT INSTRUCTIONS ?YES
THE GAME IS TIC-TAC-TOE IN A 4 X 4 X 4 CUBE.
EACH MOVE IS INDICATED BY A 3 DIGIT NUMBER, WITH EACH
DIGIT BETWEEN 1 AND 4 INCLUSIVE.   THE DIGITS INDICATE THE
LEVEL, COLUMN, AND ROW, RESPECTIVELY, OF THE OCCUPIED PLACE.
DO YOU WANT TO MOVE FIRST ?YES

YOUR MOVE ?222
MACHINE MOVES TO 111
YOUR MOVE ?211
MACHINE MOVES TO 411
YOUR MOVE ?233
NICE TRY MACHINE MOVES TO 244
YOUR MOVE ?122
MACHINE MOVES TO 414
YOUR MOVE ?422
NICE TRY MACHINE MOVES TO 322
YOUR MOVE ?121
MACHINE MOVES TO 114
YOUR MOVE ?323
NICE TRY MACHINE MOVES TO 424
YOUR MOVE ?413
NICE TRY MACHINE MOVES TO 143
YOUR MOVE ?444
MACHINE MOVES TO 141
YOUR MOVE ?142
MACHINE TAKES 112
YOUR MOVE ?113
MACHINE TAKES 223
YOUR MOVE ?141
THAT SQUARE IS USED, TRY AGAIN

YOUR MOVE ?332
MACHINE MOVES TO 441
YOUR MOVE ?241
LET'S SEE YOU GET OUT OF THIS: MACHINE MOVES TO 421
YOUR MOVE ?431
MACHINE MOVES TO 124 , AND WINS AS FOLLOWS
 421 322 223 124
DO YOU WANT TO TRY ANOTHER GAME ?YES
DO YOU WANT TO MOVE FIRST ?YES

YOUR MOVE ?111
MACHINE MOVES TO 411
YOUR MOVE ?141
MACHINE MOVES TO 414
YOUR MOVE ?441
MACHINE MOVES TO 114
YOUR MOVE ?121
NICE TRY MACHINE MOVES TO 131
YOUR MOVE ?221
NICE TRY MACHINE MOVES TO 331
YOUR MOVE ?341
NICE TRY MACHINE MOVES TO 241
YOUR MOVE ?444
MACHINE MOVES TO 144
YOUR MOVE ?222
NICE TRY MACHINE MOVES TO 333
YOUR MOVE ?213
MACHINE TAKES 232
YOUR MOVE ?434
LET'S SEE YOU GET OUT OF THIS: MACHINE MOVES TO 214
YOUR MOVE ?314
MACHINE MOVES TO 223 , AND WINS AS FOLLOWS
 241 232 223 214
DO YOU WANT TO TRY ANOTHER GAME ?NO

177

QUEEN

Description

This game is based on the permissible moves of the chess queen--i.e., along any vertical, horizontal, or diagonal. In this game, the queen can only move to the left, down, and diagonally down to the left.

The object of the game is to place the queen (one only) in the lower left-hand square (no. 150), by alternating moves between you and the computer. The one to place the queen there wins.

You go first and place the queen in any one of the squares on the top row or the right-hand column. That is your first move. The computer is beatable, but it takes some figuring. See if you can devise a winning strategy.

Source

Source and author are totally unknown.

178

PROGRAM LISTING

```
1 REM PLAYS QUEEN GAME.
2 PRINT "DO YOU WISH INSTRUCTIONS";
9 RANDOMIZE
10 DIM S(64)
11 FOR I = 1 TO 64
12 READ S(I)
13 NEXT I
14 DATA 81, 71, 61, 51, 41, 31, 21, 11
15 DATA 92, 82, 72, 62, 52, 42, 32, 22
16 DATA 103, 93, 83, 73, 63, 53, 43, 33
17 DATA 114, 104, 94, 84, 74, 64, 54, 44
18 DATA 125, 115, 105, 95, 85, 75, 65, 55
19 DATA 136, 126, 116, 106, 96, 86, 76, 66
20 DATA 147, 137, 127, 117, 107, 97, 87, 77
21 DATA 158, 148, 138, 128, 118, 108, 98, 88
22 INPUT W$
23 IF W$="NO" THEN 30
24 IF W$="YES" THEN 28
25 PRINT "INCORRECT ANSWER, PLEASE TYPE 'YES' OR 'NO'";
26 GOTO 22
28 GOSUB 5000
29 GO TO 100
30 GOSUB 5150
90 REM ERROR CHECKS.
100 PRINT "WHERE WOULD YOU LIKE TO START";
110 INPUT M1
115 IF M1 = 0 THEN 232
120 LET T1 = INT(M1/10)
130 LET U1 = M1 - 10*T1
140 IF U1 = 1 THEN 200
150 IF U1 = T1 THEN 200
160 PRINT "PLEASE READ THE DIRECTIONS AGAIN."
165 PRINT "YOU HAVE BEGUN ILLEGALLY."
170 PRINT
180 GO TO 100
200 GO SUB 2000
210 PRINT "MACHINE MOVES TO SQUARE"M
215 IF M = 158 THEN 3400
220 PRINT "WHAT IS YOUR MOVE";
230 INPUT M1
231 IF M1 <> 0 THEN 239
232 PRINT
233 PRINT "IT LOOKS LIKE I HAVE WON BY FORFEIT."
234 PRINT
235 GO TO 4000
239 IF M1 <= M THEN 3200
240 LET T1 = INT(M1/10)
250 LET U1 = M1 - 10*T1
260 LET P = U1 - U
270 IF P <> 0 THEN 300
280 LET L = T1 - T
290 IF L <= 0 THEN 3200
295 GO TO 200
300 IF T1 - T <> P THEN 320
310 GO TO 200
320 IF T1 - T <> 2*P THEN 3200
330 GO TO 200
1990 REM LOCATE MOVE FOR MACHINE.
2000 IF M1 = 41 THEN 2180
2010 IF M1 = 44 THEN 2180
2020 IF M1 = 73 THEN 2180
2030 IF M1 = 75 THEN 2180
2040 IF M1 = 126 THEN 2180
2050 IF M1 = 127 THEN 2180
2060 IF M1 = 158 THEN 3300
2065 LET C = 0
2070 FOR K = 7 TO 1 STEP -1
2080 LET U = U1
2090 LET T = T1 + K
2100 GO SUB 3500
2105 IF C = 1 THEN 2160
2110 LET U = U + K
2120 GO SUB 3500
2125 IF C = 1 THEN 2160
2130 LET T = T + K
2140 GO SUB 3500
2145 IF C = 1 THEN 2160
2150 NEXT K
2155 GO TO 2180
2160 LET C = 0
2170 RETURN
2180 GO SUB 3000
2190 RETURN
2990 REM RANDOM MOVE.
3000 LET Z=RND
3010 IF Z > .6 THEN 3110
3020 IF Z > .3 THEN 3070
3030 LET U = U1
3040 LET T = T1 + 1
3050 LET M = 10*T + U
3060 RETURN
3070 LET U = U1 + 1
3080 LET T = T1 + 2
3090 LET M = 10*T + U
3100 RETURN
3110 LET U = U1 + 1
3120 LET T = T1 + 1
3130 LET M = 10*T + U
3140 RETURN
3190 REM ILLEGAL MOVE MESSAGE.
3200 PRINT
3210 PRINT "Y O U   C H E A T . . . TRY AGAIN";
3220 GO TO 230
3290 REM PLAYER WINS.
3300 PRINT
3310 PRINT "C O N G R A T U L A T I O N S . . ."
3320 PRINT
3330 PRINT "YOU HAVE WON--VERY WELL PLAYED."
3340 PRINT "IT LOOKS LIKE I HAVE MET MY MATCH."
3350 PRINT "THANKS FOR PLAYING--I CAN'T WIN ALL THE TIME."
3360 PRINT
3370 GO TO 4000
3390 REM MACHINE WINS.
3400 PRINT
3410 PRINT "NICE TRY, BUT IT LOOKS LIKE I HAVE WON,"
3420 PRINT "THANKS FOR PLAYING,"
3430 PRINT
3440 GO TO 4000
3490 REM TEST FOR MACHINE MOVE.
3500 LET M = 10*T + U
3510 IF M = 158 THEN 3570
3520 IF M = 127 THEN 3570
3530 IF M = 126 THEN 3570
3540 IF M = 75 THEN 3570
3550 IF M = 73 THEN 3570
3560 RETURN
3570 LET C = 1
3580 GO TO 3560
3990 REM ANOTHER GAME?
4000 PRINT "ANYONE ELSE CARE TO TRY";
4020 INPUT Q$
4030 PRINT
4040 IF Q$="YES" THEN100
4042 IF Q$="NO" THEN 4050
4045 PRINT "INCORRECT ANSWER, PLEASE TYPE 'YES' OR 'NO'";
4046 GOTO 4020
4050 PRINT "OK - - THANKS AGAIN."
4060 STOP
4990 REM DIRECTIONS, ETC. . .
5000 PRINT "WE ARE GOING TO PLAY A GAME BASED ON ONE OF THE CHESS MOVES."
5010 PRINT "OUR QUEEN WILL BE ABLE TO MOVE ONLY TO THE LEFT,"
5020 PRINT "DOWN, AND DIAGONALLY DOWN TO THE LEFT."
5030 PRINT
5040 PRINT "THE OBJECT OF THE GAME IS TO PLACE THE QUEEN IN THE"
5050 PRINT "LOWER LEFT-HAND SQUARE BY ALTERNATING MOVES BETWEEN"
5060 PRINT "YOU AND THE MACHINE/  THE FIRST ONE TO PLACE THE QUEEN"
5070 PRINT "THERE, WINS."
5080 PRINT
5090 PRINT "YOU GO FIRST AND PLACE THE QUEEN IN ANY ONE OF THE"
5100 PRINT "SQUARES ON THE TOP ROW OR THE RIGHT-HAND COLUMN."
5110 PRINT "THAT WILL BE YOUR FIRST MOVE."
5120 PRINT "WE WILL THEN ALTERNATE MOVES."
5130 PRINT "YOU MAY FORFEIT AT ANY TIME BY TYPING '0' AS YOUR MOVE."
5140 PRINT "BE SURE TO PUSH THE 'RETURN' KEY AFTER EACH RESPONSE."
5150 PRINT
5160 FOR A = 0 TO 7
5170 FOR B = 1 TO 8
5180 LET I = 8*A + B
5190 PRINT S(I);
5200 NEXT B
5210 PRINT
5220 PRINT
5225 PRINT
5230 NEXT A
5240 PRINT
5250 RETURN
99999 END
```

SAMPLE RUN

```
DO YOU WISH INSTRUCTIONS ?YES
WE ARE GOING TO PLAY A GAME BASED ON ONE OF THE CHESS MOVES.
OUR QUEEN WILL BE ABLE TO MOVE ONLY TO THE LEFT,
DOWN, AND DIAGONALLY DOWN TO THE LEFT.

THE OBJECT OF THE GAME IS TO PLACE THE QUEEN IN THE
LOWER LEFT-HAND SQUARE BY ALTERNATING MOVES BETWEEN
YOU AND THE MACHINE/  THE FIRST ONE TO PLACE THE QUEEN
THERE, WINS.

YOU GO FIRST AND PLACE THE QUEEN IN ANY ONE OF THE
SQUARES ON THE TOP ROW OR THE RIGHT-HAND COLUMN.
THAT WILL BE YOUR FIRST MOVE.
WE WILL THEN ALTERNATE MOVES.
YOU MAY FORFEIT AT ANY TIME BY TYPING '0' AS YOUR MOVE.
BE SURE TO PUSH THE 'RETURN' KEY AFTER EACH RESPONSE.

81  71  61  51  41  31  21  11

92  82  72  62  52  42  32  22

103  93  83  73  63  53  43  33

114  104  94  84  74  64  54  44

125  115  105  95  85  75  65  55

136  126  116  106  96  86  76  66

147  137  127  117  107  97  87  77

158  148  138  128  118  108  98  88

WHERE WOULD YOU LIKE TO START ?81
MACHINE MOVES TO SQUARE 158

NICE TRY, BUT IT LOOKS LIKE I HAVE WON.
THANKS FOR PLAYING.

ANYONE ELSE CARE TO TRY ?YES

WHERE WOULD YOU LIKE TO START ?158
PLEASE READ THE DIRECTIONS AGAIN.
YOU HAVE BEGUN ILLEGALLY.

WHERE WOULD YOU LIKE TO START ?44
MACHINE MOVES TO SQUARE 55
WHAT IS YOUR MOVE ?65
MACHINE MOVES TO SQUARE 75
WHAT IS YOUR MOVE ?86
MACHINE MOVES TO SQUARE 126
WHAT IS YOUR MOVE ?148
MACHINE MOVES TO SQUARE 158

NICE TRY, BUT IT LOOKS LIKE I HAVE WON.
THANKS FOR PLAYING.

ANYONE ELSE CARE TO TRY ?NO

OK - - THANKS AGAIN.
```

REVRSE

Description

The game of REVERSE requires you to arrange a list of numbers
in numerical order from left to right. To move, you tell the
computer how many numbers (counting from the left) to reverse.
For example, if the current list is:

        2   3   4   5   1   6   7   8   9

and you reverse 4, the result will be:

        5   4   3   2   1   6   7   8   9

Now if you reverse 5, you win!

There are many ways to beat the game, but approaches tend to be
either algorithmic or heuristic. The game thus offers the player
a chance to play with these concepts in a practical (rather than
theoretical) context.

An algorithmic approach guarantees a solution in a predictable
number of moves, given the number of items in the list. For
example, one method guarantees a solution in $2N - 3$ moves when
the list contains N numbers. The essence of an algorithmic
approach is that you know in advance what your next move will
be. One could easily program a computer to do this.

A heuristic approach takes advantage of "partial orderings" in
the list at any moment. Using this type of approach, your next
move is dependent on the way the list currently appears. This
way of solving the problem does not guarantee a solution in a
predictable number of moves, but if you are lucky and clever,
you may come out ahead of the algorithmic solutions. One could
not so easily program this method.

In practice, many players adopt a "mixed" strategy, with both
algorithmic and heuristic features. Is this better than either
"pure" strategy?

Program Author

Bob Albrecht
People's Computer Co.
Menlo Park, CA 94025

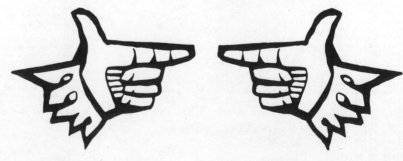

PROGRAM LISTING

```
100 PRINT\PRINT "REVERSE -- A GAME OF SKILL"\PRINT
120 RANDOMIZE
130 DIM A(20)
140 REM *** N=NUMBER OF NUMBERS
150 N=9
160 INPUT "DO YOU WANT THE RULES (YES OR NO)";A$
180 IF A$="NO" THEN 210
190 GOSUB 710
200 REM *** MAKE A RANDOM LIST A(1) TO A(N)
210 A(1)=INT((N-1)*RND)+2
220 FOR K=2 TO N
230 A(K)=INT(N*RND)+1
240 FOR J=1 TO K-1
250 IF A(K)=A(J) THEN 230
260 NEXT J\NEXT K
280 REM *** PRINT ORIGINAL LIST AND START GAME
290 PRINT\PRINT "HERE WE GO ... THE LIST IS:"
310 T=0
320 GOSUB 610
330 INPUT "HOW MANY SHALL I REVERSE";R
350 IF R=0 THEN 520
360 IF R<=N THEN 390
370 PRINT "OOPS! TOO MANY - I CAN REVERSE AT MOST"N\GOTO 330
390 T=T+1
400 REM *** REVERSE R NUMBERS AND PRINT NEW LIST
410 FOR K=1 TO INT(R/2)
420 Z=A(K)
430 A(K)=A(R-K+1)
440 A(R-K+1)=Z
450 NEXT K
460 GOSUB 610
470 REM *** CHECK FOR A WIN
480 FOR K=1 TO N
490 IF A(K)<>K THEN 330
500 NEXT K
510 PRINT "YOU WON IT IN"T"MOVES !!!"\PRINT
530 INPUT "TRY AGAIN (YES OR NO)";A$
550 IF A$="YES" THEN 210
560 PRINT\PRINT "O.K.  HOPE YOU HAD FUN!!"\GOTO 999
600 REM *** SUBROUTINE TO PRINT LIST
610 PRINT\FOR K=1 TO N\PRINT A(K);\NEXT K
650 PRINT\PRINT\RETURN
700 REM *** SUBROUTINE TO PRINT THE RULES
710 PRINT\PRINT "THIS IS THE GAME OF 'REVERSE'. TO WIN, ALL YOU HAVE"
720 PRINT "TO DO IS ARRANGE A LIST OF NUMBERS (1 THROUGH"N")"
730 PRINT "IN NUMERICAL ORDER FROM LEFT TO RIGHT. TO MOVE, YOU"
740 PRINT "TELL ME HOW MANY NUMBERS (COUNTING FROM THE LEFT) TO"
750 PRINT "REVERSE. FOR EXAMPLE, IF THE CURRENT LIST IS:"
760 PRINT\PRINT "2 3 4 5 1 6 7 8 9"
770 PRINT\PRINT "AND YOU REVERSE 4, THE RESULT WILL BE:"
780 PRINT\PRINT "5 4 3 2 1 6 7 8 9"
790 PRINT\PRINT "NOW, IF YOU REVERSE 5, YOU WIN!"
800 PRINT\PRINT "1 2 3 4 5 6 7 8 9"\PRINT
810 PRINT "NO DOUBT YOU WILL LIKE THIS GAME OF SKILL, BUT"
820 PRINT "IF YOU WANT TO QUIT, REVERSE 0 (ZERO)."\PRINT\RETURN
999 END

READY
```

SAMPLE RUN

```
REVERSE -- A GAME OF SKILL

DO YOU WANT THE RULES (YES OR NO)? YES

THIS IS THE GAME OF 'REVERSE'. TO WIN, ALL YOU HAVE
TO DO IS ARRANGE A LIST OF NUMBERS (1 THROUGH 9 )
IN NUMERICAL ORDER FROM LEFT TO RIGHT. TO MOVE, YOU
TELL ME HOW MANY NUMBERS (COUNTING FROM THE LEFT) TO
REVERSE. FOR EXAMPLE, IF THE CURRENT LIST IS:

2 3 4 5 1 6 7 8 9

AND YOU REVERSE 4, THE RESULT WILL BE:

5 4 3 2 1 6 7 8 9

NOW, IF YOU REVERSE 5, YOU WIN!

1 2 3 4 5 6 7 8 9

NO DOUBT YOU WILL LIKE THIS GAME OF SKILL, BUT
IF YOU WANT TO QUIT, REVERSE 0 (ZERO).

HERE WE GO ... THE LIST IS:

7 9 4 6 3 1 8 5 2

HOW MANY SHALL I REVERSE? 6

1 3 6 4 9 7 8 5 2

HOW MANY SHALL I REVERSE? 8

5 8 7 9 4 6 3 1 2

HOW MANY SHALL I REVERSE? 9

2 1 3 6 4 9 7 8 5

HOW MANY SHALL I REVERSE? 2

1 2 3 6 4 9 7 8 5

HOW MANY SHALL I REVERSE? 8

8 7 9 4 6 3 2 1 5

HOW MANY SHALL I REVERSE? 9

5 1 2 3 6 4 9 7 8
```

```
HOW MANY SHALL I REVERSE? 4

3 2 1 5 6 4 9 7 8

HOW MANY SHALL I REVERSE? 6

4 6 5 1 2 3 9 7 8

HOW MANY SHALL I REVERSE? 2

6 4 5 1 2 3 9 7 8

HOW MANY SHALL I REVERSE? 9

8 7 9 3 2 1 5 4 6

HOW MANY SHALL I REVERSE? 2

7 8 9 3 2 1 5 4 6

HOW MANY SHALL I REVERSE? 9

6 4 5 1 2 3 9 8 7

HOW MANY SHALL I REVERSE? 3

5 4 6 1 2 3 9 8 7

HOW MANY SHALL I REVERSE? 2

4 5 6 1 2 3 9 8 7

HOW MANY SHALL I REVERSE? 6

3 2 1 6 5 4 9 8 7

HOW MANY SHALL I REVERSE? 3

1 2 3 6 5 4 9 8 7

HOW MANY SHALL I REVERSE? 6

4 5 6 3 2 1 9 8 7

HOW MANY SHALL I REVERSE? 3

6 5 4 3 2 1 9 8 7

HOW MANY SHALL I REVERSE? 9

7 8 9 1 2 3 4 5 6

HOW MANY SHALL I REVERSE? 3

9 8 7 1 2 3 4 5 6

HOW MANY SHALL I REVERSE? 9

6 5 4 3 2 1 7 8 9

HOW MANY SHALL I REVERSE? 6

1 2 3 4 5 6 7 8 9

YOU WON IT IN 22 MOVES !!!

TRY AGAIN (YES OR NO)? YES

HERE WE GO ... THE LIST IS:

9 8 6 1 7 3 2 4 5

HOW MANY SHALL I REVERSE? 9

5 4 2 3 7 1 6 8 9

HOW MANY SHALL I REVERSE? 4

3 2 4 5 7 1 6 8 9

HOW MANY SHALL I REVERSE? 2

2 3 4 5 7 1 6 8 9

HOW MANY SHALL I REVERSE? 6

1 7 5 4 3 2 6 8 9

HOW MANY SHALL I REVERSE? 2

7 1 5 4 3 2 6 8 9

HOW MANY SHALL I REVERSE? 6

2 3 4 5 1 7 6 8 9

HOW MANY SHALL I REVERSE? 7

6 7 1 5 4 3 2 8 9

HOW MANY SHALL I REVERSE? 2

7 6 1 5 4 3 2 8 9

HOW MANY SHALL I REVERSE? 7

2 3 4 5 1 6 7 8 9

HOW MANY SHALL I REVERSE? 4

5 4 3 2 1 6 7 8 9

HOW MANY SHALL I REVERSE? 5

1 2 3 4 5 6 7 8 9

YOU WON IT IN 11 MOVES !!!
```

181

ROCKET
LAND AN APOLLO CAPSULE ON THE MOON

Description

ROCKET, known also as LUNAR, LEM, and APOLLO, is by far and away
the single most popular computer game. It exists in versions
that start you anywhere from 500 feet to 200 miles above the
moon, or other planets, too. Some allow the control of directional
stabilization rockets and/or the retro rocket. The three versions
presented here appear to be the most popular of the many varia-
tions.

ROCKET. In this program, you set the burn rate of the retro
rockets (pounds of fuel per second) every 10 seconds and attempt
to achieve a soft landing on the moon. 200 lbs/sec really puts
the brakes on, and 0 lbs/sec is free fall. Ignition occurs at
8 lbs/sec, so do not use burn rates between 1 and 7 lbs/sec.
To make the landing more of a challenge, but more closely approximate the real Apollo LEM capsule, you should make the
available fuel at the start (N) equal to 16,000 lbs, and the
weight of the capsule (M) equal to 32,500 lbs in Statement 15.

Some computers object to the series expansion calculations in
Statements 91 and 94 (as you near the lunar surface, these
numbers get very small). If yours does, substitute the expanded
form--for the expansion in Statement 91:

$$-Q*(1+Q*(1/2+Q*(1/3+Q*(1/4+Q/5))))$$

You should be able to figure the other one out yourself.

ROCKT1. In this version, you start 500 feet above the lunar
surface and control the burn rate in 1-second bursts. Each unit
of fuel slows your descent by 1 ft/sec. The maximum thrust of
your engine is 30 ft/sec/sec.

ROCKT2. This is the most comprehensive of the three versions
and permits you to control the time interval of firing, the
thrust, and the attitude angle. It also allows you to work in
the metric or English system of measurement. The instructions
in the program dialog are very complete, so you shouldn't have
any trouble.

In most versions of ROCKET, the temptation is to slow up too
soon and then have no fuel left for the lower part of the
journey. This, of course, is disasterous (as you will find out
when you land your own capsule)!

Source

To put all the conflicting stories to rest, we can say with
confidence that ROCKET was originally written in FOCAL by a
Lexington High School student back in the mid 60's.

ROCKET:
  Jim Storer
  Lexington High School
  Lexington, MA 02173

ROCKT1:
  Eric Peters
  Digital Equipment Corp.
  Maynard, MA 01754

ROCKT2:
  William Labaree II
  621 Oakley Place
  Alexandria, VA 22302

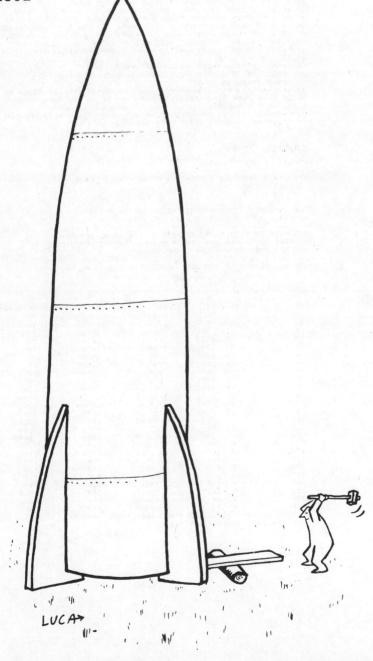

ROCKET PROGRAM LISTING

ROCKET EDUSYSTEM 30

```
2 PRINT "THIS IS A COMPUTER SIMULATION OF AN APOLLO LUNAR"
3 PRINT "LANDING CAPSULE. "\PRINT\PRINT
4 PRINT "THE ON-BOARD COMPUTER HAS FAILED (IT WASN'T MADE BY"
5 PRINT "DIGITAL) SO YOU HAVE TO LAND THE CAPSULE MANUALLY"
6 PRINT\PRINT "SET BURN RATE OF RETRO ROCKETS TO ANY VALUE BETWEEN"
7 PRINT "0 (FREE FALL) AND 200 (MAXIMUM BURN) POUNDS PER SECOND"
8 PRINT "SET NEW BURN RATE EVERY 10 SECONDS. "\PRINT
9 PRINT "CAPSULE WEIGHT 32,500 LBS;   FUEL WEIGHT 16,500 LBS"
10 PRINT\PRINT\PRINT "GOOD LUCK!!!"
11 L=0
13 PRINT\PRINT "SEC", "MI + FT", "MPH", "LB FUEL", "BURN RATE"\PRINT
15 A=120\V=1\M=33000\N=16500\G=1E-3\Z=1.8
21 PRINT L, INT(A); INT(5280*(A-INT(A))), 3600*V, M-N, \INPUT K\T=10
31 IF M-N<.001 THEN 41\IF T<.001 THEN 21\S=T\IF M>=N+S*K THEN 35
32 S=(M-N)/K
35 GOSUB 91\IF I<=0 THEN 71\IF V<=0 THEN 38\IF J<0 THEN 81
38 GOSUB 61\GOTO 31
41 PRINT "FUEL OUT AT"L"SEC"\S=(-V+SQR(V*V+2*A*G))/G\V=V+G*S\L=L+S
51 W=3600*V\PRINT"ON MOON AT"L"SEC - IMPACT VELOCITY" W "MPH"
52 IF W>1.2 THEN 53\PRINT "PERFECT LANDING! (LUCKY)"\GOTO 95
53 IF W>10 THEN 56\PRINT "GOOD LANDING (COULD BE BETTER)"\GOTO 95
56 IF W>60 THEN 58 \PRINT "CRAFT DAMAGE.....YOU'RE STRANDED HERE UNTIL"
57 PRINT "A RESCUE PARTY ARRIVES.  HOPE YOU HAVE ENOUGH OXYGEN!"\GOTO 95
58 PRINT "SORRY, BUT THERE WERE NO SURVIVORS...YOU BLEW IT!"
59 PRINT "IN FACT, YOU BLASTED A NEW LUNAR CRATER"W*.2777"FT DEEP"
60 GOTO 95
61 L=L+S\T=T-S\M=M-S*K\A=I\V=J\RETURN
71 IF S<5E-3 THEN 51\D=V+SQR(V*V+2*A*(G-Z*K/M))\S=2*A/D
73 GOSUB 91\GOSUB 61\GOTO 71
81 W=(1-M*G/(Z*K))/2\S=M*V/(Z*K*(W+SQR(W*W+V/Z)))+.05\GOSUB 91
83 IF I<=0 THEN 71\GOSUB 61\IF J>0 THEN 31\IF V>0 THEN 81\GOTO 31
91 Q=S*K/M\J=V+G*S+Z*(-Q-Q*Q/2-Q^3/3-Q^4/4-Q^5/5)
94 I=A-G*S*S/2-V*S+Z*S*(Q/2+Q^2/6+Q^3/12+Q^4/20+Q^5/30)\RETURN
95 PRINT\PRINT\PRINT\PRINT "TRY AGAIN??"\GOTO 6
99 END
```

SAMPLE RUN

ROCKET EDUSYSTEM 30

THIS IS A COMPUTER SIMULATION OF AN APOLLO LUNAR
LANDING CAPSULE.

THE ON-BOARD COMPUTER HAS FAILED (IT WASN'T MADE BY
DIGITAL) SO YOU HAVE TO LAND THE CAPSULE MANUALLY

SET BURN RATE OF RETRO ROCKETS TO ANY VALUE BETWEEN
0 (FREE FALL) AND 200 (MAXIMUM BURN) POUNDS PER SECOND
SET NEW BURN RATE EVERY 10 SECONDS.

CAPSULE WEIGHT 32,500 LBS; FUEL WEIGHT 16,500 LBS

GOOD LUCK!!!

SEC	MI + FT		MPH	LB FUEL	BURN RATE
0	120	0	3600	16500	?0
10	109	5015	3636	16500	?0
20	99	4223	3672	16500	?0
30	89	2903	3708	16500	?0
40	79	1055	3744	16500	?0
50	68	3959	3780	16500	?0
60	58	1055	3816	16500	?0
70	47	2903	3852	16500	?200
80	37	1883	3482.87	14500	?200
90	28	1191	3086.7	12500	?200
100	20	1251	2659.65	10500	?200
110	13	2549	2196.94	8500	?200
120	8	370	1692.63	6500	?200
130	4	658	1139.13	4500	?200
140	1	4203	526.598	2500	?100
150	0	4042	212.242	1500	?45
160	0	1863	84.1831	1050	?20
170	0	908	45.9129	850	?17
180	0	438	18.107	680	?12
190	0	241	8.68632	560	?11
200	0	157	2.7691	450	?9
210	0	105	4.27036	360	?9.5
220	0	46	3.65466	265	?9.8
230	0	7	1.66462	167	?9.3

ON MOON AT 233.183 SEC - IMPACT VELOCITY 1.6042 MPH
GOOD LANDING (COULD BE BETTER)

TRY AGAIN??

ROCKT1 PROGRAM LISTING

```
LIST
ROCKT1  03:37 PM      08-MAY-73
70 PRINT "LUNAR LANDING SIMULATION"
80 PRINT "----- ------- ----------"\PRINT
100 INPUT "DO YOU WANT INSTRUCTIONS (YES OR NO)";A$
120 IF A$="NO" THEN 390
160 PRINT
200 PRINT "YOU ARE LANDING ON THE MOON AND HAVE TAKEN OVER MANUAL"
210 PRINT "CONTROL 500 FEET ABOVE A GOOD LANDING SPOT.  YOU HAVE A"
220 PRINT "DOWNWARD VELOCITY OF 50 FT/SEC.  120 UNITS OF FUEL REMAIN."
225 PRINT
230 PRINT "HERE ARE THE RULES THAT GOVERN YOUR SPACE VEHICLE:"
240 PRINT "(1) AFTER EACH SECOND, THE HEIGHT, VELOCITY, AND REMAINING"
250 PRINT "    FUEL WILL BE REPORTED."
260 PRINT "(2) AFTER THE REPORT, A '?' WILL BE TYPED.  ENTER THE"
270 PRINT "    NUMBER OF UNITS OF FUEL YOU WISH TO BURN DURING THE"
280 PRINT "    NEXT SECOND.  EACH UNIT OF FUEL WILL SLOW YOUR DESCENT"
290 PRINT "    BY 1 FT/SEC."
310 PRINT "(3) THE MAXIMUM THRUST OF YOUR ENGINE IS 30 FT/SEC/SEC OR"
320 PRINT "    30 UNITS OF FUEL PER SECOND."
330 PRINT "(4) WHEN YOU CONTACT THE LUNAR SURFACE, YOUR DESCENT ENGINE"
340 PRINT "    WILL AUTOMATICALLY CUT OFF AND YOU WILL BE GIVEN A"
350 PRINT "    REPORT OF YOUR LANDING SPEED AND REMAINING FUEL."
360 PRINT "(5) IF YOU RUN OUT OF FUEL, THE '?' WILL NO LONGER APPEAR,"
370 PRINT "    BUT YOUR SECOND BY SECOND REPORT WILL CONTINUE UNTIL"
380 PRINT "    YOU CONTACT THE LUNAR SURFACE."\PRINT
390 PRINT "BEGINNING LANDING PROCEDURE....."\PRINT
410 PRINT "G O O D   L U C K ! ! !"
420 PRINT\PRINT
440 PRINT "SEC  FEET   SPEED    FUEL      PLOT OF DISTANCE"
450 PRINT
455 T=0\H=500\V=50\F=120
490 PRINT T;TAB(4);H;TAB(12);V;TAB(20);F;TAB(29);"I";TAB(H/12+29);"*"
500 INPUT B
510 IF B<0 THEN 650
520 IF B>30 THEN B=30
530 IF B>F THEN B=F
540 V1=V-B+5
560 F=F-B
570 H=H-.5*(V+V1)
580 IF H<=0 THEN 670
590 T=T+1
600 V=V1
610 IF F>0 THEN 490
615 IF B=0 THEN 640
620 PRINT "*** OUT OF FUEL ***"
640 PRINT T;TAB(4);H;TAB(12);V;TAB(20);F;TAB(29);"I";TAB(H/12+29);"*"
650 B=0
660 GOTO 540
670 PRINT "*** CONTACT ***"
680 H=H+.5*(V+V1)
690 IF B=5 THEN 720
700 D=(-V+SQR(V*V+H*(10-2*B)))/(5-B)
710 GOTO 730
720 D=H/V
730 V1=V+(5-B)*D
760 PRINT "TOUCHDOWN AT";T+D;"SECONDS."
770 PRINT "LANDING VELOCITY =";V1;"FT/SEC"
780 PRINT F;"UNITS OF FUEL REMAINING."
790 IF V1<>0 THEN 810
800 PRINT "CONGRATULATIONS!!    A PERFECT LANDING!"
805 PRINT "YOUR LICENSE WILL BE RENEWED.......LATER."
810 IF ABS(V1)<2 THEN 840
820 PRINT "***** SORRY, BUT YOU BLEW IT!!!!"
830 PRINT "APPROPRIATE CONDOLENCES WILL BE SENT TO YOUR NEXT OF KIN."
840 PRINT\PRINT\PRINT
050 INPUT "ANOTHER MISSION";A$
870 IF A$="YES" THEN 390
880 PRINT\PRINT "CONTROL OUT."\PRINT
999 END

READY
```

SAMPLE RUN

```
RUN
ROCKT1  03:39 PM      08-MAY-73
LUNAR LANDING SIMULATION
----- ------- ----------

DO YOU WANT INSTRUCTIONS (YES OR NO)? YES

YOU ARE LANDING ON THE MOON AND HAVE TAKEN OVER MANUAL
CONTROL 500 FEET ABOVE A GOOD LANDING SPOT.  YOU HAVE A
DOWNWARD VELOCITY OF 50 FT/SEC.  120 UNITS OF FUEL REMAIN.

HERE ARE THE RULES THAT GOVERN YOUR SPACE VEHICLE:
(1) AFTER EACH SECOND, THE HEIGHT, VELOCITY, AND REMAINING
    FUEL WILL BE REPORTED.
(2) AFTER THE REPORT, A '?' WILL BE TYPED.  ENTER THE
    NUMBER OF UNITS OF FUEL YOU WISH TO BURN DURING THE
    NEXT SECOND.  EACH UNIT OF FUEL WILL SLOW YOUR DESCENT
    BY 1 FT/SEC.
(3) THE MAXIMUM THRUST OF YOUR ENGINE IS 30 FT/SEC/SEC OR
    30 UNITS OF FUEL PER SECOND.
(4) WHEN YOU CONTACT THE LUNAR SURFACE, YOUR DESCENT ENGINE
    WILL AUTOMATICALLY CUT OFF AND YOU WILL BE GIVEN A
    REPORT OF YOUR LANDING SPEED AND REMAINING FUEL.
(5) IF YOU RUN OUT OF FUEL, THE '?' WILL NO LONGER APPEAR,
    BUT YOUR SECOND BY SECOND REPORT WILL CONTINUE UNTIL
    YOU CONTACT THE LUNAR SURFACE.

BEGINNING LANDING PROCEDURE.....

G O O D   L U C K ! ! !

SEC  FEET   SPEED    FUEL      PLOT OF DISTANCE

 0    500     50      120      I                                        *
? 3
 1    449     52      117      I                                     *
? 3
 2    396     54      114      I                                  *
? 3
 3    341     56      111      I                              *
? 3
 4    284     58      108      I                          *
? 7
 5    227     56      101      I                     *
? 9
 6    173     52       92      I                *
? 9
 7    123     48       83      I           *
? 8
 8    76.5    45       75      I       *
? 25
 9    41.5    25       50      I *
? 25
10    26.5     5       25      I *
? 25
*** OUT OF FUEL ***
11    31.5   -15        0      I *
12    44     -10        0      I *
13    51.5    -5        0      I  *
14    54       0        0      I  *
15    51.5     5        0      I  *
16    44      10        0      I *
17    31.5    15        0      I *
18    14      20        0      I*
*** CONTACT ***
TOUCHDOWN AT 18.6476 SECONDS.
LANDING VELOCITY = 23.2379 FT/SEC
 0 UNITS OF FUEL REMAINING.
***** SORRY, BUT YOU BLEW IT!!!!
APPROPRIATE CONDOLENCES WILL BE SENT TO YOUR NEXT OF KIN.


ANOTHER MISSION? YES
BEGINNING LANDING PROCEDURE.....

G O O D   L U C K ! ! !

SEC  FEET   SPEED    FUEL      PLOT OF DISTANCE

 0    500     50      120      I                                        *
? 5
 1    450     50      115      I                                     *
? 5
 2    400     50      110      I                                  .  *
? 5
 3    350     50      105      I                              *
? 5
 4    300     50      100      I                          *
? 5
 5    250     50       95      I                      *
? 5
 6    200     50       90      I                  *
? 5
 7    150     50       85      I            *
? 5
 8    100     50       80      I       *
? 5
 9     50     50       75      I *
? 30
10    12.5    25       45      I*
? 30
*** CONTACT ***
TOUCHDOWN AT 11 SECONDS.
LANDING VELOCITY = 0 FT/SEC
 15 UNITS OF FUEL REMAINING.
CONGRATULATIONS!!    A PERFECT LANDING!
YOUR LICENSE WILL BE RENEWED.......LATER.
```

```
7 REM LUNAR1 IS A INTERACTIVE GAME THAT SIMULATES A LUNAR
8 REM LANDING SIMILAR TO THAT OF THE APOLLO PROGRAM.
9 REM THERE IS ABSOLUTELY NO CHANCE INVOLVED.
10 LET Z$="GO"
15 LET B1=1
20 LET M=17.95
25 LET F1=5.25
30 LET N=7.5
35 LET R0=926
40 LET V0=1.29
45 LET T=0
50 LET H0=60
55 LET R=R0+H0
60 LET A=-3.425
65 LET R1=0
70 LET A1=8.84361E-04
75 LET R3=0
80 LET A3=0
85 LET M1=7.45
90 LET M0=M1
95 LET B=750
100 LET T1=0
105 LET F=0
110 LET P=0
115 LET N=1
120 LET M2=0
125 LET S=0
130 LET C=0
135 IF Z$="YES" THEN 1150
140 PRINT
145 PRINT "LUNAR LANDING SIMULATION"
150 PRINT
155 PRINT "HAVE YOU FLOWN ON AN APOLLO/LEM MISSION BEFORE#";
160 PRINT "(YES OR NO)";
165 INPUT Q$
170 IF Q$="YES" THEN 190
175 IF Q$="NO" THEN 205
180 PRINT "JUST ANSWER THE QUESTION, PLEASE";
185 GOTO 160
190 PRINT
195 PRINT "ENTER MEASUREMENT OPTION NUMBER";
200 GOTO 225
205 PRINT
210 PRINT "WHICH SYSTEM OF MEASUREMENT DO YOU PREFER ?"
215 PRINT " 1=METRIC   0=ENGLISH"
220 PRINT "ENTER THE APPROPRIATE NUMBER";
225 INPUT K
230 PRINT
235 IF K=0 THEN 280
240 IF K=1 THEN 250
245 GOTO 220
250 LET Z=1852.8
255 LET M$="METERS"
260 LET G3=3.6
265 LET N$=" KILOMETERS"
270 LET G5=1000
275 GOTO 305
280 LET Z=G060
285 LET M$="FEET"
290 LET G3=.592
295 LET N$=" N.MILES"
300 LET G5=Z
305 IF B1=3 THEN 670
310 IF Q$="YES" THEN 485
315 PRINT
320 PRINT " YOU ARE ON A LUNAR LANDING MISSION.  AS THE PILOT OF"
325 PRINT "THE LUNAR EXCURSION MODULE, YOU WILL BE EXPECTED TO"
330 PRINT "GIVE CERTAIN COMMANDS TO THE MODULE NAVIGATION SYSTEM."
335 PRINT " THE ON BOARD COMPUTER WILL GIVE A RUNNING ACCOUNT"
340 PRINT "OF INFORMATION NEEDED TO NAVIGATE THE SHIP."
345 PRINT
350 PRINT
355 PRINT "THE ATTITUDE ANGLE CALLED FOR IS DESCRIBED AS FOLLOWS-"
360 PRINT "+ OR -180 DEGREES IS DIRECTLY AWAY FROM THE MOON"
365 PRINT "-90 DEGREES IS ON A TANGENT IN THE DIRECTION OF ORBIT"
370 PRINT "90 DEGREES IS ON A TANGENT FROM THE DIRECTION OF ORBIT"
375 PRINT "0 (ZERO) DEGREES IS DIRECTLY TOWARD THE MOON"
380 PRINT
385 PRINT TAB(30);"-180,180"
390 PRINT TAB(34);"↑"
395 PRINT TAB(27);"-90 < -+- > 90"
400 PRINT TAB(34);"I"
405 PRINT TAB(34);"0"
410 PRINT TAB(23);"<< DIRECTION OF ORBIT <<"
415 PRINT
420 PRINT TAB(27);"SURFACE OF MOON"
425 PRINT
430 PRINT
435 PRINT "ALL ANGLES BETWEEN -180 AND 180 DEGREES ARE ACCEPTED."
440 PRINT
445 PRINT "1 FUEL UNIT = 1 SEC. AT MAX. THRUST"
450 PRINT "ANY DISCREPANCIES ARE ACCOUNTED FOR IN THE USE OF FUEL"
455 PRINT "FOR AN ATTITUDE CHANGE."
460 PRINT "AVAILABLE ENGINE POWER: 0 (ZERO) AND ANY VALUE BETWEEN"
465 PRINT "10 AND 100 PERCENT"
470 PRINT
475 PRINT "NEGATIVE THRUST OR TIME IS PROHIBITED"
480 PRINT
485 PRINT
490 PRINT "INPUT: TIME INTERVAL IN SECONDS ------ (T)"
495 PRINT "       PERCENTAGE OF THRUST ---------- (P)"
500 PRINT "       ATTITUDE ANGLE IN DEGREES ----- (A)"
505 PRINT
510 IF Q$="YES" THEN 535
515 PRINT "FOR EXAMPLE:"
520 PRINT "T,P,A?12,65,-60"
525 PRINT "TO ABORT THE MISSION AT ANY TIME, ENTER 0,0,0"
530 PRINT
535 PRINT "OUTPUT: TOTAL TIME ELAPSED IN SECONDS"
540 PRINT "        HEIGHT IN ";M$
545 PRINT "        DISTANCE FROM LANDING SITE IN ";M$
550 PRINT "        VERTICAL VELOCITY IN ";M$;"/SECOND"
555 PRINT "        HORIZONTAL VELOCITY IN ";M$;"/SECOND"
560 PRINT "        FUEL UNITS REMAINING"
565 PRINT
570 GOTO 670
575 PRINT
580 PRINT "T,P,A";
585 INPUT T1,F,P
590 LET F=F/100
595 IF T1=0 THEN 905
600 IF T1=0 THEN 1090
605 IF ABS(F-.05)>1 THEN 945
610 IF ABS(F-.05)<.05 THEN 945
615 IF ABS(P)>180 THEN 925
620 LET N=20
625 IF T1<400 THEN 635
630 LET N=T1/20
635 LET T1=T1/N
640 LET P=P*3.14159/180
645 LET S=SIN(P)
650 LET C=COS(P)
655 LET M2=M0*T1*F/B
660 LET R3=-.5*R0*((V0/R)↑2)+R*A1*A1
665 LET A3=-2*R1*A1/R
670 FOR I=1 TO N
675 IF M1=0 THEN 715
680 LET M1=M1-M2
685 IF M1>0 THEN 725
690 LET F=F*(1+M1/M2)
695 LET M2=M1+M2
700 PRINT "YOU ARE OUT OF FUEL"
705 LET M1=0
710 GOTO 725
715 LET F=0
720 LET M2=0
725 LET M=M-.5*M2
730 LET R4=R3
735 LET R3=-.5*R0*((V0/R)↑2)+R*A1*A1
740 LET R2=(3*R3-R4)/2+.00526*F1*F*C/M
745 LET A4=A3
750 LET A3=-2*R1*A1/R
755 LET A2=(3*A3-A4)/2+.00526*F1*F*S/(M*R)
760 LET X=R1*T1+.5*R2*T1*T1
765 LET R=R+X
770 LET H0=H0+X
775 LET R1=R1+R2*T1
780 LET A=A+A1*T1+.5*A2*T1*T1
785 LET A1=A1+A2*T1
790 LET M=M-.5*M2
795 LET T=T+T1
800 IF H0<3.287828E-04 THEN 810
825 NEXT I
810 LET H=H0*Z
815 LET H1=R1*Z
820 LET D=R0*A*Z
825 LET D1=R*A1*Z
830 LET T2=M1*B/M0
835 PRINT TAB(1);T;TAB(10);H;TAB(23);D;
840 PRINT TAB(37);H1;TAB(49);D1;TAB(60);T2
845 IF H0<3.287828E-04 THEN 880
850 IF R0*A>164.4736 THEN 1050
855 IF M1>0 THEN 580
860 LET T1=20
865 LET F=0
870 LET P=0
875 GOTO 620
880 IF R1<-8.21957E-04 THEN 1020
885 IF ABS(R*A1)>4.931742E-04 THEN 1020
890 IF H0<-3.287828E-04 THEN 1020
895 IF ABS(D)>10*Z THEN 1065
900 GOTO 995
905 PRINT
910 PRINT "THIS SPACECRAFT IS NOT ABLE TO VIOLATE THE SPACE-";
915 PRINT "TIME CONTINUUM"
920 GOTO 575
925 PRINT
930 PRINT "IF YOU WANT TO SPIN AROUND, GO OUTSIDE THE MODULE";
935 PRINT "FOR AN E.V.A"
940 GOTO 575
945 PRINT
950 PRINT "IMPOSSIBLE THRUST-VALUE ";
955 IF F<0 THEN 985
960 IF F-.05<.05 THEN 975
965 PRINT "TOO LARGE"
970 GOTO 575
975 PRINT "TOO SMALL"
980 GOTO 575
985 PRINT "NEGATIVE"
990 GOTO 575
995 PRINT
1000 PRINT "TRANQUILITY BASE HERE -- THE EAGLE HAS LANDED"
1005 PRINT "CONGRATULATIONS - THERE WAS NO SPACECRAFT DAMAGE"
1010 PRINT "YOU MAY NOW PROCEED WITH SURFACE EXPLORATION."
1015 GOTO 1100
1020 PRINT
1025 PRINT "CRASH !!!!!!!!!!!"
1030 PRINT "YOUR IMPACT CREATED A CRATER";ABS(H);M$;" DEEP"
1035 X1=SQR(D1*D1+H1*H1)*G3
1040 PRINT "AT CONTACT YOU WERE TRAVELLING";X1;N$;"/HR."
1045 GOTO 1100
1050 PRINT
1055 PRINT "YOU HAVE BEEN LOST IN SPACE WITH NO HOPE OF RECOVERY"
1060 GOTO 1100
1065 PRINT "YOU ARE DOWN SAFELY - "
1075 PRINT
1080 PRINT "BUT MISSED THE LANDING SITE BY";ABS(D/G5);N$
1085 GOTO 1100
1090 PRINT
1095 PRINT "MISSION ABORTED"
1100 PRINT
1105 PRINT "DO YOU WANT TO FLY IT AGAIN ? (YES OR NO)";
1110 INPUT Z$
1115 IF Z$="YES" THEN 20
1120 IF Z$="NO" THEN 1130
1125 GOTO 1105
1130 PRINT
1135 PRINT "TOO BAD, THE SPACE PROGRAM HATES TO LOSE EXPERIENCED";
1140 PRINT " ASTRONAUTS."
1145 STOP
1150 PRINT
1155 PRINT "OK, DO YOU WANT THE COMPLETE INSTRUCTIONS OR THE INPUT-"
1160 PRINT "OUTPUT STATEMENTS ?"
1165 PRINT "1=COMPLETE INSTRUCTIONS"
1170 PRINT "2=INPUT-OUTPUT STATEMENTS"
1175 PRINT "3=NEITHER"
1180 INPUT B1
1185 LET Q$="NO"
1190 IF B1=1 THEN 205
1195 LET Q$="YES"
1200 IF B1=2 THEN 190
1205 IF B1=3 THEN 190
1210 GOTO 1165
1215 END
```

ROCKT2 SAMPLE RUN

LUNAR LANDING SIMULATION

HAVE YOU FLOWN ON AN APOLLO/LEM MISSION BEFORE#(YES OR NO)? NO

WHICH SYSTEM OF MEASUREMENT DO YOU PREFER ?
  1=METRIC   2=ENGLISH
ENTER THE APPROPRIATE NUMBER? 0

  YOU ARE ON A LUNAR LANDING MISSION. AS THE PILOT OF
THE LUNAR EXCURSION MODULE, YOU WILL BE EXPECTED TO
GIVE CERTAIN COMMANDS TO THE MODULE NAVIGATION SYSTEM.
  THE ON BOARD COMPUTER WILL GIVE A RUNNING ACCOUNT
OF INFORMATION NEEDED TO NAVIGATE THE SHIP.

THE ATTITUDE ANGLE CALLED FOR IS DESCRIBED AS FOLLOWS-
+ OR -180 DEGREES IS DIRECTLY AWAY FROM THE MOON
-90 DEGREES IS ON A TANGENT IN THE DIRECTION OF ORBIT
90 DEGREES IS ON A TANGENT FROM THE DIRECTION OF ORBIT
0 (ZERO) DEGREES IS DIRECTLY TOWARD THE MOON

              << DIRECTION OF ORBIT <<

              SURFACE OF MOON

ALL ANGLES BETWEEN -180 AND 180 DEGREES ARE ACCEPTED.

1 FUEL UNIT = 1 SEC. AT MAX. THRUST
ANY DISCREPANCIES ARE ACCOUNTED FOR IN THE USE OF FUEL
FOR AN ATTITUDE CHANGE.
AVAILABLE ENGINE POWER: 0 (ZERO) AND ANY VALUE BETWEEN
10 AND 100 PERCENT

NEGATIVE THRUST OR TIME IS PROHIBITED

INPUT: TIME INTERVAL IN SECONDS ------ (T)
       PERCENTAGE OF THRUST ---------- (P)
       ATTITUDE ANGLE IN DEGREES ----- (A)

FOR EXAMPLE:
T,P,A?10,65,-60
TO ABORT THE MISSION AT ANY TIME, ENTER 0,0,0

OUTPUT: TOTAL TIME ELAPSED IN SECONDS
        HEIGHT IN FEET
        DISTANCE FROM LANDING SITE IN FEET
        VERTICAL VELOCITY IN FEET/SECOND
        HORIZONTAL VELOCITY IN FEET/SECOND
        FUEL UNITS REMAINING

```
 0        364800      -1.928302E+7    0          5301.638   750
T,P,A? 20,20,-90
 20       364769.7    -1.918380E+7   -3.257229   5264.209   746.0001
T,P,A? 200,10,-90
 220      358044.1    -1.821200E+7  -74.76607    5081.405   726.0002
T,P,A? 500,10,-90
 720      224322.9    -1.589872E+7 -522.3451     4709.512   676.0002
T,P,A? 500,0,0
 1040     -6773.7     -1.439553E+7 -918.728      4902.473   676.0002
```

CRASH !!!!!!!!!!
YOUR IMPACT CREATED A CRATER 6773.7 FEET DEEP
AT CONTACT YOU WERE TRAVELLING 2952.787 N.MIL/HR.

DO YOU WANT TO FLY IT AGAIN ? (YES OR NO)? YES

OK, DO YOU WANT THE COMPLETE INSTRUCTIONS OR THE INPUT-
OUTPUT STATEMENTS ?
1=COMPLETE INSTRUCTIONS
2=INPUT-OUTPUT STATEMENTS
3=NEITHER
? 3

ENTER MEASUREMENT OPTION NUMBER? 1

```
 0        111168      -5.876248E+6    0          1615.604   750
T,P,A? 500,0,0
 500      106291.7    -5.116247E+6  -19.20258    1619.915   750
T,P,A? 100,0,0
 600      104194.1    -4.963536E+6  -22.72435    1621.782   750
T,P,A? 50,90,-90
 650      102921.8    -4.890089E+6  -30.02382    1492.978   705.0001
T,P,A? 100,0,-20,0
 750      101574.9    -4.749094E+6    3.206664   1494.091   685.0002
T,P,A? 50,90,-90
 800      101326.7    -4.681730E+6  -14.90814    1359.475   640.0003
T,P,A? 100,40,-090
 900      97203.62    -4.558928E+6  -70.50644    1239.533   600.0003
T,P,A? 50,10,0
 950      93262.42    -4.500152E+6  -87.14224    1242.232   595.0004
T,P,A? 50,100,0
 1000     92036.68    -4.441169E+6   38.9189     1243.085   545.0004
T,P,A? 50,100,-90
 1050     93087.58    -4.386076E+6    1.363938   1079.071   495.0004
T,P,A? 50,100,-90
 1100     92008.52    -4.338861E+6  -46.0884      910.9774   445.0004
T,P,A? 50,100,-90
 1150     88333.39    -4.299676E+6 -102.2833      738.2616   395.0005
T,P,A? 100,100,-90
 1250     71627.24    -4.246314E+6 -236.0606      375.7879   295.0005
T,P,A? 50,100,0
 1300     62820.57    -4.228179E+6 -115.1086      377.652    245.0005
T,P,A? 50,100,0
 1350     60235.55    -4.209927E+6   12.98513     378.2053   195.0005
T,P,A? 100,50,0
 1450     64599.96    -4.173457E+6   75.8418      377.2816   145.0006
T,P,A? 100,40,-90
 1550     64756.08    -4.145499E+6  -73.66691     202.8112   105.0006
T,P,A? 50,50,-90
 1600     59156.86    -4.138397E+6 -150.5384       91.24105   80.0006
T,P,A? 10,0,0
 1610     57573.89    -4.137515E+6 -166.0619       91.32249   80.0006
T,P,A? 10,100,0
 1620     56062.7     -4.136631E+6 -136.1128       91.40043   70.00061
T,P,A? 10,100,-90
 1630     54623.65    -4.135968E+6 -151.7089       45.55091   60.00062
T,P,A? 10,100,-90
 1640     53028.37    -4.135751E+6 -167.3554        -.746715   50.00063
T,P,A? 10,0,0
 1650     51276.44    -4.135759E+6 -183.0355        -.7474552  50.00063
T,P,A? 30,0,0
 1680     45077.51    -4.135780E+6 -230.2823        -.7500852  50.00063
T,P,A? 30,0,0
 1710     37455.8     -4.135802E+6 -277.9013        -.7533445  50.00063
T,P,A? 50,0,0
 1760     21556.4     -4.135839E+6 -358.3198        -.7602341  50.00063
T,P,A? 10,100,0
 1770     18125.25    -4.135846E+6 -327.851         -.761739   40.00063
T,P,A? 30,0,0
 1800      7553.268   -4.135869E+6 -377.0488        -.7664103  40.00063
T,P,A? 10,50,0
 1810      3817.706   -4.135876E+6 -370.0578        -.7680755  35.00064
T,P,A? 5,100,-,0
 1815      2005.734   -4.135882E+6 -354.7163        -.7688858  30.00064
T,P,A? 5,100,0
 1820       270.6975  -4.135884E+6 -339.2829        -.7696634  25.00065
T,P,A? 1,100,0
 1820.8     .2621521  -4.135885E+6 -336.805         -.7697848  24.20065
```

CRASH !!!!!!!!!!
YOUR IMPACT CREATED A CRATER .2621521 METERS DEEP
AT CONTACT YOU WERE TRAVELLING 1212.501 KILOM/HR.

DO YOU WANT TO FLY IT AGAIN ? (YES OR NO)? NO---NO

TOO BAD, THE SPACE PROGRAM HATES TO LOSE EXPERIENCED ASTRONAUTS.

READY

ROCKSP

GAME OF ROCK, SCISSORS, PAPER

Description

Remember the game of rock-scissors-paper. You and your opponent
make a motion three times with your fists and then either show
a flat hand (paper), fist (rock), or two fingers (scissors).
Depending upon what is shown, the game is a tie (both show the
same) or one person wins. Paper wraps up rock, so it wins.
Scissors cut paper, so it wins. And rock breaks scissors,
so it wins.

In this computerized version of rock-scissors-paper, you can
play up to ten games vs. the computer.

Program Author

Charles Lund
The American School
Hague, Netherlands

```
LIST
ROCKSP  05:06 PM        03-MAY-73
1 PRINT "THIS PROGRAM ALLOWS YOU TO PLAY THE OLD GAME OF"
2 PRINT "ROCKS, PAPER, AND SISSORS AGAINST THE COMPUTER. "
5 RANDOMIZE
6 INPUT "HOW MANY GAMES DO YOU WANT";Q
8 IF Q<11  THEN 11
9 PRINT "SORRY, BUT WE AREN'T ALLOWED TO PLAY THAT MANY. "\GOTO 6
11 FOR G=1 TO Q
15 PRINT\PRINT "GAME NUMBER"G
20 X=INT(RND*3+1)
25 PRINT "3=ROCK...2=SISSORS...1=PAPER"
30 INPUT "1....2....3....WHAT'S YOUR CHOICE";K
32 IF (K-1)*(K-2)*(K-3)<>0 THEN PRINT "INVALID"\GOTO 25
35 PRINT "THIS IS MY CHOICE..."
40 ON X GOTO 50,60,70
50 PRINT "...PAPER"\GOTO 80
60 PRINT "...SISSORS"\GOTO 80
70 PRINT "...ROCK"
80 IF X=K THEN 155
85 IF X>K THEN 125
90 IF X=1 THEN 105
95 PRINT "YOU WIN!!!"\H=H+1\GOTO 160
105 IF K=3 THEN 115 ELSE GOTO 95
115 PRINT "WOW!  I WIN!!"\C=C+1\GOTO 160
125 IF K<>1 THEN 115
140 IF X<>3 THEN 115 ELSE 95
155 PRINT "TIE GAME, NO WINNER. "
160 NEXT G
170 PRINT\PRINT "HERE IS THE FINAL SCORE:"
175 PRINT "I HAVE WON"C"GAME(S). "
180 PRINT "YOU HAVE WON"H"GAME(S). "
185 PRINT "AND"G-(C+H)"GAME(S) ENDED IN A TIE. "
190 PRINT\PRINT "THANKS FOR PLAYING!!"
200 END

READY
```

```
THIS PROGRAM ALLOWS YOU TO PLAY THE OLD GAME OF
ROCKS, PAPER, AND SISSORS AGAINST THE COMPUTER.
HOW MANY GAMES DO YOU WANT? 20
SORRY, BUT WE AREN'T ALLOWED TO PLAY THAT MANY.
HOW MANY GAMES DO YOU WANT? 10

GAME NUMBER 1
3=ROCK...2=SISSORS...1=PAPER
1....2....3....WHAT'S YOUR CHOICE? 1
THIS IS MY CHOICE...
...PAPER
TIE GAME, NO WINNER.

GAME NUMBER 2
3=ROCK...2=SISSORS...1=PAPER
1....2....3....WHAT'S YOUR CHOICE? 2
THIS IS MY CHOICE...
...ROCK
WOW!  I WIN!!

GAME NUMBER 3
3=ROCK...2=SISSORS...1=PAPER
1....2....3....WHAT'S YOUR CHOICE? 3
THIS IS MY CHOICE...
...SISSORS
YOU WIN!!!

GAME NUMBER 4
3=ROCK...2=SISSORS...1=PAPER
1....2....3....WHAT'S YOUR CHOI'
THIS IS MY CHOICE...
...SISSORS
WOW!  I WIN!!

GAME NUMBER 5
3=ROCK...2=SIS
1....2....3
THIS IS '                    .HOICE? 1
...RO
WO'


                ...SISSORS...1=PAPER
              ..3....WHAT'S YOUR CHOICE? 2
          IS MY CHOICE...
       .PAPER
YOU WIN!!!

GAME NUMBER 9
3=ROCK...2=SISSORS...1=PAPER
1....2....3....WHAT'S YOUR CHOICE? 3
THIS IS MY CHOICE...
...SISSORS
YOU WIN!!!

GAME NUMBER 10
3=ROCK...2=SISSORS...1=PAPER
1....2....3....WHAT'S YOUR CHOICE? 1
THIS IS MY CHOICE...
...SISSORS
WOW!  I WIN!!

HERE IS THE FINAL SCORE:
I HAVE WON 5 GAME(S).
YOU HAVE WON 3 GAME(S).
AND 2 GAME(S) ENDED IN A TIE.

THANKS FOR PLAYING!!

READY
```

ROULET

Description

This game simulates a European Roulette wheel; "European" because
it has 37 number compartments (1 to 36 and 0). The American
wheel has 38 numbers (1 to 36, 0 and 00). The Bahamas, Puerto
Rico, and South American countries are slowly switching to the
American wheel because it gives the house a bigger percentage.
Odd and even numbers alternate around the wheel, as do red and
black. The layout of the wheel insures a highly random number
pattern. In fact, roulette wheels are sometimes used to generate
tables of random numbers.

In this game, you may bet from $1 to $10,000 and you may bet on
red or black, odd or even, a column, or single number.

There is no long-range winning strategy for playing roulette.
However, a good strategy is that of "doubling." First spin,
bet $1 on an even/odds bet (odd, even, red, or black). If you
lose, double your bet to $2. If you lose again, double to $4.
Continue to double until you win (i.e., you break even on a
losing sequence). As soon as you win, bet $1 again, and after
every win, bet $1. Do not ever bet more than $1 unless you are
recuperating losses by doubling. Do not ever bet anything but
the even odds bets. Good luck!

Source

Like so many other games of chance, computerized ROULET has been
around a long time in FORTRAN, LISP, and so on. Its original
author is unknown today.

```
1010 REM     TYPE RUN TO PLAY THE GAME.
1020 LET K1 = 0
1030 PRINT "    WELCOME TO MONTE CARLO AND OUR EUROPEAN ROULETTE TABLE."
1040 PRINT "    I WISH YOU THE BEST OF LUCK."
1050 PRINT
1060 PRINT
1070 PRINT "DO YOU WANT INSTRUCTIONS";
1080 INPUT Z$
1090 IF Z$ = "NO" THEN 1800
1100 IF Z$ = "YES" THEN 1130
1110 GOSUB 2790
1120 GO TO 1070
1130 PRINT "    THIS IS A GAME OF ROULETTE.  YOU ARE ALLOWED TO BET"
1140 PRINT "AN ODD OR EVEN NUMBER AND/OR A BLACK OR RED NUMBER AND/OR"
1150 PRINT "A COLUMN OF NUMBERS AND/OR A NUMBER ITSELF.  NUMBERS RANGE"
1160 PRINT "FROM 0 TO 36.  IF 0 APPEARS, THE BANK COLLECTS ALL BETS"
1170 PRINT "EXCEPT THOSE BET ON THE NUMBER 0.  THE PAYOFFS ARE AS FOLLOWS"
1180 PRINT,"ODD OR EVEN = 1 TO 1"
1190 PRINT,"RED OR BLACK = 1 TO 1"
1200 PRINT, "A COLUMN = 2 TO 1"
1210 PRINT, "A NUMBER = 35 TO 1"
1220 PRINT "    YOU ARE ALLOWED TO BET FROM $1 TO $10000, BUT THE";
1230 PRINT " TABLE WILL ONLY ACCEPT BETS OF WHOLE DOLLARS (NO CENTS)."
1240 PRINT
1250 PRINT " WOULD YOU LIKE TO SEE A PICTURE OF THE GAMBLING TABLE";
1260 INPUT Z1$
1270 IF Z1$ = "NO" THEN 1800
1280 IF Z1$ = "YES" THEN 1320
1290 GOSUB 2790
1300 GO TO 1250
1310 PRINT
1320 PRINT
1330 PRINT"    BELOW IS THE PICTURE OF OUR GAMBLING TABLE."
1340 PRINT
1350 PRINT
1360 PRINT, "   ***********"
1370 PRINT, "   *    0    *"
1375 LET U$ = "******************"
1380 PRINT,U$
1390 PRINT,"*  1  *  2  *  3  *"
1400 PRINT,"* RED *BLACK* RED *"
1410 PRINT ,U$
1420 PRINT,"*  4  *  5  *  6  *"
1430 PRINT,"*BLACK* RED *BLACK*"
1440 PRINT,U$
1450 PRINT,"*  7  *  8  *  9  *"
1460 PRINT,"* RED *BLACK* RED *"
1470 PRINT,U$
1480 PRINT,"* 10  * 11  * 12  *"
1490 PRINT,"*BLACK*BLACK* RED *"
1500 PRINT,U$
1510 PRINT,"* 13  * 14  * 15  *"
1520 PRINT,"*BLACK* RED *BLACK*"
1530 PRINT,U$
1540 PRINT,"* 16  * 17  * 18  *"
1550 PRINT,"* RED *BLACK* RED *"
1560 PRINT,U$
1570 PRINT,"* 19  * 20  * 21  *"
1580 PRINT,"* RED *BLACK* RED *"
1590 PRINT,U$
1600 PRINT,"* 22  * 23  * 24  *"
1610 PRINT,"*BLACK* RED *BLACK*"
1620 PRINT,U$
1630 PRINT,"* 25  * 26  * 27  *"
1640 PRINT,"* RED * RED *BLACK*"
1650 PRINT,U$
1660 PRINT,"* 28  * 29  * 30  *"
1670 PRINT,"*BLACK*BLACK* RED *"
1680 PRINT ,U$
1690 PRINT,"* 31  * 32  * 33  *"
1700 PRINT,"*BLACK* RED *BLACK*"
1710 PRINT,U$
1720 PRINT,"* 34  * 35  * 36  *"
1730 PRINT,"* RED *BLACK* RED *"
1740 PRINT,U$
1750 PRINT, "*COL.1*COL.2*COL.3*"
1760 PRINT,U$
1800 PRINT
1810 PRINT
1820 PRINT
1830 PRINT "DO YOU WANT TO BET AN ODD OR EVEN NUMBER";
1840 INPUT A$
1850 IF A$ = "NO" THEN 2050
1860 IF A$ = "YES" THEN 1890
1870 GOSUB 2790
1880 GO TO 1830
1890 PRINT "ODD OR EVEN";
1900 INPUT B$
1910 IF B$ = "ODD"THEN 1950
1920 IF B$ = "EVEN"THEN 1950
1930 PRINT "PLEASE TYPE ODD OR EVEN"
1940 GO TO 1890
1950 PRINT "HOW MUCH DO YOU WANT TO BET";
1960 INPUT H
1970 IF H <= 10000 THEN 2000
1980 GOSUB 2810
1990 GO TO 1950
2000 FOR H1 = 0 TO 10000
2010 IF H1 = H THEN 2060
2020 NEXT H1
2030 GOSUB 2840
2040 GO TO 1950
2050 LET H = 0
2060 PRINT
2070 PRINT "DO YOU WANT TO BET A RED OR BLACK NUMBER";
2080 INPUT C$
2090 IF C$ = "NO" THEN 2290
2100 IF C$ = "YES" THEN 2130
2110 GOSUB 2790
2120 GO TO 2070
2130 PRINT "RED OR BLACK";
2140 INPUT D$
2150 IF D$ = "RED" THEN 2190
2160 IF D$ = "BLACK" THEN 2190
2170 PRINT "PLEASE TYPE RED OR BLACK."
2180 GO TO 2130
2190 PRINT "HOW MUCH DO YOU WANT TO BET";
2200 INPUT I
2210 IF I <= 10000 THEN 2240
2220 GOSUB 2810
```

```
2230 GO TO 2190
2240 FOR I2 = 0 TO 10000
2250 IF I2 = I THEN 2300
2260 NEXT I2
2270 GOSUB 2840
2280 GO TO 2190
2290 LET I = 0
2300 PRINT
2310 PRINT "DO YOU WANT TO BET A COLUMN OF NUMBERS";
2320 INPUT B1$
2330 IF B1$ = "NO" THEN 2530
2340 IF B1$ = "YES" THEN 2370
2350 GOSUB 2790
2360 GO TO 2310
2370 PRINT "COLUMN 1, 2, OR 3";
2380 INPUT B2
2390 IF B2 = 1 THEN 2440
2400 IF B2 = 2 THEN 2440
2410 IF B2 = 3 THEN 2440
2420 PRINT "PLEASE TYPE 1, 2, OR 3."
2430 GO TO 2370
2440 PRINT "HOW MUCH DO YOU WANT TO BET";
2450 INPUT B8
2460 IF B8 <= 10000 THEN 2490
2470 GOSUB 2810
2480 GO TO 2440
2490 FOR B9 = 0 TO 10000
2500 IF B8 = B9 THEN 2540
2510 NEXT B9
2520 GO TO 2440
2530 LET B8 = 0
2540 PRINT
2550 PRINT "DO YOU WANT TO BET A NUMBER";
2560 INPUT E$
2570 IF E$ = "NO" THEN 2870
2580 IF E$ = "YES" THEN 2610
2590 GOSUB 2790
2600 GO TO 2550
2610 PRINT "WHAT IS YOUR NUMBER";
2620 INPUT F
2630 FOR M = 0 TO 36
2640 IF F = M THEN 2690
2650 NEXT M
2660 PRINT "THAT IS AN ILLEGAL NUMBER"
2670 PRINT "YOU ARE ONLY ALLOWED TO BET INTEGERS RANGING FROM 0 TO 36"
2680 GO TO 2610
2690 PRINT "HOW MUCH DO YOU WANT TO BET";
2700 INPUT G
2710 IF G <= 10000 THEN 2740
2720 GOSUB 2810
2730 GO TO 2690
2740 FOR G9 = 0 TO 10000
2750 IF G = G9 THEN 2880
2760 NEXT G9
2770 GOSUB 2840
2780 GO TO 2690
2790 PRINT "PLEASE TYPE YES OR NO."
2800 RETURN
2810 PRINT "SORRY, BUT THE TABLE CANNOT ACCEPT A BET OF THAT MUCH";
2820 PRINT " MONEY."
2830 RETURN
2840 PRINT "SORRY, BUT YOU CAN ONLY BET IN $1 INCREMENTS FROM $1 TO";
2850 PRINT " $10000."
2860 RETURN
2870 LET G = 0
2880 PRINT
2890 RANDOMIZE
2900 LET T = INT(37*RND)
2910 PRINT "THE NUMBER IS ";
2920 LET T1 = INT(T/10)+1
2930 ON T1 GO TO 2940,2950,2960,2970
2940 ON T+1 GO TO 3530,3350,3430,3390,3410,3370,3450,3350,3430,3390
2950 ON T-9 GO TO 3410,3490,3330,3470,3310,3510,3290,3490,3330,3350
2960 ON T-19 GO TO 3430,3390,3410,3370,3450,3350,3310,3510,3410,3490
2970 ON T-29 GO TO 3330,3470,3310,3510,3290,3490,3330
3290 PRINT T;" RED, EVEN, COLUMN 1"
3300 GO TO 3540
3310 PRINT T;" RED, EVEN, COLUMN 2"
3320 GO TO 3540
3330 PRINT T;" RED, EVEN, COLUMN 3"
3340 GO TO 3540
3350 PRINT T;" RED, ODD, COLUMN 1"
3360 GO TO 3540
3370 PRINT T;" RED, ODD, COLUMN 2"
3380 GO TO 3540
3390 PRINT T;" RED, ODD, COLUMN 3"
3400 GO TO 3540
3410 PRINT T;" BLACK, EVEN, COLUMN 1"
3420 GO TO 3540
3430 PRINT T;" BLACK, EVEN, COLUMN 2"
3440 GO TO 3540
3450 PRINT T;" BLACK, EVEN, COLUMN 3"
3460 GO TO 3540
3470 PRINT T;" BLACK, ODD, COLUMN1"
3480 GO TO 3540
3490 PRINT T;" BLACK, ODD, COLUMN 2"
3500 GO TO 3540
3510 PRINT T;" BLACK, ODD, COLUMN 3"
3520 GO TO 3540
3530 PRINT T
3540 IF G = 0 THEN 3610
3550 IF T = F THEN 3590
3560 PRINT " YOU LOSE $"G" FOR YOUR NUMBER BET."
3570 LET G = -G
3580 GO TO 3610
3590 PRINT " YOU WIN $"35*G" FOR YOUR NUMBER BET."
3600 LET G = 35*G
3610 IF H = 0 THEN 3800
3620 IF T = 0 THEN 3710
3630 IF B$ = "EVEN" THEN 3680
3640 FOR X = 1 TO 35 STEP 2
3650 IF T = X THEN 3750
3660 NEXT X
3670 GO TO 3710
3680 FOR X1 = 2 TO 36 STEP 2
3690 IF T = X1 THEN 3750
3700 NEXT X1
3710 PRINT " YOU LOSE $"H;
3720 GOSUB 3780
3730 LET H = -H
```

```
3740 GO TO 3800
3750 PRINT " YOU WIN $"H;
3760 GOSUB 3780
3770 GO TO 3800
3780 PRINT "FOR YOUR ODD-EVEN BET."
3790 RETURN
3800 IF I = 0 THEN 4000
3810 IF T = 0 THEN 3980
3820 FOR A1 = 1 TO 9 STEP 2
3830 IF T = A1 THEN 3970
3840 NEXT A1
3850 FOR A2 = 12 TO 18 STEP 2
3860 IF T = A2 THEN 3970
3870 NEXT A2
3880 FOR A3 = 19 TO 25 STEP 2
3890 IF T = A3 THEN 3970
3900 NEXT A3
3910 FOR A4 = 30 TO 36 STEP 2
3920 IF T = A4 THEN 3970
3930 NEXT A4
3940 IF T = 26 THEN 3970
3950 IF D$ = "BLACK" THEN 4020
3960 GO TO 3980
3970 IF D$ = "RED" THEN 4020
3980 PRINT " YOU LOSE $"I;
3990 GOSUB 4060
4000 LET I = -I
4010 GO TO 4080
4020 PRINT " YOU WIN $";
4030 PRINT I;
4040 GOSUB 4060
4050 GO TO 4080
4060 PRINT "FOR YOUR RED-BLACK BET."
4070 RETURN
4080 IF B8 = 0 THEN 4340
4090 IF T = 0 THEN 4300
4100 FOR B3 = 1 TO 34 STEP 3
4110 IF T = B3 THEN 4190
4120 NEXT B3
4130 FOR B4 = 2 TO 35 STEP 3
4140 IF T = B4 THEN 4210
4150 NEXT B4
4160 FOR B5 = 3 TO 36 STEP 3
4170 IF T = B5 THEN 4230
4180 NEXT B5
4190 IF B2 = 1 THEN 4250
4200 IF B2 <> 1 THEN 4300
4210 IF B2 = 2 THEN 4250
4220 IF B2 <> 2 THEN 4300
4230 IF B2 = 3 THEN 4250
4240 IF B2 <> 3 THEN 4300
4250 PRINT " YOU WIN $";
4260 PRINT 2*B8;
4270 PRINT "FOR YOUR COLUMN BET."
4280 LET B9 = 2*B8
4290 GO TO 4340
4300 PRINT " YOU LOSE $";
4310 PRINT B8;
4320 PRINT "FOR YOUR COLUMN BET."
4330 LET B8 = -B8
4340 PRINT
4350 LET K = (G) + (H) + (I) + (B8)
4360 IF K < 0 THEN 4400
4370 IF K = 0 THEN 4420
4380 IF K > 0 THEN 4440
4390 GO TO 4450
4400 PRINT " YOU LOST $" ABS(K)" ON THIS ROUND."
4410 GO TO 4450
4420 PRINT " YOU BROKE EVEN THIS TIME."
4430 GO TO 4450
4440 PRINT " YOU WON $"K" ON THIS ROUND."
4450 PRINT
4460 PRINT
4470 LET K1 = K1 + K
4480 IF K1 < 0 THEN 4510
4490 IF K1 = 0 THEN 4530
4500 IF K1 > 0 THEN 4550
4510 PRINT " YOU HAVE LOST A TOTAL OF $"ABS(K1)" THUS FAR."
4520 GO TO 4570
4530 PRINT " THUS FAR YOU HAVE BROKEN EVEN."
4540 GO TO 4570
4550 PRINT " YOU HAVE WON A TOTAL OF $"K1" THUS FAR."
4560 GO TO 4570
4570 PRINT
4580 PRINT " DO YOU WANT TO PLAY AGAIN";
4590 INPUT M$
4600 IF M$ = "NO" THEN 4640
4610 IF M$ = "YES" THEN 1800
4620 PRINT "PLEASE TYPE YES OR NO."
4630 GO TO 4580
4640 PRINT
4650 PRINT " THANKS FOR PLAYING."
4660 IF K1 < 0 THEN 4690
4670 IF K1 = 0 THEN 4710
4680 IF K1 > 0 THEN 4740
4690 PRINT " YOU LOST $" ABS(K1);", BETTER LUCK NEXT TIME."
4700 GO TO 4750
4710 PRINT " YOU BROKE EVEN TODAY, MAYBE NEXT TIME YOU WILL WIN";
4720 PRINT " A FORTUNE."
4730 GO TO 4750
4740 PRINT " CONGRATULATIONS, YOU BEAT THE ODDS,  YOU WON $"K1"TODAY."
4750 END
```

```
          WELCOME TO MONTE CARLO AND OUR EUROPEAN ROULETTE TABLE.
          I WISH YOU THE BEST OF LUCK.

DO YOU WANT INSTRUCTIONS ?YES
          THIS IS A GAME OF ROULETTE.  YOU ARE ALLOWED TO BET
AN ODD OR EVEN NUMBER AND/OR A BLACK OR RED NUMBER AND/OR
A COLUMN OF NUMBERS AND/OR A NUMBER ITSELF.  NUMBERS RANGE
FROM 0 TO 36.  IF 0 APPEARS, THE BANK COLLECTS ALL BETS
EXCEPT THOSE BET ON THE NUMBER 0.  THE PAYOFFS ARE AS FOLLOWS
          ODD OR EVEN = 1 TO 1
          RED OR BLACK = 1 TO 1
          A COLUMN = 2 TO 1
          A NUMBER = 35 TO 1
     YOU ARE ALLOWED TO BET FROM $1 TO $10000, BUT THE TABLE WILL ONLY A
CCEPT BETS OF WHOLE DOLLARS (NO CENTS).

WOULD YOU LIKE TO SEE A PICTURE OF THE GAMBLING TABLE ?YES

     BELOW IS THE PICTURE OF OUR GAMBLING TABLE.


                    **********
                    *   0   *
          *********************
          *  1  *  2  *  3  *
          * RED *BLACK* RED *
          *********************
          *  4  *  5  *  6  *
          *BLACK* RED *BLACK*
          *********************
          *  7  *  8  *  9  *
          * RED *BLACK* RED *
          *********************
          * 10  * 11  * 12  *
          *BLACK*BLACK* RED *
          *********************
          * 13  * 14  * 15  *
          *BLACK* RED *BLACK*
          *********************
          * 16  * 17  * 18  *
          * RED *BLACK* RED *
          *********************
          * 19  * 20  * 21  *
          * RED *BLACK* RED *
          *********************
          * 22  * 23  * 24  *
          *BLACK* RED *BLACK*
          *********************
          * 25  * 26  * 27  *
          * RED * RED *BLACK*
          *********************
          * 28  * 29  * 30  *
          *BLACK*BLACK* RED *
          *********************
          * 31  * 32  * 33  *
          *BLACK* RED *BLACK*
          *********************
          * 34  * 35  * 36  *
          * RED *BLACK* RED *
          *********************
          *COL. 1*COL. 2*COL. 3*
          *********************


DO YOU WANT TO BET AN ODD OR EVEN NUMBER ?YES
ODD OR EVEN ?ODD
HOW MUCH DO YOU WANT TO BET ?100

DO YOU WANT TO BET A RED OR BLACK NUMBER ?NO

DO YOU WANT TO BET A COLUMN OF NUMBERS ?YES
COLUMN 1, 2, OR 3 ?1
HOW MUCH DO YOU WANT TO BET ?100

DO YOU WANT TO BET A NUMBER ?NO

THE NUMBER IS  1  RED, ODD, COLUMN 1
 YOU WIN $ 100 FOR YOUR ODD-EVEN BET.
 YOU WIN $ 200 FOR YOUR COLUMN BET.

 YOU WON $ 300  ON THIS ROUND.


 YOU HAVE WON A TOTAL OF $ 300  THUS FAR.

 DO YOU WANT TO PLAY AGAIN ?YES



DO YOU WANT TO BET AN ODD OR EVEN NUMBER ?YES
ODD OR EVEN ?EVEN
HOW MUCH DO YOU WANT TO BET ?100

DO YOU WANT TO BET A RED OR BLACK NUMBER ?YES
RED OR BLACK ?RED
HOW MUCH DO YOU WANT TO BET ?100

DO YOU WANT TO BET A COLUMN OF NUMBERS ?NO

DO YOU WANT TO BET A NUMBER ?YES
WHAT IS YOUR NUMBER ?6
HOW MUCH DO YOU WANT TO BET ?10

THE NUMBER IS  9  RED, ODD, COLUMN 3
 YOU LOSE $ 10  FOR YOUR NUMBER BET.
 YOU LOSE $ 100 FOR YOUR ODD-EVEN BET.
 YOU WIN $ 100 FOR YOUR RED-BLACK BET.

 YOU LOST $ 10  ON THIS ROUND.


 YOU HAVE WON A TOTAL OF $ 290  THUS FAR.

 DO YOU WANT TO PLAY AGAIN ?YES
```

RUSROU

Description

In this game, you are given by the computer a revolver loaded with one bullet and five empty chambers. You spin the chamber and pull the trigger by inputting a "1," or, if you want to quit, input a "2." You win if you play ten times and are still alive.

Program Author

Two versions of Russian Roulette were submitted, one by John Kowalik of East Greenwich, RI and the one printed here by:

Tom Adametx
Curtis Junior High School
Sudbury, MA   01776

```
5 RANDOMIZE
8 PRINT "THIS IS A GAME OF >>>>>>>>>>RUSSIAN ROULETTE".
10 PRINT\PRINT "HERE IS A REVOLVER"
20 PRINT "HIT '1' TO SPIN CHAMBER AND PULL TRIGGER. "
22 PRINT "    (HIT '2' TO GIVE UP)"\PRINT "GO";
25 N=0
30 INPUT I
31 IF I<>2 THEN 35
32 PRINT "     CHICKEN !!!"\GOTO 72
35 N=N+1
40 IF RND(0)>0.83333 THEN 70
45 IF N>10 THEN 80
50 PRINT "- CLICK -"
60 PRINT\GOTO 30
70 PRINT "     BANG!!!!  YOU'RE DEAD!"
71 PRINT "CONDOLENCES WILL BE SENT TO YOUR RELATIVES. "
72 PRINT\PRINT\PRINT "...NEXT VICTIM..."\GOTO 20
80 PRINT "YOU WIN !!!"
85 PRINT "LET SOMEONE ELSE BLOW HIS BRAINS OUT. "
90 GOTO 10
99 END

READY


THIS IS A GAME OF >>>>>>>>>>RUSSIAN ROULETTE

HERE IS A REVOLVER
HIT '1' TO SPIN CHAMBER AND PULL TRIGGER.
    (HIT '2' TO GIVE UP)
GO?1
- CLICK -

?1
- CLICK -

?1
- CLICK -

?1
- CLICK -

?1
- CLICK -

?1
- CLICK -

?1
     BANG!!!!  YOU'RE DEAD!
CONDOLENCES WILL BE SENT TO YOUR RELATIVES.


...NEXT VICTIM...
HIT '1' TO SPIN CHAMBER AND PULL TRIGGER.
    (HIT '2' TO GIVE UP)
GO?
```

SALVO

Description

The rules are <u>not</u> explained by the program, so read carefully
this description by Larry Siegel, the program author.

"SALVO is played on a 10x10 grid or board using an x,y coordinate
system. The player has 4 ships: battleship (5 squares), cruiser
(3 squares), and two destroyers (2 squares each). The ships
must be placed horizontally, vertically, or diagonally and must
not overlap. The ships do not move during the game.

"As long as any square of a battleship still survives, the player
is allowed three shots, for a cruiser 2 shots, and for each
destroyer 1 shot. Thus, at the beginning of the game the player
has 3+2+1+1=7 shots. The player enters all of his shots and
the computer tells what was hit." A shot is entered by its grid
coordinates, x,y. The winner is the one who sinks all of the
opponent's ships.

Important note: Your ships and the computer's ships are located
on 2 <u>separate</u> 10x10 boards. For a simpler version of this game,
try SALVO1.

Program Author

Lawrence Siegel
3052 Warrington Road
Shaker Heights, OH 44120

PROGRAM LISTING

```
1000 REM *** SALVO BY LARRY SIEGEL
1010 REM *** LAST REVISION 6/9/73
1020 REM *** CHECKED OUT ON RSTS/E BY DAVE AHL, DIGITAL
1030 REM ***
1040 DIMA(10,10),B(10,10),C(7),D(7),E(12),F(12),G(12),H(12),K(10,10)
1050 LETZ8=0
1060 FORW=1TO12
1070 LETE(W)=-1
1080 LETH(W)=-1
1090 NEXTW
1100 FORX=1TO10
1110 FORY=1TO10
1120 LETB(X,Y)=0
1130 NEXTY
1140 NEXTX
1150 FORX=1TO12
1160 LETF(X)=0
1170 LETG(X)=0
1180 NEXTX
1190 FORX=1TO10
1200 FORY=1TO12
1210 LETA(X,Y)=0
1220 NEXTX
1230 NEXTX
1240 FORK=4TO1STEP-1
1250 LETU6=0
1260 GOSUB2910
1270 DEFFNA(K)=(5-K)*3-2+INT(K/4)+SGN(K-1)-1
1280 DEFFNB(K)=K+INT(K/4)-SGN(K-1)
1290 IFV+V2+V+V2=0THEN1260
1300 IFY+V+FNB(K)>10THEN1260
1310 IFY+V+FNB(K)<1THEN1260
1320 IFX+V2+FNB(K)>10THEN1260
1330 IFX+V2+FNB(K)<1THEN1260
1340 LETU6=U6+1
1350 IFU6=25THEN1190
1360 FORZ=0TOFNB(K)
1370 LETF(Z+FNA(K))=X+V2+Z
1380 LETG(Z+FNA(K))=Y+V+Z
1390 NEXTZ
1400 LETU8=FNA(K)
1410 FORZ2=U8TOU8+FNB(K)
1420 FORZ3=1TOU8-1
1430 IFSQR((F(Z3)-F(Z2))^2+(G(Z3)-G(Z2))^2)<3.59THEN1260
1440 NEXTZ3
1450 NEXTZ2
1460 FORZ=0TOFNB(K)
1470 LETA(F(Z+U8),G(Z+U8))=.5+SGN(K-1)*(K-1.5)
1480 NEXTZ
1490 NEXTK
1500 PRINT"ENTER COORDINATES FOR..."
1510 PRINT"BATTLESHIP"
1520 FORX=1TO5
1530 INPUTY,Z
1540 LETB(Y,Z)=3
1550 NEXTX
1560 PRINT"CRUISER"
1570 FORX=1TO3
1580 INPUTY,Z
1590 LETB(Y,Z)=2
1600 NEXTX
1610 PRINT"DESTROYER<A>"
1620 FORX=1TO2
1630 INPUTY,Z
1640 LETB(Y,Z)=1
1650 NEXTX
1660 PRINT"DESTROYER<B>"
1670 FORX=1TO2
1680 INPUTY,Z
1690 LETB(Y,Z)=.5
1700 NEXTX
1710 PRINT"DO YOU WANT TO START";
1720 INPUTJ$
1730 IFJ$<>"WHERE ARE YOUR SHIPS?"THEN1890
1740 PRINT"BATTLESHIP"
1750 FORZ=1TO5
1760 PRINTF(Z);G(Z)
1770 NEXTZ
1780 PRINT"CRUISER"
1790 PRINTF(6);G(6)
1800 PRINTF(7);G(7)
1810 PRINTF(8);G(8)
1820 PRINT"DESTROYER<A>"
1830 PRINTF(9);G(9)
1840 PRINTF(10);G(10)
1850 PRINT"DESTROYER<B>"
1860 PRINTF(11);G(11)
1870 PRINTF(12);G(12)
1880 GOTO1710
1890 LETC=0
1900 PRINT"DO YOU WANT TO SEE MY SHOTS";
1910 INPUTK$
1920 PRINT
1930 IFJ$<>"YES"THEN2620
1940 REM*************START
1950 IFJ$<>"YES"THEN1990
1960 LETC=C+1
1970 PRINT
1980 PRINT"TURN"C
1990 LETA=0
2000 FORW=.5TO3STEP.5
2010 FORX=1TO10
2020 FORY=1TO10
2030 IFB(X,Y)=WTHEN2070
2040 NEXTY
2050 NEXTX
2060 GOTO2080
2070 LETA=A+INT(W+.5)
2080 NEXTW
2090 FORW=1TO7
2100 LETC(W)=0
2110 LETD(W)=0
2120 LETF(W)=0
2130 LETG(W)=0
2140 NEXTW
2150 LETP3=0
2160 FORX=1TO10
2170 FORY=1TO10
2180 IFA(X,Y)>10THEN2200
2190 LETP3=P3+1
2200 NEXTY
2210 NEXTX
2220 PRINT"YOU HAVE"A"SHOTS"
2230 IFP3=ATHEN2260
2240 PRINT"THE NUMBER OF YOUR SHOTS EXCEEDS THE NUMBER OF BLANK SQUARES"
2250 GOTO2890
2260 IFA<>0THEN2290
2270 PRINT"I HAVE WON"
2280 STOP
2290 FORW=1TOA
2300 INPUTX,Y
2310 IFX<>INT(X)THEN2370
2320 IFX>10THEN2370
2330 IFX<1THEN2370
2340 IFY<>INT(Y)THEN2370
2350 IFY>10THEN2370
2360 IFY>=1THEN2390
2370 PRINT"ILLEGAL, ENTER AGAIN"
2380 GOTO2300
2390 IFA(X,Y)>10THEN2440
2400 LETC(W)=X
2410 LETD(W)=Y
2420 NEXTW
2430 GOTO2460
2440 PRINT"YOU SHOT THERE BEFORE ON TURN"A(X,Y)-10
2450 GOTO2300
2460 FORW=1TOA
2470 IFA(C(W),D(W))=3THEN2540
2480 IFA(C(W),D(W))=2THEN2560
2490 IFA(C(W),D(W))=1THEN2580
2500 IFA(C(W),D(W))=.5THEN2600
2510 LETA(C(W),D(W))=10+C
2520 NEXTW
2530 GOTO2620
2540 PRINT"YOU HIT MY BATTLESHIP"
2550 GOTO2510
2560 PRINT"YOU HIT MY CRUISER"
2570 GOTO2510
2580 PRINT"YOU HIT MY DESTROYER<A>"
2590 GOTO2510
2600 PRINT"YOU HIT MY DESTROYER<B>"
2610 GOTO2510
2620 LETA=0
2630 IFJ$="YES"THEN2670
2640 LETC=C+1
2650 PRINT
2660 PRINT"TURN"C
2670 LETA=0
2680 FORW=.5TO3.1STEP.5
2690 FORX=1TO10
2700 FORY=1TO10
2710 IFA(X,Y)=WTHEN2750
2720 NEXTY
2730 NEXTX
2740 GOTO2760
2750 LETA=A+INT(W+.5)
2760 NEXTW
2770 LETP3=0
2780 FORX=1TO10
2790 FORY=1TO10
2800 IFB(X,Y)>10THEN2820
2810 LETP3=P3+1
2820 NEXTY
2830 NEXTX
2840 PRINT"I HAVE"A"SHOTS"
2850 IFP3>ATHEN2880
2860 PRINT"THE NUMBER OF MY SHOTS EXCEEDS THE NUMBER OF BLANK SQUARES"
2870 GOTO2270
2880 IFA<>0THEN2960
2890 PRINT"YOU HAVE WON"
2900 STOP
2910 LETX=INT((RND(-1)*10)+1)
2920 LETY=INT((RND(-1)*10)+1)
2930 LETV=INT(3*RND(-1)-1)
2940 LETV2=INT(3*RND(-1)-1)
2950 RETURN
2960 FORW=1TO12
2970 IFH(W)>0THEN3800
2980 NEXTW
2990 REM*************RANDOM
3000 LETW=0
3010 LETR3=0
3020 GOSUB2910
3030 RESTORE
3040 LETR2=0
3050 LETR3=R3+1
3060 IFR3>100THEN3010
3070 IFX>10THEN3110
3080 IFX>0THEN3120
3090 LETX=1+INT(RND(-1)*2.5)
3100 GOTO3120
3110 LETX=10-INT(RND(-1)*2.5)
3120 IFY>10THEN3160
3130 IFY>0THEN3270
3140 LETY=1+INT(RND(-1)*2.5)
3150 GOTO3270
3160 LETY=10-INT(RND(-1)*2.5)
3170 GOTO3270
3180 LETF(W)=X
3190 LETG(W)=Y
3200 IFW=ATHEN3380
3210 IFR2=6THEN3030
3220 READX1,Y1
3230 LETR2=R2+1
3240 DATA1,1,-1,1,1,-3,1,1,0,2,-1,1
3250 LETX=X+X1
3260 LETY=Y+Y1
3270 IFX>10THEN3210
3280 IFX<1THEN3210
3290 IFY>10THEN3210
3300 IFY<1THEN3210
3310 IFB(X,Y)>10THEN3210
3320 FORQ9=1TOW
3330 IFF(Q9)<>XTHEN3350
3340 IFG(Q9)=YTHEN3210
3350 NEXTQ9
```

```
3360LETW=W+1
3370GOTO3180
3380IFK$<>"YES"THEN3420
3390FORZ5=1TOA
3400PRINTF(Z5);G(Z5)
3410NEXTZ5
3420FORW=1TOA
3430IFB(F(W),G(W))=3THEN3500
3440IFB(F(W),G(W))=2THEN3520
3450IFB(F(W),G(W))=1THEN3560
3462IFB(F(W),G(W))=.5THEN3540
3470LETB(F(W),G(W))=10+C
3480NEXTW
3490GOTO1950
3500PRINT"I HIT YOUR BATTLESHIP"
3510GOTO3570
3520PRINT"I HIT YOUR CRUISER"
3530GOTO3570
3540PRINT"I HIT YOUR DESTROYER<B>"
3550GOTO3570
3560PRINT"I HIT YOUR DESTROYER<A>"
3570FORQ=1TO12
3580IFE(Q)<>=1THEN3730
3590LETE(Q)=10+C
3600LETH(Q)=B(F(W),G(W))
3610LETM3=0
3620FORM2=1TO12
3630IFH(M2)<>H(Q)THEN3650
3640M3=M3+1
3650NEXTM2
3660IFM3<>INT(H(Q)+.5)+1+INT(INT(H(Q)+.5)/3)THEN3470
3670FORM2=1TO12
3680IFH(M2)>H(Q)THEN3710
3690LETE(M2)=-1
3700LETH(M2)=-1
3710NEXTM2
3720GOTO3470
3730NEXTQ
3740PRINT"PROGRAM ABORT!"
3750FORQ=1TO12
3760PRINT"E("Q")="E(Q)
3770PRINT"H("Q")="H(Q)
3780NEXTQ
3790STOP
3800REM**************USINGEARRAY
3810FORR=1TO10
3820FORS=1TO10
3830LETK(R,S)=0
3840NEXTS
3850NEXTR
3860FORU=1TO12
3870IFE(U)<1THEN4020
3880FORR=1TO10
3890FORS=1TO10
3900IFB(R,S)<1THEN3930
3910LETK(R,S)=-1000000
3920GOTO4000
3930FORM=SGN(1-R)TOSGN(10-R)
3940FORN=SGN(1-S)TOSGN(10-S)
3950IFN+M+N=0THEN3980
3960IFH(R+M,S+N)<>E(U)THEN3980
3970LETK(R,S)=K(R,S)+E(U)-2*INT(H(U)+.5)
3980NEXTN
3990NEXTM
4000NEXTS
4010NEXTR
4020NEXTU
4030FORR=1TOA
4040LETF(R)=R
4050LETG(R)=R
4060NEXTR
4070FORR=1TO10
4080FORS=1TO10
4090LETQ9=1
4100FORM=1TOA
4110IFK(F(M),G(M))>=K(F(Q9),G(Q9))THEN4130
4120LETQ9=M
4130NEXTM
4131 IF R>ATHEN4140
4132 IF R=S THEN 4210
4140IFK(R,S)<K(F(Q9),G(Q9))THEN4210
4150FORM=1TOA
4160IFF(M)<>RTHEN4190
4170IFG(M)=STHEN4210
4180NEXTM
4190LETF(Q9)=R
4200LETG(Q9)=S
4210NEXTS
4220NEXTR
4230GOTO3380
4240END
```

(grid with values)

Player's shots against the enemy. Number indicates the round of the game on which the shot was fired. The initial objective was to destroy the enemy battleship-- it took 6 rounds to accomplish this objective.

SAMPLE RUN

```
ENTER COORDINATES FOR...
BATTLESHIP
? 3,4
? 4,5
? 5,6
? 6,7
? 7,8
CRUISER
? 7,2
? 8,2
? 9,2
DESTROYER<A>
? 2,9
? 3,8
DESTROYER<B>
? 8,5
? 8,6

DO YOU WANT TO START? YES
DO YOU WANT TO SEE MY SHOTS? YES


TURN 1
YOU HAVE 7 SHOTS
? 2,5
? 3,5
? 4,5
? 5,5
? 6,5
? 7,5
? 8,5
YOU HIT MY CRUISER
YOU HIT MY BATTLESHIP
I HAVE 7 SHOTS
 1   3
 2   4
 1   5
 2   2
 3   3
 3   5
 2   6

TURN 2
YOU HAVE 7 SHOTS
? 2,6
? 3,4
? 4,6
? 5,4
? 6,6
? 7,4
? 8,6
YOU HIT MY BATTLESHIP
I HAVE 7 SHOTS
 6   3
 7   4
 6   5
 7   2
 8   3
 8   5
 7   6
I HIT YOUR CRUISER
I HIT YOUR DESTROYER<B>

TURN 3
YOU HAVE 7 SHOTS
? 2,8
? 3,7
? 3,9
? 4,8
? 5,7
? 5,9
? 6,8
YOU HIT MY DESTROYER<B>
I HAVE 7 SHOTS
 8   4
 6   4
 9   4
 7   3
 7   5
 6   6
 8   2
I HIT YOUR CRUISER

TURN 4
YOU HAVE 7 SHOTS
? 2,2
? 3,3
? 3,1
? 4,2
? 5,1
? 5,3
? 6,2
YOU HIT MY DESTROYER<A>
I HAVE 7 SHOTS
 6   2
 8   6
 5   4
 9   3
 5   5
 9   5
 7   7
I HIT YOUR DESTROYER<B>

TURN 5
YOU HAVE 6 SHOTS
? 4,4
? 6,4
? 7,3
? 7,7
? 8,4
? 9,7
YOU HIT MY BATTLESHIP
```

```
I HAVE 7 SHOTS
 8   1
 5   3
 5   6
 9   2
 10  5
 6   7
 7   1
I HIT YOUR BATTLESHIP
I HIT YOUR CRUISER
I HIT YOUR BATTLESHIP

TURN 6
YOU HAVE 4 SHOTS
? 7,8
? 8,8
? 8,7
? 8,3
YOU HIT MY BATTLESHIP
YOU HIT MY BATTLESHIP
I HAVE 4 SHOTS
 5   7
 9   1
 10  6
 4   4

TURN 7
YOU HAVE 4 SHOTS
? 2,3
2? .4
? 9,5
? 10,5
YOU HIT MY CRUISER
I HAVE 4 SHOTS
 10  4
 4   3
 4   5
 4   6
I HIT YOUR BATTLESHIP

TURN 8
YOU HAVE 4 SHOTS
? 1,3
? 3,2
? 4,1
? 5,2
YOU HIT MY CRUISER
I HAVE 2 SHOTS
 10  3
 4   7

TURN 9
YOU HAVE 4 SHOTS
? 2,1
? 4,3
? 6,1
? 6,3
YOU HIT MY DESTROYER<A>
I HAVE 1 SHOTS
 5   2

TURN 10
YOU HAVE 4 SHOTS
? 2,9
? 3,8
? 4,9
? 5,8
I HAVE 1 SHOTS
 4   2

TURN 11
YOU HAVE 4 SHOTS
? 2,7
? 4,7
? 6,7
? 6,9
I HAVE 1 SHOTS
 3   6

TURN 12
YOU HAVE 4 SHOTS
? 1,7
? 1,8
? 3,6
? 5,6
I HAVE 1 SHOTS
 3   4
I HIT YOUR BATTLESHIP

TURN 13
YOU HAVE 4 SHOTS
? 1,9
? 3,10
? 5,10
? 7,9
I HAVE 1 SHOTS
 10  2

TURN 14
YOU HAVE 4 SHOTS
? 2,10
? 4,10
? 6,10
? 1,6
YOU HIT MY DESTROYER<B>
I HAVE 0 SHOTS
YOU HAVE WON
```

195

SALVO 1

ARMY GUN BATTLE

Description

SALVO1 is played on two, 5x5 grids or boards with 25 outpost
locations numbered 1 to 25. Both you and the computer have
four platoons of troops that can be located at any four outposts on your respective grids.

At the start of the game, you locate (or hide) your four
platoons on your grid. The computer does the same on its
grid. You then take turns firing missiles or bombs at each
other's outposts trying to destroy all four platoons. The
one who finds all four opponent's platoons first, wins.

Program Author

This program was slightly modified from the original submitted by:

Martin Burdash
70 Pinetree Drive
Parlin, NJ 08859

PROGRAM LISTING

```
100 PRINT "YOU ARE ON A BATTLEFIELD WITH 4 PLATOONS AND YOU"
110 PRINT "HAVE 25 OUTPOSTS AVAILABLE WHERE THEY MAY BE PLACED."
120 PRINT "YOU CAN ONLY PLACE ONE PLATOON AT ANY  ONE OUTPOST."
130 PRINT "THE COMPUTER DOES THE SAME WITH ITS FOUR PLATOONS."
135 PRINT
140 PRINT "THE ORJECT OF THE GAME IS TO FIRE MISSILES AT THE"
150 PRINT "OUTPOSTS OF THE COMPUTER.  IT WILL DO THE SAME TO YOU."
160 PRINT "THE ONE WHO DESTROYS ALL FOUR OF THE ENEMY'S PLATOONS "
170 PRINT "FIRST IS THE WINNER."
180  PRINT
190 PRINT "GOOD LUCK... AND TELL US WHERE YOU WANT THE BODIES SENT!"
200 PRINT
210 PRINT"TEAR OFF THE MATRIX AND USE IT TO CHECK OFF THE NUMBERS."
220 FOR R=1 TO 5\PRINT\NEXT R
250 RANDOMIZE
260 DIM M(100)
270 FOR R=1 TO 5
280 I=(R-1)*5+1
290 PRINT I,I+1,I+2,I+3,I+4
300 NEXT R
350 FOR R=1 TO 10\PRINT\NEXT R
380 LET C = INT(RND(N) * 25) + 1
390 D = INT(RND(N) * 25) +1
400 E = INT(RND(N) *25) +1
410 F = INT(RND(N) * 25) + 1
420 IF C = D GOTO 390
430 IF C = E GOTO 400
440 IF C = F GOTO 410
450 IF D = E GOTO 400
460 IF D = F GOTO 410
470 IF E = F GOTO 410
480 PRINT "WHAT ARE YOUR FOUR POSITIONS";
490 INPUT G,H,K,L
495 PRINT
500 PRINT "WHERE DO YOU WISH TO FIRE YOUR MISSILE";
510 INPUT Y
520 IF Y = C GOTO 710
530 IF Y = D GOTO 710
540 IF Y = E GOTO 710
550 IF Y = F GOTO 710
560 GOTO 630
570 M = INT(RND(N) * 25) + 1
575 GOTO 1160
580 IF X = G GOTO 920
590 IF X = H GOTO 920
600 IF X = L GOTO 920
610 IF X = K GOTO 920
620 GOTO 670
630 PRINT" HA,HA YOU MISSED, MY TURN NOW"
640 PRINT\PRINT\GOTO 570
670 PRINT"I MISSED YOU, YOU DIRTY RAT, I PICKED";M;", YOUR TURN."
680 PRINT\PRINT\GOTO 500

710 Q = Q +1
720 IF Q = 4 GOTO 890
730 PRINT "YOU GOT ONE OF MY OUTPOSTS."
740 IF Q = 1 GOTO 770
750 IF Q = 2 GOTO 810
760 IF Q = 3 GOTO 850
770 PRINT " ONE DOWN THREE TO GO"
780 PRINT\PRINT\GOTO 570
810 PRINT " TWO DOWN TWO TO GO"
820 PRINT\PRINT\GOTO 570
850 PRINT " THREE DOWN ONE TO GO"
860 PRINT\PRINT\GOTO 570
890 PRINT " YOU GOT ME,I'M GOING FAST, BUT I'LL GET YOU WHEN "
900 PRINT " Y TRANSISTORS SECUPERA E"
910 GOTO 1235
920 Z=Z+1
930 IF Z=4 THEN 1110
940 PRINT "I GOT YOU.  IT WON'T BE LONG NOW. POST"X"WAS HIT."
950 IF Z=1 THEN 990
960 IF Z=2 THEN 1030
970 IF Z=3 THEN 1070
990 PRINT "YOU HAVE ONLY THREE OUTPOSTS LEFT"
1000 PRINT\PRINT\GOTO 500
1030 PRINT "YOU HAVE ONLY TWO OUTPOSTS LEFT."
1040  PRINT\PRINT\GOTO 500
1070 PRINT "YOU HAVE ONLY ONE OUTPOST LEFT."
1080 PRINT\PRINT\GOTO 500
1110 PRINT " YOU'RE DEAD.  YOUR LAST OUTPOST WAS AT"X".  HA, HA, HA!"
1120 PRINT " BETTER LUCK NEXT TIME."
1150 GOTO 1235
1160 P=P+1
1170 N=P-1
1180 FOR T = 1 TO N
1190 IF M = M(T) GOTO 570
1200 NEXT T
1210 X = M
1220 M(P) = M
1230 GOTO 580
1235 END
```

197

SAMPLE RUN

YOU ARE ON A BATTLEFIELD WITH 4 PLATOONS AND YOU
HAVE 25 OUTPOSTS AVAILABLE WHERE THEY MAY BE PLACED.
YOU CAN ONLY PLACE ONE PLATOON AT ANY ONE OUTPOST.
THE COMPUTER DOES THE SAME WITH ITS FOUR PLATOONS.

THE OBJECT OF THE GAME IS TO FIRE MISSILES AT THE
OUTPOSTS OF THE COMPUTER. IT WILL DO THE SAME TO YOU.
THE ONE WHO DESTROYS ALL FOUR OF THE ENEMY'S PLATOONS
FIRST IS THE WINNER.

GOOD LUCK... AND TELL US WHERE YOU WANT THE BODIES SENT!

TEAR OFF THE MATRIX AND USE IT TO CHECK OFF THE NUMBERS.

1	2	3	4	5
6	7	8	9	10
11	12	13	14	15
16	17	18	19	20
21	22	23	24	25

```
WHAT ARE YOUR FOUR POSITIONS? 10,15,20,25

WHERE DO YOU WISH TO FIRE YOUR MISSILE? 6
 HA, HA YOU MISSED. MY TURN NOW

I MISSED YOU, YOU DIRTY RAT. I PICKED 9 . YOUR TURN.

WHERE DO YOU WISH TO FIRE YOUR MISSILE? 7
 HA,HA YOU MISSED. MY TURN NOW

I MISSED YOU, YOU DIRTY RAT. I PICKED 23 . YOUR TURN.

WHERE DO YOU WISH TO FIRE YOUR MISSILE? 8
 HA,HA YOU MISSED. MY TURN NOW

I MISSED YOU, YOU DIRTY RAT. I PICKED 5 . YOUR TURN.

WHERE DO YOU WISH TO FIRE YOUR MISSILE? 9
 HA,HA YOU MISSED. MY TURN NOW

I MISSED YOU, YOU DIRTY RAT. I PICKED 4 . YOUR TURN.

WHERE DO YOU WISH TO FIRE YOUR MISSILE? 10
 HA,HA YOU MISSED. MY TURN NOW

I MISSED YOU, YOU DIRTY RAT. I PICKED 6 . YOUR TURN.

WHERE DO YOU WISH TO FIRE YOUR MISSILE? 11
YOU GOT ONE OF MY OUTPOSTS.
 ONE DOWN THREE TO GO

I GOT YOU.  IT WON'T BE LONG NOW. POST 25 WAS HIT.
YOU HAVE ONLY THREE OUTPOSTS LEFT

WHERE DO YOU WISH TO FIRE YOUR MISSILE? 12
 HA,HA YOU MISSED. MY TURN NOW

I MISSED YOU, YOU DIRTY RAT. I PICKED 1 . YOUR TURN.

WHERE DO YOU WISH TO FIRE YOUR MISSILE? 13
 HA,HA YOU MISSED. MY TURN NOW

I MISSED YOU, YOU DIRTY RAT. I PICKED 21 . YOUR TURN.

WHERE DO YOU WISH TO FIRE YOUR MISSILE? 14
 HA,HA YOU MISSED. MY TURN NOW

I MISSED YOU, YOU DIRTY RAT. I PICKED 8 . YOUR TURN.

WHERE DO YOU WISH TO FIRE YOUR MISSILE? 15
YOU GOT ONE OF MY OUTPOSTS.
 TWO DOWN TWO TO GO

I MISSED YOU, YOU DIRTY RAT. I PICKED 11 . YOUR TURN.

WHERE DO YOU WISH TO FIRE YOUR MISSILE? 16
 HA,HA YOU MISSED. MY TURN NOW

I MISSED YOU, YOU DIRTY RAT. I PICKED 7 . YOUR TURN.

WHERE DO YOU WISH TO FIRE YOUR MISSILE? 17
 HA,HA YOU MISSED. MY TURN NOW
```

SLOTS

Description

The slot machine or one-arm bandit is a mechanical device that
will absorb coins just about as fast as you can feed it. After
inserting a coin, you pull a handle that sets three independent
reels spinning. If the reels stop with certain symbols appear-
ing in the pay line, you get a certain payoff. The original
slot machine, called the Liberty Bell, was invented in 1895
by Charles Fey in San Francisco. Fey refused to sell or lease
the manufacturing rights, so H.S. Mills in Chicago built a
similar, but much improved, machine called the Operators Bell.
This has survived nearly unchanged to today.

On the Operators Bell and other standard slot machines, there
are 20 symbols on each wheel but they are not distributed
evenly among the objects (cherries, bar, apples, etc.). Of
the 8,000 possible combinations, the expected payoff (to the
player) is 7,049 or $89.11 for every $100.00 put in, one of the
lowest expected payoffs of all casino games.

In the program here, the payoff is considerably more liberal;
indeed it favors the player by 11%--i.e., an expected payoff
of $111 for each $100 bet. To approximate Nevada odds, reduce
the jackpot to $15 and keno to $4.

Source

Lots of slot machine programs were submitted including a very
nice one by Rob Hoffberg of Roslyn, NY. The author of the
one published is unknown.

PROGRAM LISTING

```
100 RANDOMIZE
110 DIM D(3)
120 PRINT"THIS IS A SIMULATION OF A SLOT MACHINE USING A COMPUTER "
130 PRINT "EACH TIME YOU 'PULL' I WILL ASK YOU IF YOU WISH TO PLAY AGAIN. "
140 PRINT "JUST ANSWER WITH A 'Y' FOR YES OR A 'N' FOR NO. "
150 PRINT "PLEASE PLACE 4 QUARTERS ON MY CPU FOR EACH PLAY. "
160 PRINT
170 FOR B1=1 TO 3
180 LET D(B1)=INT(RND(0)*6)+1
190 NEXT B1
200 FOR G1=1 TO 3
210 IF D(G1)=1 THEN 280
220 IF D(G1)=2 THE N 300
230 IF D(G1)=3 THEN 320
240 IF D(G1)=4 THEN 340
250 IF D(G1)=5 THEN 360
260 IF D(G1)=6 THEN 380
270 GOTO 580
280 PRINT TAB(G1*7);" BELL";
290 GOTO 390
300 PRINT TAB(G1*7);" BAR";
310 GOTO 390
320 PRINT TAB(G1*7);"CHERRY";
330 GOTO 390
340 PRINT TAB(G1*7);"APPLE";
350 GOTO 390
360 PRINT TAB(G1*7);"LEMON";
370 GOTO 390
380 PRINT TAB(G1*7);"  $";
390 NEXT G1
400 PRINT TAB(28);
410 IF D(1)<>D(2) THEN 440
420 IF D(2)=D(3) THEN 530
430 IF D(1)=D(2) THEN 460
440 IF D(1)<>D(3) THEN 490
450 GO TO 510
460 IF D(1)/2<>INT(D(1)/2) THEN 510
470 LET B=B+5\PRINT "KENO..YOU WIN $5..TOTAL=$";B;
480 GO TO 550
490 LET B=B-1\PRINT "YOU HAVE LOST $1 -- TOTAL=$";B;
500 GOTO 550
510 LET B=B+1\PRINT "YOU HAVE WON $1 --- TOTAL=$";B;
520 GOTO 550
530 LET B=B+20\PRINT CHR$(7);"JACKPOT...$20... TOTAL=$";B;CHR$(7);
540 GOTO 550
550 PRINT "AGAIN?";
560 INPUT $A\PRINT\IF A=#Y THEN 160\IF A<>#N THEN 560
570 PRINT"IT'S BEEN NICE OPERATING FOR YOU COME BACK SOON!"
580 END
```

SAMPLE RUN

```
THIS IS A SIMULATION OF A SLOT MACHINE USING A COMPUTER
EACH TIME YOU 'PULL' I WILL ASK YOU IF YOU WISH TO PLAY AGAIN.
JUST ANSWER WITH A 'Y' FOR YES OR A 'N' FOR NO.
PLEASE PLACE 4 QUARTERS ON MY CPU FOR EACH PLAY.

      BELL   APPLE   BELL   YOU HAVE WON $1 --- TOTAL=$ 1 AGAIN?Y

      APPLE  APPLE  CHERRY  KENO..YOU WIN $5..TOTAL=$ 6 AGAIN?Y

      APPLE  APPLE  APPLE   JACKPOT...$20... TOTAL=$ 26 AGAIN?Y

      APPLE   BAR   APPLE   YOU HAVE WON $1 --- TOTAL=$ 27 AGAIN?Y

       $      $    CHERRY   KENO..YOU WIN $5..TOTAL=$ 32 AGAIN?Y

      BELL  LEMON  CHERRY  YOU HAVE LOST $1 -- TOTAL=$ 31 AGAIN?Y

       $    CHERRY    $     YOU HAVE WON $1 --- TOTAL=$ 32 AGAIN?Y

      APPLE    $     BAR    YOU HAVE LOST $1 -- TOTAL=$ 31 AGAIN?Y

       $    CHERRY  BELL    YOU HAVE LOST $1 -- TOTAL=$ 30 AGAIN?Y

     CHERRY  BELL   BELL    YOU HAVE LOST $1 -- TOTAL=$ 29 AGAIN?Y

      BAR   LEMON   BELL    YOU HAVE LOST $1 -- TOTAL=$ 28 AGAIN?Y

       $    CHERRY CHERRY  YOU HAVE LOST $1 -- TOTAL=$ 27 AGAIN?Y

      BELL   BELL   BAR    YOU HAVE WON $1 --- TOTAL=$ 28 AGAIN?Y

       $    LEMON  APPLE   YOU HAVE LOST $1 -- TOTAL=$ 27 AGAIN?Y

     LEMON  CHERRY  BAR    YOU HAVE LOST $1 -- TOTAL=$ 26 AGAIN?Y

      BAR   APPLE   BAR    YOU HAVE WON $1 --- TOTAL=$ 27 AGAIN?Y

    CHERRY  LEMON  CHERRY  YOU HAVE WON $1 --- TOTAL=$ 28 AGAIN?Y

      BELL    $    LEMON   YOU HAVE LOST $1 -- TOTAL=$ 27 AGAIN?Y

      BELL  LEMON  LEMON   YOU HAVE LOST $1 -- TOTAL=$ 26 AGAIN?Y

      BELL  LEMON  LEMON   YOU HAVE LOST $1 -- TOTAL=$ 25 AGAIN?Y

     CHERRY CHERRY   $     YOU HAVE WON $1 --- TOTAL=$ 26 AGAIN?N
IT'S BEEN NICE OPERATING FOR YOU COME BACK SOON!
```

SNOOPY

Description

There must be 7,000 various computer pictures of Snoopy around dating from the ENIAC I. Just why Snoopy was universally adopted as the programmers' mascot is hard to say, but it's clear today that he was--overwhelmingly! Here are a couple of pictures of that ubiquitous dog.

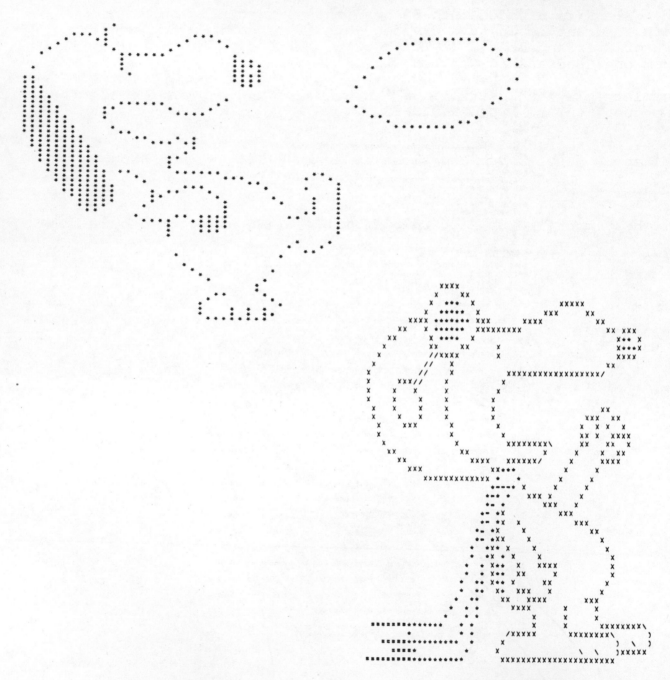

CURSE YOU, RED BARON!

SPACWR

SPACEWAR BASED ON STAR TREK

Description

This program is an incredibly complete version of spacewar.
You are Captain Kirk of the Starship Enterprise and have as
your mission to destroy a certain number of enemy Klingon
spaceships (generally around 24) and thus keep the galaxy safe
for democracy. You must complete your mission in 30 stardates
(measure of time in space--think of it as a day).

The galaxy is divided into 64 quadrants arranged in an 8x8 grid.
Each quadrant is in turn divided into 64 sectors, also in an
8x8 grid arrangement. It, of course, costs time and fuel to get
from one quadrant to another.

Complete playing instructions are given if you answer YES to
the question, DO YOU WANT INSTRUCTIONS?

Note: This program appears to have one or two minor bugs. It's
eminently usable, but occasionally funny little things happen.

Program Author

Slightly modified by Mary Cole from the original written by:

Mike Mayfield
Centerline Engineering

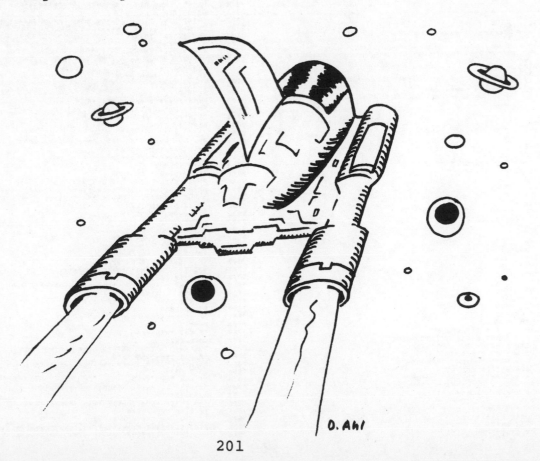

O. Ahl

```
100 REM *** PROGRAM SIMULATES IV PROGRAM STARTREK
110 REM *** WRITTEN BY MIKE MAYFIELD, CENTERLINE ENGINEERING.
120 REM *** DEBUGGING AND MINOR REVISIONS BY LEO LAVERDURE, IRA POTEL,
130 REM *** MARY COLE, AND DAVE AHL OF DIGITAL
170 RANDOMIZE
180 PRINT "              * . * STAR TREK * . * ":PRINT
200 INPUT "DO YOU WANT INSTRUCTIONS (THEY'RE LONG!)";A$
210 IF A$<>"YES" THEN 230
220 GOTO 5820
230 REM *** PROGRAM BEGINS HERE
240 Z$,R$,G$=""
260 DIM G(8,8),C(9,2),K(3,3),N(3),Z(8,8)
290 T0,T=INT(RND(1)*20+20)*100
300 T9=30:D0=0:E0,F=3000:P0,P=10:S9=20*15,H8=0
370 DEF FND(D)=SQR((K(I,1)-S1)**2+(K(I,2)-S2)**2)
380 Q1=INT(RND(1)*8+1)
390 Q2=INT(RND(1)*8+1)
400 S1=INT(RND(1)*8+1)
410 S2=INT(RND(1)*8+1)
410 J7=TIME(0)
420 C(2,1),C(3,1),C(4,1),C(4,2),C(5,2),C(6,2)=-1
430 C(1,1),C(3,1),C(5,1),C(7,2),C(9,1)=0
440 C(1,2),C(2,2),C(6,1),C(7,1),C(8,1),C(8,2),C(9,2)=1
450 MAT D=ZER
460 D$="WARP ENGINESS.R. SENSORSL.R. SENSORSPHASER CNTRL"
470 D$=D$+"PHOTON TUBESDAMAGE CNTRL "
480 E$="SHIELD CNTRLCOMPUTER"
490 B9,K9=0
491 REM *** SETS UP WHAT EXISTS IN GALAXY
500 FOR I=1TO8
510 FOR J=1TO8
520 R1=RND(1)
530 IF R1>.9A THEN 580
540 IF R1>.95 THEN 610
550 IF R1>.8 THEN 640
560 K3=0:GOTO 660
580 K3=3:K9=K9+3:GOTO 660
610 K3=2:K9=K9+2:GOTO 660
640 K3=1:K9=K9+1
660 R1=RND(1)
670 IF R1>.9A THEN 700
680 B3=0:GOTO 720
700 B3=1:B9=B9+1
720 S3=INT(RND(1)*8+1)
730 G(I,J)=K3*100+B3*10+S3
740 Z(I,J)=0
750 NEXT J
760 NEXT I
770 K7=K9
775 PRINT:PRINT
780 PRINT"YOU MUST DESTROY"K9" KLINGONS IN"T9" STARDATES WITH "B9
790 IF B9>0 THEN 810
                              " STARBASES"
800 G(Q1,Q2)=114
810 K3,B3,S3=0
820 IF Q1<1 OR Q1>8 OR Q2<1 OR Q2>8 THEN 920
830 X=G(Q1,Q2)*.01
840 K3=INT(X)
850 B3=INT((X-K3)*10)
860 S3=G(Q1,Q2)-INT(G(Q1,Q2)*.1)*10
870 IF K3<0 THEN 910
880 IF S>200 THEN 910
890 PRINT"COMBAT AREA      CONDITION RED"
900 PRINT"    SHIELDS DANGEROUSLY LOW"
910 MAT K=ZER
920 FOR I=1TO3
930 K(I,3)=0
940 NEXT I
950 G$=Z$:R$=Z$
970 S$=MID(Z$,1,48)
971 REM *** PUT ENTERPRISE SOMEWHERE
980 A$="<*>"
990 Z1=S1
1000 Z2=S2
1010 GOSUB 5510
1020 FOR I=1TOK3
1030 GOSUB 5380
1031 REM *** PUT KLINGONS SOMEWHERE
1040 A$="+++"
1050 Z1=R1
1060 Z2=R2
1070 GOSUB 5510
1080 K(I,1)=R1: K(I,2)=R2: K(I,3)=S9
1110 NEXT I
1120 FOR I=1TOB3
1130 GOSUB 5380
1131 REM *** PUT STARBASE(S) SOMEWHERE
1140 A$=">!<" Z1=R1: Z2=R2
1170 GOSUB 5510
1180 NEXT I
1190 FOR I=1TOS3
1200 GOSUB 5380
1201 REM *** PUT STARS SOMEWHERE
1210 A$=" * ": Z1=R1: Z2=R2
1240 GOSUB 5510
1250 NEXT I
1260 GOSUB 4120
1270 INPUT "COMMAND";A
1290 IF A=0 GOTO 1410
1291 IF A=1 GOTO 1260
1292 IF A=2 GOTO 2330
1293 IF A=3 GOTO 2530
1294 IF A=4 GOTO 2800
1295 IF A=5 GOTO 3460
1296 IF A=6 GOTO 3560
1297 IF A=7 GOTO 4630
1298 IF A=8 GOTO 6510
1310 PRINT:PRINT"    0 = SET COURSE"
1320 PRINT"    1 = SHORT RANGE SENSOR SCAN"
1330 PRINT"    2 = LONG RANGE SENSOR SCAN"
1340 PRINT"    3 = FIRE PHASERS"
1350 PRINT"    4 = FIRE PHOTON TORPEDOES"
1360 PRINT"    5 = SHIELD CONTROL"
1370 PRINT"    6 = DAMAGE CONTROL REPORT"
1380 PRINT"    7 = CALL ON LIBRARY COMPUTER"
1390 PRINT"    8 = END THE CONTEST":PRINT
1400 GOTO 1270
1401 REM *** COURSE CONTROL CODE BEGINS HERE
1410 INPUT "COURSE (1-9)";C1
1430 IF C1=0 THEN 1270
1440 IF C1<1 OR C1>9 THEN 1410
1450 INPUT "WARP FACTOR (0-8)";W1
1460 IF W1<0 OR W1>8 THEN 1410
1470 IF D(1)>=0 OR W1<=.2 THEN 1510
1490 PRINT"WARP ENGINES ARE DAMAGED, MAXIMUM SPEED = WARP .2"
1500 GOTO 1410
1510 IF K3=0 THEN 1560
1520 GOSUB 3790
1530 IF K3<=0 THEN 1560
1540 IF S<=0 THEN 4000
1550 GOTO 1610
1560 IF E>0 THEN 1610
1570 IF S<1 THEN 3920
1580 PRINT "YOU HAVE"E" UNITS OF ENERGY"
1590 PRINT "SUGGEST YOU GET SOME FROM YOUR SHIELDS WHICH HAVE"S" UNITS LEFT"
1600 GOTO 1270
1610 FOR I=1TO8: IF D(I)>=0 THEN 1640
1611 REM *** FIX ANY DAMAGED DEVICE
1630 D(I)=D(I)+1
1640 NEXT I
1650 IF RND(1)>.2 THEN 1810
1660 R1=INT(RND(1)*8+1)
1670 IF RND(1)>=.5 THEN 1750
1680 D(R1)=D(R1)-(RND(1)*5+1)
1690 PRINT:PRINT "DAMAGE CONTROL REPORT:";
1710 GOSUB 5610
1720 PRINT" DAMAGED":PRINT:GOTO 1810
1750 D(R1)=D(R1)+(RND(1)*5+1)
1760 PRINT:PRINT "DAMAGE CONTROL REPORT:";
1780 GOSUB 5610
1790 PRINT" STATE OF REPAIR IMPROVED":PRINT
1810 N=INT(W1*8):A$="   ":Z1=S1:Z2=S2
1850 GOSUB 5510
1860 X1=C(C1,1)+(C(C1+1,1)-C(C1,1))*(C1-INT(C1))
1870 X=S1:Y=S2
1890 X1=C(C1,1)+(C(C1+1,1)-C(C1,1))*(C1-INT(C1))
1900 X2=C(C1,2)+(C(C1+1,2)-C(C1,2))*(C1-INT(C1))
1910 FOR I=1TON:S1=S1+X1:S2=S2+X2
1940 IF S1<1 OR S1>=9. OR S2<1 OR S2>=9 THEN 2170
1950 S8=S1*24+S2*3+261 IF S8>72 THEN 1990
1970 IF MID(G$,S8,3)="   " THEN 2070
1980 GOTO 2030
1990 IF S8>144 THEN 2020
2000 IF MID(R$,S8-72,3)="   " THEN 2070
2010 GOTO 2030
2020 IF MID(S$,S8-144,3)="   " THEN 2070
2030 PRINT"WARP ENGINES SHUTDOWN AT SECTOR "S1","S2" DUE TO BAD NAVIGATION"
2040 S1=S1-X1:S2=S2-X2:GOTO 2080
2070 NEXT I
2080 A$="<*>":Z1=S1:Z2=S2
2110 GOSUB 5510
2130 E=E-N-5:IF W1<1 THEN 2150
2140 T=T+1
2150 IF T>T0+T9 THEN 3970
2160 GOTO 1260
2170 X=S1+8*X1+X1*N:Y=S2+8*Y+X2*N
2190 Q1=INT(X/8):Q2=INT(Y/8):S1=INT(X-Q1*8):S2=INT(Y-Q2*8)
2230 IF S1<>0 THEN 2260
2240 Q1=Q1-1:S1=8
2260 IF S2<>0 THEN 2290
2270 Q2=Q2-1:S2=8
2290 T=T+1:F=F-N+5
2310 IF T>T0 + T9 THEN 3970
2320 GOTO 810
2321 REM *** LONG RANGE SENSOR SCAN CODE BEGINS HERE
2330 IF D(3)>=0 THEN 2370
2340 PRINT "LONG RANGE SENSORS ARE INOPERABLE"
2360 GOTO 1270
2370 PRINT"LONG RANGE SENSOR SCAN FOR QUADRANT "Q1","Q2
2380 PRINT"-------------------"
2390 FOR I=Q1-1 TO Q1+1
2400 MAT N=ZER
2410 FOR J=Q2-1 TO Q2+1
2420 IF I<1 OR I>8 OR J<1 OR J>8 THEN 2460
2430 N(J-Q2+2)=G(I,J)
2440 IF D(7)<0 THEN 2460
2450 Z(I,J)=G(I,J)
2460 NEXT J
2470 P1$="! ### ! ### ! ### !"
2471 PRINT USING P1$,N(1),N(2),N(3)
2480 PRINT"-------------------"
2490 NEXT I
2500 GOTO 1270
2501 REM *** PHASER CONTROL CODE BEGINS HERE
2530 IF K3<=0 THEN 3670
2540 IF D(4)>=0 THEN 2570
2560 GOTO 1270
2570 IF D(7)>=0 THEN 2590
2580 PRINT " COMPUTER FAILURE HAMPERS ACCURACY"
2590 PRINT"PHASERS LOCKED ON TARGET.  ENERGY AVAILABLE="E
2600 INPUT "NUMBER OF UNITS TO FIRE:";X
2620 IF X<=0 THEN 1270
2630 IF E-X<0 THEN 2570
2640 E=E-X
2650 GOSUB 3790
2660 IF D(7)>=0 THEN 2680
2670 X=X*RND(1)
2680 FOR I=1TO3
2690 IF K(I,3)<=0 THEN 2770
2700 H=INT((X/K3/FND(0))*(2+RND(1)))
2710 K(I,3)=K(I,3)-H
2720 PRINTH" UNIT HIT ON KLINGON AT SECTOR "K(I,1)","K(I,2);
2721 PRINT"  ("K(I,3)" LEFT)"
2740 IF K(I,3)>0 THEN 2770
2750 GOSUB 3690
2760 IF K9<=0 THEN 4040
2770 NEXT I
2780 IF E<0 THEN 4000
2790 GOTO 1270
2791 REM *** PHOTON TORPEDO CODE BEGINS HERE
2800 IF D(5)>=0 THEN 2830
2810 PRINT "PHOTON TUBES ARE NOT OPERATIONAL"
2820 GOTO 1270
2830 IF P>0 THEN 2860
2840 PRINT "ALL PHOTON TORPEDOES EXPENDED"
2850 GOTO 1270
2860 INPUT "TORPEDO COURSE (1-9)";C1
2880 IF C1=0 THEN 1270
2890 IF C1<1 OR C1>=9. THEN 2860
2900 X1=C(C1,1)+(C(C1+1,1)-C(C1,1))*(C1-INT(C1))
2910 X2=C(C1,2)+(C(C1+1,2)-C(C1,2))*(C1-INT(C1))
```

```
2920  X=X1:Y=X2:P=P-1
2950  PRINT "TORPEDO TRACK:"
2960  X=X+X1:Y=Y+X2
2980  IF X<1 OR X>=9 OR Y<1 OR Y>=9 THEN 3420
2990  PRINT"        ";X;" ";Y
3010  A$="    ";Z1=X;Z2=Y
3040  GOSUB 5680
3050  IF Z3=0 THEN 3070
3060  GOTO 2960
3070  A$="+++";Z1=X;Z2=Y
3100  GOSUB 5680
3110  IF Z3=0 THEN 3220
3120  PRINT "*** KLINGON DESTROYED ***"
3130  K3=K3-1:K9=K9-1
3150  IF K9=0 THEN 4040
3160  FOR I=1TO3:IF INT(X)<>K(I,1) THEN 3190
3180  IF INT(Y)=K(I,2) THEN 3200
3190  NEXT I
3200  K(I,3)=0:GOTO 3360
3220  A$=" * ";Z1=X;Z2=Y
3250  GOSUB 5680
3260  IF Z3=0 THEN 3290
3270  PRINT "YOU CAN'T DESTROY STARS, SILLY"
3280  GOTO 3420
3290  A$=">!<";Z1=X;Z2=Y
3320  GOSUB 5680
3330  IF Z3=0 THEN 2960
3340  PRINT "*** STAR BASE DESTROYED *** ........CONGRATULATIONS"
3350  B3=B3-1
3360  A$="   ";Z1=X;Z2=Y
3390  GOSUB 5510
3400  G(Q1,Q2)=K3*100+B3*10+S3
3410  GOTO 3430
3420  PRINT "TORPEDO MISSED"
3430  GOSUB 3790
3440  IF E<=0 THEN 4000
3450  GOTO 1270
3451  REM *** SHIELD CONTROL CODE BEGINS HERE
3460  IF D(7)>=0 THEN 3490
3470  PRINT "SHIELD CONTROL IS NON-OPERATIONAL"
3480  GOTO 1270
3490  PRINT "ENERGY AVAILABLE =";E;
3500  INPUT " NUMBER OF UNITS TO SHIELDS:";X
3510  IF X<=0 THEN 1270
3520  IF E+S-X<0 THEN 3490
3530  E=E+S-X:S=X
3540  GOTO 1270
3551  REM *** DAMAGE CONTROL REPORT CODE BEGINS HERE
3560  IF D(6)>=0 THEN 3590
3570  PRINT "DAMAGE CONTROL REPORT IS NOT AVAILABLE"
3580  GOTO 1270
3590  PRINT:PRINT "DEVICE          STATE OF REPAIR"
3610  FOR R1=1TO8
3620  GOSUB 5610
3630  PRINTD(R1)
3640  NEXT R1:PRINT
3660  GOTO 1270
3670  PRINT"SHORT RANGE SENSORS REPORT NO KLINGONS IN THIS QUADRANT"
3680  GOTO 1270
3690  PRINT "KLINGON AT SECTOR ";K(I,1);",";K(I,2)"DESTROYED ***"
3710  K3=K3-1:K9=K9-1:A$="   ";Z1=K(I,1);Z2=K(I,2)
3760  GOSUB 5510
3770  G(Q1,Q2)=K3*100+B3*10+S3
3780  RETURN
3790  IF C$<>"DOCKED" THEN 3820
3800  PRINT "STAR BASE SHIELDS PROTECT THE ENTERPRISE"
3810  RETURN
3820  IF K3=0 THEN 3910
3830  FOR I=1TO3:IF K(I,3)<=0 THEN 3900
3850  H=INT((K(I,3)/FND(0))*(2+RND(1)));S=S-H
3870  PRINT" UNIT HIT ON ENTERPRISE AT SECTOR ";K(I,1);",";K(I,2)
3871  PRINT"       (";S;" LEFT)"
3890  IF S<=0 THEN 4000
3900  NEXT I
3910  RETURN
3920  PRINT "THE ENTERPRISE IS DEAD IN SPACE.  IF YOU SURVIVE ALL IMPENDING"
3930  PRINT "ATTACKS,YOU WILL BE DEMOTED TO THE RANK OF PRIVATE"
3940  IF K3<=0 THEN 4020
3950  GOSUB 3790
3960  GOTO 3940
3970  PRINT:PRINT "IT IS STARDATE"T
3990  GOTO 4020
3991  REM *** NO ENERGY LEFT
4000  PRINT:PRINT"THE ENTERPRISE HAS BEEN DESTROYED.  THE FEDERATION WILL BE
4020  PRINT "THERE ARE STILL ";K9;" KLINGON BATTLE CRUISERS"           CONQUERED"
4030  PRINT:PRINT:PRINT:PRINT "YOU GET ANOTHER CHANCE....";GOTO 230
4040  PRINT:PRINT"THE LAST KLINGON BATTLE CRUISER IN THE GALAXY HAS BEEN
4050  PRINT"THE FEDERATION HAS BEEN SAVED!!!!!";PRINT                   DESTROYED"
4075  E5=((K7/(T-T0))*1000)
4080  PRINT "YOUR EFFICIENCY RATING =";E5
4100  PRINT"YOUR ACTUAL TIME OF MISSION ="INT((TIME(0)-T7)/60);" MINUTES"
4105  PRINT:PRINT:PRINT
4106  INPUT"DO YOU WANT TO TRY AGAIN";R$
4107  IF R$ = "YES" THEN 230
4110  GOTO 6510
4111  REM *** SHORT RANGE SENSOR SCAN AND STARTING POINT CODE
4120  FOR I=S1-1TO S1+1
4130  FOR J=S2-1TO S2+1
4140  IF I<1 OR I>8 OR J<1 OR J>8 THEN 4200
4150  A$=">!<";Z1=I;Z2=J
4180  GOSUB 5680
4190  IF Z3=1 THEN 4240
4200  NEXT J
4210  NEXT I
4220  D0=0;GOTO 4310
4240  D0=1:C$="DOCKED":E=3000:P=10
4280  PRINT "SHIELDS DROPPED FOR DOCKING PURPOSES"
4290  S=0;GOTO 4380
4310  IF K3>0 THEN 4350
4320  IF E<E0 +.1 THEN 4370
4330  C$="GREEN"
4340  GOTO 4380
4350  C$="RED":GOTO 4380
4370  C$="YELLOW"
4380  IF D(2)>=0 THEN 4430
4390  PRINT:PRINT"*** SHORT RANGE SENSORS ARE OUT ***";PRINT
4420  GOTO 4530
4430  O1$="-------------------------------"
4435  PRINT USING O1$
4440  O2$="\ \ \ \ \ \ \ \ \ \ "
4445  PRINT USING O2$,MID(Q$,1,3),MID(Q$,4,3),MID(Q$,7,3),
      MID(Q$,10,3),MID(Q$,13,3),MID(Q$,16,3),MID(Q$,19,3),
      MID(Q$,22,3)
4450  O3$=O2$+"        STARDATE        #####"
4455  PRINT USING O3$,MID(Q$,25,3),MID(Q$,28,3),MID(Q$,31,3),
      MID(Q$,34,3),MID(Q$,37,3),MID(Q$,40,3),
      MID(Q$,43,3),MID(Q$,46,3),T
4460  O4$=O2$+"        CONDITION       \ \"
4465  PRINT USING O4$,MID(Q$,49,3),MID(Q$,52,3),MID(Q$,55,3),
      MID(Q$,58,3),MID(Q$,61,3),MID(Q$,64,3),MID(Q$,67,3),
      MID(Q$,70,3),C$
4470  O5$=O2$+"        QUADRANT        #"
4475  PRINT USING O5$,MID(R$,1,3),MID(R$,4,3),MID(R$,7,3),
      MID(R$,10,3),MID(R$,13,3),MID(R$,16,3),MID(R$,19,3),
      MID(R$,22,3),Q1
4476  PRINT ",";Q2
4480  O6$=O2$+"        SECTOR          #"
4485  PRINT USING O6$,MID(R$,25,3),MID(R$,28,3),
      MID(R$,31,3),MID(R$,34,3),MID(R$,37,3),MID(R$,40,3),
      MID(R$,43,3),MID(R$,46,3),S1
4486  PRINT ",";S2
4490  O7$=O2$+"        TOTAL ENERGY    ######"
4495  PRINT USING O7$,MID(R$,49,3),MID(R$,52,3),MID(R$,55,3),
      MID(R$,58,3),MID(R$,61,3),MID(R$,64,3),MID(R$,67,3),
      MID(R$,70,3),E
4500  O8$=O2$+"        PHOTON TORPEDOES ###"
4505  PRINT USING O8$,MID(S$,1,3),MID(S$,4,3),MID(S$,7,3),MID(S$,10,3),
      MID(S$,13,3),MID(S$,16,3),MID(S$,19,3),MID(S$,22,3),P
4510  O9$=O2$+"        SHIELDS         ######"
4515  PRINT USING O9$,MID(S$,25,3),MID(S$,28,3),MID(S$,31,3),
      MID(S$,34,3),MID(S$,37,3),MID(S$,40,3),MID(S$,43,3),
      MID(S$,46,3),S
4520  PRINT USING O1$
4530  RETURN
4620  REM *** LIBRARY COMPUTER CODE BEGINS HERE
4630  IF D(8)>=0 THEN 4660
4640  PRINT "COMPUTER DISABLED";GOTO 1270
4660  INPUT"COMPUTER ACTIVE AND AWAITING COMMAND:";A
4680  IF A=0 GOTO 4740
4681  IF A=1 GOTO 4830
4682  IF A=2 GOTO 4880
4690  PRINT "FUNCTIONS AVAILABLE FROM COMPUTER"
4700  PRINT "   0 = CUMULATIVE GALACTIC RECORD"
4710  PRINT "   1 = STATUS REPORT"
4720  PRINT "   2 = PHOTON TORPEDO DATA"
4730  GOTO 4660
4731  REM *** CUMULATIVE GALACTIC RECORD CODE BEGINS HERE
4740  PRINT"COMPUTER RECORD OF GALAXY FOR QUADRANT ";Q1;",";Q2
4760  PRINT "    1    2    3    4    5    6    7    8"
4770  PRINT"  ----- ----- ----- ----- ----- ----- ----- -----"
4780  FOR I=1TO8
4790  N1$="#  ### ### ### ### ### ### ### ###"
4795  PRINT USING N1$,I,Z(I,1),Z(I,2),Z(I,3),Z(I,4),Z(I,5),Z(I,6),
      Z(I,7),Z(I,8)
4800  PRINT"  ----- ----- ----- ----- ----- ----- ----- -----"
4810  NEXT I
4820  GOTO 1270
4821  REM *** STATUS REPORT CODE BEGINS HERE
4830  PRINT "     STATUS REPORT"
4840  PRINT "NUMBER OF KLINGONS LEFT =";K9
4850  V5=(T0+T9)-T
4851  PRINT "NUMBER OF STARDATES LEFT =";V5
4860  PRINT "NUMBER OF STARBASES LEFT =";B9
4870  GOTO 3560
4880  PRINT;H8=0
4881  REM *** PHOTON TORPEDO DATA CODE BEGINS HERE
4900  FOR I=1TO3
4910  IF K(I,3)<=0 THEN 5260
4920  C1=S1;A=S2;W1=K(I,1);X=K(I,2)
4960  GOTO 5010
4970  PRINT"YOU ARE AT QUADRANT ( ";Q1;",";Q2" )  SECTOR ( ";S1;",";S2" )"
4990  INPUT "SHIP AND TARGET COORDINATES ARE:";C1,A,W1,X
5010  X=X-A;A=C1-W1
5030  IF X<0 THEN 5130
5031  IF A<0 THEN 5190
5050  IF X>0 THEN 5070
5051  IF A=0 THEN 5150
5070  C1=1
5080  IF ABS(A) <= ABS(X) THEN 5110
5085  V5=C1+(((ABS(A)-ABS(X))+ABS(A))/ABS(A))
5090  PRINT "DIRECTION =";V5
5100  GOTO 5240
5110  PRINT "DIRECTION =";C1+((ABS(A)/ABS(X)))
5120  GOTO 5240
5130  IF A>0 THEN 5170
5140  IF X=0 THEN 5190
5150  C1=5;GOTO 5080
5170  C1=3;GOTO5200
5190  C1=7
5200  IF ABS(A)>=ABS(X) THEN 5230
5210  PRINT "DIRECTION =";C1+((ABS(X)-ABS(A))+ABS(X))/ABS(X))
5220  GOTO 5240
5230  PRINT "DIRECTION =";C1+((ABS(X)/ABS(A)))
5240  PRINT "DISTANCE =";SQR(X^2+A^2)
5250  IF H8=1 THEN 5320
5260  NEXT I
5270  H8=0
5280  INPUT "DO YOU WANT TO USE THE CALCULATOR";A$
5300  IF A$="YES" THEN 4970
5310  IF A$<>"NO" THEN 5280
5320  GOTO 1270
5321  REM *** END OF LIBRARY COMPUTER CODE
5380  R1=INT(RND(1)*8+1);R2=INT(RND(1)*8+1);A$="   ";Z1=R1;Z2=R2
5430  GOSUB 5680
5440  IF Z3=0 THEN 5380
5450  RETURN
5510  REM *** INSERTION IN STRING ARRAY FOR QUADRANT ***
5520  S8=Z1*24+Z2*3-26;IF S8>72 THEN 5560
5540  Q$=LEFT(Q$,S8-1)+A$+RIGHT(Q$,S8+3)
5550  GOTO 5600
5560  IF S8>144 THEN 5590
5570  R$=LEFT(R$,S8-73)+A$+RIGHT(R$,S8-69)
5580  GOTO 5600
5590  S$=LEFT(S$,S8-145)+A$+RIGHT(S$,S8-141)
5600  RETURN
5610  REM *** PRINTS DEVICE NAME FROM ARRAY***
5620  S8=R1*12-11;IF S8>72 THEN 5660
5640  PRINT MID(D$,S8,11);GOTO 5670
5660  PRINT MID(E$,S8-72,11);
5670  RETURN
```

203

```
5680    REM ***STRING COMPARISON IN QUADRANT ARRAY***
5690    S8=Z1*24+Z2*3-26:Z3=0:IF S8>72 THEN 5750
5720    IF MID(Q$,S8,3)<>A$ THEN 5810
5730    Z3=1:GOTO 5810
5750    IF S8>144 THEN 5790
5760    IF MID(R$,S8-72,3)<>A$ THEN 5810
5770    Z3=1:GOTO 5810
5790    IF MID(S$,S8-144,3)<>A$ THEN 5810
5800    Z3=1
5810    RETURN
5820    R"       INSTRUCTIONS"
5821    R:R"THE GALAXY IS DIVIDED INTO AN 8,8 QUADRANT GRID"
5822    R"WHICH IS IN TURN DIVIDED INTO AN 8,8 SECTOR GRID."
5823    R:R"THE CAST OF CHARACTERS IS AS FOLLOWS:"
5830    R"<*> = ENTERPRISE"
5840    R"+++ = KLINGON"
5850    R">!< = STARBASE":R" * = STAR"
5870    R"COMMAND 0 = WARP ENGINE CONTROL:"
5880    R"  COURSE IS IN A CIRCULAR NUMERICAL"
5890    R"  VECTOR ARRANGEMENT AS SHOWN."
5900    R"  INTEGER AND REAL VALUES MAY BE"
5910    R"  USED.  THEREFORE COURSE 1.5 IS"
5920    R"  HALF WAY BETWEEN 1 AND 2."
5930    R"
5940    R"  A VECTOR OF 9 IS UNDEFINED, BUT"
5950    R"  VALUES MAY APPROACH 9."
5960    R"
5970    R"  ONE WARP FACTOR IS THE SIZE OF"
5980    R"  ONE QUADRANT.  THEREFORE TO GET"
5990    R"  FROM QUADRANT 6.5 TO 5.5 YOU WOULD"
6000    R"  USE COURSE 3, WARP FACTOR 1"
6005    R"
6010    R"COMMAND 1 = SHORT RANGE SENSOR SCAN"
6020    R"  PRINT THE QUADRANT YOU ARE CURRENTLY IN.  INCLUDING"
6030    R"  STARS, KLINGONS, STARBASES, AND THE ENTERPRISE, ALONG"
6040    R"  WITH OTHER PERTINATE INFORMATION."
6045    R:R"COMMAND 2 = LONG RANGE SENSOR SCAN"
6060    R"  SHOWS CONDITIONS IN SPACE FOR ONE QUADRANT ON EACH SIDE"
6070    R"  OF THE ENTERPRISE IN THE MIDDLE OF THE SCAN. THE SCAN"
6080    R"  IS CODED IN THE FORM XXX, WHERE THE UNITS DIGIT IS THE "
6090    R"  NUMBER OF STARS, THE TENS DIGIT IS THE NUMBER OF STAR-"
6100    R"  BASES.  THE HUNDREDS DIGIT IS THE NUMBER OF KLINGONS."
6110    R:R"COMMAND 3 = PHASER CONTROL"
6120    R"  ALLOWS YOU TO DESTROY THE KLINGONS BY HITTING HIM WITH"
6130    R"  SUITABLY LARGE NUMBERS OF ENERGY UNITS TO DEPLETE HIS "
6140    R"  SHIELD POWER.  KEEP IN MIND THAT WHEN YOU SHOOT AT HIM,"
6150    R"  HE GONNA SHOOT AT YOU, TOO!"
6160    R:R"COMMAND 4 = PHOTON TORPEDO CONTROL"
6170    R"  COURSE IS THE SAME AS USED IN WARP ENGINE CONTROL"
6180    R"  IF YOU HIT THE KLINGON, HE IS DESTROYED AND CANNOT FIRE"
6190    R"  BACK AT YOU.  IF YOU MISS, YOU ARE SUBJECT TO HIS "
6200    R"  PHASER FIRE."
6210    R:R  NOTE:  THE LIBRARY COMPUTER (COMMAND 7) HAS AN OPTION"
6220    R"  TO COMPUTE TORPEDO TRAJECTORY FOR YOU (OPTION 2)."
6230    R:R"COMMAND 5 = SHIELD CONTROL"
6240    R"  DEFINES NUMBER OF ENERGY UNITS TO BE ASSIGNED TO SHIELDS"
6250    R"  ENERGY IS TAKEN FROM TOTAL SHIP'S ENERGY."
6251    R"  NOTE THAT TOTAL ENERGY INCLUDES SHIELD ENERGY."
6260    R:R"COMMAND 6 = DAMAGE CONTROL REPORT"
6270    R"  GIVES STATE OF REPAIRS OF ALL DEVICES.  A STATE OF REPAIR"
6280    R"  LESS THAN ZERO SHOWS THAT THE DEVICE IS TEMPORARALY"
6290    R"  DAMAGED."
6300    R:R"COMMAND 7 = LIBRARY COMPUTER"
6310    R"  THE LIBRARY COMPUTER CONTAINS THREE OPTIONS:"
6320    R"    OPTION 0 = CUMULATIVE GALACTIC RECORD"
6330    R"      WHICH SHOWS COMPUTER MEMORY OF THE RESULTS"
6340    R"      OF ALL PREVIOUS LONG RANGE SENSOR SCANS"
6350    R"    OPTION 1 = STATUS REPORT"
6360    R"      WHICH SHOWS NUMBER OF KLINGONS, STARDATES,"
6370    R"      AND STARBASES LEFT."
6380    R"    OPTION 2 = PHOTON TORPEDO DATA"
6390    R"      GIVES TRAJECTORY AND DISTANCE BETWEEN THE"
6400    R"      ENTERPRISE AND ALL KLINGONS IN YOUR QUADRANT"
6500    GOTO 230
6510    END
```

SAMPLE RUN

```
YOU MUST DESTROY 12  KLINGONS IN 30  STARDATES WITH  3  STARBASES
------------------------------------
                    <*>           STARDATE          2300
                                  CONDITION         GREEN
              *                   QUADRANT          2, 3
                                  SECTOR            2, 6
                                  TOTAL ENERGY      3000
                                  PHOTON TORPEDOES  10
                                  SHIELDS           0
------------------------------------
COMMAND:? 2
LONG RANGE SENSOR SCAN FOR QUADRANT 2 , 3

: 5 : 1 : 7 :
---------------------
: 8 : 1 : 2 :
---------------------
: 4 : 2 :104 :
---------------------
COMMAND:? 0
COURSE (1-9):? 8
WARP FACTOR (0-8):? 1
COMBAT AREA     CONDITION RED
   SHIELDS DANGEROUSLY LOW
------------------------------------
              +++
                    <*>           STARDATE          2301
                                  CONDITION         RED
         *      *         *       QUADRANT          3, 4
                                  SECTOR            2, 6
                                  TOTAL ENERGY      2997
              *                   PHOTON TORPEDOES  10
                                  SHIELDS           0
------------------------------------
COMMAND:? 5
ENERGY AVAILABLE = 2997    NUMBER OF UNITS TO SHIELDS:? 300
COMMAND:? 7
COMPUTER ACTIVE AND AWAITING COMMAND:? 2
```

```
DIRECTION = 4
DISTANCE = 1.41421
DO YOU WANT TO USE THE CALCULATOR? NO
COMMAND:? 4
TORPEDO COURSE (1-9):? 4
TORPEDO TRACK:
               1 , 5
*** KLINGON DESTROYED ***

COMMAND:? 0
COURSE (1-9):? 7
WARP FACTOR (0-8):? 3
------------------------------------
         *
                    <*>           STARDATE          2302
                                  CONDITION         GREEN
                         *  *     QUADRANT          6, 4
                                  SECTOR            2, 6
                    *             TOTAL ENERGY      2678
                                  PHOTON TORPEDOES  9
                                  SHIELDS           300
COMMAND:? 0
COURSE (1-9):? 3
WARP FACTOR (0-8):? 1
------------------------------------


                    <*>      *    STARDATE          2303
                                  CONDITION         RED
         *                        QUADRANT          5, 4
              +++        *        SECTOR            2, 6
                    *             TOTAL ENERGY      2675
                    *             PHOTON TORPEDOES  9
                                  SHIELDS           300
------------------------------------
COMMAND:? 7
COMPUTER ACTIVE AND AWAITING COMMAND:? 2

DIRECTION = 6
DISTANCE = 4.24264
DO YOU WANT TO USE THE CALCULATOR? NO
COMMAND:? 4
TORPEDO COURSE (1-9):? 6
TORPEDO TRACK:
               3 , 5
               4 , 4
               5 , 3
*** KLINGON DESTROYED ***

COMMAND:? 0
COURSE (1-9):? 7
WARP FACTOR (0-8):? 1
WARP ENGINES SHUTDOWN AT SECTOR  8 , 1.5  DUE TO BAD NAVIGATION
------------------------------------
                                  STARDATE          2307
                                  CONDITION         GREEN
                                  QUADRANT          7, 6
                                  SECTOR            7, 1.5
         <* >                     TOTAL ENERGY      2573
         >!<          *   *       PHOTON TORPEDOES  4
                                  SHIELDS           200
------------------------------------
COMMAND:? 7
COMPUTER ACTIVE AND AWAITING COMMAND:? 0
COMPUTER RECORD OF GALAXY FOR QUADRANT  7 , 7
     1    2    3    4    5    6    7    8
   ---- ---- ---- ---- ---- ---- ---- ----
1  0    5    1    7    0    0    0    0
   ---- ---- ---- ---- ---- ---- ---- ----
2  0    8    1    2    0    0    0    0
   ---- ---- ---- ---- ---- ---- ---- ----
3  0    4    2   104   0    0    0    0
   ---- ---- ---- ---- ---- ---- ---- ----
4  0    1    5    5    0    0    0    0
   ---- ---- ---- ---- ---- ---- ---- ----
5  0    7    2    5    2    0    0    0
   ---- ---- ---- ---- ---- ---- ---- ----
6  0    7    8    5    2    8    2    0
   ---- ---- ---- ---- ---- ---- ---- ----
7  0    0    1   14    6   12    6    0
   ---- ---- ---- ---- ---- ---- ---- ----
8  0    0    0    2    5  102    8    0
   ---- ---- ---- ---- ---- ---- ---- ----
COMMAND:? 0
COURSE (1-9):? 3
WARP FACTOR (0-8):? 5
------------------------------------
                                  STARDATE          2308
                                  CONDITION         GREEN
              >!<                 QUADRANT          2, 6
                                  SECTOR            7, 1
                    *             TOTAL ENERGY      2538
         <*>                      PHOTON TORPEDOES  4
              *                   SHIELDS           200
------------------------------------
COMMAND:? 2
LONG RANGE SENSOR SCAN FOR QUADRANT 2 , 6

: 6 : 2 : 3 :
---------------------
: 7 : 12 : 3 :
---------------------
: 4 : 8 : 8 :
---------------------
COMMAND:? 7
COMPUTER ACTIVE AND AWAITING COMMAND:? 1
   STATUS REPORT
NUMBER OF KLINGONS LEFT = 6
NUMBER OF STARDATES LEFT = 22
NUMBER OF STARBASES LEFT = 3

DEVICE        STATE OF REPAIR
WARP ENGINE      0
S.R. SENSOR      0
L.R. SENSOR      2.73447
PHASER CNTR      0
PHOTON TUBE      0
DAMAGE CNTR      0
SHIELD CNTR      0
```

204

SPLAT

OPEN A PARACHUTE AT THE LAST MOMENT

Description

SPLAT simulates a parachute jump in which you try to open your 'chute at the last possible moment without going splat! You may select your own terminal velocity or let the computer do it for you. You may also select the acceleration due to gravity or, again, let the computer do it in which case you might wind up on any of the eight planets (out to Neptune), the moon, or sun.

The computer then tells you the height you're jumping from and asks for the seconds of free fall. It then divides your free fall time into eight intervals and gives you progress reports on your way down. The computer also keeps track of all prior jumps in the file PARACH.UTE and lets you know how you compared with previous successful jumps.

Program Author

John F. Yegge
Oak Ridge Associated Universities
Oak Ridge,TN 37830

PROGRAM LISTING

```
30 OPEN "PARACHUTE" AS FILE 1%
40 DIM #1%,A(4000)
55 RANDOMIZE
95 PRINT "WELCOME TO 'SPLAT' -- THE GAME THAT SIMULATES A PARACHUTE"
96 PRINT "JUMP. TRY TO OPEN YOUR CHUTE AT THE LAST POSSIBLE"
97 PRINT "MOMENT WITHOUT GOING SPLAT."
118 PRINT\PRINT\D1=0\V=0\A=0\M=0\M=0\D1=INT(9001*RND(1)+1000)
119 PRINT " SELECT YOUR OWN TERMINAL VELOCITY (YES OR NO)";\INPUT A1$
120 IF A1$="NO" THEN 128 ELSE IF A1$="YES" THEN 123
121 PRINT "'YES' OR 'NO' PLEASE";\INPUT A1$\GOTO 120
123 PRINT "WHAT TERMINAL VELOCITY (MI/HR)";\INPUT V1
125 V1=V1*(5280/3600)\V=V1+((V1*RND(0))/20)-((V1*RND(0))/20)\GOTO 135
128 V1=INT(1000*RND(0))
130 PRINT "OK. TERMINAL VELOCITY ="V1"MI/HR"
131 V1=V1*(5280/3600)\V=V1+((V1*RND(0))/20)-((V1*RND(0))/20)
135 PRINT "WANT TO SELECT ACCELERATION DUE TO GRAVITY (YES OR NO)";
136 INPUT B1$
140 IF B1$="NO" THEN 150 ELSE IF B1$="YES" THEN 143
141 PRINT "'YES' OR 'NO' PLEASE";\INPUT B1$\GOTO 140
143 PRINT "WHAT ACCELERATION (FT/SEC/SEC)";\INPUT A2
145 A=A2+((A2*RND(0))/20)-((A2*RND(0))/20)\GOTO 205
150 ON INT(1+(10*RND(0)))GOTO151,152,153,154,155,156,157,158,159,160
151 PRINT"FINE. YOU'RE ON MERCURY. ACCELERATION=12.2FT/SEC/SEC"\GOTO161
152 PRINT"ALRIGHT, YOU'RE ON VENUS. ACCELERATION=28.3 FT/SEC/SEC"\GOTO162
153 PRINT"THEN YOU'RE ON EARTH. ACCELERATION=32.16 FT/SEC/SEC"\GOTO 163
154 PRINT"FINE. YOU'RE ON THE MOON. ACCELERATION=5.15FT/SEC/SEC"\GOTO 164
155 PRINT"ALRIGHT, YOU'RE ON MARS. ACCELERATION=12.5FT/SEC/SEC"\GOTO 165
156 PRINT"THEN YOU'RE ON JUPITER. ACCELERATION=85.2FT/SEC/SEC"\GOTO 166
157 PRINT"FINE. YOU'RE ON SATURN. ACCELERATION=37.6FT/SEC/SEC"\GOTO 167
158 PRINT"ALRIGHT, YOU'RE ON URANUS. ACCELERATION=33.8FT/SEC/SEC"\GOTO 168
159 PRINT"THEN YOU'RE ON NEPTUNE. ACCELERATION=39.6FT/SEC/SEC"\GOTO 169
160 PRINT"FINE. YOU'RE ON THE SUN. ACCELERATION=896FT/SEC/SEC"\GOTO 170
161 A2=12.2\GOTO 145
162 A2=28.3\GOTO 145
163 A2=32.16\GOTO 145
164 A2=5.15\GOTO 145
165 A2=12.5\GOTO 145
166 A2=85.2\GOTO 145
167 A2=37.6\GOTO 145
168 A2=33.8 \GOTO 145
169 A2=39.6\GOTO 145
170 A2=896\GOTO 145
205 PRINT
206 PRINT "     ALTITUDE          ="D1"FT"
207 PRINT "    TERM.VELOCITY      ="V1"FT/SEC +-5%"
208 PRINT "    ACCELERATION       ="A2"FT/SEC/SEC +-5%"
210 PRINT "SET THE TIMER FOR YOUR FREEFALL."
211 PRINT "HOW MANY SECONDS";\INPUT T
215 PRINT "HERE WE GO."
217 PRINT
218 PRINT "TIME (SEC)","DIST TO FALL (FT)"
219 PRINT "==========","================"
300 FOR I=0 TO T STEP (T/8)
310 IF I>V/A GOTO 400
320 D=D1-((A/2)*I*2)
330 IF D<=0 GOTO 1000
340 PRINT I,D
350 NEXT I
360 GOTO 500
400 PRINT "TERMINAL VELOCITY REACHED AT T PLUS"V/A"SECONDS"
405 FOR I=I TO T STEP (T/8)
410 D=D1-((V*2/(2*A))+(V*(I-(V/A))))
420 IF D<=0 GOTO 1010
430 PRINT I,D
440 NEXT I
450 GOTO 500
500 PRINT "CHUTE OPEN"
510 K=0\K1=0
530 FOR I=1 TO 4000
550 IF A(I)=0 GOTO 620
560 K=K+1
570 IF D>=A(I) GOTO 600
580 K1=K1+1
600 NEXT I
620 A(I)=D
630 I=I-1
650 IF K-K1<=.1*K GOTO 700
660 IF K-K1<=.25*K GOTO 710
670 IF K-K1<=.5*K GOTO 720
680 IF K-K1<=.75*K GOTO 730
690 IF K-K1<=.9*K GOTO 740
695 GOTO 750
700 PRINT "WOW! THAT'S SOME JUMPING. OF THE"K"SUCCESSFUL JUMPS"
701 PRINT "BEFORE YOURS, ONLY"K-K1"OPENED THEIR CHUTES LOWER THAN"
702 PRINT "YOU DID."
703 GOTO 2000
710 PRINT "PRETTY GOOD! " K"SUCCESSFUL JUMPS PRECEDED YOURS AND ONLY"
711 PRINT K-K1" OF THEM GOT LOWER THAN YOU DID BEFORE THEIR CHUTES"
712 PRINT "OPENED." \GOTO 2000
720 PRINT "NOT BAD. THERE HAVE BEEN"K"SUCCESSFUL JUMPS BEFORE YOURS."
721 PRINT"YOU WERE BEATEN OUT BY"K-K1"OF THEM."\GOTO 2000
730 PRINT "CONSERVATIVE AREN'T YOU?  YOU RANKED ONLY"K-K1"IN THE"
731 PRINT K"SUCCESSFUL JUMPS BEFORE YOURS."\GOTO 2000
740 PRINT "HUMPH! DON'T YOU HAVE ANY SPORTING BLOOD? THERE WERE"
741 PRINT K"SUCCESSFUL JUMPS BEFORE YOURS AND YOU CAME IN"K1"JUMPS"
742 PRINT "BETTER THAN THE WORST. SHAPE UP!!!"\GOTO 2000
750 PRINT "HEY! YOU PULLED THE RIP CORD MUCH TOO SOON.  "K"SUCCESSFUL"
751 PRINT "JUMPS BEFORE YOURS AND YOU CAME IN NUMBER"K-K1"! GET WITH IT!"
752 GOTO 2000
800 PRINT "REQUIESCAT IN PACE."\GOTO 1950
801 PRINT "MAY THE ANGEL OF HEAVEN LEAD YOU INTO PARADISE"\GOTO 1950
802 PRINT "REST IN PEACE"\GOTO 1950
803 PRINT "SON-OF-A-GUN"\GOTO 1950
804 PRINT "#$%&&%!$"\GOTO 1950
805 PRINT "A KICK IN THE PANTS IS A BOOST IF YOU'RE HEADED RIGHT"\GOTO 1950
806 PRINT "HMMM, SHOULD HAVE PICKED A SHORTER TIME."\GOTO 1950
807 PRINT "MUTTER. MUTTER. MUTTER."\GOTO 1950
808 PRINT "PUSHING UP DAISIES."\GOTO1950
809 PRINT "EASY COME, EASY GO."\GOTO 1950
1000 PRINT SQR(2*D1/A),"SPLAT"
1005 ON INT(1+(10*RND(0)))GOTO 800,801,802,803,804,805,806,807,808,809
1010 PRINT (V/A)+((D1-(V*2/(2*A)))/V),"SPLAT"
1020 GOTO 1005
1950 PRINT "I'LL GIVE YOU ANOTHER CHANCE."\GOTO 2000
2000 PRINT "DO YOU WANT TO PLAY AGAIN";\INPUT Z$
2001 IF Z$="YES" GOTO 118
2002 IF Z$="NO" GOTO 2005
2003 PRINT "YES OR NO"\GOTO 2000
2005 PRINT "PLEASE";\INPUT Z$\IF Z$="YES" THEN 118 ELSE 2007
2007 PRINT "SSSSSSSSSS."\GOTO 2046
2046 CLOSE 1%
9999 END
```

206

SAMPLE RUN

```
WELCOME TO 'SPLAT' -- THE GAME THAT SIMULATES A PARACHUTE
JUMP. TRY TO OPEN YOUR CHUTE AT THE LAST POSSIBLE
MOMENT WITHOUT GOING SPLAT.


SELECT YOUR OWN TERMINAL VELOCITY (YES OR NO)? NO
OK. TERMINAL VELOCITY = 796 MI/HR
WANT TO SELECT ACCELERATION DUE TO GRAVITY (YES OR NO)? NO
FINE. YOU'RE ON MERCURY. ACCELERATION=12.2FT/SEC/SEC

     ALTITUDE        = 9297 FT
     TERM.VELOCITY   = 1167.47 FT/SEC +-5%
     ACCELERATION    = 12.2 FT/SEC/SEC +-5%
SET THE TIMER FOR YOUR FREEFALL.
HOW MANY SECONDS? 8
HERE WE GO.

TIME (SEC)       DIST TO FALL (FT)
==========       =================
0                9297
1                9290.88
2                9272.51
3                9241.89
4                9199.02
5                9143.91
6                9076.55
7                8996.94
8                8905.09
CHUTE OPEN
CONSERVATIVE AREN'T YOU?  YOU RANKED ONLY 9 IN THE
14 SUCCESSFUL JUMPS BEFORE YOURS.
DO YOU WANT TO PLAY AGAIN? YES


SELECT YOUR OWN TERMINAL VELOCITY (YES OR NO)? NO
OK. TERMINAL VELOCITY = 971 MI/HR
WANT TO SELECT ACCELERATION DUE TO GRAVITY (YES OR NO)? NO
FINE. YOU'RE ON MERCURY. ACCELERATION=12.2FT/SEC/SEC

     ALTITUDE        = 5884 FT
     TERM.VELOCITY   = 1424.13 FT/SEC +-5%
     ACCELERATION    = 12.2 FT/SEC/SEC +-5%
SET THE TIMER FOR YOUR FREEFALL.
HOW MANY SECONDS? 80
HERE WE GO.

TIME (SEC)       DIST TO FALL (FT)
==========       =================
0                5884
10               5295
20               3527.99
30               582.97
31.6066          SPLAT
PUSHING UP DAISIES.
I'LL GIVE YOU ANOTHER CHANCE.
DO YOU WANT TO PLAY AGAIN? YES


SELECT YOUR OWN TERMINAL VELOCITY (YES OR NO)? NO
OK. TERMINAL VELOCITY = 740 MI/HR
WANT TO SELECT ACCELERATION DUE TO GRAVITY (YES OR NO)? NO
THEN YOU'RE ON NEPTUNE. ACCELERATION=39.6FT/SEC/SEC

     ALTITUDE        = 5189 FT
     TERM.VELOCITY   = 1085.33 FT/SEC +-5%
     ACCELERATION    = 39.6 FT/SEC/SEC +-5%
SET THE TIMER FOR YOUR FREEFALL.
HOW MANY SECONDS? 18
HERE WE GO.

TIME (SEC)       DIST TO FALL (FT)
==========       =================
0                5189
2.25             5089.74
4.5              4791.95
6.75             4295.63
9                3600.78
11.25            2707.4
13.5             1615.5
15.75            325.072
16.2678          SPLAT
MAY THE ANGEL OF HEAVEN LEAD YOU INTO PARADISE
I'LL GIVE YOU ANOTHER CHANCE.
DO YOU WANT TO PLAY AGAIN? YES
```

STARS

A NUMBER GUESSING GAME

Description

In this game, the computer selects a random number from 1 to 100
(or any value you set in Statement 150). You try to guess the
number and the computer gives you clues to tell you how close
you're getting. One star (*) means you're far away from the
number; seven stars (*******) means you're really close. You
get 7 guesses.

On the surface this game is very similar to GUESS; however, the
guessing strategy is quite different. See if you can come up
with one or more approaches to finding the mystery number.

Program Author

Bob Albrecht
People's Computer Company
Menlo Park, CA 94025

PROGRAM LISTING

```
100 REM *** STARS - PEOPLE'S COMPUTER CENTER, MENLO PARK, CA
110 PRINT "STARS - A NUMBER GUESSING GAME"
120 PRINT
130 RANDOMIZE
140 REM *** A IS LIMIT ON NUMBER, M IS NUMBER OF GUESSES
150 LET A=100
160 LET M=7
170 PRINT "DO YOU WANT INSTRUCTIONS (1=YES 0=NO)";
180 INPUT Z
190 IF Z=0 THEN 280
200 REM *** INSTRUCTIONS ON HOW TO PLAY
210 PRINT "I AM THINKING OF A WHOLE NUMBER FROM 1 TO";A
220 PRINT "TRY TO GUESS MY NUMBER. AFTER YOU GUESS, I"
230 PRINT "WILL TYPE ONE OR MORE STARS (*). THE MORE"
240 PRINT "STARS I TYPE, THE CLOSER YOU ARE TO MY NUMBER."
250 PRINT "ONE STAR (*) MEANS FAR AWAY. SEVEN STARS (*******)"
260 PRINT "MEANS REALLY CLOSE! YOU GET";M;"GUESSES."
270 REM *** COMPUTER 'THINKS' OF A NUMBER
280 PRINT
290 PRINT
300 LET X=INT(A*RND(0))+1
310 PRINT "OK, I AM THINKING OF A NUMBER. START GUESSING."
320 REM *** GUESSING BEGINS. HUMAN GETS M GUESSES
330 FOR K=1 TO M
340 PRINT
350 PRINT "YOUR GUESS";
360 INPUT G
370 IF G=X THEN 600
380 LET D=ABS(X-G)
390 IF D >= 64 THEN 510
400 IF D >= 32 THEN 500
410 IF D >= 16 THEN 490
420 IF D >= 8 THEN 480
430 IF D >= 4 THEN 470
440 IF D >= 2 THEN 460
450 PRINT "*";
460 PRINT "*";
470 PRINT "*";
480 PRINT "*";
490 PRINT "*";
500 PRINT "*";
510 PRINT "*";
520 PRINT
530 NEXT K
540 REM *** DID NOT GUESS NUMBER IN M GUESSES
550 PRINT
560 PRINT "SORRY, THAT'S";M;"GUESSES. NUMBER WAS";X
580 GOTO 280
590 REM *** WE HAVE A WINNER
600 FOR N=1 TO 50
610 PRINT "*";
620 NEXT N
630 PRINT "!!!"
640 PRINT "YOU GOT IT IN ";K;"GUESSES!! LET'S PLAY AGAIN..."
650 GOTO 280
660 END
```

SAMPLE RUN

```
STARS - A NUMBER GUESSING GAME

DO YOU WANT INSTRUCTIONS (1=YES 0=NO)? 1
I AM THINKING OF A WHOLE NUMBE  FROM 1 TO 100
TRY TO GUESS MY NUMBER. AFTER YOU GUESS, I
WILL TYPE ONE OR MORE STARS (*). THE MORE
STARS I TYPE, THE CLOSER YOU ARE TO MY NUMBER.
ONE STAR (*) MEANS FAR AWAY. SEVEN STARS (*******)
MEANS REALLY CLOSE! YOU GET 7 GUESSES.

OK, I AM THINKING OF A NUMBER. START GUESSING.

YOUR GUESS? 50
***

YOUR GUESS? 75
*****

YOUR GUESS? 82
****

YOUR GUESS? 67
******

YOUR GUESS? 68
*******

YOUR GUESS? 69
*************************************************!!!
YOU GOT IT IN  6 GUESSES!!  LET'S PLAY AGAIN...
```

```
OK, I AM THINKING OF A NUMBER. START GUESSING.

YOUR GUESS? 80
***

YOUR GUESS? 56
******

YOUR GUESS? 58
*************************************************!!!
YOU GOT IT IN  3 GUESSES!! LET'S PLAY AGAIN...

OK, I AM THINKING OF A NUMBER. START GUESSING.

YOUR GUESS? 20
**

YOUR GUESS? 68
****

YOUR GUESS? 80
******

YOUR GUESS? 82
*****

YOUR GUESS? 78
*******

YOUR GUESS? 77
*************************************************!!!
YOU GOT IT IN  6 GUESSES!! LET'S PLAY AGAIN...

OK, I AM THINKING OF A NUMBER. START GUESSING.

YOUR GUESS? 20
***

YOUR GUESS? 44
*****

YOUR GUESS? 50
****

YOUR GUESS? 38
******

YOUR GUESS? 40
*************************************************!!!
YOU GOT IT IN  5 GUESSES!! LET'S PLAY AGAIN...

OK, I AM THINKING OF A NUMBER. START GUESSING.

YOUR GUESS? 80
**

YOUR GUESS? 32
****

YOUR GUESS? 20
***

YOUR GUESS? 42
*****

YOUR GUESS? 46
*************************************************!!!
YOU GOT IT IN  5 GUESSES!! LET'S PLAY AGAIN...

OK, I AM THINKING OF A NUMBER. START GUESSING.

YOUR GUESS? 30
****

YOUR GUESS? 44
***

YOUR GUESS? 18
******

YOUR GUESS? 16
*****

YOUR GUESS? 20
*******

YOUR GUESS? 21
*************************************************!!!
YOU GOT IT IN  6 GUESSES!! LET'S PLAY AGAIN...
```

STOCK

Description

This program "plays" the stock market. You will be given $10,000
and may buy or sell stocks. Stock prices and trends are generated
randomly; therefore, this model does not represent exactly what
happens on the exchange. (Depending upon your point of view, you
may feel this is quite a good representation!)

Every trading day, a table of stocks, their prices, and number of
shares in your portfolio is printed. Following this, the initials
of each stock are printed followed by a question mark. You indicate your transaction in number of shares--a positive number
to buy, negative number to sell, or 0 to do no trading. A
brokerage fee of 1% is charged on all transactions (a bargain!).
Note: Even if the value of a stock drops to zero, it may rebound again--then again, it may not.

Source

A good stock market game for EduSystem 30 was submitted by John
Tieman of Adlai Stevenson High School, Prairie View, Illinois;
it was written by a student named Gidzinski. Another one was
written by G. Clayton Jobel of Concord, NH, for EduSystem 10!
The authors of the one printed are:

D. Pessel, L. Braun, C. Losik
Huntington Computer Project
SUNY
Stony Brook, NY

PROGRAM LISTING

```
100 REM STOCK MARKET SIMULATION  =STOCK=
101 REM REVISED 8/18/70 (D. PESSEL, L. BRAUN, C. LOSIK)
102 REM IMP VRBLS: A=MRKT TRND SLP; B5=BRKRGE FEE; C=TTL CSH ASSTS;
103 REM C5=TTL CSH ASSTS (TEMP); C(I)=CHNG IN STK VAL; D=TTL ASSTS;
104 REM E1,E2=LRG CHNG MISC; I=STCK #; I1,I2=STCKS W LRG CHNG;
105 REM N1,N2=LRG CHNG DAY CNTS; P5=TTL DAYS PRCHSS; P(I)=PRTFL CNTNTS;
106 REM G9=NEW CYCL?; S4=SGN OF A; S5=TTL DYS SLS; S(I)=VALUE/SHR;
107 REM T=TTL STCK ASSTS; T5=TTL VAL OF TRNSCTNS;
108 REM W3=LRG CHNG; X1=SMLL CHNG(<$1); Z4,Z5,Z6=NYSE AVE.; Z(I)=TRNSCTN.
109 PRINT TAB(20);"THE STOCK MARKET"
110 DIM S(5),P(5),Z(5),C(5)
112 REM SLOPE OF MARKET TREND:A  (SAME FOR ALL STOCKS)
113 RANDOMIZE
114 LET A=INT((RND(X)/10)*100+.5)/100
115 LET T5=0
116 LET X9=0
117 LET N1=0
118 LET N2=0
119 LET E1=0
120 LET E2=0
121 REM INTRODUCTION
122 PRINT "DO YOU WANT THE INSTRUCTIONS (YES-TYPE 1, NO-TYPE 0)";
123 INPUT Z9
124 PRINT
125 PRINT
126 IF Z9<1 THEN 200
130 PRINT "THIS PROGRAM PLAYS THE STOCK MARKET.  YOU WILL BE GIVEN"
132 PRINT "$10,000 AND MAY BUY OR SELL STOCKS.  THE STOCK PRICES WILL"
134 PRINT "BE GENERATED RANDOMLY AND THEREFORE THIS MODEL DOES NOT"
135 PRINT "REPRESENT EXACTLY WHAT HAPPENS ON THE EXCHANGE.  A TABLE"
136 PRINT "OF AVAILABLE STOCKS, THEIR PRICES, AND THE NUMBER OF SHARES"
137 PRINT "IN YOUR PORTFOLIO WILL BE PRINTED.  FOLLOWING THIS, THE"
138 PRINT "INITIALS OF EACH STOCK WILL BE PRINTED WITH A QUESTION"
139 PRINT "MARK.  HERE YOU INDICATE A TRANSACTION.  TO BUY A STOCK"
140 PRINT "TYPE +NNN, TO SELL A STOCK TYPE -NNN, WHERE NNN IS THE"
141 PRINT "NUMBER OF SHARES.  A BROKERAGE FEE OF 1% WILL BE CHARGED"
142 PRINT "ON ALL TRANSACTIONS.  NOTE THAT IF A STOCK'S VALUE DROPS"
143 PRINT "TO ZERO IT MAY REBOUND TO A POSITIVE VALUE AGAIN.  YOU"
144 PRINT "HAVE $10,000 TO INVEST.  USE INTEGERS FOR ALL YOUR INPUTS."
145 PRINT "(NOTE:  TO GET A 'FEEL' FOR THE MARKET RUN FOR AT LEAST"
146 PRINT "10 DAYS)"
147 PRINT "-----GOOD LUCK!-----"
200 REM GENERATION OF STOCK TABLE; INPUT REQUESTS
210 REM INITIAL STOCK VALUES
220 LET S(1)=100
230 LET S(2)=85
240 LET S(3)=150
250 LET S(4)=140
260 LET S(5)=110
265 REM INITIAL T8 - # DAYS FOR FIRST TREND SLOPE (A)
266 LET T8=INT(4.99*RND(X)+1)
267 REM RANDOMIZE SIGN OF FIRST TREND SLOPE (A)
268 IF RND(X)>.5 THEN 270
269 LET A=-A
270 REM RANDOMIZE INITIAL VALUES
280 GOSUB 830
285 REM INITIAL PORTFOLIO CONTENTS
290 FOR I=1 TO 5
300 LET P(I)=0
305 LET Z(I)=0
310 NEXT I
320 PRINT
330 PRINT
333 REM INITIALIZE CASH ASSETS:C
335 LET C=10000
338 REM PRINT INITIAL PORTFOLIO
340 PRINT "STOCK"," ","INITIALS","PRICE/SHARE"
350 PRINT "INT. BALLISTIC MISSILES","  IBM",S(1)
352 PRINT "RED CROSS OF AMERICA","  RCA",S(2)
354 PRINT "LICHTENSTEIN, BUMRAP & JOKE","  LBJ",S(3)
356 PRINT "AMERICAN BANKRUPT CO.","  ABC",S(4)
358 PRINT "CENSURED BOOKS STORE","  CBS",S(5)
360 PRINT
361 REM NYSE AVERAGE:Z5; TEMP. VALUE:Z4; NET CHANGE:Z6
363 LET Z4=Z5
364 LET Z5=0
365 LET T=0
370 FOR I=1 TO 5
375 LET Z5=Z5+S(I)
380 LET T=T+S(I)*P(I)
390 NEXT I
391 LET Z5=INT(100*(Z5/5)+.5)/100
392 LET Z6=INT((Z5-Z4)*100+.5)/100
393 REM TOTAL ASSETS:D
394 LET D=T+C
395 IF X9>0 THEN 398
396 PRINT "NEW YORK STOCK EXCHANGE AVERAGE: "Z5
397 GO TO 399
398 PRINT "NEW YORK STOCK EXCHANGE AVERAGE: "Z5"   NET CHANGE: "Z6
399 PRINT
400 LET T=INT(100*T+.5)/100
401 PRINT "TOTAL STOCK ASSETS ARE    $";T
403 LET C=INT(100*C+.5)/100
405 PRINT "TOTAL CASH ASSETS ARE     $";C
407 LET D=INT(100*D+.5)/100
408 PRINT "TOTAL ASSETS ARE          $";D
410 PRINT
411 IF X9=0 THEN 416
412 PRINT "DO YOU WISH TO CONTINUE (YES-TYPE 1, NO-TYPE 0)";
413 INPUT G9
414 IF G9<1 THEN 998
416 REM INPUT TRANSACTIONS
420 PRINT "WHAT IS YOUR TRANSACTION IN"
430 PRINT "IBM";
440 INPUT Z(1)
450 PRINT "RCA";
460 INPUT Z(2)
470 PRINT "LBJ";
480 INPUT Z(3)
490 PRINT "ABC";
500 INPUT Z(4)
510 PRINT "CBS";
520 INPUT Z(5)
525 PRINT
530 REM TOTAL DAY'S PURCHASES IN $:P5
540 LET P5=0
```

```
550 REM TOTAL DAY'S SALES IN $:S5
560 LET S5=0
570 FOR I=1 TO 5
575 LET Z(I)=INT(Z(I)+.5)
580 IF Z(I)<=0 THEN 610
590 LET P5=P5+Z(I)*S(I)
600 GO TO 620
610 LET S5=S5-Z(I)*S(I)
612 IF -Z(I)<=P(I) THEN 620
614 PRINT "YOU HAVE OVERSOLD A STOCK; TRY AGAIN."
616 GO TO 420
620 NEXT I
622 REM TOTAL VALUE OF TRANSACTIONS:T5
625 LET T5=P5+S5
630 REM BROKERAGE FEE:B5
640 LET B5=INT(.01*T5*100+.5)/100
650 REM CASH ASSETS=OLD CASH ASSETS-TOTAL PURCHASES
652 REM -BROKERAGE FEES+TOTAL SALES:C5
654 LET C5=C-P5-B5+S5
656 IF C5>=0 THEN 674
658 PRINT "YOU HAVE USED $";-C5"MORE THAN YOU HAVE."
660 GO TO 420
674 LET C=C5
675 REM CALCULATE NEW PORTFOLIO
680 FOR I=1 TO 5
690 LET P(I)=P(I)+Z(I)
700 NEXT I
710 REM CALCULATE NEW STOCK VALUES
720 GOSUB 830
750 REM PRINT PORTFOLIO
751 REM BELL RINGING=DIFFERENT ON MANY COMPUTERS
752 FOR I=1 TO 20
753 PRINT CHRS(135);
754 NEXT I
755 PRINT
756 PRINT "**********  END OF DAY'S TRADING"
757 PRINT
758 PRINT
755 IF X9<1 THEN 769
769 PRINT "STOCK","PRICE/SHARE","HOLDINGS","VALUE","NET PRICE CHANGE"
770 PRINT "IBM", S(1), P(1), S(1)*P(1), C(1)
771 PRINT "RCA", S(2), P(2), S(2)*P(2), C(2)
772 PRINT "LBJ", S(3), P(3), S(3)*P(3), C(3)
773 PRINT "ABC", S(4), P(4), S(4)*P(4), C(4)
774 PRINT "CBS", S(5), P(5), S(5)*P(5), C(5)
775 LET X9=1
780 PRINT
790 PRINT
810 GO TO 360
829 REM NEW STOCK VALUES = SUBROUTINE
830 REM RANDOMLY PRODUCE NEW STOCK VALUES BASED ON PREVIOUS
831 REM DAY'S VALUES
832 REM N1,N2 ARE RANDOM NUMBERS OF DAYS WHICH RESPECTIVELY
833 REM DETERMINE WHEN STOCK I1 WILL INCREASE 10 PTS. AND STOCK
834 REM I2 WILL DECREASE 10 PTS.
840 REM IF N1 DAYS HAVE PASSED, PICK AN I1, SET E1, DETERMINE NEW N1
841 IF N1>0 THEN 850
845 LET I1=INT(4.99*RND(X)+1)
846 LET N1=INT(4.99*RND(X)+1)
847 LET E1=1
850 REM IF N2 DAYS HAVE PASSED, PICK AN I2, SET E2, DETERMINE NEW N2
851 IF N2>0 THEN 860
855 LET I2=INT(4.99*RND(X)+1)
856 LET N2=INT(4.99*RND(X)+1)
857 LET E2=1
860 REM DEDUCT ONE DAY FROM N1 AND N2
861 LET N1=N1-1
862 LET N2=N2-1
898 REM LOOP THROUGH ALL STOCKS
900 FOR I=1 TO 5
910 LET X1=RND(X)
915 IF X1>.25 THEN 920
916 LET X1=.25
917 GO TO 935
920 IF X1>.50 THEN 925
921 LET X1=.50
922 GO TO 935
925 IF X1>.75 THEN 930
926 LET X1=.75
927 GO TO 935
930 LET X1=0.0
931 REM BIG CHANGE CONSTANT:W3  (SET TO ZERO INITIALLY)
935 LET W3=0
936 IF E1<1 THEN 945
937 IF INT(I1+.5)<>INT(I+.5) THEN 945
938 REM ADD 10 PTS. TO THIS STOCK;  RESET E1
939 LET W3=10
943 LET E1=0
945 IF E2<1 THEN 955
947 IF INT(I2+.5)<>INT(I+.5) THEN 955
948 REM SUBTRACT 10 PTS. FROM THIS STOCK;  RESET E2
949 LET W3=W3-10
953 LET E2=0
954 REM C(I) IS CHANGE IN STOCK VALUE
955 LET C(I)=INT(A*S(I))+X1+INT(3-6*RND(X)+.5)+W3
956 LET C(I)=INT(100*C(I)+.5)/100
957 LET S(I)=S(I)+C(I)
960 IF S(I)>0 THEN 967
964 LET C(I)=0
965 LET S(I)=0
966 GO TO 970
967 LET S(I)=INT(100*S(I)+.5)/100
970 NEXT I
972 REM AFTER T8 DAYS RANDOMLY CHANGE TREND SIGN AND SLOPE
973 LET T8=T8-1
974 IF T8<1 THEN 985
980 RETURN
985 REM RANDOMLY CHANGE TREND SIGN AND SLOPE (A), AND DURATION
986 REM OF TREND (T8)
990 LET T8=INT(4.99*RND(X)+1)
992 LET A=INT((RND(X)/10)*100+.5)/100
993 LET S4=RND(X)
994 IF S4<=.5 THEN 997
995 LET A=-A
997 RETURN
998 PRINT "HOPE YOU HAD FUN!!"
999 END
```

SAMPLE RUN

```
                    THE STOCK MARKET
DO YOU WANT THE INSTRUCTIONS (YES-TYPE 1, NO-TYPE 0)? 1


THIS PROGRAM PLAYS THE STOCK MARKET.   YOU WILL BE GIVEN
$10,000 AND MAY BUY OR SELL STOCKS.   THE STOCK PRICES WILL
BE GENERATED RANDOMLY AND THEREFORE THIS MODEL DOES NOT
REPRESENT EXACTLY WHAT HAPPENS ON THE EXCHANGE.   A TABLE
OF AVAILABLE STOCKS, THEIR PRICES, AND THE NUMBER OF SHARES
IN YOUR PORTFOLIO WILL BE PRINTED.   FOLLOWING THIS, THE
INITIALS OF EACH STOCK WILL BE PRINTED WITH A QUESTION
MARK.   HERE YOU INDICATE A TRANSACTION.   TO BUY A STOCK
TYPE +NNN, TO SELL A STOCK TYPE -NNN, WHERE NNN IS THE
NUMBER OF SHARES.   A BROKERAGE FEE OF 1% WILL BE CHARGED
ON ALL TRANSACTIONS.   NOTE THAT IF A STOCK'S VALUE DROPS
TO ZERO IT MAY REBOUND TO A POSITIVE VALUE AGAIN.   YOU
HAVE $10,000 TO INVEST.   USE INTEGERS FOR ALL YOUR INPUTS.
(NOTE:  TO GET A 'FEEL' FOR THE MARKET RUN FOR AT LEAST
10 DAYS)
-----GOOD LUCK!-----
```

STOCK	INITIALS	PRICE/SHARE
INT. BALLISTIC MISSILES	IBM	107.25
RED CROSS OF AMERICA	RCA	85.75
LICHTENSTEIN, BUMRAP & JOKE	LBJ	147.5
AMERICAN BANKRUPT CO.	ABC	137.75
CENSURED BOOKS STORE	CBS	99.25

```
NEW YORK STOCK EXCHANGE AVERAGE:  115.5

TOTAL STOCK ASSETS ARE    $ 0
TOTAL CASH ASSETS ARE     $ 10000
TOTAL ASSETS ARE          $ 10000

WHAT IS YOUR TRANSACTION IN
IBM? 20
RCA? 5
LBJ? 0
ABC? 5
CBS? 10


********** END OF DAY'S TRADING
```

STOCK	PRICE/SHARE	HOLDINGS	VALUE	NET PRICE CHANGE
IBM	107.75	20	2155	.5
RCA	83	5	415	-2.75
LBJ	145	0	0	-2.5
ABC	132.75	5	663.75	-5
CBS	95.75	10	957.5	-3.5

```
NEW YORK STOCK EXCHANGE AVERAGE:  112.85   NET CHANGE: -2.65

TOTAL STOCK ASSETS ARE    $ 4191.25
TOTAL CASH ASSETS ARE     $ 5702.45
TOTAL ASSETS ARE          $ 9893.7

DO YOU WISH TO CONTINUE (YES-TYPE 1, NO-TYPE 0)? 1
WHAT IS YOUR TRANSACTION IN
IBM? 10
RCA? 10
LBJ? 0
ABC? 0
CBS? 10


********** END OF DAY'S TRADING
```

STOCK	PRICE/SHARE	HOLDINGS	VALUE	NET PRICE CHANGE
IBM	99.75	30	2992.5	-8
RCA	78.75	15	1181.25	-4.25
LBJ	140.5	0	0	-4.5
ABC	122.75	5	613.75	-10
CBS	90.25	20	1805	-5.5

```
NEW YORK STOCK EXCHANGE AVERAGE:  106.4   NET CHANGE: -6.45

TOTAL STOCK ASSETS ARE    $ 6592.5
TOTAL CASH ASSETS ARE     $ 2808.8
TOTAL ASSETS ARE          $ 9401.3

DO YOU WISH TO CONTINUE (YES-TYPE 1, NO-TYPE 0)? 1
WHAT IS YOUR TRANSACTION IN
IBM? 0
RCA? 0
LBJ? 0
ABC? 0
CBS? 0


********** END OF DAY'S TRADING
```

STOCK	PRICE/SHARE	HOLDINGS	VALUE	NET PRICE CHANGE
IBM	92.25	30	2767.5	-7.5
RCA	75.75	15	1136.25	-3
LBJ	129.5	0	0	-11
ABC	115.25	5	576.25	-7.5
CBS	84.75	20	1695	-5.5

```
NEW YORK STOCK EXCHANGE AVERAGE:  99.5   NET CHANGE: -6.9

TOTAL STOCK ASSETS ARE    $ 6175
TOTAL CASH ASSETS ARE     $ 2808.8
TOTAL ASSETS ARE          $ 8983.8

DO YOU WISH TO CONTINUE (YES-TYPE 1, NO-TYPE 0)? 1
WHAT IS YOUR TRANSACTION IN
IBM? 0
RCA? 0
LBJ? 0
ABC? 0
CBS? 0
```

```
********** END OF DAY'S TRADING
```

STOCK	PRICE/SHARE	HOLDINGS	VALUE	NET PRICE CHANGE
IBM	87.25	30	2617.5	-5
RCA	74.5	15	1117.5	-1.25
LBJ	126.5	0	0	-3
ABC	111	5	555	-4.25
CBS	82.25	20	1645	-2.5

```
NEW YORK STOCK EXCHANGE AVERAGE:  96.3   NET CHANGE: -3.2

TOTAL STOCK ASSETS ARE    $ 5935
TOTAL CASH ASSETS ARE     $ 2808.8
TOTAL ASSETS ARE          $ 8743.8

DO YOU WISH TO CONTINUE (YES-TYPE 1, NO-TYPE 0)? 1
WHAT IS YOUR TRANSACTION IN
IBM? 0
RCA? 0
LBJ? 0
ABC? 0
CBS? 0


********** END OF DAY'S TRADING
```

STOCK	PRICE/SHARE	HOLDINGS	VALUE	NET PRICE CHANGE
IBM	89.75	30	2692.5	2.5
RCA	87.25	15	1308.75	12.75
LBJ	125.75	0	0	-.75
ABC	114	5	570	3
CBS	83.25	20	1665	1

```
NEW YORK STOCK EXCHANGE AVERAGE:  100   NET CHANGE: 3.7

TOTAL STOCK ASSETS ARE    $ 6236.25
TOTAL CASH ASSETS ARE     $ 2808.8
TOTAL ASSETS ARE          $ 9045.05

DO YOU WISH TO CONTINUE (YES-TYPE 1, NO-TYPE 0)? 1
WHAT IS YOUR TRANSACTION IN
IBM? 5
RCA? 10
LBJ? 5
ABC? 0
CBS? 10

YOU HAVE USED $ 1.52995 MORE THAN YOU HAVE.
WHAT IS YOUR TRANSACTION IN
IBM? 5
RCA? 10
LBJ? 5
ABC? 0
CBS? 9


********** END OF DAY'S TRADING
```

STOCK	PRICE/SHARE	HOLDINGS	VALUE	NET PRICE CHANGE
IBM	93.75	35	3281.25	4
RCA	95	25	2375	7.75
LBJ	130.75	5	653.75	5
ABC	122.75	5	613.75	8.75
CBS	85.75	29	2486.75	2.5

```
NEW YORK STOCK EXCHANGE AVERAGE:  105.6   NET CHANGE: 5.6

TOTAL STOCK ASSETS ARE    $ 9410.5
TOTAL CASH ASSETS ARE     $ 82.56
TOTAL ASSETS ARE          $ 9493.06

DO YOU WISH TO CONTINUE (YES-TYPE 1, NO-TYPE 0)? 1
WHAT IS YOUR TRANSACTION IN
IBM? 0
RCA? 0
LBJ? 0
ABC? 0
CBS? 0


********** END OF DAY'S TRADING
```

STOCK	PRICE/SHARE	HOLDINGS	VALUE	NET PRICE CHANGE
IBM	98	35	3430	4.25
RCA	100.5	25	2512.5	5.5
LBJ	139.5	5	697.5	8.75
ABC	130.75	5	653.75	8
CBS	89.5	29	2595.5	3.75

```
NEW YORK STOCK EXCHANGE AVERAGE:  111.65   NET CHANGE: 6.05

TOTAL STOCK ASSETS ARE    $ 9889.25
TOTAL CASH ASSETS ARE     $ 82.56
TOTAL ASSETS ARE          $ 9971.81

DO YOU WISH TO CONTINUE (YES-TYPE 1, NO-TYPE 0)? 1
```

SYNONM

WORD SYNONYMS

Description

A synonym of a word is another word in the English language
which has the same, or very nearly the same, meaning. This
program tests your knowledge of synonyms of a few common words.

The computer chooses a word and asks you for a synonym. The
computer then tells you whether you're right or wrong. If you
can't think of a synonym, type "HELP" which causes a synonym
to be printed.

You may put in words of your choice in the data statements (510-600).
The number following DATA in Statement 500 is the total number
of data statements. In each data statement, the first number
is the number of words in that statement.

Can you think of a way to make this into a more general kind of
CAI program for any subject?

Program Author

Walt Koetke
Lexington High School
Lexington, MA   02173

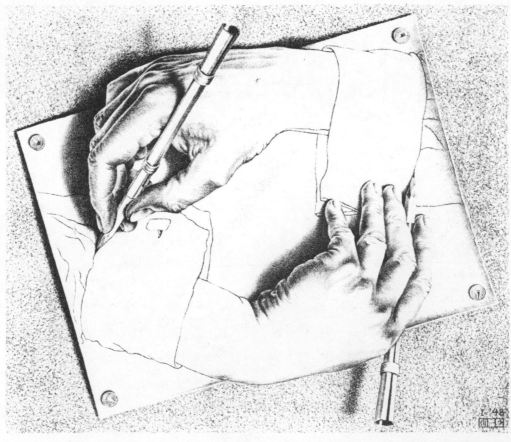

PROGRAM LISTING

```
LIST
SYNONM  03:17 PM        09-JUL-73
5 REM *** SYNONM CONVERTED TO RSTS/E BASIC-PLUS BY DAVE AHL, DIGITAL
10 DIM R$(5),W$(10),L(30),R(30)
20 R$(1)="RIGHT":R$(2)="CORRECT":R$(3)="FINE":R$(4)="GOOD!":R$(5)="CHECK"
70 RANDOMIZE:C=0:PRINT:PRINT "SYNONYMS":PRINT
90 PRINT "A SYNONYM OF A WORD MEANS ANOTHER WORD IN THE ENGLISH"
100 PRINT "LANGUAGE WHICH HAS THE SAME OR VERY NEARLY THE SAME"
110 PRINT "MEANING. ":PRINT
130 PRINT "I CHOOSE A WORD -- YOU TYPE A SYNONYM. "
140 PRINT "IF YOU CAN'T THINK OF A SYNONYM, TYPE THE WORD 'HELP'"
145 PRINT "AND I WILL TELL YOU A SYNONYM. ":PRINT
150 RESTORE:C=C+1:READ N
160 IF C>N THEN 420
170 N1=INT(RND*N+1)
174 IF R(N1)=1 THEN 170
176 R(N1)=1
180 FOR I=1 TO N1
190 READ N2
200 FOR J=1 TO N2
210 READ W$(J)
220 NEXT J
230 NEXT I
232 L(J)=J FOR J=1 TO N2
235 L(0)=N2:G=1:PRINT
237 L(G)=L(L(0)):L(0)=N2-1:PRINT
240 PRINT "     WHAT IS A SYNONYM OF "W$(G);:INPUT A$
250 IF A$="HELP" THEN 340
260 FOR J=1 TO N2
270 IF G=J THEN 290
280 IF A$=W$(J) THEN 320
290 NEXT J
300 PRINT "     TRY AGAIN. "
310 GOTO 240
320 PRINT R$(RND*5+1)
330 GOTO 150
340 G1=INT(RND*L(0)+1)
360 PRINT "**** A SYNONYM OF "W$(G)" IS "W$(L(G1))". "
365 PRINT
370 L(G1)=L(L(0)):L(0)=L(0)-1
390 GOTO 240
420 PRINT:PRINT "SYNONYM DRILL COMPLETED. ":STOP
500 DATA 10
510 DATA 5,"FIRST","START","BEGINNING","ONSET","INITIAL"
520 DATA 5,"SIMILAR","ALIKE","SAME","LIKE","RESEMBLING"
530 DATA 5,"MODEL","PATTERN","PROTOTYPE","STANDARD","CRITERION"
540 DATA 5,"SMALL","INSIGNIFICANT","LITTLE","TINY","MINUTE"
550 DATA 6,"STOP","HALT","STAY","ARREST","CHECK","STANDSTILL"
560 DATA 6,"HOUSE","DWELLING","RESIDENCE","DOMICILE","LODGING","HABITATION"
570 DATA 7,"PIT","HOLE","HOLLOW","WELL","GULF","CHASM","ABYSS"
580 DATA 7,"PUSH","SHOVE","THRUST","PROD","POKE","BUTT","PRESS"
590 DATA 6,"RED","ROUGE","SCARLET","CRIMSON","FLAME","RUBY"
600 DATA 7,"PAIN","SUFFERING","HURT","MISERY","DISTRESS","ACHE","DISCOMFORT"
999 END

READY
```

SAMPLE RUN

```
RUN
SYNONM  03:19 PM        09-JUL-73

SYNONYMS

A SYNONYM OF A WORD MEANS ANOTHER WORD IN THE ENGLISH
LANGUAGE WHICH HAS THE SAME OR VERY NEARLY THE SAME
MEANING.

I CHOOSE A WORD -- YOU TYPE A SYNONYM.
IF YOU CAN'T THINK OF A SYNONYM, TYPE THE WORD 'HELP'
AND I WILL TELL YOU A SYNONYM.


     WHAT IS A SYNONYM OF FIRST? START
CORRECT

     WHAT IS A SYNONYM OF PIT? WELL
CHECK

     WHAT IS A SYNONYM OF SMALL? TINY
CHECK

     WHAT IS A SYNONYM OF HOUSE? HOME
     TRY AGAIN.
     WHAT IS A SYNONYM OF HOUSE? DWELLING
RIGHT

     WHAT IS A SYNONYM OF MODEL? SIMULATION
     TRY AGAIN.
     WHAT IS A SYNONYM OF MODEL? HELP
**** A SYNONYM OF MODEL IS PROTOTYPE.

     WHAT IS A SYNONYM OF MODEL? STANDARD
CHECK

     WHAT IS A SYNONYM OF RED? ROSE
     TRY AGAIN.
     WHAT IS A SYNONYM OF RED? HELP
**** A SYNONYM OF RED IS FLAME.

     WHAT IS A SYNONYM OF RED? HELP
**** A SYNONYM OF RED IS RUBY.

     WHAT IS A SYNONYM OF RED? CRIMSON
CHECK

     WHAT IS A SYNONYM OF SIMILAR? SAME
CORRECT

     WHAT IS A SYNONYM OF PUSH? SHOVE
GOOD!

     WHAT IS A SYNONYM OF STOP? END
     TRY AGAIN.
     WHAT IS A SYNONYM OF STOP? HALT
GOOD!

     WHAT IS A SYNONYM OF PAIN? DISTRESS
CHECK

SYNONYM DRILL COMPLETED.
```

TARGET

DESTROY A TARGET IN 3-D SPACE

Description

In this program, you are firing a weapon from a spaceship in 3-dimensional space. Your ship, the Starship Enterprise, is located at the origin (0,0,0) of a set of x,y,z coordinates. You will be told the approximate location of the target in 3-dimensional rectangular coordinates, the approximate angular deviation from the x and z axes in both radius and degrees, and the approximate distance to the target.

Given this information, you then proceed to shoot at the target. A shot within 20 kilometers of the target destroys it. After each shot, you are given information as to the position of the explosion of your shot and a somewhat improved estimate of the location of the target. Fortunately, this is just practice and the target doesn't shoot back. After you have attained proficiency, you ought to be able to destroy a target in 3 or 4 shots. However, attaining proficiency might take a while!

Program Author

H. David Crockett
5609 Wimbleton Way
Fort Worth, TX 76133

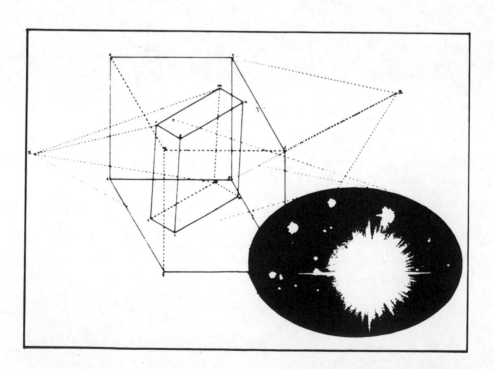

Illustration by John Nelson,
Scott, Foresman and Co.

PROGRAM LISTING

```
100 R=1\R1=57.296\RANDOMIZE
110 PRINT "YOU ARE THE WEAPONS OFFICER ON THE STAR SHIP ENTERPRISE"
120 PRINT "AND THIS IS A TEST TO SEE HOW ACCURATE A SHOT YOU"
130 PRINT "ARE IN A THREE-DIMENSIONAL RANGE.  YOU WILL BE TOLD"
140 PRINT "THE RADIAN OFFSET FOR THE X AND Z AXES, THE LOCATION"
150 PRINT "OF THE TARGET IN THREE-DIMENSIONAL RECTANGULAR COORDINATES,"
160 PRINT "THE APPROXIMATE NUMBER OF DEGREES FROM THE X AND Z"
170 PRINT "AXES, AND THE APPROXIMATE DISTANCE TO THE TARGET."
180 PRINT "YOU WILL THEN PROCEED TO SHOOT AT THE TARGET UNTIL IT IS"
190 PRINT "DESTROYED!"\PRINT\PRINT "GOOD LUCK!!"\PRINT\PRINT
220 A=RND*2*PI\B=RND*2*PI\Q=INT(A*R1)\W=INT(B*R1)
260 PRINT "RADIANS FROM X AXIS ="A"    FROM Z AXIS ="B
270 PRINT "APPROX DEGREES FROM X AXIS ="Q"    FROM Z AXIS ="W
280 P=100000*RND+RND\X=SIN(B)*COS(A)*P\Y=SIN(B)*SIN(A)*P\Z=COS(B)*P
340 PRINT "TARGET SIGHTED: APPROX COORDINATES X="X"  Y="Y"  Z="Z
345 R=R+1\IF R>5 THEN 390
350 ON R GOTO 355,360,365,370,375
355 P3=INT(P*.05)*20\GOTO 390
360 P3=INT(P*.1)*10\GOTO 390
365 P3=INT(P*.5)*2\GOTO 390
370 P3=INT(P)\GOTO 390
375 P3=P
390 PRINT "     ESTIMATED DISTANCE="P3
400 INPUT "INPUT ANGLE DEVIATION FROM X, DEVIATION FROM Z, DISTANCE";A1,B1,P2
410 PRINT\IF P2<20 THEN PRINT "YOU BLEW YOURSELF UP!!"\GOTO 580
420 A1=A1/R1\B1=B1/R1\PRINT "RADIANS FROM X AXIS ="A1"    FROM Z AXIS ="B1
480 X1=P2*SIN(B1)*COS(A1)\Y1=P2*SIN(B1)*SIN(A1)\Z1=P2*COS(B1)
510 D=((X1-X)^2+(Y1-Y)^2+(Z1-Z)^2)^(1/2)
520 IF D>20 THEN 670
530 PRINT\PRINT " * * * HIT * * *    TARGET IS NON-FUNCTIONAL"\PRINT
550 PRINT "DISTANCE OF EXPLOSION FROM TARGET WAS"D"KILOMETERS"
570 PRINT\PRINT "MISSION ACCOMPLISHED IN"R"SHOTS."
580 R=0\FOR I=1 TO 5\PRINT\NEXT I\PRINT "NEXT TARGET...."\PRINT\GOTO 220
670 X2=X1-X\Y2=Y1-Y\Z2=Z1-Z\IF X2<0 THEN 730
710 PRINT "SHOT IN FRONT OF TARGET"X2"KILOMETERS."\GOTO 740
730 PRINT "SHOT BEHIND TARGET";-X2"KILOMETERS."
740 IF Y2<0 THEN 770
750 PRINT "SHOT TO LEFT OF TARGET"Y2"KILOMETERS."\GOTO 780
770 PRINT "SHOT TO RIGHT OF TARGET";-Y2"KILOMETERS."
780 IF Z2<0 THEN 810
790 PRINT "SHOT ABOVE TARGET"Z2"KILOMETERS."\GOTO 8220
810 PRINT "SHOT BELOW TARGET";-Z2"KILOMETERS."
820 PRINT "APPROX POSITION OF EXPLOSION: X="X1"  Y="Y1"  Z="Z1
830 PRINT "   DISTANCE FROM TARGET ="D\PRINT\PRINT\PRINT\GOTO 345
999 END
```

SAMPLE RUN

```
YOU ARE THE WEAPONS OFFICER ON THE STAR SHIP ENTERPRISE
AND THIS IS A TEST TO SEE HOW ACCURATE A SHOT YOU
ARE IN A THREE-DIMENSIONAL RANGE.  YOU WILL BE TOLD
THE RADIAN OFFSET FOR THE X AND Z AXES, THE LOCATION
OF THE TARGET IN THREE-DIMENSIONAL RECTANGULAR COORDINATES,
THE APPROXIMATE NUMBER OF DEGREES FROM THE X AND Z
AXES, AND THE APPROXIMATE DISTANCE TO THE TARGET.
YOU WILL THEN PROCEED TO SHOOT AT THE TARGET UNTIL IT IS
DESTROYED!

GOOD LUCK!!


RADIANS FROM X AXIS = 6.18367    FROM Z AXIS = 1.0759
APPROX DEGREES FROM X AXIS = 354    FROM Z AXIS = 61
TARGET SIGHTED: APPROX COORDINATES X= 14882.5   Y=-1485.97   Z= 8072.02
    ESTIMATED DISTANCE= 16990
INPUT ANGLE DEVIATION FROM X, DEVIATION FROM Z, DISTANCE? 354,61,16990

RADIANS FROM X AXIS = 6.17844    FROM Z AXIS = 1.06465
SHOT BEHIND TARGET 104.188 KILOMETERS.
SHOT TO RIGHT OF TARGET 67.6549 KILOMETERS.
SHOT ABOVE TARGET 164.96 KILOMETERS.
APPROX POSITION OF EXPLOSION: X= 14778.3   Y=-1553.62   Z= 8236.98
    DISTANCE FROM TARGET = 206.505



    ESTIMATED DISTANCE= 16994
INPUT ANGLE DEVIATION FROM X, DEVIATION FROM Z, DISTANCE? 353.5,60.5,16990

RADIANS FROM X AXIS = 6.16972    FROM Z AXIS = 1.05592
SHOT BEHIND TARGET 190.291 KILOMETERS.
SHOT TO RIGHT OF TARGET 188.358 KILOMETERS.
SHOT ABOVE TARGET 294.319 KILOMETERS.
APPROX POSITION OF EXPLOSION: X= 14692.2   Y=-1674.32   Z= 8366.34
    DISTANCE FROM TARGET = 397.886



    ESTIMATED DISTANCE= 16995
INPUT ANGLE DEVIATION FROM X, DEVIATION FROM Z, DISTANCE? 354.4,61.8,16995

RADIANS FROM X AXIS = 6.18542    FROM Z AXIS = 1.07861
SHOT IN FRONT OF TARGET 23.6973 KILOMETERS.
SHOT TO LEFT OF TARGET 24.0381 KILOMETERS.
SHOT BELOW TARGET 40.9536 KILOMETERS.
APPROX POSITION OF EXPLOSION: X= 14906.2   Y=-1461.93   Z= 8031.06
    DISTANCE FROM TARGET = 53.0716



    ESTIMATED DISTANCE= 16995.7
INPUT ANGLE DEVIATION FROM X, DEVIATION FROM Z, DISTANCE? 354.3,61.9,16996

RADIANS FROM X AXIS = 6.18368    FROM Z AXIS = 1.08035
SHOT IN FRONT OF TARGET 35.9248 KILOMETERS.
SHOT TO RIGHT OF TARGET 3.45166 KILOMETERS.
SHOT BELOW TARGET 66.6372 KILOMETERS.
APPROX POSITION OF EXPLOSION: X= 14918.4   Y=-1489.42   Z= 8005.38
    DISTANCE FROM TARGET = 75.7828



    ESTIMATED DISTANCE= 16995.7
INPUT ANGLE DEVIATION FROM X, DEVIATION FROM Z, DISTANCE? 354.5,61.8,16996

RADIANS FROM X AXIS = 6.18717    FROM Z AXIS = 1.07861
SHOT IN FRONT OF TARGET 27.1035 KILOMETERS.
SHOT TO LEFT OF TARGET 49.9703 KILOMETERS.
SHOT BELOW TARGET 40.4814 KILOMETERS.
APPROX POSITION OF EXPLOSION: X= 14909.6   Y=-1436   Z= 8031.54
    DISTANCE FROM TARGET = 69.7882



    ESTIMATED DISTANCE= 16995.7
INPUT ANGLE DEVIATION FROM X, DEVIATION FROM Z, DISTANCE? 354..6,61.9
ILLEGAL NUMBER AT LINE 400
INPUT ANGLE DEVIATION FROM X, DEVIATION FROM Z, DISTANCE? 354.6,61.9,16996

RADIANS FROM X AXIS = 6.18891    FROM Z AXIS = 1.08035
SHOT IN FRONT OF TARGET 43.5186 KILOMETERS.
SHOT TO LEFT OF TARGET 74.681 KILOMETERS.
SHOT BELOW TARGET 66.6372 KILOMETERS.
APPROX POSITION OF EXPLOSION: X= 14926   Y=-1411.28   Z= 8005.38
    DISTANCE FROM TARGET = 109.14
```

3D PLOT

PLOTS A FAMILY OF CURVES

Description

3DPLOT will plot the family of curves of any function. The function Z is plotted as "rising" out of the x-y plane with x and y inside a circle of radius 30. The resultant plot looks almost 3-dimensional.

You set the function you want plotted in line 5. As with any mathematical plot, some functions come out "prettier" than others. Here are some that work nicely:

```
5 DEF FNA(Z) = 30*EXP (-Z*Z/100)
5 DEF FNA(Z) = SQR (900.01-Z*Z)*.9-2
5 DEF FNA(Z) = 30*(COS(Z/16))↑2
5 DEF FNA(Z) = 30-30*SIN (Z/18)
5 DEF FNA(Z) = 30*EXP (-COS(Z/16))-30
    (Bessel function--Summerfeld's Integral)
5 DEF FNA(Z) = 30*SIN (Z/10)
```

One of the shortest programs submitted (14 lines), 3DPLOT has to rank as perhaps the most clever.

Program Author

Mark Bramhall
Digital Equipment Corp.
Maynard, MA 01754

PROGRAM LISTING

```
5 DEF FNA(Z)=30*EXP(-Z*Z/100)
100 PRINT
110 FOR X=-30 TO 30 STEP 1.5
120 L=0
130 Y1=5*INT(SQR(900-X*X)/5)
140 FOR Y=Y1 TO -Y1 STEP -5
150 Z=INT(25+FNA(SQR(X*X+Y*Y))-.7*Y)
160 IF Z<=L THEN 190
170 L=Z
180 PRINT TAB(Z)"*";
190 NEXT Y
200 PRINT
210 NEXT X
300 END
```

SAMPLE RUN

```
10 DEF FNA(Z)=30*(COS(Z/16))↑2
RUN
```

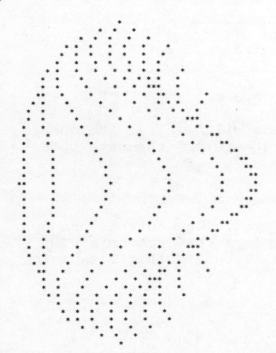

```
10 DEF FNA(Z)=30*EXP(-COS(Z/16))-30
·RUN
```

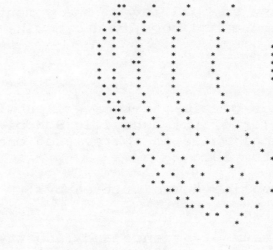

```
5 DEF FNA(Z)=30*EXP(-Z*Z/100)
RUNNH
```

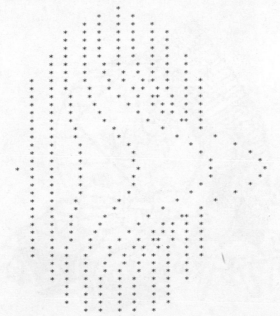

217

TIC TAC

Description

The game of tic-tac-toe hardly needs any introduction. In this
one, you play versus the computer. Moves are entered by row
number, a comma, and column number, as in the diagram below.

1,1	1,2	1,3
2,1	2,2	2,3
3,1	3,2	3,3

If you make any bad moves, the computer will win; if the computer makes a bad move, you can win; otherwise, the game ends
in a tie.

Source

Seven games of tic-tac-toe were submitted. One notable one by
Chase Ambler of the Asheville School plays the game on a VT05
CRT terminal while an abbreviated one by Dana Noftle fits into
an EduSystem 10.

The one published was written by:

Tom Kloos
Oregon Museum of Science and Industry
Portland, Oregon 97200

PROGRAM LISTING

```
120 PRINT"YOU HAVE THE OPPORTUNITY OF TRYING TO BEAT THE COMPUTER"
130 PRINT"AT TIC-TAC-TOE.  ENTER YOUR MOVES AS FOLLOWS!"
140 PRINT
150 DIM C(11)
160 DIM D(11)
170 FOR K=1 TO 11
180 READ C(K), D(K)
190 NEXT K
200 PRINT "...ROW NUMBER...COMMA...COLUMN NUMBER..."
210 PRINT
220 PRINT"ROWS ARE HORIZONTAL(ACROSS)...COLUMNS ARE VERTICAL(UP + DOWN)"
230 DIM B(9)
240 DIM A(3,3)
250 PRINT
260 PRINT "NEW GAME STARTED NOW,.........................."
270 FOR J=1 TO 3
280 FOR I=1 TO 3
290 LET A(I,J)=0
300 NEXT I
301 LET I=I-1
310 NEXT J
311 LET J=J-1
320 LET Z= 0
330 PRINT "YOUR MOVE",
340 INPUT R,C
350 PRINT
360 IF R>3 THEN 620
370 IF C>3 THEN 620
380 IF A(R,C) <> 0 THEN 620
390 LET A(R,C)=1
400 GOSUB 1660
410 IF Z =1 THEN 2070
420 REM MACHINE MOVE...
430 GOSUB 1100
440 REM TEST FOR GAME WIN...
450 GOSUB 1660
460 IF Z=0 THEN 650
470 REM PRINT GAME BOARD..
480 GO TO 490
490 PRINT
500 FOR K=1 TO 3
510 LET B=A(K,1)
520 LET D=A(K,2)
530 LET F=A(K,3)
540 GOSUB 840
550 IF K>2 THEN 570
560 PRINT "***************"
570 NEXT K
571 LET K=K-1
580 PRINT
590 IF Z <>0 THEN 2070
600 GO TO 330
610 STOP
620 PRINT "==== ILLEGAL MOVE == TRY AGAIN ===="
630 PRINT
640 GO TO 330
650 LET T2=0
660 FOR J=1 TO 3
670 FOR I=1 TO 3
680 IF A(I,J)<>0 THEN 700
690 LET T2=T2+1
700 NEXT I
701 LET I=I-1
710 NEXT J
711 LET J=J-1
720 IF  T2>0 THEN 750
730 GOSUB 1340
740 GO TO 480
750 IF T2>1 THEN 480
760 FOR J=1 TO 8
770 IF B(J)==2 THEN 800
780 NEXT J
781 LET J=J-1
790 GO TO 730
800 GOSUB 2000
810 GO TO 480
820 REM PRINT TIC-TAC-TOE BOARD ROW.....
830 REM
840 IF B<>0 THEN 910
850 PRINT "    *  ";
860 IF D<>0 THEN 940
870 PRINT "    *  ";
880 IF F<>0 THEN 970
890 PRINT "    "
900 GO TO 1070
910 IF B>0 THEN 1000
920 PRINT "YOU *  ";
930 GO TO 860
940 IF D>0 THEN 1020
950 PRINT "YOU *  ";
960 GO TO 880
970 IF F>0 THEN 1040
980 PRINT "YOU"
990 GO TO 900
1000 PRINT"PDP *  ";
1010 GO TO 860
1020 PRINT "PDP *  ";
1030 GO TO 880
1040 PRINT "PDP"
1050 GO TO900
1060 REM PRINT LEGENDS..
1070 PRINT "     *     "
1080 RETURN
1090 REM PROGRAM TO MAKE MOVE FOR THE MACHINE....
1100 LET M=INT(3.33*RND(M))
1110 LET N=INT(3.33333*RND(N))
1120 IF M=0 THEN 1100
1130 IF M>3 THEN 1100
1140 IF N=0 THEN 1110
1150 IF N>3 THEN 1110
1160 LET C(2)=M
1170 LET D(2)=N
1180 LET C(3)=N
1190 LET D(3)=M
1200 FOR I=1 TO 8
1210 IF B(I)>1 THEN 1370
1220 NEXT I
1221 LET I=I-1
1230 FOR I=1 TO 8
1240 IF B(I)<=1 THEN 1370
1250 NEXT I
1251 LET I=I-1
1260 IF R+C=0 THEN 1550
1270 FOR K=1 TO 11
1280 LET I=C(K)
1290 LET J=D(K)
1300 IF A(I,J)<>0 THEN 1330
1310 LET A(I,J)=1
1320 GO TO 1360
1330 NEXT K
1331 LET K=K-1
1340 PRINT "  ... TIE GAME ...   "
1350 LET Z=3
1360 RETURN
1370 IF I>3 THEN 1440
1380 FOR J=1 TO 3
1390 IF A(I,J)=0 THEN 1420
1400 NEXT J
1401 LET J=J-1
1410 GO TO 1360
1420 LET A(I,J)=1
1430 GO TO 1360
1440 IF I>6 THEN 1510
1450 FOR J=1 TO 3
1460 IF A(J,I-3)=0 THEN 1490
1470 NEXT J
1471 LET J=J-1
1480 GO TO 1360
1490 LET A(J,I-3)=1
1500 GO TO 1360
1510 IF I>7 THEN 1550
1520 FOR J=1 TO 3
1530 IF A(J,J)=0 THEN 1590
1540 NEXT J
1541 LET J=J-1
1550 IF A(1,3)=0 THEN 1610
1560 IF A(3,1)=0 THEN 1630
1570 LET A(2,2)=1
1580 GO TO 1360
1590 LET A(J,J)=1
1600 GO TO 1360
1610 LET A(1,3)=1
1620 GO TO 1360
1630 LET A(3,1)=1
1640 GO TO 1360
1650 REM PROGRAM TO TEST FOR GAME WINNER....
1660 LET T1=0
1670 FOR J=1 TO 9
1680 LET B(J)=0
1690 NEXT J
1691 LET J=J-1
1700 FOR J=1 TO 3
1710 FOR I=1 TO 3
1720 IF A(J,1)<>A(J,I) THEN 1750
1730 NEXT I
1731 LET I=I-1
1740 LET T1=A(J,I)
1750 NEXT J
1751 LET J=J-1
1760 FOR J=1 TO 3
1770 FOR I=1 TO 3
1780 IF A(1,J)<>A(I,J) THEN 1810
1790 NEXT I
1791 LET I=I-1
1800 LET T1=A(I,J)
1810 NEXT J
1811 LET J=J-1
1820 IF A(1,1)=A(3,3) THEN 1930
1830 IF A(3,1)=A(1,3) THEN 1970
1840 IF T1<>0 THEN 1990
1850 FOR J=1 TO 3
1860 FOR I=1 TO 3
1870 LET B(J)=B(J)+A(J,I)
1880 LET B(J+3)=B(J+3)+A(I,J)
1890 NEXT I
1891 LET I=I-1
1900 NEXT J
1901 LET J=J-1
1910 LET B(7)=A(1,1)+A(2,2)+A(3,3)
1920 RETURN
1930 IF A(2,2)=A(3,3) THEN 1950
1940 GO TO 1830
1950 LET T1=A(2,2)
1960 GO TO 1840
1970 IF A(2,2)=A(1,3) THEN 1950
1980 GO TO 1840
1990 IF T1>0 THEN 2030
2000 PRINT " ...YOU WIN THIS TIME..."
2010 LET Z=1
2020 GO TO 1850
2030 PRINT " ... THE PDP-8 WINS THIS TIME ..."
2040 LET Z=2
2050 GO TO 1850
2060 REM END OF TEST WINNER PROGRAM.......
2070 PRINT "DO YOU WANT TO PLAY ANOTHER GAME: YES(1), NO(0)",
2080 INPUT X1
2090 IF X1 = 1 THEN 250
2100 IF X1 = 0 THEN 2130
2110 PRINT "I SAID ONE OR ZERO: TRY AGAIN",
2120 GO TO 2080
2130 PRINT"IT'S BEEN FUN, COME AGAIN SOMETIME"
2140 GO TO 2160
2150 DATA 2,2,0,0,0,0,1,1,3,3,1,3,3,1,1,2,3,2,2,3,2,1
2160 CHAIN "DEMON "
2170 END
```

SAMPLE RUN

```
TICTAC   EDUSYSTEM-35

YOU HAVE THE OPPORTUNITY OF TRYING TO BEAT THE COMPUTER
AT TIC-TAC-TOE.  ENTER YOUR MOVES AS FOLLOWS:

...ROW NUMBER...COMMA...COLUMN NUMBER...

ROWS ARE HORIZONTAL(ACROSS)...COLUMNS ARE VERTICAL(UP + DOWN)

NEW GAME STARTED NOW...........................
YOUR MOVE     ?3,1


        *       *
        *       *
***************
      * PDP *
        *       *
***************
YOU *       *
        *       *

YOUR MOVE      ?1,1


YOU *       *
        *       *
***************
PDP * PDP *
        *       *
***************
YOU *       *
        *       *

YOUR MOVE      ?2,3


YOU *       *
        *       *
***************
PDP * PDP * YOU
        *       *
***************
YOU *       * PDP
        *       *

YOUR MOVE      ?1,2

   ... TIE GAME ...

YOU * YOU * PDP
      *       *
***************
PDP * PDP * YOU
      *       *
***************
YOU *       * PDP
      *       *

DO YOU WANT TO PLAY ANOTHER GAME: YES(1), NO(0)        ?0
```

TOWER

also End of the world Puzzle (how do we have)

Description

This is a simulation of a game of logic that originated in the
middle East. It is sometimes called Pharoah's Needles, but
its most common name is the Towers of Hanoi.

Legend has it that a secret society of monks live beneath the
city of Hanoi. They possess three large towers or needles on
which different size gold disks may be placed. Moving one at
a time and never placing a larger on a smaller disk, the monks
endeavor to move the tower of disks from the left needle to
the right needle. Legend says when they have finished moving
this 64-disk tower, the world will end. How many moves will
they have to make to accomplish this? If they can move 1
disk per minute and work 24 hours per day, how many years
will it take?

In the computer puzzle you are faced with three upright needles.
On the leftmost needle are placed from two to seven graduated
disks, the largest being on the bottom and smallest on the top.
Your object is to move the entire stack of disks to the right-
most needle. However, you may only move one disk at a time
and you may never place a larger disk on top of a smaller one.

In this computer game, the disks are referred
to by their size--i.e., the smallest is 3,
next 5, 7, 9, 11, 13, and 15. If you play
with fewer than 7 disks always use the largest,
i.e. with 2 disks you would use nos. 13 and
15. The program instructions are self-
explanatory. Good luck!

Program Author

Charles Lund
The American School
Hague, Netherlands

PROGRAM LISTING

```
90 PRINT
100 REM *** INITIALIZE
110 DIM T(7,3)
120 E=0
130 FOR D=1 TO 7
140 FOR N=1 TO 3
150 T(D,N)=0
160 NEXT N
170 NEXT D
180 PRINT "TOWERS OF HANOI PUZZLE"\PRINT
200 PRINT "YOU MUST TRANSFER THE DISKS FROM THE LEFT TO THE RIGHT"
205 PRINT "TOWER, ONE AT A TIME, NEVER PUTTING A LARGER ON A"
210 PRINT "SMALLER DISK."\PRINT
215 PRINT "HOW MANY DISKS DO YOU WANT TO MOVE (7 IS MAX)";
220 INPUT S\PRINT
230 M=0
240 FOR Q=1 TO 7
250 IF Q=S THEN 350
260 NEXT Q
270 E=E+1
280 IF E>2 THEN 310
290 PRINT "SORRY, BUT I CAN'T DO THAT JOB FOR YOU."\GOTO 215
310 PRINT "ALRIGHT, WISE GUY, IF YOU CAN'T PLAY THE GAME RIGHT, I'LL"
320 PRINT "JUST TAKE MY PUZZLE AND GO HOME.  SO LONG."\STOP
340 REM *** STORE DISKS FROM SMALLEST TO LARGEST
350 PRINT "IN THIS PROGRAM, WE SHALL REFER TO DISKS BY A NUMERICAL CODE."
355 PRINT "3 WILL REPRESENT THE SMALLEST DISK, 5 THE NEXT SIZE, 7 THE NEXT,"
360 PRINT "AND SO ON, UP TO 15.  IF YOU DO THE PUZZLE WITH 2 DISKS, THEIR"
365 PRINT "CODE NAMES WOULD BY 13 AND 15.  WITH THREE DISKS, THE CODE"
370 PRINT "NAMES WOULD BE 11, 13, AND 15, ETC.  THE NEEDLES ARE"
375 PRINT "NUMBERED FROM LEFT TO RIGHT, 1 TO 3.  WE WILL START WITH THE "
380 PRINT "DISKS ON NEEDLE 1, AND ATTEMPT TO MOVE THEM TO NEEDLE 3."
390 PRINT\PRINT "GOOD LUCK!!"\PRINT
400 Y=7\D=15
420 FOR X=S TO 1 STEP -1
430 T(Y,1)=D\D=D-2\Y=Y-1
460 NEXT X
470 GOSUB 1230
480 PRINT "WHICH DISK WOULD YOU LIKE TO MOVE";\E=0
500 INPUT D
510 IF (D-3)*(D-5)*(D-7)*(D-9)*(D-11)*(D-13)*(D-15)=0 THEN 580
520 PRINT "ILLEGAL ENTRY...YOU MAY ONLY TYPE 3,5,7,9,11,13, OR 15."
530 E=E+1\IF E>1 THEN 560
550 GOTO 500
560 PRINT\PRINT "STOP WASTING MY TIME.  GO BOTHER SOMEONE ELSE."\STOP
580 REM *** CHECK IF REQUESTED DISK IS BELOW ANOTHER
590 FOR R=1 TO 7
600 FOR C=1 TO 3
610 IF T(R,C)=D THEN 640
620 NEXT C\NEXT R
640 FOR Q=R TO 1 STEP -1
645 IF T(Q,C)=0 THEN 660
650 IF T(Q,C)<D THEN 680
660 NEXT Q
670 GOTO 700
680 PRINT "THAT DISK IS BELOW ANOTHER ONE.  MAKE ANOTHER CHOICE."\GOTO 480
700 E=0
705 PRINT "PLACE DISK ON WHICH NEEDLE";\INPUT N
730 IF (N-1)*(N-2)*(N-3)=0 THEN 800
735 E=E+1
740 IF E>1 THEN 780
750 PRINT "I'LL ASSUME YOU HIT THE WRONG KEY THIS TIME.  BUT WATCH IT,"
760 PRINT "I ONLY ALLOW ONE MISTAKE."\GOTO 705
780 PRINT "I TRIED TO WARN YOU, BUT YOU WOULDN'T LISTEN."
790 PRINT "BYE, BYE, BIG SHOT."\STOP
795 REM *** LOCATE DISK TO BE MOVED
800 FOR R=1 TO 7
810 IF T(R,N)<>0 THEN 840
820 NEXT R
830 GOTO 880
835 REM *** CHECK IF DISK TO BE PLACED ON A LARGER ONE
840 IF D<T(R,N) THEN 880
850 PRINT "YOU CAN'T PLACE A LARGER DISK ON TOP OF A SMALLER ONE."
860 PRINT "IT MIGHT CRUSH IT!"\PRINT "NOW THEN, ";\GOTO 480
875 REM *** RELOCATE MOVED DISK
880 FOR V=1 TO 7\FOR W=1 TO 3
900 IF T(V,W)=D THEN 930
910 NEXT W\NEXT V
925 REM *** LOCATE FIRST EMPTY SPACE ON NEEDLE N
930 FOR U=1 TO 7
940 IF T(U,N)<>0 THEN 970
950 NEXT U
960 GOTO 980
965 REM *** MOVE DISK AND SET OLD LOCATION TO 0
970 U=U-1
980 T(U,N)=T(V,W)\T(V,W)=0
995 REM *** PRINT OUT CURRENT STATUS
1000 GOSUB 1230
1010 REM *** CHECK IF DONE
1020 M=M+1
1030 FOR R=1 TO 7\FOR C=1 TO 2
1050 IF T(R,C)<>0 THEN 1090
1060 NEXT C\NEXT R
1080 GOTO 1120
1090 IF M<=128 THEN 480
1100 PRINT "SORRY, BUT I HAVE ORDERS TO STOP IF YOU MAKE MORE THAN"
1110 PRINT "128 MOVES."\STOP
1120 IF M<>2^S-1 THEN 1140
1130 PRINT "CONGRATULATIONS!! ";
1140 PRINT "YOU HAVE PERFORMED THE TASK IN"M"MOVES."
1150 PRINT\PRINT "TRY ANOTHER ONE (YES OR NO)";\INPUT A$
1160 IF A$="NO" THEN 1390
1170 IF A$="YES" THEN 90
1180 PRINT\PRINT "'YES' OR 'NO' PLEASE";\INPUT A$\GOTO 1160
1230 REM *** PRINT SUBROUTINE
1240 FOR K=1 TO 7
1250 Z=10
1260 FOR J=1 TO 3
1270 IF T(K,J)=0 THEN 1330
1280 PRINT TAB(Z-INT(T(K,J)/2));
1290 FOR V=1 TO T(K,J)
1300 PRINT "*";
1310 NEXT V
1320 GOTO 1340
1330 PRINT TAB(Z);"*";
1340 Z=Z+21
1350 NEXT J
1360 PRINT
1370 NEXT K
1380 RETURN
1390 PRINT\PRINT "THANKS FOR THE GAME!"\PRINT\END
```

SAMPLE RUN

TOWERS OF HANOI PUZZLE

YOU MUST TRANSFER THE DISKS FROM THE LEFT TO THE RIGHT
TOWER, ONE AT A TIME, NEVER PUTTING A LARGER ON A
SMALLER DISK.

HOW MANY DISKS DO YOU WANT TO MOVE (7 IS MAX)? 3

IN THIS PROGRAM, WE SHALL REFER TO DISKS BY A NUMERICAL CODE.
3 WILL REPRESENT THE SMALLEST DISK, 5 THE NEXT SIZE, 7 THE NEXT,
AND SO ON, UP TO 15. IF YOU DO THE PUZZLE WITH 2 DISKS, THEIR
CODE NAMES WOULD BE 13 AND 15. WITH THREE DISKS, THE CODE
NAMES WOULD BE 11, 13, AND 15, ETC. NEEDLES ARE
NUMBERED FROM LEFT TO RIGHT, 1 TO 3. WE WILL START WITH THE
DISKS ON NEEDLE 1, AND ATTEMPT TO MOVE THEM TO NEEDLE 3.

GOOD LUCK!!

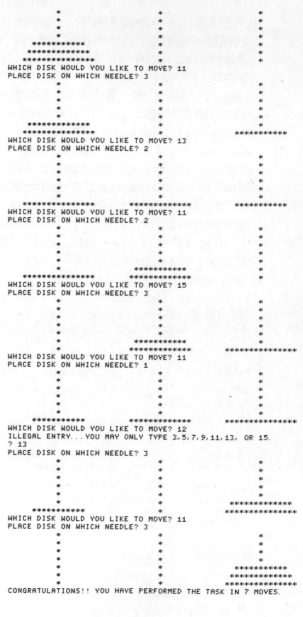

WHICH DISK WOULD YOU LIKE TO MOVE? 11
PLACE DISK ON WHICH NEEDLE? 3

WHICH DISK WOULD YOU LIKE TO MOVE? 13
PLACE DISK ON WHICH NEEDLE? 2

WHICH DISK WOULD YOU LIKE TO MOVE? 11
PLACE DISK ON WHICH NEEDLE? 2

WHICH DISK WOULD YOU LIKE TO MOVE? 15
PLACE DISK ON WHICH NEEDLE? 3

WHICH DISK WOULD YOU LIKE TO MOVE? 11
PLACE DISK ON WHICH NEEDLE? 1

WHICH DISK WOULD YOU LIKE TO MOVE? 12
ILLEGAL ENTRY...YOU MAY ONLY TYPE 3,5,7,9,11,13, OR 15.
? 13
PLACE DISK ON WHICH NEEDLE? 3

WHICH DISK WOULD YOU LIKE TO MOVE? 11
PLACE DISK ON WHICH NEEDLE? 3

CONGRATULATIONS!! YOU HAVE PERFORMED THE TASK IN 7 MOVES.

TRAIN

Description

TRAIN is a program which uses the computer to generate problems
with random initial conditions to teach about the time-speed-
distance relationship (distance = rate x time). You then input
your answer and the computer verifies your response.

TRAIN is merely an example of a student-generated problem.
Maximum fun (and benefit) comes more from <u>writing</u> programs
like this as opposed to solving the specific problem posed.
Exchange your program with others - you solve their problem
and let them solve yours.

Source

TRAIN was originally written in FOCAL by one student for use
by others in his class. It was submitted to us by:

Walt Koetke
Lexington High School
Lexington, Mass. 02173

```
4 PRINT "TIME - SPEED - DISTANCE EXERCISE"\PRINT
5 RANDOMIZE
10 C=INT(RND*25)+40
15 D=INT(RND*15)+5
20 T=INT(RND*19)+20
25 PRINT " A CAR TRAVELING"C"MPH CAN MAKE A CERTAIN TRIP IN"
30 PRINT D"HOURS LESS THAN A TRAIN TRAVELING AT"T"MPH."
35 PRINT "HOW LONG DOES THE TRIP TAKE BY CAR";
40 INPUT A
45 Y=D*T/(C-T)
50 E=INT(ABS((Y-A)*100/A)+.5)
55 IF E>5 THEN 70
60 PRINT "GOOD!  ANSWER WITHIN"E"PERCENT."
65 GOTO 80
70 PRINT "SORRY.  YOU WERE OFF BY"E"PERCENT."
80 PRINT "CORRECT ANSWER IS"Y"HOURS."
90 PRINT
95 PRINT "ANOTHER PROBLEM (YES OR NO)";
100 INPUT A$\PRINT
105 IF A$="YES" THEN 10
999 END

READY

RUN
TRAIN    04:16 PM        08-MAY-73
TIME - SPEED - DISTANCE EXERCISE

 A CAR TRAVELING 44 MPH CAN MAKE A CERTAIN TRIP IN
 14 HOURS LESS THAN A TRAIN TRAVELING AT 24 MPH.
HOW LONG DOES THE TRIP TAKE BY CAR? 16.8
GOOD!  ANSWER WITHIN 0 PERCENT.
CORRECT ANSWER IS 16.8 HOURS.

ANOTHER PROBLEM (YES OR NO)? YES

 A CAR TRAVELING 55 MPH CAN MAKE A CERTAIN TRIP IN
 10 HOURS LESS THAN A TRAIN TRAVELING AT 34 MPH.
HOW LONG DOES THE TRIP TAKE BY CAR? 16.2
GOOD!  ANSWER WITHIN 0 PERCENT.
CORRECT ANSWER IS 16.1905 HOURS.

ANOTHER PROBLEM (YES OR NO)? YES

 A CAR TRAVELING 40 MPH CAN MAKE A CERTAIN TRIP IN
 11 HOURS LESS THAN A TRAIN TRAVELING AT 24 MPH.
HOW LONG DOES THE TRIP TAKE BY CAR? 15.5
SORRY.  YOU WERE OFF BY 6 PERCENT.
CORRECT ANSWER IS 16.5 HOURS.

ANOTHER PROBLEM (YES OR NO)? NO
```

```
READY
```

TRAP

TRAP A MYSTERY NUMBER

Description

Another of the family of "guess the mystery number" games, in
TRAP the computer selects a random number between 1 and 100
(or other limit set in statement 20). Your object is to find
the number. On each guess, you enter 2 numbers trying to
trap the mystery number between your two trap numbers. The
computer will tell you if its number is larger or smaller
than your trap numbers or if you have trapped the number.

To win the game, you must guess the mystery number by entering
it as the same value for both of your trap numbers. You get
6 guesses (this should be changed in statement 10 if you
change the guessing limit in statement 20).

After you have played GUESS, STARS, and TRAP, compare the
guessing strategy you have found best for each game. Do you
notice any similarities? What are the differences? Can you
write a new guessing game with still another approach?

Program Author

TRAP was suggested by 10-year old when he was playing GUESS.
It was originally programmed by Steve Ullman and extensively
modified into its final form by:

> Bob Albrecht
> People's Computer Co.
> Menlo Park, CA. 94025

PROGRAM LISTING

```
TRAP    EDUSYSTEM 30

10   G=6
20   N=100
30   REM-TRAP
40   REM-STEVE ULLMAN, 8-1-72
50   PRINT "WANT INSTRUCTIONS (1 FOR YES)";
60   INPUT Z
70   IF Z<>1 THEN 180
80    PRINT "I AM THINKING OF A NUMBER BETWEEN 1 AND";N
90    PRINT "TRY TO GUESS MY NUMBER. ON EACH GUESS,"
100   PRINT "YOU ARE TO ENTER 2 NUMBERS, TRYING TO TRAP"
110   PRINT "MY NUMBER BETWEEN THE TWO NUMBERS. I WILL"
120   PRINT "TELL YOU IF YOU HAVE TRAPPED MY NUMBER, IF MY"
130   PRINT "NUMBER IS LARGER THAN YOUR TWO NUMBERS, OR IF"
140   PRINT "MY NUMBER IS SMALLER THAN YOUR TWO NUMBERS. "
150   PRINT "IF YOU WANT TO GUESS ONE SINGLE NUMBER, TYPE"
160   PRINT "YOUR GUESS FOR BOTH YOUR TRAP NUMBERS. "
170   PRINT "YOU GET";G;"GUESSES TO GET MY NUMBER. "
180   X=INT(N*RND(0))+1
190   FOR Q=1 TO G
200    PRINT
210    PRINT "GUESS #";Q;
220    INPUT A,B
230   IF A<>B THEN 240
235   IF X=A THEN 400
240   IF A<=B THEN 260
250    GOSUB 360
260   IF X<A THEN 300
270   IF X<=B THEN 320
280   PRINT "MY NUMBER IS LARGER THAN YOUR TRAP NUMBERS. "
290   GOTO 330
300   PRINT "MY NUMBER IS SMALLER THAN YOUR TRAP NUMBERS. "
310   GOTO 330
320   PRINT "YOU HAVE TRAPPED MY NUMBER. "
330   NEXT Q
340   PRINT "SORRY, THAT'S";G;"GUESSES. NUMBER WAS";X
350   GOTO 410
360   R=A
370   A=B
380   B=R
390   RETURN
400   PRINT "YOU GOT IT!!!"
410   PRINT
420   PRINT "TRY AGAIN. "
430   PRINT
440   GOTO 180
450   END

READY
```

SAMPLE RUN

```
TRAP    EDUSYSTEM 30

WANT INSTRUCTIONS (1 FOR YES)?1
I AM THINKING OF A NUMBER BETWEEN 1 AND 100
TRY TO GUESS MY NUMBER. ON EACH GUESS,
YOU ARE TO ENTER 2 NUMBERS, TRYING TO TRAP
MY NUMBER BETWEEN THE TWO NUMBERS. I WILL
TELL YOU IF YOU HAVE TRAPPED MY NUMBER, IF MY
NUMBER IS LARGER THAN YOUR TWO NUMBERS, OR IF
MY NUMBER IS SMALLER THAN YOUR TWO NUMBERS.
IF YOU WANT TO GUESS ONE SINGLE NUMBER, TYPE
YOUR GUESS FOR BOTH YOUR TRAP NUMBERS.
YOU GET 6 GUESSES TO GET MY NUMBER.

GUESS # 1 ?33,67
MY NUMBER IS SMALLER THAN YOUR TRAP NUMBERS.

GUESS # 2 ?11,22
MY NUMBER IS LARGER THAN YOUR TRAP NUMBERS.

GUESS # 3 ?25,28
MY NUMBER IS SMALLER THAN YOUR TRAP NUMBERS.

GUESS # 4 ?23,23
YOU GOT IT!!!

TRY AGAIN.


GUESS # 1 ?33,67
MY NUMBER IS SMALLER THAN YOUR TRAP NUMBERS.

GUESS # 2 ?11,22
MY NUMBER IS LARGER THAN YOUR TRAP NUMBERS.

GUESS # 3 ?25,28
YOU HAVE TRAPPED MY NUMBER.

GUESS # 4 ?26,26
MY NUMBER IS LARGER THAN YOUR TRAP NUMBERS.

GUESS # 5 ?27,27
YOU GOT IT!!!

TRY AGAIN.


GUESS # 1 ?33,67
YOU HAVE TRAPPED MY NUMBER.

GUESS # 2 ?44,56
MY NUMBER IS SMALLER THAN YOUR TRAP NUMBERS.

GUESS # 3 ?37,40
YOU HAVE TRAPPED MY NUMBER.

GUESS # 4 ?38,38
MY NUMBER IS SMALLER THAN YOUR TRAP NUMBERS.

GUESS # 5 ?37,37
YOU GOT IT!!!
```

23 MTCH

GAME OF 23 MATCHES

Description

In the game of twenty-three matches, you start with 23 matches
lying on a table. On each turn, you may take 1, 2, or 3 matches.
You alternate moves with the computer and the one who has to
take the last match loses.

The easiest way to devise a winning strategy is to start at
the end of the game. Since you wish to leave the last match
to your opponent, you would like to have either 4, 3, or 2
on your last turn so you can take away 3, 2, or 1 and leave
1. Consequently, you would like to leave your opponent with
5 on his next to last turn so, no matter what his move, you
are left with 4, 3, or 2. Work this backwards to the beginning and you'll find the game can effectively be won on the
first move. Fortunately, the computer gives you the first
move, so if you play wisely, you can win.

After you've mastered 23 Matches, move on to BATNUM and then
to NIM.

Program Author

Raymond Burhitt of Plainedge H.S., N. Massapeque, N.Y. submitted
one version of 23 Matches, however, the one published is from:

> Bob Albrecht
> People's Computer Co.
> Menlo Park, CA. 94025

PROGRAM LISTING

```
100 REM ***23 MATCHES
110 PRINT "LET'S PLAY 23 MATCHES. WE START WITH 23 MATCHES."
115 PRINT "YOU MOVE FIRST. YOU MAY TAKE 1,2 OR 3 MATCHES."
120 PRINT "THEN I MOVE...I MAY TAKE 1,2 OR 3 MATCHES."
125 PRINT "YOU MOVE, I MOVE AND SO ON. THE ONE WHO HAS TO"
130 PRINT "TAKE THE LAST MATCH LOSES."
135 PRINT "GOOD LUCK AND MAY THE BEST COMPUTER (HA HA) WIN."
140 PRINT
150 LET M=23
200 REM ***THE HUMAN MOVES
205 PRINT
210 PRINT "THERE ARE NOW";M;"MATCHES."
215 PRINT
220 PRINT "HOW MANY DO YOU TAKE";
230 INPUT H
240 IF H>M THEN 510
250 IF H<>INT(H) THEN 510
260 IF H<=0 THEN 510
270 IF H>=4 THEN 510
280 LET M=M-H
290 IF M=0 THEN 410
300 REM ***THE COMPUTER MOVES
305 IF M=1 THEN 440
310 LET R=M-4*INT(M/4)
320 IF R<>1 THEN 350
330 LET C=INT(3*RND(0))+1
340 GO TO 360
350 LET C=(R+3)-4*INT((R+3)/4)
360 LET M=M-C
370 IF M=0 THEN 440
375 PRINT
380 PRINT "I TOOK";C;"...";
390 GO TO 210
400 REM ***SOMEBODY WON (SEE LINES 290,305,370)
410 PRINT
420 PRINT "I WON!!! BETTER LUCK NEXT TIME."
430 GO TO 140
440 PRINT
450 PRINT "O.K. SO YOU WON. LET'S PLAY AGAIN."
460 GO TO 140
500 REM ***THE HUMAN CHEATED! (SEE LINES 240 THRU 270)
510 PRINT "YOU CHEATED! BUT I'LL GIVE YOU ANOTHER CHANCE."
520 GO TO 215
999 END

READY
```

SAMPLE RUN

```
23MTCH   EDUSYSTEM 30

LET'S PLAY 23 MATCHES. WE START WITH 23 MATCHES.
YOU MOVE FIRST. YOU MAY TAKE 1,2 OR 3 MATCHES.
THEN I MOVE...I MAY TAKE 1,2 OR 3 MATCHES.
YOU MOVE, I MOVE AND SO ON. THE ONE WHO HAS TO
TAKE THE LAST MATCH LOSES.
GOOD LUCK AND MAY THE BEST COMPUTER (HA HA) WIN.


THERE ARE NOW 23 MATCHES.

HOW MANY DO YOU TAKE?3

I TOOK 3 ...THERE ARE NOW 17 MATCHES.

HOW MANY DO YOU TAKE?1

I TOOK 3 ...THERE ARE NOW 13 MATCHES.

HOW MANY DO YOU TAKE?2

I TOOK 2 ...THERE ARE NOW 9 MATCHES.

HOW MANY DO YOU TAKE?1

I TOOK 3 ...THERE ARE NOW 5 MATCHES.

HOW MANY DO YOU TAKE?1

I TOOK 3 ...THERE ARE NOW 1 MATCHES.

HOW MANY DO YOU TAKE?0
YOU CHEATED! BUT I'LL GIVE YOU ANOTHER CHANCE.

HOW MANY DO YOU TAKE?1

I WON!!! BETTER LUCK NEXT TIME.


THERE ARE NOW 23 MATCHES.

HOW MANY DO YOU TAKE?2

I TOOK 1 ...THERE ARE NOW 20 MATCHES.

HOW MANY DO YOU TAKE?3

I TOOK 1 ...THERE ARE NOW 16 MATCHES.

HOW MANY DO YOU TAKE?3

I TOOK 2 ...THERE ARE NOW 11 MATCHES.

HOW MANY DO YOU TAKE?2

I TOOK 3 ...THERE ARE NOW 6 MATCHES.

HOW MANY DO YOU TAKE?1

I TOOK 3 ...THERE ARE NOW 2 MATCHES.

HOW MANY DO YOU TAKE?1

O.K. SO YOU WON. LET'S PLAY AGAIN.
```

UGLY

Description

This program draws on the terminal the profile of a woman. It gives you an opportunity to specify the "dimensions" of your woman (termed SPECIAL) or take your chances (CHANCE).

The computer draws your figure and then makes a determination whether or not to call your woman ugly or just leave it up to your own judgement.

Program Author

Mark Maslar
231 Appletree Drive
Media, PA. 19063

PROGRAM LISTING

```
5 PRINT "PROGRAM 'UGLY'"\PRINT
6 D=1\E=1\F=1\PRINT "DO YOU WANT CHANCE(1), OR SPECIAL(2)";
7 INPUT G
8 IF G=2 THEN 17
9 RANDOMIZE
10 A=INT(40*RND)+15
11 B=INT(40*RND)+10
12 C=INT(40*RND)+15
13 PRINT "A=",A,"B=",B,"C=",C
14 PRINT "DO YOU STILL WANT CHANCE -- 1 FOR YES, 2 FOR NO";
15 INPUT H
16 ON H GOTO 19, 6
17 PRINT "WHAT ARE YOUR VALUES FOR A, B, AND C";
18 INPUT A,B,C
19 PRINT\PRINT\PRINT TAB(20)"XXX"
20 PRINT TAB(19)"XXXXX"
25 PRINT TAB(20)"XXX"
30 PRINT TAB(21)"X"
35 PRINT TAB(15)"X";
40 D=D+1
45 PRINT "X";
50 IF D>=A-2 THEN 60
55 GOTO 40
60 PRINT "X"
65 PRINT TAB(15)"X";
70 D=1
75 D=D+1
80 PRINT "X";
85 IF D=A-1 THEN 95
90 GOTO 75
95 PRINT "X)."
100 PRINT TAB(15)"X";
105 D=1
110 D=D+1
115 PRINT "X";
120 IF D>=A-2 THEN 130
125 GOTO 110
130 PRINT "X"
135 PRINT TAB(15)"X";
140 E=E+1
150 PRINT "X";
155 IF E=B-1 THEN 165
160 GOTO 140
165 PRINT "X"
170 PRINT TAB(15)"X";
175 E=1
180 E=E+1
185 PRINT "X";
190 IF E=B-1 THEN 205
200 GOTO 180
205 PRINT "X"
210 PRINT TAB (15)"X";
215 E=1
220 E=E+1
225 PRINT "X";
230 IF E=B-1 THEN 240
235 GOTO 220
240 PRINT "X"
245 PRINT TAB(15)"X";
250 F=F+1
255 PRINT "X";
260 IF F>=C-2 THEN 270
265 GOTO 250
270 PRINT "X"
275 PRINT TAB(15)"X";
280 F=1
285 F=F+1
290 PRINT "X";
295 IF F=C-1 THEN 305
300 GOTO 285
305 PRINT "X"
310 PRINT TAB(15)"X";
315 F=1
316 GOTO 320
317 F=F+3
320 F=F+1
325 PRINT "X";
327 IF F=7 THEN 329
328 GOTO 331
329 PRINT "()";
330 GOTO 317
331 IF F=C-1 THEN 340
335 GOTO 320
340 PRINT "X"
345 PRINT TAB(19)"XX     XX"
350 PRINT TAB(18)"XX      XX"
355 PRINT TAB(17)"XX      XX"
360 PRINT TAB(16)"XX       XX"
365 PRINT TAB(15)"XX        XX"
370 PRINT TAB(13)"XXXX        XXXX"
380 PRINT\PRINT
385 IF B<A THEN 6
395 FOR X=1 TO 48
400 PRINT "UGLY! ";
405 NEXT X
407 PRINT\PRINT
410 GOTO 6
415 END

READY
```

SAMPLE RUN

```
PROGRAM 'UGLY'

DO YOU WANT CHANCE(1), OR SPECIAL(2)? 1
A= 21          B= 46          C= 52
DO YOU STILL WANT CHANCE -- 1 FOR YES, 2 FOR NO? 1


                    XXX
                   XXXXX
                    XXX
                     X
          XXXXXXXXXXXXXXXXXXXX
          XXXXXXXXXXXXXXXXXXXX).
          XXXXXXXXXXXXXXXXXX
          XXXXXXXXXXXXXXXXXXXXXXXXXXXXXXXXXXXXXXXXXX
          XXXXXXXXXXXXXXXXXXXXXXXXXXXXXXXXXXXXXXXXXX
          XXXXXXXXXXXXXXXXXXXXXXXXXXXXXXXXXXXXXXXXX
          XXXXXXXXXXXXXXXXXXXXXXXXXXXXXXXXXXXXXXXXXXX
          XXXXXXX()XXXXXXXXXXXXXXXXXXXXXXXXXXXXXXXXXX
              XX      XX
               XX    XX
                XX    XX
                 XX    XX
                  XX    XX
                 XXXX    XXXX


UGLY! UGLY! UGLY! UGLY! UGLY! UGLY! UGLY! UGLY! UGLY! UGLY! UGLY! UGLY!
UGLY! UGLY! UGLY! UGLY! UGLY! UGLY! UGLY! UGLY! UGLY! UGLY! UGLY! UGLY!
UGLY! UGLY! UGLY! UGLY! UGLY! UGLY! UGLY! UGLY! UGLY! UGLY! UGLY! UGLY!
UGLY! UGLY! UGLY! UGLY! UGLY! UGLY! UGLY! UGLY! UGLY! UGLY! UGLY! UGLY!

DO YOU WANT CHANCE(1), OR SPECIAL(2)? 1
A= 19          B= 25          C= 24
DO YOU STILL WANT CHANCE -- 1 FOR YES, 2 FOR NO? 2
DO YOU WANT CHANCE(1), OR SPECIAL(2)? 1
A= 25          B= 26          C= 24
DO YOU STILL WANT CHANCE -- 1 FOR YES, 2 FOR NO? 2
DO YOU WANT CHANCE(1), OR SPECIAL(2)? 2
WHAT ARE YOUR VALUES FOR A, B, AND C? 22,15,22


                    XXX
                   XXXXX
                    XXX
                     X
          XXXXXXXXXXXXXXXXXXXX
          XXXXXXXXXXXXXXXXXXXX).
          XXXXXXXXXXXXXXXXXX
          XXXXXXXXXXXXXXXX
          XXXXXXXXXXXXXXXX
          XXXXXXXXXXXXXXXX
          XXXXXXXXXXXXXXXXXXXX
          XXXXXXXXXXXXXXXXXXXX
          XXXXXXX()XXXXXXXXXXXXX
              XX      XX
               XX    XX
                XX    XX
                 XX    XX
                  XX    XX
                 XXXX    XXXX
```

229

WAR

Description

This program plays the card game of War. In War, the card deck is shuffled, then two cards are dealt, one to each player. Players compare cards and the higher card (numerically) wins. In case of tie, no one wins. The game ends when you have gone through the whole deck (52 cards, 26 games) or when you decide to quit.

The computer gives cards by suit and number, for example, 5-7 is the 7 of spades.

Note: The ↑G in some of the PRINT statements(470,650) indicates the ringing of the teletype bell.

Source

This program showed up on a DIGITAL in-house DECsystem-10 one day. The author is unknown.

PROGRAM LISTING

```
1 REM  THIS PROGRAM PLAYS THE CARD GAME OF WAR.  THE ONLY CHANGE
2 REM IS THAT A TIE MAKES NO SCORE AT ALL.  THE PACK IS READ IN
3 REM AND THEN SHUFFLES IN A RANDOM WAY.  THE COMPUTER THEN DEALS THE
4 REM CARDS TWO AT A TIME AS LONG AS THE GAME CONTINUES.  A RUNNING
5 REM SCORE IS KEPT.
100 PRINT "THIS IS THE CARD GAME OF WAR.  EACH CARD IS GIVEN BY SUIT-#";
110 PRINT "AS S-7 FOR SPADE 7.  ";
120 PRINT "DO YOU WANT DIRECTIONS";
130 INPUT B$
140 IF B$="NO" THEN 210
150 IF B$="YES" THEN 180
160 PRINT "YES OR NO, PLEASE.  ";
170 GO TO 120
180 PRINT "THE COMPUTER GIVES YOU AND IT A 'CARD'.  THE HIGHER 'CARD' ";
190 PRINT "(NUMERICALLY) WINS.  THE GAME ENDS WHEN YOU CHOOSE NOT";
200 PRINT " TO CONTINUE OR WHEN YOU HAVE FINISHED THE PACK."
210 PRINT
220 PRINT
230 DIM A$(52), L(54)
240 FOR I=1 TO 52
250 READ A$(I)
260 NEXT I
270 RANDOM
280 FOR J=1 TO 52
290 LET L(J)=INT(52*RND(X)+1)
300 FOR K=1 TO J-1
310 IF L(K)<>L(J) THEN 340
320 LET J=J-1
330 GO TO 350
340 NEXT K
350 NEXT J
360 LET P=P+1
370 LET M1=L(P)
380 LET P=P+1
390 LET M2=L(P)
400 PRINT
410 PRINT
420 PRINT "YOU: ";A$(M1), "COMPUTER: ";A$(M2),
430 LET N1=INT((M1-.5)/4)
440 LET N2=INT((M2-.5)/4)
450 IF N1>=N2 THEN 490
460 LET A1=A1+1
470 PRINT "COMPUTER WINS.^G^G^G^G^G  YOU HAVE";B1;"; COMPUTER HAS";A1
480 GO TO 540
490 IF N1=N2 THEN 530
500 LET B1=B1+1
510 PRINT "YOU WIN.   YOU HAVE";B1;"; COMPUTER HAS";A1
520 GO TO 540
530 PRINT "TIE.  NO SCORE CHANGE."
540 IF L(P+1)=0, THEN 610
550 PRINT "DO YOU WANT TO CONTINUE";
560 INPUT V$
570 IF V$="YES" THEN 360
580 IF V$="NO"THEN 650
590 PRINT "YES OR NO, PLEASE.  ";
600 GO TO 540
610 PRINT
620 PRINT
630 PRINT "YOU HAVE RUN OUT OF CARDS.  FINAL SCORE:  YOU--";B1;
640 PRINT "; COMPUTER--";A1
650 PRINT "THANKS FOR PLAYING.  IT WAS FUN.^G^G"
660 DATA S-2,H-2,C-2,D-2,S-3,H-3,C-3,D-3,S-4,H-4,C-4,D-4,S-5,H-5,C-5
670 DATA D-5,S-6,H-6,C-6,D-6,S-7,H-7,C-7,D-7,S-8,H-8,C-8,D-8,S-9,H-9
680 DATA C-9,D-9,S-10,H-10,C-10,D-10,S-J,H-J,C-J,D-J,S-Q,H-Q,C-Q,D-Q
690 DATA S-K,H-K,C-K,D-K,S-A,H-A,C-A,D-A
700 END
```

SAMPLE RUN

```
THIS IS THE CARD GAME OF WAR.  EACH CARD IS GIVEN BY SUIT - #
AS S-7 FOR SPADE 7.  DO YOU WANT DIRECTIONS ?YES
THE COMPUTER GIVES YOU AND IT A 'CARD'.  THE HIGHER 'CARD'
(NUMERICALLY) WINS.  THE GAME ENDS WHEN YOU CHOOSE NOT
 TO CONTINUE OR WHEN YOU HAVE FINISHED THE PACK.


YOU: D-3      COMPUTER: D-2
YOU WIN.   YOU HAVE 1 ; COMPUTER HAS 0
DO YOU WANT TO CONTINUE ?YES


YOU: H-3      COMPUTER: D-8
COMPUTER WINS.  YOU HAVE 1 ; COMPUTER HAS 1
DO YOU WANT TO CONTINUE ?YES


YOU: H-9      COMPUTER: C-8
YOU WIN.   YOU HAVE 2 ; COMPUTER HAS 1
DO YOU WANT TO CONTINUE ?YES


YOU: D-J      COMPUTER: C-10
YOU WIN.   YOU HAVE 3 ; COMPUTER HAS 1
DO YOU WANT TO CONTINUE ?YES


YOU: S-10     COMPUTER: D-9
YOU WIN.   YOU HAVE 4 ; COMPUTER HAS 1
DO YOU WANT TO CONTINUE ?YES


YOU: C-5      COMPUTER: D-4
YOU WIN.   YOU HAVE 5 ; COMPUTER HAS 1
DO YOU WANT TO CONTINUE ?YES


YOU: C-6      COMPUTER: S-A
COMPUTER WINS.  YOU HAVE 5 ; COMPUTER HAS 2
DO YOU WANT TO CONTINUE ?YES


YOU: S-K      COMPUTER: H-10
YOU WIN.   YOU HAVE 6 ; COMPUTER HAS 2
DO YOU WANT TO CONTINUE ?YES


YOU: S-4      COMPUTER: D-A
COMPUTER WINS.  YOU HAVE 6 ; COMPUTER HAS 3
DO YOU WANT TO CONTINUE ?YES


YOU: C-3      COMPUTER: S-2
YOU WIN.   YOU HAVE 7 ; COMPUTER HAS 3
DO YOU WANT TO CONTINUE ?YES


YOU: C-J      COMPUTER: H-K
COMPUTER WINS.  YOU HAVE 7 ; COMPUTER HAS 4
DO YOU WANT TO CONTINUE ?YES


YOU: H-6      COMPUTER: C-A
COMPUTER WINS.  YOU HAVE 7 ; COMPUTER HAS 5
DO YOU WANT TO CONTINUE ?YES


YOU: C-Q      COMPUTER: C-2
YOU WIN.   YOU HAVE 8 ; COMPUTER HAS 5
DO YOU WANT TO CONTINUE ?YES


YOU: S-5      COMPUTER: C-7
COMPUTER WINS.  YOU HAVE 8 ; COMPUTER HAS 6
DO YOU WANT TO CONTINUE ?YES


YOU: H-5      COMPUTER: D-10
COMPUTER WINS.  YOU HAVE 8 ; COMPUTER HAS 7
DO YOU WANT TO CONTINUE ?YES


YOU: H-A      COMPUTER: C-9
YOU WIN.   YOU HAVE 9 ; COMPUTER HAS 7
DO YOU WANT TO CONTINUE ?YES


YOU: H-Q      COMPUTER: D-6
YOU WIN.   YOU HAVE 10 ; COMPUTER HAS 7
DO YOU WANT TO CONTINUE ?YES


YOU: H-8      COMPUTER: D-K
COMPUTER WINS.  YOU HAVE 10 ; COMPUTER HAS 8
DO YOU WANT TO CONTINUE ?YES


YOU: S-7      COMPUTER: H-4
YOU WIN.   YOU HAVE 11 ; COMPUTER HAS 8
DO YOU WANT TO CONTINUE ?YES


YOU: S-J      COMPUTER: H-J
TIE.  NO SCORE CHANGE.
DO YOU WANT TO CONTINUE ?YES


YOU: S-Q      COMPUTER: D-Q
TIE.  NO SCORE CHANGE.
DO YOU WANT TO CONTINUE ?YES


YOU: C-4      COMPUTER: H-2
YOU WIN.   YOU HAVE 12 ; COMPUTER HAS 8
DO YOU WANT TO CONTINUE ?YES


YOU: S-3      COMPUTER: S-6
COMPUTER WINS.  YOU HAVE 12 ; COMPUTER HAS 9
DO YOU WANT TO CONTINUE ?YES


YOU: H-7      COMPUTER: S-8
COMPUTER WINS.  YOU HAVE 12 ; COMPUTER HAS 10
DO YOU WANT TO CONTINUE ?YES


YOU: C-K      COMPUTER: D-5
YOU WIN.   YOU HAVE 13 ; COMPUTER HAS 10
DO YOU WANT TO CONTINUE ?YES


YOU: D-7      COMPUTER: S-9
COMPUTER WINS.  YOU HAVE 13 ; COMPUTER HAS 11


YOU HAVE RUN OUT OF CARDS.  FINAL SCORE:  YOU-- 13 ; COMPUTER-- 11
THANKS FOR PLAYING.  IT WAS FUN.
```

WAR·2

Description

In this game, you are fighting a small-scale war with the computer. You have 72,000 troops which you first must distribute into your Army, Navy, and Air Force. You may distribute them in any way you choose as long as you don't use more than 72,000.

You then attach your opponent (the computer) and input which service and the number of men you wish to use. The computer then tells you the outcome of the battle, gives you the current statistics and allows you to determine your next move.

After the second battle, it is decided from the total statistics whether you win or lose or if a treaty is signed.

Program Author

Bob Dores
70 Summer Street
Milton, MA.   02186

PROGRAM LISTING

```
1 REM BOB DORES/WAR
2 PRI "I AM AT WAR WITH YOU."
4 PRI "WE HAVE 72000 SOLDIERS A PIECE."
5 PRI "DISTRIBUTE YOUR FORCES."
6 PRI ,"ME","YOU"
7 PRI"ARMY","30000",
8 INPUT A
9 PRI"NAVY","20000",
10 INPUT B
11 PRI"A.F.","22000",
12 INPUT C
13 IF A+B+C>72000 THE 5
14 D=30000
15 E=20000
16 F=22000
17 PRI "YOU ATTACK FIRST. TYPE 1 FOR ARMY  2 FOR NAVY"
18 PRI "AND 3 FOR AIR FORCE."
19 INPUT Y
20 PRI "HOW MANY MEN"
21 INPUT X
22 IF X<0 THEN 20
23 ON Y GOTO 100,200,300
100 IF X>A THEN 20
105 IF X<A/3 THEN 120
110 IF X<2*A/3 THEN 150
115 GOT 270
120 PRI "YOU LOST "X" MEN FROM YOUR ARMY."
125 A=INT(A-X)
130 GOTO 500
150 PRI"YOU LOST "INT(X/3)" MEN, BUT I LOST "INT(2*D/3)
155 A=INT(A-X/3)
160 D=0
165 GOTO 500
200 IF X>B THE 20
210 IF X<E/3 THEN 230
215 IF X<2*E/3 THEN 250
220 GOT 270
230 PRI "YOUR ATTACK WAS STOPPED!"
232 B=INT(B-X)
235 GOTO 500
250 PRI "YOU DESTROYED "INT(2*E/3)" OF MY ARMY."
255 E=INT(E/3)
260 GOTO 500
270 PRI"YOU SUNK 1 OF MY PATROL BOATS, BUT I WIPED OUT 2"
275 PRI"OF YOUR A.F. BASES, AND 3 ARMY BASES."
280 A=INT(A/3)
285 C=INT(C/3)
290 E=INT(2*E/3)
293 GOTO 500
300 IF X>C THEN 20
310 IF X<C/3 THEN 350
320 IF X<2*C/3 THEN 370
330 GOT 380
350 PRI "YOUR ATTACK WAS WIPED OUT."
355 C=INT(C-X)
360 GOTO 500
370 PRI "WE HAD A DOGFIGHT- YOU WON - AND FINISHED YOUR MISSION."
375 D=INT(2*D/3)
377 E=INT(E/3)
378 F=INT(F/3)
379 GOT500
380 PRI "YOU WIPED OUT ONE OF MY ARMY PATROLS, BUT I"
381 PRI "DESTROYED 2 NAVY BASES, AND BOMBED 3 ARMY BASES."
385 A=INT(A/4)
387 B=INT(B/3)
390 D=INT(2*D/3)
500 PRI
501 PRI,"YOU","ME"
510 PRI"ARMY",A,D
520 PRI"NAVY",B,E
530 PRI"A.F.",C,F
1000 PRI "WHAT IS YOUR NEXT MOVE?"
1010 PRI "ARMY=1 NAVY=2  AIR FORCE=3"
1020 INPUT G
1030 PRI "HOW MANY MEN"
1040 INPUT T
1045 IF T<0 THE 1030
1050 ON G GOTO 1600,1700,1800
1600 IF T>A THE 1030
1610 IF T<D/2 THE 1630
1615 PRI"YOU DESTROYED MY ARMY!"
1616 D=0
1617 GOTO 2000
1630 PRI "I WIPED OUT YOUR ATTACK"
1635 A=A-T
1640 GOTO 2000
1700 IF T>B THEN 1030
1710 IF T<E/2 THEN 1750
1720 GOT 1770
1750 PRI "I SUNK 2 OF YOUR BATTLESHIPS, AND MY AIR FORCE"
1751 PRI "WIPED OUT YOUR UNGUARDED CAPITOL."
1755 A=A/4
1760 B=B/2
1765 GOTO 2000
1770 PRI "YOUR NAVY SHOT DOWN 3 OF MY XIII PLANES ,"
1771 PRI"AND SUNK 3 BATTLESHIPS."
1775 F=2*F/3
1780 E=(E/2)
1790 GOTO2000
1800 IF T>C THEN 1030
1810 IF T>F/2 THEN 1830
1820 GOT 1850
1830 PRI "MY NAVY AND AIR FORCE IN A COMBINED ATTACK LEFT"
1831 PRI "YOUR COUNTRY IN SHAMBLES."
1835 A=A/3
1837 B=B/3
1840 C=C/3
1845 GOTO 2000
1850 PRI"ONE OF YOUR PLANES CRASHED INTO MY HOUSE. I AM DEAD."
1851 PRI"MY COUNTRY FELL APART."
1860 GOTO 2010
2000 PRI
2001 PRI "FROM THE RESULTS OF BOTH OF YOUR ATTACKS,"
2002 IF A+B+C>3/2*(D+E+F) THE 2010
2005 IF A+B+C<2/3*(D+E+F) THE 2015
2006 PRI"THE TREATY OF PARIS CONCLUDED THAT WE TAKE OUR"
2007 PRI"RESPECTIVE COUNTRIES, AND LIVE IN PEACE."
2008 GOT2020
2010 PRI "YOU WON, OH! SHUCKS!!!!!"
2012 GOTO 2020
2015 PRI "YOU LOST-I CONQUERED YOUR COUNTRY. IT SERVES YOU "
2016 PRI "RIGHT FOR PLAYING THIS STUPID GAME!!!"
2020 END
```

SAMPLE RUN

```
I AM AT WAR WITH YOU.
WE HAVE 72000 SOLDIERS A PIECE.
DISTRIBUTE YOUR FORCES.
                  ME           YOU
ARMY           30000        ? 30000
NAVY           20000        ? 20000
A.F.           22000        ? 22000
YOU ATTACK FIRST. TYPE 1 FOR ARMY  2 FOR NAVY
AND 3 FOR AIR FORCE.
? 1
HOW MANY MEN
? 2
YOU LOST  2  MEN FROM YOUR ARMY.

                  YOU          ME
ARMY           29998        30000
NAVY           20000        20000
A.F.           22000        22000
WHAT IS YOUR NEXT MOVE?
ARMY=1  NAVY=2  AIR FORCE=3
? 1
HOW MANY MEN
? 2.34
I WIPED OUT YOUR ATTACK

FROM THE RESULTS OF BOTH OF YOUR ATTACKS,
THE TREATY OF PARIS CONCLUDED THAT WE TAKE OUR
RESPECTIVE COUNTRIES, AND LIVE IN PEACE.

READY

RUN
I AM AT WAR WITH YOU.
WE HAVE 72000 SOLDIERS A PIECE.
DISTRIBUTE YOUR FORCES.
                  ME           YOU
ARMY           30000        ? 72000
NAVY           20000        ? 300000
A.F.           22000        ? 34
DISTRIBUTE YOUR FORCES.
                  ME           YOU
ARMY           30000        ? 2333
NAVY           20000        ? 54322
A.F.           22000        ? 74633
DISTRIBUTE YOUR FORCES.
                  ME           YOU
ARMY           30000        ? 3455
NAVY           20000        ? 6344
A.F.           22000        ? 27700
YOU ATTACK FIRST. TYPE 1 FOR ARMY  2 FOR NAVY
AND 3 FOR AIR FORCE.
? 2
HOW MANY MEN
? 17899
HOW MANY MEN
? 3000
YOUR ATTACK WAS STOPPED!

                  YOU          ME
ARMY            3455        30000
NAVY            3344        20000
A.F.           27700        22000
WHAT IS YOUR NEXT MOVE?
ARMY=1  NAVY=2  AIR FORCE=3
? 2
HOW MANY MEN
? 3344
I SUNK 2 OF YOUR BATTLESHIPS, AND MY AIR FORCE
WIPED OUT YOUR UNGUARDED CAPITOL.

FROM THE RESULTS OF BOTH OF YOUR ATTACKS,
YOU LOST-I CONQUERED YOUR COUNTRY. IT SERVES YOU
RIGHT FOR PLAYING THIS STUPID GAME!!!

READY

RUN
I AM AT WAR WITH YOU.
WE HAVE 72000 SOLDIERS A PIECE.
DISTRIBUTE YOUR FORCES.
                  ME           YOU
ARMY           30000        ? 2000
NAVY           20000        ? 30000
A.F.           22000        ? 6444
YOU ATTACK FIRST. TYPE 1 FOR ARMY  2 FOR NAVY
AND 3 FOR AIR FORCE.
? 3
HOW MANY MEN
? 6443
YOU WIPED OUT ONE OF MY ARMY PATROLS, BUT I
DESTROYED 2 NAVY BASES, AND BOMBED 3 ARMY BASES.

                  YOU          ME
ARMY             500        20000
NAVY           10000        20000
A.F.            6444        22000
WHAT IS YOUR NEXT MOVE?
ARMY=1  NAVY=2  AIR FORCE=3
? 3
HOW MANY MEN
? 5
ONE OF YOUR PLANES CRASHED INTO MY HOUSE. I AM DEAD.
MY COUNTRY FELL APART.
YOU WON, OH! SHUCKS!!!!!

READY
```

WEKDAY

Description

This program gives facts about your date of birth (or some other day of interest). It is not prepared to give information on people born before the use of the current type of calendar, i.e. year 1582.

You merely enter today's date in the form - month, day, year and your date of birth in the same form. The computer then tells you the day of the week of your birth date, your age, and how much time you have spent sleeping, eating, working, and relaxing.

Source

WEKDAY was adapted from the GE timesharing program by:

Tom Kloos
Oregon Museum of Science and Industry
Portland, Oregon 97200

PROGRAM LISTING

```
10 PRINT""
120PRINT
124 LET Y1 = 1970
130 PRINT" ENTER TODAY'S DATE IN THIS FORM: MONTH,DAY, YEAR";
140 INPUT M1,D1,Y1
150 IF Y1>100 THEN 170
160 LET Y = Y1 + 1900
170 DEF FNA(A)=INT(A/4)
180 DIM T(12)
190 DEF FNB(A)=INT(A/7)
210 FOR I= 1 TO 12
220 READ T(I)
230 NEXT I
240 PRINT
241 PRINT"THIS PROGRAM DEMONSTRATES PDP-11 BASIC AND ALSO GIVES "
242 PRINT"FACTS ABOUT A DATE OF INTEREST TO YOU"
244 PRINT
245 PRINT"ENTER DATE OF BIRTH IN THIS FORM: MO,DAY,YEAR";
250 INPUT M,D,Y
260 PRINT
270 IF Y - 75 >0 THEN 280
275 LET Y = Y+1900
280 LET I1 = INT((Y-1500)/100)
290 IF Y-1582<0 THEN 1300
300 LET A = I1+5+(I1+3)/4
310 LET I2 = INT(A-FNB(A)*7)
320 LET Y2= INT(Y/100)
330 LET Y3 = INT(Y-Y2*100)
340 LET A = Y3/4+Y3+D+T(M)+I2
350 LET B = INT(A-FNB(A)*7)+1
360 IF M>2 THEN 470
370 IF Y3= 0 THEN 440
380 LET T1 = INT(Y-FNA(Y)*4)
390 IF T1<> 0 THEN 470
400 IF B<>0 THEN 420
410 LET B = 6
420 LET B = B-1
430 GOTO 470
440 LET A = I1-1
450 LET T1 = INT(A-FNA(A)*4)
460 IF T1 = 0 THEN 400
470 IF B <> 0 THEN 490
480 LET B = 7
490 IF (Y1*12+M1)*31+D1<(Y*12+M)*31+D THEN 550
500 IF (Y1*12+M1)*31+D1=(Y*12+M)*31+D THEN 530
510 PRINT M;"/";D;"/";Y;" WAS A ";
520 GOTO 570
530 PRINT M;"/";D;"/";Y;" IS A ";
540 GOTO 570
550 PRINT M;"/";D;"/";Y;" WILL BE A ";
570 IF B<>1 THEN 590
580 PRINT "SUNDAY"
590 IF B<>2 THEN 610
600 PRINT "MONDAY"
610 IF B<>3 THEN630
620 PRINT "TUESDAY"
630 IF B<>4 THEN 650
640 PRINT "WEDNESDAY"
650 IF B<>5 THEN 670
660 PRINT "THURSDAY"
670 IF B<>6 THEN 690
680 GOTO 1250
690 IF B<>7 THEN 710
700 PRINT "SATURDAY"
710 IF (Y1*12+M1)*31+D1=(Y*12+M)*31+D THEN 1120
720 LET I5=Y1-Y
730 PRINT
740 LET I6=M1-M
750 LET I7=D1-D
760 IF I7>=0 THEN 790
770 LET I6=I6-1
780 LET I7=I7+30
790 IF I6>=0 THEN 820
800 LET I5=I5-1
810 LET I6=I6+12
820 IF I5<0 THEN 1310
830 IF I7<>0 THEN 850
835 IF I6<>0 THEN 850
840 PRINT "****HAPPY BIRTHDAY*****"
850 PRINT " "," ","YEARS","MONTHS","DAYS"
860 PRINT "YOUR AGE          ",I5,I6,I7
870 LET A8= (I5*365)+(I6*30)+I7+INT(I6/2)
880 LET K5=I5
890 LET K6=I6
900 LET K7=I7
920 LET E=Y+65
940 LET F=.35
950 PRINT "YOU HAVE SLEPT ",
960 GOSUB 1370
970 LET F=.17
980 PRINT "YOU HAVE EATEN ",
990 GOSUB 1370
1000 LET F=.23
1010 IF K5 > 3 THEN 1040
1020 PRINT"YOU HAVE PLAYED ",
1030 GOTO 1080
1040 IF K5 > 9 THEN 1070
1050 PRINT "YOU HAVE PLAYED/STUDIED",
1060 GOTO 1080
1070 PRINT "YOU HAVE WORKED/STUDIED",
1080 GOSUB 1370
1090 PRINT "YOU HAVE RELAXED ",K5,K6,K7
1100 PRINT
1110 PRINT " ","**YOU MAY RETIRE IN";E;"**"
1120 PRINT
1130 PRINT" CALCULATED BY THE BEST MINICOMPUTER TODAY - THE PDP-11"
1140 FOR Q=1 TO 2
1150 PRINT
1160 NEXT Q
1170 PRINT
1240 GOTO 240
1250 IF D=13 THEN 1280
1260 PRINT "FRIDAY "
1270 GOTO 710
1280 PRINT "FRIDAY THE THIRTEENT#----BEWARE!"
1290 GOTO 710
1300 PRINT "NOT PREPARED TO GIVE DAY OF WEEK PRIOR TO MDLXPXII ="
1305 PRINT "    THE CURRENT CALENDAR DID NOT EXIST BEFORE THAT YEAR."
1310 GOTO 1140
1330 DATA 0, 3, 3, 6, 1, 4, 6, 2, 5, 0, 3, 5
1370 LET K1= INT(F*A8)
1380 LET I5 = INT(K1/365)
1390 LET K1= K1-(I5*365)
1400 LET I6 = INT(K1/30)
1410 LET I7 = K1-(I6*30)
1420 LET K5 = K5-I5
1430 LET K6 = K6-I6
1440 LET K7 = K7-I7
1450 IF K7 >= 0 THEN 1480
1460 LET K7 = K7+30
1470 LET K6 = K6-1
1480 IF K6 > 0 THEN 1510
1490 LET K6 = K6+12
1500 LET K5 = K5-1
1510 PRINT I5,I6,I7
1520 RETURN
1530 IF K6 = 12 THEN 1550
1540 GOTO 1090
1550 LET K5 = K5+1
1560 LET K6=0
1570 GOTO 1090
1580 END
```

SAMPLE RUN

```
ENTER TODAY'S DATE IN THIS FORM: MONTH,DAY, YEAR? 646,12,73

THIS PROGRAM DEMONSTRATES PDP-11 BASIC AND ALSO GIVES
FACTS^C

READY

RUN
WEKDAY   02:16 PM       12-JUN-73


 ENTER TODAY'S DATE IN THIS FORM: MONTH,DAY, YEAR? 6,12,73

THIS PROGRAM DEMONSTRATES PDP-11 BASIC AND ALSO GIVES
FACTS ABOUT A DATE OF INTEREST TO YOU

ENTER DATE OF BIRTH IN THIS FORM: MO,DAY,YEAR? 5,17,39

 5 / 17 / 1939  WAS A WEDNESDAY
```

	YEARS	MONTHS	DAYS
YOUR AGE	34	0	25
YOU HAVE SLEPT	11	11	7
YOU HAVE EATEN	5	9	18
YOU HAVE WORKED/STUDIED	7	10	5
YOU HAVE RELAXED	8	5	25

```
                **YOU MAY RETIRE IN 2004 **

 CALCULATED BY THE BEST MINICOMPUTER TODAY - THE PDP-11



THIS PROGRAM DEMONSTRATES PDP-11 BASIC AND ALSO GIVES
FACTS ABOUT A DATE OF INTEREST TO YOU

ENTER DATE OF BIRTH IN THIS FORM: MO,DAY,YEAR? 9,24,48

 9 / 24 / 1948  WAS A FRIDAY
```

	YEARS	MONTHS	DAYS
YOUR AGE	24	8	18
YOU HAVE SLEPT	8	7	27
YOU HAVE EATEN	4	2	13
YOU HAVE WORKED/STUDIED	5	8	10
YOU HAVE RELAXED	6	1	28

```
                **YOU MAY RETIRE IN 2013 **

 CALCULATED BY THE BEST MINICOMPUTER TODAY - THE PDP-11
```

WORD

Description

WORD is similar to Hangman in that the player must guess
a word with clues as to letter position furnished by the
computer. However, instead of guessing one letter at a time,
in WORD, you guess an entire word (or group of 5 letters,
such as ABCDE). The computer will tell you if any letters
in your word are in the mystery word and if any of them are
in the correct position. Armed with these clues, you go on
guessing until you get the word or, if you can't get it,
input a "?" and the computer will tell you the mystery word.

You may change the words in Data Statements 512 and 513, but
they must be 5-letter words.

Program Author

Charles Reid
Lexington High School
Lexington, MA. 02173

PROGRAM LISTING

```
2 PRINT:PRINT:PRINT:PRINT "PROGRAM 'WORD'"
3 REM *** WRITTEN BY CHRIS REID, LEXINGTON HS, CLASS OF '73
5 DIM S(7),A(7),L(7),D(7),P(7)
10 PRINT:PRINT "I AM THINKING OF A WORD -- YOU GUESS IT.  I WILL GIVE YOU"
15 PRINT "CLUES TO HELP YOU GET IT.  GOOD LUCK!!":PRINT:PRINT
20 RANDOMIZE
30 PRINT:PRINT:PRINT "YOU ARE STARTING A NEW GAME..."
35 RESTORE
40 READ N
50 C=INT(RND*N+1)
60 FOR I=1 TO C
70 READ S$
80 NEXT I
90 G=0
100 CHANGE S$ TO S
110 FOR I=1 TO 5
120 A(I)=45
130 NEXT I
140 FOR J=1 TO 5
144 P(J)=0
146 NEXT J
150 PRINT "GUESS A FIVE-LETTER WORD";
160 INPUT L$
170 G=G+1
172 IF L$=S$ THEN 500
180 CHANGE L$ TO L
190 IF L(1)=63 THEN 300
200 IF L(0)<>5 THEN 400
205 M=0:Q=1
210 FOR I=1 TO 5
220 FOR J=1 TO 5
230 IF S(I)<>L(J) THEN 260
231 P(Q)=L(J)
232 Q=Q+1
233 IF I<>J THEN 250
240 A(J)=L(J)
250 M=M+1
260 NEXT J
265 NEXT I
270 A(0)=5
272 P(0)=M
275 CHANGE A TO A$
277 CHANGE P TO P$
280 PRINT "THERE WERE"M"MATCHES AND THE COMMON LETTERS WERE... ",P$
285 PRINT "FROM THE EXACT LETTER MATCHES, YOU KNOW............ ",A$
286 IF A$=S$ THEN 500
287 IF M>1 THEN 289
288 PRINT:PRINT "IF YOU GIVE UP, TYPE '?' FOR YOUR NEXT GUESS"
289 PRINT
290 GOTO 150
300 CHANGE S TO S$
310 PRINT "THE SECRET WORD IS "S$:PRINT
320 GOTO 30
400 PRINT:PRINT "YOU MUST GUESS A 5-LETTER WORD.  START AGAIN"
410 PRINT:G=G-1:GOTO 150
500 PRINT "YOU HAVE GUESSED THE WORD.  IT TOOK"G"GUESSES!":PRINT
510 INPUT "WANT TO PLAY AGAIN";Q$
520 IF Q$="YES" THEN 30
530 DATA 12,"DINKY","SMOKE","WATER","GRASS","TRAIN","MIGHT","FIRST"
540 DATA "CANDY","CHAMP","WOULD","CLUMP","DOPEY"
999 END

READY
```

SAMPLE RUN

```
PROGRAM 'WORD'

I AM THINKING OF A WORD -- YOU GUESS IT.  I WILL GIVE YOU
CLUES TO HELP YOU GET IT.  GOOD LUCK!!




YOU ARE STARTING A NEW GAME...
GUESS A FIVE-LETTER WORD? ABCDE
THERE WERE 1 MATCHES AND THE COMMON LETTERS WERE...      C
FROM THE EXACT LETTER MATCHES, YOU KNOW............      -----

IF YOU GIVE UP, TYPE '?' FOR YOUR NEXT GUESS

GUESS A FIVE-LETTER WORD? CFGHI
THERE WERE 1 MATCHES AND THE COMMON LETTERS WERE...      C
FROM THE EXACT LETTER MATCHES, YOU KNOW............      C----

IF YOU GIVE UP, TYPE '?' FOR YOUR NEXT GUESS

GUESS A FIVE-LETTER WORD? CJKLMN

YOU MUST GUESS A 5-LETTER WORD.  START AGAIN

GUESS A FIVE-LETTER WORD? CJKLM
THERE WERE 3 MATCHES AND THE COMMON LETTERS WERE...      CLM
FROM THE EXACT LETTER MATCHES, YOU KNOW............      C----

GUESS A FIVE-LETTER WORD? COLMN
THERE WERE 3 MATCHES AND THE COMMON LETTERS WERE...      CLM
FROM THE EXACT LETTER MATCHES, YOU KNOW............      C--M-

GUESS A FIVE-LETTER WORD? COLMP
THERE WERE 4 MATCHES AND THE COMMON LETTERS WERE...      CLMP
FROM THE EXACT LETTER MATCHES, YOU KNOW............      C--MP

GUESS A FIVE-LETTER WORD? CLUMP
YOU HAVE GUESSED THE WORD.  IT TOOK 6 GUESSES!

WANT TO PLAY AGAIN? YES


YOU ARE STARTING A NEW GAME...
GUESS A FIVE-LETTER WORD? ABCDE
THERE WERE 0 MATCHES AND THE COMMON LETTERS WERE...
FROM THE EXACT LETTER MATCHES, YOU KNOW............      -----

IF YOU GIVE UP, TYPE '?' FOR YOUR NEXT GUESS

GUESS A FIVE-LETTER WORD? FGHIJ
THERE WERE 2 MATCHES AND THE COMMON LETTERS WERE...      FI
FROM THE EXACT LETTER MATCHES, YOU KNOW............      F----

GUESS A FIVE-LETTER WORD? FIKLM
THERE WERE 2 MATCHES AND THE COMMON LETTERS WERE...      FI
FROM THE EXACT LETTER MATCHES, YOU KNOW............      FI---

GUESS A FIVE-LETTER WORD? FINOP
THERE WERE 2 MATCHES AND THE COMMON LETTERS WERE...      FI
FROM THE EXACT LETTER MATCHES, YOU KNOW............      FI---

GUESS A FIVE-LETTER WORD? FIRST
YOU HAVE GUESSED THE WORD.  IT TOOK 5 GUESSES!

WANT TO PLAY AGAIN? NO

READY
```

YAHTZE

DICE GAME OF YAHTZEE

Description

Yahtzee may be played by up to 15 people. The object of the game is to get the highest grand total score. Each player on his turn receives from the computer the values of 5 pseudo dice. He may then roll as many of them as he wants to again. This may be repeated once again (3 rolls maximum). To roll again, you tell the computer how many dice you want to re-roll or change and the number of each die. You play 13 rounds for a complete game.

After you have finished rolling, you must decide how you want to score the five dice. Typing "SUMMARY" will show you which categories have been used, otherwise, you must decide on one of 13 categories or "ZERO" to eliminate a category with no score.

Category	How Scored
ACES	Count and add all ones.
TWOS	Count and add all twos.
THREES	Count and add all threes.
FOURS	Count and add all fours.
FIVES	Count and add all fives.
SIXES	Count and add all sixes.
THREE OF A KIND	Total all 5 dice (assuming 3 of a kind).
FOUR OF A KIND	Total all 5 dice (assuming 4 of a kind).
FULL HOUSE	25 Points (3 of one kind, 2 of another).
SMALL STRAIGHT	30 Points (Sequence of 4).
LARGE STRAIGHT	40 Points (Sequence of 5).
YAHTZEE	50 Points (5 of a kind).
CHANCE	Total of all 5 dice.
ZERO	Zero out any category above.

If your accumulated score of the first six categories ever reaches 63 points, you receive a bonus of 35 points.

Source

Unfortunately, the program author of this extremely comprehensive game is unknown.

```
1000 A(0)=5
1010 FOR U=1 TO 5
1020 A(U)=7
1030 NEXT U
1040 CHANGE A TO C$
1060 DIMA(15,15),T(15,15),F(15,15),S(15,15),L(15,15),K(15,15),H(15,15)
1070 FOR I=1 TO 5
1080 B(I)=0
1090 Q(I)=0
1100 A(I)=0
1110 NEXT I
1120 RANDOM
1130 PRINT "HOW MANY PLAYERS [TYPE: '0' FOR INSTRUCTIONS]";
1140 INPUT P
1150 IF P>15 THEN 1180
1160 IF P=0 THEN 4980
1170 GO TO 1200
1180 GOSUB 5710
1190 GO TO 1130
1200 IF P=.01 THEN 1220
1210 GO TO 1240
1220 GOSUB 5730
1230 GO TO 1140
1240 FOR I=1 TO P
1250 A(1,I)=-5
1260 A(1,I)=-5
1270 T(2,I)=-5
1280 F(1,I)=-5
1290 F(2,I)=-5
1300 S(1,I)=-5
1310 T(3,I)=-5
1320 F(3,I)=-5
1330 F(4,I)=-5
1340 S(2,I)=-5
1350 L(1,I)=-5
1360 Y(I)=-5
1370 C(I)=-5
1380 K(1,I)=0
1390 K(I)=0
1400 M(I)=0
1410 PRINT "NAME";
1420 INPUT N$(I)
1430 IF N$(I)="WHAT?" THEN 1450
1440 GO TO 1470
1450 GOSUB 5580
1460 GO TO 1410
1470 NEXT I
1480 H=0
1490 R=R+1
1495 IF R>13 THEN 6470
1500 PRINT
1510 PRINT
1520 PRINT "ROUND";R
1530 PRINT
1540 FOR I=1 TO P
1550 PRINT
1560 PRINT
1570 PRINT N$(I);"'S TURN"
1580 FOR L=1 TO 5
1590 A(L)=INT(6*RND(=1)+1)
1600 NEXT L
1605 GOSUB 1610
1607 GO TO 1700
1610 G=0
1620 FOR X=1 TO 5
1630 IF A(X)>=A(X+1) THEN 1680
1640 H=A(X)
1650 A(X)=A(X+1)
1660 A(X+1)=H
1670 G=1
1680 NEXT X
1685 IF G=1 THEN 1610
1690 RETURN
1700 PRINT "YOU HAVE A ";A(1);A(2);A(3);A(4);A(5)
1710 PRINT "THIS IS YOUR 2ND OF 3 ROLLS,"
1720 PRINT "HOW MANY DO YOU WANT TO CHANGE";
1730 INPUT Z
1740 IF Z=.01 THEN 1760
1750 GO TO 1780
1760 GOSUB 5600
1770 GO TO 1730
1780 IF Z=0 THEN 2620
1790 IF Z=5 THEN 1890
1800 FOR S=1 TO Z
1810 PRINT "WHICH";
1820 INPUT B(S)
1830 IF B(S)=.01 THEN 1850
1840 GO TO 1870
1850 GOSUB 5620
1860 GO TO 1810
1870 NEXT S
1880 GO TO 1930
1890 FOR S=1 TO 5
1900 A(S)=INT(6*RND(=1)+1)
1910 NEXT S
1920 GO TO 2050
1930 FOR L=1 TO 5
1940 FOR L1=1 TO 5
1950 IF B(L)=L1 THEN 1970
1960 GO TO 1980
1970 A(L1)=Q(L1)
1980 NEXT L1
1990 NEXT L
2000 FOR S=1 TO 5
2010 IF A(S)=0 THEN 2030
2020 GO TO 2040
2030 A(S)=INT(6*RND(=1)+1)
2040 NEXT S
2050 GOSUB 1610
2140 PRINT "YOU HAVE A ";A(1);A(2);A(3);A(4);A(5)
2150 PRINT "THIS IS YOUR LAST ROLL,"
2160 PRINT "HOW MANY DO YOU WANT TO CHANGE";
2170 INPUT Z
2180 IF Z=.01 THEN 2200
2190 GO TO 2220
2200 GOSUB 5600
2210 GO TO 2170
2220 IF Z=0 THEN 2620
2230 IF Z=5 THEN 2360
2240 FOR E=1 TO 5
```

```
2250 B(E)=0
2260 NEXT E
2270 FOR S=1 TO Z
2280 PRINT "WHICH";
2290 INPUT B(S)
2300 IF B(S)=.01 THEN 2320
2310 GO TO 2340
2320 GOSUB 5620
2330 GO TO 2280
2340 NEXT S
2350 GO TO 2400
2360 FOR S=1 TO 5
2370 A(S)=INT(6*RND(=1)+1)
2380 NEXT S
2390 GO TO 2520
2400 FOR L=1 TO 5
2410 FOR L1=1 TO 5
2420 IF B(L)=L1 THEN 2440
2430 GO TO 2450
2440 A(L1)=Q(L)
2450 NEXT L1
2460 NEXT L
2470 FOR S=1 TO 5
2480 IF A(S)=0 THEN 2500
2490 GO TO 2510
2500 A(S)=INT(6*RND(=1)+1)
2510 NEXT S
2520 GOSUB 1610
2610 PRINT "YOU HAVE A ";A(1);A(2);A(3);A(4);A(5)
2620 PRINT "HOW DO YOU WANT THIS ROUND SCORED";
2630 INPUT Z$
2640 IF Z$="WHAT?" THEN 2680
2650 IF Z$="SUMMARY" THEN 2670
2660 GO TO 2700
2670 GOSUB 6140
2675 GO TO 2620
2680 GOSUB 5650
2690 GO TO 2630
2700 IF Z$="ACES" THEN 2850
2710 IF Z$="TWOS" THEN 2940
2720 IF Z$="THREES" THEN 3030
2730 IF Z$="FOURS" THEN 3120
2740 IF Z$="FIVES" THEN 3210
2750 IF Z$="SIXES" THEN 3300
2760 IF Z$="THREE OF A KIND" THEN 3390
2770 IF Z$="FOUR OF A KIND" THEN 3440
2780 IF Z$="FULL HOUSE" THEN 3520
2790 IF Z$="SM. STRAIGHT" THEN 3620
2800 IF Z$="LG. STRAIGHT" THEN 3660
2810 IF Z$="YAHTZEE" THEN 3730
2820 IF Z$="CHANCE" THEN 3820
2830 IF Z$="ZERO" THEN 3890
2840 GO TO 2620
2850 IF A(1,I)<>-5 THEN 3870
2860 A(1,I)=0
2870 FOR S=1 TO 5
2880 IF A(S)=1 THEN 2900
2890 GO TO 2910
2900 A(1,I)=A(1,I)+1
2910 NEXT S
2920 M(I)=A(1,I)
2930 GO TO 4690
2940 IF T(1,I)<>-5 THEN 3870
2950 T(1,I)=0
2960 FOR S=1 TO 5
2970 IF A(S)=2 THEN 2990
2980 GO TO 3000
2990 T(1,I)=T(1,I)+2
3000 NEXT S
3010 M(I)=T(1,I)
3020 GO TO 4690
3030 IF T(2,I)<>-5 THEN 3870
3040 T(2,I)=0
3050 FOR S=1 TO 5
3060 IF A(S)=3 THEN 3080
3070 GO TO 3090
3080 T(2,I)=T(2,I)+3
3090 NEXT S
3100 M(I)=T(2,I)
3110 GO TO 4690
3120 IF F(1,I)<>-5 THEN 3870
3130 F(1,I)=0
3140 FOR S=1 TO 5
3150 IF A(S)=4 THEN 3170
3160 GO TO 3180
3170 F(1,I)=F(1,I)+4
3180 NEXT S
3185 M(I)=F(1,I)
3190 GO TO 4690
3210 IF F(2,I)<>-5 THEN 3870
3220 F(2,I)=0
3230 FOR S=1 TO 5
3240 IF A(S)=5 THEN 3260
3250 GO TO 3270
3260 F(2,I)=F(2,I)+5
3270 NEXT S
3280 M(I)=F(2,I)
3290 GO TO 4690
3300 IF S(1,I)<>-5 THEN 3870
3310 S(1,I)=0
3320 FOR S=1 TO 5
3330 IF A(S)=6 THEN 3350
3340 GO TO 3360
3350 S(1,I)=S(1,I)+6
3360 NEXT S
3370 M(I)=S(1,I)
3380 GO TO 4690
3390 IF T(3,I)<>-5 THEN 3870
3400 T(3,I)=0
3410 T(3,I)=A(1)+A(2)+A(3)+A(4)+A(5)
3420 M(I)=T(3,I)
3430 GO TO 4690
3440 IF F(3,I)<>-5 THEN 3870
3450 IF A(1)<>A(4) THEN 4960
3460 IF A(2)<>A(3) THEN 4960
3470 F(3,I)=0
3480 F(3,I)=A(1)+A(2)+A(3)+A(4)+A(5)
3490 M(I)=F(3,I)
3500 F(3,I)=0
3510 GO TO 4690
```

```
3520 IF F(4,I)<>=5 THEN 3870
3530 IF A(1)<>A(2) THEN 4960
3540 IF A(4)<>A(5) THEN 4960
3550 IF A(3)<>A(2) THEN 3570
3560 GO TO 3590
3570 IF A(3)<>A(4) THEN 4960
3580 GO TO 3590
3590 F(4,I)=25
3600 M(I)=F(4,I)
3610 GO TO 4690
3620 IF S(2,I)<>=5 THEN 3870
3630 S(2,I)=30
3640 M(I)=S(2,I)
3650 GO TO 4690
3660 IF L(1,I)<>=5 THEN 3870
3670 IF A(1)<>A(5)+4 THEN 4960
3680 IF A(2)<>A(4)+2 THEN 4960
3690 IF A(3)<>A(5)+2 THEN 4960
3700 L(1,I)=40
3710 M(I)=L(1,I)
3720 GO TO 4690
3730 IF Y(I)<>=5 THEN 3870
3740 FOR O=1 TO 5
3750 FOR O1=1 TO 5
3760 IF A(O)<>A(O1) THEN 4960
3770 NEXT O1
3780 NEXT O
3790 Y(I)=50
3800 M(I)=Y(I)
3810 GO TO 4690
3820 IF C(I)<>=5 THEN 3870
3830 C(I)=A(1)+A(2)+A(3)+A(4)+A(5)
3840
3850 M(I)=C(I)
3860 GO TO 4690
3870 GOSUB 4650
3880 GO TO 2620
3890 PRINT "WHAT DO YOU WANT TO ZERO";
3900 INPUT Z$
3920 IF Z$="SUMMARY" THEN 3940
3930 GO TO 3970
3940 GOSUB 6140
3945 GO TO 2620
3950 GOSUB 5680
3960 GO TO 3900
3970 IF Z$="ACES" THEN 4110
3980 IF Z$="TWOS" THEN 4150
3990 IF Z$="THREES" THEN 4190
4000 IF Z$="FOURS" THEN 4230
4010 IF Z$="FIVES" THEN 4270
4020 IF Z$="SIXES" THEN 4310
4030 IF Z$="THREE OF A KIND" THEN 4390
4040 IF Z$="FOUR OF A KIND" THEN 4430
4050 IF Z$="FULL HOUSE" THEN 4430
4060 IF Z$="SM. STRAIGHT" THEN 4470
4070 IF Z$="LG. STRAIGHT" THEN 4510
4080 IF Z$="YAHTZEE" THEN 4550
4090 IF Z$="CHANCE" THEN 4590
4100 GO TO 3890
4110 IF A(1,I)<>=5 THEN 4630
4120 A(1,I)=0
4130 M(I)=A(1,I)
4140 GO TO 4690
4150 IF T(1,I)<>=5 THEN 4630
4160 T(1,I)=0
4170 M(I)=T(1,I)
4180 GO TO 4690
4190 IF T(2,I)<>=5 THEN 4630
4200 T(2,I)=0
4210 M(I)=T(2,I)
4220 GO TO 4690
4230 IF F(1,I)<>=5 THEN 4630
4240 F(1,I)=0
4250 M(I)=F(1,I)
4260 GO TO 4690
4270 IF F(2,I)<>=5 THEN 4630
4280 F(2,I)=0
4290 M(I)=F(2,I)
4300 GO TO 4690
4310 IF S(1,I)<>=5 THEN 4630
4320 S(1,I)=0
4330 M(I)=S(1,I)
4340 GO TO 4690
4350 IF T(3,I)<>=5 THEN 4630
4360 T(3,I)=0
4370 M(I)=T(3,I)
4380 GO TO 4690
4390 IF F(3,I)<>=5 THEN 4630
4400 F(3,I)=0
4410 M(I)=F(3,I)
4420 GO TO 4690
4430 IF F(4,I)<>=5 THEN 4630
4440 F(4,I)=0
4450 M(I)=F(4,I)
4460 GO TO 4690
4470 IF S(2,I)<>=5 THEN 4630
4480 S(2,I)=0
4490 M(I)=S(2,I)
4500 GO TO 4690
4510 IF L(1,I)<>=5 THEN 4630
4520 L(1,I)=0
4530 M(I)=L(1,I)
4540 GO TO 4690
4550 IF Y(I)<>=5 THEN 4630
4560 Y(I)=0
4570 M(I)=Y(I)
4580 GO TO 4690
4590 IF C(I)<>=5 THEN 4630
4600 C(I)=0
4610 M(I)=C(I)
4620 GO TO 4690
4630 GOSUB 4650
4640 GOTO 2620
4650 PRINT "YOU HAVE ALREADY USED ";Z$;" AS A CATEGORY";C$
4660 PRINT
4670 RETURN
4680 GOTO 2620
4690 PRINT N$(I);" YOU GET A SCORE OF ";M(I);" FOR THIS ROUND"
4700 GO TO 5750
4710 NEXT I

4720 PRINT
4730 FOR J=1 TO P
4740 IF M(J)=A(1,J) THEN 4810
4750 IF M(J)=T(1,J) THEN 4810
4760 IF M(J)=T(2,J) THEN 4810
4770 IF M(J)=F(1,J) THEN 4810
4780 IF M(J)=F(2,J) THEN 4810
4790 IF M(J)=S(1,J) THEN 4810
4800 GO TO 4920
4810 K(1,J)=K(1,J)+M(J)
4820 GO TO 4830
4830 IF K(1,J)>=63 THEN 4860
4840 K(J)=K(J)+M(J)
4850 GO TO 4930
4860 K(1,J)=K(1,J)+35
4870 PRINT C$;N$(J);" HAS ACCUMULATED AT LEAST 63 POINTS"
4880 PRINT "IN THE FIRST SIX CATEGORIES,"
4890 PRINT "HE SCORES A BONUS OF 35 POINTS!";C$
4900 K(J)=K(J)+M(J)
4910 GO TO 4930
4920 K(J)=K(J)+M(J)
4930 PRINT N$(J);" HAS ";K(J);" POINTS"
4940 NEXT J
4950 GO TO 1490
4960 PRINT "IT IS ILLEGAL TO USE ";Z$;" THIS ROUND";C$
4970 GO TO 2620
4980 PRINT
4990 PRINT
5000 PRINT
5010 PRINT "INSTRUCTIONS FOR PLAYING YAHTZEE";C$
5020 PRINT
5030 PRINT "YAHTZEE MAY BE PLAYED BY UP TO 15 PEOPLE."
5040 PRINT "THE OBJECT OF THE GAME IS TO GET THE HIGHEST SCORE"
5050 PRINT "EACH PLAYER ON HIS TURN RECEIVES FROM THE COMPUTER"
5060 PRINT "THE VALUES OF THE 5 PSEUDO-DICE, HE MAY THEN ROLL"
5070 PRINT "AS MANY OF THEM AS HE WANTS TO AGAIN, HOWEVER,"
5080 PRINT "HE IS ENTITLED UP TO BUT NO MORE THAN THREE ROLLS"
5090 PRINT "OF THE DICE,"
5100 PRINT "     YOU TELL THE COMPUTER  MANY DICE YOU"
5110 PRINT "WANT TO CHANGE, THEN TELL IT WHICH ONES IN THE FOL-"
5120 PRINT "LOWING MANNER:"
5130 PRINT
5140 PRINT " TYPE: '1' FOR THE 1ST DIE, '2' FOR THE 2ND, ETC"
5150 PRINT "     AFTER THE THIRD ROLL THE PLAYER MUST DECIDE HOW"
5160 PRINT "HE WANTS TO SCORE HIS FIVE DICE."
5170 PRINT "TYPING 'SUMMARY' WILLL SHOW WHAT CATEGORIES"
5180 PRINT "HAVE BEEN USED, OTHERWISE,"
5190 PRINT "YOU HAVE 13 CHOICES, TYPE 1 OF THE FOLLOWING"
5200 PRINT "DEPENDING ON HOW YOU WANT YOUR DICE SCORED,"
5210 PRINT "THE CHOICES ARE:"
5220 PRINT "ACES,TWOS,THREES,FOURS,FIVES,SIXES"
5230 PRINT "THREE OF A KIND,FOUR OF A KIND,FULL HOUSE, SM. STRAIGHT,"
5240 PRINT "LG. STRAIGHT, YAHTZEE,CHANCE."
5250 PRINT "WHAT THE COMPUTER WILL DO:"
5260 PRINT "FOR ACES IT WILL COUNT AND ADD ALL OF YOUR ONES."
5270 PRINT "FOR TWOS IT WILL COUNT AND ADD ALL OF YOUR TWOS,"
5280 PRINT "THE SAME IS TRUE THROUGH THE SIXES,"
5290 PRINT "THREE OF A KIND WILL TOTAL ALL OF THE DICE PRO-"
5300 PRINT "VIDED THAT YOU HAVE THREE OF A KIND"
5310 PRINT "FOUR OF A KIND IS THE SAME AS THREE OF A KIND EXCEPT"
5320 PRINT "THAT YOU MUST HAVE FOUR OF A KIND"
5330 PRINT "FULL HOUSE [3 OF ONE NO, AND 2 OF ANOTHER] WILL YIELD"
5340 PRINT "25 POINTS, SM. STRAIGHT WILL GIVE YOU 30 POINTS BUT"
5350 PRINT "YOU MUST HAVE A SEQUENCE OF FOUR."
5360 PRINT "LG.STRAIGHT WILL YIELD 40 POINTS BUT YOU MUST HAVE A SE-"
5370 PRINT "QUENCE OF FIVE."
5380 PRINT "YAHTZEE WILLL GIVE 50 POINTS IF YOU HAVE FIVE OF A KIND."
5390 PRINT "CHANCE WILL TOTAL ALL OF YOUR DICE AND USE THAT AS YOUR SCORE."
5400 PRINT "CHANCE IS USEFUL WHEN YOU DON'T HAVE ANYTHING WORTH SCORING."
5410 PRINT "ANOTHER CATEGORY, 'ZERO' WILL ZERO OUT A CATEGORY"
5420 PRINT "IF YOU DON'T HAVE ANYTHING WORTH SCORING"
5430 PRINT "BUT HAVE PERHAPS ALREADY USED YOUR CHANCE."
5440 PRINT
5450 PRINT "IF YOUR ACCUMULATED SCORE OF THE FIRST SIX CATEGORIES"
5460 PRINT "EVER REACHES AT LEAST 63 POINTS YOU WILL RECEIVE"
5470 PRINT "A BONUS OF 35 POINTS!";C$
5480 PRINT
5490 PRINT "FOR INSTRUCTIONS DURING THE RUNNING OF THE PROGRAM"
5500 PRINT "TYPE 'WHAT?' WHEN THE COMPUTER ASKS FOR A WORD, OR,"
5510 PRINT"'.01' WHEN IT WANTS A NUMBER, AND YOU WILL RECEIVE"
5520 PRINT "FURTHER NOTES RELATED TO WHAT THE COMPUTER ASKED FOR,"
5530 PRINT
5540 PRINT
5550 PRINT
5560 PRINT "GOOD LUCK!!!!!!";C$
5570 GO TO 1070
5580 PRINT "WHAT DO YOU WANT ONE OF THE PLAYERS CALLED BY"
5600 PRINT "HOW MANY DICE DO YOU WANT TO ROLL AGAIN";
5610 RETURN
5620 PRINT "WHICH DIE DO YOU WANT TO CHANGE"
5630 PRINT "TYPE: '1' FOR THE 1ST DIE, '2' FOR THE 2ND DIE, ETC."
5640 RETURN
5650 PRINT "IN WHICH CATEGORY DO YOU WANT THIS ROUND SCORED"
5660 PRINT "TYPING: 'SUMMARY' WILL TELL YOU WHICH CATEGORIES YOU HAVE USED";
5670 RETURN
5680 PRINT "WHICH CATEGORY DO YOU WANT ZEROED"
5690 GO TO 5660
5700 RETURN
5710 PRINT "A MAXIMUM OF 15 PLAYERS IS ALLOWED"
5720 RETURN
5730 PRINT "HOW MANY PEOPLE WISH TO PLAY";
5740 RETURN
5750 IF Z$="ACES" THEN 5880
5760 IF Z$="TWOS" THEN 5900
5770 IF Z$="THREES" THEN 5920
5780 IF Z$="FOURS" THEN 5940
5790 IF Z$="FIVES" THEN 5960
5800 IF Z$="SIXES" THEN 5980
5810 IF Z$="THREE OF A KIND" THEN 6000
5820 IF Z$="FOUR OF A KIND" THEN 6020
5830 IF Z$="FULL HOUSE" THEN 6040
5840 IF Z$="SM. STRAIGHT" THEN 6060
5850 IF Z$="LG. STRAIGHT" THEN 6080
5860 IF Z$="YAHTZEE" THEN 6100
5870 IF Z$="CHANCE" THEN 6120
5880 H(I,R)=1
5890 GO TO 4710
5900 H(I,R)=2
5910 GO TO 4710
5920 H(I,R)=3
5930 GO TO 4710
```

```
5940 H(I,R)=4
5950 GO TO 4710
5960 H(I,R)=5
5970 GO TO 4710
5980 H(I,R)=6
5990 GO TO 4710
6000 H(I,R)=7
6010 GO TO 4710
6020 H(I,R)=8
6030 GO TO 4710
6040 H(I,R)=9
6050 GO TO 4710
6060 H(I,R)=10
6070 GO TO 4710
6080 H(I,R)=11
6090 GO TO 4710
6100 H(I,R)=12
6110 GO TO 4710
6120 H(I,R)=13
6130 GO TO 4710
6140 PRINT N$(I);" HAS USED THE FOLLOWING CATEGORIES:"
6150 FOR S=1 TO (R-1)
6160 IF H(I,S)>7 THEN 6180
6170 ON H(I,S) GO TO 6190,6210,6230,6250,6270,6290,6310
6180 ON H(I,S)-7 GO TO 6330,6350,6370,6390,6410,6430
6190 PRINT "ACES, ";
6200 GO TO 6440
6210 PRINT "TWOS, ";
6220 GO TO 6440
6230 PRINT "THREES, ";
6240 GO TO 6440
6250 PRINT "FOURS, ";
6260 GO TO 6440
6270 PRINT "FIVES, ";
6280 GO TO 6440
6290 PRINT "SIXES, ";
6300 GO TO 6440
6310 PRINT "THREE OF A KIND, ";
6320 GO TO 6440
6330 PRINT "FOUR OF A KIND, ";
6340 GO TO 6440
6350 PRINT "FULL HOUSE, ";
6360 GO TO 6440
6370 PRINT "SM. STRAIGHT, ";
6380 GO TO 6440
6390 PRINT "LG. STRAIGHT, ";
6400 GO TO 6440
6410 PRINT "YAHTZEE, ";
6420 GO TO 6440
6430 PRINT "CHANCE, ";
6440 NEXT S
6445 PRINT
6446 PRINT "HE HAS ";K(I);" POINTS,"
6447 PRINT "AND ";K(1,I);" OF THE 65 POINTS NEEDED FOR THE BONUS";
6450 PRINT "."
6460 RETURN
6470 G=0
6480 FOR X=1 TO P
6490 IF S(X)>=S(X+1) THEN 6540
6500 H=S(X)
6510 S(X)=S(X+1)
6520 S(X+1)=H
6530 G=1
6540 NEXT X
6550 IF G=1 THEN 6470
6560 PRINT "THE GAME IS OVER."
6570 PRINT
6571 FOR X=1 TO P
6572 IF K(X)=S(X) THEN 6580
6573 NEXT X
6580 PRINT "THE WINNER IS ";N$(1);" WITH ";K(1);" POINTS."
6585 IF P=1 THEN 9999
6586 PRINT "OTHER FINAL SCORES ARE:"
6590 FOR Y=1 TO P
6600 IF K(Y)=S(X) THEN 6620
6610 PRINT N$(Y);" FINISHES WITH ";K(Y);" POINTS."
6620 NEXT Y
9999 END
```

241

```
KEN'S TURN                                    KEN'S TURN
YOU HAVE A 5 5 3 3 1                          YOU HAVE A 5 3 2 2 1
THIS IS YOUR 2ND OF 3 ROLLS,                  THIS IS YOUR 2ND OF 3 ROLLS,
HOW MANY DO YOU WANT TO CHANGE ?1             HOW MANY DO YOU WANT TO CHANGE ?1
WHICH ?5                                      WHICH ?3
YOU HAVE A 5 5 3 2 1                          YOU HAVE A 6 5 3 2 1
THIS IS YOUR LAST ROLL,                       THIS IS YOUR LAST ROLL,
HOW MANY DO YOU WANT TO CHANGE ?1             HOW MANY DO YOU WANT TO CHANGE ?1
WHICH ?2                                      WHICH ?1
YOU HAVE A 5 3 2 1 1                          YOU HAVE A 5 3 2 1 1
HOW DO YOU WANT THIS ROUND SCORED ?ACES       HOW DO YOU WANT THIS ROUND SCORED ?SUMMARY
KEN YOU GET A SCORE OF  2 FOR THIS ROUND      KEN HAS USED THE FOLLOWING CATEGORIES:
                                              TWOS, ACES, SM. STRAIGHT, LG. STRAIGHT, SIXES, FIVES, THREES, FOURS, FUL
DAVE HAS  65  POINTS                          L HOUSE,  THREE OF A KIND,
KEN HAS  4  POINTS                            HE HAS  151  POINTS,
                                              AND  45  OF THE 65 POINTS NEEDED FOR THE BONUS.
                                              HOW DO YOU WANT THIS ROUND SCORED ?CHANCE
ROUND 3                                       KEN YOU GET A SCORE OF  12 FOR THIS ROUND

                                              DAVE HAS  182  POINTS
                                              KEN HAS  163  POINTS

DAVE'S TURN
YOU HAVE A 6 5 4 4 1                          ROUND 12
THIS IS YOUR 2ND OF 3 ROLLS,
HOW MANY DO YOU WANT TO CHANGE ?2
WHICH ?4
WHICH ?5                                      DAVE'S TURN
YOU HAVE A 6 5 5 5 4                          YOU HAVE A 6 4 4 3 2
THIS IS YOUR LAST ROLL,                       THIS IS YOUR 2ND OF 3 ROLLS,
HOW MANY DO YOU WANT TO CHANGE ?2             HOW MANY DO YOU WANT TO CHANGE ?2
WHICH ?1                                      WHICH ?1
WHICH ?5                                      WHICH ?2
YOU HAVE A 5 5 5 5 3                          YOU HAVE A 6 4 3 3 2
HOW DO YOU WANT THIS ROUND SCORED ?FOUR OF A KIND   THIS IS YOUR LAST ROLL,
DAVE YOU GET A SCORE OF  23 FOR THIS ROUND    HOW MANY DO YOU WANT TO CHANGE ?2
                                              WHICH ?1
KEN'S TURN                                    WHICH ?3
YOU HAVE A 6 4 3 2 1                          YOU HAVE A 4 3 2 2 2
THIS IS YOUR 2ND OF 3 ROLLS,                  HOW DO YOU WANT THIS ROUND SCORED ?SM. STRAIGHT
HOW MANY DO YOU WANT TO CHANGE ?0             DAVE YOU GET A SCORE OF  30 FOR THIS ROUND
HOW DO YOU WANT THIS ROUND SCORED ?SM. STRAIGHT
KEN YOU GET A SCORE OF  30 FOR THIS ROUND
                                              KEN'S TURN
DAVE HAS  88  POINTS                          YOU HAVE A 6 4 4 1 1
KEN HAS  34  POINTS                           THIS IS YOUR 2ND OF 3 ROLLS,
                                              HOW MANY DO YOU WANT TO CHANGE ?3
                                              WHICH ?1
ROUND 4                                       WHICH ?4
                                              WHICH ?5
                                              YOU HAVE A 5 4 4 2 1
DAVE'S TURN                                   THIS IS YOUR LAST ROLL,
YOU HAVE A 6 5 3 2 1                           HOW MANY DO YOU WANT TO CHANGE ?3
THIS IS YOUR 2ND OF 3 ROLLS,                  WHICH ?1
HOW MANY DO YOU WANT TO CHANGE ?1             WHICH ?4
WHICH ?1                                      WHICH ?5
YOU HAVE A 5 5 3 2 1                          YOU HAVE A 5 4 4 4 3
THIS IS YOUR LAST ROLL,                       HOW DO YOU WANT THIS ROUND SCORED ?ZERO
HOW MANY DO YOU WANT TO CHANGE ?1             WHAT DO YOU WANT TO ZERO ?YAHTZEE
WHICH ?1                                      KEN YOU GET A SCORE OF  0 FOR THIS ROUND
YOU HAVE A 5 5 3 2 1
HOW DO YOU WANT THIS ROUND SCORED ?FIVES      DAVE HAS  212  POINTS
DAVE YOU GET A SCORE OF  10 FOR THIS ROUND    KEN HAS  163  POINTS

KEN'S TURN
YOU HAVE A 5 4 3 2 1                          ROUND 13
THIS IS YOUR 2ND OF 3 ROLLS,
HOW MANY DO YOU WANT TO CHANGE ?0
HOW DO YOU WANT THIS ROUND SCORED ?LG. STRAIGHT
KEN YOU GET A SCORE OF  40 FOR THIS ROUND     DAVE'S TURN
                                              YOU HAVE A 5 4 3 1 1
DAVE HAS  98  POINTS                          THIS IS YOUR 2ND OF 3 ROLLS,
KEN HAS  74  POINTS                           HOW MANY DO YOU WANT TO CHANGE ?3
                                              WHICH ?1
                                              WHICH ?2
ROUND 5                                       WHICH ?3
                                              YOU HAVE A 5 2 1 1 1
                                              THIS IS YOUR LAST ROLL,
                                              HOW MANY DO YOU WANT TO CHANGE ?2
DAVE'S TURN                                   WHICH ?1
YOU HAVE A 6 6 3 3 2                          WHICH ?2
THIS IS YOUR 2ND OF 3 ROLLS,                  YOU HAVE A 4 3 1 1 1
HOW MANY DO YOU WANT TO CHANGE ?1             HOW DO YOU WANT THIS ROUND SCORED ?ZERO
WHICH ?5                                      WHAT DO YOU WANT TO ZERO ?YAHTZEE
YOU HAVE A 6 6 4 3 3                          DAVE YOU GET A SCORE OF  0 FOR THIS ROUND
THIS IS YOUR LAST ROLL,
HOW MANY DO YOU WANT TO CHANGE ?1             KEN'S TURN
WHICH ?3                                      YOU HAVE A 6 6 5 4 2
YOU HAVE A 6 6 5 3 3                          THIS IS YOUR 2ND OF 3 ROLLS,
HOW DO YOU WANT THIS ROUND SCORED ?SIXES      HOW MANY DO YOU WANT TO CHANGE ?3
DAVE YOU GET A SCORE OF  12 FOR THIS ROUND    WHICH ?3
                                              WHICH ?4
KEN'S TURN                                    WHICH ?5
YOU HAVE A 6 5 3 2 2                          YOU HAVE A 6 6 6 4 2
THIS IS YOUR 2ND OF 3 ROLLS,                  THIS IS YOUR LAST ROLL,
HOW MANY DO YOU WANT TO CHANGE ?3             HOW MANY DO YOU WANT TO CHANGE ?2
WHICH ?1                                      WHICH ?4
WHICH2 ?                                      WHICH ?5
WHICH ?3                                      YOU HAVE A 6 6 6 5 2
YOU HAVE A 6 6 4 2 2                          HOW DO YOU WANT THIS ROUND SCORED ?ZERO
THIS IS YOUR LAST ROLL,                       WHAT DO YOU WANT TO ZERO ?FOUR OF A KIND
HOW MANY DO YOU WANT TO CHANGE ?3             KEN YOU GET A SCORE OF  0 FOR THIS ROUND
WHICH ?3
WHICH ?4                                      DAVE HAS  212  POINTS
WHICH ?5                                      KEN HAS  163  POINTS
YOU HAVE A 6 6 6 4 3                          THE GAME IS OVER.
HOW DO YOU WANT THIS ROUND SCORED ?SIXES
KEN YOU GET A SCORE OF  18 FOR THIS ROUND     THE WINNER IS DAVE WITH  212  POINTS.
                                              OTHER FINAL SCORES ARE:
DAVE HAS  110  POINTS                         DAVE FINISHES WITH  212  POINTS.
KEN HAS  92  POINTS                           KEN FINISHES WITH  163  POINTS.
```

ZOOP

BASIC PROGRAMMER'S NIGHTMARE

Description

ZOOP is designed to imitate the system commands of a BASIC compiler, however, it gives totally meaningless and frustrating results. For example, to the command:

CAT

ZOOP responds with:

TRY MONTGOMERY WARD's

To the command:

SCRATCH

ZOOP responds with:

GOT AN ITCH?

Computer Limitations

The version of ZOOP printed here was written for DIGITAL Edusystems 15/30/35 and immediately decodes the first two characters input and carries on from there. It is a simple matter to convert ZOOP to a system which has string handling, however, it was felt that this version is more creative. It also happens to be the original.

Program Author

Tom Kloos
Oregon Museum of Science and Industry
Portland, Oregon 97200

```
100PRINT\PRINT"READY"\PRINT
110 INPUT $A\IF A=253 THEN 300\INPUT $B\IF B=253 THEN 300
120LETK=10*A+B
130IFK<>2313THEN140\PRINT"N  NO FILE YOU BOOB"\GOTO100
140IFK<>2143THEN150\PRINT"TALOG  TRY MONTGOMERY WARD'S"\GOTO100
150IFK<>2241THEN160\PRINT"STNH  I DON'T FEEL LIKE IT"\GOTO100
160IFK<>2257THEN170\PRINT"W YES I'M QUITE NEW"\GOTO100
170IFK<>2274THEN190\PRINT"D I'M NOT THAT OLD, BUT I'M OLD ENOUGH!!!"
180GOTO100
190IFK<>2297THEN210\PRINT"NAME  WHY? I LIKE MY NAME"\GOTO100
200IFK<>207THEN210\PRINT"NAME  WHY? I LIKE MY NAME"\GOTO100
210IFK<>2157THEN220\PRINT"BUG  GET A CAN OF RAID"\GOTO100
220IFK<>2322THEN230\PRINT"OP THE FUN IS JUST STARTING"\GOTO100
230IFK<>2303THEN240\PRINT"VE I DON'T LIKE BANKS"\GOTO100
240IFK<>2336THEN250\PRINT"SAVE O.K., THE WHOLE DEC TAPE"\CHAIN "ZOOP  "
250IFK<>2305THEN260\PRINT"RATCH  GOT AN ITCH?"\GOTO100
260IFK<>2166THEN270\PRINT"IT  THIS IS NO NEWSPAPER"\GOTO100
270 INPUT $C\IF C=253 THEN 300
280IFC<>141THEN270
290PRINT\PRINT"WHAT??"\GOTO100
300 PRINT " WIPED OUT COMPLETELY!!!"
310 CHAIN "DEMON "
320END
```

Appendices

FAMILIES OF GAMES

Number or Letter Guessing
1. GUESS
2. HI-LO
3. LETTER
4. TRAP
5. STARS

Piles of Objects
1. 23MTCH
2. BATNUM
3. EVEN
4. NIM

Matrix
BATTLE
HURKLE
MUGWMP
PIZZA
SALVO
SALVO1

Cybernetics (Artificial Intelligence)
ANIMAL
DIGITS
EVEN1
HEX

Land Management, Government, History
CIVILW
FURS
HMRABI
KING
STOCK

Plotting
BOUNCE
BUNNY
DIAMND
SNOOPY (2)
3DPLOT
UGLY

Logic
AWAR1
BAGLES
BULCOW
CHOMP
CUBE
FIPFOP
HI-Q
1CHECK
QUBIC
QUEEN
REVRSE
TICTAC
TOWER

Casino, Gambling, Betting
BINGO
BLKJAK, BLKJAC
CRAPS
DOGS
HORSES
POKER
ROULET
SLOTS

Card and Board
ACEYDU
CHECKR
GOMOKO
MNOPLY
WAR
YAHTZE

Sports
BASBAL
BASKET
BOWL
BOXING
BULEYE
CANAM
FOOTBL, FOTBAL
GOLF
HOCKEY

Space
ORBIT
ROCKET, ROCKT1, ROCKT2
SPACWR
TARGET

CAI, Quiz
CHEMST
CHIEF
HELLO
KINEMA
LITQZ
MATHD1
TRAIN

War
BOAT
BOMBER
GUNNER, GUNER1

Word
BUZZWD
HANG
SYNONM
WORD

Dates
CALNDR
WEKDAY

Miscellaneous
AMAZIN
BUG
BULL
CHANGE
DICE
LIFE
LIFE-2
NUMBER
POETRY, POET
ROCKSP
RUSROU
SPLAT
ZOOP

APPENDIX B – GAME DIAGRAMS

Grids for playing BATTLE, HURKLE , MUGWMP, and SALVO.

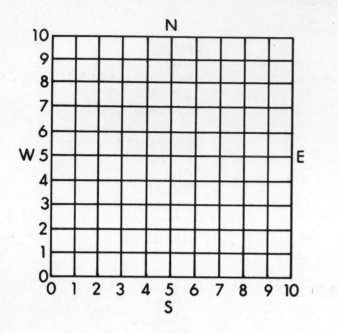

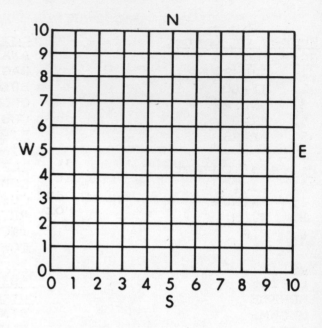

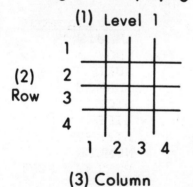

Use this scale with a compass for MUGWMP.

Diagram for playing QUBIC.

(1) Level 1

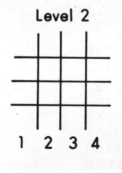

Level 2

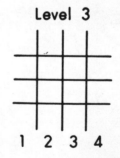

Level 3

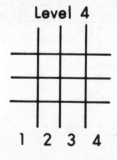

Level 4

(2) Row 1 2 3 4

1 2 3 4

(3) Column

Blanks for playing DIGITS

1st 10 — — — — — — — — — —

2nd 10 — — — — — — — — — —

3rd 10 — — — — — — — — — —

APPENDIX C

INSTRUCTIONS TO GAME AUTHORS

1. Programs must be <u>complete</u> and <u>debugged</u>, BASIC language only.

2. Please submit:
   A. One program listing and
   B. Two sample runs the way an average person would play.

3. Listing and run must be on <u>white</u>, <u>unlined</u> paper. If you have lined paper, turn it around to the unlined side. We <u>absolutely</u> cannot handle submittals on pink, yellow, blue or gray paper. Xerox, Ditto, or other copies are also unacceptable. Make as few folds in the output as possible.

4. Listing and run must be done with a <u>fresh black</u> ribbon. Not a purple or blue ribbon and especially not a used ribbon.

5. The Teletype type ball must be clean and produce crisp copy. Clean the ball with typewriter type cleaner or a stiff toothbrush.

6. If possible, submit a paper tape of the program. Unoiled fan-fold tape is preferable. If you have oiled paper tape (as from a Teletype), fan fold it (folds are 8½" apart), leave at least 17" blank leader and 8½" trailer tape. Rolled paper tape or fan folds much greater or less than 8½" cannot be handled on our high-speed readers and are unusable for making copies. <u>Be sure</u> to wrap oiled paper tape in kitchen plastic wrap or waxed paper when you mail it. If you don't the oil seeps out and smears the output. Oil seepage has ruined any number of otherwise excellent submittals.

7. We also have to know:
   A. Your name
   B. Complete address
   C. Telephone
   D. School affiliation
   E. Your age
   F. Computer system used
   G. Original source of program (if not you)

8. By submitting a program, you are giving Digital Equipment Corp. the right to publish, reprint, distribute, or use your program in any other way. You will, of course, always be cited as the author.